The Horseman's International Book of Reference

A Lipizanner of the Spanish Riding School, Vienna,
in *pesade*.

The Horseman's International Book of Reference

Edited by *Jean Froissard*
and *Lily Powell Froissard*

Stanley Paul · London
London Melbourne Sydney Auckland Johannesburg

Dedication

In memory of and in tribute to Reggie
R. S. Summerhays, father of this book

Stanley Paul & Co. Ltd
An imprint of the Hutchinson Publishing Group

3 Fitzroy Square, London W1P 6JD

Hutchinson Group (Australia) Pty Ltd
30–32 Cremorne Street, Richmond South, Victoria 3121
PO Box 151, Broadway, New South Wales 2007

Hutchinson Group (NZ) Ltd
32–34 View Road, PO Box 40–086, Glenfield,
Auckland 10

Hutchinson Group (SA) Pty Ltd
PO Box 337, Bergvlei 2012, South Africa

First published 1980
© Stanley Paul & Co. Ltd 1980
Dictionary of Technical Terms
© Jean Froissard and Lily Powell Froissard 1980

Set in Monotype Garamond

Printed in Great Britain by
The Anchor Press Ltd, and bound by
Wm Brendon & Son Ltd, both of
Tiptree, Essex

ISBN 0 09 132400 9

Contents

APPENDICES

List of Photographs

The following breeds appear on pp. 432–9 in alphabetical order within their respective countries:

Haflinger, Lipizzaner, Noriker, Ardennais, Canadian Cutting horse, Frederiksborg, Knapstrup, Boulonnais, Anglo-Arab, French Trotter, Percheron, Selle Français, Cleveland Bay, Clydesdale, Cob, Dales pony, Dartmoor pony, Exmoor pony, Fell pony, Hack, Hackney horse, Highland pony, Heavyweight Hunter, New Forest pony, Shetland pony, Shire, Suffolk Punch, Welsh Cob (Section C), Welsh Cob (Section D), Welsh Mountain pony, Welsh pony (Section B) Hungarian Half-Bred, Muraközi, Nonius, Connemara pony, Irish Draught, Salerno, Dutch Draught, Friesian, Gelderland, Hucul ponies, Konik pony, Wielkopolski, Andalusian, Swedish Warm Blood, Eisiedler, Quarter horse, Standardbred, Morgan, Tennessee Walking horse, Akhal-Teke, Budyony, Don, Karabair, Lithuanian Heavy Draught, Orlov Trotter, Tersk, Vladimir, Oldenburg, Schleswig, Trakehner, Hanoverian, Holstein.

COLOUR SECTION

Between pages 136 and 137

A Lipizzaner of The Spanish Riding School, Vienna in *pesade* (*frontispiece*)

James Ward, RA, *Coursing in Sussex* (Roy Miles Fine Paintings, London)

George Stubbs ARA, *Phaeton with Cream Ponies and Stable Lad* (Yale Center for British Art)

French Trotters in action at St Malo

Flat Racing at Deauville

Coming out of the stalls on a dirt racetrack in America

Racing over hurdles at Sandown Park, one of England's premier courses

Janou Tissot, twice ladies' world show jumping champion, competing at the All-England jumping course, Hickstead

The German event rider, Klaus Wagner, jumping into the lake at the Badminton Horse Trials

A Hackney pony competing in a show class at Hickstead

HRH The Prince Philip, Duke of Edinburgh, competing in the marathon at a combined driving event at Windsor

Lipizzaner liberty horses presented by Mary Chipperfield, a member of the renowned circus family

Switzerland's Christine Stückelberger riding Granat to victory in the Grand Prix Dressage at the 1976 Olympic Games

The ancient game of polo in a modern setting, Smith's Lawn, Windsor

The Old Surrey and Burstow foxhounds

A drum horse of the Household Cavalry Regiment in ceremonial attire

Heavy horses demonstrating an age-old farming technique at a ploughing match in Oxfordshire

List of Line Drawings

Acknowledgements

From the editors: Our gratitude to the contributors – who became our friends – and the friends – who became our contributors – for giving their very best in writing on often complex subjects within the necessarily limited space allowed.

Lt. Col. M. A. Q. Darley, Mr Robert Dumas-Hermès, Gen. Jean Herlem, Mr János Pál, Messrs Jean and Louis Romanet, Col. Jean de Saint-André, and the late Mr E. A. Sarasin have donated their work in a gesture of personal friendship. The articles of Mr Dumas-Hermès and Col. de Saint-André, in particular, have been a labour of love, since, until granting our request, they had strictly and consistently refused to write for publication.

Prof. Igor Bobylev, Col. Jacques Bois, Sir John Glubb, Mr François de La Sayette, and the Lady Anne Lytton have donated many beautiful photographs to choose from, not only for the illustrations of their own, but of other contributors' articles.

Prof. J. K. Anderson, Mr Marcel Delzons, Mr Anthony A. Dent, Mr Charles Chenevix Trench and Mr and Mrs Sanders Watney have given us their untiring, patient help and advice.

Mr Anthony A. Dent and the late Mr André Monteilhet have been invaluable aside from giving us their writings and advice – as expert translators, while the late Mr André Vannier presented us with his time and bilingual gifts for friendship's sake alone, expecting no more than these heartfelt words which, alas, can no longer reach him: thank you.

The publishers would also like to thank Judith Draper for her invaluable help and advice, also Niki Fagg and Norman Ball, and Christine Bousfield for the beautiful drawings.

Translators: André Vannier, André Monteilhet, Anthony Dent, Jean Froissard, Lily Froissard

Introduction

Jean Froissard and Lily Powell Froissard

This book is an invitation to you to attend a forum on almost all subjects concerning the horse. If we say almost, it is because we are quite aware that there are regrettable gaps, as there are in all works of this kind, if for different reasons. It is not, here, a question of oversight, not even in all cases necessarily of a lack of space. The reason in our case resides in the fact that it is indeed a forum to which we have invited, for your benefit, the top authorities to discuss their particular fields. In fact, the word 'discussion', of which you are the auditorium, has been chosen quite consciously, and this is also why we have been using the word 'forum'.

We know that readers and critics alike will find that some of the subjects are dealt with somewhat sketchily. First of all, there is the handicap of space limitations in a work such as this; secondly, we consider that the person interested in an in-depth treatment of any one subject will quite naturally turn to a book specializing in it. Above all, this *is a forum* where each specialist touches on the aspects which to *him* or *her* seem essential in a brief 'lecture' which necessarily must be more succinct than a complete 'dissertation'. We hope you will leave this forum with the feeling that you have received the most competent guidelines available in the world today, enabling you to pursue further studies in whatever subject interests you most.

If the title of this work includes the word 'reference', it is not meant in the sense that if you wish to inform yourself on a given equestrian term you will find that term with a brief explanation of its meaning in alphabetical order. Several encyclopedias of that sort are available. The word in our case signifies that for the true meaning of the main subjects you can refer to the opinions of those who know them most thoroughly, from the equestrian as well as historical points of view.

We are also certain that the English-French index which completes this work will be a welcome addition for those who read both languages; but, above all, for the ever-increasing number of those who cross their own frontiers for international competition and who, for communication with their foreign colleagues, are in need of the basic vocabulary making up the two official languages of the FEI. And we do not forget the non-competitive traveller who, with a basic knowledge of both technical languages, will be able to make his or her way anywhere in the equestrian world. Again critics may be dissatisfied and readers disappointed in not finding an occasional term they are looking for. But do not forget that a complete technical dictionary is a voluminous work in itself; our index simply lists every technical term appearing in this book. Fortunately, the vastness of subjects and the literacy of our contributors render the vocabulary virtually complete.

Let us not finish without acknowledging with gratitude the many, and not the least famous, collaborators who have contributed to this work purely *pour l'amour de l'art*, and the enormous enthusiasm brought to this work by the cream of equestrian society.

Part One

The Prehistoric Horse

Anthony A. Dent

The most striking thing about horses, distinguishing them above all from their near relations the asses and zebras, is their great climatic adaptability; their tolerance of various extremes of heat and cold, damp and drought, at various altitudes. There are mountain, swamp, desert and tundra horses. And yet there are limits to the tolerance, definable in degrees of latitude, within which the horse will live 'of its own free will': they are, very roughly, 36° and 51° N. Within these limits it once lived as a wild animal, overstepping them only when assisted or constrained by man, and there it would re-establish itself most successfully as a feral population of runaway horses or the descendants of such. The corresponding parallel in the southern hemisphere is the area to which the horse is not native but has been introduced by human agency.

What the horse 'wants', as a species, is a mild, medium-dry climate on a plain, but rolling hills will do quite well; only the craggiest mountains or dense forests are unacceptable. On such a plain, within these boundaries north and south, the species evolved in North America, and its migration over a land bridge into Eurasia, which took place some time before the human migration by the same route counterwise, from Siberia to Alaska, brought it into a land mass not essentially different from its old habitat. Whereas the old one had been bisected by the Rockies, through the gaps in which infiltration would have been slow, now the only considerable horse-stopping feature was the Himalayan massif and its prolongations east and west, and this effectively formed the southern boundary of the wild horse territory. In any case, beyond it the soil and climate were unfavourable to the species. Most recent research indicates the boundary dipped slightly before reaching the Caspian, and the Iranian plateau seems to have formed part of the original wild-horse country.

But the climatic limits are more absolute on one side than on the other. Horses can stand excessive cold better than excessive heat, excessive drought better than excessive damp, high altitudes better (though not with impunity) than low. Thus the race has advanced towards the pole from its first bridgehead in Eurasia to the latitudes of Verkhoyansk and Yakutsk, where it can exist wild, well up in the 60s.

Domestic horses in Iceland winter quite well on the fells at above this latitude, but although the climate is tempered by oceanic influences here, Iceland must be very near the wet-cold limit of tolerance for horses. The combinations wet-cold and wet-hot are less tolerable to them than dry-cold and dry-hot: negative altitudes, that is, depressions below sea-level, appear to be lethal. Very high altitudes, even those which support adequate vegetation, are never a permanent habitat, if only because the horse, unlike the ass and the llama, suffers from altitude sickness to a greater extent than humans, the yak replacing the pack-horse in the high Himalayas. Horses in marsh areas live and breed only in climates no less temperate than the Mediterranean. Life at abnormal altitudes in excessive humidity produces after some generations symptoms of degeneracy, including large heads, an excessively narrow body, and dwarfing. The mountain horse has always shorter legs than the plains horse of the same overall mass.

The only surviving authentic wild horses, the Mongolian Taki (*Equus przevalskii poliakoff*) have now, as a restricted habitat, an environment most hostile to mammalian life because of the scarceness and salinity of the water, the scanty and innutritious vegetation, and the extreme cold of the nights all the year round, not to mention the biting cold winds of winter days. One hopes that the present tense is correctly employed, for the Taki is to the domestic horse as the wolf is to the dog: it has never subscribed to '*le pacte des villes/Que l'homme a fait avec les animaux serviles . . .*'; and it alone, according to Western zoological ideas. It is questionable whether the sub-arctic horses of Yakutia, not yet dignified by a specific Latin title, are feral domestic horses (then why are they all of one colour?) or direct descendants of the white horses whose remains are occasionally recovered from the Siberian permafrost along with those of mammoths. It can only be solved by Soviet scientists, and perhaps soon. In particular they may determine whether the chromosome count of the white sub-arctic horse is identical with that of the domestic horse (64) or with that of Przevalsky's Taki (66), since hitherto this factor has been taken as the one sure indication of specific difference (the domestic ass has the count 62, Asiatic wild asses 56, Somali zebras 46, for instance).

The horse, by reason of its physical conformation, is better able to get at snow-covered grazing than any other domestic animal except the reindeer. Its forefeet can be used as shovels and its nose, which is not naked, can finish the snow-clearing process which none of the naked-snouted bovids and cervids, only the hairy-nosed reindeer, can do. The fact that all horses, even pure-bred Arabs, know what to do about snow when confronted with it for the first time, is sufficient proof that the homeland to which all horses trace back must have been one of regular, and heavy, winter snowfall.

Time was when all horses were thought to be descended from an ancestor identical with the Taki of Mongolia, but it is now realized that some of the Taki's characteristics have been acquired since its restriction to the hostile environment of the Djungarian saline desert; i.e., it has become specialized for survival in that particular environment. Moreover, such restriction has only taken place within the period during which Mongolian man has been practising a nomadic stock-rearing economy: the Taki has been driven into the worst grazing country by the pressure of domestic herds on grazing and water – specifically of domestic horse-herds – within the last ten thousand years or so. That a period of time so short by geological standards should have sufficed to produce this modification in the wild race is yet another facet of the extreme genetic plasticity of horses, domestication *per se* always producing a greater degree of plasticity than natural selection.

Since the early nineteenth century scientific fashion concerning the ancestry of the horse has run a chequered course, postulating at various times anything between one *Equus przevalskii poliakoff* and seven different wild varieties. If I adopt the theory currently most favoured, it is with the realization that it will be greatly modified if not exploded within my own expectation of longevity, and also gratefully acknowledging it as the one that most neatly accounts for all facts known at this writing about horses living and extinct. The theory was formulated jointly by J. G. Speed (Edinburgh), Edward Skorkowski (Cracow) and F. Ebhardt (Stuttgart) and it relies extensively on X-ray analysis of bone structure, and of dental formation – the latter enabling conclusions to be drawn about the nutriment, whether browsing or grazing, upon which the animal subsisted.

This evidence indicates that there were four distinct equine sub-species in the Old World, co-existing, over a larger or smaller territory, with human populations before the moment of domestication. At least one of these has been identified with remains in Alaska, and it is at least possible that all became differentiated before the migration from the New to the Old World. They were:

The four early types of wild pony and horse probably resembled the four modern breeds shown here: however no modern breeds totally equate to these types since all are a cross of one or more of the wild varieties.

Pony Type I (Exmoor)

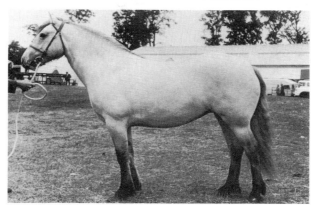

Pony Type II (Highland)

Horse Type III (Akhal-Teke)

Horse Type IV (Caspian pony)

Pony I (also in Alaska) Unspecialized, similar in size and conformation to the Exmoor pony, eventually establishing itself in north-west Europe. Resistant to wet.

Pony II Slightly taller, much heavier, adapted to soft ground (at least in summer), resembling the Taki but without its comparatively recent attributes mentioned above. Resistant to cold. Principal habitat: north Eurasia. Wiry, stiff mane and tail.

Horse III The tallest wild variety, up to 14.3 h.h., with a long narrow head, forehead much narrower than I above, sparse lank mane and tail, goose rump, 'split-up behind', long neck, long ears, slab sides, shallow body. Principal habitat: Central Asia. Resistant to heat.

Horse IV The 'proto-Arab'. Smaller than all the others, the size of a Welsh Mountain pony (Section A). Principal habitat: western Asia. Resistant to drought. Possibly surviving in relatively unmixed form as the recently re-discovered Caspian pony of Iran, just within the bounds of the wild-horse habitat.

Opinions differ as to the former existence of wild hybrids but if one was possible then all were, and at the moment of domestication there would have existed, besides these four local races, a further nine possible fifty per cent crosses alone; readers may compute their own total of possible less simple crosses involving three or all four of the original wild races. The one that practically concerns us is the I × IV half-bred, occurring wild in European Russia as the Tarpan until the nineteenth century, since it was the principal ancestor of the Carpathian pony, the Polish Konik, the Prussian Schweike, and many Balkan breeds. A dwarf variant of I, seen wild among cave-paintings in Spain, was the 'Shetland' pony, whose habitat first shrank to northern Scotland, then reexpanded in domestication over most of the civilized world. A giant variant of I is so far unknown.

Giant variants of II are readily produced in the wild, usually in swampy environments with abundant grazing. The tallest domestic races are largely an amalgam of II and III, and the only prehistoric horses of size comparable with these occurred in swampy lake country on the borders of the Alps (so-called Forest horse or Diluvial: a now unfashionable term is *Equus germanicus*). Since mobility is what the horse, wild or tame, is all about, outliers of every race will have been present within the territory of every other defined above. After domestication, the obvious partnership for a species of such propensities was with human tribes which were themselves nomadic, and whose capabilities as stockbreeders (say, of cattle) were greatly expanded by their adoption of the horse. These two facts account for such anomalies as the fact that Horse III, originally domiciled about Bactria, is today represented by a domestic race called the Sorraia, on the Spanish/Portuguese border. Of all living horses this most closely resembles the primeval III, warts and all, but also, paradoxically, it represents the principal element in the ancestry of the handsome Andalusian; while Horse III itself, despite the aesthetically unpleasing exterior described before, must have contributed through more than one channel to the ancestry of the Thoroughbred.

For the above reasons, among others, ascriptions of modern breeds to exclusive derivation from one of these types is impossible, and to hybrids of such is, to say the least, uncertain. If an attempt must be made, then:

European native ponies of the lighter types are either I or I × IV. Heavier pony type are either II × I or II. Heavy draught horses, including British and those in the entire region between Brittany and Jutland and south down the Rhine to the Danube region, are derived from the giant variant of II, with some element of III. It should be noted that both these primeval types had or could have the Roman nose characteristic of many heavy breeds. It has been explained as part of the apparatus for life in a cold climate, since the nasal passages being curved are longer, giving time to pre-heat the air slightly before it reaches the lungs. Horses native to China and the Pacific coast of Asia with its offshore islands are predominantly of type II. The Arabian horse can only be IV, despite the small size of the latter, with an admixture of III which ranges from the infinitesimal in the Seglawi to the perceptible in the Muniqi and despite a fundamentalist belief in the Separate Creation of the Arab horse, which surely may be discounted.

The Barb horse in its pre-Arabized form, however, must be of very different ancestry. As Wilfrid Scawen Blunt long ago observed, the fact that there are two desert breeds about the same size need not mean that both derive from the same aboriginal desert stock; indeed there are deserts and deserts, and the Barb probably derives, like the Andalusian, from III. The question whether or not there ever were wild horses in North Africa is no nearer solution now than fifty years ago when it was arousing such heated controversy, since the fossil evidence is nil, and that of prehistoric art enigmatic. If a positive answer should finally be proved on the basis of indisputable skeletal remains, the question would still remain: by what route did they arrive, and when? It is known that about 5000 years ago the climate of the Central Sahara was less (and in comparison with the Arabian desert much less) arid than now. Prehistoric rock pictures show cattle grazing where camels cannot live today and even such water-loving fauna as hippopotami are pictured on the walls of wadis in Tassili n'Adjer, dry these many centuries.

In any case there can have been but a small fringe horse population, since the south shore of the Mediterranean lay so far outside the original wild-horse habitat, as did Syria, that wild migration via Suez and Sinai seems unlikely. On the other hand, there were wild horses in Spain, but originally no wild asses. Now, the presence of occasional representations of asses, unquestionably of North African type, among Iberian rock paintings of the Old Stone Age, supports the theory that the present Strait of Gibraltar was passable from south to north. When this occurred, Iberian wild horses could have crossed into Africa. It would follow that the horse in Africa would be about as rare as the ass in prehistoric Spain, or only slightly less so since its reproduction rate is faster: eleven and not twelve months' gestation. It would also mean that the Barb and the Andalusian had substantially the same ancestry, and this is consistent with what is known of the conformation of both breeds in quite recent times, before the Arabizing of both at the demand of fashion in at least the upper price brackets.

It is worth remarking here that fashion is one of the most baneful factors working against the historian in this field, since it so often dictates both the suppression of the truth and the suggestion of the false in the matter of ancestry. But it requires a lot of Arab blood to put a high-set tail on the goose rump of the primeval Barb or the massive sloping croup of the real old 'Carthusian' Andaluz. It takes diligent enquiry among natives of the region to establish what the 'old-fashioned sort' really did look like. But in any domestic horse population kept on free range and not hand-fed or housed in winter, there will always be a proportion of brood mares of the original type. They alone are able to withstand the climate and live off the local food supply, which will not suffice to nourish the alien stallions introduced as 'improvers' or their cross-bred progeny. As Sir Berkeley Piggott has said of the New Forest,

which has been subjected to more than its share of extraneous stallions, the horse population is always 'ground down' by the weather, the soil and the vegetation to that type which alone can thrive in this environment. Half-breds with less than their share of local characteristics either perish in the first bad season or are sold away quickly. This is as true of Exmoor as of Siberia or of the Camargue.

Here is the point at which we must look back to the demonstrable conditions of primitive domestication and horse breeding. It is extremely unlikely that horses were first tamed by people who had not already got some other domesticated herbivores. The reason is the virtual impossibility, for dismounted men, of capturing alive and undamaged any but those foals too young to graze. Even then it is very difficult; it could perhaps be done by relays of men driving wild herds to the point at which young foals begin to drop out, exhausted. This has been done in this century, but much more easily, by mounted hunters employed to capture the foundation stock of the 150 or so Przevalsky horses now in the world's zoos. But the foals once captured would have to be suckled, which means the possession of tame nanny-goats, ewes, or perhaps reindeer does. With the single exception of the pig, all early domestication had as its object the supply of milk and the meat of the young, usually killed in the first autumn. Neolithic pictures on the rock-walls of Levantine Spain may be interpreted as an illustration of such horse-keeping. At this stage no males were kept in captivity, the herdsmen relying for reproduction on tethering the oestrous female at some spot where the wild male would come out of the forest or the desert or the marshes to cover her. A famous rock drawing from Ferghana in Bactria seems to show this happening; so do similar drawings (of asses) in the eastern desert of Egypt.

At this stage only fillies are kept beyond weaning time, and selection is for tractability. Large animals are not desired as they are too difficult to handle. Thus the first symptom of domestication is dwarfing, combined with a diminution in brain size and presumably intelligence, because the animal no longer has to think for itself, and the unpractised herdsmen cannot provide as well for the herd as it did for itself in freedom. Grass husbandry does not exist; hay is not made; other food there is none. When the pasture is eaten down, the tribe, human and animal, must move on, and there is usually a seasonal cycle of migration, often to summer pastures at a higher altitude. In the case of the reindeer the herdsmen are virtually the prisoners of their charges, bound to the same migratory cycle of the herds which prevailed before domestication. The moose (European elk) was certainly domesticated in early times in north Eurasia; moose-herders' lives were spent entirely in the forests, and only in those swampy forests with ponds in which grew the aquatic plants on which the elk feeds at certain seasons. As an alternative, the horse was a liberator and not a jailer of mankind, since it would willingly migrate in any direction in which grass grew. It seems likely that the earliest horse-herders were ex-reindeer-herders, who already rode reindeer before domesticating Pony II. But the truth of this assumption would not exclude the possibility of the independent domestication of other varieties of horse in other regions.

The syndrome which leads from mare and foal domestication to riding runs as follows: 1) packing tents, tools, etc., on quiet mares; 2) carrying lame, old, sick people, pregnant women and children too young to walk, on quiet mares; 3) carrying healthy but tired or idle men on the same conveyance; 4) able-bodied men riding fit animals.

At about stage 3 selection for tractability, and for small size, ceases to operate so stringently. When all the people can ride, the speed of the herd is not reduced to that of a man on foot, access to grazing is improved, and the animals grow bigger because they are better fed – though their brains do not grow back to the wild size.

Riding alone is characteristic of the earliest use of horses in the Central Asian region. Driving alone characterizes early stages in western Asia, using Horse IV (see p. 19). But the use of wheeled vehicles did not first arise among horse-nomads. The chariot derives from the pole and yoke ox-cart invented in Mesopotamia in the third millennium, probably not in its original form but as adapted by the Sumerians to be drawn by pairs of onagers. At some point where contact was made between horse-riding nomads from the north-east, the Sumerians were able to discard onagers, whose temperament seems to have been difficult, in favour of horses. This is when the chariot-driving era characteristic of all the great civilizations of the Near East, and consequently of classical Mediterranean Europe, begins.

Celtic Europe north of the Alps adopted the chariot either from Greek or from western Asiatic sources, and it was many centuries before the Celts rode. But everywhere in Europe the custom of riding demanded something bigger than the 11 or 12 h.h. pony which worked in pairs under the yoke. A contributory factor to riding was the impossibility, the further into Europe one went, of hunting from the chariot over rugged country, quite feasible, say, in the flat Euphrates plain, or even the Danube Valley. Significantly, one of the earliest and most striking European statuettes of the ridden horse is a little Iron Age equestrian group of figures mounted on a wheeled platform, the spearman riding after a wild boar: it comes from Merida in Spain, made perhaps at that stage in Celtiberian history when the Hallstatt culture was giving place to that of La Tène.

From this use of the ridden horse for hunting, the Celtic nobleman passed to its use in the other prestige-gaining occupation of his class. On the day when he defied tradition by leaving his war-chariot at home and mounting his tall (say, 14 h.h.) hunter to ride out to battle, the typical hero-figure of Atlantic Europe was born. We then entered what we may regard as the historical period, and a trend in Western culture leading directly to medieval chivalry began. This in its turn imposed yet another standard of selection on horse-breeders: from this point onwards, the bigger the better was the rule of the day.

Hippology

Jean Froissard

The horse, *Equus caballus*, is a monungulate mammal belonging to the equidae, of which only one genus survives in our time, consisting of six species. These vary from the domestic horse and the closely allied wild species *Equus przevalskii*, to the domestic ass and the wild asses of Africa, the hemiones or wild asses of Asia (onagers), and the three species of zebra. The relationship between *E. caballus* and the *true* wild horses is only sub-specific. But in popular parlance 'wild horses' fails to distinguish semantically between the latter and feral horses, such as the American Mustang descended from the escaped horses of the conquistadores and from runaways of every successive wave of equine immigration, or the Brumbies of the Australian outback.

The last authentic European wild horse (tarpan) died in Munich Zoo in 1870. At the beginning of the nineteenth century it was still fairly common in south-western Russia and eastern Poland. Specimens have been 'bred back' on more than one system of crossing ponies of 'primitive' physique in Germany, Poland and Russia.

If the Asiatic wild horse still exists, it is in a restricted area of Djungaria, near the frontiers of China, Mongolia and Russia, which is also the habitat of the Asiatic wild ass, specifically of the local race known as Kulan. This and other local races of onager or hemione which were formerly distributed as far west as Sinai, but now no farther west than the highlands of Persia, represent a compromise between the horse on the one hand and the African wild ass on the other: the smallest sub-races stand 12 h.h., the largest over 14 h.h.

The two species of African wild ass, the Nubian and the Somali, have become very rare, though formerly distributed over all Africa north of the Sahara. A few Nubian asses survive in the Sudan, slightly more of the other race in Somalia. They are the ancestors of the domestic ass, proved by the fact that the progeny of their cross-breeding with the latter is fertile, unlike the mule.

Zoologists disagree about the classification of races of zebra besides the extinct quagga. The Mountain zebra, now rare and confined to the south of the continent; Burchell's zebra, more widely distributed; and Grevy's zebra, the chief habitat of which is Ethiopia and Somaliland, and which most resembles the horse, are the three species most commonly recognized by English-speaking zoologists.

It is possible to trace the genus *Equus* back for sixty million years by the study of fossils, and it is remarkable that there are no gaps. The cainozoic era consists of the tertiary and quaternary periods, the first of which falls into five epochs, beginning with the most distant: palaeocene, eocene, oligocene, miocene, pliocene. The quaternary begins with the pleistocene, followed by what is known as the recent or holocene era in which we live. The pleistocene corresponds with the Ice Age, a million years before our time: that gives an idea of the timescale.

In the second stage of the tertiary period (eocene) the *eohippus* flourished. It is the most distant recognizable ancestor of the horse. Dog-sized, about 41 cm high, it had four toes in front, each of which ended in a hoof. These were the second, third, fourth and fifth digits,

The evolution of the skeleton of the foot

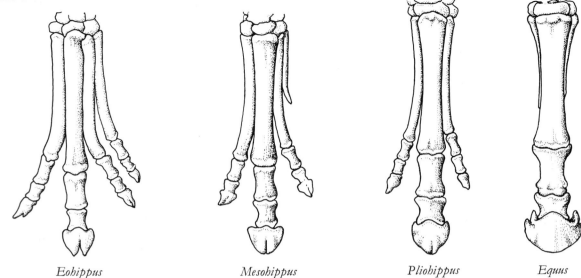

| *Eohippus* | *Mesohippus* | *Pliohippus* | *Equus* |

the first having already disappeared. On the hind limbs it had only three digits, the first and fifth having vanished. It is the third digit (middle finger) both before and behind, that is strongest and most important. This little creature lived in America and Eurasia until the middle of the eocene when it was replaced by the *orohippus* and by the *epihippus* at its end; the skeletal differences were not considerable. In the succeeding oligocene period we find *mesohippus*, which was rather larger than *eohippus* but which only had three toes all round, and had already begun to resemble a horse though it was only 61 cm high. From this *mesohippus* sprang many branches, of which *miohippus* most resembled the parent stock. Early in the miocene era we find *parahippus*, which was very similar to the preceding save that its teeth were considerably more horse-like. Those of *merichippus* were even further developed in the same direction, and it stood as high as 102 cm, but still had three toes, though only the middle one supported any weight. *Pliohippus*, with only one toe, appeared in the pliocene era, the remaining two toes being atrophied to the point where they no longer appeared outside the skin.

Late in the pliocene or early in the pleistocene, that is at the beginning of the quaternary era, *Equus* appeared. Not taking account of sundry migrations over this whole period of some sixty million years, all evidence points to North America as the cradle of the equine race, from which it disappeared completely some eight thousand years ago, not to return except in human company with the Spanish conquistadores.

The paces of the horse

A horse moves in three different ways: naturally, artificially and defectively. For convenience of study, the following are the most generally used terms:

Front pair: the two forelegs; back pair: the two hind legs; left lateral pair: left (near) fore and hind leg; right lateral pair: right (off) fore and hind leg; left diagonal pair: left (near) fore, right (off) hind leg; right diagonal pair: right (off) fore, left (near) hind leg.

A horse placing its hind foot in the print of the fore on the same side tracks up; if it places it further forward, it overtracks; or farther back, it undertracks. The hoofprint is the mark left by the foot on the ground; the track is the composite pattern of such prints and those of the hind feet ought to be on the same line as those of the fore on each side: the horse is then said to go straight on one track. If when moving in a straight line the print of the hind feet fall outside those of the forefeet the animal is said to 'walk in dog fashion'.

The stride is the amount of ground covered by a complete stride measured from tip to tip of successive prints of the same hoof. According to the amount by which the horse lifts its feet, the action may be low or high.

Natural paces

The walk is in four-time, each limb being separately moved; e.g., near fore, off hind, off fore, near hind.

The trot is a sprung pace, in two-time, with the weight alternately on each diagonal, with a pause between each double-beat, longer or shorter in accordance with the speed of the trot; the faster the trot the longer the horse is in suspension. A horse trots on the road at about 14 kph or 1 kilometre in 4 minutes. Maximum speeds in trotting races are of the order of 1 minute and 16 seconds per km. But note that at the racing trot there is a moment when the pairs are separated.

The canter is a swinging, sprung, unsymmetrical pace, in three-time, plus a moment of suspension. Unlike the walk and trot, which are symmetrical, the feet come to the ground in a different order according to whether the horse is leading with the off fore or near fore. When cantering to the left the order is: off hind, right diagonal, near fore, followed by a moment of suspension. Note that during the second beat (when the diagonal comes to the ground)the hind foot comes down very slightly before the forefoot, but the interval is so short as to be negligible. The average speed is 24 kph, with a stride spanning 3 to 4 m; racing speeds of 60 kph and upward involve strides of 8 m. The speed at all paces of horses moving at liberty can be measured in terms of their height at the withers. Thus at a walk the horse moves forward by the space of its own height in one second; at the trot by a space twice its height; at the canter four times its height, or up to ten times its own height in one second.

The gallop is a pace in four-time plus a mo-ment of suspension longer than that in the canter. Taking the same example of leading with the near fore, the order of footfalls is as follows: off hind, near hind, off fore, near fore. Note that the near hind is still on the ground when the off fore comes down and that the latter is still on the ground when the near hind is already in the air.

The rein back is a two-time walking pace in reverse, on successive diagonals.

Artificial paces

These are taught to the horse and in general are contrary to the physical mechanism. Although the horse will occasionally execute the passage and the piaffe by itself – the latter very rarely – these two paces, derived from the trot, may be styled artificial, since the rider can only produce them at will after prolonged training (see *High School: A Judge's View*). We should bear in mind the Spanish walk and trot, the canter on three legs, etc., all feats of the fantasia. The pace or amble is nowadays considered an artificial and defective way of going, though it was once widely cultivated throughout Europe, by a combination of breeding and training, and is now seen mostly in the Americas (see *The Story of Harness Racing in America*). If not purposely taught it is the result of a defensive measure by the horse to avoid engagement of the hind legs. At the pace or amble both feet on the same side move together in two-time; like the rack, it is much more comfortable for the rider than the trot. Other things being equal, pacers on the racetrack go faster than trotters.

The rack and its variants, fast and slow, known by the Anglo-American terms flat-footed walk, slow gait, running walk, the Hispano-American *paso fino*, etc., are all derived from the trot and pace, mostly a broken pace: they differ not only in speed but also in the height to which the feet are picked up and the length of stride. As in certain classes of show trotting, a high action can be imparted by feet grown long, very heavy shoes and, in training, weights attached to the pasterns, and even by some sorts of rather cruel operations.

Defective paces

Apart from the pace and the broken pace (dis-association of lateral pairs) mentioned above, there is a broken trot called foxtrot. Some draft horses, for reasons of fatigue, canter in front and trot behind, or occasionally do the reverse. There are, besides, defective forms of the gaits, for instance, dishing, in which the forelegs swing outward. Its opposite is the pigeon-toed gait. Forging derives its name from the noise caused by the hind toe striking the fore heel. A horse can injure itself, sometimes severely, by brushing, hitting one leg with the foot of the other; such treads are most common on the pasterns but also occur on the heels, most serious when reaching the point of speedy cutting.

There are faults peculiar to the gallop or canter, such as the disunited one in which the horse goes on the near fore and the off hind or vice versa. There is the four-time canter, in the second phase of which the pairs do not come together: this usually happens when the rider is trying to slow down excessively without due warning to the horse. There is the false canter, not exactly defective in itself, since the feet move in the right order, but running contrary to the balance of the horse when, on turning left it has to canter on the near fore, and vice versa, or run the risk of falling down if the pace is fast and the turn sharp. This is not to be confused with the counter-canter, a classical training exercise to set up the horse, rendering it supple and improving the balance.

To these various gaits, natural, artificial, defective, should be added rearing in which the horse raises its forehand off the ground, standing on its hind legs. This is a movement characteristic of the entire male, or used as a defence, when the horse is afraid, when the back is sore, or when the hocks hurt. Lashing out behind is almost the only means of self-defence the horse commands. The head is lowered to bring all the weight on to the fore-hand, the horse gathers the hind feet under the body and violently shoots them up and back. Buckjumping, a device to rid the horse of an unwanted burden (today rider or packsaddle, before domestication probably a large feline) is a leap in which the four legs are gathered under the body, the back is rounded, all four feet leave the ground together and the head goes down. This is sometimes done sportively, mostly by foals. These three motions have been stylized and exploited in the manège of the high school (see *High School*, p. 138).

The jump

This has three main phases: the rise (take-off), the summit (suspension), and the descent (landing). The raising of the forehand is preceded by one or two strides during which the horse makes ready by gathering up its forehand before rising; the hind legs, which have been brought well forward under the mass, drive the whole body strongly forward and upward. Once the shoulders are over the obstacle the head and neck are stretched forward and downward to tilt the hind quarters over the obstacle (summit phase). During the descent (landing), the head and neck are raised while the forelegs come down, followed by the hind legs, and the stride is resumed.

The foot and shoeing

Besides supporting the weight of the body, the foot also has to deaden the violent shock arising from the rapid motion characteristic of the horse. The foot consists of two principal parts: one internal, the other external, the latter being the hoof. This is composed of horny matter, having the form of a cylindrical box serving to protect the sensitive internal part. The outer surface of the wall is composed of periople which grows out from the perioplic ring around the coronet, from which the rest of the wall is also produced by continual growth; below (on the surface which is to the ground) are the sole and the frog. The internal parts consist of three bones, the second and third phalanxes and the navicular bone, which are jointed together to form the skeletal foot; the ligaments joining these bones; the tendons; lateral cartilages; and

The foot

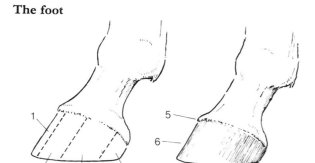

1 Toe; 2 Quarters; 3 Quarters; 4 Heel
5 Perioplic ring; 6 Wall

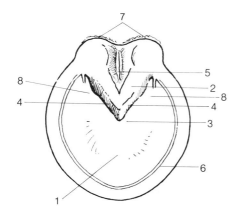

1 Sole; 2 Frog; 3 Apex of the frog; 4 Lateral
groove of the frog; 5 Central groove of the frog;
6 White line; 7 Bulbs of heel; 8 Bars

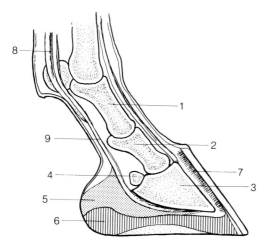

1 First phalanx or long pastern bone; 2 Second
phalanx or short pastern bone; 3 Third phalanx or
pedal bone or coffin bone; 4 Navicular bone; 5 Plantar
or digital cushion; 6 Corium; 7 Sensitive laminae;
8 Superficial flexor tendon; 9 Deep flexor tendon

the plantar cushion. Their main function is that of shock-absorbers, of which the external complement is the frog. The sensitive laminae spread out from in front of the pedal bone forming flanges separated by deep grooves corresponding to those on the internal surface of the wall. The whole forms a tissue rich in blood vessels surrounding the plantar cushion, the lower surface of the foot, which is the organ from which the sole and the frog grow: this is known as the corium. In order to act as a shock-absorber, the frog must come in contact with the ground and the heel must be open enough not to prevent the foot spreading as it takes the weight. Further, the hoof must not be too long or too short, otherwise the third phalanx will not be in its right position, which would cause additional fatigue and hence lesions dangerous to the tendons and to various parts of the foot. It is to the foot and adjacent parts that the deep and superficial flexor tendons are attached, as well as the suspensory ligament. The former is attached to the third phalanx; the second, to the second phalanx; and the third branches in two to join the two sesamoid bones.

The blacksmith has a double task: to prepare the foot by removing excessive horn-growth and level the bearing-surface ('trimming the hoof'); and to forge the shoe and fit it to the hoof, which is called 'hot-shoeing', or else simply to make the necessary adjustments to a ready-made shoe which is of the right size ('cold-shoeing'). Whether it is worn or not, a shoe should be taken off at least once a month in order to trim the hoof, since the horn grows $\frac{1}{4}$ in. (6 mm) in that time; if the old shoe is not worn it can be re-used, which is called a 'remove'. It is better not to cut into the wall of the hoof to receive the clip, and too much use should not be made of the rasp on the wall, because this exposes the ends of the horn tubes, which causes the horn to dry out or else to absorb too much water according to whether the going is wet or dry: either can have vexatious consequences.

There are many different kinds of shoe, quite apart from those used for remedial purposes. They can be classified as of plain iron

Shoes

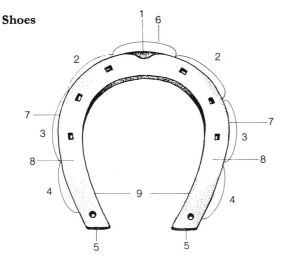

Left foreshoe – foot surface   1 Toe clip; 2 Inside and outside toe; 3 Quarters (inside and outside); 4 Inside and outside heel; 5 Heels; 6 Toe; 7 Outside edges; 8 Internal and external branches; 9 Inside edges

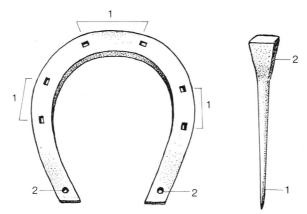

Left foreshoe – ground surface   1 Nail holes; 2 Screw holes for studs
Shoeing nail   1 Bevel; 2 Head

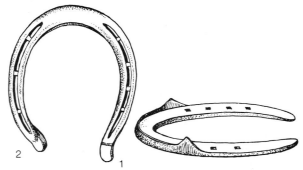

Hind shoe, fullered iron   1 Calkin outside; 2 Wedge inside
Hind shoe with side clips

or of fullered iron, the latter being lighter and affording a better grip. Often the inner branch is feathered, to avoid brushing. Hind shoes, of which the toes are not so rounded as in front shoes, are also longer: the practice of providing them with quarter clips is very widespread, as is that of rolling the toe, to avoid damage by forging (the hind toe striking the front heel). Very often in hind shoes the end of the outer branch is turned up in an outside calkin, while that of the inner branch is formed into an inside wedge. Finally, and especially for hunters, it is advisable to finish the foreshoes with heels, slightly bevelled or pencilled; this mitigates the risk of their being torn off by the toe of the hind shoe. Some shoes have threaded holes in them for fixing screw studs.

The white line which marks the junction of the wall with the sole also serves as a guide to the thickness of the former, and the points of the nails should enter along this line, never inside it. Coarse nailing, i.e., aiming the points too high, means pricking the sensitive 'quick'; while fine nailing bringing the points out too low, does not give enough purchase to the clench.

Colours and markings

Body colours

The principal colours are black, brown, bay and chestnut. Where there is any doubt as to the colour, the muzzle and eyelids should be carefully examined for guidance.

Black: Where black pigment is general throughout the coat, limbs, mane and tail, with no pattern factor present other than white markings.

Black-brown: Where the predominating colour is black, with muzzle, and sometimes flanks, brown or tan.

Brown: Where there is a mixture of black and brown pigment in the coat, with black limbs, mane and tail.

Bay-brown: Where the predominating colour is brown, with muzzle bay, black limbs, mane and tail.

English farrier's tools

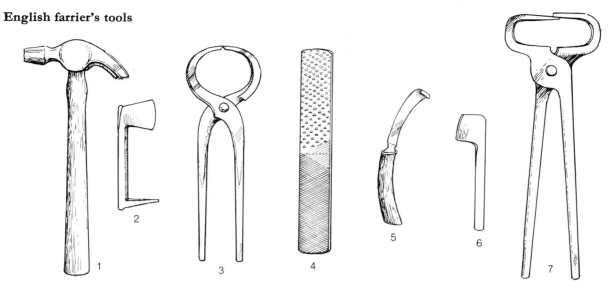

1 Driving hammer; 2 Buffer; 3 Pincers; 4 Rasp; 5 Drawing knife; 6 Toeing knife; 7 Hoof cutters

French farrier's tools

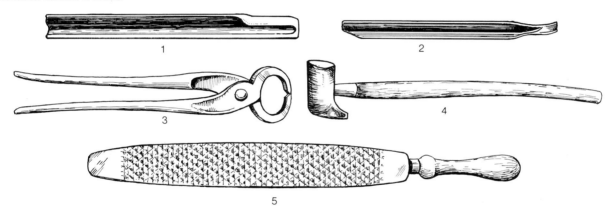

1 Rogne-pied (no equivalent in English); 2 Stamp; 3 Hoof cutters; 4 Driving hammer; 5 Rasp

Bay: Bay varies considerably in shade from dull red approaching brown, to a yellowish colour approaching chestnut, but it can be distinguished from the chestnut by the fact that the bay has a black mane and tail and almost invariably has black on the limbs.

Chestnut: This colour consists of yellow-coloured hair in different degrees of intensity, which may be noted if thought desirable. A 'true' chestnut has a chestnut mane and tail which may be lighter or darker than the body colour. Lighter-coloured chestnuts may have flaxen manes and tails.

Blue dun: The body colour is a dilute black evenly distributed. The mane and tail are black.

There may or may not be a dorsal band (list) and/or a withers stripe. The skin is black.

Yellow dun: Where there is a diffuse yellow pigment in the hair. There may or may not be a dorsal band (list), withers stripe, and bars on the legs. The striping is usually associated with black pigment on the head and limbs. The skin is black.

Cream: The body coat is of a cream colour, with unpigmented skin. The iris is deficient in pigment and is often devoid of it, giving the eye a pinkish or bluish appearance.

Grey: Where the body coat is a varying mosaic of black and white hairs, with the skin black. With increasing age the coat grows lighter in colour. As there are many variations according to age and season, all of them should be described by the general term 'grey'.

The flea-bitten grey may contain three colours or the two basic colours, and should be so described.

Roans: Roans are distinguished by the ground or body colours, all of which are permanent.

Blue roan: Where the body colour is black or black-brown, with an admixture of white hair, which gives a blue tinge to the coat. On the limbs from the knees and hocks down the black hairs usually predominate; white markings may be encountered.

Bay or *red roan:* Where the body colour is bay or bay-brown with an admixture of white hairs which gives a reddish tinge to the coat. On the limbs from the knees and hocks down the black hairs usually predominate; white markings may be encountered.

Strawberry or *chestnut roan:* Where the body colour is chestnut with an admixture of white hairs.

Piebald: Where the body coat consists of large irregular patches of black and of white. The line of demarcation between the two colours is generally well defined.

Skewbald: Where the body coat consists of large irregular patches of white and of any definite colour except black. The line of demarcation between the colours is generally well defined.

Odd coloured: Where the body coat consists of large irregular patches of more than two colours, which may merge into each other at the edges of the patches.

NOTE: The term 'whole coloured' is used where there are no hairs of any other colour on the body, head or limbs.

Head

Star: Any white mark on the forehead. Size, shape, intensity, position and coloured markings (if any) on the white to be specified. Should the marking in the region of the centre of the forehead consist of a few white hairs only it

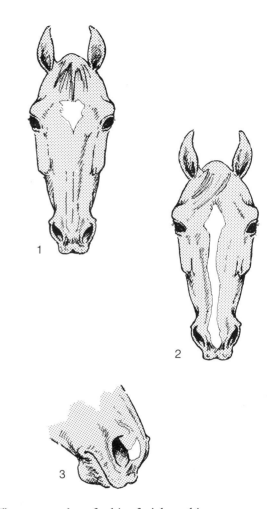

Three examples of white facial markings:
1 star; 2 stripe; 3 snip

should be so described and not referred to as a star.

Stripe: Many terms have been used to describe the narrow white marking down the face, not wider than the flat anterior surface of the nasal bones, e.g. rase, race, rache, reach, streak, stripe, strip, etc.

The Sub-Committee of the Royal Veterinary College recommend for the sake of uniformity that one term only be used and they select as being most useful for the purpose the term 'stripe'. In the majority of cases the star and stripe are continuous and should be described as 'star and stripe conjoined': where the stripe is separate and distinct from the star it should be described as 'interrupted stripe'; where no star

Overall spots, one example of the type of body colouring where small collections of hairs differing from the general body colour occur.

is present the point of origin of the stripe should be indicated. The termination of the stripe and any variation in breadth, direction and any markings on the white should be stated, e.g. 'broad stripe', 'narrow stripe', 'inclined to left/right'.

Blaze: A white marking covering almost the whole of the forehead between the eyes and extending beyond the width of the nasal bones and usually to the muzzle. Any variation in direction, termination and any markings on the white should be stated.

White face: Where the white covers the forehead and front of the face, extending laterally towards the mouth. The extension may be unilateral or bilateral, in which cases it should be described accordingly.

Snip: An isolated white marking, independent of those already named, and situated between or in the region of the nostrils. Its size, position and intensity should be specified.

Lip markings: Should be accurately described, whether embracing the whole or a portion of either lip.

White muzzle: Where the white embraces both lips and extends to the region of the nostrils.

Wall-eye: This term should be used exclusively where there is such a lack of pigment,

either partial or complete, in the iris as usually to give a pinkish-white or bluish-white appearance to the eye. Any other important variations should be noted.

Showing the white of the eye: Where some part of the white sclerotic of the eye shows between the eyelids.

Body

Grey-ticked: Where white hairs are sparsely distributed through the coat in any part of the body.

Flecked: Where small collections of white hairs occur distributed irregularly in any part of the body. The degrees of flecking may be described by the terms 'heavily flecked', 'lightly flecked'.

Black marks: This term should be used to describe small areas of black hairs among white or any other colour.

Spots: Where small, more or less circular, collections of hairs differing from the general body colour occur, distributed in various parts of the body. The position and colour of the spots must be stated.

Patch: This term should be used to describe any larger well-defined irregular area (not covered by previous definitions) of hairs differing from the general body colour. The colour, shape, position and extent should be described.

Zebra marks: Where there is striping on the limbs, neck, withers or quarters.

Mane and tail: The presence of differently coloured hairs in mane and tail should be specified.

Limbs

Hoofs: Any variation in the colour of the hoofs should be noted.

White markings on limbs: It is recommended that any white markings on the limbs should be accurately defined and the extent precisely stated, e.g. 'white to half pastern', 'white to below the fetlock', etc. The use of such terms as 'sock' and 'stocking' should be discontinued.

The teeth

The horse develops two sets of teeth: the temporary, milk or deciduous teeth and the permanent or persistent teeth. The former appear in the following order: centrals, laterals and corners. They are progressively replaced by the permanent teeth which come out in the same order. The milk teeth are smaller than the permanent ones. It may be said that between four and a half and five years all permanent teeth are present and in contact. A full set comprises forty teeth, twenty in each jaw: six incisors; two canines or tushes; twelve molars.

The spaces between the first molars and the last incisors are called the bars.

Mares do not usually have canines and thus generally have only thirty-six teeth.

At the age of seven the dovetail or hook appears. The last incisors (corners) of the upper jaw show at the back a broken line, the wear of this tooth not being equal along its full length.

A horse's age is easily and safely determined up to the age of five; first by the appearance of the milk teeth, then by their falling out and substitution of permanent teeth. From that age on, judgment is passed after particular examination of the incisors of the lower jaw. The table of the crown undergoes transformations as concerns shape and wear. The jaw itself changes gradually; the profile view of the incisive angle (formed by the incisors of both jaws), rounded in the young horse, flattens out with age.

Incisor teeth

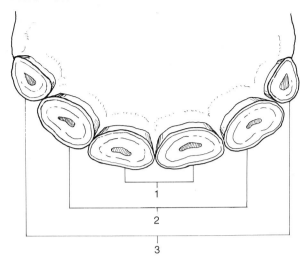

1 Centrals; 2 Laterals; 3 Corners

Section of incisor tooth

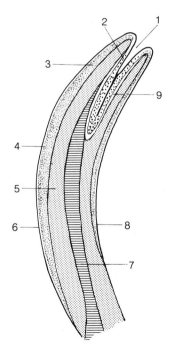

1 Infundibulum ('cup'); 2 Central cement; 3 External enamel; 4 Peripheral cement; 5 Dentine; 6 Front of tooth; 7 Central dentine; 8 Back of tooth; 9 Central enamel

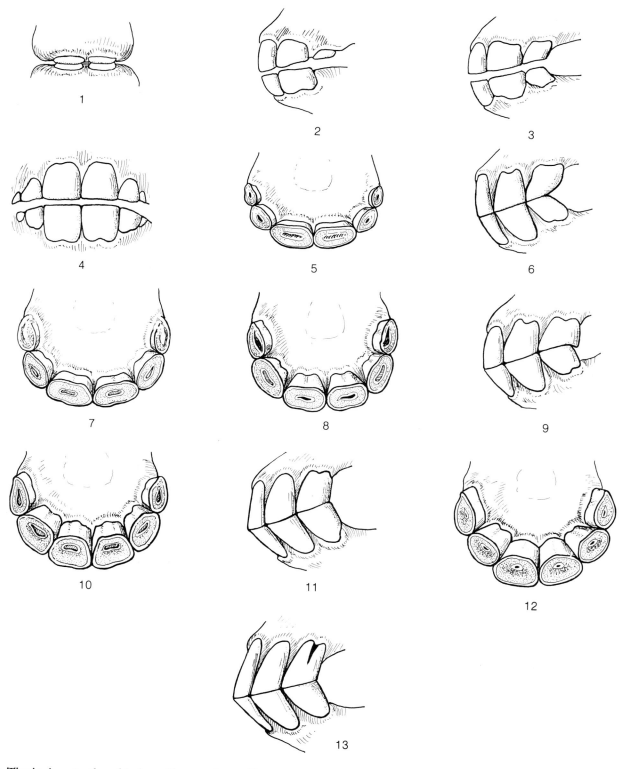

1 The incisor teeth at birth; 2 Six months; 3 Two years; 4 Three years; 5 Three years; 6 Five years;
7 Five years; 8 Six years; 9 Seven years. Note the notch or hook on posterior edge of top corner incisor tooth;
10 Seven years; 11 Ten years; 12 Ten years; 13 Fourteen years

Anatomy of the Horse

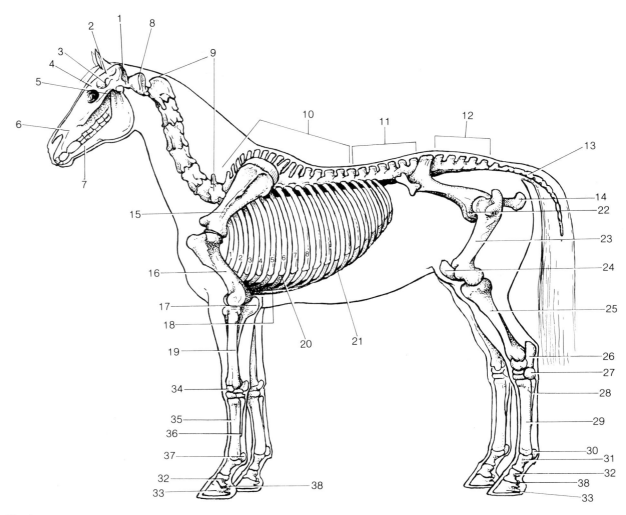

Skeleton of the horse

1 Occipital; 2 Parietal; 3 Temporal; 4 Frontal; 5 Zygomatic bone; 6 Upper jaw; 7 Lower jaw; 8 Atlas; 9 Cervical vertebrae (seven including atlas); 10 Dorsal vertebrae (eighteen); 11 Lumbar vertebrae (six or five); 12 Sacral vertebrae (five); 13 Caudal vertebrae (fifteen to eighteen); 14 Ischium; 15 Scapula; 16 Humerus; 17 Olecranon; 18 Sternum or breast bone; 19 Radius; 20 True ribs (eight); 21 False ribs (ten); 22 Ilium; 23 Femur; 24 Patella; 25 Tibia; 26 Os calcis; 27 Tarsus (including os calcis); 28 Small metatarsal bones or splint bones (two); 29 Large metatarsal bone or cannon bone; 30 Sesamoids; 31 Long pastern bone or first phalanx; 32 Short pastern bone or second phalanx; 33 Pedal bone or third phalanx; 34 Carpus; 35 Large metacarpal bone or cannon bone; 36 Small metacarpal bones or splint bones (two); 37 Sesamoids; 38 Navicular bone or 'shuttle bone'

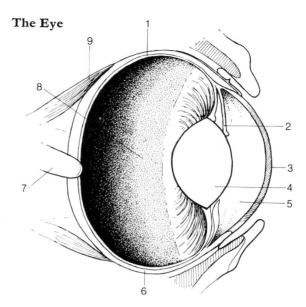

The Eye

1 Retina; 2 Iris forming the pupil; 3 Cornea;
4 Crystalline lens; 5 Front chamber; 6 Sclera;
7 Optic nerve; 8 Back chamber; 9 Muscles

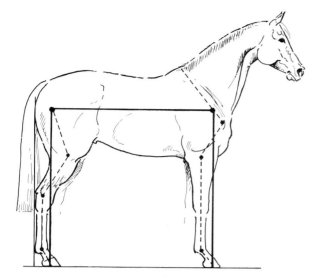

Perfect direction of the limbs, horse standing square and true

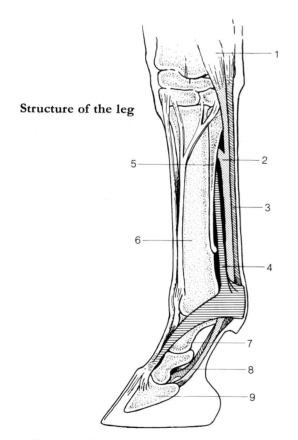

Structure of the leg

1 Muscle; 2 Deep flexor tendon; 3 Superficial flexor
tendon; 4 Suspensory liagment; 5 Splint bone.
6 Cannon bone; 7 Long pastern bone; 8 Short pastern
bone; 9 Pedal bone

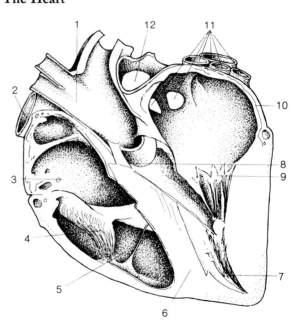

The Heart

1 Aorta; 2 Vena cava; 3 Right atrium; 4 Valves
between right atrium and ventricle; 5 Right ventricle;
6 Dividing septum; 7 Left ventricle; 8 Aortic valves;
9 Valves between left atrium and ventricle; 10 Left
atrium; 11 Pulmonary veins; 12 Pulmonary artery

The conformation of the fore limbs – side view

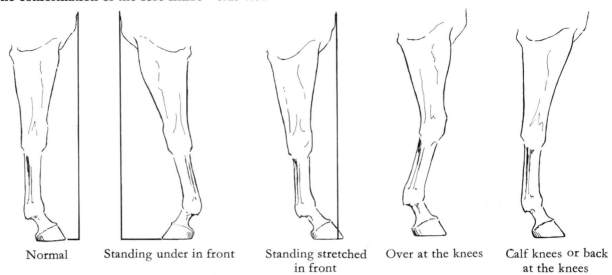

Normal   Standing under in front   Standing stretched in front   Over at the knees   Calf knees or back at the knees

The conformation of the fore limbs – front view

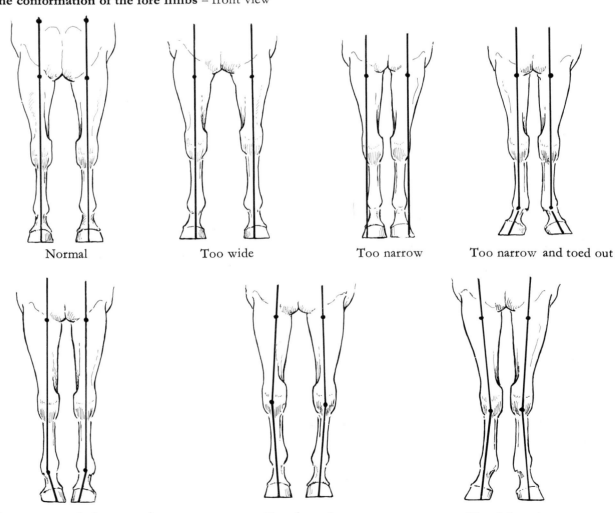

Normal   Too wide   Too narrow   Too narrow and toed out

Too narrow and pigeon-toed   Bow legged   Knock-kneed

The conformation of the hind limbs – side view

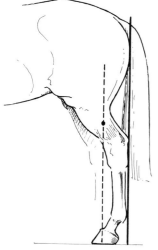

Normal

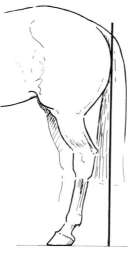

Standing under behind

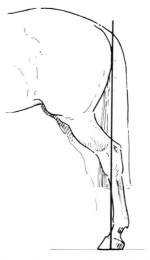

Standing stretched behind

Sickle hocks

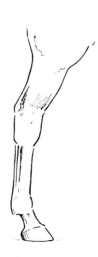

Hocks too straight

The conformation of the hind limbs – hind view

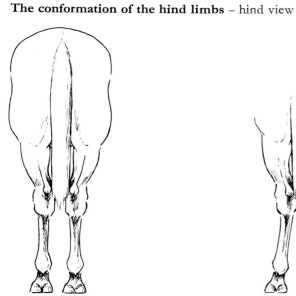

Normal

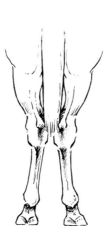

Cow hocks

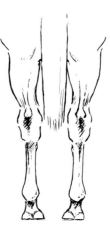

Bow-legged

Conformation of the foot

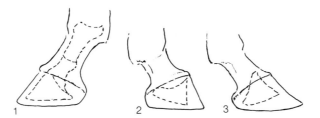 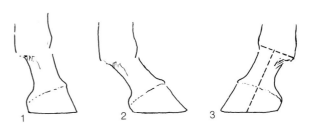

1 Normal; 2 Angle of toe too steep; 3 Toe too long

1 Upright pastern; 2 Sloping pastern; 3 Normal and correct slope

External locations of the principal blemishes

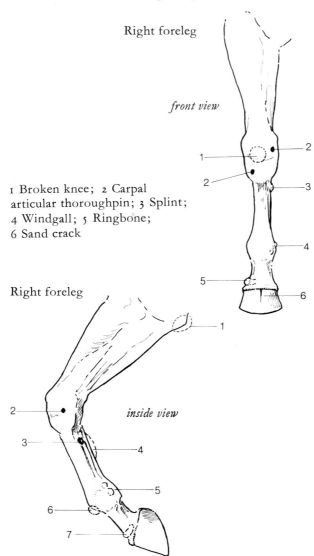

Right foreleg

front view

1 Broken knee; 2 Carpal articular thoroughpin; 3 Splint; 4 Windgall; 5 Ringbone; 6 Sand crack

Right foreleg

inside view

1 Capped elbow; 2 Carpal articular thoroughpin; 3 Splint; 4 Sprained tendon; 5 Windgall; 6 Hygroma at the fetlock; 7 Ringbone

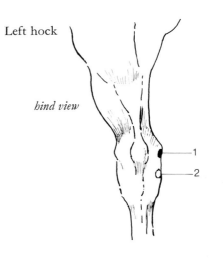

Left hock

hind view

1 Curb; 2 Bone spavin

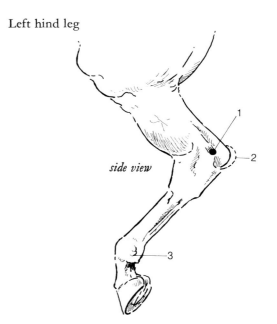

Left hind leg

side view

1 Thoroughpin; 2 Capped hock; 3 Windgall

Internal locations of the principal blemishes

Foreleg

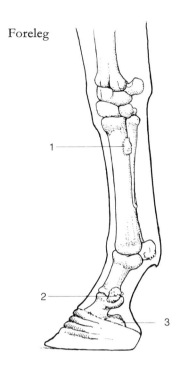

1 Splint; 2 High ringbone; 3 Low ringbone

Hind leg

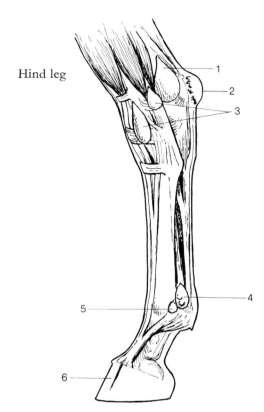

1 Tendinous thoroughpin; 2 Capped hock; ___
3 Articular thoroughpin; 4 Tendinous windgall;
5 Articular windgall; 6 Sand crack

Right hock

hind view

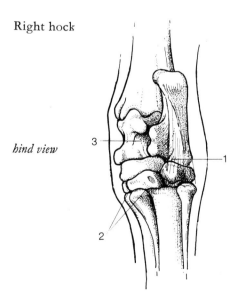

1 Curb; 2 Bone spavin; 3 Bog spavin (in front)

Right hock

inside view

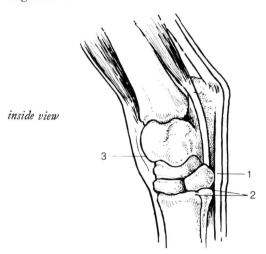

1 Curb; 2 Bone spavin; 3 Bog spavin

The points of the horse

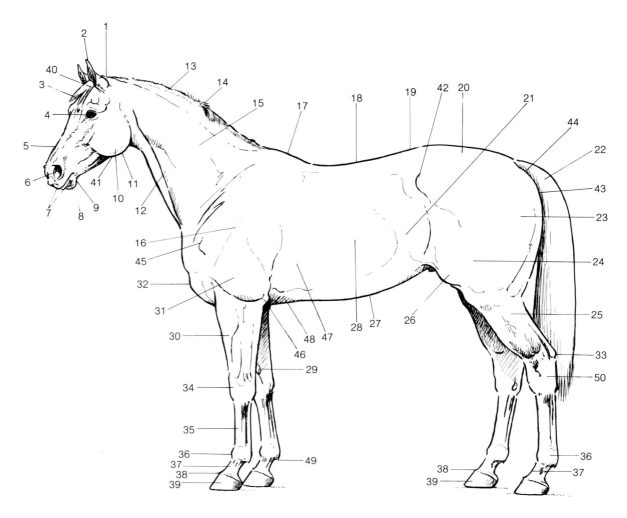

1 Poll; 2 Ear; 3 Forehead; 4 Eye; 5 Nose; 6 Nostril; 7 Lips; 8 Mouth; 9 Chin: 10 Cheek; 11 Lower jaw; 12 Jugular groove; 13 Crest; 14 Mane; 15 Neck; 16 Shoulder; 17 Withers; 18 Back; 19 Loins; 20 Croup; 21 Flank; 22 Tail; 23 Buttock; 24 Thigh; 25 Gaskin or 'second thighs'; 26 Stifle; 27 Belly; 28 Ribs; 29 Chestnut; 30 Forearm; 31 Arm; 32 Breast; 33 Point of hock; 34 Knee; 35 Cannon bone; 36 Fetlock; 37 Pastern; 35 Coronet; 39 Hoof; 40 Forelock; 41 Vascular groove; 42 Point of hip; 43 Point of buttock; 44 Dock; 45 Point of shoulder; 46 Elbow; 47 Chest; 48 Brisket; 49 Ergot; 50 Hock

Ailments and Unsoundness of Horses

Dr Peter D. Rossdale

Horses are kept for a purpose. If they suffer disease or injury which interferes with that purpose they are unsound. Unsoundness, which may be permanent or temporary, can be discussed under the headings of: 1) Physical injuries; 2) infectious diseases; 3) parasitic infestations; 4) non-infective conditions; 5) genetic and predisposing factors; 6) environmental factors.

Physical injuries

These may be extrinsic as in cuts, bruises, burns, firing (cautery) and irritant blisters, or intrinsic as in sprain of a ligament, tendon or muscle. Injuries to bony structures (arthritis, osteitis and periostitis) are recognized by horsemen as swollen joints, ringbone, splints and sore shins. Fractured bones cause great pain until their ends are firmly united by a bridging callus.

Sprains result from tearing of small fibres. For example, a sprained tendon or ligament consists of a number of broken fibres, and periostitis of a tearing of the fibres in the periosteum, the fine membrane that covers the outside of bone.

These injuries are caused by excessive tension imposed by a sudden abnormal movement, as in stumbling or where the limb's normal function is altered by muscular fatigue. Repetitive strain may occur where a part is consistently used abnormally, such as if the conformation is faulty. For example, splints often result from excessive concussion transmitted,

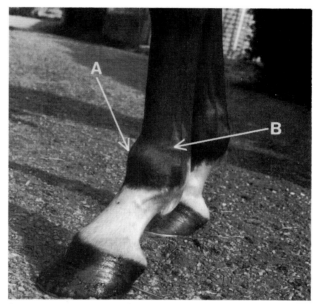

A three-year-old filly showing evidence of arthritis of the left fetlock joint, with a swelling at A (osselets) and an articular windgall at B.

abnormally, through the inner or outer aspect of the cannon bone.

Sprains and similar injuries invoke the body's inflammatory response. This is an increase in blood flow to the injured part, bringing with it special cells to deal with the damaged tissue. Inflammation is associated with heat, swelling, pain and redness, though the latter may not be apparent in animals because of the hair covering the skin. Pain causes a change in behaviour, recognized as lameness. This interferes with normal function and may therefore reduce the individual's capacity to fulfil the desired purpose; i.e., it is unsound.

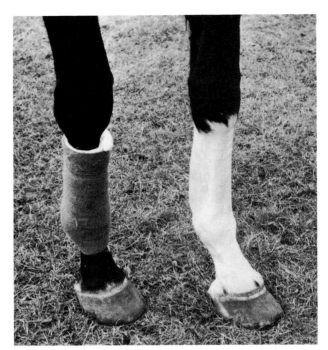

Sprained superficial flexor tendon on left fore limb, causing swelling at back of cannon bone between knee and fetlock.

The treatment of physical injuries depends on their nature and the structures involved. In general injuries to bones, tendons and ligaments require rest, such as afforded by confinement to a loose box, whereas injury to muscle may be best treated with controlled exercise. In all cases measures to reduce the inflammation and promote healing should be applied. Alternate applications of hot and cold, by means of poultices and electrothermia (short-wave inductothermia, etc.) for heat, and ice-packs, freezing lotions and cold water hosing for cold, are recommended. Cortisone and other anti-inflammatory drugs (phenylbutazone-Bute-, oxyphenbutazone, etc.) help to reduce pain and restore normal function.

Infectious diseases

Horses are surrounded by microbes, which are microscopic animals or plants called bacteria, virus or fungus. The body's natural resistance deals with these potentially harmful micro-organisms by making it difficult for them to enter. Beneath the skin and mucous membranes lining the body cavities, such as the mouth and vagina, special blood cells produce protective substances (antibodies) which cause the microbes to clump together or break up. White blood cells 'consume' bacteria and fungus, eliminating them from the tissues. Viruses may be neutralized by special substances present on the outside of the cells. All these processes are part of the body's immunity or resistance to infection. But the situation is not one-sided and microbes vary in their capacity to cause infection and disease; i.e., to overcome the body's resistance.

Common infectious diseases of horses caused by bacteria are strangles, salmonellosis, lymphangitis, tetanus and summer pneumonia of foals and venereal infection (klebsiellosis). Conditions once prevalent but now relatively rare include tuberculosis and glanders.

Bacteria are also responsible for pus found in abscesses, the nasal discharge (catarrh) in snotty nose, pneumonia, peritonitis, pleurisy, cystitis (infection of the bladder) and metritis (infection of the uterus). These infections are often secondary to viral infection, injury such as wounds or damage caused by migrating parasites.

Viral conditions include influenza (epidemic cough), arteritis (pink eye) and infections of the respiratory tract characterized by occasional cough, watery nasal discharge, pneumonia and bronchitis. These are caused by rhino- and reo-viruses and certain members of the group herpes (rhinopneumonitis) which occasionally cause abortion. Virus is also responsible for Western, Eastern and Venezuelan encephalomyelitis (inflammation of the brain), African horse sickness, infectious anaemia, coital exanthema (spots) and warts.

Fungus is responsible for skin infections such as ringworm, rain scald and certain types of heel bug. Allergy to fungal spores is the basis of broken wind (heaves, chronic pulmonary emphysema).

New-born foals are particularly vulnerable to bacterial and viral infections because they are

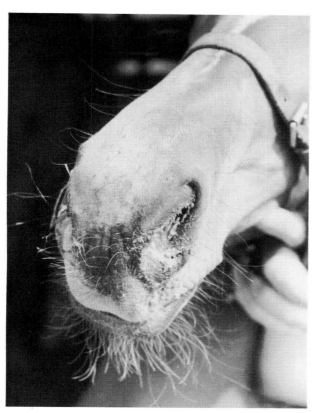

'Snotty nose' (catarrhal) condition caused by virus infection.

which they occur. Antibiotic drugs help to combat bacterial infections and ringworm, but are not usually effective against virus. Cortisone may help to reduce the effects of viral disease but has no specific action against the virus itself. Specific serums are sometimes used but vaccines to prevent disease are better. Vaccines can protect against tetanus (lockjaw), strangles, viral encephalomyelitis, herpesvirus I (rhino-pneumonitis), abortion, influenza and African horse sickness. Vaccines act by stimulating the body to produce protective substances (antibodies), but they must be used annually or bi-annually to give continuing protection.

Parasitic Infestations

A parasite is an animal or plant which lives at the expense of another, on the skin (ecto-parasites) or inside the body (endo-parasites). Parasites may live all or only part of their lives on or in their equine host.

Ecto-parasites such as lice, ticks and mange or harvest mites irritate and cause loss of hair, weeping sores and scabs. These infestations respond to treatment with derris, gamma benzene hexachloride or other parasiticidal lotions and powders.

The chief endo-parasites of the horse are red worms. These are nematode worms belonging to the strongyle group. Their life cycle consists of free living forms (larvae) which develop from the eggs passed in the horse's faeces on to the pasture. After a period of development these larvae are ready to infect their equine host. The horse swallows the larva which enters the small intestine. Here it develops further before reaching adult maturity, when the female lays eggs. The eggs pass out in the faeces thus completing the cycle. The most harmful member of the group is *Strongylus vulgaris* because the larvae wander through the blood vessels of the gut, sometimes causing loss of condition and fatal colic. The larvae of *Strongylus edentatus* migrate into the peritoneum and may cause similar trouble. Adult strongyles

born without immunity. But they gain immunity from the mare's first milk (colostrum) which contains protective substances (antibodies). These are absorbed into the foal's blood stream through its stomach during the first twenty-four hours of life. For various reasons this transference may not occur. The foal is then vulnerable to infection for two or three months, before it can develop active immunity by responding to contact with microbes, in the same way as the body responds to infection of the vaccine. As a foetus, it is protected from microbes because most of them cannot cross the placental barrier even though the mare may be infected. Exceptions are herpesvirus I (rhino-pneumonitis) infection and certain bacterial and fungal infections of the placenta. Infection during foetal life may cause abortion, or illness in the first few days after birth.

Infections must be treated according to the particular causal microbes and the positions in

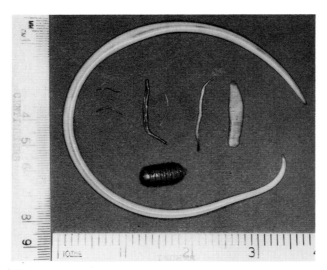

Some common parasites of the horse: a white worm surrounds and, from left to right: small red worms, large red worm (strongyles), a seat worm, a tape worm and below: a bot fly maggot.

Bot flies (*Gasterophilus* species) attach their eggs to the horse's coat. The horse licks off the eggs which then hatch and develop into maggots in the stomach. The maggots which cling to the stomach lining can ulcerate or even rupture the organ. In summer the maggots leave the stomach and pass out in the faeces, hatching into flies to complete the life cycle.

Warble flies (*Hypoderma bovis*) are really cattle parasites, but sometimes they lay eggs on horses. The eggs develop into maggots which crawl beneath the skin to reach the back, from where they emerge in summer. They cause painful abscesses, usually in the saddle region.

Non-infective conditions

Colic is a common condition in horses. They sweat, paw the ground, get up and down, lie on their backs and roll. This is because they feel pain as a result of some disturbance in the gut. There are many different types and causes of colic, ranging from a simple stoppage consisting of dry food to a fatal twist of the gut or damage to its wall. Some colics are caused by migrating red worm larvae, and others by improper diet. Treatment is based on a diagnosis of the type of colic. A simple stoppage is treated by fluid and 'softening' substances introduced through a stomach tube; twists must be relieved surgically. In all cases pain-relieving drugs are injected.

Liver disease may be caused by parasites, toxic substances in poisons and poisonous plants, anaesthetics or other drugs. Signs include wasting, poor appetite and/or diarrhoea.

Heart disease usually consists of damaged valves or inflammation of the heart muscle. Coronary thrombosis is rare. Heart conditions in horses are seldom so severe as to cause serious disability or even death. Their effect on athletic performance is usually a matter of debate in each particular case, due to the difficulties in diagnosis and the heart's ability to adapt. For example, the heart may increase its pumping power to overcome the conse-

live in the large colon and caecum, where they feed from the gut wall, causing small haemorrhages, ulcers, and irritation. They may be responsible for anaemia and diarrhoea, especially in foals.

Strongyle infestation can be treated with thibendazole, mebendazole, phenothiazine and other anthelmintics. These drugs are effective only on the adult forms living in the gut and do not kill the larval stages in the blood vessels or peritoneum.

White worms (*Ascaris equorum*) live in the small intestine, where the females lay eggs which pass out in the faeces. The eggs are swallowed by a new host and hatch into larvae which penetrate the liver. After passing through the lungs they migrate up the windpipe to the throat, from where they are swallowed to reach the small intestine. Here they complete the cycle by developing into adults. White worms affect the horse only if present in excessively large numbers. They may cause digestive disturbances, colic and diarrhoea. The larval forms can damage the liver and lungs but in general this applies only to foals and, especially, yearlings. Older horses appear relatively immune to this type of infestation.

quences of a leaking valve which might otherwise make the organ less efficient.

Urinary disease is comparatively uncommon, although bladder stones may occur in geldings and occasionally in mares and stallions. Nor are horses particularly prone to tumours. The most common tumours are warts of the simple (milk) variety and their more serious counterpart the angleberry (sarcoid). Grey horses suffer from pigmented tumours (melanomata). Ovarian tumours occur in Thoroughbreds and cause infertility if not removed surgically.

Dental disease is uncommon and horses' teeth rarely suffer from decay but sometimes the angle of growth causes sharp edges which need attention.

Laminitis and allergic conditions may be responsible for lameness, swollen legs or nettle-rash-type swellings on the skin (urticaria).

External or internal injuries of the eyeball may produce cataracts with partial or complete loss of vision. Moon blindness (periodic ophthalmia) is a condition in which repeated attacks of increasing severity affect the eyes, often ending in blindness. The cause is unknown although infection with worms, bacteria or virus has been suggested.

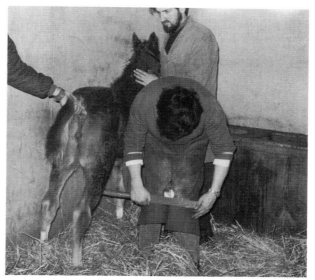

Proper attention to the feet may help avoid limb injuries due to bad conformation. Here a foal at Derisley Wood Stud, Newmarket, receives the farrier's attention for the first time.

skin (photosensitization); and some are prone to the effects of parasitic and microbial infections. A susceptibility may be inherited and act through conformation or gait, as is frequently the case in leg unsoundnesses, especially those involving sprains of the superficial and deep flexor tendons.

Genetic and predisposing factors

Some conditions may be directly inherited. Others are congenital in that they arise from defects in development brought about by the environment during foetal life. For example, they are caused by virus, bacteria, malnutrition or drugs which affect the foetus.

However, many horses become unsound because they are basically susceptible to conditions which affect them during early or adult life. For example, faulty conformation of the mare's vulva and perineum does not cause infertility, but it may allow air to enter the genital tract, setting up infection and so causing infertility; some horses with white markings are prone to inflammatory conditions of the

Environmental factors

Abuse of function may cause trouble in any system. The horse's body is no exception. Its form and structure evolved over many millions of years to meet special needs: namely those of speed and size in order to outrun its enemies. Its eating habits and digestive system adapted to meet the relatively hard fibrous diet on which it was forced to feed. We cannot change the basic needs nor distort the true function of the body without imposing strains which lead to disease and unsoundness. The horse is equipped for a certain type of environment, a particular way of life; alter this too drastically and the weakest link in the chain may snap.

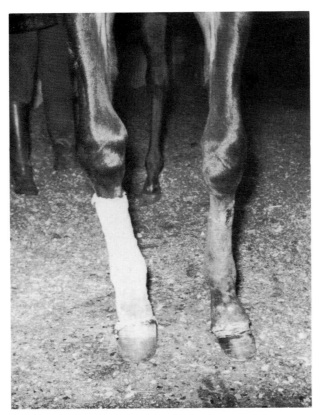

Significant factors in the environment include methods of feeding and the diet, pasture management, shelter, over-concentration leading to parasitic, bacterial or viral infections and, just as important, the way we use the horse for work. A man on its back and a control of its actions imposes unnatural stresses which the body was not evolved to meet. These forces inevitably result in injury and limit the purposes to which we put the horse.

Diseases in which management plays a decisive role are red worm infestation, rickets and other bone diseases based on malnutrition, certain types of diarrhoea in foals and adults, bacterial and viral epidemics, broken wind and lymphangitis. Conditions directly or indirectly related to management include sprained tendons and ligaments, torn muscles, laminitis and many forms of dermatitis.

A yearling with bowed forelegs due to faulty nutrition.

Horse Breeding

Dr Edouard Pouret

The horse has followed in the trail of every great human migration. Allied to man in all his triumphs of war, one may say that the modern horse is the product of Mediterranean civilization. Some Central Asian breeds first made up the nucleus used by man, but it was oriental horses, Arabians, and Barbs, which invaded all Europe when the barbarians finally overran the Roman Empire.

The Crusaders of the twelfth and thirteenth centuries, mounted on horses which were a cross between oriental and north European strains, were in a position to bring back to western Europe swift eastern horses. They had long passed the stage where the horse was regarded as a wild animal that could be tamed. It had become the means of locomotion and it remained so until the nineteenth century, not being finally replaced by the internal combustion engine until the twentieth century.

The only true wild horses to survive by then were on the borders of Mongolia and Asiatic Russia, discovered in 1870 by Przevalsky and bearing his name.

The horse is the only animal that has been able to adapt itself to all climates without difficulty and still remains the servant of man. Better still, it has adapted itself physiologically without loss of strength or willingness to very limited areas compared with the open spaces of its ancestors.

This result has been achieved by simple breeding methods which we call traditional because they are based on human experience and orally transmitted from one generation to the next by men who knew how to make use of this knowledge. Those societies that were unable to pass on this lore or were ignorant of it, were invaded and colonized by others, and their own civilization was erased.

Nevertheless, all stages of this progressive knowledge may be observed universally today, for in all countries there are breeders who let their horses go back to more or less a state of nature, while at the same time other breeders use the most scientific methods.

The horse is a herbivore by nature and under wild conditions selects the kind of pasture that suits him. One is forced to think that the early and wide ranging migrations by mounted peoples, who did not encounter at every stage the grazing they required, compelled them to have recourse to some portable form of horse feed. Grain was the only one which could be carried by the individual horseman or by a packhorse, or by a wagon which followed. Thus it was discovered that hard grain feeds gave better energy and that oats and barley were the best feed for the horse.

When they passed through countries where grain was grown for human and animal consumption and hay was made to keep stock over the winter, then the conquering nomads could survive on local resources and 'live off the country'.

In more recent times scientific research has been brought to bear on breeding, and thus between 1920 and 1940 much work was done on quantitative production, and actually other investigations are carried out on glandular functions, bacteriology as it affects reproduction, and other aspects of physiology.

Since 1940 research has borne on qualitative production of horses, it is now understood that no time must be lost in enabling the high-performance horse to develop as rapidly as possible within the bounds which nature has set by his genetic inheritance.

Research technique, therefore, is exerted on every aspect that may increase the strength and early development in breeds that are kept for racing, etc., and on all that may keep down the cost of production in stock that is bred for common work in harness or under the saddle.

Quantitative production

The horse in modern times is genetically an immigrant, inhabiting countries where soil and climate are utterly different from those of the cradle of the race. Acclimatization implies also providing for his needs according to the place, the altitude, the humidity, the rainfall, the temperature, etc. Moreover, he is only permitted to breed during a short part of the year which may or may not coincide with the equally limited breeding season of wild ancestors; bad climate or dietetic conditions inhibit the capacity of the horse to breed.

There is a characteristic female standard of desirable points varying from breed to breed, but there is an overall feminine make and shape which can be judged by eye. The head should be small, the body long, there should be breadth from hip to hip, the mane and the skin should be fine, and the disposition gentle. The male type presents contrasting characteristics: but mare and stallion must have in common a good development of the external genital organs.

Selection by performance does not necessarily correspond to selection for quantitative production; on the contrary. Athletic characteristics often fail to coincide with those required for quantitative reproduction. It is worth while to remark that the influence of sporting events on reproduction is unfavourable, at least as regards females.

Efforts demanded on the racecourse tire out the organism and are evidently a handicap for present or potential breeding stock. We should therefore not be surprised to find that great performers are not necessarily great sires and dams.

Quantitative production can be expressed in percentages, which can be good or bad for a series of factors which are cumulative.

In every country some districts are more favourable for breeding than others. This may apply either to the nature and quality of the topsoil or the acreage of ground available for breeding.

Good health of mares and stallions is a *sine qua non*.

Parasitism is undoubtedly Reproductive Enemy Number One, for it debilitates the animals, exhausts them, and leads to intestinal troubles.

Horses are subject to microbic or viral ailments; some can be avoided through vaccination. Soil may be deficient in an incalculable number of trace elements such as iodine, magnesium, iron, cobalt, copper, potassium, manganese, etc. Man also has been responsible for forced reproduction of bad producers. It is admitted that bad quantitative reproduction is heritable. When horses were bred on free range – wild – the bad breeders were eliminated by natural forces. Nowadays, by different treatment, it is possible to correct cases of sterility, and to use shy breeders.

In our day we have a conception of management which implies the co-ordination of all methods of quantitative production and of all elements capable of improving the conditions of life of the animals, their feeding and state of health.

Gynaecological care

It is necessary to prepare the next covering season by an examination of all barren and maiden mares at the beginning of October, for the percentage of mares in foal next spring will be just as high among mares now barren or not yet covered as among mares in foal on 1 October.

Empty mares and maiden fillies are examined and classified. The maidens are listed as normal, as slow developers (that is, those which will be in foal, but late, next season), as difficult maidens whose percentage of fertility is doubtful, or as 'impossible maidens' whose development does not allow reproduction yet.

Empty mares are classified as follows: 1) normal barren mares up to twelve or fourteen years old; 2) normal old mares over twelve or fourteen years old; 3) mares which demand special care as the result of bacteriological infection; 4) mares which are bacteriologically infected and which cannot be treated with any prospect of success; 5) infected mares needing complicated or expensive treatment but with whom, as they have already produced very good horses, the impossible must be attempted.

One must take into account the fact that the older a mare is the slimmer are her chances of conceiving. Five-year-old maidens will be in foal in more than ninety per cent of cases, whereas twenty-year-old mares will be in foal in five to ten per cent of cases.

This classification of barren and maiden mares is a great saving to owners, for bringing them to a first-class stallion is an expensive business. One must know in advance which mares have the best chance of conceiving in order to send them to the best horses.

It is at this October season that maximum care is taken and all measures put in hand for the successful running of the next covering season.

It is sometimes necessary in December or January to re-examine the mares about which there is doubt in order to draw up the final list of mares to be covered.

These lists have been drawn up the previous autumn, after the examination of a veterinary surgeon expert in palpation of the ovaries, of the genital organs, and the inspection of the vaginal cavity. It is an enormous advantage to be able to palpate the ovaries through the rectum. It gives as well an idea about the shape and tonicity (quality of fibres) of the uterus, the consistence of the ovaries, the formation of follicles that will produce ova.

Examination of the vaginal cavity permits the observation of colour, traces of infection, inflammation or dilation. The surgeon can also determine by palpation of the ovaries whether ova are developing in the ovaries or not. He can forecast within a few hours when ovulation will take place: that is, the moment when the ovaries send eggs into the uterus. This last is very important because it allows one to spare the stallions by presenting them only with mares whose chances of conception are good. Such gynaecological tests should not be too frequent since they are not always necessary and may hinder ovulation. A good method is to examine the mare on the seventh day after parturition, and at the same time the organs can be checked for possible lacerations or other birth injuries.

Stud work

In order to find out which mares to bring to the stallion, the stud grooms confront each mare with a teaser, to whom she will indicate her own wishes in this respect.

Men entrusted with this task must have experience and ability to judge the mare's psychology, and take into account her possible shyness and determine whether or not it is time to bring her to the stallion.

The stallion is in the charge of the stallion-man, who must take great care of the valuable horse entrusted to him, know his needs with regard to exercise and feeding and be well aware of his good health. It is his duty to lead the stallion when he is serving the mares alloted to him.

The stallion-man should have a good idea of equine hygiene and be ready to wash the horse's genitals before and after every service to avoid the possibility of bacteriological infection of the horse or the contagion to other mares.

The foal

Foaling generally takes place at night, and several rules must be followed. There must be a minimum of noise, and the groom in charge

Mares and foals at grass.

of foaling must be calm, gentle with the mares, and helpful in an intelligent way. Hygiene is extremely important at birth, both for the safety of the foal and of the mare. A foal at birth weighs nearly a hundred pounds and the weight of the foal plus the placenta and the liquids it contains comes to 180 to 200 lb. It is thus a vast cavity that is being emptied, and this must not be reached by germs from the outside. The stud groom in attendance should also take note of tearing or lesions of the genital organs that may occur at birth and know if it is necessary to call for help or to call the veterinary surgeon in case of difficulty.

Veterinary surgeons working in studs are not only gynaecologists and obstetricians but also consultants on the general running of covering, knowing at which moments the stallions should be spared or used frequently.

They should also be able to perform a quick fertility test or to give a firm opinion whether or not a mare brought for service is capable of conception. The stud staff must have confidence in him.

He also practises diagnosis of pregnancy by examination of the uterus, as well as carrying out biological tests.

The stud veterinary surgeon in his advisory capacity is very important in relation to the in-foal mares since while at work in the stud he may notice that their fare is not right for pregnant females, or that one or another looks a little off colour. In the case of an abortion he should be alerted at once, in order to make an instant check for contagious abortion. This is of crucial importance, for many a breeder has been brought to ruin by contagious abortion, and the veterinary surgeon must decide what to do and the enquiries to be pursued. The feeding of in-foal mares has been the subject of much study by specialists. It is impossible to give an exhaustive list of indispensible nutritional minima for the good formation of the foetus or the good health of the mare.

The care of the new-born foal is equally important; the utmost cleanliness should be observed, and the quarters housing it should be meticulously disinfected. The state of its bowels should be minutely observed in the hours following birth to find out whether or not it is eliminating the black embryonic faeces known as meconium. In some countries it is customary to give an antitetanus injection automatically. In any case the foal should be under continuous observation by the staff of the stud. As an individual the infant horse is closely examined: the eyes, ears and, especially, the limbs, so as to determine their normal or abnormal conformation and the possible means of correction. The new-born foal may be plagued by all sorts of ailments requiring the attention of a veterinary surgeon. During delivery it may have remained too long in the genital canal, resulting in respiratory troubles or lesions on limbs, chest or abdomen. Prenatal infection is also possible, and this can be observed at the moment of birth or in the few hours or few days after it. Such infections may affect the umbilical cord, the intestine, or the nervous or articular system.

Qualitative production in the horse

Many of the points raised hitherto have their bearing on qualitative production, for we have already said that ill health in the mare did not favour quantitative output, but it is certain that good health favours qualitative output.

Basic breeding method, the outlook of the breeder, the grazing in its quality and exposure to sunlight etc., the feed, the fencing, the morale of the horses, veterinary and technical resources, the eradication of sickness and systematic prophylaxy; all are factors as important for quantity as quality. Equally, methods of selection, pedigree, and the right matching of sire and dam produce the same effects.

But the great point to emphasize in qualitative production of horses is that after making the best choice of pedigree on the side of sire as of dam, and after assuring the best possible conditions of parturition, so that a totally healthy foal is born from a perfectly fed mare, the problem is still not solved; because we have to maintain the optimum growth-rate for the foal from birth onwards to the moment when he goes into training, and here again the best possible methods of nutrition must come into play if the young horse is to develop to the maximum extent possible within the limits of his biological potential.

A good racehorse is one that can run faster than others of the same age. It is time we found out to what extent precocious horses and the great racehorses of recent years have been better developed than their contemporaries. Mill Reef, Sir Ivor, Nijinsky, Nonoalco have all been conspicuous recent examples.

Thus with the introduction into modern feeding of vitamin and mineral compounds, in order to give young stock all possible chances of optimum development, the whole process must be subjected to close observation by those conversant with all the problems.

Alas, *vita brevis ars longa*, no man in his time can discover all he would wish to know about breeding, and nobody concerned with horses, when he comes to die, does not regret that he has only found out less than half the knowledge he would have desired.

Genetics and the Horse

Dr P. J. Gazder

Compared with other domestic and laboratory animals, the horse must be considered a less satisfactory subject for genetical research, as it is expensive to keep, has relatively few off-spring, and is slow to mature. Nevertheless, it is remarkable how much knowledge has been accumulated about heredity in the horse, and this may be conveniently considered under two headings: the mechanism of inheritance of particular factors or genes – qualitative inheritance; and the inheritance of factors within a particular population – quantitative inheritance. Qualitative inheritance has mainly been studied in three areas: studies of coat colour and markings; inherited and developmental abnormalities; and studies of blood proteins, sometimes referred to as biochemical polymorphism. Quantitative inheritance studies have centred around two areas: heritability estimates – the frequency of a factor or a group of factors in a population; and breed studies, which have considered inbreeding and 'inter se' relationships within a breed.

Coat colour was an obvious subject for early inheritance studies. The work of early pioneers such as Andersen, Crewe, Buchanan Smith, Klemola, Wreidt and others, was consolidated by later studies of Castle and Salisbury into the present generally accepted position that the common coat colours are produced by the interaction of a small number of genes, controlling pigmentation, distribution, etc., whose presence or absence determine coat colour in the mature animal. For example, a pair of genes control pigmentation: the B gene produces black/brown pigment, while the b gene produces red/yellow pigment. These alternative forms are located at the same point on each one of a pair of chromosomes, and are therefore *alleles* or variants of each other. If both are present, B is *dominant*, b is *recessive*, and the individual shows black/brown pigmentation. If only b is present, as in a double recessive bb, the individual shows red/yellow pigmentation. Another group of genes limit the production of pigment to particular parts of the body, chiefly dorsal and peripheral. The dominant A gene produces the bay pattern, and its recessive allele a uniform colour all over the body, which, in conjunction with the b gene, produces chestnut. There is also a third gene, a^t, in this allelic series, recessive to A, but dominant to a, which probably occurred as a change or mutation, and which produces the brown colour. Grey coat colour is produced by the dominant gene G which overrides genes A and B and is therefore epistatic to them. There are other genes such as E and its alleles which also control the extension of pigmentation, D which produces dilution, S which is similar in action to D and produces silver dapple in Shetland ponies, R which produces roan, and W which produces a white colour, which is different from grey as the foals are white at birth. The external appearance (*phenotype*) and actual genetic constitution (*genotype*) of the common equine coat colours are shown below in tabular form. Following the usual custom, dominant genes are capitalized, recessive genes are in lower case.

Coat colours

Phenotype	Genotype
BAY	
dark or mahogany bay	A – B – E – d d
red or blood bay	A – B – e e d d
BLACK	
intensive dominant black	A – B – E^d d d
recessive black, uniform all over	a a B – E – d d
recessive black, with darker mane and tail	a a B – e e d d
SEAL BROWN	a^t a^t B – E – dd
LIVER CHESTNUT	
uniform	a a b b E – d d
with lighter mane and tail	A – b b E – d d
SORREL CHESTNUT	
uniform	a a b b e e d d
with lighter mane and tail	A – b b e e d d
light chestnut	a a b b e e D d
DUN	A – B – E – D d
BUCKSKIN	A – B – e e D d
PALOMINO	A – b b E – D d
Epistatic genetic effects	
GREY	G
ROAN	R
WHITE	W
SILVER DAPPLE (in Shetland ponies)	S

Markings on horses vary from white markings on the extremities found in most breeds, to the extensive markings of Pintos, and the colourful patterns of Appaloosa and Knapstruper. Inheritance studies in this area have produced confusing, occasionally conflicting, results and more work is clearly needed. Blunn and Howell considered the blaze to be controlled by three genes, for star, stripe, and snip, inherited as dominants and modified by general factors for white markings. They considered chin spot to be a recessive, but this has been recently disputed. Studies on paint horses have suggested the possibility of two groups of factors, one dominant, the other recessive. White areas are mainly dorsally distributed in the dominant group, referred to as 'Tobiano'. In the other group, sometimes called 'splashed white' or 'Overo', white areas are ventrally distributed, and wall eyes are often associated

with this pattern. The spotted pattern of the Appaloosa is complex in inheritance, but there are at least two groups of genes, one for the overall spotting, another for the blanket hip pattern, each with several modifiers to control the size, shape and extent of spotting.

Inherited abnormalities in horses are a difficult area for investigation. Data may be scanty or incomplete, environmental factors must be considered, experiments to prove hypotheses may not be possible. Also, considerable time may have elapsed since the introduction of the carrier, as in the case of the Percheron stallion Superb exported from America to Japan in the latter part of the nineteenth century. He was shown by Yamane in 1927 to have carried a lethal factor for *atresia coli* (closed colon), but by that time he had left a large number of descendants. Sometimes the presence of an abnormality has to be deduced from an abnormal foal or a reduced number of foals. It was observed that white (W) foals occurred in a ratio of 2 to 1 instead of the expected 3 to 1. Further investigation showed that the homozygous (uniform) dominant WW foals died before birth and that all white foals had the genotype Ww. This is an example of a gene which has more than one (pleiotropic) effect, on coat colour and on viability. Other inherited abnormalities reported in the literature include deformed forelegs, spinal ataxia, epitheliogenesis imperfecta, cerebellar hypoplasia, and haemophilia.

Blood protein studies have increased in significance because of their value in blood testing for identification. Differences in haemoglobin, transferrins, esterases, albumens, prealbumens, and isoagglutinins have been studied. The isoagglutinin genes, which have many alleles, have proved particularly useful in parentage identification work. Seventeen genes, each with two or more alleles, have been located so far in blood proteins; more will undoubtedly be found in the near future.

Quantitative inheritance studies have involved analysis of national breeds and famous studs. The first breed to be studied was the Clydesdale, in which it was observed that inbreeding within the breed gradually increased to 6.5 per cent by 1925, mostly due to breeders trying to obtain sons or grandsons of famous sires to head their studs. A similar pattern could be seen in breeds studied in America, such as the Quarter horse, the Tennessee Walking horse and the Arabian; relationship to famous sires was high. Studies were made on a stud of Belgian horses inbred to Farceur and on the Quarter horses of the King Ranch in Texas. After fifteen years, inbreeding in the Belgian stud reached an average of 12.8 per cent with a relationship of 43.6 per cent to Farceur, without any apparent decrease in the quality of the stock. At the King Ranch, foals of 1941–2 had a similar level of relationship to Old Sorrel.

Heritability estimates, the ratio of the additive genetic variance to total variation, have been made for a number of factors affected by many genes. Results so far have been variable, perhaps due to sample size, but in general, characters developed early in life have greater heritability. This may be because characters which develop late are more susceptible to environmental influences.

Knowledge of the principles of inheritance is necessary for successful selection. Minimum culling levels may be used to eliminate defects or undesirable characters, but this is essentially a negative method, contributing little to positive advancement unless the intensity of selection is kept at a high level. This is unlikely in horse breeding, for while only a few colts may be retained for the breeding herd, most pure-bred fillies are kept for breeding, which results in low selection pressure. Selection for one factor at a time, or more usually, a group of factors producing a particular effect such as show-ring performance ability, is only possible if all these factors are independently inherited and positively associated, and this is unlikely. It is better to consider all the desirable traits required, rate them according to their relative value, assess each animal, give it an index figure which represents its value for these traits, and then compare animals directly.

There are three ways in which the inheritance of an animal may be approached. Before birth, or soon after, the way must be through the pedigree: an evaluation of the ancestors, but mainly of the quality of parents and grand-parents. Obviously, this evaluation depends on the amount of knowledge of the good and bad points of these ancestors and their capacity for reproducing them. When the individual is old enough, assessment may be made directly on conformation and performance; one can see if the characters sought for have, in fact, been inherited. In the breeding herd the way to determine whether the desired inheritance is being passed on is through the progeny.

However, although much is known, much still remains to be discovered. Many records are anecdotal, incomplete, or inaccurate, while stud book data are often unreliable with regard to colour and markings. This may be due to linguistic difficulties, to differences due to lack of standardization or to errors in interpretation. It seems certain that many of these difficulties will be resolved in the near future and that more will be added to our present knowledge of equine genetics.

Part Two

A History of Veterinary Medicine

Dr Edouard Pouret

Veterinary medicine has been practised from remote antiquity; in ancient India sick horses and elephants were treated and hospitals opened for various kinds of animals; texts were written on diseases of animals. In Mesopotamia King Hammurabi, about 1800 BC, laid down a code of fees for treating asses and oxen.

In 1900 BC the Egyptian papyrus of Kahun gave formulae for sicknesses of dogs and oxen.

Among the Greeks horse doctors were called *hippiatori* and the first physicians, among whom was Hippocrates, the first and greatest of all, had systems for treating sick animals (400 BC).

Of course, the Romans were interested in animal medicine, but in Rome they employed Greeks in this capacity. It was thus that the term *Veterinarius* came into use for a practitioner of animal medicine and *Veterinarium* for a horse hospital.

The Greek veterinary surgeons of the Roman army had great renown, and the best of them at the beginning of the Byzantine period (about AD 330) was Aspyrtus who wrote texts which were re-published in the tenth century under the title of *Hippiatrika*.

Vegetius, about AD 450, wrote *The Veterinary Art*, which for almost ten centuries remained the basic document on animal medicine. It was thus that the prophylaxis of contagious diseases became known, for at that period there raged at Rome epidemics of virus diseases which seem to have been identical with the equine influenza and African horse sickness of our time.

In the Middle Ages, and almost into modern times, the care of sick animals was confided to farriers who in Roman times had only shod horses but afterward practised such veterinary medicine and surgery as there was. Down to the eighteenth century veterinary medicine was in a complete decline, except for a single author, the Roman Carlo Ruini with his *Anatomia del Cavallo*, written in 1598.

The warlike policy of Louis XIV, the war of the Spanish Succession, combined with political and economic difficulties, the needs of the army, the court and commerce, all gave a vital stimulus to horse breeding. It became imperative to cure equine epidemics by studying their causes, instead of treating their symptoms. Thus it came about that the first veterinary school was founded at Lyons in 1762 by Jean-Baptiste Bertin, Intendant of the Generality of Lyons; Bourgelat was the first principal.

The novelty of this school drew the curious from France and from abroad, and in 1765 Bertin founded a second school at Alfort.

Visitors came to the schools from all over Europe. One was founded in London in 1791, others at Edinburgh in 1825, at Glasgow in 1863, at Dublin in 1900, at Liverpool in 1904, at Bristol and Cambridge in 1945. The whole world followed suit: in the United States, Iowa State College dates from 1879, the University of Pennsylvania from 1884, Ohio State University from 1885, and so on.

Schools were set up in other countries, such as Italy, Sweden, Austria and Germany.

Bourgelat, at the Lyons school, wished to get away from empiricism and the farriers' rule-of-thumb in favour of rational thought about animal ailments. Along these lines more

Claude Bourgelat (1712–79), founder of the Royal Veterinary School at Lyons.

than 180 veterinary schools have been founded throughout the world.

The horse was taken as the basic animal for research, being a soliped (single-hoofed), then other species with more than one toe and a different digestive system were studied, and since then every species has become the subject of a different medical discipline. Instead of specializing in particular organs, as physicians do, veterinarians at this stage of the twentieth century specialized in one animal.

In France they have received the title of Doctor since the 1930s because they have to sustain a doctoral thesis before a board of examiners in human medicine in order to practise legally on animals.

Persons who previous to that carried on the calling of animal doctor without a diploma were allowed to continue in practice, but no newcomers were able to set up in the profession.

In the USA the title of DVM was at the same time conferred on graduates of veterinary schools, meaning Doctor of Veterinary Medicine, and in the United Kingdom the recognized degrees are MRCVS or FRCVS, standing, respectively, for Member or Fellow of the Royal College of Veterinary Surgeons.

However, veterinary medicine now finds itself at the beginning of a new age, and as in antiquity it is overtaking human medicine. The necessity for experiment on animal subjects before the application of drugs or treatment to human beings, techniques of heart surgery, new drugs, the exploration of space, all offer to veterinary medicine a new field of activity which is vital to the human race.

Greater and greater consumption of animal protein means that the inspection of foodstuffs of animal origin has become very important to human health.

Virus diseases, which can be better studied in animals than in man, because it is possible to let an illness develop, or induce it without curing it, in order to study its development in the animal, open up new possibilities in animal medicine which are consistent with the philosophy held by Bourgelat at the time when he founded the French veterinary schools.

Bone surgery, abdominal surgery, new ways of surgical stitching, grafting of organs, all must pass through an experimental stage on animals before being applied to man.

Finally, genetics can best be studied in animals and the information so gained is invaluable to the human species.

Horsemanship of Antiquity

Prof. J. K. Anderson

The Bronze Age

Horses and the Greek language probably entered Greece together, brought by invaders shortly after 2000 BC. Horse bones found in excavations are not accompanied by harness, or pictorial evidence, and it is disputed whether the horse was already used for war, or merely as a pack-animal. Evidence for war chariots comes from crudely carved gravestones found above the Shaft Graves at Mycenae (*c.* 1550–1500 BC), and a gold signet from the graves shows a stag pursued by a two-horse chariot carrying a charioteer and an archer.

At this period chariots were used in large numbers for war and hunting by the kings of the Egyptian Eighteenth Dynasty. Many objects

Horses of Seti I of Egypt (*c.* 1321–1300 BC) being driven in drop nosebands.

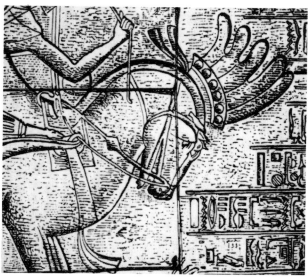

from the Shaft Graves show Egyptian influence, but this may have been transmitted indirectly through Crete, where the horse was unknown before the coming of Greek-speaking warriors in the Late Minoan period. Horses, mares, foals and chariots are recorded in large numbers on the 'Linear B' tablets from Knossos (perhaps shortly before 1400 BC). Chariots are associated with armour in these records, but the terrain of Greece is not suited to the massed chariot charges of contemporary Hittite and Egyptian warfare. Hunting from chariots is frequently represented in Egypt and south-west Asia, but does not reappear in Minoan or Mycenean art, though two young ladies drive out to watch a boar-hunt on a fresco from Tiryns (fourteenth century BC).

Vase paintings are schematic, but establish that the chariot was light, two-wheeled, normally with two occupants, and drawn by two horses harnessed on either side of a central pole. A rigid yoke was carried just in front of the withers on a yoke-saddle, and was normally secured by a belly-band. The horse exerted its tractive effort through a flexible collar, which bore upon the lower part of the throat rather than upon the bony structure of the shoulders, and its pressure upon the windpipe limited the effective load. Horses were unshod. Bronze snaffle bits, sometimes with twisted mouthpieces, or with short spikes inside the cheeks, were used during the Late Bronze Age, but the Egyptian monuments show that horses were also driven in drop nosebands.

Horses were sometimes ridden, but representations of mounted men are few and do not suggest great skill in horsemanship or the existence of effective cavalry. Saddles were unknown, and the means of control were inadequate.

The Early Iron Age

Little evidence for Greek horsemanship survives from the period following the collapse of Mycenean civilization (*c.* 1200 BC), which marked the transition to the Iron Age. Sketches of horses appear on a few vases, and a pair of snaffle bits was found in an Athenian grave of about 1000 BC. A vase from Crete (*c.* 900 BC) bears a crude picture of an armed rider. It is probable that the war chariot retained its importance; when pictorial evidence again becomes common on vases decorated in the Late Geometric style (second half of the eighth century BC) chariots are still more common than mounted men, and constructional details suggest descent from Bronze Age chariots rather than re-introduction. Processions of chariots, each containing a single armed man, appear on large Attic vases that served as grave markers, and the funerals of great men were perhaps followed, as in Homer's *Iliad*, by chariot races.

Chariot racing was also a feature of athletic festivals. The traditional date for the first Olympiad is 776 BC, but the origin of the Games was also traced to the race in which Pelops, the legendary ancestor of the Bronze Age kings of Mycenae, overcame King Oenomaus and won his daughter and kingdom. Many bronze tripods, dating from the eighth century BC, have been found at Olympia and other sanctuaries, and some have statuettes of horses on their handles.

Homer's race was run across the plain, round a distant landmark, and back.

> Mark then the goal, 'tis easy to be found;
> Yon aged trunk, a cubit from the ground;
> Of some once stately oak the last remains,
> Or hardy fir, unperished with the rains.
> (Homer *Iliad* 23. 327–8.)

Later races consisted of many laps, with 180° turns round markers, on a regular course. Crashes were frequent.

> Then the Aenian hero's hard-mouthed colts
> Bolted in turning for the seventh lap
> And crashed into a Cyrenean team.
> And from this one disaster team on team
> Collided headlong, and the wrecks of chariots
> Filled all the plain of Crisa.
> (Sophocles *Electra* 721–7.)

Most famous courses had a bogy – at Olympia the ghost of Oenomaus' charioteer – who, unless propitiated, would fill the horses with panic.

Therefore the charioteers offer sacrifices and pray to Taraxippus [the terror of horses] to be gracious to them. . . . Another story is that Pelops made a cenotaph for Myrtilus [whom he had murdered after the race] and sacrificed to him and called him Taraxippus because he had contrived to terrify the horses of Oenomaus. . . . I have also heard the blame given to Alcathus the son of Porthaon, who was said to have been a suitor of Hippodamia, and killed and buried here by Oenomaus. From his own bad luck at the racecourse, his ghost bears a spite against the charioteers. . . . There is also a Taraxippus at the Isthmus, Glaucus, son of Sisyphus, killed by his own horses at his father's funeral games. At Nemea there was no ghost which made the horses shy, but above the turning point a red rock, the light from which was like a fire and frightened the horses. (Pausanias 6.20. 16–9.)

In the *Iliad*, heroes come to war in chariots, driven by a charioteer of lesser rank. Princely opponents often jump down to fight on foot with spear and sword.

From his proud car the prince impetuous springs,
On earth he leaps: his brazon armour rings.
Two shining spears are brandished in his hands.
Thus arm'd, he animates his drooping bands.
(Homer *Iliad* 5. 494–6.)

The spear is sometimes thrown from the chariot, but generally unsuccessfully and there is little evidence for manoeuvres by large formations. Cavalry is unknown, though heroes mount and ride away on chariot horses that they are carrying off by night from the enemy's

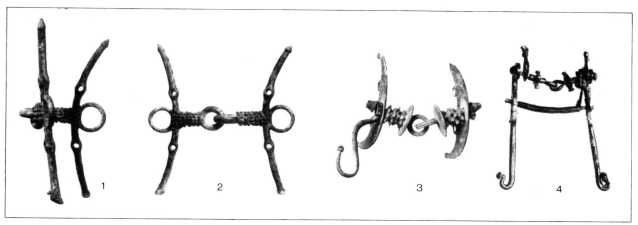

1 and 2 Asiatic bits with rough mouthpieces, sixth century BC (?). (The Ashmolean Museum, Oxford)

3 Greek bit, fourth century BC (?). (The Trustees of the British Museum)
4 Celtic curb bit, early third century BC.

camp (Homer *Iliad* 10. 512 ff.) and Ulysses, astride the keel of his capsized ship, is compared to a horseman. (Homer *Odyssey* 5. 371.) The epics probably date from the late eighth century BC, and contain ancient traditions, descriptions drawn from contemporary life, and poetic fictions. The proportion in which these are mingled is disputed by scholars.

Archaic Greece

The seventh century BC saw the rise of Greek urban civilization, supported by revived commerce and contacts with Egypt and Asia.

> Look there;
> The race horse is Venetic, but the hair
> Of Hagesichora shines like pure gold,
> Her face is like silver – why need that be told
> Which all the world must know?
> Here's Hagesichora, in beauty's course
> She who runs second after Agido,
> A Colaxaean to an Iberian horse.
> (Alcman *Partheneion* 15 ff.)

Cavalry, which had been an effective branch of the Assyrian army since the ninth century BC, replaced the war chariot, and Assyrian influence may be seen in the introduction of severe bits with spiked mouthpieces.

Asiatic and other foreign horses are noted by the poets (e.g. Alcman *Partheneion* 1. 50 ff.), but there is no evidence for the development of an improved breed of riding horse by the systematic introduction of foreign blood. Stallions were normally run with herds of mares which were maintained where pasture was available (notably in Thessaly and Elis). The selection of a particular mare to be covered by a particular stallion was unusual, and though a few strains were traced back to exceptional (and often legendary) ancestors, pedigrees were not recorded. Gelding was not practised (probably for fear of infection), and stallions were preferred to mares as war horses. Greek horses remained at all periods small (perhaps generally about 14 to 15 h.h.), fine-limbed and fine-headed. A solid body, with the spine sunken between well-developed dorsal muscles, was desirable in an age of bareback riders (though saddle cloths were already in use in Assyria, and are occasionally shown in Greek art from the sixth century BC onwards). Heavy breeds were not developed, as the form of harness remained basically unchanged and curtailed the horse's use for heavy draught. Mules were bred for the plough (more often drawn by oxen) and to pull carts.

The development of cavalry did not increase the importance of the horse in warfare, as in most Greek states a disciplined infantry drawn from the middle class henceforth provided the chief part of the army and imposed its rights at

Horses being trained on long reins, Attic vase, late sixth century BC.

the expense of the horse-owning aristocracy. Vase paintings of the sixth century BC show horsemen, equipped with infantry armour and attended by unarmed youths on spare horses, who apparently formed an elite corps of mounted infantry. Light cavalry, equipped with javelins, are also portrayed, and set the pattern for the future.

In sport, stag-hunting by mounted youths with javelins is shown on vases of the late sixth century. The chariot kept its place in processions, and on the racecourse, where four-horse chariots now appeared (in 680 BC at Olympia; on Attic vases a generation earlier). In Greece, the extra horses were attached to the chariot by single traces, and probably contributed little traction, but added to the magnificence and expense of a rich man's sport. Two poles were fitted to the heavy Asiatic chariot, so that all four horses were brought under the yoke, but this system was not introduced into Greece, though it was known in Cyprus, where such vehicles, with the skeletons of the teams that drew them, have been found in royal graves in the Greek city of Salamis.

The race for ridden horses was introduced at Olympia in 648 BC and was run on the same course as the chariot races, with similar chances for accidents. A statue commemorated a mare who threw her rider at the start but continued to race round the turning point, and on hearing the trumpets (signalling the last lap) quickened her pace, reached the judges first, knew she had won, and stopped. She was declared the winner (Pausanias 6. 13. 9–10) – but the story suggests that a loose horse galloping on past the winning post would be disqualified.

Classical Greece

The Greek classical age begins with the defeat of the Persian invasion of 480–479 BC. The Medes and the Persians were descended from Central Asiatic nomads and were excellent horsemen. Their ancestors had overthrown the Assyrians in the late seventh century BC, and Persia became an empire after the defeat of Lydia by Cyrus the Great (546 BC); the Lydian cavalry horses stampeded at the sight and smell of the Persian baggage camels (Herodotus 1.80). The Nisaean horses, pastured on the lucerne of Media, were larger and faster than the best in Greece (Herodotus 7.40), Persian cavalry was superior, and the Greek victories over the barbarian were won by their infantry, or at sea. But Greek horsemanship was nobly commemorated by the artists of the classical period, notably on the Parthenon frieze (c. 440 BC), and was described in the technical treatises of Simon (c. 430 BC?, now mostly lost), and Xenophon (c. 430–356 BC); his *Art of Horsemanship* was written late in life, after an outstanding career as a professional soldier, to offer to his 'younger friends' the fruits of his experience.

Xenophon's book is an outline, addressed to the wealthy amateur, and he deliberately excludes the breaking in of colts – best left to professionals. He covers the selection and handling of colts, stable management, equitation in the school and across country, advanced equitation for parade and display, and cavalry armour. He presents, clearly and directly, principles that are still of fundamental importance.

A horse can obviously learn nothing by mere words. If when he behaves as you wish you show him some kindness in return, and when he disobeys you punish him, in this way he will most readily serve you as he ought. (Xenophon 8.13.)

Association of ideas is to play its part even in the education of the unbroken colt, who is to learn to 'associate hunger and thirst and the attacks of insects with solitude, and food and drink and freedom from pests with men', and so become quiet to handle. (8.23.)

Good sense and moderation are everywhere apparent:

as for sudden application of the aids, a spirited horse is alarmed by sudden sights, sounds or sensations, just like a man. . . . Quiet prolonged rides settle the spirited horse and make him gentle without exciting him. . . . When the horse suspects some object and is unwilling to approach, you must make it clear that there is nothing to be afraid of . . . and if this fails you must yourself touch the object and lead him up gently. Those who compel the horse with blows make him more frightened than ever. (6.14-15, 9.7, 9.40)

Above all, 'Never lose your temper in dealing with horses; this is the one best precept and custom in horsemanship'.

Technically, Xenophon was limited by the want of saddle and stirrups (though he assumes that cavalry will use saddle cloths; 12.8). Bits had become still more severe, with revolving 'hedgehogs' and sharp-edged discs fitted to the mouthpiece to prevent the horse from taking the bit between his teeth. Xenophon recommends using a smooth bit on the made horse, so that 'he may be pleased by its smoothness and perform in it the lessons taught by the rough one'. (10.6) The curb chain was unknown, but the psalion, a metal cavesson, was used to supplement the bit. Spurs had been recently introduced.

Xenophon offers advice on obtaining the correct lead at the canter (7.11.), but does not seem to have practised flying changes of leg. His advice on jumping is directed to the safe crossing of small obstacles in war or hunting, and not to steeplechasing or show jumping, which were unknown. Hunting provided good training, when conditions permitted, but Xenophon's other writings indicate that, though he

Horse and Groom from Xanthus in Lycia (*c.* 480 BC).

had himself enjoyed big-game hunting in the Asiatic manner when serving in 401 BC under the rebel Persian prince Cyrus (*Anabasis* 1.5.1–3.), opportunities were rare in Greece. The Athenian landowner might ride to and from his farm but he would hunt on foot (*Oeconomicus* 5.5 ff.). Agriculture restricted sport; Xenophon tells even the hunter on foot to respect the crops (*Cynegeticus* 5.34.).

For parade, Xenophon directs that the rider should not try to show off by pulling at the horse's mouth, spurring and whipping, but should reproduce as far as possible the manner in which the horse naturally displays himself 'especially in front of mares' (Ch. 10). The exceptional horse is to be trained to rear, not under compulsion ('Such actions are no more beautiful than if one were to teach a dancer by whipping or spurring') but 'following the indication of the aids to display of his own free will his most beautiful and brilliant qualities' (Ch. 11). Once again, the limited technical means at Xenophon's disposal must have stopped his achievement short of that of the modern masters of dressage and *haute école*, who acknowledge themselves his successors. Of his predecessors, Simon is little more than a name, but much of Xenophon's practice must have been anticipated in the archaic period. Several attic vases of the later sixth century BC show horses being taught to rear by means of long reins, and the story was told (*Athenaeus* 12.

520 d.) that the luxurious city of Sybaris fell (509 BC) because its cavalry horses had been taught to 'dance' to a tune which was revealed to the enemy before the fatal battle.

Macedonians, Celts and the rise of Rome

Within a generation of Xenophon's death, the Greek city states and Persian empire were both conquered by the Macedonians under Philip II and his son Alexander the Great. Alexander's skill in horsemanship was shown as a boy, when he mastered the unmanageable Bucephalus, not by force, but by observing that the horse was shying at his own shadow. As king he led his cavalry in person, repeatedly killing enemy commanders with his own hand. In the first of his Persian victories, at the Granicus (373 BC) his helmet was broken by a blow from a battle-axe, and a horse killed under him. Bucephalus survived, to die at the age of thirty in India, where a city was founded in his honour (325 BC: Plutarch *Alexander* 6; 61). The horse is said to have known the royal saddle-cloth, and to have allowed none but the king to mount when it was on his back (Pliny *Natural History* 8.154).

Alexander's victories were not won solely by personal prowess, but by the skilful combination of all arms, based on the phalanx of heavy infantry. After his death (323 BC), his empire was torn to pieces by the wars of his generals, under whom the relative importance of cavalry decreased, though different types – mailed lancers, light cavalry and horse-archers – were developed. The different regiments of King Antiochus's army impressed the Romans, until they were reminded that pork cooked in different ways was still pork, and Syrians were Syrians, however equipped (Plutarch *Flamininus* 17). The Parthians, Iranians who had recovered their independence, were later to prove more formidable enemies.

Italian horsemanship seems to have developed along the same lines as Greek, though its origins are less clear. The 'Troy Games', apparently a sort of mounted carousel still practised by young Roman nobles in the early Imperial period, were said by Virgil (*Aeneid* 5. 545–603) to have been brought to Italy by the legendary Aeneas, but were probably derived from an Etruscan ritual. Graves of the Villanovan period (eighth century BC) often contain pairs of bits, as though for chariot teams. Cavalry played an important part in the early wars of Romans, Etruscans and Latins. Livy represents it as a point of honour for commanders to engage in person (Livy 2. 6. 6–11), but not all the duels that he describes need be accepted as historical.

In the third century BC, during their war with Carthage, the Romans encountered African cavalry, including Numidians, who rode bareback and without bridles, controlling their horses by cords looped round the neck. The Romans at first regarded these ill-equipped riders and their awkward ponies with contempt, which the Numidians deliberately encouraged by tumbling off their horses in view of the enemy (Livy 35.11). But under Hannibal the African cavalry proved its superiority and was largely responsible for the Roman disaster at Cannae (216 BC). The Romans did not adopt Numidian methods, though Numidians were

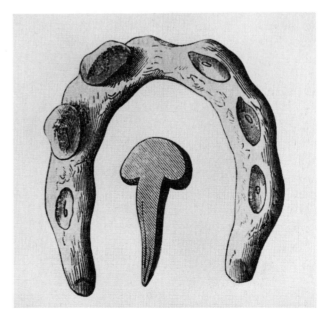

Horseshoe from Gaul, *c.* 200 BC.

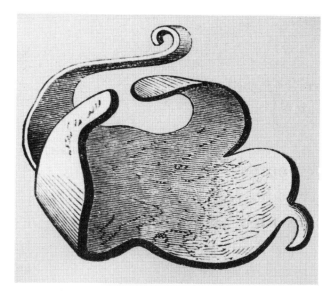

A Roman hipposandal.

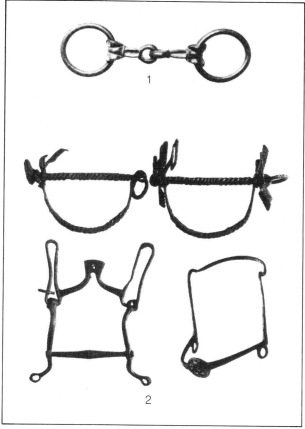

1 Celtic ring snaffle, early first century AD. (The Trustees of the British Museum)
2 Bits and metal *psalim* from the Roman cavalry port of Newstead, second century AD.

later recruited for the Roman armies. Their unbridled horses are noted by authors of the Imperial period (Gratius Faliscus *Cynegeticon* 1. 496 ff; Nemesianus *Cynegeticon* 204 ff.) and depicted on Trajan's column.

European horsemanship was more strongly influenced by the Celts, who, though un-civilized, were expert metal workers. The iron of Noricum (roughly modern Austria) was famous, and its smiths may have invented the horseshoe. Horseshoes from ancient sites are generally suspect, as they may have been lost by chance, or during mediaeval quarrying; but a few specimens have been excavated from sealed deposits antedating the Roman conquest of the Alpine region (late first century BC). There is no reason to carry the antiquity of the horse-shoe further back or to credit it with the Gauls' defeat of the Romans at the Allia (390 BC). Its use seems to have been restricted to draught and pack-animals; it is not found in Roman cavalry camps of the Imperial period, or mentioned by writers on veterinary medicine, though Roman veterinarians used a detachable metal shoe, nowadays called hipposandal, for the protection of injured feet.

The curb bit with a rigid metal chain, un-like the modern version and usually with a spiked mouthpiece, was also possibly invented by the Celts. Roman examples are known, but they are preceded in date by a specimen from a Celtic mercenary's grave of the third century BC. More certainly of Celtic origin is the ring snaffle, with two- or three-piece jointed mouth-piece, but this was perhaps used for driving rather than riding. (The light war chariot remained in use in Britain until the Roman conquest.)

The Celts perhaps also helped to transmit the saddle from its nomad inventors to western Europe. On the 'Gundestrup Cauldron' (pro-bably second century BC) appear saddled ponies ridden by Celtic cavalrymen wearing spurs and breeches (another introduction from the steppe: the English word is derived from the Latinized Celtic *bracae*). Similar saddles, secured by girth,

Battle between Roman and Gaulish cavalry (note the saddle of the fallen horse). Detail from the Mausoleum of St Rany de Provence at Glaumium, *c.* late first century BC.

crupper and breast-plate, and without stirrups, appear regularly upon Roman monuments from the late first century BC (the mausoleum at Glanum) onwards, but the date of their adoption by the Roman cavalry is uncertain. They were probably standard equipment in Caesar's day, since he notes (*De Bello Gallico* 4. 2) the contempt of the Germanic Suebi for enemies who used saddles. Caesar was himself a noted horseman from his childhood, and used to ride at full gallop with his hands clasped behind his back. During his campaigns he would dictate dispatches while on horseback, to two or more secretaries simultaneously (Plutarch *Caesar* 17).

Roman Imperial period

In the army of the Emperor Augustus (BC 27-AD 14) and his successors, cavalry units were raised from the subject peoples of the empire. But these 'auxiliaries' were officered by young Romans of equestrian rank; and members of the senatorial class, whose careers advanced from staff appointments through the command of legions to the government of provinces, also rode in the discharge of their military duties. Upper-class Romans accordingly continued to practise horsemanship, including hunting. Martial (late first century after Christ) warns a friend:

> Why gallop so? Bold riding, I declare
> Breaks up the horseman oftener than the hare
> (Martial 12.14)

He suggests that the boar, hunted on foot with spears, hounds and nets, is a nobler antagonist. But the Emperor Hadrian (AD 117–38) hunted big game on horseback; the epitaph of his favourite hunter (*CIL XII* 122) records the horse's achievements against the boars of Pannonia (modern Hungary). Mosaics of the fourth century after Christ, from Africa and Sicily, show horsemen pursuing big game, including lions, and the development of this eastern sport has been seen as a symptom of the gradual transformation of the Roman Principate into an 'oriental monarchy'.

For the Roman people, the massacre of wild beasts in the amphitheatre was rivalled as a spectator-sport by chariot racing. Outside the circus, carriages of different sorts were used for travel on the excellent Roman roads, and light chariots were driven by young men of fashion, to the admiration of their mistresses and the scandal of the public.

> His fortune's spent on horses, but some day
> He hopes to mend it with a colonel's pay.
> Meanwhile young Jehu takes the reins and goad
> Himself, in public, on the Great North Road,
> And rattles through the country, to impress
> His girl-friend, dolled up in a coachman's dress.
> (Juvenal 1. 58–62.)

The imperial post linked the provinces to Rome, but the use of the horse for heavy draught was still limited by the want of suitable harness. For travellers, the mule was the usual mount, but ambling *theldones* were imported from Spain, the smoothness of whose 'alternate unfolding of the legs' is praised by Pliny. (*Natural History* 8. 166). Parthian hackneys (*trepidarii*) were trained to pick their feet up by trotting over transverse furrows. The practice of weighting the feet of trotters was also known (Vegetius *Mulmedicus* 1. 56.37–9).

Large Imperial studs, which provided remounts for the army and post, encouraged more systematic breeding, and the fourth century saw the collection of professional writings (the *Corpus Hippiatricorum Graecorum*) by veterinary officers. By this time the legionary system had been abandoned, and cavalry played a greatly increased part in the Roman armies, which included large numbers of more or less romanized Germans and Sarmatians. Heavily armoured lancers (*clibanarii*) were copied from Sassanian Persia. Being still without stirrups, they wielded the lance in both hands instead of couching it. These fore-runners of the medieval knight mark the approaching end of the ancient world.

Riding Through the Dark Ages

Prof. J. K. Anderson

In the history of horsemanship, the Dark Ages following the fall of the Western Roman Empire are marked by the introduction of the stirrup. It is agreed that without the stirrup neither the shock tactics of medieval and later cavalry nor cross-country riding in the modern sense could have been possible, and that the stirrup has profoundly influenced every form of equitation. But its potentialities were very gradually realized, and, partly for this reason, even the date of its introduction remains doubtful. No immediate major change in the design of bits or saddles, as compared with those of late antiquity, can be shown to accompany the stirrup. There is no one point at which cavalry tactics are revolutionized. Works of art continue to show riders without stirrups until an unexpectedly late date, perhaps because the artists were working in a derivative formal tradition rather than drawing from life.

The barbarian invaders of the fourth and fifth centuries after Christ cannot be proved to have had stirrups. The Huns, who had ridden out of the wilderness, driving the other nations before them, are described in detail by contemporary historians. They could not plant their feet firmly on the ground, but lived and slept on their horses (Zosimus 9. 20.4). They were offspring of Scythian witches and demons of the wilderness; squat, bow-legged, beardless, flatnosed, with long unkempt hair. They remained continuously on horseback, even turning themselves sideways, like women, instead of dismounting, in order to ease nature (Ammianus 31.2.6). Their horses were like themselves; tough but ugly to the point where the contra-diction of all normal standards of beauty had its own inverted symmetry (Vegetius 3. 6.5). Like other steppe peoples they had saddles, apparently with wooden trees. The saddles of Attila's host, defeated at Châlons (AD 451), were heaped into a pyre, on which the beaten king would have been burned himself if he had not been spared by Roman policy (Jordanes *Getica* 40. 213). But stirrups were never mentioned.

Armoured horse-archers, described by Procopius (1. 1.12–15), guarded the Byzantine Empire and in the middle of the sixth century reconquered much of the West. Their opponents, Persians, Vandals and Goths, were also horsemen. But stirrups are not found in Byzantine literature before the *Strategicon* of the Emperor Maurice (reigned AD 582–602; the authorship and date are disputed). Maurice directs (p. 22 of J. Scheffer's edition: Upsala, 1664) that cavalry saddles should be fitted with two iron stirrups (*scalae*, literally 'steps'). The orderlies detailed to save men wounded or unhorsed in action are to have an extra stirrup attached to the cantle on the near side, to help

Byzantine horsemen riding without stirrups, seventh century AD. (The Trustees of the British Museum)

the rescued to mount behind their rescuers (p. 64). Much of the equipment that Maurice recommends (though not expressly the stirrups) is said to be 'of Avar type'. It is inferred that the stirrup reached Europe about a century after its invention in the eastern steppe, with the Avars – nomads of Turkish stock – who attacked the northern frontiers of the Byzantine Empire about AD 560 and subsequently founded a kingdom in modern Hungary. Cast-iron stirrups have been found in supposedly Avar graves.

By the early seventh century the stirrup had apparently reached Spain; Isidore, Archbishop of Seville, knew *scansuae*, 'the iron by which a horse is mounted'. (*Stapes*, the usual medieval Latin word, appears to be a later introduction.) Evidently the stirrup was at first valued as a help in mounting rather than for the security that it gives the rider once in the saddle. The writer of the *Souda*, a tenth-century antiquarian dictionary, finding no classical word for stirrup, gave *scala* – stirrup – as one definition of *anaboleus*: properly a groom who gives his master a leg-up. Roman emperors had still been helped to mount in this way in the fourth century. Julian, when his groom slipped, saw it as a symbol of the fall of his rival Constantius, who had earlier helped him into power. Valentinian ordered the right hand to be struck from a clumsy groom; but the man was hidden by the Master of the Horse until the Emperor recovered his temper (Ammianus Marcellinus 22. 1.2; 30. 5.19).

Archaeological evidence from Western Europe is rare and doubtful until stirrups appear in Viking graves of the ninth century and later, but Christian warriors did not receive large grave offerings, and we cannot assert positively that the Vikings brought the stirrup to France and Britain.

Jutes, Angles, Saxons and Franks were, however, exceptional among the conquerors of the Western Empire in that their strength originally lay in their infantry. In Britain the invaders –

Horsemen riding with stirrups, ninth century AD. (Musée de Cluny)

despite their White Horse banner and their leaders, Hengist (cf. Hengst: stallion) and Horsa – fought on foot; the Britons, who retained, with Christianity, a fading remnant of Roman civilization, were led by men whose ancestors had served in the Imperial cavalry. King Arthur and his Knights embody traditions of this time, overlaid by medieval and Victorian romance, and a glimpse of the last British chivalry, about the beginning of the seventh century, seems to be given by the *Gododdin* (cf. Votadini, a tribe from beyond Hadrian's Wall who had provided the Romans with auxiliaries). In this poem the bard Aneirin laments the death at the battle of Cattraeth (Catterick?) of three hundred comrades, a band of specially-trained horsemen.

The Franks who attacked the Byzantines in Italy after AD 552 are said by Procopius (6. 25.3–4) to have been, except for a few mounted body-guards, all infantry, armed with sword, buckler and throwing-axe. By AD 732, when between Tours and Poitiers Charles Martel defeated the Arabs, whose horsemen had in the previous century overrun Syria, Egypt, North Africa and Spain, the importance and quality of Frankish cavalry had increased. With Charles Martel's grandson, 'Charlemagne and all his peerage', the Age of Chivalry dawns (see p. 81).

Horsemanship and Breeding in Central Asia

Lt. Col. Gerald Morgan

The origins of horse breeding and riding in Central Asia are hazy and speculative in such a vast region where relevant archaeological finds are rare. Pastoral nomads in particular had no written language and few artefacts. The earliest written records of breeding horses come from China and India. The Hittites wrote treatises on breeding in the fourteenth century BC. An Egyptian statuette of a mounted man is dated at between 1800 and 2500 BC.

It can be assumed that the horse was first used as a pack animal, and in Central Asia it would therefore have contributed to the development of the Silk Road running through the Ili River valley, possibly the oldest trade, cultural and invasion route in the world. In Egypt chariot driving for war preceded riding and that presupposes a knowledge of breeding; but the influence of the horse on culture and war did not make itself felt to the fullest extent till it was bred for riding. There are grounds for believing that Central Asia was where such breeding began.

In the Northern Hemisphere the reindeer culture was supreme from the last Ice Age until the climate warmed up and the moss lichen, which is the reindeer's sole food, retreated northwards, followed perforce by the reindeer and their herders. But the grass steppes which replaced the moss suited sheep and horses too, provided there was adequate water. So nomads began to exploit the new fodder, and their livestock grew in stature. Alfalfa (lucerne), together with barley, no doubt contributed to their superior size and quality. Supplies of it accompanied them when

they were first imported: subsequently it was cultivated in China for their special use. That would have benefited the cold-blood breeds from the north as well. We know from recent days how in China ponies imported for racing put on weight and height when fed on it.

There were several breeds of indigenous horse (most of which we would now call ponies); all of them were originally wild and hunted for food before they were domesticated. Small breeds existed in the forests from China through Siberia to northern Europe, as well as in Tibet and the hill states bordering India's northern frontiers; larger breeds inhabited western Central Asia. The smaller, slower draught types are distinguished as 'cold-bloods', the Mongol being typical, as well as historically important. The larger and faster riding types are called 'warm-bloods' (the difference is in temperament not body temperature), and they were the ancestors of the Arab, Iranian and Bactrian breeds. True ponies apart, in Central Asia the dividing line between the two types was approximately the mountain ranges running south-westwards from the Altay through the Tien Shan to the Pamir: that is, from Mongolia to Afghan Badakhshan.

It is impossible to say with certainty on which side of this line horse breeding was first practised. If it was in Egypt or Assyria, a possibility suggested by the early use of war chariots, then horses would have needed some degree of skilled care, including stabling, to enable them to flourish in the relatively hot climate.

It is most likely, however, that riding was

first practised on the Mongol type east of the dividing line, in Dzungaria and Mongolia; this was suggested in 1911 by D. Carruthers, the British naturalist and explorer of the Sayan range west of Mongolia. There, by a peculiar climatic quirk, reindeer moss continues to grow, and he observed reindeer herding being carried on in the mountains, alongside horse culture in the valleys below. Owen Lattimore reported both cultures still being practised in 1970. The reindeer herdsmen of Sayan are the only ones who ride their deer and the inference is that they had passed their skill on to the horsemen.

If riding was practised as early as this it must have been in order to exploit better pastures and improved herding methods and so to increase stocks, which represented wealth. The steppe region of Mongolia with its low snowfall, affording winter as well as summer grazing, was particularly suitable for stock raising. So in this land of climatic extremes, the hardy Mongol horse was evolved by the equally tough, hardy nomad tribes. This habitat so well suits the wild cold-blood *Equus przevalskii* (named after the Russian explorer and naturalist), that the sighting of a small herd was reported near the Mongolian border with China as recently as 1965. Wild warm-bloods died out much earlier, probably through earlier amelioration of the climate. Nevertheless, a rock drawing of a warm-blood stallion serving a mare, discovered in Fergana, is dated at about the first century BC, that is, several thousand years later than those depicted in the Upper Palaeolithic cave paintings of Le Portel and Altamira.

But perhaps the strongest evidence, supporting not only the theory that riding first began in the region of Mongolia but suggesting that it was also the cradle of the domesticated horse, is that the earliest and greatest migrations and invasions known to historians all emanated from this region. Such tidal waves could only have occurred through a combination of vast herds of horses and the ability to ride. Not only did the Mongol breed provide the essential mobility, but it was also a complete source of sustenance for the nomads in the form of *kumis* (fermented

mares' milk), and necessities such as leather for clothing and harness. Their only other basic needs were provided by sheep which, besides meat, produced wool for their felt tents.

Increased mobility provided economic advantages, but it also brought less desirable results. Pressure on local pastures led to more distant grazing being sought, and that led inevitably to fighting another tribe for possession. The weaker tribe either perished, moved on or, as often happened, it combined with the stronger tribe to gain greater strength; the process was then repeated on a larger scale. After herding, fighting became the chief preoccupation of pastoral nomads. No doubt aggressive young men, bored with herding, easily found excuses such as horse thieving for a foray against a neighbouring tribe. The keyword was mutability: tribal alliances were formed and as quickly broken; the rights and wrongs of the cause were of no account. When a khan summoned his followers to 'mount', as the expression was, for a campaign, they quickly assembled, each with several spare horses: every man was self-supporting. Only a few men were left to guard the flocks and families in their temporary settlements. Naturally a successful leader easily attracted allies, with the promise of victory followed by pillage and debauchery.

These campaigns led gradually to the great migrations which were always eastwards and westwards within the latitudes suitable for horse culture. As they extended they reached the rich oases of the settled agrarian races, in China and westwards beyond the Tien Shan. As nomads scorned all settled races and had no use for their products, they indulged in massacre and wanton destruction before withdrawing. Of all the Mongoloid invaders out of Central Asia, only Genghis Khan had the wisdom to encourage commerce and culture and thus consolidate his vast empire, though some cities, such as Balkh, remained in ruins.

With the accent on mobility, every improvement in horsemanship and horse breeding was an important development. Originally horses everywhere must have been ridden bareback:

but on the evidence of the Sayan it is possible that the saddle originated there with the reindeer culture, and was copied by the later horse culture. The same type is used by both; it consists of a pad on either side of the spine joined across the front and back by two X-shaped wooden forks, and covered with a felt numnah; a breast-plate and a crupper helped to keep it in place. All saddles used in Central Asia later had high pommels and cantles. Sayan reindeer herdsmen use only a halter: the bit, giving greater control, may have enabled horse herders to begin riding.

Stirrups were a relatively late additional aid to mobility and accurate bowmanship. They are first seen in Chinese statuettes of the eighth century AD on warm-blood horses. The Chinese may have invented them, but more likely they originated in the equestrian society of Central Asia. Mongol stirrups weighed $1\frac{1}{2}$ kilos or more and had a wide oval tread to accommodate the big felt or fur boots. Some were decorated with silver inlaid motifs.

Much evidence about riding and horse equipment, and indeed about the whole equestrian civilization of Central Asia, comes from the astonishing finds in the Pazyryk Burial Tombs discovered in the western Altay Mountains between 1926 and 1946. These burials date from the fourth century BC. Frost had preserved intact not only the bodies of men and horses but saddlery for the riding horses, ornate harness and light carts for the draught horses, and much else besides. They prove that for these High Altaians, and by inference throughout Central Asia, the horse was the chief source of wealth. The fully evolved saddles of Scythian type show how advanced this equestrian civilization was in its horsemanship. The lasting influence of the reindeer culture is, however, suggested by the ceremonial reindeer masks worn by some of the horses. This is further inferential support for the Sayan theory.

A ceremonial reindeer mask, dating from the fourth century BC, one of the astonishing finds discovered in the Pazyrik Burial Tombs in the Altay Mountains.

Horse wearing a reindeer mask.

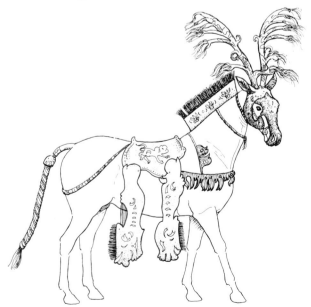

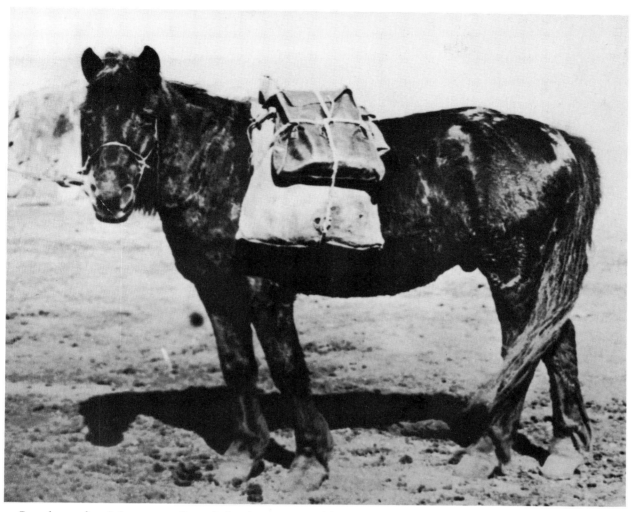

The Mongol pony which was and still is noted for its stamina and weight-carrying ability. Animals of this type were found in the Pazyrik Tombs along with warm-blood saddle horses.

In these burials were found both warm-bloods, described as of Thoroughbred type, as well as cold-bloods, of Mongol type. The latter were used for draught, the former, all gelded, were saddle horses. The difference between the two types of blood here found side by side is of great significance.

The Mongol pony, as we know, was, and still is, a short-legged, stocky animal between 12 and 13 h.h. 2 in. in height, with a thick neck and heavy head and able to carry weight; but it was not fast. Mongols were bred for stamina and races were commonly run over twelve miles or more just as they are today. They stayed in herds until wanted for riding. At about three years old they were caught by lasso for breaking in. Nomads – perhaps because of their heavy felt boots – lived in the saddle and would ride even a hundred yards rather than walk.

When the first Mongol hordes crossed the Altay and the Pamir they found a less harsh climate with lush grazing, barley and lucerne growing in the valleys and rich prosperous cities in the oases. This land lay chiefly in the regions now comprising the Soviet Socialist Republics of eastern Kazakhstan, Kirghizia, Tadzhikistan and Uzbekistan; that is, from Bactria, south of the Oxus, to north of the Jaxartes. Most importantly, they found the superior type of warm-blooded horse which, following whatever race dominated the region, has successively been called the Bactrian, Turanian, Turk and most recently Turkoman. On the evidence of the Pazyryk Burials it stood 15 h.h. or more in height with fine clean limbs and the intelligent head of a Thoroughbred. It was as fast as its Arab cousin bred further west, but it had more stamina. It is believed that mares in season were run with wild stallions; if so, this could have contributed to the known strong prepotency of the breed. The semi-nomad tribesmen of the region, whose sole wealth and currency it was, took pride in its breeding and kept vast herds. Moreover they were formidable fighting men and hence valuable as mercenaries.

Inevitably, Central Asia was a cockpit. All the great invasions had this land for an objective since, apart from the wealth of its cities, these horses and their riders conferred notably superior mobility and fighting power on their possessors. Huns, Mongols and others came from the east, but there were invaders from elsewhere too: thus the powerful Scythians came from the north and west and Cyrus the Great from Iran. But the greatest was Alexander of Macedon who, in about 330 BC, founded Greek colonies in Bactria (Balkh) and Sogdiana before conquering India. He was the first great commander to exploit these horses and their riders as true cavalry. His famous charger Bucephalus may well have been a Bactrian. They were exported to Greece, as friezes of the period show, and they reached western Europe. Centuries later, together with Arabs, they were to form the root stock of the modern Thoroughbred.

China first began to import warm-bloods only after the Greeks had abandoned Bactria. For centuries the Huns, also making use of them, had been raiding into China's northern provinces and the Chinese had no answer to these 'thousand league'* horses. In 126 BC the

*An oriental league was 360 steps.

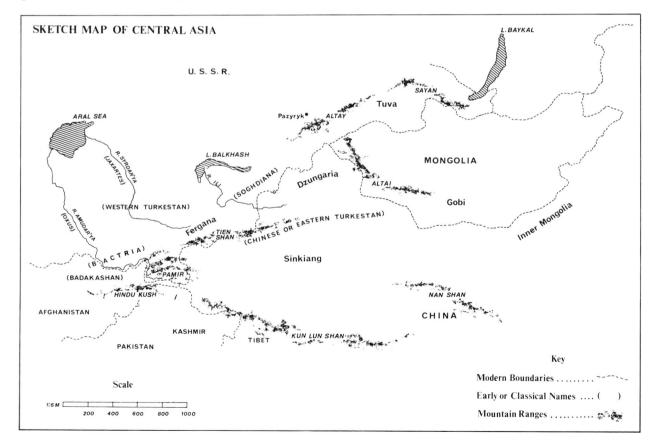

SKETCH MAP OF CENTRAL ASIA

U.S.S.R.

L. BAYKAL

SAYAN

Tuva

ARAL SEA

Pazyryk•   ALTAY

L. BALKHASH

MONGOLIA

(WESTERN TURKESTAN)

Dzungaria

ALTAI

Gobi

(SOGHDIANA)

Fergana   (CHINESE OR EASTERN TURKESTAN)

Inner Mongolia

TIEN SHAN

Sinkiang

(BADAKASHAN)   PAMIR

NAN SHAN

HINDU KUSH

CHINA

AFGHANISTAN

KASHMIR

KUN LUN SHAN

PAKISTAN   TIBET

Scale

1:6 M

200   400   600   800   1000

Key

Modern Boundaries ....

Early or Classical Names .... (   )

Mountain Ranges ....

Emperor Wu Ti heard of a fabulous strain of horse in Fergana. Nearly twenty years later, after a costly military campaign, about thirty 'superior' horses and some three thousand of 'middling or lower quality' were brought back. It was the former that the Emperor named the Heavenly Horses, which he believed would carry him to heaven. They were long known for sweating blood, but this is now generally accepted as due to a parasite. Both superior and middling types were imported and bred from thereafter, but whether in sufficient numbers to deter the Hun, who finally turned westwards to eastern Europe, is not certain. It is more likely that mounted mercenaries from border tribes, including perhaps even Hunnish tribes, armed with the Chinese cross-bow, ultimately achieved superiority over the Hun long-bow-men. Han (native) Chinese were never natural horsemen.

The Heavenly Horses were in great demand by Chinese dignitaries for drawing their mis-called chariots, which in reality were pro-cessional carriages; hence the commonly depicted ceremonial umbrella.

Genghis Khan was the last and incomparably the greatest exploiter of both Mongol and Bactrian horses within the period of this review: but, though Bactrian blood lived on in the favourable climate of western Central Asia and Europe, it gradually died out in Mongolia and China. Long before then the equestrian culture of Central Asia had had its incalculable effect on civilization.

Equestrian History of the Middle East

Lt. Gen. Sir John Glubb

I do not know whether horses were indigenous to the Middle East, or whether they were imported. The first mention of horses in the Bible is in Gen. 49:17, in connection with the death of Jacob, perhaps 1750 BC. We may assume that horses were fairly common from then onwards. Their principal use was for war, whether in chariots or as cavalry.

Domestic and transportation duties were mostly performed by other animals. The ass was the principal civilian riding animal from the earliest times, almost to the beginning of the present century. At an early date, the mule supplemented the ass for longer distances. In 2 Sam. 13:29, in connection with the rebellion of Absalom, it is stated that every man mounted his mule and fled (*c.* 970 BC).

For longer distances or in desert areas the riding and baggage animal was the camel. Horses were rarely used in the Middle East for ploughing, a task commonly performed by oxen. The horse was pre-eminently used for war, and as such was the pampered darling of his or her master.

The military arm which dominated the Middle East for many centuries was the horse-archer. These originated from the nomadic tribes of the steppes, from areas which are now southern Russia, Turkestan and Mongolia. These immense grassy plains supported great numbers of horses. When the Turkoman or Mongol went to war, he rode one horse, while three or four loose horses followed behind. By frequently changing horses, he was able to cover long distances. Common report alleged that these nomads lived, ate and slept on the backs of

Middle Eastern rider with falcon.

their horses. Their way of life made them the finest horsemen in the world. From early infancy, the boys spent most of their time practising archery.

Almost all the shooting done by the Turkomans was from horseback and at full gallop. They used short, specially stiffened bows, easy to handle on horseback. When the nomad horse-archer was about to attack an enemy formation, he placed an arrow on his bowstring and held two more in his left hand, which also grasped the bow. He then advanced at a collected hand-gallop, leaning slightly forward. The reins, which had been knotted, were dropped on the horse's neck. The rider was thereafter obliged to control his horse by using only his legs.

When about two hundred yards from the enemy, he pressed his horse into a full gallop and stood up in his stirrups. From a distance of seventy yards, he shot his three arrows in quick succession at the enemy. Meanwhile, still at full gallop, he wheeled about sharply to the right and galloped away at full speed. As he did so, he drew a fourth arrow from his quiver, and shot it back at the enemy over his horse's hind quarters.

The expression 'a parting shot', is one frequently used in English, usually meaning the last word in an argument. It has, however, been suggested that the original expression was 'a Parthian shot', and that it referred to the last arrow shot over the horse's tail.

The attack of a wave of horse-archers lasted only a few seconds, after which they galloped away out of range. There they regained their breath and replenished their arrows, while other echelons galloped in and out of action. By this means, a continuous stream of arrows was poured onto the enemy.

The most famous battle of this kind was the defeat of the Romans at Carrhae (the modern Harran) in Syria in 55 BC. Crassus was marching against Parthia with seven legions, that is to say thirty-five thousand infantry and four thousand cavalry. In the open plains between the Tigris and the Euphrates, he was attacked by the Parthian commander, Surena, with an army consisting solely of horse-archers.

The Parthians attacked all four flanks of the Roman army at the same time, galloping up and shooting their arrows continuously. The Roman infantry stood in solid ranks and were shot down, without being able to reply. Crassus was killed and his army was virtually destroyed.

Curiously enough, the same process was exactly repeated more than a thousand years later, on 19 August 1071, at Malazkirt, only 250 miles north-east of Carrhae. The Byzantine Emperor, Romanus Diogenes, had drawn up his army in two lines of heavy infantry. The Seljuq Turks, commanded by Alp Arslan, enveloped the Byzantines in a cloud of light horse-archers, who galloped up, shot their arrows and raced away in their usual manner. The Byzantine army was shot to pieces and eventually overrun, the Emperor being taken prisoner.

The tactics of the horse-archers were never mastered by Western armies. They needed for their execution wide open plains where the horses could gallop without obstruction. The Levantine countries overlooking the Mediterranean – Lebanon, Syria and Palestine – were mountainous, and obstructed by villages, orchards and cultivation. Here the horse-archers could not practise their tactics. Hostile mounted troops in country of this kind rode at one another with lance, sword or battleaxe, in conditions similar to those prevalent in Europe.

The contrast between the two systems was apparent in the Crusades. The Crusaders wore armour, and rode in saddles with high pommels and cantles, on large, heavy horses. In the words of Anna Comnena, the daughter of the Byzantine Emperor, 'a charge of Frankish knights would burst through the great wall of Babylon'. When the Crusaders entered the plains beyond the Euphrates, they were defeated by the horse-archers, but the latter could not tackle them in the broken country or in the mountains.

In 1219, the terrible Mongols, led by Genghis Khan, burst into Persia, massacring the whole population. Their armies consisted solely of cavalry, but (though they too were originally steppe nomads) they were more sophisticated than the original horse-archers. Their principal weapon was the bow, but they also carried swords and lances.

Meanwhile a new variety of horsemen had seized Egypt and Syria. The Mamlukes were a military dictatorship, which built up a great Middle East empire, including both Egypt and

Syria. Every recruit in the Mamluke army had to have been born among the nomadic tribes of the steppes. The Mamlukes likewise were horse-archers, but when they were established in Egypt and Syria, they were obliged to adopt more varied tactics. The bow remained their favourite weapon, but it could be slung at the rider's belt, enabling him also to use the lance, mace, axe or sword.

Horsemanship was the occupation of the Mamluke's life. Day after day, from morning until night, he galloped round the training field, shooting his arrows at targets. As shooting a bow required both hands, they also presumably controlled their horses solely with their legs. A deadly enmity existed between the Mongols and the Mamlukes, all of them horsemen from the steppes.

The Mamlukes exterminated the Crusaders and remained undefeated until 1517, when they were destroyed by the Ottoman Turks using artillery.

We thus find two widely different styles of Middle East horsemanship, produced by varied military tactics. On the one hand there were the Crusaders and the people of the mountains and settled areas who rode in heavy saddles and used powerful bits. These were needed to keep the horse always collected to enable the rider to use lance, sword or mace. The alternative style was that used by the horse-archers, in which the reins played only a minor part, and the rider relied on his legs. The Mamlukes seem to have evolved a compromise, which combined the best of both systems.

As we have already seen, Middle Eastern horsemanship was almost entirely dominated by war. But during the Mamluke period (1250–1517) horses also played the leading part in sport. The origin of polo is lost in antiquity, but the earliest accounts of the game are Persian. The Mamlukes were passionately dedicated to polo, and all of them, from the sultan downwards, were constant players.

Horse racing was also a Mamluke speciality, and sultans and ameers would pay very high prices for racehorses. It has been stated that the ass was the commonest riding animal in the Middle East and this remained true for the normal Egyptian civilian. But the Mamluke would never ride any animal but the horse, and the streets of the towns in their days were crowded with horsemen. Another favourite Mamluke sport was shooting birds with bows and arrows. They often rode out of Cairo on horseback to shoot water birds on the lakes and lagoons of the Delta. The Mamluke Sultan Malik-al-Nasir was alleged to have four thousand brood mares on his stud farm.

Unlike the vast grassy plains of Central Asia, the Arabian deserts seem to be utterly unsuitable to the breeding and maintenance of the horse. A thin crop of grass appears in the desert from December to April, but thereafter everything is dry and parched for eight or nine months. For some time, the horses continue to graze the dry grass, which might be called 'growing hay'. When this is finished, they are reduced to nibbling the leaves of the sparse desert shrubs. Yet, under these adverse conditions, the Arab horse has, for thousands of years, been recognized as the most beautiful horse in the world. Its most striking characteristics are the fine, lean head and the tail held high. It is the father of the Thoroughbred of the racing world of the West today.

By the autumn, the bedouin horses are thin and weak-looking. As their owners do not groom them seriously, their coats are dusty and matted. But if an alarm were raised and the Arab leaped on to the back of his mare, she would suddenly spring to life. Ears pricked, head and tail high, she would stride away to the battle as though she had been trained as a racehorse.

The bedouins only ride mares. In the open desert, where there are no stables, stallions would be a constant nuisance. As a result, most of the stallions are sold, a fact which has enabled the beauties of the Arab horse to spread to the outer world. Curiously enough, the bedouins do not geld their horses, though they practise gelding on camels.

The mares, in the days of raiding, were the

Drinker of the Wind. The mare is breathing in the air, a favourite trick of Arabian horses.

queens of the bedouin tribe. The camel is too ungainly to be used in close fighting and camel-riders normally dismount before battle and fight on foot. As a result, the galloping horse dominated the skirmishes and the charges of raiders.

To maintain a mare was a heavy expense on the Arab family. A prosperous bedouin would carry a small supply of barley on a camel, in order to feed the mare when grazing was non-existent. On the move, water for the mare to drink would also be carried on camels.

When moving camp, or setting out on a raid, the Arab nomad always rode on a camel, leading his mare on a long leading rope. The mare was never mounted, except when the battle was about to begin.

The Arabian deserts included open rolling plains, like those of Central Asia. The bedouins, however, do not seem to have used bows and arrows as the Mongol horse-archers did. Probably the special kinds of wood required for bows were not available in the desert. Their

mounted battles were open galloping affairs, where the horsemen, armed with lances and swords, raced, swerved, wheeled and chased one another. In the early part of the twentieth century, light cavalry carbines were much in demand, and were fired from horseback.

Perhaps for reasons of expense or lack of materials, the bedouin used only a pad on his horse's back, fastened by a webbing girth and without stirrups. Neither had he a bit, bridle or reins, but only a webbing halter and a single headrope.

I was somewhat alarmed the first time I was invited to ride on a pad without stirrups, and with only a rope round the mare's nose, but I found it less difficult than I had expected. The Arab mare answers readily to the rider's legs and to the use of his weight. She is extremely handy at bending, swerving and turning at a gallop. To hold her with only a rope round her nose requires 'hands', as much as do a curb and snaffle. In neither case is it a matter of brute force, but rather of mutual understanding.

One of the most delightful qualities of desert horses is their intimacy with people. Nomads who live in tents cannot shut their horses away in stables. Normally the mares are tied up to the tent pegs in front of the tent, but if the night is wet and cold, the mare will come into the tent and lie down among the people.

By day, the mares' forefeet are shackled together, and they are turned loose in the open desert to graze. Before sunset, the mares can be seen coming home. When they reach the camp, they separate, each one going to her own tent. Even if the tents had not yet been pitched when they were turned out to graze, each mare knows her tent. In Europe, people often say that horses are stupid when compared to dogs. Perhaps this is because, unlike the bedouins, we do not have our horses with us in our houses.

The most beautiful horses in the world emanated from the hostile environment of the Arabian desert. In addition to their physical attributes, they possess the qualities of sweetness and intelligence, which result from their constant intimacy with human beings.

In brief, the equestrian art has a long and varied history in the Middle East. The principal, indeed almost the sole use of horses, was for war. The many domestic duties entrusted to horses in Europe – travel, transportation or agricultural work, for example – were mostly performed by other animals, such as asses, camels or oxen.

Two types of horsemanship were developed in the Middle East, according to the nature of the weapons and the terrain. On the great plains east of the mountains of Syria, the horse-archers developed a style of horsemanship in which the rider made great use of his legs; on the Mediterranean shores, the Crusaders used powerful bits and deep saddles, from which the rider could not easily be thrown. The Mamlukes, obliged to fight alike in mountains and in open plains, devised a compromise between these two techniques.

The Age of Chivalry

Charles Chenevix Trench

There was not much written in the Middle Ages about horsemanship. Indeed there was not much written about anything. But this does not mean that there was no science of equitation. After all, there are no medieval manuals of cathedral-building, but they contrived then to build tolerably good cathedrals. Since the world of chivalry was, as the word implies, centred on the horse and its rider, and execrable roads compelled all travellers to walk or ride, we can assume that a great deal of thought was given to equitation and horsemastership. About medieval horsemastership one can learn something from the Rules of the Templars and Hospitallers, and from the works of travellers such as Marco Polo and the Sieur Bertrandon de la Brocquière, who in the fourteenth century rode disguised from Jerusalem to Constantinople. But of equitation in the Age of Chivalry we must infer what we can from contemporary pictures and from the works of masters of horse in the Renaissance period who described, probably, an established science, not methods they had just invented.

Since it loomed largest in the chivalric mind, let us first examine military equitation. Until the fourteenth century the mailed, mounted knight was master of the battlefield, for the best infantry missile weapon, the crossbow, though long-ranged, accurate and hard-hitting, took far too long to re-load when the arbalester had 'shot his bolt'.

The knight, with his arms, armour and saddlery, probably weighed on average between 224 and 238 lb., which is appreciably less than the weight of the average French,

A medieval knight by Dürer.

German or British cavalry trooper in 1914. There was thus no reason for him to ride a horse heavier than the 1914 troop horse, which was generally a fairly well-bred animal of about 15.3 h.h., weighing some 1000 lb.

Medieval pictures confirm this: knights are depicted riding lightish horses and charging at the gallop; when a horse was struck down he might (as in the Bayeux Tapestry) turn a complete somersault. The knights of Outremer favoured light breeds such as Spanish, Turkoman and even Arab horses. The popular idea of a knight riding the ponderous prototype of the modern Shire horse has no validity before the development of heavy plate-armour in the late fourteenth century. What is rather strange is that the knight's destrier was invariably a stallion. However formidable a stallion's teeth and hooves may be in a mêlée (perhaps rather exaggerated), one would have thought that this was definitely outweighed by the drawbacks of riding in war an animal which was apt to neigh loudly when silence was desirable, to become unmanageable and even to desert in the presence of the enemy if the enemy happened to be riding mares, as was the common practice of Arabs and Turks.

The knight had two great advantages denied to cavalrymen of the ancient world – a wooden saddle-tree, with high pommel and cantle, and stirrups. These enabled him to charge with couched lance and to fight hand-to-hand without falling off. But in his right hand he wielded a long, heavy lance or sword, and on his left arm he carried a heavy, kite-shaped shield which in the early chivalric period was as much as three feet long, though it was later made shorter and handier. So he had to hold both reins in the left hand, far higher than is now the practice, in a position where he had very little control of a spirited horse. Thus encumbered, he needed the mechanical advantage of a powerful curb bit, with long cheeks. The use of the indirect rein must have been almost impossible, so he probably had to turn his horse by vigorous leg-action, aided by long, sharp spurs.

He rode with an absolutely straight leg, feet thrust forward, buttocks braced against the rounded cantle, like the nineteenth-century cowboy. Since he was no fool and rode much more than we do, there must have been good reason for this. Two mishaps could unseat him in a charge: he could be thrown forward with the shock of impact or if his horse suddenly propped; he could be knocked back by the thrust of an enemy's lance. Very high pommel and cantle helped to keep him in place, but more was needed. We believe that the best safeguard against going 'out of the front window' is a shortened leather and a sloping thigh, rather than the 'sugar-tongs' seat. The knight thought otherwise, believing (as Bertrandon de la Brocquière wrote of the Turkish short-legged seat) that a man riding short 'could not support the least blow of a lance without being unhorsed'. Without actual experience of headlong charges, lance-to-shield, one can hardly dispute this expert opinion, and the present writer is disinclined to experiment. So the knight rode long lest he be bowled over backwards, and with his legs braced stiffly forward, feet in stirrups which were hung well in front of the girth, lest he be thrown or severely damaged in a delicate region by the high pommel when his horse came to a sudden, jarring halt. In the context of medieval battle this made sense. The surprising thing is that the seat was retained long after its original purpose had disappeared.

At the time of the great Norman conquests of southern Italy, Sicily, England and Syria the knight was merely a fighting man rich enough to own a war horse and calf-length mail hauberk: there was as yet no ceremony or mystique of knighthood, no concept of chivalry. The idea of the knight as a gallant gentleman dedicated to the service of God and the oppressed – unless, of course the oppressed got ideas above their station – developed during the twelfth century, with all the attendant panoply of golden spurs and heraldic insignia to distinguish him in battle. The Church encouraged this as a civilizing influence and one which directed surplus energies towards the capture and defence of the Holy Land. But it also developed in a direction which had absolutely no relish of salvation.

For war was all very well, but almost as much renown, and substantial fringe benefits, could be won at almost as much risk but with much less inconvenience and discomfort, in tournaments. These at first were miniature battles, fought between gangs of knights roughly equal in numbers, across open countryside.

They developed into single combats, on regular tournament grounds, in the presence of enormous crowds of spectators, fought often to the death but according to strict rules which forbade, for instance, the wounding of an opponent's horse, or a blow below the belt. Semi-professional knights errant toured the tournament circuit between May and September, challenging all comers: so expert were they in horsemanship and skill-at-arms that an ordinary knight had about as much chance against them as a club boxer against Muhammad Ali. They acquired wealth in prizes, and the horses, arms and armour of the vanquished. Fringe benefits included amatory favours, for central to the chivalric tourney was the concept of courtly love, or aristocratic adultery. A knight would select some lady, beautiful, accomplished, and preferably married to someone of a higher social status than himself (Lancelot and Guinevere being the most celebrated examples in romance), and fight in her honour wearing some emblem more or less intimate, which she had bestowed upon him. It was 'not done' for her to disappoint him if he distinguished himself, which was why the Popes so disapproved of tournaments but were never able to stop them.

According to *Breviare d'Amour*, at less serious medieval tournaments the ladies of easy virtue would sometimes don the knights' armour and ride around on their horses.

In the fourteenth century the whole character of war was altered by the development of the longbow, man's first weapon of mass destruction. The bodkin-pointed arrow, falling steeply from the sky, pierced mail at two hundred yards, and so quickly could a company of trained bowmen shoot that, so long as their ammunition supply did not fail, their 'arrow-hail' produced a beaten zone through which no mailed cavalry could pass. So mail was gradually replaced by plate-armour, for man and horse; but to be effective, this had to be almost complete and extremely heavy, and the destrier now had to carry anything up to 420 lb. The war horse became heavier and heavier, slower and slower, until he could hardly be spurred into a ponderous, earth-shaking trot. To make this elephantine creature relatively handy in a mêlée, curb bits were used with cheeks fifteen and eighteen inches long and horrific spiked mouthpieces, with which the charger was grotesquely over-collected and over-bent. But it was all rather bogus, for the knight seldom ventured his expensive Great Horse in battle where a single arrow could kill him or turn him mad with pain and fear, but generally fought on foot. So the armoured horseman was no longer master of the battlefield, but had been driven from it by peasants skilled in the use of the longbow costing about one shilling and sixpence, and, later, the arquebus.

In these circumstances it could hardly be claimed that the tournament was of value for military training. Losing all contact with reality, it became a ludicrously formal, highly expensive spectator-sport, in which the contestants were separated in 'the lists' by a stout wooden barrier, lest by collision they hurt one another. Fighting now with blunt weapons, the object was no longer to kill or incapacitate your opponent, but to topple him off his horse, or simply to break your lance on his shield, thus proving the impetuosity of your charge. These objects were facilitated by slender, brittle lances and by saddles without a cantle, from which one could fall without being hurt. There had to be some extraordinary accident to cause death or serious injury. The Age of Chivalry, of Saint Louis and Richard Coeur de Lion, was over; that of Don Quixote had begun.

Of course not all equitation was military. Knights spent much of their time hunting. Pictures indicate that – for no reason, apparently, but habit – their hunting seat was also straight-legged, their hunting bit also a severe curb. Although from contact with the horsemen of Islam and eastern Europe they were familiar with a more relaxed, bent-legged riding style, they did not themselves adopt it, save in Spain, where cavaliers learned from the Moors to ride *a la gineta*. Ladies, too, hunted, riding astride in divided skirts; on journeys they seem generally to have ridden pillion or sat sideways on broad pads, though in *The Canterbury Tales* the Wife of Bath seems to have ridden astride.

In the twelfth century we first hear of running horses, *equites cursores*. They were rare and expensive, no doubt partly of Arabian blood. Richard Coeur de Lion owned two, described as swifter than destriers or dromedaries, which he declared he would not sell for a thousand pounds. Probably the principal use of these valuable animals was for kings' messengers and despatch riders; but all horsemen in all ages like to race, and no doubt there were many informal races such as was described at Smithfield in Richard's reign, where the jockeys 'clapped spurs to their willing horses, brandished their whips and cheered them on with their cries'. It arouses interesting speculation that an early fifteenth-century painting of a race through the streets of Florence shows the jockeys riding (bareback) with bent legs, crouched forward over their horses' necks, much as in the modern racing-seat.

The Age of the Charger

Col. John R. Elting

The cavalryman should live only for his horse, which is his legs, his safety, his honour, and his rewards. . . . I repeat it, the strength and vigour of his horse are the cavalryman's fortune.*

Before the charger came the chariot. In fact, the first clumsy Sumerian War vehicles (*c.* 3000 BC) were dragged by little onagers. We do not know when the horse was first used for warfare, but apparently it was among the wandering peoples out of Central Asia something before 2000 BC. One chariot-fighter clan, the Hyksos of uncertain origin, held Egypt *c.* 1730–1570 BC, introducing the domesticated horse to North Africa. Similar conquering migrations spread chariot warfare from China to Britain. Among the Aryan invaders of Europe the chariot was primarily a means of transport for the chiefs, who usually dismounted to fight. Sumerians, Assyrians, and Hittites employed them much like modern tanks, to smash enemy infantry; their chariots were high and strongly built to carry several men. Egyptians favoured lighter, swifter chariots with only an archer and a driver, relying on their arrows to throw the enemy into disorder before their final assault. Their chariot force was the elite of their armies; a field army might have a total of 2500 chariots, organized in basic units of ten.

These organized chariot forces shattered the more primitive armies of militia spearmen. The Book of Job echoes the panic they inspired:

Hast thou given the horse strength? Hast thou clothed his neck with thunder? . . . The glory of his nostrils is terrible. He paweth in the valley, and rejoiceth in his strength: he goeth on to meet the armed men. He mocketh at fear, and is not affrighted; neither turneth he back from the sword. . . . He swalloweth the ground with fierceness and rage. . . . He saith among the trumpets, Ha, ha; and he smelleth the battle afar off, the thunder of the captains, and the shouting.

The chariot fighter, however, required years of training to handle his springless vehicle at the gallop across country and to shoot accurately from it – let alone to control a chariot unit in action. Professional soldiers were required, and these evolved as a military aristocracy, holding land in return for service. An elaborate logistical service was needed to support them – factories for chariot manufacture, repair shops along the army's line of communications, maintenance detachments with the troops. Forage, water, and spare horses must be always available. Stallions were used for chariot teams: one Egyptian army almost broke up when the enemy drove a mare in heat in among its chariots.

Individual horsemen appear in Egyptian art around 1400 BC, but these seem to be only grooms or messengers. Horses were small, lacking the size and strength to carry a warrior. Then, sometime during 1000–800 BC, mounted archers appear in the Assyrian army. Both the idea and the mounts probably came from Media (northern Iran) which was already breeding superior horses. As recorded on bas-reliefs, these first Assyrian efforts seem almost

*De Brack, Antoine F., *Avant-Postes de Cavalerie Légère*, Breda, 1834, pp. 61, 179

comic – each archer had a mounted attendant to lead his horse so that he might use both hands to work his bow. These apprentice troopers rode bareback and also bare legged and barefoot. However, the Assyrians – who combined scientific curiosity with utter ruthlessness – set up drill fields and technical schools for their cavalry. Later inscriptions show Assyrian horse-archers riding free, their reins resting on their horses' necks. These men are armoured and booted; they sit on elaborate horsecloths, and their horses appear to be protected by light bards. Other cavalrymen are armed with spears instead of bows, some with both bow and spear. But the chariot, now specialized into light and heavy types, remained Assyria's principal mounted arm.

After Assyria came the Medes and Persians. Persian gentlemen were brought up to ride, to shoot with the bow, and to tell the truth. They were gallant horsemen and great conquerors, but for some reason they later abandoned the bow for the shorter-ranged javelin. Moreover, they never developed an effective infantry to form a pivot for their cavalry manoeuvres.

All of these early cavalrymen rode without saddles or stirrups. Consequently only the very best of them could handle long lances or swords without the risk of losing their balance. If they lanced an opponent solidly head on, the impact was likely to send them back over their own horse's tail. A cavalry engagement tended to be a confused scrimmage in which the most effective weapon was a short stabbing-spear. Cavalry might scatter light infantry skirmishers, but had no chance against heavy infantry whose long spears could outreach the cavalryman's weapons. Also it was easy to pull a cavalryman off his mount. Mounted archers – the best known were the Scythians of southern Russia – could inflict casualties from a distance, but usually ran out of arrows before they hurt the enemy seriously.

The Parthians, who seized control of Persia in 250 BC, worked out a new system. Being master horse breeders, they improved the already excellent Nesaean stock (developed by the Medes and Persians) into great, swift chargers like the medieval destriers. These were for the Parthian aristocracy who fought with the lance, both men and horses covered with flexible lamellar armour. Their retainers, mounted on lighter horses, served as mounted bowmen. A Parthian army, therefore, was entirely cavalry: the mounted archers harassed and weakened the enemy, the armoured lancers (cataphracts) then rode him down. Given open terrain, this system was almost irresistible. At Carrhae in 53 BC some 10000 Parthians destroyed a Roman army of 30000 (the Parthian commander had an 'ammunition train' of camels to keep his horse-archers supplied with arrows). This system spread across Asia. The Sarmatians (who had conquered the Scythians) gave the Romans considerable trouble during the first century AD, their cataphracts being especially dreaded.

Rugged and rocky, Greece was infantry country. When Athenians wanted to get an important message to Sparta, they sent it by runner, not mounted courier. Battles were won by push of heavy infantry. In the semi-feudal northern kingdoms of Thessaly and Macedonia however, the nobility and their retainers fought on horseback. By careful training and hard campaigning Philip II of Macedon (382–336 BC) formed them into professional heavy cavalry: the Macedonian 'Companion cavalry', which habitually took position on the right of Philip's massive infantry phalanx, and the Thessalian cavalry who covered its left. (The outer flanks of both were, in turn, covered by allied or mercenary light horsemen.) Philip's battles were affairs of calculated manoeuvre, designed to create a gap in the enemy's line through which he could ram his heavy cavalry to take the disorganized enemy in flank and rear.

Alexander, Philip's son, was one of history's greatest cavalry generals. Quick to see and seize an opportunity, relentless in pursuit, he had an inspiring personal valour that lifted his troopers forward against any odds and kept them firmly in hand through every shift of action. His heavy cavalry were picked veterans, fired with a sense of national superiority. Even so, their battles (334–331 BC) with the renowned

Persian horse were desperate affairs, won largely through Alexander's leadership and the superior organization of the Macedonian army as a whole. Had Darius III of Persia not been a complete coward, Alexander's epic well might have been far shorter.

Alexander dead (323 BC), his generals – 'the Successors' – divided his empire and army among themselves and soon came to blows. They kept up and even elaborated Alexander's cavalry tactics, but they could not get recruits of the quality of his companions. They also made much use of elephants to suppress enemy cavalry, horses being terrified of those great beasts unless very carefully trained. Carthage also organized its cavalry after the Macedonian fashion, using native levies from Numidia (Algeria) as their light horse. Hannibal certainly knew how to use cavalry. In all his victories in Italy (218–203 BC) his cavalry was the decisive arm, riding down the Roman cavalry and then attacking the Roman infantry from behind.

Italy, like Greece, was not cavalry country, and comparatively few Romans seem to have been enthusiastic horsemen. Originally each Roman legion included a small cavalry detachment, but their idea of combat frequently was to wrestle their opponent off his horse and finish him off on the ground. During the Punic Wars a series of defeats by Carthaginian cavalry forced them to improve their mounted arm. Publius Scipio also won over many of the Numidians; his Roman and Numidian cavalry had a decisive part in his victory over Hannibal at Zama (202 BC). Victory and peace, however, saw these veteran cavalrymen disbanded. Thereafter the Romans depended on allies and mercenaries for most of their cavalry – Gauls, Spaniards, Germans, Batavians, and Thracians – either enlisted in regular 'auxiliary' squadrons or in temporary tribal levies. These were efficient enough; even at Carrhae, Gallic horsemen mauled the Parthian cataphracts before being overwhelmed by arrows. Cavalry gained in importance in the second century AD, after Rome's wars of conquest ended. The army's mission had become frontier security. Mobile forces were needed to intercept raiding bar-

barians, and so the Romans increased their cavalry and raised units of mounted infantry. These cavalrymen were famous for the splendour of their parade dress. Some units had leather saddles, though without stirrups. Standards of equitation must have been high: Hadrian (emperor AD 117–138) praised their jumping. Sarmatian troopers served in Britain; Moors in Dacia (Rumania); Spanish, Syrian, and German horsemen in North Africa. But in AD 378 the Emperor Valens bungled an attack on a Gothic encampment near Adrianople. Caught unexpectedly in flank and rear by Gothic cavalry, Valens and two-thirds of his army were killed. It was only a temporary victory for the Goths (fresh Roman troops methodically rounded them up), but Adrianople nevertheless marked a major change in warfare. For many reasons, Rome could no longer muster legions of the old come-what-may breed; existing legions were too slow and inflexible; light infantry could not stand against the barbarian assaults. For lack of other suitable troops, Rome recruited increasing numbers of barbarian cavalry. These were mostly Goths and other Germans, armed with long spears, but also included horse-archers from the Huns and related eastern peoples. As Rome crumbled such 'war bands' gradually settled throughout western Europe, setting up small states and fighting among themselves.

This process was gradual; Goths and Franks rallied to Aetius, the last great West Roman general, to break the devastating invasion of Attila's Huns at Châlons (AD 451). In Britain King Arthur and his knights of the Round Table must have been a Roman-British war band, reinforced by adventurers and refugees of many nations, which fought the Saxon invaders to a standstill during 470–500. Possibly some of Arthur's men had cataphract-type armour; probably they rode without stirrups; but the Saxons were barbarian spearmen, without armour or discipline. Arthur's small force of trained cavalry scattered them – and still lives in legend.

Some time in that dark period after Rome, the stirrup came into common use. Its invention has been attributed to the Sarmatians of the first century AD, or to the Scythians several centuries earlier, or to China or India; some writers claim that the Goths rode with stirrups at Adrianople. All this remains magnificently unproven. Being a common sense piece of equipment, the stirrup must have been developed independently by several nations. Western Europe probably adopted it during the fifth century.

Whatever its unknown history, the stirrup vastly increased the cavalryman's efficiency. He sat his horse more securely and could cut and thrust in all directions without danger of overbalancing himself; even better, he could use long lances and swords effectively. Massed shock action, horses at the dead run, troopers closed up knee-to-knee, became possible. Caught among infantry, the horseman was in far less danger of being dragged from his horse. And with all this came greater personal comfort: the incidence of hernias among cavalrymen must have declined considerably.

Iron horseshoes of the modern type appeared at an equally uncertain time during the next few centuries. Horses then could be ridden hard over rocky ground.

Cavalry now was dominant throughout Europe, but it took various forms. In the enduring East Roman Empire, the cavalryman was a long-service regular, recruited from the empire's more warlike districts. Termed a 'cataphract', he was actually an armoured horse-archer, capable of both fire and shock action, and the decisive arm of the empire's carefully organized, highly professional army. Through the centuries he defeated Goths, Vandals, Bulgars, Russians, Persians, and – after their first fanaticism ebbed – the Arabs. He held the Seljuk Turks until a niggard bureaucracy, an incompetent general, and a traitorous subordinate brought the East Roman field army to destruction at Manzikert (1071). Even then, later emperors made some head against the Turk with mercenary Norman and Asiatic cavalry until the empire's end in 1453.

In Britain and Scandinavia cavalry was slower to take definite form. Warriors might ride to battle, but they usually fought on foot (a servant held the horse ready in case of defeat). Once ashore, Viking raiders were quick to 'horse' themselves for advances inland and the easier transport of their booty, but they likewise fought dismounted. The Norman conquest brought the feudal system's armoured cavalry to England, but the Normans themselves seem to have adopted the earlier English practice: all through the Middle Ages, English cavalry tended to fight dismounted, especially when on the defensive. (There are occasional indications that England bred too few horses suitable for medieval heavy cavalry.) Along the troublesome border between England and Scotland there developed an equally troublesome breed of light horsemen, raiders and reivers, whose favourite weapon was the 'horseman's staff' (light lance) with which they were so expert they could spear salmon from horseback. Their horses were highly bred to their purpose – small, hardy, swift, sure-footed across crags and bogs where infantry hesitated to go, and able to travel seventy miles a day.

Spanish horses were prized throughout Europe, but most Spanish cavalry were 'genetours' – lightly armoured riders armed with javelins – useful only against similarly equipped Moors. Spanish heavy cavalry was good, but its habit of lancing its opponents' horses was damned as 'unknightly'.

France, western Germany, and Lombardy saw the greatest development of feudal cavalry. Their mailed knights broke repeated attacks by Avars, Saracens, Vikings, and Magyars, with energy left over for constant internal wars. Feudal armies were loose assemblies of war bands, but gifted commanders could – especially during foreign expeditions – impose enough order to manoeuvre their individualistic horsemen effectively. By the fourteenth century, however, strong kings had restricted local wars. Thus deprived of practical military experience, French knighthood developed an overweening pride that threw battles away by bull-headed assaults on prepared enemy positions, as at Courtrai, Crecy, and Nicopolis. Eventually, after a period of futile dismounted action, they relearned the art of war. Charles VII of France organized (1439–44) regular companies of heavy cavalry, *gendarmerie* of the *Compagnies d'Ordonnance*, to replace feudal levies and mercenaries.

A knight normally rode an easy-gaited 'palfrey'; just before action he mounted his 'destrier'. Destriers were clean-limbed, powerful stallions – a larger version of the modern hunter. Squires and men-at-arms had somewhat lighter 'rounseys' of lesser breeding. An armoured knight did not weigh much more than a fully equipped nineteenth-century cavalryman. In his carefully fitted armour, he could use his weapons easily and mount and dismount without assistance.

The great cavalrymen of the Middle Ages were Genghis Khan (*c.* 1162–1227), Tamerlane (*c.* 1333–1405), and their generals, who rode to the conquest of most of Asia and Russia. Carefully organized, savagely disciplined, their vast armies of horse-archers and armoured lancers combined barbarian hardihood with professional military skills. Each of their troopers had several extra horses – originally the tough, stocky Mongol pony, later the finest animals of conquered nations.

Sixteenth-century European infantry developed a formidable combination of pikes and arquebuses that was almost impossible for cavalry to break. Cavalry therefore replaced its lances with wheel-lock pistols. German *schwarz-reiters* often employed the 'caracole': successive ranks would trot slowly up to the enemy, fire their pistols, then wheel to the rear to reload. Even cavalry engagements tended to become pistol fights. Light cavalry – stradiots, Croats, hussars, argoulets – were used increasingly for scouting and raiding. Dragoons also appeared. Originally they were simply infantrymen, mounted on small horses for outpost, escort, and advance-guard service. However, their colonels tended to get them better horses so that they could fight mounted.

Gustavus Adolphus of Sweden (1594–1632) restored dash to cavalry movements, training his troopers to charge at the fast trot, firing their pistols point-blank and then using their swords. His methods were imitated by Oliver Cromwell's 'New Model' cavalry. Armour by now had been reduced to an open helmet and cuirass; during the early eighteenth century it practically disappeared. Marlborough's English cavalry charged at the trot with the sword; Charles XII of Sweden (1681–1718) led his cavalry against anything at the gallop. Frederick the Great's (1712–86) cavalry operated in tight formations at high speed. His cavalry commanders, Seydlitz and Ziethen, insisted on realistic training; their horsemen repeatedly saved Frederick from defeat. Nevertheless, Frederick was frequently baffled by Austrian irregular cavalry which cut his communications and smothered his reconnaissances.

French cavalry did not officially adopt swift shock action until 1764. Even thereafter, officers complained that instruction in equitation remained too elaborate, as if cavalry warfare could be learned in the riding hall. The French Revolution crippled the cavalry: its officers were nobles and practically all of them emigrated. Volunteers preferred to join showy new hussar regiments rather than regular units. Cavalry regiments were parcelled out to infantry divisions and much used up as escorts and orderlies. Revolutionary bureaucrats sent the stallions from the royal stud farms to the armies for remounts. In 1801, First Consul Napoleon Bonaparte used a temporary peace to reorganize the much-frayed army.

Napoleon assigned a brigade of light cavalry to each army corps for local reconnaissance; the rest of his horsemen formed his 'Cavalry Reserve'. Most of the heavy cavalry were re-equipped as cuirassiers with steel helmets and complete cuirasses; dragoons were trained – not very successfully – for both mounted and dismounted combat. During 1811 Napoleon formed more lancer regiments, both Polish and French. Finally, there were the picked veterans of his Guard cavalry.

In war, a 'screen' of light cavalry (hussars and chasseurs) from the leading corps and the Reserve concealed the *Grande Armée*'s advance and sought out the enemy. Divisions of dragoons reinforced this screen and covered the army's flanks. Cuirassiers were battlefield cavalry, committed (with dragoons and lancers) in mass for the decisive attack. Light cavalry led the pursuit.

Napoleon's system gave cavalry a strategic and tactical role not seen since Genghis Khan. However, his involvement in Spain (1808–14) seriously reduced the dragoons and light cavalry available for service with his main army. The Russian campaign (1812) ruined his cavalry; in 1813–14 his green troopers frequently could neither manoeuvre nor gallop.

France did not produce horses enough to mount Napoleon's cavalry. The shortage had to be made up by purchases in Denmark and Germany and by capture. Austria was stripped of horses in 1805 and 1809, Prussia in 1806–7. Cuirassiers were especially hard to mount since they required tall, powerful animals. (A well-cared-for cavalry horse can carry up to one-fourth of his own weight: a fully equipped cuirassier averaged 309 lb. These great horses suffered more from changes of feed and weather than did the light cavalry's smaller mounts. French horsemanship and horse-mastership were comparatively poor: Marshal Murat, commander of the Cavalry Reserve, never learned how to take care of men and horses; some regimental commanders were equally slipshod. But there were many officers and men like the dragoon who cherished his horse 'Cadet' through eight years with twelve battles and thirty engagements.

Napoleon's enemies attempted to copy his system. Austrians were brave but – except for Hungarian hussars – lacked determination and dash. Prussians were tough, especially their light cavalry. Russians, individually and collectively, were clumsy; their Cossacks harriers and hecklers, always alert, more interested in loot than glory. English cavalry was splendidly mounted, but had more courage than skill. Germans in general, it was agreed, took the best care of their horses.

Cavalry history in the Western Hemisphere began with European colonization.* In North

America its development was slow: the forested eastern seaboard offered scant opportunity for shock action. Cavalry had no real part in the Colonial Wars (1689–1764). During the American Revolution (1775–83) the new United States painfully developed effective light cavalry but by European standards their largest operations were outpost bickerings. From 1784 to 1815 the US Army was authorized to enlist a few cavalrymen during major crises; from 1815 to 1833 it had none at all. Thereafter, expansion into the western prairies made increasing numbers of cavalry necessary.

United States regular cavalry developed into the ideal dragoon, effective alike in dismounted combat and shock action. By 1850 the revolver was replacing the sabre as its primary weapon for mounted engagements. Mounted militia and volunteers from the frontier areas tended to serve as 'rangers' or 'rifles'. Armed with long rifles and tomahawks, they used their horses primarily for transportation and fought dismounted, Indian fashion. Highly mobile, but often undisciplined, their effectiveness depended on their commanders.

The American Civil War (1861–5), together with concurrent Indian campaigns, saw cavalry in action across the entire United States – a front greater than the distance from Lisbon to Moscow. Much of this territory was still wooded; cultivated areas were cut up by fences, seriously limiting cavalry action. Infantrymen were equipped with the new 'rifle-musket', which had an effective range three times that of the Napoleonic smoothbore musket. Under such conditions both Federal and Confederate cavalrymen had to learn their profession on the battlefield. Northern volunteers were mostly untrained riders on green horses. By contrast, the average Confederate trooper had ridden since boyhood; most of them provided their own mounts. They therefore had a definite initial advantage, especially in raids and outpost clashes. By late 1862, however, Federal cavalry began to get the upper hand. Northern industry provided breechloading carbines; commanders like Buford and Wilson worked out tactics to exploit this increased firepower. At Gettysburg

*See *Riders of the Far West*, page 200.

(1863) Federal cavalrymen dismounted to repulse superior numbers of Confederate infantry; then defeated Confederate cavalry in mounted engagements with sabre and revolver.

Civil War cavalry was invaluable for reconnaissance and screening. If it seldom risked a charge on unbroken infantry, it could check infantry movements and seize and hold important terrain. It also was much employed in long-distance raids against enemy communications, sometimes with great strategic effect, but often a fruitless wasting of men and horses. In 1865 a separate Federal cavalry corps (12000) marched across Alabama and Georgia, routing an equal Confederate force of all arms and storming fortified cities. Providing such forces with horses was increasingly difficult. Federal cavalry reportedly required 500 remounts a day. One regiment reported half its men riding 'small, active' mules. The Confederates suffered far worse since their cavalrymen were expected to find their own remounts.

In Central and South America cavalry was a major factor in the Spanish conquests and every subsequent war. It retained its Spanish heritage, including a reliance on skirmishing tactics and the lance. Regular cavalry of the various states was organized and equipped much on the European fashion, but was supplemented by irregulars raised among the wild backcountry herdsmen – *gauchos*, *llaneros*, or *rancheros* – who often carried the lasso as a secondary weapon.

The two American cavalry systems clashed briefly during the Mexican War (1846–8). The better training and leadership of the United States cavalry – and the greater size and strength of its men and horses – gave it an almost uninterrupted series of successes. Though superior in number, the Mexicans seldom charged home. Their rancheros enveloped American armies, but troubled their own countrymen more than American detachments.

The horse intensified Indian warfare. In North America struggles between different tribes raged through the eighteenth and nineteenth centuries.* Strong groups, such as the

*See *Riders of the Far West*, page 200.

Sioux, seized the hunting grounds of weaker neighbours. Commanche, Kiowa, and Apache raided northern Mexico and Texas methodically for generations. Young warriors with reputations to win rode hundreds of miles to lift scalps and horses from any unwary stranger. After 1850 the western expansion of white settlements brought these 'horse Indians' into conflict with the US Army. These 'wars' were many small actions, fought by isolated units which had to win – or die messily – on their own. The cavalry horse carried a trooper, his weapons, equipment, ammunition, and rations. The Indian rode light, lived off the country, and usually had spare ponies. But in winter, with Indian villages snowed in and their horses weak from feeding on cottonwood bark, the cavalry and its grain-fed mounts had the advantage.

Such Indian wars were minor affairs compared to those of South America. There, the Araucanians of southern Chile secured horses in the early sixteenth century. The Araucanians had gifted leaders, courage, and tactical skill. They halted the Spaniards; Chile could not subdue them until about 1890. Many tribes in the Argentine and Chaco similarly became mounted warriors, adopting the Spanish lance and horse gear, but retaining their native *bola*. The speed and stealth of their attacks (made when possible during the settlers' siesta) was terrible, overrunning unwary villages in minutes. However, a small ditch or wall would stop them since they never trained their horses to jump.

In Africa and Asia, cavalrymen were the spearheads of the European conquests. In both continents the native forces included swarms of irregular cavalry. To deal with these, Europeans organized new cavalry, including prideful native regiments. Their names still echo: *Chasseurs d'Afrique*, 'God's Own Guides', Spahis, the 'yellow boys' of Skinner's Horse, Cossacks of the Don, Bengal Lancers, *Cavalerie de la Légion Étrangère*. Well into the twentieth century this was cavalry service in the ancient tradition of high adventure and regimental pride.

Studying the American Civil War, several European observers realized that its new cavalry tactics exploited recent improvements in military firearms. However, their views gained little credence: American cavalry was largely dismissed as 'mounted infantry' lacking the true cavalry spirit. European cavalry continued to rely on the lance and sabre, though these weapons accomplished nothing during the Austro-Prussian War (1866): the Franco-Prussian War (1870–1) pitted them against breechloading rifles and improved artillery. Massed cavalry charges were bloody failures. Prussian light cavalry reconnoitered aggressively but was baffled by *franc-tireurs*; French horsemen proved gallant fumblers. American observers were not impressed.

Despite this defeat, French cavalry continued to stress shock action. The Germans began instruction in dismounted tactics (amid a teapot

tempest concerning what dismounted uhlans should do with their lances). The British received a liberal education (1899–1902) in modern cavalry tactics from the Boers, who were natural mounted infantry. Their 'commandos' rode rings around the British until the latter vastly increased their mounted forces.

Then came World War One, and masses of cavalry – over 100 divisions, plus corps and divisional cavalry – took the field. In general, the smaller units gave excellent service, mounted and dismounted, in the first months; larger formations, held intact for massed mounted action that never developed, killed their horses by useless forced marches. Once a continuous front was established from Switzerland to the English Channel, French and British cavalry waited to exploit a breakthrough (never quite achieved) of the German lines: meanwhile, they proved useful as a mobile reserve that could be shifted cross-country to plug gaps in the Allied defences.

A Russian cavalryman during the last war.

In Palestine the ancient battle plain of Megiddo again heard the sound of many horses running furiously to battle. British, Anzac, and Indian cavalry made amazing desert marches to ride down Turkish infantry and guns. Allenby's final offensive (1918) was one of history's most masterful cavalry operations. A French cavalry brigade distinguished itself in the Balkan mountains during the final Salonika offensive (1918). But it was in Poland and Russia – too wide a front for continuous trench lines – that cavalry fought in the old way by divisions and corps.

Large-scale mounted warfare continued through the Russian Civil War (1918–20). Wrangel's 'White' cavalry charged victoriously, standards flaunting, bands playing; cavalry helped to drive Bolshevik invaders from Poland and the Baltic states. In the West, however, tanks replaced horsemen. World War Two's beginning justified this change: German *Panzers* scattered Polish lancers and overran French cavalry in the Ardennes. But in Russia, distance, bad roads, and winter clogged armoured units, while Russian cavalry moved freely through marsh and woodlands. Hitler hastily increased his mounted arm, to include SS divisions and Cossack volunteers. In the Far East a Philippine Scout cavalry regiment covered MacArthur's withdrawal to Bataan. In Italy, American divisions improvised cavalry reconnaissance units, and Moroccan *goumiers* of the French Expeditionary Force seeped through the roughest mountains.

Today only a few horse cavalry remain, and these are largely ceremonial units. Armies now have 'armoured cavalry' and 'sky cavalry' instead – yet such formations follow 3000 years of horse-cavalry tradition.

'Never be daunted. Rely on yourself and a little good luck – and always go forward.'*

*Unidentified Napoleonic cavalryman.

Part Three

A History of Academic Equitation

André Monteilhet

Naples, the cradle of modern equestrian art

Sixty years after the Roman Empire had vanished from the western world – officially in 476 – Belisarius had reconquered Naples and Rome along with a part of the provinces lost: North Africa, Dalmatia, Italy and her islands and south-east Spain; a reconquest decided by Justinian in Constantinople. Narses finished the ultimate campaign in 552. By and by these territories were lost again; but the *basileis* of an oriental empire (the Byzantine) which spoke Greek, while preserving the Roman Imperial tradition to the very end, held on to peninsular and insular Italy for several centuries. Their final bastions there were Sardinia, Sicily and the far south, including Naples, the last to slip away, in 1139, although her Duke Sergius VII was by then already only nominally dependent on Constantinople.

Five years earlier, in 1134, a group of Byzantine equestrians set foot on Neapolitan ground where they founded a riding academy (see Treccani's *Italian Encyclopedia*). The great equestrian masters of the Renaissance were to be their direct heirs in time and place, just as, under the Roman Republic in the same land, well before the Median Wars, the *desultores* of the campagna had inherited the equestrian science of the Greek Euboean *hippobotoï*.

The entire Hellenistic and Roman periods had practically subsisted on Xenophon's *The Art of Equitation* which to this day remains the simplest and clearest expression – the most Greek in the best sense of the word – of equestrian principles, even considering the ulterior advent of the saddle complete with tree, along with the stirrup, the curb bit, the horseshoe nail and the pillars. In this respect we only need refer to modern equestrian judges, such as d'Aure, Nolan, Ruy d'Andrade, Armand Charpentier, W. Sidney Felton, Waldemar Seunig, Alois Podhajsky, Edouard Delebecque, Lily Powell-Froissard and J. K. Anderson. General Decarpentry was quite right in seeing the birth of academic equitation at the great riding schools of the Italian Renaissance. Indeed, from the twelfth to the sixteenth centuries we can closely follow the trail of that academy founded by the Byzantine equestrians at Naples in the times of *basileus* John Comnenus, a road dotted with the landmarks of equestrian authors; of uneven worth, granted, but in an uninterrupted chain: Giordano Ruffo di Calabria (Jordanus Ruffus, *Hippiatria*, written in Sicilian between 1240 and 1250); Pier de' Crescenzi, a senator from Bologna having taken refuge in Naples (Petrus de Crescentiis, *Opus ruralum commodorum*, between 1300 and 1309); Lorenzo Rusio, master farrier in Rome (Laurentius Rusus de Urbe Marescalcum, *Liber Marescalcie Equorum*, Latin or Sicilian manuscripts prior to 1340); Leone Battista Alberti (1404–72), in turn – great architect, eminent humanist, precursor of da Vinci, nicknamed 'the Florentine Vitruvius', author of two famous treatises (*Della Pittura*, 1436; *De re aedificatoria*, 1425) – has left us *De Equo animante*, written about 1440, printed in 1556.

In the Maieutics of modern equitation, the first Byzantine gift dates from the twelfth century. In the times of Alberti Italy reaped the second and last benefit of the moribund eastern empire: the arrival of refugees from Constantinople and ancient Greece swamped by the Ottoman tidal wave. Alberti was a member of the Medici Neoplatonists of the Camaldolese, where he had had occasion to hear Chrysoloras, Plethon, perhaps Bessarion, who taught him who had served in the cavalry to read Xenophon in the text. That was the way it was throughout Italy and, by sublime capillarity, in the rest of Europe, in all artistic and cultural disciplines; equitation was no exception. By the late fifteenth century there sprang up the concept of transcendency in equitation, painful and stimulating at once.

The Turkish invasion had inseminated into Italy the antique equestrian knowledge enriched by a thousand years of warlike, commercial or philosophical contacts with Asia, where the Silk Road had transported both ways, from the Bosphorus to Pe-tchi-li, the Greco-Buddhist art, Confucian or Platonist thought, the stirrup, the saddle and Christianity. The Pico de la Mirandolas and Erasmuses of the rein, however, still lacked the educator without whom they probably would never have developed the rules of higher equitation towards which the best of them were bent – knowing that it alone could preserve that fragile secular capital – and towards teaching it perhaps, some far-off day, the world over.

Still another war was needed to confer this third and decisive benefit, a war opposing in and for the Realm of Naples from 1495 to 1504 Ferdinand the Catholic, King of Aragon, Castile and Sicily, and the kings of France, Charles VIII and Louis XII, who successively pulled out their stakes. Naples remained Spanish from 1504 to 1713.
Diogo de Bragance writes,

It was then that the Renaissance Italians discovered the horses come from the Iberian peninsula. Unable to obtain from theirs what they saw done with seemingly great ease by the Spaniards, they were led to invent rules bringing their mounts up to the degree of concentration observed in the peninsular horses which, in that balance, handled themselves with the greatest of ease.*

The collection of the Andalusian or Spanish horses proceeded, aside from a millenary selection, from the seven hundred years of war fought by the Christians to expel the Moors, as well as from the tauromachy. These exercises eventually endowed the horses with

such a concentrated attitude that the halts, the rein backs, the turns, the side-steps, the sudden starts, became easy and lent their riders an extraordinary weapon, mobility in all directions.

The foundations had been laid. Without major trouble the work between the pillars then came to join them, as well as the work on two tracks, the appearance of the English Thoroughbred and the forward seat, first across country, later over big fences.

Italia, mater et magistra

Thus Italy became direct heir to the original Greek formulation which, twice over with an interval of fifteen hundred years she had put to work and redistributed. She remained from the sixteenth to the twentieth century the mother and schoolmistress whose children would train, personally or by the interposition of their disciples, prestigious foreign masters, showing the worthiest among them often unexpected methods and ways to promote on their own, and to their own credit, some discipline or matter equestrian.

In the sixteenth century Naples, Ferrara and Padua were teachers' colleges where legions of future masters sought instruction. Some of them – Italian or alien – shed their personal and particular brilliance on the equestrian history of the Holy Roman Empire, Spain, France, England and northern Europe. The work between pillars, for example, brought home by Pluvinel from the academy of his master,

*L'Equitation de Tradition Française, Le Livre de Paris, 1975

Pignatelli, was to lead one century later to the French invention of shoulder-in.

At the turn of the eighteenth and nineteenth centuries it was once more up to Naples to prepare the modern seat over fences, which a young lieutenant, Caprilli, trained at Piedmont, would pick up again in the campagna one hundred years later. In Napoleon's time, young François Baucher would be storing up in obscurity the principles of his future method in Milan. 'Mother and schoolmistress' Italy remained, explicitly from Grisone's *Ordini* to Caprilli's *sistema*, implicitly from the pillars at the Louvre to those at the Hofburg, from Welbeck to Saumur.

In 1532 Federico Grisone, 'a Neapolitan nobleman', opened a riding school which quickly gained celebrity all across Christendom. In 1550 his fellow citizen, the publisher Giovan Paulo Suganappo, published *Gli Ordini di Cavalcare* (The Rules of Riding), a bestseller which got underway the huge modern equestrian literature, with the benediction of Pope Julius III and the help of the mass media created by the relatively recent use of the printing press. The work was successively translated into French, Spanish, Portuguese, German and English. It saw eight new Italian editions between 1550 and 1600, an enormous figure for the times.

There has been considerable mockery concerning some of his recipes, admittedly worthy of the *Commedia dell' Arte*: hitting the horse with a stick, throwing water into its eyes, placing flaming straw or a furious hedgehog or cat between the thighs of one loath to advance: '*Ha traditore! ha ribaldo!*' Yet Grisone mentioned such practices as deterrents, stating that the true horseman had no need for them. He was to alternate caress and punishment and, above all, seek 'the gentle, good contact at the mouth, foundation of the entire doctrine'.

Cesare Fiaschi, practically Grisone's contemporary, who had opened his own riding academy at Ferrara two years after Grisone's at Naples, published in Bologna in 1556 his *Trattato dell' imbrigliare, maneggiare e ferrare cavalli &c.* (A Treatise of Bridling, Managing

Federico Grisone.

and Shoeing Horses). Aside from his rules for shoeing, unsurpassed until the second half of the eighteenth century, Fiaschi had the original distinction of training his horses to music, the notes of which are on hand, saying that nothing good could be achieved 'without beat and measure', a somewhat controversial theory. The horse recognizes the sound of certain instruments, such as the cavalry trumpet or the hunting horn; it does lack a sense of the musical staves of solfeggio.

Fiaschi – and probably Grisone – taught Pignatelli, that 'Third Man' at whose academy La Broue, Pluvinel, Saint-Antoine (future equerry to James I and Charles I of England), the German Fayser, Vargas and Paolo d'Aquino of Spain were to receive their schooling. The young Pluvinel arrived at Naples a year or two before the publication in 1567 of the masterful

Gloria del Cavallo by Pasquale Carraciolo. In 1571 or 1572, before he was twenty, he returned to Paris. Georg Engelhardt von Löhneysen, Palatine equerry to the Elector of Saxony, was to go off to teach at Strömsholm on the banks of the Mälar. It is uncertain whether he ever went to school at Naples, but his thick treatise of 1588 (*Die neu eröffnete Hof- Kriegs- und Reitschule*) copies almost literally entire pages of Grisone, so that he may be looked upon as a direct disciple of the Neapolitan riding schools of his century, the brilliant Cinquecento. There was to follow the publication of the *Cavalerice* by Claudio Corte (1575) and, in Spain, the *Libro de ejercicios de la gineta* by Bernardo de Vargas (1599) who, too, was, as we have seen, trained at the School of Naples.

In 1810 an adolescent François Baucher went to learn horsemastership and rudimentary equitation at the side of his uncle, who headed the stables of Prince Camillo Borghese in Milan. At that time the city was distinguished by the presence of the famous equestrian Federigo Mazzuchelli who, in 1805, had published a *Scuola Equestre, Elementi di Cavalle-*

François Baucher.

rizza. In it we find, almost word for word, the basic formula – revived by Baucher thirty years later – concerning the destruction of the horse's instinctive forces which were to be replaced by the transmitted forces: '*è della più grande importanza*', Mazzuchelli wrote already, '*di distruggere ogni volontà nel cavallo, e de convertirla in quella di fare l'altrui.*' Thus, Baucherism – which revolutionized training from about 1840 on and caused such flows of ink – owes a great deal to what the young man had observed and read in Milan; he was later to hint, without naming him, at the *maestro* whose work he had so fruitfully watched and whose book he had most probably read.

Federico Caprilli, born in 1868 in Leghorn, became a student at the Military College of Florence in 1881. He graduated to the Cavalry Section of the Military School of Modena in 1886, rising to the rank of second lieutenant at Saluzzo in 1888. Federico Caprilli made his debut at the Cavalry School of Pinerolo before being sent, in 1891, to attend the training course at Tor di Quinto, newly created at the gates of Rome by Colonel Avogadro, the director of Pinerolo. From 1894 to 1896 he returned there as a lieutenant instructor, then was transferred to the *Lancieri di Milano*, garrisoned at Nola in the campagna plain, 25 km from Naples, 20 km from Maddaloni.

At Pinerolo, with Paderni (an Austrian-trained Venetian), and even at Tor di Quinto, across all sorts of country, with Roccagiovine, Caprilli had a strong hunch of the advantage to the rider of not encumbering his horse at the moment of the jump. He had done away with the martingale but not renounced the contact with the mouth at take-off. Thus, returning from Nola, in 1898, and with his regiment at Parma, he was using his new method, the famous *sistema* of the forward seat which he was to continue to perfect until his death. It is almost certain that this Tuscan equestrian genius met in the campagna one or several former officers of the excellent Bourbon cavalry schooled in accordance with the principles of *la Nunziatella* which had disappeared in 1860. By the final years of the century some of those men might not yet have reached their sixties and would have been able to pass on their ideas to Caprilli who had not reached his thirties. Such advice would surely not have been wasted on him.

He had dumbfounded everyone in 1893, at Tor di Quinto, negotiating a 1.40 m fence. Back from the campagna, by 1898 he jumped 1.60 m with Bagongo; by 1901, 1.85 m with Vecchio; by 1902 2.08 m with Melopo. Captain Instructor at Pinerolo in 1904 and at Tor di Quinto in 1906, he won the first Italian Military in the spring of 1907 with the unforgettable Pouff.

Exhausted by his double life of playboy and sportsman, he fainted on horseback on a Turin street, breaking his neck on the pavement and dying, a few hours later, during the night of 5 to 6 December 1907.

He had seen his *sistema* adopted by the Italian cavalry and had some foreknowledge of its adoption abroad. Indeed, Caprillism triumphed definitively after World War One, among civilians as well as the military. In 1967 Major Piero Santini compiled, translated and published Caprilli's manuscript notes in London under the title, *The Caprilli Papers, Principles of Outdoor Equitation*.

From the Euboean *hippobotoï* of the sixth century before our era to Caprilli in the early twentieth century, the golden thread of Naples was never broken.

Von dem Belt bis an die Donau. . . Von der Maas bis an die Memel. . .

The Holy Roman Empire

In the mid-sixteenth century – at the time of the publication of Grisone's and Fiaschi's works, 1550 and 1556, respectively – the Holy Roman Empire (*Heiliges römisches Reich deutscher Nation*) had been brought to its zenith by Maximilian I and Charles V. The Habsburgs, having chased the Valois from Italy, were ruling Spain, Mexico, Peru and the Philippines, and they were outright owners of the Austrian lands,

Flanders and Franche-Comté, 'circles' of the Holy Roman Empire widening all the way to the Baltic Sea. Vienna had already repulsed the the Turks in 1529; and in 1550, Johann Tscherte had built the *Stallburg* there, where in 1565 the first horses of the Court were installed, today the dwelling of the Lipizzaners. The Imperial studs of Kladrub in Bohemia (1562) and of Lipizza near Trieste (1580) provided remounts for the Spanish School whose first wooden riding hall functioned in 1572 with horses directly from Andalusia or via the Kingdom of Naples and the studs which the treaty of Granada (1500) had ceded to the Venetian Republic between Bari and Brindisi: as, for example, Conversano.

The end of the century witnessed the rise of the great studs of Dillenburg (Hessen-Nassau) and Graditz (Saxony).

Löhneysen, Italianizing as we have seen, has left us not only his training treatise of 1588, but one on the art of being the perfect knight (*How to Educate Young Noblemen*), inspired by Castiglione's *Cortegiano*. While he contradicted Grisone on more than one count, he usually followed the Neapolitan teachings up to the higher airs and school leaps of the cavalry soldier.

After him, the Rhenish equestrian, Johan Jacob Wallhausen – who at Siegen near Dillenburg organized a military school at the service of Maurice of Nassau, Prince of Orange and Stadholder of Holland – published in 1616 in Frankfurt *Art of Chivalry* and *Military Art*. About the same time, Geissert and Lieb were teaching at the *Spainischer Reithstall* in Vienna and in 1628, the German translation of *L'Instruction du Roy* by Pluvinel appeared. These were followed by Wallhausen-inspired works from the pens of Johann Pinter von der Au (1664) and Georg Winter von Aldersflügel (1674).

Let us not forget that the seventeenth century was a frightful age for a Germany devastated almost from end to end by the Thirty Years War. It took the decisive victory of Prince Eugene over the Turks at Zenta in 1697, and the Peace of Carlowitz in 1699, to return Hungary and Transylvania to Christendom.

The Emperor Charles VI.

Only thereafter did Germany for a time breathe somewhat more easily. Thus Emperor Charles VI was able to busy himself with the arts and the hereditary provinces, while George I, Elector of Hanover, became king of England at the death of Queen Anne in 1714. Vienna and Hanover became the two great poles of the equestrian upswing in Germany, and so, despite wars and revolutions, they have remained to this day.

In 1729 there appeared in Germany *Hof-Kriegs-und Reitschul* (Court-War-and Riding School) by Valentin Trichter, first instructor, in 1736, at the riding school of the University of Göttingen, 'Georgia-Augusta', founded in 1734. Its first principal was Baron Gerlach-Adolf von Münchhausen, cousin of the great teller of tall tales.

In 1733 in France, François Robichon de La Guéninière published *École de Cavalerie*, which

was to become the 'equestrian Bible' of the School of Vienna where Adam von Weyrother, the first of a 'dynasty', was to become director that same year.

It was a memorable decade, indeed: in 1727 Baron Eisenberg, a Thuringian horseman, former student at the School of Vienna, published in London *Description du Manège moderne*, a publication underwritten by such personages as Louis XV, George II and Prince Eugene. The inauguration of the riding school was in 1735 at the *Hofburg*, Fischer von Erlach's masterpiece, where the noble Lipizzaners have been working in unwavering accordance with the principles of the old French school for almost two and a half centuries, without any interruptions other than the French occupations of 1805 and 1809 and the withdrawal to Upper Austria from 1945 to 1955.

Meanwhile, in 1760, at Göttingen, Münchhausen was fortunate to hire as instructor Johann Heinrich Ayrer (1732–1817). Born in Coburg, also schooled at Vienna, Ayrer, Sr., was one of the greatest horsemen not only of Germany but Europe. His prestige, a determining factor in the renown of the Georgia Augusta in the eighteenth century, caused him to be raised to the rank of Member of the Faculty. In 1784 he founded the Göttingen Veterinary School after the pattern of that of Lyons. Goethe, a fine outdoor horseman, went to pay him homage in 1801.

With Ayrer at Göttingen, the austere and indispensable manège work was practised, as it was at Vienna and Versailles. Two men of war, two Germans, one of whom ended up as Marshal of France, were the basic promoters of the turnabout in cavalry tactics: the Prussian, Friedrich-Wilhelm von Seydlitz; and Maurice, Count of Saxony, the latter to be mentioned again once we get to the subject of France.

Seydlitz (1721–73) was to Frederick the Great what Lasalle and Murat were to Napoleon: a leader of men. He initiated the *all-out* charge which surprised and overran the Franco-German cavalry at Rossbach in 1757, the Russians at Zorndorf in August 1758 and the Austrians at Hochkirch in October 1758, before he himself, severely wounded, was carried off in the disaster of Künersdorf in 1759. The French came across to the system a little later, with d'Auvergne at the *École Militaire de Paris* (1756–88) and with the Carabineers at Saumur (1771–88).

Two German authors distinguished themselves during the second half of the eighteenth century: Baron J. B. von Sind, disciple of La Guérinière, and of Regenthal in Vienna, published in 1762 *Art du Manège*, first in Bonn, then in a new edition in Paris in 1774. In Cassel, in 1791 (the same year which saw the first German edition of La Guérinière), the Hessian Ludwig Hünersdorf (1748–1813) published *Anleitung zu der natürlichen und leichtesten Art, Pferde abzurichten* (A Guide to the Natural and Easiest Way of Training Horses).

In 1804 the Holy Roman Emperor Francis II of Habsburg assumed the title of Francis I, Emperor of Austria. After Austerlitz (2 December, 1805) he renounced, on 6 August, 1806, the secular title first created by the Senate of Rome and her population, then restored by Charlemagne. The Holy Roman Empire had come to an end.

Several German nineteenth-century horsemen deserve mention.

Louis Seeger (1794–186?), former pupil of the Spanish School in the time of Max von Weyrother, ran his own equestrian establishment in Berlin, the 'Seegershof'. In 1844 his book, *System der Reitkunst* (A System of Equestrian Art), was published with a dedication to Prince William of Prussia. After Baucher's tour in Berlin, he wrote, in 1852, a pamphlet against his method, *Herr Baucher und seine Künste. Ein ernstes Wort an Deutschlands Reiter* (Mr Baucher and his Artifices. A Serious Warning to Germany's Horsemen).

Seeger's contemporary and rival was Seidler (1798–1865) who was entrusted with the direction of Berlin's *Lehr-Eskadron* (Instruction Squadron). He had taken an interest in Baucher's method and taken lessons from that '*Scharlatan*' (sic); thus Seeger, who considered himself the only person worthy of the post at the *Lehr-*

Gustav Steinbrecht.

Eskadron, actually took aim at Seidler in his pamphlet against Baucher.

Gustav Steinbrecht (1808–85) was by far the most famous of all Germanic horsemen of his time. He was studying veterinary science when Seeger, who gave him riding lessons, persuaded him to become an instructor. He was only twenty-six years old when he ran a riding school in Magdeburg. In 1842 he returned to Berlin. Meanwhile he had married Seeger's niece and succeeded the uncle as head of the Seegershof in 1849. Ten years later he had an occasion to purchase an 'institute' at Dessau. This was to be the heyday of his success, when he gave himself up exclusively to training dressage horses, becoming a veritable purveyor to circuses like Renz and Herzog. One of his pupils was the famous circus equestrienne Elisa Petzold. He left behind an important book – 'kollosal', it might be called – *Das*

Gymnasium des Pferdes (The Gymnasium of the Horse). Death in 1885 prevented him from finishing it himself, and the task was accomplished by his pupil Plinzner who published it during the same year.

Paul Plinzner (1852–192?) was one of Steinbrecht's favourite pupils and the one to whom Steinbrecht entrusted the compiling and finishing of his book. Plinzner's talent caused him to be employed as a high-grade instructor at William I's private stables; later he became equerry to William II. He wrote several books on equestrian subjects.

Gebhardt (1842–1918) was born in Berlin of a Prussian family. He spent a great part of his career in Vienna. Towards 1863 or 1865 he went to study at the Spanish School. He was sufficiently gifted for the Austrian Emperor to appoint him chief instructor of that academy in 1887, despite the recent memory of Sadowa (1866). He gave him proof of even greater trust by appointing him equerry to the Empress Elisabeth. For various reasons, some of them political, he returned to Germany in 1906, and although a civilian became chief instructor of the Hanover Cavalry School.

Let us close this list with von Heydebreck (1866–1935), a field artillery officer. Passionately interested in teaching, he added numerous footnotes to the fourth edition of Steinbrecht's *Das Gymnasium des Pferdes*.

The Dual Monarchy

From 1806 to 1918 Austria and Hungary lived in cohabitation filled with often stormy household scenes (1848–9), followed by reconciliations (the 1867 Compromise), accompanied by occasional meddling on the part of other peoples of Habsburg origins: Czechs, Poles, Slovaks, Rumanians, Croats, Triestinos. Chased from Germany and practically all of Italy in 1866, the monarchy became resolutely Danubian in outlook, turning its eyes toward the Balkans (Bosnia, 1878). Below we shall be dealing with what the diplomats of the *Belle Époque* called 'Austro-Hungarian'.

This political complex already had control over several great studs of international reputation: Kladrub (1562) in Bohemia; Lipizza (1580) in Carniola; Piber (1798) in Styria; Mezöhegyes (1785) and Bábolna (1789) in Hungary, the most celebrated of all, hosting the most famous foundation sires – *Gidran* in 1812, *Nonius* in 1816, *Obajan* in 1853, and so on; Mezöhegyes had sheltered the Lipizzans in 1809. Piber became a state stud in 1858 and from then on produced a type of Lipizzan lighter than the large coach-horses, for the specific needs of Hungary, Croatia, and Transylvania.

Until 1808 the Spanish School of the Viennese Court (*Spanische Hofreitschule Wien*) was the only institution giving part-training to young cavalry officers. It fulfilled this function up to the demise of the Imperial and Royal cavalry, without neglecting its role of 'Riding Teachers' College', under the birch rod (*Birkengerte*) of a Pleiad of chief instructors (*Oberbereiter*), such as the last two Weyrothers: Gottlieb (1810–15) and his brother Max (1815–33), von Nadosy (1859–65), Niedermaier (1865–87), Meixner (1897–1916) and Lindenbauer (1942–51); of directors (*Leiter*), such as Holbein von Holbeinsberg (d. 1910), author of the precious *Directives* published in 1898, van der Straten-Pontholz who saved the School in 1918, and Alois Podhajsky, along with General Patton its saviour of 1945, and author of several books, chiefly *Die Klassische Reitkunst* (The Complete Training of Horse and Rider in the Principles of Classical Horsemanship).

Three officers deserve separate mention because they exercised considerable influence as military riding instructors: Oeynhausen, Edelsheim and Josipovich.

Börries Christian von Oeynhausen (1812–75), alumnus of the Göttingen manège (he was Westphalian) taught from 1844 to 1850 at the Central Riding Institute of Salzburg, then at Vienna (1850–75) where that institution had been transferred. He has left several valuable textbooks.

Colonel, later General, Leopold von Edelsheim, a brilliant combat officer in 1859 and

1866, taught in Vienna Cesare Paderni, future instructor of Caprilli.

General Sigmund von Josipovich (1869–1945), before 1914 instructor at the *Militär-Reitlehrerinstitut* of Vienna, went to the Higher Institute of Military Equitation in Budapest in 1922 and in 1930 was transferred to Örkeny, where he taught brilliantly till 1942. Having taken refuge in Vienna, he perished there during a bombing raid in January 1945.

Notwithstanding its radiance, the Spanish School did not, indeed, impart military instruction to a modern cavalry worthy of the name. Austria acquired such a school in 1808, the *Militär-Equitations-Institut* at Wiener-Neustadt, organized by Archduke Charles, the following year's hero of Essling and Wagram. Dissolved in 1823, the Institute was replaced in 1836 by the *Militär-Zentral-Equitations-Institut* at Salzburg, set up by Radetzky. Chief instructor there in 1844, Oeynhausen followed it in 1850 to the Ungargasse in Vienna. Rechristened *Zentral-Kavallerieschule* in 1860, *Zentral-Kavallerie-Kurs* in 1870, it became in 1875 the famous *Militär-Reitlehrerinstitut* (Military Riding Instructors' Institute) – whose best alumni were admitted for additional training to the Spanish School – which till 1914 trained practically all Austro-Hungarian cavalry and field artillery officers, offering a programme of racing, long-distance rides from Vienna to Berlin, international dressage tests, puissances, stag hunting, and the rest.

The *Militär-Reitlehrerinstitut* lived on for a short time (1919–38) at Schlosshof. Then came the *Anschluss* and with it the end of the glorious Austrian cavalry.

But the Spanish School lives on!

In France

When 'the father of French equitation', Antoine de Pluvinel (1555–1620), was a young man, Monsieur de Sourdis, prime equerry to Charles IX, brought him back with him from Naples. His outstanding training at Pignatelli's school caused him, in turn, to be appointed prime

equerry to the King's brother, the Duke of Anjou and future Henri III whom he accompanied to Poland when the Prince was elected that country's king in 1573. When Charles IX died in 1574, his brother made his way back from Cracow on horseback in the company of Pluvinel and two other French noblemen. Pluvinel was rewarded with a number of trusts and benefices which were confirmed by Henri IV (1589–1610). Notably, in 1594 he was authorized to open the Parisian riding academy near the Louvre where he had the honour of instructing his fourth sovereign, young Louis XIII (1610–43). One of the happy results was *L'Instruction du Roy en l'Exercice de monter à Cheval* (1625), a posthumous publication splendidly illustrated by Crispin de Pas. Many times over Pluvinel quotes his master Pignatelli, 'sparing the rod and generous with caresses', having inherited his tact and discretion which left the horses all their 'gentle kindness'. His co-alumnus at Naples, Salomon de la Broue,

Shoulder-in, from *École de Cavalerie* by La Guérinière.

had published *Le Cavalerie françoys*. He seemingly inaugurated, 250 years prior to Baucher, the flexions at the neck which he had undoubtedly learned at Pignatelli's.

There followed Menou de Charnizay, an old friend of Pluvinel, Pierre de la Noüe (publ. 1620), Jacques de Solleysel (publ. 1664), Fouquet de Beaurepaire (publ. 1671), du Breuil-Pompée, Saunier Sr. and Jr., and Monsieur de Vendeuil, La Guérinière's 'illustrious master'. La Guérinière himself was the paragon of the masterful classical equitation of France. His *École de Cavalerie* remains to this day the 'equestrian Bible' of dressage not only at the Spanish School of Vienna but for many European, American, even Japanese specialists.

François Robichon de La Guérinière (1688–1751), riding master by royal appointment in 1715, director of the royal manège of the Tuileries from 1730 to 1751, was the first to describe the essential lesson of shoulder-in (where he developed on the straight line Newcastle's circular work on two tracks) and the more subtle one of the *descente de main* (yielding of finger pressure on the reins on a balanced horse which is not to change its pace or alter its attitude). His treatise of 1729–30, written in the impeccable French peculiar to the eighteenth century, illustrated with the famous engravings by Parrocel, no less than his abridgement, *Élémens de Cavalerie* (1740), has gone through several new editions and complete or partial translations in the principal vernaculars.

Administratively, La Guérinière depended on the *Grand Écuyer* of France resident at Versailles. After his time, the manège of the Tuileries lost much of its brilliance. Later it sheltered the Revolutionary Assemblies and eventually, in 1803–4, was demolished on the orders of the First Consul to make room for the rue de Rivoli.

What for simplicity's sake is today called the School of Versailles (Great and Small Stables) was installed in 1682 in the royal city by Louis XIV; but the institution had long since been functioning in Paris. The first known of the Grands Écuyers of France was Xaintrailles,

M. de Nestier, Premier Écuyer of Louis XV.

former companion-in-arms of Joan of Arc. Until the end of the *ancien régime*, Versailles, whose last Grand Écuyer was the Prince of Lambesc, was working under the direction of eminent masters, such as Cazeau de Nestier (d. 1754), François de Salvert, Montfaucon de Rogles, Lubersac, the Marquis de la Bigne or the d'Abzac brothers. In 1793, in order to save the royal horses, la Bigne, the only one not to have emigrated yet, obtained from the *Convention* permission to establish an '*École Nationale d'Équitation*' (National School of Equitation), transformed in 1798 into an '*École d'Instruction des Troupes à Cheval*' (School for the Instruction of Mounted Troops). The teaching there was entrusted to former *piqueurs* (subordinates in charge of breaking in green horses and similar chores) of the Royal Stables (Jardin, Gervais and the Coupés), till its transfer, in 1809, to Saint-Germain-en-Laye, where it disappeared in 1814.

At Versailles, however, an entirely novel doctrine and method of cavalry use was now to see the light: on the advice of Marshal de Saxe, one of his former aides-de-camp, Louis-Hector Drummond de Melfort (1721–88) had submitted in 1749 to the war minister, d'Argenson, a report advocating simplification of cavalry manoeuvres and, above all, the application of the all-out charge, instead of charging, as before, at the trot, which Maurice de Saxe had successfully inaugurated at Fontenoy in 1745. The following year Drummond de Melfort, Lubersac and Montfaucon de Rogles were gathered at the manège of the *chevau-légers* of the Royal Household where the younger Jacques-Amable d'Auvergne (1729–98) was also working at the time. At any rate, in 1751 (the year of La Guérinière's demise) Louis XV decided to found the *École Militaire de Paris* which opened its gates in 1756. D'Auvergne was to be its only chief instructor until its closure, for lack of funds, in 1788. This had given him time to train a Pleiad of horsemen who were to teach at Saumur: Boisdeffre, Livron before, and Ducroc de Chabannes after the Revolution.

After the lessons of the Seven Years War, Choiseul and Madame de Pompadour persuaded Louis XV to create, in 1764, five cavalry schools of which only a single one, Saumur, was ever to function, from 1771 to 1788. It, too, was going to endow the French cavalry with an officer corps, many of whose members were to be met up with again in the armies of the First Empire.

In 1814 Louis XVIII re-established two of the pre-1789 schools: Versailles and Saumur. The former disappeared definitively in 1830. Pierre-Marie d'Abzac had still had time there to train his successor, Antoine Cartier d'Aure (1799–1863). An analogous role was played at Saumur, from 1814 to 1817, by the Marquis Ducroc de Chabannes, former pupil of d'Auvergne and, to a point by Messrs Rousselet and Cordier, former pupils of the *piqueurs* of Versailles, as well as of the older d'Abzac. Political circumstances – a Bonapartist plot – closed Saumur from 1822 to 1825.

D'Aure, who unofficially practised the '*trot à l'anglaise*', the rising trot, established himself on his own account in 1830. In 1834 he dedicated his *Traité d'Équitation* to Lord Henry Seymour, taught the Orléans Princes and carried on an acerbic controversy with Baucher from 1842 to 1855. Chief instructor at Saumur from 1847 to 1855, he promoted racing and outdoor equitation across all sorts of rough country. His famous *Cours d'Équitation* (1850) constituted the basis of French military equitation at the time, its author playing a role comparable to that played by d'Auvergne between 1756 and 1788. He resigned for reasons of ill health (the scrape about the circus equestrienne, Madame Isabelle, who was to conduct an experiment at Saumur, served solely as a pretext) and finished his career as inspector general of the Imperial Studs in 1861, dying at Saint-Cloud on 6 April, 1863.

François Baucher, son of a Versailles wine merchant, learned horsemastership and the rudiments of equitation in Milan (1810–14) at the side of his uncle, who was Prince Camillo Borghese's *First Piqueur*. There he watched *maestro* Federigo Mazzuchelli and retained his idea of the destruction of the horse's instinctive forces, as well as perhaps the flexions inherited from the Neapolitan School. Returning to France, he brilliantly developed his 'first manner' (too difficult for whoever lacked his physical capacities), first in Le Havre and Rouen, in 1820, then in Paris, in 1834, where, in association with such famous circus riders as Pellier and the Franconis, he went from triumph to triumph. It was no different abroad, until his accident of 1855. In 1842 his *Méthode d'Équitation* poured oil on the fires: the great 'Romantic quarrel' between his own partisans and those of d'Aure who accused him of 'dulling' his horses.

The 1855 accident (the tent's chandelier broke loose, fracturing one of his legs and severely hurting his torso) set an end to his public career. But by a *tour de force* he succeeded in working out his 'second manner', far more accessible to the average rider. He died in March 1873, giving his ultimate and movingly

Alexis François L'Hotte (from a painting by Col. Margot).

reported advice to his friend, Colonel L'Hotte.

General Faverot de Kerbrech (1837–1905), a pupil of Baucher, wrote a book, *Dressage méthodique du cheval de selle d'après les derniers enseignements de Baucher* (1891), an exposé of the principles advocated by his master at the end of his teaching career.

General L'Hotte (1825–1904) had been remarkably wise in becoming the friend and disciple of both d'Aure and Baucher. Besides, he had been lucky in finding for his first riding instructor an obscure Major Dupuis who, in Portuguese exile, had received the ultra-classical schooling 'à la Marialva' which was as traditional as that imparted at old-time Versailles. A career officer, when a second lieutenant at Saumur in 1846, Alexis L'Hotte had the benefit of the venerable Rousselet's advice to set his horse *straight*. In 1849 he became friendly with Baucher in Lyons; d'Aure was his chief instructor at Saumur from 1850 to 1851. He himself was to be chief instructor from 1864 to 1870 and colonel of Dragoons from 1870 to 1871. Promoted to brigadier general in 1874, he commanded the cavalry school from 1875 to 1880. Major-general and inspector-general of cavalry, he entered the reserve in 1890 and retired to his native town of Lunéville where he died in February, 1904. Sent on important missions to Austria, he had returned with the elements of the famous rules of the French cavalry, dated 1876. His two posthumously published works – *Un Officier de Cavalerie* (1905) and *Questions Équestres* (1906) (A Cavalry Officer and Equestrian Questions, respectively) are inexhaustible mines of the history of equitation and the equestrian knowledge of 1900.

A brilliant Pleiad of artists was formed by several highly gifted contemporaries or near-contemporaries of Generals L'Hotte and Faverot de Kerbrech. All, to varying degrees, combined riding and writing talent, producing several important books.

Captain Raabe (1811–89), a pupil of Baucher, brought some interesting modifications to the method of his master, and the explanations of his own practice turned the pupil into a master in his own right who developed the talents of two pupils of his own, Major Bonnal and Barroil who each left us a book approved by 'Father Raabe'. He himself produced *Manuel Équestre* (1845), *Nouvelle Méthode d'Équitation* (1848), *Traité de Haute Équitation* (1863), three books constituting the essence of his writings. He was a giant of a man, sarcastic, wielding a pen as sharp as his hands were light and his legs powerful. He used to say that 'the horse must carry the Good Lord on its back and have the devil under its belly'. During the Crimean War he proved this saying when he bet Captain Nolan that he would make his horse jump into the Black Sea off a forty-five-foot high cliff in order to show the point to which training could render a horse submissive to its rider's will. While Nolan never got off the ground, Raabe's training method let him win the wager, the rider being rescued *in extremis*, the horse drowning, alas.

Colonel Guérin (1817–84) spent a great part of his life at the School of Saumur. Since he was a *sous-maître* (non-commissioned officer) there at the time of the experiment with Baucher's method at the cavalry school in 1843, the master, aware of young Guérin's gifts, introduced him to it in person. He was just as adroit in assimilating the method of d'Aure, who became chief instructor in 1847. As skilful in the riding school as he was bold outdoors, he was able to give signal proof that one and the same horse could meet the requirements of both kinds of equitation. His early recognized talent let him climb in less than a decade from non-commissioned to field officer. When d'Aure left, he was appointed chief instructor. He was, aside from an excellent rider, a remarkable teacher, 'his oral teaching was luminous'. Unlike his successor to the chief instructor's post, General L'Hotte, he developed a number of brilliant horsemen. He also was the first and one of the most able '*fusionnistes*' of the two methods, leaving us several books, chiefly *Cours d'Équitation*, 'where the combination of the methods of his two masters is skilfully presented'.

Major Dutilh (1828–79), Guérin's pupil, became chief instructor (1874–7), having started off as a private. Guérin's teaching had likewise made of him a '*fusionniste*' of the methods of Baucher and d'Aure. Rightly considering that only complete control of the horse's neck allowed it to make the best possible use of its powers in manège and outdoor work, as different as they might be, Dutilh explained gymnastics of the neck enabling the rider to obtain its complete raising combined with a corresponding ramener; or, conversely, to obtain its stretching for outdoor work. In brief, the neck, through its acquired flexibility, developed by such gymnastics, permitted a permanent contact of mouth with bit. When the hand was lowered the neck stretched, when it was raised the neck raised and arched itself. A born teacher, he gave his pupils excellent oral explanations of his principles which he set down in a book, *Gymnastique Équestre*.

Captain Beudant (1863–1949) was, according to General Decarpentry, 'the most dazzling horseman I have ever known'. The modesty of this sorcerer was equalled only by his talent. He, too, had come up through the ranks. He became aware of Baucher's method (second manner) through his commanding officer, General Faverot de Kerbrech, as well as indirectly. He assimilated it so well that he found it the easiest to apply, saying, 'It is in fact because I am not a true horseman that I am using the means most within my capabilities.' He obtained the unlikeliest airs from his horses, and this with seemingly extraordinary ease. Faithful to the principle 'hand without legs, legs without hand', he eventually no longer even used his legs; and this was why he called his last book *Hand Without Legs* (1945). Others of his writings are *Extérieur et Haute-École* (1923) and *Dressage du Cheval* (1929).

Captain de Saint-Phalle (1867–1908) combined the fortunes of high birth, intelligence, wealth and talent. He was a meteorite streaking through the equestrian world of his time, whatever the profusion of its men of talent. Admitted simultaneously to *Polytechnique* and *St-Cyr*, he opted for the latter and graduated sufficiently near the head of his class to have his choice of the cavalry. Stationed with the 2ème Hussars at Senlis, he undertook the training of *Mademoiselle d'Etioles*. In 1899 he published his first book, *Dressage et Emploi du Cheval de Selle*, the result of notes written down during his training of that mare. In 1902 he won the first 'military' championship (ancestor of the three-day event) with another Thoroughbred mare, *Marseille II*. Appointed captain instructor at the cavalry school in 1902, he spent his days on horseback, without neglecting his regular service duties. It was at that time that he paid his somewhat stormy call on General L'Hotte in Lunéville and that Fillis defied him in a wager to execute certain airs he had described in his book. The overwork involved in training his horses, *Théo* and *Iran*, alongside his military duties, got the better of his health. He won his bet but had to leave the school to take care of himself. He still had time to finish his second book, *Équitation*, published in 1907, but also to see the death of Mademoiselle d'Etiolles who had determined his voc-

General Decarpentry.

ation. He himself died the following year, at the age of forty-one, giving the lie to his own axiom: 'Riding has never yet caused anyone's death.'

This knowledge, enriched by a half-century of practice and observation, was set down on paper by General Albert Decarpentry (1878–1956), equerry at the Cadre Noir from 1907 to 1914, severely wounded at Verdun in 1916, president of the Olympic Dressage Jury, where he used to 'leave his nationality in the cloakroom', and who died in Paris on 29 May 1956. He left important writings, such as *Baucher et son École* (Baucher and His School, 1948) and *Équitation Académique* (Academic Equitation, 1949, and another, posthumous, edition in 1957) the sum total of all current equestrian knowledge.

The cavalry school of Saumur pursued its brilliant career after World War One, under Chief Instructors Wattel (1919–29); Danloux (1929–33), who perfected and introduced in France Caprilli's jumping system; Wallon (1933–5); Lesage (1935–9), who won the Olympic gold medal in dressage at Los Angeles in 1932; Margot (1945–72); Lair (1958–64); Saint-André (1964–72); Boisfleury (1972–5);

Bouchet (1975), who died in line of duty; and since then Durand.

In 1973 the *École d'Application de l'Arme Blindée et de la Cavalerie* (School of Instruction in Armoured and Cavalry Warfare), or *EAABC*, became the *École Nationale d'Équitation*, or *ENE* (National School of Equitation), a large-scale civilian institute where the Cadre Noir, detached to serve equestrian instruction, is hiring by and by not only military but civilian instructors and 'sous-maîtres' (subordinate instructors) who, except for a few details such as special braids and no epaulets, are wearing the very same uniform.

Spain and Portugal

Cradle of horses that have been famous since antiquity, at the dawn of the modern age (Columbus's first voyage and the reconquest of Granada in 1492), the Iberian peninsula owned a horse which at the time was unique in Europe: the Andalusian, also called 'the Spanish jennet' (*jinete*, or *alfario* from the Arab *alfaraz*). Until the end of the eighteenth century this horse was the great favourite of princes, warriors, breeders and the greatest horsemen of Europe and America. A descendant of the Iberian horse favoured by Hannibal and Caesar in turn, infused with oriental and Barb blood of horses originating in Bactria, it had been introduced by the Moors. Its high collection had been developed over seven centuries of *reconquista* carried on by sword-armed horsemen and by a tauromachian equestrian tradition dating back to the Cid Campeador of the eleventh century. Thus the peninsular horses had become incomparable mounts for dressage, for battle or the *rejoneo* so perfectly defined by Diogo de Bragance, whose book we mentioned earlier.

We have already seen, apropos the Neapolitan School, the way the Italian Renaissance horsemen, past masters in the matter, had turned those marvellous Iberian horses to the best account, benefiting their cosmopolitan pupils and enabling the Andalusian horse to circulate throughout the Holy Roman Empire, Denmark, France, England and the Americas.

As early as 1381 *O Livro de Alveitaria*, by the Portuguese monk Mestre Giraldo, had opened the way for the Iberian authors. Then, towards 1434, ahead of his age, King Duarte of Portugal (1401–38) had written *O Livro da Ensynnança de Bem Cavalgar Toda Sella*, a training treatise, with an eye to the very best outdoor use of the horse, which is remarkable for its sparing use of the aids. Later Portugal saw the publication of the *Livro de Cavallaria* by Fernando Teles de Meneses (1605); *Tratado da Gineta* by Frei Pedro Galego (1629); *Tratado de Cavallaria da Gineta* by Pinto Pacheco (1670); and, eventually, the valuable *Luz da Liberal e Nobre Arte de Cavallaria* (1790) by Manoel Carlos de Andrade, a contemporary of the great Marialva.

During the same period the Spaniards produced their own equestrian literature: *Lo Cavaller* by Ponz de Menaguer (1532); *Tractado de la cavallería de la gineta* . . . by Pedro Aguilar (1570); *Tratado de la cavallería de la gineta y brida* by Juan Suárez de Peralta (1580); *Libro de la gineta en España* . . . by Pedro Fernández de Andrade (1599); *Teoría y exercicios de la gineta* . . . by Vargas Machuca (1600); and *Palestra particular de los ejercicios del cavallo* . . . by Andrés Dávila y Heredia (1674).

The Andalusian horse, which has not degenerated since, is bred chiefly in the provinces of Cádiz, Córdoba, Huelva and Sevilla, as well as in Spanish and Portuguese Estramadura, in Portugal chiefly north of Alentejo. Today the capital of the Spanish Andalusian is Jerez de la Frontera where in 1740 the Carthusian Reverend Fathers founded their famous stud producing the no less famous Cartujano horse, remount of the new Escuela Andaluz established by the Spanish government in 1974. Breeding stock had been scattered during the War of Independence (1808–13); but the large *ganaderías*, emptied during the Napoleonic Wars, were quite quickly restored in the nineteenth century. They did not suffer during the Carlist Wars and very little during the 1936–39 Civil War, since most of the Andalusian Plain was under Nationalist control from the start.

Nowadays, Spanish breeding keeps three great stud books: the *Andalusian* (also called 'the Spanish Pure-bred'); the *Arabian* and the *Anglo-Arab*. Almost all Andalusian and Arab breeding is carried on in Andalusia; there are two studs in Madrid, one in Mallorca. Andalusia also boasts twenty Anglo-Arab studs, while there are seven in Madrid and one in Biscay. Olympic champion Paco Goyoaga's famous *Vergel*, though foaled at Salamanca, was of Andalusian Cartujano origin.

The art of *rejoneo* obliges the horse trained in the Andalusian manner, when facing the bull in the arena, to execute all figures – *suertes* – up to the decisive stab – *rejón* – . . . . needless to dwell on the training, submissiveness and obedience, let alone suppleness, required of these horses . . . (General Sebastián Díez Rumayor).

Andalusian training excludes the rising trot and includes direct flexions, using the cavesson.

From the fourteenth century onwards Portugal had been purchasing Andalusian horses in Castile; but after sixty years (1580–1640) of *Cativeiro* under Spanish overlordship, it was only by the end of the reign of Dom Joâo V (1706–50) that the great studs were born which were the glory of the Lusitanian realm till the late eighteenth century and which eventually allowed for the preservation and restoration of the breed called *Alter de Châo*, the Portuguese counterpart of the Spanish *cartujano*.

The first stud was the royal one of Portel. It was founded in 1749 and merged in 1757 with that of Alter de Châo near Portalegre, founded in 1751. Gradually other studs of Alentejo were annexed by it, the most important being the Vila Boïm stud, near Elvas. The 'Alter horses' were of pure-bred Andalusian origin and remained so till the last third of the eighteenth century, when as, elsewhere, 'utilitarian' crossings were attempted in Portugal. Nevertheless, the *haute école* horses ridden by a 'Portuguese La Guérinière' were pure 'Alter horses'. This great man was Pedro José de Alcântara Antonio Luis de Meneses, fourth Marquis de Marialva (1713–99), Master of the Horse (*estribeiro mor*) from 1770 to 1797, whose name has remained the eponym of *haute école* on the banks of the Tagus.

After the departure of the French in 1812, the tardy return from Brazilian exile in 1821 of King João VI and the Miquelet War (1828–34), the recovery of breeding was slow: at the Mafra stud, Alter mares were crossed with Arab, Barb and Thoroughbred stallions; at the Sintra stud and the Ajuda, Portuguese and Spanish horses were bred. At last a 1911 law concerning remounts retrieved the fortunes of the Mafra stud where three pure-bred Arabs and ten Andalusian mares in 1921 practically restored the traditional Alter breed.

In 1939 Mafra received the cavalry squadron of the School of Torres Novas whose riders had distinguished themselves in international competition, although it was progressively to be mechanized until its transfer in 1957 to Santarem where it became an armoured vehicle school.

At Mafra, the remount station continued to break in and train horses for the eight still mounted regiments, four of which subsisted in 1946 when Captain de Saint-André of the Cadre Noir was detached to instruct them. In 1949 the remount station became the *Escola Nacional de Equitação*; and after the departure of the by then Major de Saint-André in 1951, the school became, in 1957, the *Centro Militar de Educação Fisica e Desportes Equestres* which by 1965 kept only a score of horses.

Upholding the tradition of the *Picaria Real* of Belem, there remains, however, the civilian riding school of Joaquim Gonçalves de Miranda whose disciple, Nuno Oliveira will, it is hoped, safeguard and pass on the heritage of the glorious Portuguese School.

England

In the equestrian history of the United Kingdom, it is England which took the lead. Etienne Saurel writes:

aside from Newcastle, equestrian art owes little to England; but due to her creation of the Thorough-bred, king of horses, breeding and equestrian sport owe her their very essence.*

The American critic, W. Sidney Felton (*Masters of Equitation*, 1962) observes in turn that school riding, clearly at its zenith with Newcastle, had, in contrast with the Continent, made no further progress since, at least not in the same way.

Prior to Newcastle, Thomas Blundeville had published in 1534 *The Art of Riding* and around 1566 *The fower chiefyst Offices belonging to Horsemanshippe . . .*, in which he copied Federico Grisone. This was not a bad thing in itself, since the teachings of the same Neapolitan School were perpetuated later by the chevalier de Saint-Antoine who, like Pluvinel, was an alumnus of Pignatelli's, and was sent by Henri IV of France to serve James I, becoming chief equerry to the early Stuarts, thus having a decisive influence on academic equitation in the England of his time.

From 1593 on, Gervase Markham, the poet in great contemporary rivalry with Shakespeare, and a faithful follower of Essex, who rode in front of Queen Elizabeth I, deluged England with a series of equestrian works. The first was *A Discourse of Horsemanshippe* in 1593; many were repetitions under different titles, and in 1617 the booksellers extorted his promise not to write any more on the subject. However, the works of this remarkably modern-minded horseman embraced (somewhat like Xenophon's *The Art of Equitation*) the choice of the colt or mature horse, the progression of breaking in and training, including higher equitation, feed and care; and this not only for the manège horse but for the charger, hunter, running and coach horse.

William Cavendish (1592–1676), Baron of Bolsover, Viscount Mansfield, Earl, Marquess and finally Duke of Newcastle, Knight of the Garter, Lord Warden of Sherwood and Lieutenant of Nottingham, as well as Lord Lieutenant of Derbyshire, poet, playwright, breeder and horseman, not only raised a cavalry troop but otherwise helped finance Charles I's

Histoire de l'Équitation, 1971.

William Cavendish, Duke of Newcastle.

warfare against Cromwell. In the world's equestrian history he remains the author of a work on *haute école* splendidly illustrated by a pupil of Rubens, Abraham van Diepenbeke. He was the first and last of the truly 'great' riding masters in his country until – in the mid-nineteenth century – academic equitation once more raised a timid head in a nation which for almost three hundred years had remained nearly exclusively oriented towards hunting, the great charges of Mont-Saint-Jean (Waterloo) or Balaclava, and of course racing, which beyond any doubt saw its beginnings in England.

Newcastle published *Méthode et Invention Nouvelle de Dresser Les Chevaux* in French at Antwerp in 1658 during his self-imposed exile

The Duke of Newcastle's riding school at Bolsover Castle.

there, following the defeat at Marston Moor. In 1667 another book, *A New Method to Dress Horses and Work Them According to Nature*, followed his return to Welbeck after the Restoration.

The Duke's writings, though tempered with a nice dose of humour, were somewhat grandiloquent in their huge pride; but let us concentrate on their technical excellence, as expressed in maxims such as that art must ever follow nature, never oppose it. Then there is the work on two tracks with the bend of shoulder-in, but on the circle, hemming in the forehand. We have seen that La Guérinière was to give the horse the same bend, though on the straight line.

Indeed, La Guérinière was to mention Newcastle, along with La Broue, as one of the only two authors having remained valid in his time. But after Newcastle night fell over academic equitation in England – a night which lasted till the nineteenth century when a man was born who was English by birth but French in spirit, much like Newcastle, that 'cavalier', a derisive nickname proudly carried. His name was James Fillis, of whom we shall hear more later. But first let us mention a few fine horsemen who aimed a little higher than the tips of their hunting whips.

Lord Herbert, tenth Earl of Pembroke (1734–94), a career soldier, published in 1761 *A Method of Breaking Horses and Teaching Soldiers to Ride for the Use of the Army*, serving the British cavalry rules in force at the beginning of the hostilities ensuing from the American Revolution, then with the armies of the French Revolution and the First Empire. Pembroke was a great admirer of Baron d'Eisenberg and Claude Bourgelat, father of the veterinary schools of Lyons and Alfort. He visited both and was much taken with higher equitation, although – as did his French counterpart of Scottish origin, Drummond de Melfort, in 1749 – he simplified military equitation and kept manège work (pillars, shoulder-in) for future instructors.

Richard Berenger published in 1771 in London *History and Art of Horsemanship*, the

Lord Herbert, tenth Earl of Pembroke.

last English-language classic, with the meritorious addendum of a fine translation of Xenophon's *The Art of Equitation*.

The work of Philip Astley (see *The Circus*) is of interest here only because his two books, *The Modern Riding Master* (1774) and *System of Equestrian Education* (1800), are results of his experience as a circus rider in England, as well as in France with the Franconis.

In 1805 there appeared in London *The Analysis of Horsemanship* by 'one John Adams', as Felton puts it. It has the merit of defining for us the 'auld hunting seat' of the eighteenth century foxhunters.

After *The Art of Horsemanship* (1806) by Sir Sidney Meadows there was nothing till the *Treatise of Equitation Simplified* by J. G. Peters, published in English, French and German. Peters, former pupil of Ayrer at Göttingen, ex-lieutenant colonel of the Scots Greys, deplored England's lack of any school comparable to those of Vienna, Versailles, Saumur or Hanover. Having read La Guérinière, he mocked the young squires who, according to him, only knew what their fathers' grooms had taught them.

There was also Lewis Edward Nolan, killed in action with the Light Brigade at Balaclava, who wrote *The Training of Cavalry Remount Horses* in 1852. He was an avid reader of Xenophon, while considering Pluvinel, Newcastle and La Guérinière obsolete; he was however somewhat taken with Baucher, being acquainted with his 'first manner', although for him the first thing remained to ride his horse forward.

Four decades later we begin to find a series of books by Veterinary Captain Matthew Horace Hayes (1842–1904), a polyglot Woolwich graduate. Having spent nine years in the Indian Army, he returned to civilian life but ran the military equitation courses in England, then in India, the Far East and South Africa. He published *Riding: on the Flat and Across Country* in 1882; *Among Men and Horses* in 1894; *The Points of the Horse* in 1891; *Riding and Hunting* in 1901. He was an outdoor rider who respected Baucher but found him obscure.

James Fillis (1834–1913), English by birth, French by choice, even perhaps by naturalization, practised an equitation of *haute école* that was entirely French and which made him famous. He himself stated so straight out in the dedication of his book, *Principes de Dressage et d'Équitation* (1890) to François Caron:

It is to you, dear master and friend, that I dedicate this book. It rightfully belongs to you, even if gratitude were not offering it to you. You have guided my first steps in the difficult art of equitation; you have watched over, encouraged, helped me in my entire career.

A very gifted horseman, he cannot be said to have shone by his elegance. But he was truly obsessed with forward movement, an obsession which he knew how to convey to his horses. Curiously, his 'dear master and friend', François Caron, had been a pupil of Baucher whom Fillis attacked in his book. He even happened to claim credit, possibly in good faith, for discoveries which in reality were nothing but rediscoveries of principles enunciated by Baucher in his 'second manner' with which Fillis may not have been acquainted.

Georges Clemenceau.

A remarkable circus rider whose talent had reached maturity, he wished, just like Baucher, to become chief instructor at Saumur. He was recommended for it by Georges Clemenceau, one of his pupils, yet ran up against the inflexible veto of General L'Hotte who at the time (in 1889) was president of the Cavalry Committee. Fillis's book was published the following year; and it is rumoured that Clemenceau had a ghost writer's hand in it.

Thanks to the support of François Caron – who himself had at one time held that position – Fillis went from 1898 to 1910 as chief instructor to the Imperial Cavalry School of St Petersburg. Returning from Russia he published the last of three books, *Règlement pour le Dressage du Cheval d'Armes*, rules adopted by the School of St Petersburg in 1908. The second book had been a *Journal de Dressage* dedicated to the city of Paris.

English equitation in general took the turn of the century in one cantering stride, indifferent to manège work. It was World War One which put a goodly number of His Majesty's officers in touch with their French and Italian counterparts, then with the refugees of the Imperial Russian cavalry. The Army Equitation School of Weedon, founded in 1919, kept working conscientiously till 1939.

This was a period of transition which was to end after three decades or more with the re-implantation and definitive adoption of the idea of classical dressage in the country of fox-hunters.

The pioneer of this revival was Maxwell Fielding McTaggart (1874–1930) whose books are still up to date: *Mount and Man, A Key to Better Horsemanship* (1925); *From Colonel to Subaltern, Some Keys for Horseowners* (1928); *Stable and Saddle* (1929). Having bravely fought the Afridis at the Khyber Pass, the Boers at Ladysmith and the Germans 'somewhere in France', Lieutenant Colonel McTaggart, DSO, wrote the foreword to Santini's *Riding Reflexions*, in full agreement with the latter's Caprillism.

Lieutenant Colonel John Edward, alias Jack Hance (1887–1960) was one of the first British equestrian authors to renounce the martingale and recognize the importance of manège work in horse training for outdoor riding. He practised flexions à la Baucher on the advice of a French friend, Henri de Morville, whom he met at St John's Wood in 1916. A civilian riding instructor from 1923 to 1939, he was then called back into service and stationed at Weedon where, he stated somewhat tongue-in-cheek, 'I must admit some of the instructors were horsemen for whom I entertained a considerable personal regard'.

It fell to a foreign-born civilian horseman to introduce Great Britain to dressage and higher equitation: Henry Wynmalen, born Wijnmalen in the Netherlands in 1889; industrialist, inventor, aviation pioneer, besides being a passionate amateur rider, he settled in Britain in 1927. On several occasions he rode dressage in front of the Royal Family and in 1961 received the gold medal of the British Horse Society. Having written *Equitation* in 1938 and *Horse Breeding and Stud Management* in 1950, he published in 1953 his masterwork, *Dressage: A Study of the Finer Points of Riding*, and in 1954 *The Horse in Action*, 'a careful study,' writes Felton,

of what the horse does while moving at his various gaits, how he accomplishes the transition from one gait to another and how a horse's movements may be interfered with so that his gaits are no longer 'pure'.

'At this he became an authority,' wrote Mrs Julia Wynmalen to this author, 'and it is fair to say that he has had an incalculable influence in the awareness and importance of dressage for the British rider.'

Equitation

E. Hartley Edwards

If we accept General L'Hotte's definition of equitation as 'the art of managing the powers of the horse', it follows that its foundations lie in first developing the powers and then in directing those powers towards the purposes to which the horse is to be put.

Both will be achieved by a system of progressive training that will begin early in the horse's life and continue until the required level is reached or, which will more often than not be the case, until the horse has advanced as far as his individual limitations allow.

The very talented horse, like his human equivalent, will benefit from advanced schooling, designed in the case of the horse to fit him for the specialist disciplines of jumping, eventing or dressage; but every horse, whether highly talented or not, requires a basis of education up to a secondary level if he is to lead a useful working life of reasonable duration.

The schooling of the horse is, indeed, similar in its divisions to that of the human child. The equine training is naturally condensed into a shorter period of time and is necessarily more concerned with the physical development than is human education, although the mental conditioning and the animal's span of concentration is of equal importance.

Like the child's, the young horse's education begins in what we may term the 'nursery school'. This first stage, undemanding of physical or mental effort, occupies the time between foalhood and the age of three years. At three the young horse is sufficiently mature to enter primary education, which involves physical training preparing him for the acceptance of the rider's weight upon his back, and in which he will become accustomed to light work, acquainted with rudimentary aids, and learn the habit of obedience to his trainer. This period will not exceed some six months, after which the horse will be rested and allowed to 'grow on' naturally until he attains the age of four, at which time his secondary education will begin.

It is not possible here to do more than outline the basic schooling of the riding horse, and this will be more easily achieved if the work involved is examined in general terms under the headings of Stage 1 ('nursery', up to three years), Stage 2 ('primary', taking place at three) and Stage 3 ('secondary', involving the four-year-old schooling). At the outset, however, it should be stressed that while it is convenient to think of the horse's schooling as being thus divided, each stage will, to a degree, overlap its neighbour, and the success of further stages is dependent upon the firm establishment of the objectives achieved in the preceding stage.

Stage 1

The objectives are as follows: 1) to accustom the young foal to the presence of human beings and to encourage the establishment of a relationship between the two; 2) to accustom the youngster to a very elementary form of discipline; 3) to develop the natural growth by proper feeding and management.

Foals should be handled early in their life,

and most will soon submit to being patted and stroked. It will be necessary for the foal to be fitted with a head slip when only a few weeks old, and when this is accomplished he can be taught to be led in hand. The foal will always follow the dam, and it is a fairly easy matter to get him used to being led, in sight of the mare, by holding the strap of the head slip while the mare is being led to or from the stable. He will naturally follow and will hardly be conscious of any restraint.

In the stable, where he can be given regular feeds, handling can be continued until his feet can be lifted up individually and, of course, he is also learning to accept the confinement of a box for short periods.

Up to the age of three the young horse needs the freedom of ample and good grazing, supplemented by artificial foods, if he is to reach his full potential. As a guide, a foal should receive 1 lb. of concentrates, consisting of nuts, bran, oats, linseed, apples, carrots, etc., for each month of his age up to a maximum of 5 to 6 lb. according to his size. To this ration should be added powdered milk (2 to 8 oz. per day) and cod-liver oil, in one form or another, to promote bone growth. In winter he will also need as much hay as he will eat.

Stage 2

At three years the horse is sufficiently mature for schooling proper to begin. In Europe, the young horse is usually brought up in April, worked lightly up to August and then turned out until the following year when he attains his fourth year. The objectives in this stage are: 1) to accustom the horse to the acceptance of discipline and to being handled more intensively; 2) to prepare him physically to carry weight; 3) to teach him to *accept* weight on his back; 4) to teach him to *carry* weight, which involves the horse in making adjustments to his natural balance; 5) to teach the rudiments of control by the rider.

Feeding is gradually increased until the horse may be receiving as much as 9 lb. of concentrates per day. In the stable handling is

intensified until the horse can be groomed and trimmed thoroughly without showing resentment, and he is taught stable manners, such as learning to move over when requested. Very importantly, a regular routine, which should include a few hours of relaxation in his paddock each day, is implemented.

Initially, exercise is no more than being led about the place, but in the process the young horse learns how to walk in hand, striding freely forward with, if necessary, an assistant behind to emphasize what is required. Until the horse is used to walking calmly forward in hand it is not much good attempting the physical exercises on the lunge which follow. Within three weeks or so it should be possible to effect a change from exercise to work and the lungeing exercises are begun.

Lungeing has both physical and mental objectives.

Physically, the exercise will promote the build-up of muscles without their being formed in opposition to the rider's weight. It will assist the lateral suppling of the horse by equal stretching (and, therefore, contraction) of the dorsal, neck and abdominal muscles on each side. A 'tension', or a rounding, of the spine will be induced by encouraging an extension of head and neck combined with the engagement of the hind legs. This latter is always more easily obtained on the circle, since the inside leg is bound to be actively engaged beneath the body. The flexion of the joints will be increased as the result of greater and more supple muscular development. The spine, as far as possible, can be flexed to correct the natural curvature, thus encouraging 'straight' movement, with hind legs following the track of the forelegs. The necessary engagement of the hocks on the circle will contribute to improved balance.

Mentally, the exercise inculcates calm in the horse. Additionally, he learns the habit of discipline and of obedience to the voice. Finally, the horse is taught to go forward, which is a combination of both mental and physical qualities.

Initially the lungeing periods should be

short so as not to impose strain on the horse, but, as he becomes stronger and more proficient, they can be increased in duration.

Once the horse works freely on the lunge no time should be lost in introducing a bit to his mouth. Carried out with intelligence and tact this need not cause difficulties. A carrot sliced and placed in the hand with the bit will usually obtain the co-operation required. For some days the horse can wear the bit for a short time in his stable to get used to its presence. It can also be worn under his lunge cavesson while he works.

It is now necessary to make use of a roller, which will prepare the horse for the feel of a saddle, and to which side-reins can be attached. Initially these are fastened to the cavesson rings and later on to the bit itself. The object is not to force the horse into contact but to encourage him to follow and 'seek out' his bit. To this end, side-reins, instead of being shortened, should, in fact, be left long and the horse encouraged to reach forward to his bit, extending his head and neck to make contact with it. Later, the higher head carriage can be encouraged by shortening the reins, but not until the stretching process (on which depends the ability to contract) has been established. The stretching of the head and neck, the rounding of the 'top line' and the further engagement of the hocks will be encouraged by trotting over poles on the ground.

Saddling will cause no trouble if the horse is first worked in a roller, but it is advisable to let him work under the saddle before attempting to back him. Backing, similarly, is not difficult if the horse is prepared in advance by an assistant lying across the saddle and gradually placing more weight on the back.

Once the horse accepts the rider he can continue to work on the lunge in obedience to the trainer's voice and is gradually taught the basic rein and leg aids until he circles the school, off the lunge, and under the rider's control.

At this point a further set of objectives arise. The horse now has to learn how to adjust his balance under the rider's weight and he must learn how to walk, trot and canter under saddle. He will also acquire a knowledge of the elementary aids and will have his first lessons in jumping on the lunge. The first three will be achieved by riding the horse out in the open on straight lines. Circles and school figures are premature at this point and will only impose strain and restriction. Undulating ground crossed at trot or canter demands constant adjustments of balance and is the natural and most effective way of teaching the requirements of balance under the rider.

Jumping training on the lunge is done by progressing from poles on the ground to low cavalletti and finally by arranging a grid of the latter so that the last element forms a small fence. Towards the end of this primary training period, when the horse has learned to jump small fences on the lunge, without being hampered by weight, it should be possible for him to be ridden over small fences and, if a loose school is available, no harm will be done by letting the pupil jump a few slightly bigger fences unmounted.

In late August or early September the horse can be roughed off gradually and put out. But, of course, it is necessary to continue feeding. Whether or not a horse benefits from long-reining during his three-year-old period is a matter of some controversy. One suspects that those who are not very expert at the exercise are against it and those who are more proficient, or think they are, are in favour.

It is possible to produce good results by long-reining, even by the rather unsophisticated English method – so long as the trainer is capable and experienced.

There is, however, rather more to be said for the French method in which the trainer, walking directly behind the horse, pushes him into acceptance of the bit and obtains a higher head carriage by encouraging the engagement of the quarters. Personally, I believe this rather advanced form of long-reining is most beneficially employed in the later stages of the four-year-old training, since the shortened 'outline' induced would be beyond the capacity of a younger horse.

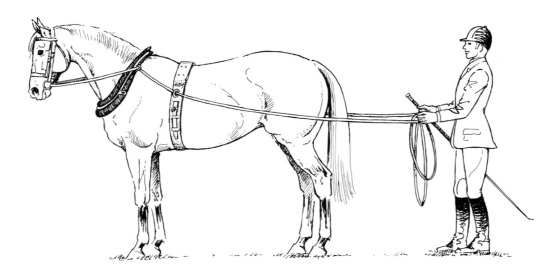

Long-reining in the French manner

Stage 3

At four years the horse is bigger, stronger and capable of more sustained physical effort. The objectives in the continuing schooling are these: 1) progressive physical conditioning by the combination of feeding, exercising and grooming; 2) the furtherance of the horse's mental development and powers of concentration; 3) placing the horse on the bit and the hand; 4) the increase of lateral and longitudinal suppleness by the gymnastic exercises contained in the riding of school figures, etc.; 5) teaching the aids up to a secondary standard; 6) inducing a greater degree of straightness in the horse by perfecting, as far as possible, the school figures and obtaining more control of the quarters; 7) continuing and extending the jumping training; 8) the final introduction of the double bridle.

While hacking out is very necessary for the horse's relaxation and interest, regular school periods are incorporated in the work.

Initially, these are confined to the simple changes of rein, accomplished by a transition from the opening rein to the more effective direct rein of opposition and work on large circles. Longitudinal suppling is encouraged by exercises alternately shortening and lengthening the frame of the horse, initially practised by 'slow-ups' of the pace followed by 'speed-ups'.

The canter departs are best taught outside the school where large circles can be ridden, but once established they can be incorporated in the school movements. More advanced schooling movements can be introduced gradually and as the horse begins to make greater use of the hind legs the head carriage will rise almost automatically. However, it will still be necessary to strengthen the neck and assist the rounding of the top-line by regular periods of stretching. This is best accomplished by 'rein-combing'. The rider holds the end of the reins at his chest with one hand while with the other he 'combs' the reins upwards, changing hands as the 'combing' one reaches the chest. Stretching muscles is followed by their relaxation and when the muscles relax the head lowers. Until this relaxation can be obtained it is not possible to ask for the contraction of the muscles required in a higher carriage of the head.

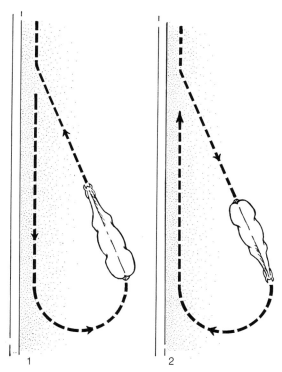

1 The half-volte, an exercise used as a preliminary to the turn on the quarters.
2 The reversed half-volte, which is used as a preliminary to the turn on the forehand.

Once the head is capable of being carried in a raised position attention is turned to lightening both ends. To reach that goal it is necessary to obtain the mobility of the quarters which begins with teaching the horse to move his quarters away from the action of the single leg

and finally to moving them around the pivot of one foreleg in a 'half turn on the forehand'. Exercises encouraging obedience to the single leg and leading to the half turn on the forehand are the zig-zag and the reversed half-volte. The half circle involved in the latter is reduced gradually until the quarters move around the forehand in the finished half turn.

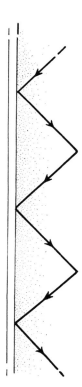

The zig-zag, an exercise which encourages obedience to the single leg.

At the other end lightness is encouraged by the half turn on the quarters, which cannot be attempted until the head is raised and more weight is distributed over the hind legs. This movement is approached from the half-volte.

The half turn on the forehand lightens the quarters, the half turn on the quarters acts in the opposite fashion; both contribute to better balance. The half turn on the forehand supples the hind legs, the half turn on the quarters supples the shoulders. Both lead to greater control and towards eradication of basic resistances.

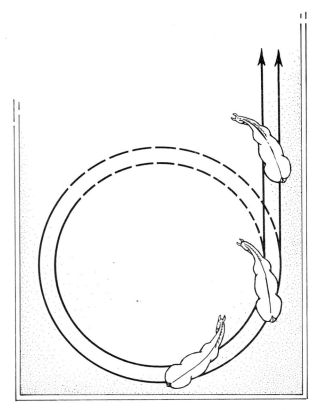

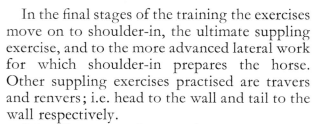

Left shoulder-in made from a circle, one of the exercises employed in the final stages of training.

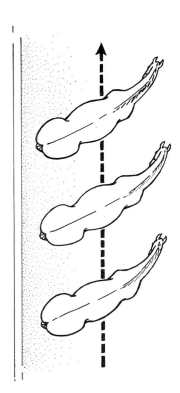

Tail to the wall or renvers, one of the suppling exercises practised when moving on to the more advanced lateral work.

In the final stages of the training the exercises move on to shoulder-in, the ultimate suppling exercise, and to the more advanced lateral work for which shoulder-in prepares the horse. Other suppling exercises practised are travers and renvers; i.e. head to the wall and tail to the wall respectively.

Schooling over fences advances similarly, and as the horse becomes more supple and obedient the exercises involving distances, that is the doubles and trebles, can be tackled with more certainty of success.

Correctly carried out a progression on these lines produces a strong, willing horse, obedient and comfortable to ride and less inclined to unsoundness caused by strain – in fact, the sort of horse everyone wants and which will be a pleasure to ride.

Equestrian Instruction and Dressage

Col. Jean de Saint-André

The author riding Steamer in the pas d'École.

Teaching a man to ride used to be a simple thing. Riding was intrinsically the utilization of the horse for transport. Over the centuries, equitation has taken on a more learned and complex form, having become both an art and a sport. Equestrian instruction, empirical to begin with, has been drawing gradually nearer to pedagogy in definition and structure.

Attila's rude companions, in spreading at a gallop east to west, just needed to be saddle-fast, and doubtless learned to ride by just imitating their elders. By the Middle Ages a handier horse was required for the thrust and parry of combat and joust. The aspiring knight was taught in castle courts to manage the forehand and control the haunches.

Renaissance Italy was to lend to equitation its first artistic touch, although still tainted by the rigour of the period, and the eighteenth century was to endow it with its studied grace. By the nineteenth century the Continent received an influx of equestrian sports from England, adding novel aspects to the ways of using a horse.

Consequently, the twentieth century instructor's field of action has become very vast, comprising classical equitation (currently called dressage) and sports equitation of all sorts, from hunting to show jumping including racing and eventing.

Needless to say, the learner's horizons should be widened, albeit progressively, apace with increasing knowledge and capabilities in striving for higher aims. Therefore, the instructor builds up his teaching phase by phase.

First comes the initiation, intended to shape a stable, energetic, confident rider able to manage his horse by simple aids on the flat and over small fences – called by the riding manuals, 'elementary equitation'.

The second phase is devoted to improvement, aiming at a steadier seat and balance and giving the rider the complete knowledge of the aids by which he will manage his horse with authority and reflection in the proper attitude. At this point, the student should be able to enter any sort of competition (racing, horse trials, show jumping, dressage) on a national level. This is the 'secondary (or complementary) equitation'.

The third phase, 'higher equitation', implies the rider specializing in the branch of equitation best suited to his aptitudes and tastes. Indeed, at this stage of international competition even the exceptionally gifted horseman cannot shine equally in manège riding, on a steeplechase course and over show jumping fences. If he were to scatter himself among several specialities, the time factor in itself would keep him from getting to the core of his doctrine, from mastering his aids and improving the training of his horse. So he must take his choice, and still will find it difficult enough to attain deep knowledge and perfect control in one single discipline.

The instructor

Detailed discussion of instruction is necessarily preceded by that of the instructor.

Handbooks complaisantly enumerate the qualities he requires: he simply must possess one and all, particularly those which appear to be in conflict with each other. He should, for instance, be energetic and demanding, yet gentle and mindful; clear and precise in teaching, yet full of imagination; concise in explanation, yet able to emphasize the whys and wherefores of everything. He is expected to be his pupils' friend, yet without undue familiarity, to impose discipline and yet keep this clear of any sense of constraint, and so on.

Of course, the perfect instructor is non-

A class being addressed by the instructor in a well-equipped covered school.

existent and each one's teaching bears the hall-mark of his own personality; his force as well as his foibles. The former can be developed, the latter attenuated, but only if, rather than being a mere working pedagogue, he gives himself up totally to his calling. If he does so, his pupils will 'take to him', because they will recognize the validity of his knowledge and method and his ability to serve them as a living example, but above all because they sense his faith and the motivation that animates it.

His essential quality, however, is to be methodical, i.e. aware of the successive goals he is striving for. He must define the intermediate stages which lead, *lesson by precisely planned lesson*, to these goals through day-by-day 'novel instruction'.

A prototype hour of such equitation might, for example, be broken down as follows:

Ten minutes for setting the horse on its legs and 'warming up' both horse and rider.

Fifteen minutes for the repetition and inculcation of exercises already known, particularly the preceding day's 'new teachings'.

Twenty-five minutes of daily new teaching, announced, performed and demonstrated by the instructor on his own horse, who explains, analyses, and then makes his students perform it: individually, collectively, first at slow, then at lively paces.

Ten minutes for critical commentary, which also constitutes, for both horses and riders, the 'return to calm'.

This commentary determines indeed the plan for the following lesson: if the work has been well done the ground is cleared for another step ahead; if not, the same subject will require additional 'hammering in'.

Depending on whether the new teaching deals with making the pupil saddle-fast, or with the application of the aids, or with the preliminaries for work over the fences, etc., the lesson is adjusted to the subject's leading idea.

The learner should also be encouraged to consult a simple and precise handbook where he will find his instructor's teachings in somewhat different terms. He should undertake some study of hippology as well.

Learning to mount.

Elementary equitation

Let us imagine face to face for the first time a pupil who knows nothing and an instructor who is to teach him everything. No doubt, the neophyte feels quite apprehensive faced with a discipline and an animal equally unknown to him. So the first thing to do is to give him confidence, which will do away with that psychological tenseness which necessarily produces its physical equivalent.

The school of confidence

In a preparatory lesson on foot, the pupil learns to saddle and unsaddle, bridle and un-bridle his horse, get in and out of the saddle, adjust his stirrups, place his feet into the irons as he should, hold the reins, and lead his horse in hand. He will receive some explanations of the use of his legs for the walk, and of his hands for the halt, but the main object of this initial lesson is, by allowing the aspiring rider to handle the horse on foot, to create a first physical contact between them, the beginning of their mutual trust.

Ideally, a covered school will be available where a small group of beginners on calm horses align themselves behind an assistant instructor; for watching others ride quickly brings with it a sense of emulation. If the pupil is alone, he may be initiated on the lunge line or led by the hand of his mounted instructor; but the initial problem remains the same: doing away with mental and physical tenseness.

'Recreational suppling exercises' are meant to, and do, entertain the pupil by making him stir. They are based on imagination and a bit of humour, ranging from patting the horse all over or lighting a cigarette, to juggling with a ball or writing a postcard!

Hacks at the walk, calling attention to the world around, contribute to a more relaxed mood. 'Managing exercises', simple ones such as riding the horse forward, halting, turning by the opening rein, demonstrate that a horse is indeed manageable.

Stretches of sitting trot, very brief, promote the free play of the pupil's loins if he holds on to the pommel, the stirrups giving him a sense of stability. The rising trot, taught as early as possible, conveys a feeling of comfort while bringing the joints into play.

The canter is eventually approached on the lunge line, the learner holding on to the handles of a vaulting surcingle, but letting go of them as soon as practicable, patting, instead, the horse's neck and croup at the cadence of the canter.

The young rider, thus, is now confident and rid of his initial tenseness and the moment has arrived when we can give him more steadiness by developing his 'seat'. Let us emphasize, however, that this confidence we have given him is not definitive but must be refreshed at every new exercise, such as going across country or jumping.

The earliest lessons of horsemanship

These lessons are intent on giving the novice a certain stability and pliancy in the saddle. So the instructor looks, successively, for:

Suppleness; that is, relaxed joints whose play allows the rider to be and remain 'with his horse' in movement.

Steadiness; that is, absence of involuntary or useless movements produced by reaction.

Suppleness and steadiness combined produce *ease*; that is, a freedom of attitude and spirit.

Correctness; that is, the placing of the different parts of the body where they are at once most efficacious for managing the horse and most elegant in attitude.

The best means for achieving these three aims is the use of suppling exercises, provided they are not a product of routine but carried out with a view to a precise goal known to the pupil when carrying them out. So, since we have three goals, we also use three sorts of exercise.

General suppling exercises. These exercises serve our pursuit of suppleness itself, making the joints acquire on horseback the free play they possess on foot. The lower part of the body is first brought into play, and subsequently the upper part. What, indeed, would be the use of a supple upper body if the loins remained stiff and the legs drawn up!

The seat is put in its appropriate place by raising the thighs and stretching them forward. The coxo-femural joint is brought into play by swinging the thighs and setting them down with the inside muscle flattened.

The knees are brought into play by flexing the legs; the ankles by rotating, raising and lowering them; the loins by flexing, stretching and rotating them; the shoulders by shrugging them alternately or simultaneously, hands behind the back; arms and head by rotating, flexing, swinging them.

After each exercise the seat is shifted forward to its proper place, the thighs are set down with the inside muscle flattened, feet kicking downward, thus pulling down the thighs.

Suppling exercises are of great value. Here the pupil practises rotating the arms whilst on the lunge.

faults and therefore vary from pupil to pupil. After careful analysis, they are adapted to each individual. The rider whose leg is placed excessively forward, for instance, is made to flex it one hundred times, since only repetition of this movement will bring about the required change.

By and by, through such suppling practices, the instructor will help the pupil to attain the classical position. It is, above all, a *natural* one: that of a man standing up, legs spread as wide as the width of a horse, knees bent, holding in his hands an open book; hence all joints are in a position intermediate between complete flexion and extension. This guarantees efficacy, since it situates the different parts of the body in the sort of attitude conducive to each one's most effective action on the horse. More often than not, moreover, it is elegant, the consequence of effectiveness without artifice. Needless to say, it must not be static and the rider must constantly move as does the horse, yet do so as little as possible. If position is like a still photo, equitation is like a moving picture where the personage is involved in constant action.

In this work the instructor is ever intent on effectiveness and variety and lets his pupils use the pommel and cantle for a temporary sense of security.

Suppling exercises for independence. Such exercises of the different parts of the body are intended to eliminate involuntary and useless movements.

They are the same as above, except that the instructor now insists on the immobility of any other part of the body not concerned with the current suppling exercise, thus calling a halt to any reflex gestures. While, for example, the right arm is being rotated, he sees to it that the the left elbow remains still. Dissymmetry of gestures may also be of use; for instance, flexing the left leg while rotating the right foot.

Corrective suppling exercises. These exercises combat conformational or attitudinal

The application of the aids

Stability on horseback is not everything; managing the horse must be learned by means of the 'aids'; that is, by the means which 'aid' the rider to make himself obeyed.

Hence the horse is driven forward on a straight line, or sped up, by both legs acting at their regular place with back to front pressure from hip to heel, a more effective procedure than knocking the calves, heels up, backward. This pressure is repeated till obedience ensues, in cadence with the pace, and later this may be reinforced by the pressure (or 'pinch') of the spurs.

To slow down or halt (later to rein back) both hands act by an increase of rein tension. Whatever the way of holding the reins, the thumb (closed at the end of the first phalanx) is the *bolt* holding the rein adjusted, preventing its loosening; the tension is produced by closing the lower fingers, turning the nails down, rounding the wrist and raising the hand vertically. Conversely, the hand's yielding lifts this block progressively.

The co-ordination of the aids is taught as early as is feasible.

When the leg acts the hand yields and vice versa. But the motion of the hand's contact with the mouth, through a sort of constant elastic bond, precedes all; and this in preference to leaving the beginner with dangling reins, which are conducive to 'not having any hand' at all.

To turn. Fingers closing and the right hand shifting to the right, the rider draws in that direction the head and neck of the horse which will turn right provided the left hand previously yields and then maintains the contact: the *direct* or *opening* rein, or *first effect*.

Closing the fingers and shifting the right hand to the left, the rider draws the horse's nose to the right but causes the neck's weight to flow back to the left, provided the left hand yields, then keeps the contact: the *contrary* or *neck* rein, or *second effect*. The learner in performing it cannot cheat if he is made to hold both reins in one hand.

With these notions, the instructor can – first in a group at the walk, then at the trot, eventually individually – obtain the performance of movements which, while lacking interest in themselves, reveal the effectiveness of the student's aids by the precision of their execution. This way, changes of pace and speed-ups and slow-downs allow us to check up on the action of both hands and both legs, as well as on their co-ordination. Turns down and across the school, changes of hand, broken lines, half voltes, voltes, etc., are helpful in checking up on both the action of the legs and on a rein effect.

To shift the haunches. The pupil learns that retraction of one heel followed by the entire leg's perpendicular pressure against the horse's flank causes the haunches to shift to the opposite side: the effect called of the 'single leg'; for, obviously, both legs acting simultaneously in this way cannot achieve anything.

A good straight halt.

The instructor can also lend variety to his programme by using the same exercises, but now including haunches out and haunches in, and hence progressively lead up to half turns on the forehand (then on the haunches), at the walk, and to placing the horse so as to canter off on a pre-determined lead.

Preparation and management over the fences

In elementary equitation, the sole aim is to negotiate the fence without encumbering the horse: 'the first manner' of jumping.

The preparation consists of shortening the rider's stirrups a little, having him lean forward from the waist, leaving the seat in constant contact with the saddle. Holding this attitude, he speeds up, slows down, turns.

The approach consists of orientating the horse towards the obstacle, using the legs at a distance

The instructor (Bertalan de Nemethy) demonstrates the positioning of the horse at a fence.

of about ten metres (but *without* boring towards it), hands resting on the neck so as not to handicap it during the take-off and the basculating movement.

The logical progression is as follows: poles on the ground, then a cavalletto, then a maximum 80-cm obstacle; first taken in Indian file, horse following horse, thus ensuring impulsion and management; later one by one, the obstacle alongside the wall, then free-standing.

Refusal is punished by an abrupt speed-up (designed to restore impulsion) and not by hitting the horse at the halt, which too closely resembles vengeance.

Running out is punished by making the horse turn, with an outward orientation of the haunches, by the rein effect it has disobeyed.

Secondary equitation

The pupil has become a stable but quite 'uneducated' horseman; the question now is to improve him, make him more learned, more effective and more refined; that is, to turn him into a 'complete horseman' – the goal of 'secondary equitation'. Teaching now bears primarily on his theoretical knowledge which, as it increases, improves the use of the aids, leading to dressage; but it also improves his riding over fences through the improvement of seat and balance combined with a sense of 'approach'.

The notion of the proper attitude the horse is to assume regarding the exercise to be carried out, its pace and speed, must become clear and an object of permanent effort, meaning that the pupil must become a trainer in addition to an improved utilizer.

Since he cannot achieve either of these objectives unless his ideas are clear and well-ordered, let us begin by defining a doctrine and a method for him. Among various teaching approaches, we naturally advocate that of Saumur: it is the fruit of the reflections of selected instructors whose task it has been for over one and a half centuries to shape hundreds of 'complete horsemen' and who, by this very fact, have brought to maturity a way of teaching best suited to the majority of cases and impregnated with the ideas of d'Aure.

Doctrine and method

A *doctrine* is 'a body of principles accepted as truths'. They may be summed up in two basic principles that we owe to General L'Hotte: the horse must be 'calm, forward and straight'; the pursuit of 'flexibility of all its springs' must be through suppling exercises, not by work of sheer force.

A *method* is 'the logical succession of performance procedures where the principles are applied in practice'.

We have said that all springs must be rendered flexible: those of the quarters by engagement; those of the spine by their free play; those of the forehand through the 'permeation' of the poll.

How is this done? We have three possible solutions:

The solution of 'the imposed attitude', where on the lunge line, the training whip prompts the horse to engage its hind legs and, being on such a small circle, to bend its spinal column. The side reins produce the ramener,* a solution of constraint where the attitude, not commanded by the aids, is stark and stiff and hence to be rejected.

The solution of 'longitudinal suppling', where variations of speed and paces on the straight line obtained by alternate leg and hand effects, together with riding over all sorts of country, will bring about the wished for changes of attitude. But this is long-term 'oscillometric training', while we are looking for less empiricism and greater efficacy.

The solution of 'lateral suppling' is our choice. The guidelines are as follows:

Divide the difficulty. If we cause the hind legs to engage one by one, we shall ultimately obtain the engagement of both. Wishing to give flexibility to the poll, we make it bend to one side, then the other so as eventually to obtain its direct yielding. Since the spine is to be brought into play, we make extensive use of turns.

Work in motion, so as to work the *whole* horse, not just parts of him, and to make use of impulsion, but this at low speed, since resistances are a dependent variable of the speed.

Point the shoulders to one side, the haunches to the other for the muscular correlation to bring into play their opposition.

Once obedience is shown to an initial constraining exercise, replace this with ever easier ones to be obeyed by analogy.

The progression therefore is as follows:

Starting exercise, at the walk, the half turn on the forehand, placer† to the inside. The bending of the poll to the inside makes it yield to the rein. The inside hind leg, driven outward, crosses in front of the other, making engagement artificial perhaps, but real.

Just at first, two reversed pirouettes may be necessary to obtain this yielding, but soon a single one or a half, a quarter or an eighth of a turn will suffice. As soon as the horse yields, ride it forward and have it make a speed-up, the horse stretching its neck: the half turn on the forehand is a means, not an end.

Substitute for the half turn on the forehand a very small volte, placer to the inside, haunches out. By analogy with the half turn on the forehand, the horse will yield at the end of one, then a half, a quarter volte, and so on.

Substitute for the volte haunches out with placer to the inside a simple volte. Substitute for this volte a drawing aside of the hand on a straight line. Substitute this drawing aside with a mere closing of the fingers.

---

*'The *ramener* means the closing of head-and-neck angle, the poll remaining the highest point of the neck.'

†The *placer* is a lateral flexion of the poll, making the horse look slightly left or right, the top of the head remaining horizontal so as to prevent a twist at the poll.

By analogy, the horse will be yielding ever more readily.

So far this has been performed in the direct placer. Now we shall try to obtain yielding in the contrary placer which affords more balance, since the neck bends less and the weight is carried over on to the other shoulder.

A similar progression will bring about lateral yielding by a starting exercise at the walk: a half turn around the centre of gravity, using the neck rein, leg shifting the haunches to the side opposite that of the shoulders.

This is replaced by a small volte, placer reversed, haunches out, to be replaced by a normal volte, contrary placer. This is replaced, on the straight line, by a crossing over of the hand, then replaced by a closing of the fingers.

Changing hand and the direct and contrary effects (broken line and shoulder-in) lead to where closing the legs, then the fingers will suffice for the horse to yield on both sides at once: the horse 'on the bit', i.e., in ramener through the flexibility at the poll.

These exercises should alternate with speed-ups restoring impulsion and straightness and with neck stretching, because a spring that no longer bends without stretching ceases to be a spring.

At the trot, half turns on the forehand or small voltes are obviously not possible. Work on the circle, placer to the inside or outside (haunches out or in), broken lines, shoulder-in will bring the horse on to the bit on a straight line.

At the canter, shifting the haunches is out of the question, but bringing the horse on to the bit is first obtained by work on the circle with placer to the outside, then neck stretching, then placer to the inside.

Schooling the aids

Back to our pupil now. If he is to profitably apply the method above, he will improve his aids, rendering them more precise and multi-shaded.

Management on the straight line. In elementary equitation the pupil has grown accustomed to respecting the following management principles which have intentionally been kept very simple:

When both legs *act*, the hands must *yield*; when both hands *act*, the legs must remain *passive*.

Applied this way, the horse performs variations of speed and paces in a practically unchanged attitude. If so, we may now add the *concept of resistance* (exerting, in Baucher's words, 'a slow force').

When both legs *act*, the hands can *resist* and the horse goes on to the bit. When both hands *act*, the legs can *resist* and the horse engages its hind legs.

Depending on what he wishes to obtain, the rider has at his disposal an entire scale in the different ways he proportions action, resistance or yielding of both legs and both hands.

The half-halt combats the horse's 'weight resistances', whether it puts itself involuntarily on the forehand, plunges or wilfully overbends. The rein in contact, the very swift raising of one hand (or both), nails up, followed by a no less rapid lowering, the suddenness of this movement lets us raise the neck in such a way as could not be done by a slow gesture. The half-halt may be repeated till all weight on the hand has vanished.

Vibration combats the 'force resistances', of the horse which wilfully pulls, since in principle it is less easy to pull at a mobile rather than a static site. This vibratory use of the fingers consists of horizontal oscillations on a rein in contact, feebly and in cadence with the pace. After a few seconds, if the resistance fails to diminish, we act the same way with the other hand.

Managing turns. The preponderant rein gives the bend (direct or contrary placer) and determines the turn, the horse bending on the curved line it is following.

We have taught the *simple rein effects*: the opening or direct rein = first effect; and the contrary or neck rein = second effect.

Now the moment has come for acquaintance with the third effect:

The *Direct Rein of Opposition* is an opening rein whose action is felt in the direction of the haunch on the same side, parallel to the horse. It draws the shoulders to one side and shifts the haunches to the other.

The Contrary Rein of Opposition in front of the withers, or fourth effect, is a contrary rein whose action makes itself felt in the direction of the opposite shoulder, pushing the forehand to one side and drawing the haunches to the other.

The Contrary Rein of Opposition behind the withers, fifth effect, or 'intermediate rein' (between the third and fourth effects), makes its action felt in the direction of the opposite haunch. It takes from the two previously mentioned reins their predominant result. Issuing from the third effect, it shifts the quarters to the side opposite to its action and, issuing from the fourth effect, it pushes the forehand to the side opposite to its action: the horse moves obliquely sidewards, bent on the side where it is not headed.

Any effect obtained by the reins of opposition can be obtained by a simple rein effect combined with an effect of the single leg. Therefore we ask our pupil not to use the reins of opposition in normal action. If he does so, it should be to *enforce* obedience, demanding a shift of the quarters by the leg and by opposition at the same time: this way, the leg commands obedience to the rein and vice versa.

If he uses it rather than retract his hand he should block it in the chosen direction and redouble the impulsion by his legs: so channelled, the horse will on its own exert the required opposition.

The non-preponderant outside rein must, first of all, yield so as to allow for the bend given by the preponderant rein. Then it must resist so as to limit a possible bending of the neck. The half-halt we have previously defined can balance the horse if it is on the forehand and return the head to the vertical if the poll were to incline outward. By vibration, also previously defined, it can produce relaxation.

It should be noted, indeed, that on the 'outside' the bit is in firmer contact with the corner of the mouth than on the side of the preponderant rein, which makes for greater effectiveness. By its touch on the neck, provided this does not tamper with the bend, it can reinforce the action of the preponderant rein: the expression, neck rein, is to be understood in this sense.

The Single Leg, as already indicated in elementary equitation, permits superposition when turning with an inside or outside placer, the position of the quarters either in or out.

Certain management principles arise. Any hand action must be preceded by leg action; that is, impulsion. Position must be imposed before action; that is, by *flexibility*, not by force. The poll must always be the uppermost point for the horse to be in balance. The attitude must correspond to pace and speed to produce gesture. All horses are dissymmetrical and must be managed by a different form of aids, right or left, so as to re-establish rectitude.

Application exercises. We have analysed a didactic mechanism, but the student himself must feel which are the aids required for the movement (or for opposing resistance) and its proper dosage, and this demands constant thought and a persuasion that, after all, it is the head which is the best of aids.

Under such conditions all movements of the national dressage tests are but application exercises. If the flexibility of the springs has been obtained under impulsion, the chosen combinations of aids will produce speed-ups and slow-downs, rein backs, shoulder-in and half-pass, pirouettes at the walk, counter-canter, departures at the canter, and single flying changes of leg. Their detailed study is not within the framework of this writing.

Improvement of horsemanship and preparation for jumping

Using cavalletti, where the rider feels the hardest jolts, helps him to improve his seat on the one hand and his jumping balance on the other.

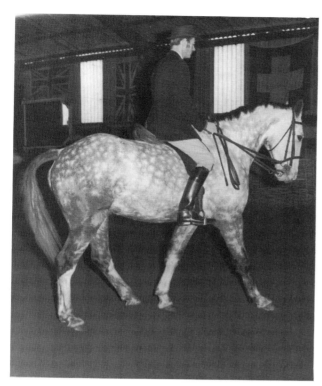

The rein-back.

These cavalletti are initially placed at a 3-m distance for the stride to be 'right' and their number will vary from one to five or six, depending on the dimensions of the long side of the school. Subsequently, two or three may be grouped at tricky distances in order to make the reactions harder to take.

The learner should not look upon these as obstacles but as stronger reactions of the horse and therefore should go over without looking, executing the same suppling exercises as during his initiation to the saddle, reins on the horse's neck.

Cavalletti negotiated without stirrups produces improvement of suppleness, particularly at the loins, if the rider negotiates them seated, upper body straight, toes dropping; improvement of the steadiness of the lower leg (in heading for the obstacles) if the rider negotiates them seated, but upper body forward, toes up, calves adhering and contracted; improvement of pliancy, if care is taken that the pupil allows the upper body its forward play and straightens up at touchdown; the

cavalletti may be replaced by true obstacles negotiated without reins and under the same conditions.

When cavalletti are negotiated with stirrups, the play of the joints (particularly ankles and knees) is developed by the rider's seeking to remain in balance on his irons, seat close to the saddle. Jumping true obstacles, without reins, hand sliding in the direction of the mouth, will solidify this exercise and afford independence of the hand. The play of the joints and the balance of the upper body have previously been developed on the flat by the 'Arab' trot where the rider draws away and approaches the saddle without ever touching down, hands behind his back or on his hips; or by inclination, straightening or rotation of the upper body, under the same conditions.

Management over the fences. The second manner of jumping where the aim is to aid the natural jump should incorporate a course on the flat with speed-ups, checks, turns, rein backs, in the pursuit of impulsion, engagement and balance, which pre-supposes a horse 'on the bit'.

Maintain these conditions during the approach: standing off at normal speed is achieved by impulsion. Up to 10 m away close the fingers to obtain engagement and balance. From 10 m away up to the take-off close the legs and allow the hands to be drawn forward by the mouth. On landing, check and ride the horse forward.

Adjust the take-off to suit the obstacle as follows. On an upright, push and tauten the rein contact so as to stand off if the approach is bad. On a spread, canter faster and do not tauten the reins so as to let the horse get nearer if the approach is bad.

On doubles, involving good distances (7.5 and 10.5 m) ride 'with' or ride 'counter', depending on whether the take-off at the first was close or distant, in order to restore proper distance at the second.

Our pupil having assimilated the teachings of 'secondary equitation' is now well-prepared to enter national competition in any discipline:

horse trials, show jumping, dressage. In doing so, he has occasion to see, compare and ponder. He will also be able to judge whether his aptitude or taste runs to a particular branch of equitation and pick his speciality. At this point he must still widen his knowledge and get to the core of his method, whether he wishes to reach the international level of competition or become an 'artist' in his speciality.

Higher equitation

Shaping a specialist in dressage or show jumping, therefore, is the current goal of 'higher equitation'. In the case of horse trials, its difficulty consists rather more in the high average to be produced among several tests than in the problems of any single one. The norms of secondary equitation suffice for this.

The dressage specialist

One may be content, as is often seen, with an engaged horse on the bit. But if the reaching of a high level is intended – the level of equitation as an art – this will no longer suffice. The horse must above all be collected and light, the French concept of artistic equitation to which Baucher has profitably contributed. These two novel notions require a rather more in-depth exposé of 'doctrine and method' than has sufficed for the stage of secondary equitation.

Doctrine. To the principle 'calm, forward and straight' we now must add the tenet, 'light'.

Lightness is, in L'Hotte's words, 'the exclusive use of such forces as are useful for the movement', and this calls for comment.

If the dressage horse, engaged and on the bit, continues to be properly developed by gymnastics at low speed within its paces, ensures its engagement by lowering its haunches, tautens its topline, raises its withers, 'grows'

and holds up its neck, and advances its poll to where it finds itself vertically just above its mouth, it takes on the attitude of *collection*.

This attitude enables it to employ its forces in all directions, moving as though at liberty. It responds to the aids with a minimum of effort, balanced, supple and light. This suppleness is achieved by degrees and reaches the mouth when the hand acts, before changing attitude or speed; the horse relaxes at the jaw, then closes its mouth, placing the bit, then yields at the poll. This lightness, located at the mouth, has received the name of '*mise en main*': 'horse in hand'.*

In the past method of schooling this could be produced empirically, through a well carried out training taking years; produced – or not produced if the horse lacked sensitivity and thus stayed endlessly 'on the bit'. We owe to François Baucher (whose work is not to be analysed here) the idea that rightfully the jaw should be suppled by appropriate exercises, no less than all other parts of the horse. He actually used to begin by this, which we have not done, though at the degree of training we are now concerned with we shall, in order to have a 'light' horse, adopt such suppling of the mouth which Baucher called 'flexions'.

Method. The method does not differ from what it used to be in secondary equitation, whether it is for obtaining collection, or *mise en main*, we first work for results on one side, then the other, so as later to obtain them on both at once.

The progression is as follows:

The quest for mise en main. This means striving for the mobility of the mouth.

Flexions on foot by drawing the snaffle and bit to one side, then to both, ending up with mobility of the jaw at our command. However, those flexions are not indispensable.

Working in the saddle, performing again, scrupulously and in their proper order, all exercises recommended for this *mise en main*

---

*The *mise en main* is the relaxing at the mouth in the position of *ramener*; that is, the closing of the angle of the head in relation to the neck, the poll remaining the uppermost point.

Harry Boldt of West Germany, an Olympic medallist, riding Chevalier. The horse is in balance, the head and mouth are steady and, although this is a young horse, impulsion is clearly evident.

(half turn on the forehand, volte haunches out, volte, drawing aside of the hand, first in direct, subsequently in contrary placer), but now producing the lateral bend by one rein, the opposite rein keeping it from going all the way. Accustomed to yielding laterally by bending its poll and unable to do, the horse will yield at the mouth on this side. If the work has been carried on methodically, the horse will acquire the habit of yielding at the jaw before it yields at the poll. We have begun by d'Aure and end up with Baucher.

The quest for collection. The lowering of the haunches is achieved by the work on the circle at the three paces, haunches in, placer to the inside, pushing this exercise on to pirouettes. The rein back, the departure from the halt or from the rein back at the trot or canter are also helpful to the same end.

The necessary half-halts produce the proper neck carriage by the progressive raising of the poll in ramener.

Turns, haunches out, are executed by the rider acting with the inside leg when the corres-

ponding hind leg rises, thus increasing the crossing step. He then acts with the outside leg as the outside hind leg rises in order to limit the spread. Through this 'swing of heels' in cadence with the pace, a first equality of both steps is achieved. If he then further limits the spread, the gesture will tend upward.

The 'stride' behind and the diagonalization at the walk in cadence with the pace emerge therefrom; that is, the road to the collected paces, piaffe and passage. In normal work, the lofty and cadenced or 'school' paces are a direct consequence.

It is quite obvious that, more than ever, the exercises dealing with the horse on the bit and the collection must alternate with speed-ups and work with neck stretched in order to restore impulsion and to change attitude in accordance with the speed.

The aids must acquire great finesse and precision: the hand, as the horse is growing light, replaces actions (half-halt, vibration) by simple resistances, and it must yield even before the horse has yielded.

The leg must learn to resist when the hand acts, else engagement and collection won't persist. It must also act more slowly than the cadence of the pace, this being the way to the slower and more ample strides characteristic of 'school' paces. Send the horse from heel to heel, this swing of heels being the key to the counter-changes of hand, flying changes of leg in close sequence and, eventually, the lofty airs.

Finally, having acquired the habit of engaging the hind legs at the action of both legs at the girth, the horse will engage on one side only if only one leg is acting and, so to speak, bending around it. This 'inside leg' or 'direct heel' takes care of impulsion, on one hand, and the position of the haunches on the other. The 'diagonal aids' are thus replaced by the 'lateral inside aids', felicitously applied in the departures at the canter, the flying changes of leg and even half-passes and pirouettes.

The weight can be used in the longitudinal sense: upper body backward, weighing on the seat produces increased balance. Upper body forward, weighing on the stirrups burdens the shoulders. And in the lateral sense: rotation of the shoulders in the direction of the turn, leaning on one buttock or on one stirrup – that is, the weight on the side concerned.

In principle, the weight helps the lateral shift but tends to shorten and precipitate the stride; the 'counter-weight', on the contrary, gives more balance and cadence.

The seat is an active aid, if the rider, by a rapid drawing back of the upper body pushes from the crotch toward the pommel, in cadence with the pace. The lateral action is produced by 'rolling' the pelvis. It is an effective aid but must remain discreet if it is not to become ungraceful.

Application exercises. With a horse in impulsion, collected and light, all *haute école* movements are the logical consequence of an accurate demand made by the aids, at the service of an erudite and observant 'head'. Needless to say, such erudition requires a knowledge of all classical works: the same things expressed in other words sometimes throw light on a point so far obscure.

Counter-changes of hand and pirouettes at the three paces, flying changes of leg including those at every stride, piaffe and passage are the summits to be reached.

The show jumping specialist

The 'third manner' of riding is to start off 'right'.

The size of the fences in big-time show jumping will not allow for just any sort of approach. The horse must approach them under *impulsion* and in *balance*, undoubtedly, yet that alone is not enough. It must, in addition, start 'right'; that is, neither standing off, nor taking off too close, but in such a way that its last stride will take it to the best possible point for the take-off, at about 1.5 metres from the fence. The trajectory of the jump will thus be symmetrical in relation to the centre of the fence, diminishing the risk of a fault and best adapting the effect to the jump to be performed.

Certain horses when arriving wrong shorten their ultimate strides on their own. All the better, they can be ridden 'between leg and fence'. The majority won't, and must be aided, but not in a haphazard way at the last moment: in this resides the entire problem of 'intervention'.

Developing his eye to 'see' the coming approach is one of the rider's tasks. Jumping without reins makes him look and see the top of the fence coming on and, so to speak, make him project the ensuing forward strides in the rhythm of the canter, telling himself beforehand, 'well' or 'badly' done, depending on the way the jump materializes. By and by he will make less and less mistakes and 'see' from an ever greater distance.

This is the moment for trying to 'arrive right' by modifying the last strides once he 'sees' his approach.

If he is 'gaining impulsion', he lengthens the last strides, driving and tightening up his horse in cadence.

If he is 'losing impulsion', he shortens the last strides, going counter to the normal play of the neck by closing his fingers at the third beat of the canter pace.

To do this, the indications of the aids must obviously 'go all the way through'; that is, the horse must engage its hind legs and rise when 'checked', speeding up at its rider's urging without putting itself on the forehand; in brief, it must be 'on the bit'.

Jumping uprights transversely allows a proper arrival if the angle of incidence is correctly judged. It also saves time. The wish to see the approach must, however, not cause a slow-down.

The influence of weight and seat consists in the rider bringing into play the right inclination of his upper body and the driving of his seat, just as was explained for dressage. To do this, he must sit back in the saddle and, consequently, ride on longer stirrups than was done some years ago, at the time of the 'Danloux Balance'. Nevertheless, the pliancy of knee and ankle in that balance lends efficacy to leg action and ought to be preserved, an impossibility on exceedingly long stirrups.

James Ward RA
Coursing in Sussex.
(Roy Miles Fine
Paintings, London)

George Stubbs ARA
*Phaeton with Cream
Ponies and Stablelad.*
(Yale Center for
British Art)

Left: French trotters in action at St. Malo.

Right: Coming out of the stalls on a dirt racetrack in America.

Below left: Flat racing at Deauville.

Below: Racing over hurdles at Sandown Park, one of England's premier courses.

Top left: Janout Tissot, twice Ladies' World Show Jumping Champion, competing at the All-England Jumping Course, Hickstead.

Above: A Hackney pony competing in a show class at Hickstead.

Left: The German event rider, Klaus Wagner, jumping into the lake at the Badminton Horse Trials.

Right: HRH The Prince Philip, Duke of Edinburgh, competing in the marathon at a combined driving event at Windsor.

Above: Lipizzaner liberty horses presented by Mary Chipperfield, a member of the renowned circus family.

Top right: The ancient game of polo in a modern setting, Smith's Lawn, Windsor.

Right: The Old Surrey and Burstow Foxhounds.

Left: Switzerland's Christine Stückelberger riding *Granat* to victory in the Grand Prix Dressage at the 1976 Olympic Games.

A drum horse of the Household Cavalry Regiment in ceremonial attire.

Heavy horses demonstrating an age-old farming technique at a ploughing match in Oxfordshire.

The good distances of combinations (not entirely alike when the fences are uprights or spreads and, likewise, varying depending on their height) must be perfectly understood. If there is a bad distance between two fences in a combination, a 'good' one must be restored on the second by taking the first long or short. An excellent exercise consists of jumping a double separated by a 9 m distance in one or two strides at will, according to how the first one has been jumped. This helps to restore the situation in case of a 'surprise take-off'.

The time must constantly be kept in mind if one intends to win, not just the jumping of a clear round. Time is saved in turning short, in jumping transversely (this requires a trained horse), as well as by taking risks which experience renders ever more reasoned and reasonable.

Little by little, the student has caught up with his master; the instructor's part has been diminishing apace with the development of the pupil's talents, and the bird has taken wing, flying on his own. The teacher is left with the profound joy of having transmitted what he knows but often can no longer perform himself. Yet, isn't this transmission, in a way, a continuation of self beyond time?

The value and efficacy of such instruction, no matter how high or low the goal, resides in the motivating faith: the pupil's faith in his instructor; the instructor's faith in his mission; faith of both in shared doctrine and method.

It is this faith which needs to be preserved in an age when doubt and contestation are attitudes all too easy for those who do not want to learn or those who do not know how to teach.

High School: A Judge's View

Col. Gustaf Nyblaeus

'A horse which is not absolutely supple, loose and flexible cannot conform to the will of man with ease and carriage.'

François Robichon de La Guérinière, *École de Cavalerie*, 1733.

If you venture to add, neither can a horse do so without attention, confidence and impulsion, you will arrive as close as possible to the purport of the term *Classical Equitation*,

the aim of which is solely to make horses supple, loose, flexible, compliant and obedient, and to make them lower their quarters, without all of which a horse – be he meant for military service, hunting or dressage – will be neither comfortable in his movements nor pleasurable to ride.

You don't have to plunge deeper into the ages before or after La Guérinière to discover anything that better corresponds to the present *Rules for Dressage Events of the Fédération Équestre Internationale* (14th edition 1975), where, in Chapter I, it states:

The object of Dressage is the harmonious development of the physique and ability of the horse. As a result, it makes the horse calm, supple, loose and flexible, but also confident, attentive and keen, thus achieving perfect understanding with his rider. These qualities are revealed by:

the freedom and regularity of the paces;
the harmony, lightness and ease of the movements;
the lightness of the forehand and the engagement of the hind quarters, originating in a lively impulsion;
the acceptance of the bridle, with submissiveness throughout and without any tenseness or resistance.

The horse thus gives the impression of doing of his own accord what is required of him. Confident and attentive, he submits generously to the control of his rider.

It takes a long time, usually about four to five years, depending on the conformation and the natural disposition, to carry out 'the harmonious development of the physique and ability of the horse' through the different training/competition stages – Preliminary, Novice, Elementary, Medium and Advanced – until finally reaching the Expert or Grand Prix level.

The Grand Prix and the Grand Prix special of the Fédération Équestre Internationale (FEI) are, so far, the only official dressage tests, published on the authority of the Bureau of the FEI, which comprise the fundamental airs of the Classical High School, such as passage, piaffe and pirouettes at the canter. These tests are therefore also the only official dressage tests that can be put under the heading of Classical High School.

Some movements, which otherwise form part of this school (e.g., levade and the school leaps), obsolete, however, and long since abandoned in a great many countries, do not for this reason figure in the Grand Prix and the Grand Prix special; nor do some fantasy paces, based on a more or less artificial extension of the forelegs, which never really belonged to this school.

The most delicate and difficult part of the training and development of the horse begins when reaching the Medium level. At the Preliminary, Novice and Elementary levels the main object is, step by step, to improve the 'freedom and regularity of the paces' and 'the harmony, lightness and ease of the movements', and to restore and improve the equilibrium, which has been more or less impaired by the weight of the rider. This object is mainly achieved by slowly bringing the horse more and more on the bit; that is, working him in such a way that – keeping his head and neck in a position suitable to the actual training level – with confidence and without any tenseness or resistance he accepts the bridle with a supple poll and a slight flexion at the jaw and willingly responds to the various aids of the rider.

The importance of bringing the horse successively more and more on the bit during the early stages of his training appears clearly when reading the following words of Hans Handler, late director of the Spanish Riding School:

The structure of the horse may be compared to a bridge with a given span, the legs serving as terminal supports. Any movement is influenced by the elastic bond connecting the haunches, the back, the neck, and the mouth. If this elastic connection is blocked at any point – by stiff haunches, a tense back, rigid jaws or a neck not anchored at the withers – the interplay between leg, seat and rein aids can have no effect.

If during the early stages of training you should put too much effort on the collection of the horse (making him lower his quarters, as La Guérinière says), instead of concentrating on making him supple, loose and flexible, you stand a great risk of ruining your chances ever to build that correct 'bridge'.

During these stages most of the training should therefore be executed in working instead of collected paces. In the working paces the horse should show himself properly balanced, with a supple poll and remaining on the bit. He should go forward with even, elastic steps (trot) and light and cadenced strides (canter) and good hock action; the latter not meaning that he has to lower the quarters, but merely that the impulsion should originate in the activity of the hind quarters.

The best means, during these stages, of making the horse supple, loose and unconstrained – for the benefit of the freedom, elasticity and regularity of his paces and the harmony, lightness and ease of his movements – is the lateral movement of leg-yielding, which does not require any collection; merely, when necessary, a restored and proper balance.

As has been said before, the most delicate and difficult part of the training and development of the horse begins when reaching the Medium training/competition level, because from this level onwards a step-by-step increased collection is required to be able to execute the Medium, Advanced and Grand Prix tests in the correct way.

The best means to improve the collection is, according to La Guérinière, shoulder-in and half-halt. The former because, if performed in the right way, the horse slightly bent from poll to tail round the inside leg of the rider, the horse must at every step move his inside hind leg underneath his body and place it in front of the outside, which he is unable to do without lowering the inside hip.

The latter because

it makes the contact with the mouth light; it can be repeated without interrupting the pace, and as the horse by this aid is brought back into balance and his forehand is slightly reined in, he consequently is obliged to lower his quarters, which is exactly what you want him to do.

What is of great importance in the execution of half-halts is, however, that the almost simultaneous conjoint action of the seat, the legs and the hand of the rider is performed in such a way that the horse is more 'pushed' on to a more or less passive, standing hand – which thereby automatically gets a reining in effect – than held back by a hand too active and resisting. A sensitive variation, alternation and interchange of the aids mentioned above, adopted and accommodated to the ever-varying reactions of the horse, should, however, not only be the mark of the execution of half-halts, but, indeed of dressage as a whole. At this stage of reading you may say: but all of this belongs to the low school and certainly not to the high school of equitation, doesn't it? The answer to this far from groundless question is: in theory, yes; in practice, no. Because, if you do not work and build up the horse in the right way throughout the early stages of his training, and slowly but steadily develop his qualities, you will never be successful in your endeavour to reach the top of the Classical High School.

Before the three tests of the Juniors' Continental Dressage Championship, introduced in 1973 (one of the Elementary and two of the Medium stage of training), the F E I had already instituted, in 1929, the first International Dressage Event in which three successive phases in the study of equitation were introduced (recently joined by the Intermediate Dressage Test, Section II), in order

to preserve the Equestrian Art from the abuses to which it can be exposed and to preserve it in the purity of its principles, so that it could be handed on intact to generations of riders to come.

Prix St-Georges (Medium stage): comprises, like the two medium competitions of the Juniors' Dressage Championship, collected as well as medium and extended paces, apt to show the standard of physical development that is required at this stage of classical equitation. The test is, however, a little more difficult than the Juniors' medium tests, as it contains flying changes of leg at every third stride and, the only high school movement, half-pirouettes at the canter to the right and to the left.

Intermediate Dressage competitions (Advanced stage): It appears clearly from the title that these are competitions to lead horses on progressively – without any physical or other harm – from the Prix St-Georges to the Grand Prix. The Section I test comprises two full pirouettes at the canter and flying changes of leg at every second stride. The Section II test comprises changes at every and every second stride, several steps of the piaffe, obligatorily advancing about 1 m. This forward piaffe is designed to prepare the horses for the piaffe in the Grand Prix tests, and at the same time to

get them into the habit of keeping their forward impulsion even later on at the piaffe on the spot in these tests.

Grand Prix (Expert stage): comprises passage, piaffe and pirouettes at the canter. Included are also flying changes of leg up to every stride, as well as all the school paces.

Summary survey of 'right and wrong' concerning the execution of some of the paces and movements included in the competitions mentioned above:

At the *collected walk* the horse should go resolutely forward with his neck raised and arched, the head approaching the vertical position, each step being higher and covering less ground than at the medium walk (the hind feet touching the ground behind, or at the utmost in, the hoofprints of the forefeet). Common faults: The neck is not sufficiently raised and arched; the steps cover almost as much ground as at the medium walk; the walk is hurried and irregular (ambling).

At the *extended walk* the horse should move energetically but calmly and without haste, each step covering as much ground as possible (the hind feet touching the ground clearly in front of the hoofprints of the forefeet). The rider should let the horse stretch his head and neck without, however, losing the contact with his mouth. Common faults: the walk is hurried, resulting in steps too short and, sometimes, irregularity (ambling); the shoulders are not free enough or the quarters are trudging; the rider maintains either too much contact with the mouth or gives the horse too much freedom, losing the contact completely.

At the *collected trot* the horse should move with his neck raised and arched, and with lively but properly balanced and elastic steps, originating in a supple back and well engaged hind quarters. Common faults: not enough impulsion, resulting in insufficient lightness of the forehand and sluggish quarters; not accepting the bridle in the right way, either being above or behind the bit or, which is not quite as bad, behind the vertical; no proper balance, with a speed either too fast or too slow as a result.

At the *extended trot* the horse should remain on the bit with such a light contact that it allows him to lower and extend his head and neck. Through great impulsion originating in his quarters and a marked freedom of his shoulders, the horse should cover in each step as much ground as possible, without his action becoming higher. Common faults: the rider does not allow the horse to lower and extend his head and neck adequately often resulting in a hollow or stiff back, in an insufficient engagement of the quarters and a too high action of the forelegs (the cannon bones of the diagonal fore- and hind legs are not parallel, and the forefeet are not touching the ground on the spot towards which they are pointing

Dr Reiner Klimke riding Mehmed in extended trot.

but often far behind). If the elastic bond connecting the haunches, the back, the neck and the mouth is blocked, the extended trot often becomes short and 'running'.

At the *collected canter* the horse should move, properly balanced, with his neck raised and arched, his strides light and cadenced, his shoulders supple, free and mobile and his quarters very active. Common faults: same as for collected trot, plus the fact that lack of impulsion can often result in an irregular pace (four-time beat).

At the *extended canter* the horse – remaining

on the bit, although allowed to slightly lower and extend his head and neck – should clearly lengthen his strides without, however, losing his lightness and calm, keeping his body straight even at the transition to a lesser pace. Common faults: the transition to extended canter is sometimes not executed in a precise yet still smooth way, but rather like a start from a catapult, usually resulting in a movement characterized by strides too short and hurried and an evident lack of calm.

At the *flying changes of leg* – which are usually executed at a collected canter, although, when performed in a series (e.g., at every fourth, third, second or every stride) the collection should be slightly less than otherwise – the horse should be properly balanced and remain light, straight and calm, notwithstanding a lively impulsion. Because, when executing a flying change of leg, the horse must hop up and down on the inside legs to be able to let the outside legs pass to become the new inside legs, it is of great importance to have the horse properly balanced and to give the aids at the right moment: an instant before the inside forefoot touches the ground. Common faults: the movement, especially when executed in a series, is not sufficiently light and fluent; the head and neck or, more often, the quarters are swinging from one side to the other; the hind feet are changing with one foot a moment after the other or, because the rider does not give his aids exactly at the right moment, usually before the outside forefoot has touched the ground, changes with the forefeet one moment before the hind feet.

At the *half-pass* the horse should be slightly bent, mainly at the neck, round the inside leg of the rider, properly balanced and as close as possible parallel to the long sides of the arena. He should move with supple and mobile shoulders and well engaged quarters, looking in the direction in which he is moving. Common faults: the horse shows resistance to the inside rein, sometimes in connection with resistance also to the outside leg, resulting in a tense and excessively straight inside, often with a protuberant inside shoulder, and sluggish quarters. Lack of engagement of the inside hind leg

Col. J. A. Brau on Quai des Brumes performing a half-pass.

usually deprives the movement of both ease and carriage. The rhythm is too hurried.

At the *pirouette at the canter* the forelegs and the outside hind leg should move round the inside hind foot, which should form the pivot, returning almost to the same spot, or slightly in front of it, each time it leaves the ground. The horse, slightly bent in the direction in which he is turning, should remain smoothly on the bit and, with well engaged hind quarters maintain the exact cadence and sequence of footfalls of his pace, executing the pirouette in about six to seven strides. Common faults: the horse is too free, not bent enough and with insufficient collection, resulting in an insufficiently elevated, unbalanced and too swift movement, sometimes executed in only four strides. Sometimes the horse, usually at the end of the pirouette, loses his balance, deviates sideways or moves backwards with irregular

Jennie Loriston-Clarke and Kadett performing a
pirouette.

steps with his hind feet. In some cases the
pirouette is performed on a circle instead of
almost on the spot and sometimes the horse is
crooked instead of straight when approaching
the place for the execution of the pirouette.

At the *passage*, which is a very collected,
elevated and cadenced trot, with a prolonged
suspension, the horse, remaining light on the
bit, with his neck raised and arched and with a
pronounced engagement of the hind quarters,
moves forward with an accentuated flexion of
the knees and the hocks (the toe of the raised
foreleg being level with the middle of the cannon bone of the other foreleg – the toe of the
raised hind leg being slightly above the fetlock
joint of the other hind leg). Common faults:
crossing the forelegs or swinging the forehand
or the quarters from one side to the other;
insufficiently raised forelegs, sluggish hind legs
and irregular steps by the hind feet.

Col. Alois Podhajsky, former director of The
Spanish Riding School, riding a Lipizzaner in passage.

Col. Danloux on Fou du Prince performing a piaffe.

At the *piaffe*, a highly measured, very collected, elevated and cadenced trot on the spot, with a slightly prolonged suspension, the horse, remaining light on the bit with his neck raised and arched and his head perpendicular, moves up and down, with a pronounced engagement of the hind quarters, which are slightly lowered, the fore- and hind legs being raised in the same way as is prescribed for the passage. Common faults: crossing the forelegs or swinging the forehand or the quarters from one side to the other; insufficiently raised hind or forelegs; lack of impulsion, which sometimes leads to the consequence that the horse, in order to restore a temporarily lost balance, takes one or two short steps backwards: the horse fails to lower his quarters at all, this sometimes resulting in a kind of mechanical 'stamping' up and down, without any moments of suspension; irregular steps, mostly with the hind feet; not executing the piaffe on the spot but in a slight forward movement.

Finally a few words about judging.

Dressage judging means the self-conquest of the judge for the benefit of truth and justice.

Gustav Rau

It is a great burden of responsibility. Competitors rely on the judge completely for a true and fair assessment of their horses' training and its result in competition. Therefore a judge must have a strong personality which is fair – neither overbearing nor obstinate. He must also have a generous, unbiased straight-mindedness, unaffected by personalities or previous performances.

He must have a quick eye to form an accurate assessment of the whole picture, like an instamatic camera automatically taking in and recording the whole general impression and not just petty details. He must endeavour to maintain the same standard, the same scale, throughout the whole competition, and must therefore step by step improve his ability to remember 'what it looked like' when he gave, for example, a four or an eight for a specific movement earlier in the competition.

He must always take his commission as a judge seriously. He must be firm, but at the same time humble.

Finally, he must remember that a judge, as well as a rider, will never reach perfection – although both should always endeavour to do so.

Note that the classical school leaps of the eighteenth century are the following, with explanations taken from La Guérinière's *Élémens de Cavalerie*, 1768, and from commentaries written by General Decarpentry.

The *pesade* (called *levade* at Vienna) consists of the raising of the forehand, haunches greatly bent, the horse in perfect balance on its hocks. This air is not truly a school leap, since all four limbs are not raised off the ground. It is rather the exercise preparatory to the school leaps.

The *courbette* is a veritable leap executed by the horse departing from the pesade by a release of the hocks. The courbette as practised nowadays at the Spanish School of Vienna is slightly different. Actually, the horse performs two or three consecutive leaps, remaining in one and the same attitude and without the forefeet returning to the ground.

The courbette at Saumur is totally different; it is not really a leap, but the horse balancing itself on its hind legs, as in the pesade, although

The pesade (left) and the courbette, from La Guérinière's *École de Cavalerie*.

The croupade (left) and the ballotade, from *École de Cavalerie*.

The capriole, from *École de Cavalerie*.

Top: The capriole as performed at Saumur.
Left: The courbette at Saumur.
Above: The croupade at Saumur.

The pesade performed by a horse of The Spanish Riding School.

The courbette, Spanish Riding School.

here the hocks are completely stretched; it is a 'high pesade'.

The *croupade* is a leap where all four limbs leave the ground, the horse tucking its hind legs under its belly, without showing its shoes. It was performed this way in the eighteenth century and still is seen at Vienna today.

At Saumur, as with the courbette, it is not truly a leap, the horse performing a high kick while supporting itself on its forelegs.

The *ballotade* is a leap differing from the classical croupade only by a slighter advance of the hind legs under the body of the horse which shows its hind shoes. This leap is still performed at Vienna, not at Saumur.

The *cabriole* or *capriole* is a leap where the horse kicks at the moment when its body is just about horizontal, 'the loftiest and most perfect of all leaps'. Both Vienna and Saumur have preserved this leap in its classical form.

Profiles in the Side-Saddle

Princesse Thérèse de Caraman Chimay

The 'Pasionaria' of the French Revolution, Théroigne de Méricourt, was the daughter of a rich Belgian farmer. Seduced by a nobleman, she had a grudge against the aristocracy, and her salon on the rue de Tournon in Paris soon became the meeting place of men like Danton, Mirabeau and Sieyès. When she heard that the Bastille was being stormed, she galloped through the streets of Paris in her scarlet riding habit and large plumed hat and was deeply offended when Suleau, the journalist, made fun of her.

Recognizing the cuplrit in the midst of the insurrection of 10 August 1792, her screams of abuse incited the mob to tear him to pieces, and she was known thereafter as '*l'Amazone de la Liberté*'. Her offer to give her jewels and money for the building of a '*Palais de la Constituante*' having produced more jealousy than gratitude, she was accused of moderation by new Revolutionary leaders and, less than a year later, was torn from her horse and almost beaten to death by angry fishwives. The experience completely shattered her unbalanced mind, and she was sent to the Salpétrière where she died insane in 1817.

This is perhaps the goriest image in the side-saddle; and at the other end of the scale we have the most frivolous:

Firmly seated, both legs to one side, and visibly unconcerned by the antics of a mettlesome bay, a fair rider wearing a thick veil drew everyone's attention one fine morning when cantering along one of the sandy avenues of Vienna's fashionable Prater. A group of cavalry officers lost no time in setting off in hot pursuit

of the charmer, but, alas, vicious kicks from the bay discouraged any close approach. It became a daily entertainment, to the delight of spectators, and might have gone on for a very long time. Unfortunately, when it was rumoured that the mysterious '*Reiterin*' could only be a particularly prank-loving ADC of His Imperial Majesty Franz Josef, the bay and its bold rider ceased to appear and were never seen again.

Some hesitation was felt about including this deceiver within these pages, but surely so spectacular a figure deserves a mention in the company of those who, since 1382, have followed the example set by Richard II's first wife, Anne of Bohemia, who brought the first, clumsy, side-saddle to England.

Catherine de Médicis improved the contraption by the addition of a well-padded roll, but this did not prevent her from having two bad falls when out hunting, resulting in a fractured skull and a broken thigh. Her daughter-in-law, Mary of Scotland, had a lesser mishap when swept off her horse by the bough of a tree, as reported by the British Ambassador in Paris, Sir Nicholas Throgmorton, in a letter to Queen Elizabeth in December 1559.

Diane de Poitiers, born in 1499, started hunting when aged six and almost up to the time of her death in 1566 kept to her habits of early rising, cold baths and long rides. She is sometimes depicted riding pillion behind Henri II, her lifelong friend and admirer, notwithstanding her nineteen years' seniority.

Another namesake of the huntress, Diane d'Andoins, was born in 1556. She is better known as '*La Belle Corisande*', loved by Henri de Navarre, for whom she raised and equipped an army. The beautiful widow of Philibert de Gramont reminds one of Chaucer, inasmuch as 'upon an amblere easily she sat', but she was certainly more decorative, being magnificently attired and followed by a retinue, including ladies in waiting, men at arms, blackamoors, a Basque page with a monkey, another with her favourite hounds (she was very fond of animals) and various other attendants.

Spanish Infantas, sitting stiffly on palfreys so richly caparisoned that they have been rendered invisible, can hardly be called horsewomen, and it is doubtful if they ever did more than let themselves be led at a walking pace.

This was very far from the style of riding adopted by Elizabeth I who, in April 1556, is described as leaving Hatfield House for a day's hunting followed by her ladies, rather surprisingly clad in white satin. One wonders if the latter were able to keep up with the then

Princess Elizabeth who had ordered the Earl of Leicester, Master of the Horse, to send to Ireland for what he describes as 'speedie riding horses which she spareth not to try as fast as they can go', adding, 'I fear them much, yet she will prove them.' Later, in 1600, Rowland White reports, 'Her Majesty is well and excellently disposed to hunting, for every second day she is on horseback and continues the sport long.' She was then sixty-seven.

Newmarket, forever associated with horses, attracted many famous horsewomen of the gay court of the Restoration. Foremost among these was Frances Theresa Stuart, grand-daughter of Lord Blantyre, '*La Belle Stuart*' who lost no time in ousting from royal favour the termagant Barbara Villiers, Duchess of Cleveland, before eloping with the Duke of Richmond and

Lady Lade, a famous horsewoman of the late eighteenth century.

galloping from Westminster to Epsom to get married. It was during a previous gallop, when riding in a race on Newmarket Heath, that Philip Rôtier made a sketch which later immortalized her as the Britannia on English pennies.

Louise de Kéroualle, the 'baby-faced Breton' and ace of secret agents, participated in all royal sports and pastimes, and no doubt her elegance on horseback contributed largely to the success of the future Duchess of Portsmouth.

Christina of Sweden was both intelligent and beautiful, but she had received a man's rather than a woman's education, and were it not for her lovely portrait in the Prado Museum – where she is depicted riding side-saddle – she would not be included here. Entering Rome after her abdication (she had been crowned with the title of *King* in 1650), she is described as riding like an Amazon, therefore astride.

From the Court of Louis XIV, '*la Grande Mademoiselle*', Henrietta of England (the unfortunate wife of the King's younger brother '*Monsieur*') and pretty Marie Mancini now join our pageant. It was a broken-hearted Marie, however, who rode beside the King to welcome his prospective bride, Marguerite de Savoie, followed by the Queen Mother and all the court. Although her spirits rose when the project was abandoned, the respite was brief: Spain offered a better deal – an Infanta along with a peace treaty.

Hailed as the best woman to hounds of her day, Letitia Darley came of humble origin but had considerable charm. Her first love having been hanged at Tyburn ('Sixteen String Jack' was a celebrated highwayman), she then married Sir John Lade, an intimate friend of the Prince of Wales. She was portrayed by both Stubbs and Joshua Reynolds. The most memorable of her many achievements in the hunting field was a run of two hours and forty minutes which 'Lady Lade kept up the whole time.'

Was Letty the inspiration for Surtees's 'Lucy Glitters', or was it 'Skittles', *née* Catherine Walters, almost a national figure in the equestrian England of the 1860s? Pretty, kindhearted, uninhibited as to language, she had the reputation of being the greatest horsewoman of the age. In her scarlet jacket and black skirt, she rode with the Quorn and the Fitzwilliam, her mount a horse who had been second in the Grand National, whom she had put over the railings of Hyde Park for a bet and on whom she later cleared the eighteen-foot water jump at the Grand National Hunt Steeplechase.

Skittles shares equestrian honours with two empresses who were her contemporaries, and although an observer in Paris declares that nothing in the Imperial stables could rival Skittles's pony chaise and black cobs, which were the talk of Paris, this does not detract from the beautiful Empress Eugénie's prowess as a horsewoman or the ease with which she rode the high-spirited chestnut which was the first, and much commented upon, gift the enamoured Napoleon III had made her.

Elizabeth, Empress of Austria, was more than an accomplished rider: riding was her passion, her whole life. Unlike Eugénie, who always feared possible damage to her complexion or hands, Elizabeth would gallop through sleet or snow, her bare hands raw from holding a puller, exulting in breakneck pursuit over the most celebrated hunting counties of England or Ireland, where the best riders in the world, Kinsky, Bay Middleton, Larisch and Prince Rudolf of Liechtenstein, to mention but a few, were hard put to keep up with their goddess. In Hungary, Elizabeth would ride bareback, perform every circus act and break in any new arrivals at the Imperial stables. The beautiful Empress spent her life in the stables; in Vienna alone there were about a hundred Thoroughbreds and the Viennese, shocked by her disregard for accepted Court etiquette, would remark acidly that she had missed her profession.

Fashions in feminine apparel have varied much since the steeple head-dresses and flowing robes of Anne of Bohemia and the billowing petticoats of Catherine de Médicis, but one of the most colourful may possibly be the attire thought up in 1840 by Mrs Thornton who won races at York where 100000 racegoers were assembled. It consisted of a purple waistcoat,

Elizabeth, Empress of Austria, a renowned rider to hounds, pictured with the Emperor Franz Josef I, hunting at Gödölo in 1878.

purple cap and purple shoes, nankeen-coloured skirt and embroidered stockings.

There are few things more beautiful than a horse, and no one can have greater *panache* than an expert side-saddle rider in our mechanized age; and should anyone doubt this, they ought to go and see Her Majesty Queen Elizabeth II at the Trooping the Colour.

Side-Saddle Riding Today

Jennie Loriston-Clarke

The side-saddle horse should have a good shoulder, a long neck, with high withers and a strong back. He should not be too round over the ribs and should have reasonably sloping pasterns. He should have a smooth stride and on no account hit the ground with a jar. The elasticity of movement is the most important point in the perfect side-saddle ride.

The side-saddle is usually made for the rider and most have an all-purpose tree. The saddle is fitted to the rider, and is measured by the length of the seat from the front of the top pommel to the back of the saddle: this should be the rider's measurement from inside the bent knee to the back of the seat when sitting. The saddle has two girths and fastens on the off side. The stirrup is fully adjustable and also has a safety catch so that it would come off in the event of a rider having a fall. The side-saddle has two pommels, the top one for the rider's right leg to hook over and the bottom one for the rider's left leg to hook under. The bottom pommel is slightly adjusted to suit the rider's choice of length of stirrup. There is a balance strap which is buckled to the front strap on the near side and does up to the balance strap on the off side which is the furthest strap and fastens just below the rider's seat.

When saddling, the saddle should be placed on the withers and slid back into position, then the girth should be done up normally, followed by the balance strap; on some saddles there is a surcingle which is fastened last on top of the other girths with a catch which clips on to the saddle flap to prevent it moving around.

When fitting the saddle on the horse, care

must be taken to see that the saddle looks completely level with the ground when on the horse's back. It should not slope backwards as this puts excessive weight over the loins and also causes a sore back; on no account should the saddle press on the horse's spine. Many saddles will need extra stuffing to ensure a correct fit, and care must be taken to see that the girths are tight enough when the rider is mounted.

When mounting the rider should stand facing the horse's croup, place the left foot in the stirrup and swing up holding on to the top pommel with the left hand, twisting in mid-air and sliding the right leg through in front of the pommels between herself and the saddle before resting gently on to the seat of the saddle. The rider then places her right leg over the right pommel with her left knee following into position under the lower left pommel.

The easiest way is to be given a leg-up when the rider stands facing the horse's head, takes up the reins in the left hand and puts the right hand on the back of the saddle while the assistant takes the rider's left foot with his left hand and puts his right hand just below the knee to support her. Then, on the required signal, he should ease the rider up into the seat of the saddle with her leg coming into position over the right pommel.

When sitting in the saddle the rider's shoulders should be directly over the seat in an upright position. The head must be carried upright and should not be tilted forward as this will loosen the seat and cause loss of balance. The weight should be evenly distributed on both seat bones and the rider must make sure that she is sitting centrally over the horse's backbone. The right thigh should lie directly forward and hook over the pommel in front with the calf dropped straight down and the toe up. The left leg should hang in the normal riding position with the toe up and the heel down and placed firmly in the stirrup. The hands should be carried just above the right thigh. To begin with, most people feel happier carrying their hands on either side of the right leg with the stick resting against the horse's side.

When moving on the horse the seat should not leave the saddle except when jumping. The rider should be able to sit comfortably at the walk and later in sitting trot and should not allow herself to be pulled forward, nor to twist round to the left, as this will immediately unbalance her. Great care should be taken to keep the right hip back and the left forward when riding side-saddle. Beginners often draw up the left leg and grip on to the lower pommel. This is incorrect.

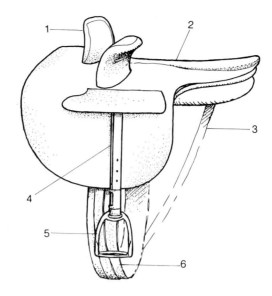

1 Pommels; 2 Seat; 3 Balance strap;
4 Stirrup leather; 5 Stirrup iron; 6 Girth

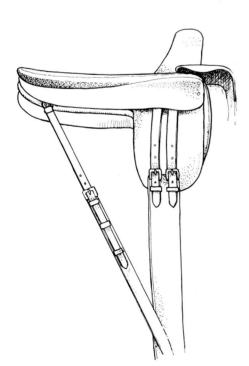

The side-saddle from the off side, showing the balance strap in position.

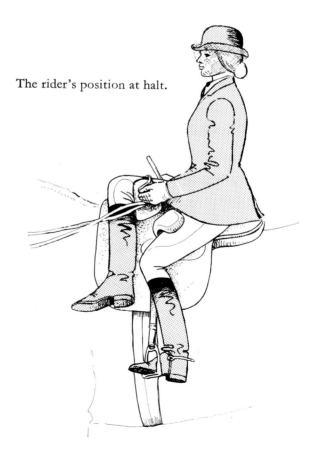

The rider's position at halt.

The author in the show ring, wearing the correct side-saddle habit.

When fitting the stirrup leather allow enough space for the hand to fit between the left leg and the lower pommel when in the normal relaxed position with the foot in the stirrup.

When riding correctly balanced the left leg should rest firmly but effortlessly in the stirrup with the heel down. The leg should only come into contact with the pommel in an emergency and when jumping.

When cantering the rider should teach the horse to canter on either leg with an aid from the left leg touching the horse well behind the girth to canter right and just behind the girth to canter left. The rider's seat should not leave the saddle at the canter but move slightly with the movement of the horse.

The rider should not attempt to jump until completely confident with the horse at all paces on both reins. When jumping, the rider should allow the body to lean forward with the hands following the reins towards the horse's mouth. The grip should come over the right pommel and the left leg should stay in the normal position. The head should look straight forward in order to help control the seat.

The correct dress when riding side-saddle is a bowler hat, collar and tie, a habit consisting of coat and skirt (also called an apron) which covers both knees, breeches, boots, waistcoat, gloves and a stick or cane.

Part Four

Training the Jumper

Lt. Col. Maurice Gudin de Vallerin

The aims of the horseman who aspires to competitive jumping, whether as a part of eventing or in show jumping, may be summarized as follows:

To follow a winding course over a series of fair but difficult fences without knocking any over, and with the greatest possible safety, comfort and dispatch; that is to say, by keeping up the impulsion through energetic action of the legs and moderating this by judicious action of the hands and the use of simple aids.

The horse will then be approaching the obstacles in a balanced manner, with the impulsion and speed that their nature may demand, taking off at the most favourable point, either of its own choice or under the influence of the rider.

It is only possible to realize this aim by methodical, systematic, and rational work which must be carried out steadily and patiently. Its duration depends on the age of the horse and how much experience it has already acquired.

The young horse is first of all broken in and accustomed to obedience by work on the lunge line; it is then introduced to the saddle, and as soon as it has been backed and mouthed the time has come to hack it out over country of varying kinds, alongside an older and well-trained horse, trotting for stretches which are progressively increased in length in order to muscle it up, and cantering for the sake of the wind at about 450 m to the minute over a distance of 160 m, changing the lead every 800 m.

The rider will endeavour to keep his horse balanced on light contact, and to paraphrase Colonel Weldon, the rider will improve himself as well as his horse when hacking out.

It is necessary to condition the young horse so that it can stand up to the efforts and fatigue to which it will be subjected at later stages. Work of the same kind will be substituted later on in order to keep it in condition during its years of competition.

Obedience to the aids demands action within close limits which are afforded by the dressage arena 60 × 20 m). The help of an enclosure is useful to begin with, but after a while it should be ignored in so far as the horse is taught to go straight parallel with the rails but 1.8 m inside them, lengthways.

The first period of training is devoted to the search for regularity of paces: a lively walk, an even trot and canter, as well as instant obedience in changes of direction, taught by performing voltes at the ends of the short sides.

In the second period, attention is paid to the changes from one pace to another, and within these paces to the lengthening and shortening of the stride.

In conformity with the advice given by General Decarpentry, all movements should be asked for always at the same point, until they are instantly and faultlessly executed: lengthening of stride at the start of the long sides, shortening at the end, voltes at the end of the short side, turns across the school, halts at the centre, striking off at a canter from the middle of the short side.

The vocal signals which the horse has been accustomed to obey on the lunge line will be of great use during the lessons and are great

A young horse being jumped on the lunge over an improvised fence. The 'form' of the horse, with the extended head and neck being used to full advantage, is excellent.

time-savers. In fact, it is important to reach, as soon as possible and with a minimum of fatigue, that point of willing obedience which constitutes perfect understanding between horse and rider.

Introducing the horse to jumps can be done under saddle, at liberty, or on the lunge line. It is logical to exploit all three possibilities.

It may begin as soon as the horse has put on a little condition and is really responsive on the lunge, which may be used to spare him the weight – and much more so the hands – of the rider.

It begins with crossing poles on the ground. The horse is led in hand beside the trainer, then in a small circle and finally at the full length of the lunge, at a walk and trot, over fixed bars which are raised little by little.

Repeated jumping from the trot develops the jumping muscles and inculcates respect for the fences. It obliges the horse to raise its shoulders and use its neck and to use the bascule effect, by depriving it of the impetus which it would have at the canter. It forces it to adopt the best style to enable it to exploit its resources to the limit, but with a minimum of effort.

Lessons should take place after a hack or some work in the arena or a long relaxed limbering up on the lunge line. It is imperative for the young jumper to be calm and attentive in order to obtain the greatest benefit while avoiding useless fatigue.

These lessons should be given sometimes on

International show jumper David Broome schooling a horse over sleepers.

the right hand and sometimes on the left and should always be followed by some form of reward, such as stroking, titbits, and above all immediate return to the stables, the supreme reward.

The jumps to be used are two poles, one above the other, and a square oxer with a falsely placed ground rail at the foot. They are not raised until the horse can be kept at the trot and from this can take jumps 1 m high. It is not possible to reach this stage in less than about thirty lessons which should not consist of more than ten jumps each. In fact, young horses are easily tired by this novel work, just like children who might be asked to do exercises on the horizontal bar, of which they can manage only a few at a stretch after progressive practice.

The horseman in a hurry will give two sessions a week and will finish this basic preparation in about three months. But the prudent trainer will space them out to spare his pupil.

After this elementary education the horseman may tackle small fences from the trot in all confidence, in order to perfect the style and obedience of his mount.

Some sessions at the canter, jumping freely in a jumping lane, preferably oval, or in a small indoor ring, are useful but not mandatory, before beginning mounted work at the canter over fences where the jumps are varied, well spaced and low.

The rider tackles them at a hand gallop, keeping the horse balanced and under impulsion but leaving him considerable freedom.

When the jumps are bigger, the rider will help to achieve the right approach: this will consist of opening the fingers before the jump and using pressure of the legs, in order to lengthen two or three strides and place the horse correctly for the most favourable take-off.

The introduction to fences is by now practically over. It remains to tackle short stretches of a course in order to be able to do them twice over, with a few moments' rest between, and thus to remedy deficiencies found at the first attempt. Longer courses are not to be thought of until perfection has been achieved, as excessive fatigue would result from repetition.

During hacks across country the young jumper will learn to jump small banks and ditches, with a schoolmaster giving the lead, or, in case of difficulty, led in hand by the rider, who must dismount to impart confidence.

At this stage the young horse may be entered in competition for experience. The commonest mistake is to attempt to place it near the top in competition straight away and to try it beyond its natural powers. This is imprudent, both in the short term and from the point of view of its future. The horse cannot take such a test unless it can 'listen' to what the rider is telling it and shorten its stride on approaching the fence. This shortening becomes indeed essential if it is not to stand off too much, to flatten out and lose the style on which so much patient and systematic work has been expended. What is more, it will get into the habit of snatching at the bit and thus escaping the rider's hand. It will also lead to the horse hollowing its neck.

A good jumper should always be well in hand and ready to respond to every signal of hand and heel, 'those mysterious and invisible actions', as Colonel Talbot-Ponsonby has so justly said.

It is then capable of specializing in show jumping or eventing. The latter demands, above all, special training to impart stamina and endurance over long distances.

Show Jumping
Chevalier d'Orgeix

With the expansion of outdoor equestrian activities at the end of the nineteenth century (point-to-points, steeplechases, hunting and cross-country events), some horsemen had the idea of simulating within the bounds of a small arena a selection of natural fences that would enable them to judge the jumping potential of any horse: thus show jumping was born.

These beginnings were not planned as such, the competitions being merely devised to assess and classify hunters, and it was only little by little that these exhibitions became a sport in their own right with its own rules and a spirit proper to it.

Throughout the initial period before 1914 show jumps were mostly a facsimile of what might be encountered outdoors, such as banks, walls, stationatas, water jumps, and they were not very high.

The rules varied from country to country and from organization to organization. Competitors were often placed according to style notes made by judges. Slats which a mere breath would dislodge were placed on all the jumps; more points were deducted for touching with the forefeet than with the hind feet. If the courses were small, high-jumping championships were greatly prized, and jumps were high in those days.

In 1906, Captain Crousse riding Conspirateur set up the first height record of 2.35 m after a very near miss at clearing 2.50 m, Conspirateur having just grazed the top bar with his hind feet. There was to have been, that year, a match between Conspirateur and the American jumper Heather Bloom who had unofficially cleared 2.44 m: but unfortunately this did not come off. In 1912 René Ricard on Montjoie III and F. de Juge-Montespieu on Biskra both jumped 2.36 m. But the most important formative years of the horse show were those

Capt. Crousse jumping Conspirateur in front of King Alfonso XIII of Spain at San Sebastian.

Capt. Larraguibel on Huaso clearing 2.47 m at Viña del Mar in 1947.

between 1920 and 1935, those in which the sport took on its personal character.

Little by little rules became standardized. Slats were done away with, as well as the judges' notes on style. Now three chief varieties of competition began to take shape: jumping against the clock, with the emphasis on speed, handiness and adroitness; grands prix, also against the clock, but over bigger jumps presenting problems of technique; and puissances, with their jump-offs.

There was also a tremendous development of fences. Many of them differed from 'natural' obstacles in height, colour, shape and construction. Combinations increased in number and this is a point worth noting. If equestrian

Pierre Jonquères d'Oriola of France, winner of two individual Olympic gold meals, riding Moët et Chandon at Dublin.

terminology has come to use the word 'combination' rather than speaking simply of doubles and trebles, this is due to the discovery that such a type of obstacle lends itself to a great variety of combinations. Ingenious course-builders began to vary the distances separating different fences, as well as their shapes, thus setting problems for riders, which could not be solved except by means of horses better and better trained, clever and under control.

One may say that from 1925 to about 1955 or 1960 the ruling spirit of the tests set by the show jumping course remained unaltered. But sometime between 1955 and 1960 there was another turn of the evolutionary wheel, at least in some countries and in such official competitions controlled by the FEI, as the Olympics and world championships.

The balance which up to that time had been

maintained between the three main types of fence – uprights, oxers and inclined planes such as the Jacob's Ladder – was upset in favour of the oxer which became by far the most important. Now, there is no doubt that a really big oxer is easier to tackle than a bare upright, but that it requires greater strength in the horse.

All these developments tended to minimize the importance of the rider in major competitions, and thus the art of equitation, in favour of the strength of the horse.

Complicated spacing between doubles and trebles was abolished, and these were now so built that the internal spaces corresponded to a number of natural strides. Thus the rider was no longer obliged to shorten the horse's stride as required, but on the other hand the use of wide oxers immediately subsequent to a multiple fence raised questions of power, because only a horse of great muscular capacity can cover enough ground at that stage.

Since the actual approach of the jumps was simpler after they had become more massive, it was necessary to make them higher in order to have riders incur sufficient faults. We had thus reached a stage where the quality of the tests was levelled down and where the strength of the horse took priority over the rider's ability.

Is this a good or a bad thing? However it may be, since change is inevitable, there must be further developments in years to come. Will the trend still be towards the massive and the colossal in the way of obstacles, or will the tendency grow towards more sophisticated riding techniques and a greater variety of problems set?

That is the question, and it is up to the FEI to take a stand, unequivocally, because, according to the stated demands made on competitors in such events, policies will be shaped not only in systems of riding but also of breeding.

Over the past ninety years the riding style has changed considerably, too. At the end of the nineteenth century, the only laws valid for all riding were those bequeathed by the great masters of dressage and 'learned equitation'.

There was no realization of the fact that to get over a fence a rider must do something else than sit upright in the hollow of the saddle, leaning well back to take the weight off the forehand and holding the reins extremely long, so as not to interfere with the horse's mouth when the latter has to make use of its neck.

Then, about 1900, the first American jockeys came to Europe, Tod Sloan in the lead. On the racecourse they rode very short, perched over the withers. Of course, hunting and show jumping men began in their turn to shorten their stirrup leathers and their reins and to lean along the horse's neck.

This was one step toward what became known as the 'forward seat'. But it was still confined to individual horsemen, not recognized by any official school until 'Caprilli's revolution' which was, and still is, a landmark in the history of riding.

It was more than the attempt to find a position for the horseman that would enable the horse to retain its natural balance: it was a facing of the fact that what is necessary to get a horse over jumps in the way of sport or competition is not the same as the requisites for performance in learned equitation. Thus, without doing violence to the unity of equitation, Caprilli pioneered the principles proper to riding for sporting purposes without referring and deferring at every turn to the precepts allowed by the tradition of academic equitation.

This radical turn of thought and its official application ensured that for twenty years the Italian army was supreme in equitation. Over quite low courses with fences that were on a 'natural' scale, this 'natural' style of riding did wonders; and riders who practised it did rounds that were swifter, more flowing and more elegant than anything performed by riders faithful to old-fashioned principles.

However, from that moment in the history of the sport when the courses began to present greater difficulties and more formidable obstacles, this style of riding began to lose its effectiveness. Now it was not enough for a horse to be balanced when approaching a difficult

combination or a big upright. The great riders of that day realized that their problems were no longer identical with those of the rider across country. Walking the course beforehand, they had time to decide on the best way to overcome this or that difficulty: it was up to them to communicate their tactical decisions to the horse, fence by fence, and to regulate the approaching strides in order to take off at the optimum distance. Such riders came to be known as 'meddlers', and in some countries there was argument, often violent, between those who proclaimed the necessity of 'meddling' and those who still held that the rider on a jumping horse was a 'necessary evil' who should leave all the initiative to his mount.

But little by little the 'meddlers' gained the upper hand in most countries in the face of the increasing severity of courses in international contests, though they often did this in very different ways. So much so that one of the great riders of the inter-war years, Colonel Gudin de Vallerin, was able to write a very interesting work on the 'international riding style' whose principles were common to the top flight of all nations.

Yet the trend in course-building over the past fifteen years has inevitably influenced riding style. As the fences came more and more to resemble those used in puissance competitions and the importance of the stopwatch waned, many of the younger riders no longer felt the need for close contact with the horse's mouth but, on the other hand, attempted a firmer seat, thus reverting to longer reins and longer leathers. It is interesting to observe today the different 'equestrian profile' presented by riders of the generation just past and that of today.

If riding style has undergone several changes, the same has been true of the stamp of horse most commonly employed.

The prime requisite in a show jumper was originally safety. Let us not forget that show jumping was devised as a means of testing and

One of the greatest show jumping riders since the war, Italy's Piero d'Inzeo riding Easter Light.

judging hunters and their capabilities. It is certain that across country or in the hunting field the first thing one requires of a horse is that he should not hit the rail. Not only is there the possibility of being injured in a fall, but also the further inconvenience that the rider may have to walk home, an occupation to which he is ill-suited by nature and disinclined for reasons of prestige! Thus the show jumper, like the hunter, was expected above all to be well balanced, to be able to size up an obstacle during the approach and, when taking it in its stride, to know how to raise its shoulders so as to avoid rapping it with the forefeet; a touch with the hind foot was considered a venial fault because it could not be the cause of a fall. This was the reason why touching with the forefoot was penalized by the loss of more points than touching with the hind.

Many of the horses ridden over show jumps at that period were cobby types, short-backed, compact and thick-set, not making much use of their forehand but full of courage and clever at getting themselves out of trouble.

As competitive jumping developed, this conception became blurred. The fault ceased to symbolize the fall which it would have caused at a solid fence but became simply a minus mark in adjudication. In the interests of speed, and in the face of certain difficulties, horses had to jump willingly standing off and describe an arc of lower trajectory. Thus naturally riders went in for lighter, handier and more highly bred horses. This was just the period when Thoroughbreds often became great show jumpers, as did Anglo-Arabs which as a breed were eminently suited to this style.

The new trend in course-building had the effect of favouring a very tall horse of great power, and breeding developed along corresponding lines.

What of the future? Prognostication is difficult, but it seems probable that we shall soon see another turn of the evolutionary wheel.

A gigantic frame and enormous muscle power cannot remain the chief criteria; this would not be fair, nor would it be mentally or

Germany's leading rider, Hans Günther Winkler, winner of no fewer than five gold medals (four team, one individual), riding Torphy at the 1976 Olympics where he won a team silver medal.

aesthetically satisfying, for its consequence would be a neglect of the art of riding. In fact, the breeder can produce remarkable jumpers without concentrating on enormous size. Think only of horses bred in South America. Nor would it ultimately be good for the unity of world riding, leading as it might conceivably do to a schism between groups of countries holding divergent views on what should constitute equestrian sport in this field.

It seems to us likely that the spirit and aims of international horse shows will be redefined so that the problems set by courses at CSIOs (official international jumping shows) shall correspond to these aims.

What, then, is one entitled to ask of the show jumper? Essentially, four things: free action, power, handiness and generous submissiveness to the demands of the rider.

And what may one ask of the rider? To be capable, by the training he has given his horse and by his accurate riding, to clear all obstacles without upsetting them, no matter what problems they pose. These problems may, indeed must, be very varied.

First, there are those inherent in the nature of the fences which are of three main sorts:

Uprights, which the horse by nature finds the most difficult to jump, having a tendency, if unaided, to approach too near and take off too late.

Oxers, comprising two uprights of substantially equal height. A type of obstacle for which the horse has a natural respect,

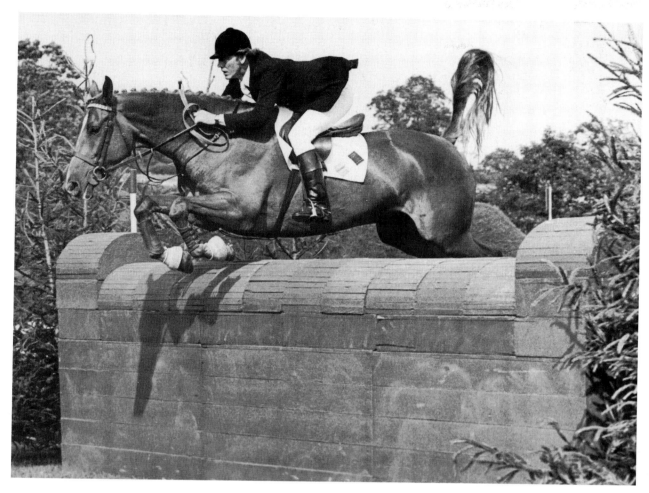

The stylish young Irish rider, Eddie Macken, riding the brilliant ex-show hunter Kerrygold (formerly Pele).

fearing as it does to get hurt if it touches it: if it is very broad it poses the problem of length of trajectory.

Inclined planes (Jacob's Ladder) which demand if they are wide enough, a different approach, since the take-off ought to be close up.

In addition to these three categories there are composite or multiple ones, having none of the characteristics of the foregoing, usually without a ground line and thus easy.

Lastly, there are special sorts such as water jumps, banks and ditches. There is a whole range of such single items, but placed close together they can form doubles, trebles, even quadruples, all comprised under the heading *combinations*.

Clearing such obstacles in combination presents no problem to the horse, always provided the distance between them is measurable in terms of its stride. They are really only interesting if the distance separating their component parts obliges horse and rider either to increase the length of the first trajectory to cover more ground or to land deliberately short in order to make room for another stride inside the combination. By changing the interior spacing and the component parts it is possible to graduate and vary the difficulties almost to infinity and to judge the capacity of the rider and the degree of training of his horse.

We have spoken hitherto of the challenge presented by single fences in isolation (counting a combination as one); but there is also that presented by the course as a whole – changes of rhythm imposed by the alternation of uprights and spreads; changes of direction – and by the necessary speed, either because the obligatory pace is quite fast, or because one is running against the clock. Indubitably, accuracy is easier to achieve if the rider can take his time. On the other hand, such precision at a faster pace asks much of horse as well as rider, including a more rapid calculation of strides, greater docility in the horse, prompt reactions, and so on.

As may be seen, there is a great range of problems that can be set to competitors in a jumping contest, and it is this very diversity that makes the whole thing worth while.

The course-builder must know how to graduate severity according to the style of each contest: giving greater weight to free action and cleverness on the part of the horse in competitions where the jumps are lower but more difficult and where speed is demanded; in others, rightly called 'puissance', to the power exerted by the horse and the way in which this is exploited by the rider.

Thus grands prix should constitute a synthesis in which a balance is maintained between all problems *without letting any single one preponderate.*

If a course really presents great difficulties other than those that can be met by the strength of the horse, then the rider is obliged in the nature of things to practise advanced equitation.

He must be able to clear an obstacle at will, the horse wholeheartedly putting its physical powers at his disposal without reserve, by varying the trajectory as required, taking off early or late, lengthening or shortening stride very quickly; he must be able, within the compass of a combination, to vary the number of strides by appropriate gymnastics on the part of the horse. And for this he will need a horse totally and perfectly trained, which is just what is meant by advanced equitation.

It is the sort of equestrian skill on which competitive jumping events should set a premium; for it and it alone sets the final seal on the age-old, almost miraculous partnership of man and horse.

Designing Show Jumping Courses

Pamela Carruthers

Designing show jumping courses is a very interesting and rewarding occupation, but few people have any idea just how much work goes into the preparation to produce a really good course.

Between the two world wars show jumping in Western Europe was far more advanced than in England or the USA. In Europe there was not the foxhunting which occupied English cavalry officers, so that show jumping was far more popular. The cavalry officers took part, there were wonderful facilities available, and naturally amongst those officers there were always some interested enough to design the courses. There was unlimited labour available to put up the courses, and because they hadn't the natural fences in the countryside, they constructed them as permanent fences in their show jumping arenas. In this period the French, Germans and Italians were supreme in the sport.

England, however, was fortunate in having Colonel Sir Michael Ansell who was largely responsible for putting this country on the map as a show jumping nation. She was also fortunate enough to have Phil Blackmore as course designer. He really was an artist at his job, and certainly it was largely his tact and understanding of what was required that helped English riders to make the transition from very dull courses, with small strips of wood on each top pole, to the present-day type. There were still in Europe, and in Colonel Talbot-Ponsonby in England, cavalry officers who had competed and who could design courses. But now the days of mounted cavalry are over, and where are the people who can design these courses to come from? Obviously amongst the present-day riders there are a few who may take up the challenge, but it is doubtful that it will ever become a full-time occupation. And nowadays it is difficult to fit the demands of course designing into the time available from full-time work of another sort.

To be really good at designing it is necessary to watch horses performing frequently. The course designer must know the form he can expect from the horses and the questions he can ask of them. He has three means at his disposal to obtain a result. Firstly, the track he is asking the horse to follow; secondly, the intelligent use of different kinds of fences at his disposal; and lastly, and possibly most important, the distance he uses between the fences. And it is only by working himself and watching the work of others, that he will gain real knowledge of distances and how to use them.

The designing of courses for novice horses is every bit as important as big international competitions, as it is here that future international horses, riders and course designers gain experience. It is all important that these courses be straightforward and free flowing. The entries are generally numerous and the temptation is great to employ either a trick fence or distance to keep the clear rounds down. The person who does this may well be praised by not very knowledgeable management, but he must realize that he has probably spoilt the confidence of many young horses.

Building big courses in indoor arenas, such as this one at Wembley, calls for particularly careful planning.

The aspiring course designer really needs to love horses and have the idea that every course he designs will help to bring out the best in good horses and riders. He must appreciate the work that is needed before a show to work out the different tracks for each competition on each day, so that the change from one course to another can be made without waste of time, and that each competition has a varied track suitable for the type of horse for which the competition is intended. He must bear in mind where the audience will be sitting, and make sure they all have something to watch. It depends as much on the course designer as it does on the riders, whether a competition has crowd appeal.

As in all occupations, some people have more flair for, and dedication to, the work than others, and it is from these that we get the international designers.

The course designer can afford to make mistakes in distances between fences up to 1.40 m, but when designing for top horses and riders the questions that must be asked are such that the success of a competition depends on the designer being correct to within a few centimetres on the distances, heights and spreads of all the fences on the course, and this is a very big responsibility. At an international show of four or more days' duration, the courses for the first day should be straightforward and simple, building up the horses' and riders' confidence to meet a really testing course in the grand prix at the end of the show. In this the scope, obedience and jumping ability of the horse should be tested to the full, but again without using trick fences (false ground lines, etc.) or trick distances. Obviously some distances must be long and some short, but neither carried to extremes; a short distance to a wide spread is an extreme, for obvious reasons, whereas a short distance to a vertical is a very fair problem. There is an unfortunate tendency at some shows to have too many very important competitions to attract the public. For any athlete the ultimate should not be asked too often or he will go stale, and the same is true of a horse. So the unfortunate course designer must keep in mind that he will get the best results by building up to the final big competition, while trying to keep the horses' and riders' interest by variety in the way he uses his fences and distances. But certainly this practice of many big competitions at a show means that the rider really needs at least two top horses at these shows, or his horses will not last the season, and it is a soul-destroying job to design courses for tired horses.

Any course designer of international calibre needs to take every opportunity to go and see what his fellow course designers are doing. At international level designers develop their own characteristics. It would be very dull for spectators and competitors alike if they were always presented with the same problems. Conversely it is dull for the designer to work always with the same horses and riders. In

A good example of a spread.

countries where there are few competitors this is a very real problem. Recently the Fédération Équestre Internationale has realized the present-day problem of course designing and is encouraging the national federations to invite course designers to attend and assist at their international shows. Naturally the interchange is comparatively easy in Europe, but the USA, Australia and South Africa, to name but a few for whom it is not so easy, have become conscious of the necessity of this also. And certainly this will help enormously to improve the standard of jumping courses throughout the world. There has always been great interest and friendship between international riders, and now possibilities are arising for the same sort of association amongst course designers. Show jumping is an ever expanding sport, and I am sure with the right riders and horses, and good fair courses for them to jump, it will go from strength to strength as a spectator sport all over the world, especially with the advent of television to bring the sport into everyone's home.

The balustrade at Hickstead, a well-constructed upright fence.

The water jump, basically an easy obstacle for a horse, but one which requires a careful approach. The obstacle can be made easier by placing a hedge on the take-off side and a rail over the water itself.

A fence of Olympic proportions: parallel bars over a water ditch, used during the Individual Show Jumping Grand Prix at the Montreal Olympic Games, 1976.

Some arenas have a variety of permanent obstacles which can be incorporated into courses in various ways. Here a competitor takes a fence off one of the banks at the Royal Dublin Showground at Ballsbridge.

Horse Trials

Commandant Guy Lefrant

Eventing is the passion of countless sportsmen, both participators and spectators. Initially it was a test for soldiers, whence its original name, 'The Military', which is still retained in some countries.

In France, the first 'Military' (*Championnat du Cheval d'Armes*), instituted by a War Office order, took place in 1902. Captain de Saint-Phalle, a famous horseman attached to the Cadre Noir at Saumur, was the winner.

One may wonder at a government department setting up a sporting event, but in fact the principle was already admitted that the springs of progress rise out of competition, and the cavalry, the arm which excelled at reconnaissance, was trying by means of the championship to reward those teams of horse and rider which seemed fittest to accomplish the tasks that might be allotted to them. This applied especially to bold horsemen – mounted on horses that were capable of swift movement over long distances and were undaunted by any obstacle – who could obtain information about the enemy and bring it back quickly to the commander for immediate action.

The mechanization of the cavalry and the entry of civilian competitors to these tests was the reason for changing the name to three-day event in English and *concours complet d'équitation* in French. The French title has the advantage of expressing the combination of disciplines practised – dressage, speed and endurance and show jumping – whereas the English title merely describes the time taken over the whole competition.

Dressage: The dressage test is meant to demonstrate the impulsion and paces of the horse intelligently used and accurately executed. No lofty paces are required, for it is not a matter of high school but of low school – without any derogatory overtones in the adjective.

Speed and endurance: The speed and endurance test is to show the speed of the horse over a steeplechase course and its ability and willingness to tackle cross-country obstacles such as might be encountered in the field. The first section of roads and tracks is meant to condition the horse before the steeplechase, while during the course of the second section it must demonstrate its powers of recuperation before tackling the cross-country.

Show jumping: The only aim of the show jumping is to demonstrate how fresh the competitors are after their fast 30 km the day before. None of the fences are over 1.20 m high.

Some hold these events to be the supreme test, while others consider them only a secondary activity, open to horses and riders of medium ability. Without wishing to take sides, I would simply say that one either likes or does not like eventing, but it is worth remembering that while top event horses and riders have achieved success in other spheres it has yet to be proved that the contrary is true.

Development of the horse trial

Since 1956, there have been some changes in the dressage test and in the way in which the cross-country and show jumping courses have

Capt. Mark Phillips riding Columbus in the dressage test, which is designed to demonstrate the impulsion and gaits of the horse.

been planned. With regard to dressage it seems that different criteria of assessment on the part of judges of exercises performed by one and the same combination of horse and rider have led to the Fédération Équestre Internationale simplifying the requirements of performance and cutting down the range of marks. The utter impartiality of the judges being admitted, their adherence to different 'schools' (German, French or what you will) may explain these differences in part, but one cannot totally overlook the aesthetic aspect to which all human judgments are subject; and in fact the overall marks awarded for each pace – its regularity, the degree of submission, the correctness in the use of the aids by the rider – will increase or diminish the appreciation accorded to each movement.

The show jumping phase, which demonstrates how fresh the competitors are after the speed and endurance, should consist of the most natural fences possible.

I do not think the present tendency is such as to encourage unanimity of adjudication: in fact, the simpler the movements are, the more narrowly must appreciation be limited to the precision of the figures, to the detriment of brio in their execution.

I remember a presentation by Colonel Margot, put on for the sole benefit of the rider who was to bring out the horse in question at the London Olympics. Watching from the little window in the school, I was dazzled by the perfection and brio of the movements. But the chief instructor of Saumur was performing the figures only when the horse was well prepared for them; that was the great art, that was the real treat. I have never since seen comparable perfection in the classic sequence of the event dressage repertoire. In fact, the test in these events is nothing but a competition in figures which are laid down, as in skating. I prefer a free presentation.

As for the speed and endurance test, apart from a few hundred yards more or less in the length of roads and tracks and the steeplechase course, the only change that has taken place is in the building of fences for the cross-country, and the use of more or less uneven ground.

Starting from the concept of really natural obstacles, such as were commonly encountered by cavalrymen in the field on patrols or reconnaissance, or by hunting men pursuing deer, boar or fox, the stage was reached of presenting problem obstacles, really out of the ordinary from the point of view of spectators, but as far removed from the natural as could be. I would even go so far as to say, such 'fences' were shocking to behold in the context of their setting, demanding such acrobatics to tackle them that the first care of the rider wishing to save time and spare his horse would simply be to go round them.

This tendency reached its climax in a veritable carnage at the Stockholm Olympics of 1956 and provoked a lively reaction on the part of animal welfare societies, and on the part of the majority of the spectators who like risks but have no stomach for butchery.

Four years later a new tendency made itself felt at the Rome Olympics, at which games two falls, however, conveyed a more proper notion of the difficulties confronting the horses.

Except for Mexico (or rather Avandaro), where the downpour that descended during the event there in 1968 made the course almost impossible for competitors who started during the second half, and for Kiev in 1973 where one of the fences was ill-conceived, this tendency to return to simpler, clearer, more open fences seems to have been maintained, notably in the recent European Championships held, over no more than rolling ground, at Lumühlen. It was a pleasure to see horses not scarred by their encounters with 'unfair' obstacles, and this pleasure was shared by some 80 000 spectators, not to mention television viewers in their (possibly) millions, who must have been impressed by the aesthetic qualities of the perfect course. Finally, the veterinary inspection authorizing the horses to proceed on the cross-country is a welcome new departure which cannot but improve the quality of sport in horse trials.

The show jumping phase, forming the third part of the event, has hardly changed at all, but it is appropriate to welcome a clear return to the source: that is, to present competitors with the most natural fences possible, so solid as to be all but fixed.

Of course, such tests cannot be performed with any prospect of success by just any sort of horse, and this leads us to consider the choice of a mount.

Without engaging in the unprofitable wrangle between the partisans of the jumper that can gallop and of the racehorse that can jump, between those who swear by the half-bred, and by the Anglo-Arab, and by the Thoroughbred, I would simply say that what is required is a very fine horse endowed with good paces; a gifted jumper, hence one that is well balanced; a fast galloper with staying power, soundness and hardiness, good temperament, a big heart and, if possible good looking. All these qualities can be found in the Anglo-Arab, the Thoroughbred and the Selle Français, to mention only three possibilities.

Simple it may be to recite the qualities required, but it is much less easy to lay one's hand on the exceptional horse that combines them.

No doubt one can impart many of them by good training, but one should always remember that there are limits to possibilities in this way, and though it is possible to improve a given horse's manner of tackling a jump, these improvements will fade away as soon as one changes the pace in approaching a fence, especially in the cross-country. Therefore, at the chosen moment, the horse must be put into the most natural situation possible. I consider it essential to be quite sure that the chosen horse does not develop at the outset a marked aversion to obstacles involving either ascending or descending banks, or else to ditches. Once the horse has been found, he must be brought progressively to such a stage of preparation that the trial for which he is being prepared does not prove a trial for his life or career.

Training

The training of event horses must be conducted so as to take account of certain categorical rules: 1) Look for endurance before developing toughness. Make such experiments as will eliminate the risk of a heart attack; 2) try to achieve a perfect and permanent balance

Olympic Games, Stockholm, 1956: Bertie Hill trying to free his mount, HM Queen Elizabeth the Queen Mother's Countryman III, from the notorious twenty-second fence on the three-day event cross-country course. This fence caused twelve falls and thirty-one refusals. One horse sustained a broken leg when being pulled free after falling.

between the specialized work for the three phases. To avoid a problem is not to solve it; in particular, the way to calm an excitable horse is not to refrain from galloping it – there is always a way to restrict his galloping work by interrupting it with other exercises to distract him. Never force the speed of a horse, as this only excites him; 3) finally, it is essential never to take a step forward in training before one has attained physical and psychological balance on the part of the horse in the pre-

European Three-day Event Championships, Kiev, 1973: Baccarat ridden by Debbie West refusing at the controversial second fence.

Badminton 1973: Cornishman V and Mary Gordon-Watson at the Ski Jump.

Jane Starkey on Topper Too, jumping confidently from a bank into water.

ceding stage, taking account of the work required and the feed given.

Constant care must be taken to keep up the morale of the horse. This presupposes a very careful study of dietary requirements. Taking as the basis the stable food (oats, hay, chaff) generally recognized, it is necessary to ensure that the horse retains his appetite and to increase it by adding fresh cereals, fruits, molasses, milk, maize, and so on. The veterinary surgeon plays an essential part: analyses of blood, among other things, will give priceless indications of the supplementary vitamins required to supply any minerals that may be lacking in the diet. The condition of the heart should be methodically checked. Worming should be performed twice a year, and the teeth checked as often. Analysis of droppings is

likewise indispensable. Finally, the rider should be able to assess the condition of his horse just by the look of him.

Training should begin by what is commonly known as conditioning; that is, the development of muscle and suppleness and the improvement of wind, with practice in tackling the essential features of an event course: banks, ditches, some jumps over fixed obstacles.

Progressively lengthen the distances of cantering (endurance); make the voltes smaller, having particular regard to impulsion, cadence and the rounding-off of the voltes; combine poles with banks and ditches; practise over some elements of the show jumping phase.

When endurance seems adequately developed slightly step up the pace over the shorter distances, to a speed of 550 m a minute over

2500 or 3000 m and finish the canters by taking, in the course of them, one or two uprights, on flat ground at first and reasonably far apart. Begin work over doubles for the show jumping phase. Begin to mobilize the haunches, with increased regard to impulsion.

Bring the horse gradually to the perfect performance of the required figures, increase the duration of trotting, over level ground at average speeds: 240 m a minute, 4 min. 10 sec. to the km. Keep up the rhythm of the gallop twice a week, over 4000 to 6000 m. Outdoor jumps sited on slopes; doubles less than 1 m high with a few bounce strides over 80 cm or so complete the show jumping programme.

Every day combine the practice of the three phases and increase the duration of work to three or four hours daily.

If the horse is still in perfect condition at this stage, then he is ready to embark on the final stages of preparation for major trials.

To finish off, replace one of the two weekly gallops for two weeks by a steeplechasing gallop over distances progressing to 3800 m. Increase work at a canter to 8000 or 9000 m, including some longish but not too steep inclines. Practise the dressage phase again. Sometimes take one or two show jumping fences after dressage or after cantering. The last week before the trial, cease work on the steeplechase and the very long canters, going into a period of 'general revision' in which every day the horse works at dressage, on some element of the test, takes one or two jumps of a cross-country course, or one or two of a show jumping course.

The training of the horse presupposes a 'born horseman'. Indeed, a horse is not a machine and no valid progression can be followed unless the horse profits by it. His progress will not be continual, for reasons which reason fails to grasp, so that often one must settle for some modification of said progression. Because of the variety of skills which the event rider must practise, he must have a considerable equestrian education, but above all he must be a true sportsman, physically and morally. If the length of the trial is not an obstacle in itself, it is important to be in perfect condition so that at any moment of the cross-country the reflex instincts carefully cultivated during training shall come into play: rather like a fencer who, in a flash, finds the right parry to get him out of an awkward situation.

If the choice of a horse for eventing is tricky, it is just as difficult to say at the outset whether such and such a horseman is the requisite type; but to convince oneself, one only has to take a look at the riders in major three-day events to see how much they vary. However, it is advisable not to exceed the recommended weight of 75 kg, all up, which will spare the horse needless exertion, and to be in good condition physically so as not to be hindered by exhaustion during the contest (as when one has to run with the horse in hand to spare him over the roads and tracks). One should know the horse 'by heart' in order to be able to exploit his potential to the full. Finally, and above all, one must love the sport and have faith in one's star.

Taking account of the changes brought about in the light of the mistakes at Stockholm in 1956, I think in all sincerity that the three-day event constitutes a basic discipline as much for riders as for mounts, and offers no more risks than do show jumping, rugby or association football, provided that no one be allowed to enter without thorough preparation, and only after making a realistic appraisal of the capacity of horse and rider. The preparation demands a great deal of time, and this demands an element of dedication; but what a joy it is to reach the stage of making the horse one's other self, with whom one can embark in all confidence on any ride, in the expectation that he will give the unreserved co-operation which is the result of perfect work in all three disciplines.

It is essential that the event horse should not develop an aversion to banks and ditches.

Interval Training

Prof. Igor F. Bobylev

Modern competition requires a horse to show itself exceedingly apt for effort, a condition which depends not on its natural abilities alone but also largely on its training. The history of equestrian sports, including that of racing, proves that a trainer, by his knowledge and experience, is capable of 'making' champions of horses seemingly no better than others, sometimes worse. The pre-Revolutionary era in Russia offers an excellent example; the famous Orlov trotter Krepysh was hard put, at the age of two, to find a buyer because of his apparently egregiously defective hind legs. Yet Mr Shapshal's training method, combined with the skill of its driver, made of Krepysh the great champion of the Orlov breed, famous even beyond the Russian borders. A similar case occurred during the post-Revolutionary period. Another Orlov trotter, of the same age, Ulov, in poor state, with bad paces, devoid of any visible quality, passed unnoticed by all experts. And yet, in the 1930s he became a national and European champion thanks to the skill and experience of his driver, N. R. Semichev. One wonders whether Ulov would have become that great champion if Mr Semichev had not happened to be his driver.

Another case is Anilin, an English Thoroughbred who stood out by nothing but his defects and who, nevertheless, became a Triple Crown winner. Let us thank his jockey, N. Nasibov, for understanding him so well in the first place, and so well training him thereafter. In the more recent past, no one would have dreamed that the horses Ikor and Pepel might become top-class dressage horses, winners of many international competitions. One may say, without fear of exaggeration, that they were brought up to this level by the skill of their trainer and the patience and know-how of their riders, Ivan Kizimov and Helena Petushkova. The famous German jumper, Meteor, is, I feel, one more example of the importance of good training.

On the other hand, I could, alas, give even more examples where irrational and/or badly executed training has killed many a fine horse. A conclusion emerges therefrom: champions are not only well-chosen horses (heredity, conformation), but also the products of the sum total of work expended on them and of the knowledge and experience which a man puts into their training. This has led to the adage that 'Nature makes the foal, man makes it a champion'.

Conditioning a competition horse has always been arduous work and it has become particularly complex in our day when the level of competition is exceedingly high and there are continuous new 'developments'. This is why preparing horses for competition can no longer remain empirical. This preparation must be based on science which, nowadays, is advancing with giant strides, clearing up many points, including the way a competition horse should be trained. However, until every aspect has been thoroughly explored, careful observation must still be devoted to all these discoveries. But it is also true that many observations based on science, which yesterday were still unknown, have helped us achieve a better understanding of the training problems and, consequently, to train better. The principal task of training a competition horse is to improve and develop his functional capacity with a view to obtaining a greater yield which, in turn, allows the rider to compete successfully without damage to the horse's organism.

Among the training methods leading to good results in a relatively brief period of time there is one known as *interval training*.

Interval training, based on physiological experiments, emerged in the late 1950s and was applied to different sports. Note, however, that with humans this sort of training spread mostly among light athletes: swimmers, skaters, cyclists.

Interval training takes on the character of repetition of a specific effort, of the scope of work it demands (distance to be covered and the speed used), and of the limited rest 'periods' (partial recovery) between efforts. Repetition of effort is an essential principle in this method of improvement of the functional activity and thereby of the horse's strength. This method of training is based on the following principle:

The improvement of the respiratory and circulatory systems in order to avoid an accumulation of carbonic and lactic acids in the muscles originating in muscular efforts (combustion) and liable to 'tetanize' the muscles. In this latter state, having lost their elasticity, the muscles can no longer function normally. If at this stage, constituting a veritable intoxication, the horse must continue to exert himself, the most serious accidents, and even death, may ensue. If, on the contrary, there is sufficient oxygen in the blood, this accumulation of acids will be less and take more time to develop. Moreover, a period of partial rest (i.e., where the muscular effort demanded, without dwindling to nothing, lessens) allows the organism to 'recover'. Thus, one endeavours progressively to activate the organic functions, lessening by and by the rest periods following the efforts, both being well-determined; or, conversely, to increase the intensity or duration of the effort or both, without increasing the rest periods.

Interval training may be used in the various equestrian sports wherever the horse's training is based on a repetition of specific efforts demanded, following an equally specific 'period of recovery'.

The essential factors endowing interval training with its entire value are, in my opinion, the following: the endurance and intensity of the effort demanded, and which are expressed by indices indicating, on one hand, the distance and the speed used in covering it, the number and size of the obstacles, the shape of the course, the difficulty of the exercises and the time used to perform them; on the other hand, the rest periods granted between the efforts demanded. To sum up, this means that the shorter the distances, the less the speed, the simpler the course, the lower the obstacles, the easier the exercises, the less is the horse's effort and consequently the rest periods will be briefer and the repetitions of effort will be more frequent. Vice versa, the longer the distances, the greater the speed, the harder the course, the higher and wider the obstacles, the harder the exercises, the harder is the work for the horse and consequently the repetition will be less frequent and the rest periods more prolonged.

We thus have quite a variety of possibilities to act upon the horse's organism by producing a variation in all these factors.

The chief problem in applying interval training is one's ability to determine, on one hand, the effort both in its intensity and duration, and on the other, the duration of the rest period – and all this for each individual horse. It must be noted that the duration of the rest periods depends not only on the work demanded (intensity and length), but also on the state of the horse, his condition, age, sex, and other items. If we take, for example, a horse which by its youth is necessarily unprepared to undergo without damage a prolonged effort of great intensity, the preparatory programme consists of relatively feeble efforts of short duration, including a certain amount of repetition but also relatively long rest periods. If, on the contrary, we are dealing with a healthy eight- or ten-year-old, already used to exerting himself, but whose physical abilities are to be improved, greater efforts are demanded and shorter rest periods granted.

Obviously, trainers and riders may and should be assisted in this form of training by veterinary specialists who alone are able to determine the work to be demanded, proceeding from accurate premises: clinical, haematological, biochemical and other check-ups. To my mind, such check-ups are very important, since the intensity of the effort does not always determine the actual reaction of the horse's organism. One and the same type of work has varying repercussions, depending on the age, the degree of preparation, and the functional and physiological state of the subject. Hence, it is of the essence to know as accurately as possible the way each reacts to a specific or to different types of work.

The qualities of the physiological functioning of the horse, the level of its training and the character of its reactions to the various phases of work can be determined with some certitude by the pulse and respiration rate, by haematological and biochemical check-ups, by temperature and weight. Thus, with a subject having already undergone training for some time, the following observations may ensue: 1) A certain diminution of the organic functions of the circulatory and respiratory systems during the rest periods; 2) a lesser variation in the clinical index after specific work; 3) a functional capacity of the organism well superior during a limited muscular and nervous effort in the course of competition; 4) after an effort, the return of temperature, pulse and respiration rate to those of normal physiological conditions requires less time.

This allows us to use successfully the method of the clinical index in the practice of equestrian sports in order to evaluate the functional state of the horses and their form with a view to establishing optimum organization for their training and utilization.

Haematological and biochemical check-ups enable us to discover differences in the index outside of any considerations of state or training. Such differences have, indeed, also been found in a state of rest, as well as after an effort varying in intensity and duration. Nevertheless, it must be understood that all haematological and biochemical indices are not equally significant in judging the capacity of a competition horse. Such indices – as the haemoglobin and erythrocyte counts, the alkaline, sugar, lactic acid reserves, and the blood sedimentation rate (BSR) – furnish far more useful information concerning the level of the horse's training than the number of leucocytes, calcium, phosphorus and carotin contents.

For a better and more objective estimate of the form reached by the horse, and, in order to lend a certain value to the haematological index, we must make two or three check-ups. While they are definitely meaningful in themselves, their results do not suffice to form an exact opinion of the horse's degree of preparedness.

It has been found that for horses in good form there is an increase of haemoglobin content in the blood; an increase in the number of erythrocytes; a slight increase in the number of leucocytes; a decrease in the BSR; an increase in alkaline reserve; an increase of the oxygen level in the blood.

Use can be made of the haematological and biochemical indices for an evaluation of the horse's condition and form, for the dosage of work to be required and for the rest periods to be granted after each effort. The weight of the horse in training is an important factor in judging its preparedness. It has been observed that the weight of a healthy adult horse, in excellent form, undergoing rational training and being correctly fed, does not vary greatly, whether in light or heavy work. The unprepared horse, on the contrary, is subject to far greater weight changes, depending on whether or not it finds itself at rest.

The loss of weight at rest during training must be looked upon as an unfavourable sign. Depending on the type of competition, the energy output varies. Thus, following a dressage test there will be an average of 0.70 per cent weight loss: after a CSO course on the national level, 2.5 to 3 per cent; and after a horse trials performance, 4.5 to 5 per cent.

The greater the horse's form, the less the weight loss and the faster its recovery. Hence, in the framework of interval training, it is normal for the weight factor to be taken into consideration in order to determine the length and intensity of the effort, as well as the recovery time granted.

Never must the trainer in the course of training ask for an effort (be it in duration or intensity) greater than that which the horse is prepared to furnish at a given moment. But, on the other hand, competition horses must be able to endure without damage a constant work increase, its peak to be reached at the moment of the competition. We should not be afraid to demand such efforts; what is important is to prepare the animal's organism so as to stand these efforts which, in turn, must correspond to its degree of preparedness.

Despite the scientific side, which is of greater importance in interval training than in other aspects of training, it is certain, and will always remain so, that to the trainer each horse is a novel subject which must be understood so as to be able to determine the very best way to train it in order to obtain the greatest yield without jeopardizing its organism. A progressive increase of the efforts demanded improves the organic functions and lets us achieve a good result safely and quite easily. On the contrary, premature work for which the horse is as yet not ready not only fails to improve the animal but blemishes it, often for ever.

We should add to the principle of 'progressiveness' in the work that of its 'regularity'. It has been seen that more or less lengthy cut-offs during training diminish the working capabilities and impair the reflexes connected with the nervous system. Consequently, systematic work (that is, progressive and regular) is the essential condition if one is to succeed in interval training.

Building a Course for Cross-Country

W. W. Thomson

In Britain the old concept of a steeplechase course was to line up a number of braver-than-wise citizens beneath the steeple of their parish church on their hunting horses and tell them that the first one to reach the steeple of the church in the next parish was the winner of the race. Perhaps that is a slight exaggeration, for way back at the turn of the century the French cavalry was already organizing a basic form of the *concours complet d'équitation*, or horse trials, principally to train their officers in the various disciplines of horsemanship and horse-mastership, to encourage the breeding of the best types of horses and to enable the cavalry to acquit itself with the utmost distinction in battle.

Prior to the last war competition in the *concours complet d'équitation* was virtually confined to the military. It was not until about 1950 that civilians came into the sport in any number. However, once this had come about, the scope of these competitions was enormously broadened. Until then the *concours complet d'équitation* had always been held over three days, but once civilians took a hand condensed versions were organized which took place over one, two or three days. Standards were fixed for the various grades and degrees of experience of horses and riders.

At the present time the design and construction of cross-country courses has become almost a science that must, however, always be leavened with an artistic approach. When the good Lord made the earth He did not waste much time about it, with the result that few hectares of land bear any detailed resemblance to each other, so that cross-country fences always have to be adapted to the ground available and blended into their surroundings with ingenuity to make the best of constantly varying circumstances.

The Fédération Équestre Internationale lays down the rules and conditions under which all international *concours complets* are conducted. The rules concerning national competitions are set up by the respective national federations, with some changes and variations, but still and ever in the spirit of the FEI. It is absolutely and utterly essential that a course designer knows exactly for which standard he is catering before he even begins to think of a single fence. In the various countries where horse trials are held the distances of the courses and the heights and spreads of the fences vary considerably. In Britain a course at novice level may be as short as 1646 m, while international cross-country courses vary from 7410 to 8100 m. Equally, the speeds demanded differ a great deal from the lowest grade to that of international competition. The heights of the fences may be as low as 0.985 m at training level in the United States to 1.20 m at the top level. The degree of severity of any cross-country course must correspond to the quality and degree of preparedness of those who are going to compete over it.

Before starting to design a course there are various factors that must be taken into account. The position of the dressage and jumping arenas, which all require flat ground, bear strongly on the position of the start and finish of the course. For the more spread out are the various centres of a horse trials course, the more difficult it is to control and the more inconvenient it is both for competitors and officials, to say nothing of spectators. It is a prerequisite that the start and finish of the course must be in the same place. Such an arrangement greatly facilitates the arduous task of time-keeping. At the initial stage, the planning of the course is the important thing; the exact position of the start and finish area can come later.

Initially, a large scale map of the area must be obtained and then a general examination of the available ground is made either on foot or from a vehicle. Any areas that are forbidden either from an agricultural point of view or because of the unsuitability of the going should be carefully marked on the map. Once an appreciation of the general layout has been gained a much more detailed examination of the land must be made, almost certainly on foot. The ground may be parkland with no fences at all, or it may be farmland with a lot of natural fences. When all the fences have to be artificial it is often difficult to blend them into their surroundings. If there are a lot of natural fences the problem is overcome, but often in any given area the fences are all of exactly the same nature and become an embarrassment by their very repetition.

At the second and more detailed investigation, all the interesting features of broken ground, ditches and streams should be marked on the map with an arrow indicating from which direction they would produce the better jump. It should soon become possible to link these features together on the map to form a continuous course which may be roughly measured against the scale and if necessary altered until its length falls within the maximum and minimum distances demanded. From the arrows against the features marked on the map it is possible to decide whether the course will go in a clockwise or an anti-clockwise direction. This decision will always be a question of balancing the merits of one group of fences against another, but never is it worth spoiling the continuity of a course to include

a particular feature, however intriguing it is, if it is remote from the main body of the course. Apart from one or two angled fences which are designed to reward good control, all turns should be wide and sweeping. Novice courses in particular should be free flowing and forward going.

Competitors will always ride the shortest distance from one fence to the next, therefore it will be necessary to construct a fence on the furthest limit of each turn in order to prevent riders from shortening the bends and gaining an unwarranted time advantage. On every cross-country course all red flags must be placed on the right and all white flags on the left, thus it is always possible to define the turns with the different coloured flags. However, they can be a nuisance, since an official has to stand by them to ensure that their message is observed and in the heat of the competition some are bound to forget them and find themselves eliminated in a fury of anguish.

It may seem strange that planning has got so far without the position of the start and finish being exactly fixed. Nevertheless, there are still a number of factors to consider. The first two or three fences should be fairly simple and straightforward, to allow horses to settle into their stride. Equally the last fence should be close enough to the finish to prevent any rider from urging his tiring horse into a wild gallop.

Course design is such a wide subject to cover in so short a contribution that it is impossible to describe, in detail, the very many different sorts of jumps that may be constructed, or how they are put together. The rules issued by the FEI govern the conduct of all international events, but they are a meaningful guide to course designers and constructors at whatever level of training.

Firstly, all fences should be so constructed that any horse making a serious mistake while jumping should suffer the minimum of injury. Parallel rails illustrate this directive well. Should a horse jump short at such a fence he may well become trapped with the rail lodged above his stifle (patella). If there should be a

Three fences on the 1978 Olympic course at Bromont, showing how water can be incorporated into a cross-country course.

lower rail on the second element his hind legs might become fixed between the upper and lower rails. Some arrangement must be made for the top rail, although rigid, to be quickly detachable and there should never be a lower rail fixed beneath it, which is anyway quite unnecessary. Drop fences constructed so that the landing is on horizontal ground are limited to two in number in international events, therefore in lesser events probably one is sufficient. Where the ground continues to slope downwards on the landing side the strain on a horse's tendons is much reduced and this type of landing is preferable. At whatever level of training, horses must never be asked to jump into water with a depth of more than 50 cm. In lower grades 15 cm is sufficient. It must be stressed that if horses are asked to jump into water, the ground beneath the water must be absolutely sound; if there is any doubt whatsoever the fence must be discarded.

It is recommended that no more than ten per cent of the total number of fences on the course should be double or multiple obstacles.

The actual ruling is rather more complicated than that, but the intention is clear. Obstacles must never constitute an acrobatic feat of jumping for the horse, nor be designed or intended to give an unpleasant or unfair surprise to the rider. Horse trials obstacles are, of course, fixed and solid and they must be imposing in appearance, which means that post and rail fences must be made out of timber about 20 cm in diameter. It has often been said, and rightly so, that flimsy fences are extremely dangerous. Horses do not treat them with any sort of real respect. By the same token, never must any fixed or solid part of a fence, at height, be concealed by flimsy material such as a thin screen of foliage. The reason for this is obvious but sometimes a situation does arise where a fence cannot be made strong enough without some sort of backing. In such a case it is best not to use the fence rather than succumb to this temptation. My earnest advice to all those who make courses and, indeed, ride over them is to learn to the last line the rules and conditions that govern their conduct.

A typically difficult sheep pen.

A good example of an obstacle presenting alternative routes. The quickest and most difficult is to take the 'V' in one jump as this competitor has decided to do, but it is also possible to take the outer sections of the obstacle in two jumps with a non-jumping stride in between.

This photograph illustrates how gradients can be incorporated into cross-country courses. Here Hugh Thomas and Playamar approach the second fence in the Montreal Olympic Three-day Event at Bromont (top left).

Fence fourteen at Bromont, showing how a fence may be sited on an uphill gradient (bottom left).

Endurance Riding

Elizabeth Anderson

As a necessary part of man's working life, the horse has long since proved its capacity for hard work. Tales of its great stamina abound; we have records from 1793 of a trotter going a hundred miles in eleven hours and fifty minutes, and of another who did thirty miles in only two hours and ten minutes. In 1880, Boston Blue went from New York to Philadelphia, eighty miles, in a day. After a few days he trotted back, ostensibly none the worse. A party led by the famous Kit Carson rode from Los Angeles to San Francisco, six hundred miles in six days. Only two of the men changed horses.

In 1897, The United States Bureau of Animal Husbandry conducted tests to compare the stamina of Thoroughbreds and Arabs. Carrying 200 to 245 lbs., and covering 300 miles in five days, it was generally decided that Arabs proved to be the fittest. This was important, for it should be remembered that troop horses had to be very hardy – a unit sometimes travelled from 250 to 300 miles in a week.

It is no longer necessary to have a horse that can do a hundred miles in a day – yet the challenge of the past remains. Wendell Robie, an expert on Californian history, began the first competitive ride in America in 1955 in an attempt to equal the records set by the famous Pony Express riders. Although relay stations were generally only ten to fifteen miles apart, there are many tales of these riders and the distances their tough horses covered. 'Pony Bob' Haslam once rode 190 miles and, after a break of nine hours, started back, found his relief station destroyed, and returned the entire

distance at one stretch. (Haslam can also be remembered for the fastest run: 120 miles in only just over eight hours.) Another rider, Ben Holladay, rode from Folsom, California to Atchison, Kansas, a distance of just over 2000 miles in twelve days.

In an attempt to prove their mounts equal to those of these riders, Robie and four other men endeavoured to finish a hundred-mile ride over an old mail route in the Sierra Mountains in less than twenty-four hours. Four of the men completed the ride. By the next year so many people had expressed interest in repeating this feat that an organized ride – the Western States Trail Ride (the Tevis Cup) – was begun. This gave encouragement to a sport that is now enjoyed all over the world.

Today, rides are classified as 'Endurance' and 'Competitive Trail' rides which have different goals and standards of judging.

According to rules set out by the North American Endurance Ride Conference (established 1971), an endurance ride is usually longer than a trail ride – fifty to one hundred miles rather than thirty to fifty – and there is no minimum time limit in which to finish. Each horse must be at least five years old and carry no less than 150 lbs. Although minor medications, such as ointments for abrasions and leg washes, are permitted, all stimulants and tranquillizers are strictly forbidden. There are no restrictions regarding the type of shoeing that may be used.

Horses are judged on speed, soundness and ability to proceed, with numerous veterinary checks along the trail. The horse's manners

A competitor fording a deep river during an endurance ride in Nevada.

are not considered unless he is a menace to examining officials or other riders. A trophy is given to the first horse to finish in acceptable condition, breed awards to the first registered horse of each breed to finish, a trophy to the best-conditioned horse among the first ten in, and awards such as belt buckles or plaques to all who complete the ride.

In England, the Endurance Horse and Pony Society has suggested the following rules for its rides: horses must be a minimum of five years old and 14 h.h. All riders must wear hard hats. No medications, bandages, boots or leather pads are allowed. No spurs are permitted, and only riders of stallions may carry riding whips. Children over ten may

compete, but all those under twelve must be accompanied by an adult sponsor. Recently the British Horse Society has formed a Long Distance Riding Group which is responsible for the annual Golden Horseshoe Ride and the qualifying rides which lead up to it.

The seventy-five-mile Golden Horseshoe Ride (held annually in England since 1965) has an interesting award system. In order to encourage true fitness and minimize the chance of the ride turning into a race, there are no outright winners. Prizes are given on a scale of speed and condition; a gold award to each horse that averages 8 mph with maximum veterinary marks (20), at each of the veterinary inspections held at the end of the first day's 50 miles and the second day's 25 miles. A silver is awarded to a horse with 14 marks averaging 8 mph or 20 points averaging

7 mph, a bronze to each with 14 marks averaging 7 mph or 20 points and 6 mph, and rosettes to those gaining 14 marks at 6 mph. It is perhaps interesting to note that in 1976 seven gold awards were given, five of which were won by Arabs or Part-bred Arabs.

Competitive trail riding in North America is regulated by the North American Trail Ride Conference, (established in 1961). They have set out the following objectives for their rides: 1) To stimulate greater interest in the breeding and use of good horses possessed of stamina and hardiness and qualified to make good mounts for trail use; 2) to demonstrate the value of type and soundness and proper selection of horses for a long ride; 3) to learn and demonstrate the proper methods of training and conditioning for a long ride (. . . without the use of artificial methods or stimulants); 4) to encourage horsemanship in competitive trail riding.

Rides are divided into two classes: 'A' – 25 to 40 miles daily for two consecutive days, and 'B' – 25 to 40 miles in a single day, with a minimum and maximum time limit to finish in: a rider who comes in too early or too late is penalized. Riding time is generally 6½ to 7 hours with a one-hour lunch break. Over rugged terrain, the ride may be shortened to keep within this limit.

There are three classes of entrants – 'Heavyweight' – rider and tack weigh 190 lbs. or over, 'Lightweight' – 140 to 189 lbs., and 'Junior', riders ten to seventeen years old, with no weight limit. All horses must be five years of age or older, except in novice classes over shortened courses, where four-year-olds may be used. No pads are allowed which cover the sole and frog of the foot, and no medications. Juniors are not permitted to ride stallions.

Judging is based on condition 40 per cent, soundness 40 per cent, manners 15 per cent, and way of going 5 per cent. In each division,

A veterinary surgeon checking a competitor before the start of a competition.

trophies and ribbons to sixth place are given to the best horses. The high-point horse also wins a sweepstakes trophy.

During the ride, competitors must care for their own mounts, as horsemanship awards are given, judged on handling, grooming, trail and stable care of horses, care of tack, trail courtesy, and 'proper equitation as it applies to trail riding'.

In both endurance and competitive trail rides, the horses receive numerous veterinary checks. Before the ride they are given a general inspection for fitness, adequate shoeing and signs of lameness. Old scars and blemishes are recorded, as are any existing wounds. Pulse and respiration are taken under normal conditions for later comparison. During the ride, horses are generally rechecked three to four times. A veterinarian notes their general condition, muscle tone, interest in food and water, ability to urinate, and pulse and respiration recovery rates. The average heart-beat of a horse is 36–50 times a minute, the average respiration 8–24. When he works, these all naturally climb, but if he is in good condition they should begin to drop when he comes to rest, and be nearly normal after fifteen minutes. Although a pulse in excess of 100, and respiration in excess of 80 are usually danger signals,

Competitors in a Golden Horseshoe Ride qualifier tackle wintry conditions on Exmoor in 1975.

A rider on the Tevis Ride in 1972.

the most important factor is the recovery rate. The vet also looks for signs of muscular soreness, lameness, sore backs, dehydration and chafing from inadequately fitting tack. Horses which do not meet established criteria are usually rechecked every ten minutes and are given thirty minutes before disqualification. A final, post-ride examination makes sure all animals have come through the ride in reason-

able form and enables the judges to choose the best conditioned horses.

As most rides are over rough country and in widely changing altitudes (the Tevis Cup starts at Tahoe City, six thousand feet above sea level and finishes at Auburn, one thousand feet above sea level, with extremes in temperature ranging from snow to heat over 100°F in the valleys), it is important that both horse and rider are extremely fit. To have a horse at the peak of condition, work begins many weeks before the competition. The horse is gradually taken on longer and longer rides until he is fit, and learns to use a steady pace, conserving his energy and wind. He is trained over hazards he may encounter, steep banks, streams, fallen logs and washed out trails. Good feeding is important, as is careful shoeing, for a lame horse is certain to be disqualified.

The rider, too, must be very fit. Just riding a hundred miles is an exhausting feat, but many endurance riders walk part of the way to conserve their horse's energy, 'tailing' up hills.

Qualified endurance horses can now be registered with the Endurance Horse Registry of America. All breeds are eligible, but to be considered a horse must complete 250 miles in a single year on rides sanctioned by the American Endurance Ride Conference, finish in the top ten of an AERC ride with fifty or more entries, or be the offspring of two registered endurance horses. The registry encourages the breeding of tough, hardy horses.

Today major rides include the *Western States Trail Ride,* held in California; the *Florida Ride,* the 100 *Mile Three-Day Ride*, held in Virginia; the *Quilty* 100 *Mile Ride* and the *Shahwai Memorial*, held in Australia; the *Golden Horse-shoe* held in England; the Canadian *Interprovincial Trail Ride*; and numerous other rides in practically every American state.

Riders of the Far West

Col. John R. Elting

The horseman came to North America with the Spanish conquistadors. He was a major factor in their conquests, probably more important than their few inaccurate – if thunderous – firearms. To Indians, the horse was a monster, the relationship between horse and rider something supernatural, the impact of armoured riders utterly irresistible.

To maintain this military superiority the Spaniards forbade the conquered Indians the use of horses. Such laws, however, proved impractical: there were too few Spaniards to control the reaches of New Spain. Indian auxiliaries were indispensable and gradually were issued mounts. Horses bred rapidly; increasing numbers of them ran wild or were stolen by hostile Indians. Eventually the Spaniards began rewarding tribes not under Spanish authority with horses for military assistance.

From Mexico horses spread northward from tribe to tribe. By 1720 the Pawnee, whose territory now is western Nebraska, owned hundreds of them. Ten years later, mounted Snake warriors out of modern Wyoming were raiding the Blackfeet in southern Alberta. The Sioux (Dakota) did not become 'horse Indians' until about 1770, after the Chippewa drove them westward out of the woodlands. The canoe tribes of the northwest coast and the degenerate 'Diggers' of the Nevada desert did not keep horses. (The Diggers liked horsemeat and so became a menace to travellers.)

With the horse, the Indian developed a new nomadic culture. He could hunt across wider areas and kill more game; he could transport more possessions and move his villages easily. Some tribes abandoned their agricultural skills. The horse became the standard of value, especially for such transactions as purchasing a wife. Mounts with the wind and sure-footedness for running buffalo were specially prized: 'medicine' rites were performed over them to make them lucky; in winter, they might be brought into their owners' lodges.

The Indian copied his horse equipment from the whites, making it of leather, wood, and horn. Most Indian saddles had high pommels and cantles, much like a Spanish medieval saddle which undoubtedly was their original model. Unable to make bits, they substituted a rawhide loop around the horse's lower jaw. For hunting and war most warriors rode with a light pad saddle or bareback; they might tie a rawhide rope, through which they could thrust their knees and feet, around their horse's barrel. Instead of spurs they used a quirt (a special kind of whip), and so could be distinguished from white riders at a considerable distance. Also, Indians always mounted from the right – a custom that gave both Indians and whites trouble when using one another's horses.

Indians practised gelding, but only the Sahaptin group – Nez Percé, Umatilla, Palouse, and Cayuse – understood selective breeding. From them came the much-prized 'Palouse horse', now famous as the Appaloosa. Most Indian horses were actually ponies, though some could outrun Kentucky Thoroughbreds.

The white westerner was equally dependent on the horse. It was a big, empty country, full of sudden dangers. What with thirst, hunger, and Indians, a man left afoot had a short life expectancy. A horse thief therefore was considered the lowest of criminals. When caught, he was shot or hanged out of hand.

The westerner used the horse primarily as a saddle animal. Mules were better pack animals; mules or oxen were more efficient for wagon trains, though horses were preferred for stage coaches. Well into the mid-nineteenth century the average western horse was still a 'Mustang' of the original Spanish stock – agile, tough, somewhat pot-gutted, and differing little from the better Indian horses. Few stood much over 14 h.h. or weighed more than 800 lb. American settlers in Texas brought some blooded stock from Kentucky and Tennessee, but over-all improvement was gradual as most of these settlers were farmers. The influx of 'American horses' increased after the Civil War and included Quarter horses, noted for their strength and handiness. Such bigger mounts were required by the introduction of heavier breeds of cattle and the opening of ranges in the rugged north-west. Some ranchers experimented at breeding range mares to draft-horse sires, especially Clydesdales, but offspring were too often clumsy 'bigfoots'.

Probably the most spectacular episode of western horsemanship was the Pony Express (1860–1) which carried mail 1966 miles from St Joseph, Missouri, to San Francisco in ten days. The average rider was eighteen years old, small and wiry. Mail was carried in the locked pockets of a *mochila* (shabraque) which could be shifted quickly from saddle to saddle at each relay. Some riders went unarmed, trusting entirely to their speed. Despite storms and Paiute war parties, very few of them failed to get through.

Cattle ranches, however, were the real schools of western horsemanship. The Spaniards introduced cattle raising in Texas and California, and its equipment and trade language always retained a Spanish influence. After the Civil War (1861–5) the cattle business spread northward into Canada, co-existing with the last furious years of the horse-Indian culture. Much Texas range was mesquite country,

full of thorny brush. Texas riders therefore preferred a short 30- to 40-ft manila rope ('lariat', 'riata', or 'lasso'); they tied one end of it to their saddle horn, and 'swung a small loop'. Their 'chaps' (*chaparreras*) were of heavy leather, usually fringed along the outer seams. Riding round-bellied Mustangs, they favoured saddles with two cinches ('rim-fire' or 'double-rigged') and low pommels and cantles.

The Californian rider came from a more open range with – apparently – larger horses and cattle. He used a single-cinch ('centerfire') saddle with a higher horn and cantle and elaborate *tapaderos* (leather stirrup hoods). His rope was a 60- to 65-ft rawhide, and he 'swung a big loop' which he tightened at the last moment to fit a hoof or horn. Instead of tying his rope to his saddle horn, he 'took a dally' (hitch) around it after making his throw, thereafter shortening or letting out rope as necessary. His chaps were usually of fur; a dandy would have matching saddle bags. Californians were noted for their 'pretty' silver-plated bits and spurs, silver *conchas* on saddle, bridle, and chaps.

The original 'cowboy' ('vaquero', 'cow puncher', 'hand', or 'buckaroo') was a specialist who worked with a horse and a rope. He would not cut hay or 'steal milk from a calf' (milk a cow). His clothing was equally specialized – a good hat, usually stiff-brimmed and low-crowned; a large silk handkerchief around his neck; a vest or short jacket over his shirt; wool pants, possibly reinforced with leather; knee-high boots with high, sloping heels that give a good grip on the stirrup (or the ground, if he were roping dismounted); heavy spurs with large, dull rowels. Short boots, big hats, denim jeans, cotton bandannas, and 'fancy' chaps came later.

The cow saddle was a heavy (30 to 40-lb. working platform. Early styles were much like the conquistadors' saddles, with the addition of a large, flat-topped ('dinner plate') horn. Later saddles had wider skirts and higher and fuller pommels and cantles. The smaller 'apple horn' appeared during the 1880s. Most cowboys used a simple curb ('grazing') bit and open reins; horses were trained to stand when

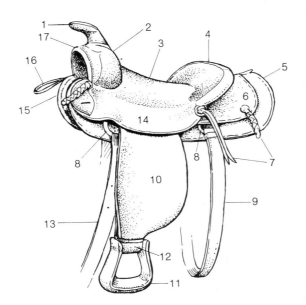

An example of a western stock saddle 1 Horn;
2 Fork; 3 Seat; 4 Cantle; 5 Skirt; 6 Back housing
or back jockey; 7 Lace strings; 8 Dee rings; 9 Leather
flank girth; 10 Fender or sudadero; 11 Stirrup;
12 Stirrup leather; 13 Front tie strap or cinch strap;
14 Front jockey and seat jockey, one piece; 15 Wool
lining; 16 Rope strap; 17 Pommel

Rodeos, which incorporate many of the old cowboy
skills, are a popular feature of the horse world in
America. 'Bronco busting' is a dangerous pastime and
professional riders who tour the rodeo circuit can earn
large sums of money.

the rider dismounted and dropped the reins.
Variations in this equipment were endless;
boots and saddles were frequently made to
order.

The cowboy rode with long stirrups, his
weight on the arch of his foot: rising to the
trot was effeminate. A favoured gait was the
'lope', an easy, distance-eating canter. Ordin-
arily the cowboy did not own the horse he
rode: it belonged to his employer, who assigned
each rider a 'string' of several horses. During
a roundup ('rodeo' or 'cow hunt') riders would
change horses three times a day, the extra
horses being herded in a 'remuda' or 'cavvy' by
a 'wrangler' during daylight and a 'nighthawk'
after dark.

Geldings were best for range work; mares
were likely to slip back to their home ranch.
'Cutting horses' with the intelligence and
quickness to force a designated cow out of a
milling herd were the elite of the remuda.
'Roping horses' also rated highly; properly
selected and trained, they would take their

rider into the most advantageous position for
throwing his loop, brace against the impact as
the lassoed animal hit the end of the rope, and
thereafter keep the rope taut, even if the rider
dismounted. Good cutting and roping horses
worked instinctively, guided only by the lightest
touch of the reins or pressure of the rider's leg.
'Night horses' were selected for their reliability,
night vision, and sure-footedness to carry a
rider safely out of a midnight stampede. For
long-distance cattle drives willing 'swimming
horses' were essential. The average 'cow horse'
was suitable only for routine herding.

In winter, only the best horses were kept at
the ranch and fed hay, the rest being turned out
to shift for themselves. Horses were usually
broken by professional 'bronc riders', but this
breaking was somewhat nominal. Many horses
remained 'snaky', always likely to buck.

Texas cowboy roping longhorn in the 1870s by Charles M. Russell.

The cattle business still flourishes, but the cowboy and his special skills are gone, except for professional rodeo riders. The rodeo grew out of informal contests between cowboys during roundups into a type of public fair. The first one to charge admission and award prizes was in Prescott, Arizona, in 1888. Rodeos now are annual features in several western states and Canada. Typical events are calf and steer roping, horse racing, bull dogging, and buck-ing horses and Brahman steers. There has been a marked revival of popular interest in western riding. Conventionalized 'cowboy' dress is common in the western states, and horse breeding has regained some of its former importance.

Part Five

The History of Racing

Jean and Louis Romanet

The history of horse racing is closely linked to the evolution of the most noble animal subject to man, to a sport, an unmatchable spectacle, a considerable industry – and a certain sector of human society.

Despite the diversity of these elements, they have one invariable factor in common whose permanence has assured the quality of matches between horses, and that is the love which men bear for that extraordinary animal, the horse. Today more than in any other age, it receives the respect and honour due to it, not because it gallops or jumps or trots better, but because modern contests are devised in a spirit quite different from that of past times.

Before the seventeenth century, which is to say before the genesis of the Thoroughbred, races had no other object than to prove the athletic prowess, the skill and the courage of the horseman. It suffices to recall the huge popularity of chariot drivers in antiquity to determine that the art of driving a team completely overshadowed the quality of the horses themselves. Coming closer in time, the steeplechase in its early days had no course marked out; the riders simply had to make, by the quickest possible means, for an objective which was visible from the starting-point. Here again the judgment and skill of the rider were more important than the quality of his mount.

And what of today? Everything is changed. It is the horses who have become the stars – some of them receive copious fan-mail – and they are treated with the honours due to the great ones of this world. One would be ill-advised to disregard this change, for it is of prime significance.

One effect of the Crusades was the great impression which oriental horses made on the Frankish knights who brought them back to the West. Above all, the English valued these wiry little light horses, swift runners whom Richard I and, long afterwards, Henry VIII and Charles II, imported in considerable numbers. By crossing them with the best of the native mares, with the consistent object of increasing speed, a new breed was founded in England, crystallizing in the reign of William III, when pedigrees were recorded in the *General Stud Book* first published by James Weatherby. The races enjoyed royal favour under monarch after monarch. But it was the racing men themselves who, from 1750, set themselves the task of imposing discipline on the racecourses by founding the Jockey Club. Newmarket, Doncaster, Epsom, and later Ascot are only some of the high places where the élite of English horse-flesh were gathered together.

But a new spirit came over racing. Competition, created by the granting of considerable prize money on established courses, took on a quite different character because it was organized by the breeders with the object of comparing the respective values of their produce. They themselves put up the purse (stakes or pools) which in some way represented the total of private wagers made by each owner-breeder.

From what had been simply an athletic contest for men, the English thus contrived a system of comparative values for horses, for which racing became an essential means of selection. Supreme ability no longer consisted in showing off one's physical prowess on horseback, but one's ability to produce a racer more brilliant than the others. The races of our time have inherited this tradition, even if the distinction between owners and breeders nowadays has given it another slant.

This is why the perennial wrangle between those who maintain that the true motive of racing is financial and those who hold it to be the improvement of horse breeding is of minor interest. It is clear that in the eighteenth and nineteenth centuries the horse regained that status in human esteem which it had once enjoyed in the Near East (Mahomet had enjoined men to treat horses with respect, because the pure-bred was preferred above all other creatures by the Most High). And so breeders behaved as the heirs of an ancient art to which they brought their contribution of science while still remaining within the bounds of tradition.

Francis Sartorius (1702–52). *A private match for 1000 guineas, with the Marquis of Rockingham's Bay Malton beating the Hon. Richard Vernon's Otto at Newmarket, 21 April 1766.* (Messrs Arthur Ackerman & Son, London)

It is interesting to consider how the main breeding countries have set about practising this selection.

Great Britain and Ireland

The Thoroughbred was born in England. It is there that the greatest races have been run, and it is perhaps the only country in the world where you are thought peculiar if you do not like horses.

Until the middle of the nineteenth century, the quality of the English Thoroughbred was unequalled, first because no other country had the same standards of assessment, and secondly because the prize money was not so considerable or the races followed with such sustained interest elsewhere.

One basic element in this evolution was the creation of what are known as the Classics:

At Newmarket in April, the One Thousand Guineas (first run in 1814) and the Two Thousand Guineas (1809); at Epsom in June, the Derby (1780) and the Oaks (1779); at Doncaster in September, the St Leger (1776).

These represented, and still do, the climax

of a racehorse's career, but obviously there are a great many more, of less importance, which have gone to make England the magnetic pole of Thoroughbred breeding.

There are towns, such as Newmarket, entirely devoted to this activity. Newmarket is the headquarters of the Jockey Club, whose function gave it a dominant position because it drew up the programmes, organized the meetings, laid down the Rules of Racing and ensured that they were obeyed.

Even today it is burdened by responsibility respecting breeding policy, with all the difficulties which this implies. The most significant example of this concerns handicapping. In handicap races, horses carry weights fixed by the handicapper with the aim of giving all an even chance of winning. It is thus very difficult to pick the winner, and thus bettors have an obvious interest in it. But breeders derive no useful hints from the result because the essential role of selection has vanished. It is the province of the Jockey Club to decide in what measure this necessary evil shall be tolerated.

Another very serious problem which aroused violent controversy in the last century was the question of two-year-old racing. When it is realized that the Thoroughbred does not attain full maturity until five, the dangers of running an animal which is still developing become clear. But it will surprise no one to learn that the costs of breeding and training soon became such that it was imperative, from the middle of the nineteenth century onwards, to select as early as possible.

These two examples show that selection is far from simple, and the results in 1865 made it sadly subject to criticism: the French horse Gladiateur won the Triple Crown; i.e., the 2000 Guineas, the Derby and the St Leger in the same year, and sixteen years later the American Iroquois won the Derby and the St Leger.

This was the first time that the Triple Crown had eluded an English runner, and this falling-off in quality was to be interpreted as the result of a programme too heavily loaded with races of minor importance (notably with handicaps) and too much beamed at precocity.

The total picture, in fact, reflected a singular dearth of races leading up to the big events and lacked coherence. But that was not the essential reason for the falling-off. Since the beginning of the nineteenth century other countries had been buying stock heavily in England and many breeders found there an ideal market sustained by such a strong demand that even mediocre animals commanded high prices. The demand for quantity at the expense of quality and the sale abroad of first-class stallions brought in its train the inevitable impoverishment. Unfortunately, the reaction was equally harmful, for political protectionism on the Disraeli model had its counterpart a generation afterwards in the Jockey Club's Jersey Act, whereby the title of Thoroughbred was denied to any animal all of whose forebears were not registered in the *General Stud Book*. This barrier against the importation of American horses, which were now achieving alarming performances, deprived British breeders of an important genetic potential.

But even after its repeal in 1949 the situation still remained critical because prize money was augmented more slowly than in France or in the United States, thus materially hindering the importation of Thoroughbreds of the first rank. Furthermore, the introduction of events over 10 f. for mature horses – such as the Coronation Cup – had been too timid; the great majority of breeders went on producing fast youngsters, lured on by the profusion of races for two-year-olds over 5 or 6 f. But still the paradox remained that the 12 f. Derby remained the supreme test of a three-year-old.

However, this quality of speed which English breeding was able to conserve afforded an excellent point of departure, combined with the importation of very good stallions from France and America, and a better balance between speed and staying power. The endowment of races like the King George VI and Queen Elizabeth Stakes served to highlight a spectacular recovery from the 1960s onwards, in which Vaguely Noble and Levmoss marked a climax by winning the Prix de l'Arc de Triomphe in 1968 and 1969.

France

In France, the first real attempt at organized racing on the English model took place under Louis XVI at the instigation of the Comte d'Artois who was to become Charles X, and the Duc de Chartres, with the support of Queen Marie Antoinette. From 1776 onwards these races were run on a course laid out on the Plaine des Sablons, to which were quickly added those of Fontainebleau and Vincennes; it must also be noted that the king himself deigned to put up considerable prize money for some races, and rules were issued for the conduct of racing.

All these efforts were swept away by the Revolution, and it was Napoleon who undertook to restore horse breeding and regularize racing practice by introducing official racing codes. A decree setting up races in those departments which specialized in the breeding of horses was promulgated on 31 August 1805, and supplemented by an order in 1806 which was to become the basic charter of racing (horses were to be between five and seven years old, born and bred in France); courses were long and meetings arranged in a rigidly hierarchic scale which culminated in the grand prix (40000 francs) to be run at Paris.

The sum total of these measures, albeit too inflexible, being based on the administrative government framework, did nevertheless provide all the support which up to that time had been lacking for the institution of racing in France.

Under the *Restauration* breeding and racing experienced a true revival, marked by the opening in 1833 of the French Stud Book by Royal Ordinance, and the foundation of a private society of twelve members under the patronage of the Duc d'Orléans and known as the 'Société d'Encouragement pour l'Amélioration des Races de Chevaux en France.'

Commonly known as the Société d'Encouragement, it was founded by a group of sportsmen who were convinced that the improvement of local breeds could only be achieved by upgrading stock with an infusion of Thoroughbred blood and by the institution of open races.

The Society did not see eye to eye with the management of the National studs whose power was firmly based on Napoleonic institutions, and which held the twofold monopoly of the direction of breeding policy and the organization of racing; they were much attached to the half-bred type and to regional meetings at various levels.

As from May 1834 the Société d'Encouragement began to organize flat racing which went on expanding as the Society was encouraged by various benefactors. The Revolution of 1848 passed over the racecourses without doing any damage, and the advent of the Second Empire served to consolidate their prosperity.

At this juncture two new parent societies were formed: the Société des Steeple-Chases de France, which Prince Murat founded in 1863, to run races over fences, and the Société pour l'Amélioration du Cheval de Demi-Sang (1864) which was to organize trotting races; both published their rules immediately.

The Société d'Encouragement soon gained pre-eminence, for its sponsors, grouped round the Duc de Morny, were powerful, and its popularity was great. The Imperial Equerry, General Fleury, also gave proof of a realistic attitude in his report to Marshal Vaillant, Minister of the Imperial Household and of Fine Arts, who drafted the decree of 16 March 1866. Its text transferred the powers of regulation and arbitration on various matters to the three parent societies, each in their respective sphere.

The Société d'Encouragement was the answer to the Jockey Club across the Channel, and in its programme of races, which was a carbon copy of the English model, the Derby became the Prix du Jockey-Club, which had been run since 1836 over the Chantilly track.

Of course, even if only French horses actually ran, breeding stock imported from Britain was numerous. Thus remarkable results were achieved very quickly, since in 1853 in the Goodwood Cup Jouvence gained the first French victory in England, while another French mare, Hervine, finished second.

A similar victory was achieved by Monarque in 1857, the third time that he had run in this race.

The same year, the Champ de Mars was replaced by Longchamp which gained international fame in 1863 by the creation of the Grand Prix de Paris, more prestigious even than the Prix du Jockey-Club: open to three-year-old colts and fillies of all countries, its prize money was richer, and the distance (1 mi. 7 f. or 2870 m) made it a most exacting test at the end of June.

Gladiateur won it in 1865, and in the same year he won the English Triple Crown, thus showing the world the quality of French-bred stock.

But the British blamed the French for only opening a few races to foreign horses, whereas in Britain the attitude had been most liberal. These protectionist devices were not given up until 1946 when almost all French racecourses were opened to foreign-bred horses.

In France the racing societies participated actively in working out the law of 2 June 1891, which was to allow racing to continue its meteoric course by the more strict control of betting.

Exchange of blood continued, and the importation of Flying Fox, winner of the English Triple Crown in 1899, allowed his buyer, M. Edmond Blanc, to take first place among owners and breeders up to World War One. This war put a severe curb on breeding which could not withstand the assault of the English, and when racing started again the first three post-war Grand Prix and the new Prix de l'Arc de Triomphe (1920) were won by English horses.

But the victories of Ksar in 1920 and 1921 when he won the Prix de l'Arc de Triomphe signalled the end of French convalescence and the dawn of a long reign of glory, exemplified by M. Marcel Boussac.

At the end of World War Two, French breeding had lost nothing in quality, for between 1946 and 1949 its representatives had many wins among the English Classics.

However, the programme laid principal stress on middle-distance races, and the Grand Prix, which long remained the crowning goal of breeding, was little by little deposed by the growing prestige of the Prix de l'Arc de Triomphe (October, over $1\frac{1}{2}$ mi.) but this change was not accompanied by any fundamental modification of the desired type. There were still rather few sprints.

Over the past five years French breeding has had some serious setbacks and one cannot help noticing that these are not without resemblance to those suffered by English breeding in the last century: impoverishment due to a boom market.

It seems to be very hard not to fall into the trap of vain glory and to resist the temptation to plunder the genetic potential of a country for the sake of instant financial gain. Breeders see in this the just reward of their efforts; but unfortunately such a drain of blood can never be offset in quality by imports of equivalent value.

Breeding is the more sensitive to these setbacks as competition has never been keener. The prize money at French meetings, thanks to the Pari-Mutuel Urbain and the creation of the Tiercé in 1954. has reached a level which has made it worth while for many foreign stables to come and set up in France.

Evidently this is an excellent stimulus to breeding in France and the quality of the sport has benefited greatly.

The authorities on matters of racing and breeding in all the leading countries now work in close collaboration, but it is certain that harmony will be attained more easily between Great Britain and France than by either with the United States, which today dominates the world breeding scene.

The United States

The United States attracts superlatives in all things; and racing is no exception. Statistics concerning gate money, horses and auctions are impressive.

The international results also are such that one wonders how the English Jockey Club came to regard the American horse as a social pariah. From the beginnings in the eighteenth century the British influence was considerable, but it was not long before the American taste for comfort and regard for practical considerations led to smaller tracks of which the whole could be seen from the grandstand.

After the Civil War the sport was considered more as a pastime than one that might bring profit, and handicaps crept into the programmes. Very early the accent was on precocity and sprinting, even more so than in England, and the 10 f. Kentucky Derby, first run in 1875, is a prime example.

Many Europeans had thought there was no such thing as American breeding until the appearance of Iroquois and of Foxhall, who between them won the Derby, the St Leger, the Grand Prix de Paris (1881) and the Ascot Gold Cup (1882).

Unfortunately, at just that time, the internal reputation of American racetracks suffered a considerable decline due to the outbreak of several scandals. Some states even banned racing, and indeed it is still illegal in many; the Jockey Club had to confine itself to the role of counsellor and manager of the stud book. The reaction was keenly felt by breeders, many of whom found an outlet for their produce in Europe. The Jersey Act was only one of various measures taken to repel this invasion.

Before the outbreak of World War Two, the resumption of racing was accompanied by a total ban on bookmakers. This decision ensured a substantial revenue by the medium of a Tote levy. Thus the future of racing could be envisaged with confidence.

But in the blackest hour some breeders had yet managed to keep up their spirits and retain good stock: and they were justified by the birth of Man O' War in 1917; the quality of this stallion was to make its mark in the annals both of the *Racing Calendar* and the stud book.

Having discovered in France the two greatest stallions in its history, Sir Galahad and Bull Dog, the American breeding industry stocked itself regularly from Europe by the power of the dollar: Blenheim, Mahmoud, Bahram (the latter had won the Triple Crown in England), Nasrullah and Princequillo, to mention only the greatest; after that Ribot and Sea Bird visited the States. If the results were tardy, they nevertheless showed remarkable qualities, as was demonstrated by the four American-bred winners of the Epsom Derby – Sir Ivor in 1968, Nijinsky in 1970, Mill Reef in 1971 and Roberto in 1972.

However, bearing in mind the lack of common policy in the drawing up of programmes – for these are arranged at state level, sometimes by individual racetracks – and the very great number of races which means that very mediocre animals can be kept in training (half the horses in training win at least one race, compared to something between a third and a quarter in England) and the number of very short races, it is strange to find that the American Thoroughbred has become the best in the world over Classic distances despite the great disparity of breeding methods as between, say, Kentucky and California.

The United States still presents to the outside world the spectacle in racing terms of a pioneer country where the best of ideas rub shoulders with the worst: because the Americans have managed to breed Thoroughbreds in deserts, because the amenities of their racetracks are extraordinary, and finally because American stock crossed with that of the Old World has done wonders. That is why they stand in the front rank today.

Italy

Horse racing on a regular basis began in Italy in 1837 at Florence and Naples; but Milan, five years later, became the centre both of racing and breeding. Rome, where there were no races until 1868, was to be the venue of the Italian Derby, first run on 19 April 1884.

King Victor Emmanuel II showed these racing centres much favour and contributed lavishly towards the large imports required to provide for them. His stable thus became very powerful and won all the big races.

New courses were opened, notably at Turin and Pisa, in the second half of the nineteenth century.

Thus the foundations of racing and breeding had been laid before the advent of the man who was to give them international fame: Federico Tesio, who founded the Dormello stud in 1898 on the shores of Lake Maggiore.

It is thanks to him that Italian breeding today figures in the pedigrees of the best blood in the world, his two aces, Nearco, foaled in 1935 and Ribot, 1952.

The Italian Thoroughbred, bred on purpose to conform to the selective requirements of the racing programme, is essentially a horse for Classic distances.

In fact, the two great spring races, the Derby for three-year-olds, the Gran Premio d'Italia for three-year-olds, the Gran Premio di Milano for three-year-olds and above, and the Gran Premio del Jockey-Club and the Coppa d'Oro for the same in the autumn are all run over 12 f.

Today the Italians can only with difficulty resist the challenge of foreign competition which is attracted by the rather rich prize money, and there is a certain tendency to protectionism; but the arrival of new owners and breeders and the purchase of quality young stock from abroad would appear to herald an imminent revival.

Germany

Germany was one of the first countries to organize horse racing on the English model; the German Derby, run at Hamburg, was initiated in 1869, fifteen years earlier than the Italian Derby. But it was not until the inter-war period that the many imports which took place at the turn of the century from Britain and France bore fruit and that the German Thoroughbred began to score international victories.

Unfortunately, World War Two left German racing and breeding in a lamentable state and recovery has been very slow.

But racing has regained international class, notably with the institution of the Grosser Preis von Europa, run at Cologne in October by three-year-olds and upwards, which now stands on a par with the Grosser Preis von Baden.

Since then German horses have scored many successes abroad but no great Classic victory, whereas foreign horses have often carried off the prizes in German races of international class.

It is to be hoped therefore that a policy of imports which was so beneficial to German breeding between the wars will be resumed and enable them one day to win a Classic.

Argentina

By reason of the number of foals born there every season, South America holds an important place in the world of breeding; and because of its temperate climate Argentina has the lion's share.

There, too, British influence was decisive: it inspired the founding of the Jockey Club in 1882 and the shaping of programmes on the basis of Classic distances of 12 f. So that the ideal Argentine horse unites speed with staying power, as their Quadruple Crown, summit of a successful racing career, shows:

Polla de Potrillos (2000 Guineas) over 1 mile, August
Gran Premio Jockey-Club over 10 furlongs, September
Gran Premio Nacional over 12½ furlongs, October
Gran Premio Carlos Pellegrini over 15 furlongs, November

(The apparent disparity of dates as against European practice is due to the inversion of seasons in the Southern Hemisphere.)

To say that nine horses in the present century have won this very high distinction is to acknowledge the value of Argentine breeding. But these successes, even if they are often spectacular, as Forli demonstrated in 1966, are very rare.

The rather low level of prize money allied to over-production is the principal drawback. It follows that breeders are forced to rely heavily on foreign demand, which is spasmodic to the extent of hampering any long-term policy. The situation is made more difficult because Argentine breeders have to import breeding stock of very high quality to keep up the standard of their studs.

However, thanks to the staying power of local stock, mating with American sprinters has paid off. Argentina occupies a very important place because it is a considerable genetic reservoir and provides that robust constitution which is the essential basis of the intricate artificial creation that is the Thoroughbred: Europe and the United States have found new blood there, blood which is constantly being refreshed by importations, principally from Europe.

South Africa

The Republic of South Africa, formerly the Union of South Africa, which was a Dominion of the Commonwealth made by the amalgamation in 1909 of the former British colonies of the Cape and Natal with the Orange and Transvaal Republics, was the scene of horse racing in early colonial times.

In accordance with the usual form, the stimulus to breeding was given by the addiction to the sport of such members of the ruling class as Lord Charles Somerset, an early nineteenth-century governor.

Further, the mineral wealth of the country was conducive to betting, and all the auguries seemed favourable. But a programme which laid great stress on handicaps and short distances, with very few races open to four-

year-old and older horses, soon put the emphasis on precocity and sprinting power.

Happily the 1960s, thanks to excellent stallions like Colorado King, Sea Cottage and Hawaii, have seen the reward of the great efforts made by breeders to improve the quality of their output.

The advent of these three gives ground for hope that one day South African horses will play an important part in the world market when they have become capable of competing at the great international meetings.

Australia and New Zealand

The relative proximity of these two countries (Sydney to Wellington 1233 miles) has tended to fuse their racing and breeding so that despite certain perceptible differences Australia and New Zealand present a certain unity, at least to the non-British external observer.

The difference is principally one of climate: temperate and with abundant rainfall in New Zealand, arid to dry over the greater part of Australia. Despite this climatic disadvantage, Australia has managed to produce excellent Thoroughbreds, just as has New Zealand. The Australian Jockey Club has since the nineteenth century given racing the necessary incentive to produce quality by laying down a programme based on Classics and prestige handicaps over long distances.

Top quality imports included Fisherman, winner of sixty-nine races in England, including the Ascot Gold Cup twice.

Thus by 1900 there had appeared a typically Australian stamp of Thoroughbred remarkable for its stamina, for which there were two reasons: the undoubted prestige of the very difficult handicaps in which every horse of consequence had to distinguish himself by carrying a heavy weight; and a policy of wholesale participation, every horse running many and frequent races.

However that may be, this view was modified by the repeated successes of New Zealand horses.

It seems that the climate was not solely responsible, but that the heavy emphasis laid on races for two-year-olds in Australia had its effect also.

New Zealand had imported excellent sires and dams from Australia at first, then from Europe, with a marked preference for horses with staying power like Hurry On and Le Filou. Results were rapid and New Zealand attained an envied stature among breeding countries, notably in Australia where Carbine continued his spectacular career; Trenton, Phar Lap and Tulloch subsequently confirmed New Zealand's success in the eyes of the world.

Japan

The unparalleled expansion of Japan following World War Two permitted racing and breeding to develop there at an extraordinary speed thanks to the enthusiasm of the public for racing and gambling and to the ardour of owners and breeders in investing part of their profits in Thoroughbreds.

It is certain that the owner there is treated better than in any other country, for almost every starter gets at least a consolation prize and a part of training expenses is covered by the Japan Racing Association.

It is understandable, under these conditions, that there should be a boom in breeding, and a rapid saturation of the home market. Unfortunately, the export market is relatively weak, and exports are limited to Malaysia, the Philippines and California.

In fact Japan has not yet managed to prove the worth of her breeding internationally, despite regular imports of very high quality from the great breeding countries.

Conclusion

Why horse racing?

To judge by its immense popularity, racing has become a social phenomenon of immense importance. Be it at Sydney, Johannesburg, Paris, Ascot, Milan or New York, crowds throng to admire this drama with its unexpected denouement, though the setting and plot never vary.

Apart from betting, the beauty of the scene and admiration for the effort exerted, the lure of racing depends partly on its being a marvellous hotbed of heroes. In our day which is singularly lacking in heroes, due more to the fact that we have become blasé than that men have become less admirable, it is curious to observe the fervour of the crowd when the winner outdistances his rivals by ten lengths or so. The title of 'unbeaten' involuntarily goes to the head. The breeder of winners is sorely tempted to look upon himself as a wizard.

Moreover, if, as that misogynist Anatole France wrote, we put the infinite into love it was not the fault of women, and one may as well say today that if the races are still one of the world's finest spectacles by virtue of the quality of the emotion they provoke, this is undoubtedly because the horse more than any other animal satisfies our aesthetic desires while at the same time so gallantly carrying our hopes.

Because racing demands observation, systematic checking and experiment in breeding, because it awakens our sense of beauty, it is at once a science and an art of which Henri Poincaré said that they constituted 'l'unique valeur des civilisations', the sole value of civilizations.

Bloodlines: A French Example

David Powell

In practice it is impossible to separate 'bloodlines' from 'racing'. A pedigree is only a compendium of races won or lost, and bloodlines as a whole are but a map of racing history. As mentioned in the entry on French flat racing, the kinds of races available determine what kind of horses will be bred. Likewise each race contested changes the map of the breed, just a little; the winner becomes a credit mark for his sire, his dam, his female line, and makes each of these just a little more valuable.

The concept of *direct male* or *direct female* line has come in for some criticism, especially from geneticists, who maintain that chromosomes are all. Apart from the fact that some genes (particularly to do with temperament) are sex-linked, there are both practical and logical reasons for classifying Thoroughbreds by direct male or female lines.

Practically, it is the only way to handle the mass of information available. A stallion can cover forty-odd mares a year, while a mare can produce at best one foal to race per year. It stands to reason that forty females are required for reproduction to every male who is retired to stud. Since they are selected on racing ability, thirty-nine times out of forty the male partner will be superior to the female.

A chain is only as strong as its weakest link, and the direct female line is presumably a chain of mostly weak links. Strength in the direct female line then is especially significant, all the more so since the mares have fewer opportunities.

So the male line, conversely, flourishes more easily: a stallion can have over five hundred foals in a lifetime of covering, and his good sons may have the same opportunity.

So much for the male and female line. Let us have a look at the most successful male lines in France.

St Simon.

The St Simon lines: St Simon, a sharp-tempered, elegant, if smallish, brown by the excitable Galopin, was never beaten. One of the best runners of all time, he developed into the mightiest sire of the nineteenth century. Several of the best male lines in France in the last fifty years descend from him.

Rabelais (by St Simon) was a fiery-tempered little fellow with his hocks well away from him. He sired Rialto, a hardy campaigner, liver chestnut with a lot of white about him, who in turn got Wild Risk. The latter was something of a 'Cinderella case', who won his first seller at 100 to 1 and then became a champion hurdler. Even this seemed hardly sufficient to make him a stallion, but he became a leading sire: Worden, Vimy and the massive chestnut Le Fabuleux have carried on the line.

The handsome chestnut Worden turned out a whole brigade of good stallions: Devon, Bel Baraka, Marino and Armistice among them.

Wild Risk frequently transmitted his straight shoulder and his club foot, but also his guts and ability to stay for ever, act in the heavy ground, and to jump.

Prince Rose (who was three generations removed from St Simon) was a high-class runner in Belgium and was killed all too young by a bomb in 1944. He had time, however, to sire three sons who bred on: Princequillo (who influenced American breeding to a marked degree), the elegant Prince Chevalier (exported to England, where he did well) and Prince Bio, an extremely common brown who broke a fetlock early in his third year.

In spite of his looks Prince Bio was an excellent stallion, and got several Classic winners, although he probably did not really stay himself. His most influential son was the St Simon-saturated Sicambre (out of a Rialto mare), a tall, elegant brown with an attractive blaze and a white eye. An extremely good-tempered horse (his produce even inclined to laziness), Sicambre won seven of his eight starts and was France's premier sire for a decade.

Sicambre's sons at stud include the good filly sire Shantung, Celtic Ash, Cambremont, Hauban, Diatome, Roi Dagobert and Barbare.

Like his sire, Prince Bio, Sicambre was also

Sicambre.

successful as a sire of brood mares. He was a high-class two-year-old himself, and won both the Prix du Jockey-Club and the Grand Prix de Paris at three. His produce are essentially mile-and-a-half runners, i.e., Classic material.

Prince Bio's highly bred son, Prince Taj (out of Nasrullah's sister), was far from a top class racehorse, but led France's sire list two years in a row, when his progeny flooded the Classic placings: Astec, Taj Dewan, Tidra, Rajput Princess, etc. He was then re-exported to the USA where he had already failed when sent to race there, presumably because of his feet.

Vatout, who descended from St Simon through the unconsidered Prince Chimay, was a small, neat and rather dandy sort with bent hocks. He was sold through a seller, but became a good racer and the sire of the Epsom Derby winner Bois Roussel (whose produce had a lot of ability but a temper to match) and Vatellor (a hardy campaigner who transmitted his excellent temperament and his ability to act in the mud), both of whom inherited and passed on Vatout's hocks.

Vatout himself was a reasonably good two-year-old, but his descendants have been noted for their stamina. The Bois Roussels had quality and were generally squat and short-legged, while the Vatellors were brown, plain, with more depth than quarters, and very honest. Little remains of the direct male line, even though Vatellor sired two successive Epsom Derby winners.

The Teddy line. Teddy was unbeaten in five starts; his career was restricted by World War One. His grandsire, Flying Fox, won the Triple Crown in England and was sold for a then record 37500 guineas to the French sportsman, Edmond Blanc. The purchase proved a wise one and, from his first crop on, Flying Fox was a success. His son, Ajax, got Teddy, a very masculine, perfectly balanced individual to whom one can inbreed as much as one likes with no risk.

Teddy was a top class sire of runners and brood mares, and his sons, Astérus and

Teddy.

Aethelstan, kept his male line alive. Astérus was more refined, due to the influence of Rabelais on the dam's side of his pedigree, while Aethelstan was more the robust Teddy sort, and resembled his sire a lot. He got the lucky Grand Prix de Paris winner Deux pour Cent, a common, lop-eared sort who lacked class and was exported to Czechoslovakia. Before going into 'exile', he had the chance to sire Tantième, a true champion who won the Prix de l'Arc de Triomphe twice.

Tantième's influence was wielded principally through his huge, imposing son Tanerko, who campaigned successfully as a three-, four- and five-year-old, and won both the Prix Ganay and the Grand Prix de Saint-Cloud twice.

Tanerko got several Classic winners, the best being Relko, who was more precocious than most of his stock, and subsequently won a Triple Crown of sorts: the Poule d'Essai des Poulains, the Epsom Derby and the Prix Royal Oak. A leggy, highly strung bay, Relko sired the Grand Critérium winner, Breton, in his first crop.

The first crop syndrome is a bizarre characteristic of the Teddy line: from Flying Fox down, all the links in the chain we have just gone through came from their sire's first or second crop. This is not a line of sprinters but of mile-and-a-half runners, and whereas Teddy was renowned as an influence for good temperament (Vatellor was out of a Teddy mare), with Tantième (who was a bad traveller) some nerves crept in, and they have continued down to Relko and his progeny. Size, scope and substance were characteristics of Tantième's descendants, while the produce of Tanerko and Relko tended to be leggy. Breton, on the other hand, was smallish and close to the ground.

Tanerko also got two three-parts brothers to Relko (all out of Reliance, by Relic), the globe trotter Match, who won an international Triple Crown of the Grand Prix de Saint-Cloud, the King George VI and Queen Elizabeth Stakes, and the Washington D.C. International, and the crack Reliance, who took both the Prix du Jockey-Club and the Grand Prix de Paris, and met his only defeat when second to Sea Bird in the Prix de l'Arc de Triomphe.

Match died too young, but Reliance (hardly an example of equine beauty, with his plain head, lop ears and twisted leg) has become a very good stallion of stayers in England.

Tanerko's young son, Djakao, an unlucky loser of the Prix du Jockey-Club, is much more like his maternal grandsire, Ribot.

The Tourbillon line. The story of the Tourbillon line is closely associated with the success of the Marcel Boussac studs. Tourbillon was a high-class racehorse, but not a champion, by the crack Ksar, and renowned for his fiery temper, which he transmitted liberally. The fact that most of his Boussac-bred descendants were inbred to him may not have helped.

High quality, a light frame, sound forelegs and hocks set well away were characteristics of the Tourbillon breed, along with the proverbial nervous influx. He sired so many Classic winners that we can only mention a few of them: Goya, Djebel, Esmeralda, Tornado, Caracalla, Coaraze, Tourment and Ambiorix.

Tourbillon gave his progeny plenty of speed and many of them were good as two-year-olds. Even the crack Djebel was probably essentially a miler. A small, sharp horse with the characteristic hind legs, Djebel has bred on through several unexpected channels: the small, bow-legged Clarion, a speedy sort who in turn got the miler and leading sire, Klairon; the sprinter, Le Lavandou, sire of the enigmatic Le Levanstell; and Hugh Lupus, the high class if unlucky sire of Hethersett.

The Blandford line. Blandford was probably high class, but virtually impossible to train because of his joints. His French son, Brantôme, was a neat, athletic little horse of great spirit, and a champion on the racecourse, from two to four years, at all distances. Brantôme was fairly lively, but his Grand Prix de Paris winner, Vieux Manoir, was remarkably good-tempered and passed on his quiet disposition to many of his colts.

Several of these became leading sires, as their sire had been. Mourne, whose career was interrupted by injury, sired many good winners, including Snob, a massive bay out of Sicambre's full sister, who headed the sire list himself in 1969. Snob got the Prix du Jockey-Club winner, Goodly, before being exported to Japan.

Le Haar, from the same crop as Mourne, has also been a very successful stallion. His sons at stud include the big, extremely handsome stayer, Ramsin, and the tiny, exquisite Exbury, both chestnuts like their sire.

Exbury reached his peak at the age of four, when he showed a dazzling turn of speed to win all five of his starts, the Prix de l'Arc de Triomphe included. Exbury's progeny have earned a reputation for unreliability, but the fact remains that he has produced a very high level of class.

Vieux Manoir was a neat, medium-sized, perfectly balanced bay with a blaze and four white socks, short cannon bones and absolutely straight hocks. Of his sons at stud Val de Loir was the most faithful to the above-mentioned traits, both in himself and in his progeny. Val de Loir was a tough and consistent colt, and won the Prix du Jockey-Club. He was a marvellous sire, both in respect to Classic elements and number of winners. His best sons were Val d'Aoste, Beaugency, Chaparral and

Tennyson, his best daughters La Lagune and Comtesse de Loir.

As you may have gathered from Vieux Manoir's Grand Prix de Paris victory, this is a line of Classic to staying runners. The colts are generally good-tempered, the fillies perhaps less so. Many of the best stallions of this line are ridglings.

Fine Top's line. The line of Hyperion never developed much in France, but an alternate line from his sire, Gainsborough, has flourished with Fine Top.

A tall, rangy, strikingly handsome black of high quality, Fine Top had lots of speed, and held the Longchamp record for seven furlongs.

He was tough, genuine and consistent, winning sixteen times and being placed sixteen times from thirty-two starts. His stock often stayed further than he did, but also were more excitable. In fact he got a Prix de l'Arc de Triomphe winner in Topyo, a Prix de Diane winner in Fine Pearl, while his ultra-nervous son, Sanctus, won both the Prix du Jockey-Club and the Grand Prix de Paris.

A small, strong-quartered, rather Araby brown of lovely quality, Sanctus has passed on the family 'nerves' (his dam is by Tourment) but has proved a good stallion all in all.

Fine Top's dam was by Vatellor, and this is a line which frequently acts well on soft or even heavy ground.

Flat Racing in Britain and Ireland

Peter Willett

Despite the stormy history of Anglo-Irish political relations, the socio-economic links between Britain and Eire have been close for many centuries. Some of the strongest links have been forged in the spheres of horses and equine sports, the mutual interest in these matters being securely rooted in the fact that large tracts of both countries are favourable for horse breeding.

Each country had a breed of racing horses for centuries before the evolution of the Thoroughbred which resulted from importation of horses of Eastern blood in the late seventeenth century and in the eighteenth century. The Hobbies of Ireland corresponded to the Galloways of Britain. The development and improvement of the Thoroughbred was due to the activities of breeders in both countries, which have shared a common stud book, the *General Stud Book*, for the breed of the racehorse since the end of the eighteenth century. In the first half of the nineteenth century Eire was producing horses like Bird-catcher (1833), Harkaway (1834), The Baron (1842) and Faugh-A-Ballagh (1844) who matched the best of the British products in racing ability and/or influence on the evolution of the breed. Eire is primarily a pastoral country, and for this reason has been able to produce many more Thoroughbreds in relation to human population than industrialized Britain. With only five per cent of the combined human population of the two countries, Eire has been able to raise its share of their joint Thoroughbred production to forty-six per cent in the twentieth century, and has usually found a ready market for its output in Britain.

In racehorse breeding selection is determined by the racing system for which production is intended. Because Irish breeders have had an eye on the British market, besides sharing the sporting inclinations of their British counterparts, the Irish racing system has always borne a close resemblance to the British. In the eighteenth century the King's Plates introduced in the reign of Charles II were the principal races in both countries. They were endurance tests in which mature horses of at least four years of age carried heavy weights over distances of from 2 to 4 miles. In the late eighteenth century and in the nineteenth century the trend towards shorter races contested by younger horses carrying lighter weights became pronounced. By the second decade of the nineteenth century the British series of five Classic races for three-year-olds had been established as the supreme tests of excellence. They have continued without significant alteration down to the present day, and are the Two Thousand Guineas for entire colts and fillies and the One Thousand Guineas fillies, both run over 1 mi. at Newmarket; the Derby for entire colts and fillies and the Oaks for fillies run over $1\frac{1}{2}$ mi. at Epsom; and the St Leger for entire colts and fillies run over $1\frac{3}{4}$ mi. 127 yds. at Doncaster. A similar Classic series was introduced in Eire.

Although the Classic races became the ultimate criteria of merit, the cult of speed and early maturity in the racehorse did not stop with these races for three-year-olds. The racing of two-year-olds forms a vital part of the racing programmes of both Britain and Eire throughout the flat racing season which extends from

March to November, and two-year-old races account for about thirty per cent of all flat races decided in Britain. These races are restricted to 5 f. during the months of March, April and May, but their distances are increased progressively during the remainder of the season. Two-year-olds may run over 1 mi. from September onwards, and there are a few races for them over as long a distance as 10 f. in the late autumn.

The most important two-year-old races in Britain are the Flying Childers Stakes at Doncaster, the Cheveley Park Stakes, the Middle Park Stakes and the Dewhurst Stakes at Newmarket and the William Hill Futurity at Doncaster; and the Phoenix Stakes, the National Stakes and the Beresford Stakes are the most important two-year-old races in Eire. Of these races the Cheveley Park Stakes alone is confined to fillies.

The similarity of the racing systems of the two countries is increased by the fact that they both have broad expanses of open heathland, providing resilient stretches of turf, for their principal racecourses and training centres, which are surrounded by excellent stud farming land containing some of the most important Thoroughbred nurseries. These are Newmarket Heath in Suffolk, England, and the Curragh of Kildare in Eire. With their racing and breeding complexes these two are the veritable racing and breeding headquarters of their respective countries. They stage flat racing only. There are two separate courses at Newmarket, where in 1976 the Rowley Mile course had eight days' racing in spring and nine in autumn and the July Course had eleven days' racing between June and August. The single course at the Curragh had seventeen days' racing.

In the same year (1976) flat racing took place on thirty-seven courses in Britain and only nine fewer in Ireland. However these figures give a false impression of the volume of racing in the two countries. Many of the Irish courses were sparsely utilized and others, like Sligo and Killarney, staged only mixed meetings with programmes divided between flat and jumping races. The British total of 2898 flat races during the 1975 season was about three and a half times the Irish total. Important Irish flat racing was confined to four courses: the Curragh, Leopardstown, Phoenix Park and Naas.

The Curragh has the monopoly of the five Irish Classic races, but in Britain the Classic series is shared between Newmarket, Epsom and Doncaster. None of these three British courses provides racing of concentrated high quality to compare with the four-day Royal Ascot meeting in June or the three-day York August meeting. Of the 100 British Pattern races (the races officially designated as composing a comprehensive system of tests for the best horses of all types) fifteen are run at Royal Ascot. These include the Ascot Gold Cup ($2\frac{1}{2}$ mi.), the supreme test of stayers, and the King's Stand Stakes (5 f.), the supreme test of sprinters. The York August meeting stages six 'Pattern' races, including the Benson and Hedges Gold Cup (10 f.), one of the most important middle distance tests for three-year-olds and older horses, and the Yorkshire Oaks ($1\frac{1}{2}$ mi.), one of the most important stamina tests for three-year-old fillies.

Other British courses which stage races of the greatest importance in the Pattern of Racing are Goodwood with the Sussex Stakes and Sandown Park with the Eclipse Stakes. Goodwood, whose course extends along a ridge of the South Downs, commands wide views of rolling downland, woods and the south coast. It is the most beautiful of British racecourses and its principal meeting, which covers five days at the end of July and the beginning of August, is popular with holiday makers.

In addition to its two Classic races, Epsom stages the Coronation Cup over the same course as the Derby and the Oaks. This forms part of the series of important European middle-distance races, as does the King George VI and Queen Elizabeth Stakes run at Ascot in July, which in 1974 became Britain's first

An aerial view of the huge crowds at Epsom on Derby day.

Ascot, one of Britain's premier courses. Queen Anne inaugurated the first meeting in 1711.

£100000 race, thanks to the sponsorship of De Beers.

The most important race run at Newmarket apart from the two Classic races and the three big two-year-old races is the Champion Stakes, run over its unique 10 f. straight course 'Across the Flat' in mid-October. This is one of the key European races in which three-year-olds meet older horses over this distance, and it is invariably contested by an international field.

Newbury, with a circuit of 1¾ mi., a straight 1 mi. course and an alternative 1 mi. course round a bend, provides one of the fairest tests of a racehorse apart from Newmarket. And, like Newmarket, it plays a part of special importance in the organization of British racing on account of its proximity to the second biggest training centre, Lambourn. Newbury had fifteen days' flat racing in 1976 and, although it has no races of the highest grade of import-

ance (Group I of the Pattern) it has four races of Group II, these being the John Porter Stakes, the Lockinge Stakes, the Geoffrey Freer Stakes and the Mill Reef Stakes, the last-named race being for two-year-olds only.

The body that has controlled British racing for more than two centuries is the Jockey Club. Formed about 1750, the Jockey Club originally was an association of persons enjoying the sport of horse racing, mostly wealthy land-owners, for purely social purposes. Before long it acquired property and built a clubhouse in Newmarket, and gradually extended its land-holding to embrace the whole of Newmarket Heath. As the members of the Club were also the most influential persons in the sport, more and more power began to accrue to the Jockey Club as an institution, while ownership of Newmarket racecourse and its adjacent training grounds supplied an absolute sanction for its edicts and regulations. The executive powers of the Club were vested in a panel of three

The blue riband of flat racing – the Epsom Derby.
Sir Ivor storms home on the outside to win the 1968 race.

'stewards' elected by the membership, the senior steward being the chief executive officer of the Club. Although stewards were elected for periods of three years, retiring stewards were eligible for re-election, and as a result of this system strong personalities like Sir Charles Bunbury, Lord George Bentinck and Admiral Rous were enabled to wield continuous power for lengthy periods. Between 1768, when Bunbury became a steward for the first time, and 1877, when Rous died, the Jockey Club extended its authority from its Newmarket base to cover the whole of British racing, imposing a uniform set of rules, legislating for each new set of circumstances as they arose, and licensing racecourses, officials, trainers and jockeys. The Turf Club was the counterpart of the Jockey Club in Eire and exercised similar control over Irish racing.

The Jockey Club and the Turf Club evolved as self-perpetuating oligarchies in the spheres of flat racing in their respective countries.

Their powers and privileges were unchallenged until after World War Two, when it became apparent that these traditional, amateur bodies were no longer adequate to cope with all the needs of racing, which had become an industry as well as a sport. The courses and their amenities were mostly in serious need of modernization, and as the years passed there was an ever more pressing demand for the introduction of technical innovations like public address systems, photo-finish cameras, electrical timing and camera patrols, besides expensive services like security and dope testing. Moreover there was an urgent requirement for greatly increased prize money if the standard of racing in Britain and Eire were to be improved, or even maintained. All these aims could be achieved only if much larger sums were made available to the racing industry through new institutions founded to raise and distribute them.

Eire was the first to take action, and in 1945 the Dail set up the Racing Board to take over the conduct of racing in all its aspects except discipline, which was to remain the responsibility of the Turf Club. The Racing Board was to draw its revenue from the Totalizator (Pari-Mutuel) and from a levy on on-course betting with bookmakers. Its early priority was the improvement of racing by increasing prize money, reducing entry fees and paying for the transport of horses to race meetings.

Progress was much slower in Britain. It was not until 1961 that the Betting Levy Act became law and set up the Horserace Betting Levy Board with powers to raise funds from the Totalizator and the bookmakers, and to distribute them for the benefit of horse racing and breeds of horses and for the promotion of veterinary research.

Racing in Britain and Eire has survived only as a result of the formation of these new statutory bodies. The effects have been more dramatic in Eire, where the value of prize money and the standard of racing have made marked advances in comparison with its neighbour. Since World War Two there have been more good horses in training in Eire than ever before, and more of them have raided the big races in Britain with success. Orby, in 1907, was the first Irish-trained horse to win the Derby. No other Irish-trained horse won the Derby until Hard Ridden in 1958. But in the next nineteen years the Irish-trained horses Santa Claus, Sir Ivor, Nijinsky, Roberto and The Minstrel all followed the example of Hard Ridden successfully at Epsom.

Moreover in 1962, thanks to sponsorship by the Irish Hospitals Sweepstakes, the Irish Derby became for the first time ever one of the important European Classic races. Eire has become not only one of the leading Thoroughbred breeding countries but also one of the principal horse-racing countries anywhere in Europe.

Steeplechasing in Britain and Ireland

Peter Willett

Steeplechasing, as horse racing over obstacles is called, plays a more important part in the overall structure of racing in Britain and Eire than in any other country. In the season of 1974–5 3255 races over fences and hurdles were run in the two countries combined and, although the total may be reduced severely in a season which includes a hard winter, the amount of racing over jumps is usually not much less than the amount of racing on the flat.

Steeplechasing originated in the twin passions of the farming and land-owning classes of Britain and Eire for foxhunting and horse racing. The drive to improve the speed of racehorses in the second half of the eighteenth century was communicated to the hunting field in the form of the fast riding to hounds pioneered by men like Childe of Kinlet Hall in Shropshire. And the competitive spirit roused by fast riding soon spilled over into the desire to match horse against horse in races over the obstacles encountered in the hunting field, but without the inhibiting presence of hounds.

The term 'steeplechase' was derived from the practice of running the early cross-country races from church to church, as the church steeples often provided the best landmarks. The first steeplechase of which the record has survived took place in Eire in 1752, when two friends, O'Callaghan and Blake, raced from Buttevant Church to the steeple of St Leger Church.

At first steeplechases were run as matches between two horses only. In the first half of the nineteenth century these races lost their original meaning and became contests between larger numbers of horses over marked courses. The 1830s were a period of rapid evolution of steeplechasing in Britain, and the decade ended with the running of the first Grand National at Aintree near Liverpool. The Grand National (called the Grand Liverpool Steeplechase in its early years) was organized by a committee whose members included Lord George Bentinck, then one of the most influential members of the Jockey Club, though the Jockey Club exercised no control over steeplechasing at that time.

The Grand National, won in its inaugural year by Lottery, soon became extremely popular in Britain and the most famous race of its kind in the world. The size and severity of the fences and the long distance (4 mi. 856 yds. have made it the most demanding test of both horse and rider. In the early years the obstacles included stone walls, banks, posts-and-rails and hurdles, besides brooks and growing hedges, and some of the race was run across ploughed fields, not grass. But as steeplechasing became an organized spectator sport and regular steeplechase meetings multiplied at many places in Britain and Eire in the second half of the nineteenth century, and horses of superior speed and breeding were trained as jumpers, a degree of uniformity of the obstacles was required, and in time these became artificial fences constructed of tightly bound birch or thorn branches. In order to provide full racing programmes, races over hurdles – smaller and less formidable obstacles usually made of chestnut bars – were introduced because horses recruited from flat racing

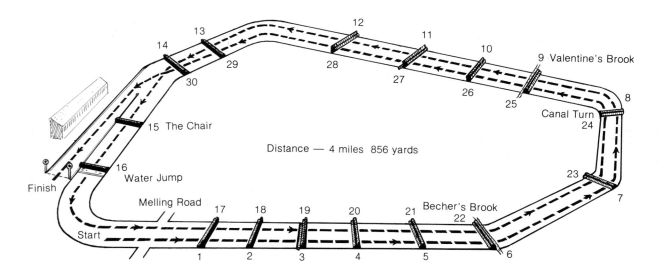

The Grand National Course at Liverpool (Aintree) as it is today.

Height of fences
No. 1 & 17 - 4 ft 6in. fence
No. 2 & 18 – 4 ft 7 in. fence
No. 3 & 19 – Open ditch – ditch 6 ft, fence 5 ft
No. 4 & 20 – 4 ft 10 in. fence
No. 5 & 21 – 5 ft fence
No. 6 & 22 – 'Bechers Brook' – 4 ft 10 in. fence,
                5 ft 6in. brook with drop
No. 7 & 23 – 4 ft fence at angle

No. 8 & 24   – 5 ft fence
No. 9 & 25   – 'Valentine's Brook' – 5 ft fence,
                 5 ft 6in. brook
No. 10 & 26 – 5 ft fence
No. 11 & 27 – Open ditch – 6 ft ditch, 5 ft fence
No. 12 & 28 – 5 ft fence followed by 5 ft 6 in. ditch
No. 13 & 29 – 4 ft 7 in. fence
No. 14 & 30 – 4 ft 6 in. fence
No. 15   – 'The Chair' – Open ditch – 6 ft;
                 fence – 5 ft 2 in.
No. 16   – 'The Water Jump' – 12 ft 6 in.
                 (width) × 2 ft 6 in. (depth)

could more easily be trained to jump them than fences.

For a long time hurdle racing was regarded with good-natured contempt by steeplechasing purists, who considered every step away from natural obstacles as a symptom of degeneracy. Until World War One the Grand National towered above every other steeplechase in public esteem, and the equine heroes of the sport were all winners of the Grand National, like Manifesto, successful twice in 1897 and 1899, and Cloister and Jerry M, who carried top weight of 175 lbs. to victory in 1893 and 1912, respectively. The Grand National was a handicap and there were no races intended to discover the best horses at even weights. Nevertheless public interest was widespread, and in 1920 steeplechasing took place on seventy-one courses in Britain and thirty in Eire.

In the 1920s the need to provide a championship test of the best horses at even weights was recognized, and in 1924 the Cheltenham Gold Cup 3¼ mi. was instituted for this purpose. The winner, Red Splash, earned only £685, compared with the £8240 earned by Master Robert for winning the Grand National the same year. But the championship principle appealed to the imagination of the racing public, and in the 1930s Golden Miller owed his reputation of being the greatest 'chaser ever seen up to that time at least as much to his achievement of winning the Cheltenham Gold Cup five times (1932–6) as to his one victory in the Grand National (1934) under the big weight of 170 lbs.

Hurdling had gained enhanced prestige from the brilliant performances of horses like Wrack shortly before and Trespasser immediately after World War One. The success of the Cheltenham Gold Cup led to the introduction three years later of the Champion Hurdle (2 mi.) at the same meeting held at Cheltenham in March. The Champion Hurdle revealed no hurdler of an excellence corresponding to that of Golden Miller in the first twenty years of its existence, but its acceptance as the test of the best hurdlers was never in doubt. After World War Two it was won by some exceptionally talented horses like National Spirit, Sir Ken and Persian War, who were as popular as the best chasers of their day.

Many small steeplechase courses did not survive World War Two, and during the next quarter of a century rising costs drove more of them out of business. In the season of

1974–5 steeplechasing took place on only forty-four courses in Britain and twenty-five in Eire, but the popularity of the sport, stimulated by excellent television coverage, had certainly not waned. The Cheltenham Gold Cup advanced steadily in value and brilliant 'chasers like Cottage Rake and Arkle, who won it three times each, were never risked over the bigger and more dangerous fences of the Grand National. In 1975 Ten Up earned £17 757 by winning the Gold Cup and L'Escargot earned £38 005 by winning the Grand National, so the differential between the two races had changed fundamentally in a period of fifty years.

The Gold Cup was supported by other valuable non-handicap steeplechases like the King George VI Steeplechase (3 mi.) and the National Hunt Two-Mile Champion Steeplechase (2 mi). Further opportunities for high class 'chasers were created by valuable new sponsored steeplechases like the Hennessy

Cheltenham, set against the backdrop of the Cotswold Hills, is the mecca of steeplechasing. The Cheltenham Gold Cup, steeplechasing's blue riband, and the hurdling equivalent, the Champion Hurdle, are run here every March during the National Hunt Festival.

Gold Cup (3¼ mi.) and the Whitbread Gold Cup (3 mi. 5 f.).

After the Betting Levy Act became law in 1961 racing over jumps, like flat racing, became the beneficiary of funds derived from a levy on betting, and was granted a system of Pattern races designed to provide a properly graded system of tests for the best horses over fences and hurdles. In the 1974–5 season the jumping Pattern received £108 250 from Levy Board Funds, and this sum was divided between thirty-three hurdle races and twenty-two steeplechases. Increased prize money in general, and the Pattern races in particular, attracted more top class horses from the flat than ever before, but this influx has not entirely compensated for the decline, for economic reasons, in the traditional breeding of specialized horses for jumping, mostly in Eire.

Although the end of the Grand National was threatened repeatedly during the late 1960s and early 1970s, the race has been run continuously, except for breaks during the two World Wars, since its inception and has commanded a world-wide television audience in modern times. The thirty fences have been modified from time to time in the interests of the safety of horses and riders, but the race has remained a rigorous test of stamina and jumping skill. The most formidable obstacle, 'The Chair' fence, is made of thorn branches faced with gorse and is 5 ft high with a ditch 6 ft wide in front of it.

The size, construction and frequency of obstacles on all other courses are regulated officially. Fences must be at least 4½ ft high and situated at a frequency of six in every mile with one fence in every mile having a ditch 6 ft wide in front of it. A water jump must be jumped at least once in every steeplechase. Hurdles must be 3¾ ft high and be situated at a frequency of four in every mile.

Steeplechasing in Britain acquired its own governing body, the National Hunt Committee, in 1866. This remained the sole authority for racing over jumps, though co-operating closely with the Jockey Club, until 1968, when the two bodies were amalgamated under the title of the Jockey Club.

Racing over jumps in Eire had its corresponding authority, the Irish National Hunt Committee. Irish steeplechasing evolved on similar lines to British, and Irish breeders have been the prime producers of horses for racing over jumps. However, low prize money in Eire was responsible for most of the best jumpers being exported to Britain until after World War Two, when powerful Irish stables like those of Vincent O'Brien (later to change to training for the flat exclusively) and Tom Dreaper began to retain more of them in their native land. The Irish Grand National is run at Fairyhouse on Easter Monday, and other important Irish races include the Leopardstown Handicap Steeplechase and the Irish Sweeps Hurdle.

Numerous mixed meetings at which both flat and jumping races are run are a feature of Irish racing. As a result there is no closed season for Irish steeplechasing, but there is a short closed season in Britain from Whitsuntide to the beginning of August.

Steeplechasing is an independent, flourishing sport. But its roots in the hunting field have never wasted away. Races for certified hunters are run at nearly all steeplechase meetings from February to the end of the season, and hunt meetings (about 180 each year) called point-to-points still prove useful recruiting grounds for steeplechasing proper in Britain.

Probably the most famous obstacle on any racecourse, Becher's Brook at Aintree, home of the Grand National Steeplechase.

Point-to-Point Racing

Michael Williams

Someone – it was, of course, 'a foreigner' – once wrote a book called *The English – Are They Human?* Well, anyone visiting the English countryside on a Saturday in February could be forgiven for thinking that they aren't. He will see on the hillside overlooking a miniature steeplechase course massed ranks of cars, many of them with open boots, behind which stand little groups of people munching chicken legs, eating salad lunches off improvised tables, downing whiskies at a rate of knots, and stamping their feet on the ground to keep themselves from freezing.

The English are starting the point-to-point season; and similar enjoyment, with pro-gressively less need for feet-stamping and sheepskin coats, is available to them right up to the end of May or the first week in June, by which time some 180 of Britain's hunts will have held their annual race meetings for horses certified to have been hunted during the current season.

Besides providing a growing public with an afternoon's sport in agreeable surroundings, it is a way of earning money to keep the hunts in business. Without the income from an annual point-to-point, many hunts would be in

A typical scene at a point-to-point, where informality is the keynote.

serious financial difficulties; and some of the smaller and less fashionable ones might be hard put to survive. Although the special regulations for point-to-point racing laid down by the Jockey Club do not permit a charge for admission to be made to spectators, a substantial profit is obtained from car-park fees (which usually range from £1 to £4) and from the sale of race-cards; while more money comes from direct donations from bookmakers, and from the annual grant made by the Horserace Betting Levy Board to which both Tote and bookmakers contribute.

Point-to-point racing, in both England and Ireland, is a traditionally amateur sport with a long history. But the exact origins are somewhat obscure, wrapped up as they are in the origins of steeplechasing. One thing we can be sure of, however, is that the point-to-point, as its name suggests, was originally a race across country from one point to another; and that in those early days there were no made-up courses or marking flags, the riders having to find their own line of country.

Needless to say, no holds were barred and a great deal of skulduggery went on, such as that which occurred during the match that took place in Leicestershire between Lord Kennedy's Radical and Captain Ross's Clinker in 1826. The race was over four miles, from Barkby Holt to Billesdon Coplow, and the wager was 2000 guineas, Lord Kennedy putting up a Captain Douglas on his horse and Ross riding his own.

Before the race, Lord Kennedy, secure in the knowledge that it wasn't his own neck he was risking, made it plain that the riders could bump, bore and jostle each other as much as they pleased. 'In short,' said Ross, 'I understand that we may ride over each other and kill each other if we can.' His Lordship was quick to agree, and Ross took him at his word, ensuring that when they came to the first obstacle, a five-bar gate, Douglas should take the obstacle without his horse. 'I stuck the spurs in,' he said later, 'and knocked Douglas over the gate.' Radical finished up lying on the take-off side; and though Douglas was eventu-

ally able to remount, having taken the precaution of fastening the rein to his wrist, by the time he did so Clinker was so far ahead that it was impossible for him to be caught.

It used to be claimed that the parent of point-to-point racing was a four-and-a-half-mile race ridden after dinner one moonlit night in 1803 by a group of cavalry officers stationed at Ipswich; and there is a series of paintings by Henry Alken depicting the scene, with the riders wearing night-shirts over their uniforms and white night-caps on their heads. But it is unfashionable nowadays to suppose that this race took place outside Alken's admittedly vigorous imagination. A pity, perhaps, because the event embodies the spirit of point-to-point racing if not the actuality.

It is certain, however, that some kind of point-to-point racing took place throughout the first half of the nineteenth century, and the annals of the Worcestershire Hunt reveal that a point-to-point meeting was staged in Worcestershire as early as 1836. But evidence of this sort is not easy to come by, which no doubt accounts for the Lonsdale Library volume on steeplechasing putting the start of point-to-point racing as 'probably about 1885 or a little later'.

In the 1850s, Robert Smith Surtees was writing in *Mr Sponge's Sporting Tour*:

In the early days of steeple-chasing a popular fiction existed that the horses were hunters; and grooms and fellows used to come nicking and grinning up to masters of hounds at checks and critical times, requesting them to note that they were out, in order to ask for certificates of the horses having been 'regularly hunted' – a species of regularity than which nothing could be more irregular.

Surtees, of course, was biased. He disliked all forms of steeplechasing and made no secret of the fact. In one way or another, this bias has shown itself in the succeeding years. Thus, in 1946, the hunting correspondent of the *Daily Telegraph* wrote in *The Horseman's Year*:

The point-to-point has become a species of bastard race-meeting, run for profit and with prizes competed for by horses principally kept for the purpose,

Point-to-pointers in action at Tweseldown. Natural fences have over the years largely been replaced by National Hunt type obstacles.

and barely qualified as hunters (even under the very lax rules imposed for such qualification).

That is as may be. The fact remains that, in order to run in point-to-points, horses are required to have been hunted and certificates to this effect must be produced for inspection. There will always be die-hards hankering after the 'good old days' and the 'natural' courses when little or no attention was paid to the needs of the public, who could have seen little more than the rumps of the horses disappearing over the horizon.

Like most other things, point-to-point racing has moved with the times, and most people would say that it has changed for the better. There are now properly constructed courses, adequate (sometimes perfect) viewing facilities and a high standard of racing, with a strong governing body.

The prize money, however, even though raised by ten pounds in 1977 and again in 1979, remains at a grossly uneconomic level. The total prize money awarded by the Jockey Club is £100 for an open event, £75 for all other races (to be allocated at the Committee's discretion). No owner is going to get rich on this. In the circumstances, it is remarkable that so many of the horses running in point-to-points these days are valuable blood horses. Some of them have been distinguished hurdlers and steeple-chasers in their prime. Some are discards from flat-racing stables. Others – and these are the ones that make point-to-point racing so exciting – are young horses on the way up, many of them bred on their owner's farms.

So there is a two-way traffic between the professional racecourse and the point-to-point field. And it is worth mentioning that, over the years, many of the horses who started their racing careers in point-to-points have gone on to win high class steeplechases, even including the Grand National and the Cheltenham Gold

Cup. The point-to-points in Britain and Ireland are, in fact, the scene of much budding talent; and quite often at the end of the season a young horse from the point-to-point field will fetch several thousand pounds at the sales.

The average fee for entering a horse in a point-to-point is £3, though some hunts will refund the entrance fee if the horse is a runner on the day. The minimum distance permitted by the regulations is three miles, although I foresee the day when it will be reduced to two and a half. The races are limited to six in number (unless one or more of them has to be divided owing to a very large entry, as happens quite often at the early-season meetings); and, generally speaking, the average card would comprise one race confined to horses qualified with the promoting hunt, an adjacent hunts' race, an adjacent hunts' maiden race, a ladies' open race, a men's open race, and a restricted

open race for horses which have never won an open point-to-point or a race on a professional course.

Although the prize money is uniform throughout the country, there are certain races which, by tradition, have established themselves as Classics. The open race for the Lady Dudley Cup at the Worcestershire Hunt meeting, for instance, is generally acknowledged to be the point-to-point equivalent of the Cheltenham Gold Cup; while the point-to-point equivalent of the Grand National is the four-and-a-half-mile open race for the Ralph Grimthorpe Gold Cup at the Middleton Hunt meeting in Yorkshire.

There are also, nowadays, two national point-to-point championships held on a professional racecourse. The present sponsors of these championships are BMW Concessionaires (GB) Ltd., who have their finals, one for men and one for women, at Chepstow. They are held towards the close of the season and there are qualifying races at selected meetings

A ladies' point-to-point race in 1931. Note the 'natural' fence and the lady riding side-saddle.

during the season. In addition to these national championships, there are a number of regional championships, of which the pioneers were the French champagne firm of Laurent Perrier.

Lady riders also have a national championship with a final on a point-to-point course. The sponsor in this instance is the Agricultural Division of ICI, who hold the final of their Ladies' Nitram Championship at the Melton Hunt Club point-to-point at Garthorpe, Leicestershire, in late May; this fixture is always one of the highlights of the season. Another is the mid-week fixture staged by the Heythrop Hunt at Stow-on-the-Wold in the Cotswolds. This is a beautiful setting and the racing there lives up to it.

So far as the riders are concerned, the most coveted individual trophies are the *Daily Telegraph* Cup for the leading male rider of the season, and the *Sporting Life* Cup for the leading lady rider of the season. These, together with the Grand Marnier Trophy for the owner winning the most races with one horse, are presented out of season in London at a national point-to-point dinner which serves as a splendid get-together for point-to-point enthusiasts from all over Great Britain.

Although Ireland is also a stronghold of point-to-point racing, far fewer races are held there, an average of fifty-six per season over the last ten years. These fixtures are held under the auspices of the Irish National Hunt Committee; and though the rules are largely the same as in Britain, there are some differences.

To take the major ones: in Ireland the ladies are permitted to ride against the men in *all* races. In England, Scotland and Wales they may not ride against them in open events other than those restricted to horses which have never won under the Rules of Racing nor an open race at a point-to-point, and which are known as 'restricted opens'. In Ireland a girl under the age of sixteen may ride in point-to-points; in England she may not, and the same applies to boys. In Ireland a horse may run in point-to-points if he is in a professional trainer's yard. In England he may only do so if he is the property of the trainer or his wife. In Ireland, but not in England, a four-year-old may run in point-to-points.

And in Ireland there is point-to-point racing on Sundays. Indeed, the majority of point-to-point races in that country are now run on Sundays. This would be unthinkable in England at the present time, though it will no doubt come to pass in the course of time.

Flat Racing in France

David Powell

The French flat racing which counts is centred around Paris, and takes place on several beautiful courses: Longchamp is the principal theatre for Classics, but the Derby and Oaks take place at Chantilly, while Maisons-Laffitte, the newly created Evry, and Saint-Cloud, are also major tracks.

The only exception comes in August, when racing emigrates to Deauville for an agreeable interlude of international events, and for the yearling sales. So 'Paris conscious' are racing people, however, that Deauville, in spite of its location on the Normandy coast, is considered for technical purposes as a '*hippodrome parisien*',

France's top flat race jockey, Yves St Martin, with Mrs Arpad Plesch and her horse Sassafras who had just beaten the English Triple Crown winner Nijinsky in the 1970 Prix de l'Arc de Triomphe.

Funny Hobby winning the Grand Prix de Paris in 1977.

as opposed to the numerous lesser courses which dot the French map, and which are considered a world apart.

'Parisians' will occasionally descend upon the 'provincials' in order to rob them of a local prize – one of the richer grands prix at Marseilles, Lyons, Bordeaux or Nantes for example. Most of the runners at 'Paris' tracks are trained at the two beautiful training centres, Chantilly and Maisons-Laffitte. The former has most of the Classic stables, while the latter is mostly populated by jumpers.

There is only incentive to breed Thoroughbreds for whom there are races to be won. Obviously then the programme of racing shapes the breed, in terms of relative precocity and speed versus stamina index and the ability to act on a certain kind of course – more or less sharp or galloping, with or without

gradients, with a long or short final straight, and so on.

The French programme, a particularly well conceived one (especially in contrast to the rather haphazard American or English ones) is first and foremost designed to produce a three-year-old capable of winning off a strong pace at $1\frac{1}{2}$ miles.

The two-year-old programme is quite simple. The Prix Robert Papin ($5\frac{1}{2}$ f.) in July is usually contested by the same sort of speedy early developer as the Prix Morny (6 f.) at Deauville in August. Then another month and another furlong bring in the future Classic contenders for the Prix de la Salamandre at Longchamp in September, and on the same course a month later comes the premier juvenile race, the 1-mi. Grand Critérium. Its winner is almost always top-weighted on the Handicap Optional, the official two-year-old free handicap.

The following spring the newly turned three-year-olds have a series of trials for the

The finish of the 1974 Prix de l'Arc de Triomphe, won by the mare Allez France, in the sheepskin noseband. The 'Arc' is the most important race in the French calendar and the richest in Europe.

Classics to run at Longchamp, in the course of April and May. With the Guineas equivalents, namely the 1-mi. Poule d'Essai des Poulains (colts) and Poule d'Essai des Pouliches (fillies) excepted, most of these take place over distances between $1\frac{1}{4}$ and $1\frac{1}{2}$ mi. The Prix Greffulhe ($10\frac{1}{2}$ f.), the Prix Daru ($10\frac{1}{2}$ f.) the Prix Noailles (11 f.) and the Prix Hocquart (12 f.) for colts culminate in a super Classic trial, the Group I Prix Lupin, which is so rich that it has become a kind of pre-Derby.

The fillies have the mile-and-a-quarter Prix St Alary as a stepping stone between their Poule d'Essai and the Prix de Diane ($10\frac{1}{2}$ f.), or French Oaks, run at Chantilly in June.

The Prix du Jockey-Club, or French Derby, is a particularly cogent test with Chantilly's sweeping turns and long up-hill straight. The colts with undoubted stamina can tackle nearly 2 miles three weeks later at Longchamp, in the Grand Prix de Paris.

The latter race has been called particularly murderous and it is true that many of its winners did not train on. Subsequently its return match is the Prix Royal Oak, run over exactly the same course in September: it is also the French St Leger.

The fillies' St Leger is the $1\frac{1}{2}$ mi. Prix Vermeille, also at Longchamp. Its excellent place in the calendar and generous prize money have made it more than that: the Prix Vermeille is now a kind of 'European Oaks'.

The three-year-olds take on their elders at the top level for the first time in July, in the Grand Prix de Saint-Cloud, at $12\frac{1}{2}$ f. The real championship race, however, is the Prix de l'Arc de Triomphe ($1\frac{1}{2}$ mi.) at Longchamp in October. A large field always insures a hell-for-leather pace, and the winner of this Classic immediately has claim to the title of 'world champion'.

Those who remain in training as four-year-olds are usually thinking of another tilt at the 'Arc' in the autumn, via a series of stakes races in the spring, foremost the Prix Ganay (10 f.), as well as the Grand Prix de Saint-Cloud and one of the 'Arc' preps at Longchamp in September.

For stayers, the Prix de Barbeville and the Prix Jean Prat prepare for the Prix du Cadran, or French Gold Cup (2½ mi.).

Auxiliary programmes exist for sprinters and milers, but they are just what the term 'auxiliary' implies: out of the mainstream. They culminate, symbolically, at Longchamp on Prix de l'Arc de Triomphe day in October with the Prix de l'Abbaye de Longchamp and the Prix du Moulin de Longchamp.

We have seen (*Bloodlines, a French Example*) what kind of breed this well-balanced programme has produced.

Prize money is excellent in France, thanks mainly to the 'Tiercé' a national form of wagering which requires bettors to indicate the first three to finish, and also to the Tote (PMU) monopoly, which ensures that a lot of money is channelled back into racing. Both flat and jump racing have benefited tremendously, although there has been a temporary drawback: the riches have made French racing so attractive to foreign horses that local breeders have suffered from the surfeit of outside competition. A highly endowed system of breeders' incentive awards has provided them with some compensation.

Steeplechasing in France

André Gareau

It is during the reign of Charles X that we first find mention of races over fences. Henry Lee wrote on this subject:

It is thus that a rather difficult course had been laid out in the park at Raincy – chosen by the Duc d'Orléans because it was closed to the public. The Grand Prix was marred by a serious accident: the winner was Toy, ridden by Mr Le Coulteux; Mr d'Hédouville came in second on Alexander. At the dry ditch, which was very wide, Count Walewski on Tarragone, owned by the Comte de Morny, came a cropper and was unconscious for six hours. But he recovered from this terrible fall, not without the affair making such a stir that it came to the royal ears, which sealed the fate of the racecourse at Raincy.

Nevertheless, Charles X was undoubtedly the original patron of racing and of the Thoroughbred in France. In his reign, as it had previously in the twilight of the Old Régime, Anglomania raged. On 4 March 1830, a race was run under the title of *Course au Clocher*, an accurate and sufficiently elegant translation of the English word, steeplechase. The French were not innovators in this matter. Before them, the Anglo-Irish and then the English had promoted steeplechases, in which the field consisted of hunters. This *Course au Clocher* took place at Jouy, then in the department of the Seine, over two leagues – nine kilometres! There were nine starters. From 1834 onward these events became more popular and spread into the provinces.

Ferdinand Riant wrote:

Unfortunately there is no encouragement for racing over fences, and more emphasis is placed on the danger which some of the jumps present than on the good side of this embryo sport. There is much criticism of the course at Croix-de-Berny. It is echoed by journalists who are far from being

A hunt steeplechase at Le-Croix-de-Berny in 1880.

A painting showing steeplechasing in France in the early days of the sport.

horsemen and who repeat that the steeplechase is cruel and ridiculous, a spectacle more suited to the declining Roman Empire. So, for almost twelve years, there have been few races around Paris, or none: and in those which did take place only Englishmen rode. Brittany and Normandy, being more independent, have kept pluckily on, and their efforts met with such success that in 1851 the State Stud management at Le Pin rescued steeplechasing from discredit and even oblivion and rid it of its ill repute. . . . As the varied terrain and natural obstacles in France are far from as suitable for steeplechasing as they are in England, we had to lay out courses and build fences; in other words, create race tracks. This task began in 1850. From that date onward, the importance of racing over fences began to grow and has never stopped since.

Nowadays, racing over fences, and steeplechasing in particular, is very fashionable. What was once upon a time known as 'the outlaw sport' has now become socially acceptable.

It is true that the Société des Steeple-Chases de France has done all that was necessary to that end.* It was founded in 1862 but did not operate until 1863. Its first headquarters was to the east of Paris, on the Plateau de Gravelle. Ten years later it acquired the lease of Auteuil. A racecourse was laid out there, but was not without its troubles, which Ferdinand Riant describes as follows:

Much work involving clearing land and drainage of a marshy soil was put in hand, and circular courses built. But Colonel de Biré, a member of the committee, who commanded a regiment of cuirassiers, used it as an exercise ground for them, and they did it so well that it could be used as of November 1. The grandstand was sited on a feature just made for the purpose, the heap of spoil thrown up when the two lakes in the Bois de Boulogne were dug out under Napoleon III. This mound, known as the Butte de Mortemart, took its name from the monument once on this site, the Croix de Mortemart, commemorating Gabriel de Mortemart (1600–1675), Ranger (*Capitaine de Chasse*) of the Bois de Boulogne. The ground was so swampy that the first stands had to be built on piles.

Today, large stands, begun in 1921, can accommodate great numbers of racegoers.

Mention is made of the Société des Steeple-Chases de France and its racecourse because it is the mother-club of racing over fences in France and because Auteuil is the leading

*At first the name was Société Générale des Steeple-Chases, then Société Anonyme des Steeple-Chases, finally Société des Steeple-Chases de France.

The present-day steeplechase course at Auteuil.

A notable feature of French steeplechase courses is
the variety of fences which include the following:

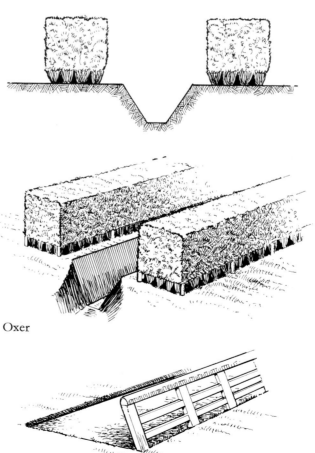

Oxer

Open ditch

Water jump with fixed barrier

course of that kind in France. Nothing can be done without the Society's consent; and everything is done, on every course in France, according to the Code des Courses à Obstacles which it laid down and which corresponds to National Hunt rules. At Auteuil also, where the fences are not at all like those of Aintree, the most important steeplechases are run. The greatest of all, run for the first time in 1874 on 25 May, under the name of Grand National de France, became known in the following year, and ever after, as the Grand Steeple-Chase de Paris. The Grande Course de Haies d'Auteuil is the finest race of its kind in the country.*

But there is not only Auteuil. There are races over fences at Enghien, north of Paris; on the suburban racecourses of Compiègne, Fontainebleau and Rambouillet; and in the country, where the most important meetings, in terms of severity of courses, are Craon, Dieppe, Pau, Le Pin, Verrie-Saumur and Granville. All of these are courses where magnificent cross-country obstacles are well-built and less dangerous than those of Pardubice in Czechosolvakia and attract big crowds who come to watch Thoroughbreds, Selles Français (AQPS)

and Anglo-Arabs tackle fences that are often formidable.

Two hundred other provincial courses have cross-country or steeplechase tracks.† That should suffice to emphasize the interest the French have in this sport. And happily so; for it offers a much-needed outlet for the Thoroughbred that has not enough class to make the grade on the flat. Among second-class horses, some have jumping potential inherent in their make and shape. Ridden over obstacles, they become veritable champions at the 'brushwood' or the 'bits of timber' (trainers' slang for hurdles and fences respectively). They also justify the opinion of my old friend, the vet Robert Lesaffre, who, in a remarkable work entitled, *Connaissance et Utilisation du Cheval de Course*, has said: 'Performance over the sticks is much more a question of aptitude than a question of class.'

In the matter of races there are no absolutes, and of course there are exceptions. Have we not all heard of a horse called Le Paillon that won the Grande Course des Haies at Auteuil and the Prix de l'Arc de Triomphe! It is exceptions that prove the rule.

---

*The programme at Auteuil in 1973 allowed for 335 races, of which 140 were steeplechases and the rest over hurdles for a total purse of 34 797 900 Frs. allocated as follows: 18 030 000 to owners of winners; 13 522 500 to owners of horses placed; 3 245 400 to the breeders of the horses.

†In the provinces where, in 1972, 1301 races were run (519 being steeplechases, 207 cross-country, 557 over hurdles), the total prize money was Frs. 22 650 000, of which 14 100 000 Frs. was put up by the Société des Steeple-Chases de France. Of this, different portions were awarded to the owners and breeders of horses placed among the 6462 starters in the first two categories and among the 5638 starters in the third.

Steeple-chase — Cross-Country and the Grand Pardubice

François de La Sayette
Jean Froissard

Steeple-chase—cross-country

A certain class of races over fences is termed in France *'steeple-chase — cross-country'*, in accordance with official usage of the Société des Steeple-Chases de France which is the parent association of all such races there and the sole arbiter, regulating matters principally by means of the rule book which it has set up, modifies and publishes.

But, in fact, the class of sport which is our subject here, the 'cross-country', consists of a horse race taking place quite literally across country, over natural fences or a close simulation thereof.

Whereas a steeple-chase consists only of fences to be taken in the stride, placed across an almost dead flat, practically straight course, and marked right and left with flags or pegs, in a cross-country the riders simply proceed from fence to fence, and the fewer flags and guideposts, it is said, the better.

It was born about a century ago when certain horsemen devoted to bold and sporting feats (hunting men, small landlords, army officers), took to occupying their leisure with impromptu matches across country, often arising from a bet.

In 1848, a poster proclaimed that the Craon

Crossing a road during a steeple-chase — cross-country race at Craon.

Agricultural Show on 10 September would be followed by one galloping and two trotting races, mentioning that 'the Committee hopes that following these races some gentlemen riders will come forward for a sweepstake race across country, the stakes to be at their own discretion'. This phrase in itself contains the entire origin of the Craon races.

Thus arose, for instance, the famous cross-country at Craon (Mayenne) run over what is undoubtedly the finest and most typical course in France, set as it is in a huge natural bowl surrounded by hills intersected by hedges and gullies: one jumps out of a field of lucerne into a ploughed field, and from there into one of maize or potatoes, before crossing, by way of a severe double-bank, the main Angers–Rennes highway strewn just a few minutes in advance with earth for the occasion – while the gend-armes hold traffic back to let the horses pass.

The first gentlemen riders to race over this course which, by its varied nature, has served to establish the reputation of the La Touche race track, were Baron de Pierre, later equerry to the Empress Eugénie; M. de La Motte, inspector of state studs; and his friend, Count Greffulhe. Both race and course were full of surprises. Count Greffulhe was unseated going up a slope; Baron de Pierre and his horse fell at a big bank; only M. de La Motte finished the course in style, to the cheers of an elegant and already numerous crowd.

Every year at mid-September, on the day of the Grand Cross de Craon, 25 000 spectators from France and abroad flock to the course and bet something like F 2 400 000 at the Pari-Mutuel, in an atmosphere combining local colour and great sport.

A true race of this nature, therefore, ought to be run on 'unimproved' ground, in a real agricultural setting, one in which the terrain is varied and comprised of obstacles of many types: steep gradients, big banks, open ditches without guard rails, moats, road crossings and fords and gullies. At Nuillé sur Vicoin, the field plunges into the River Vicoin up to the

*See *French Breeds*, under *Selle Français*, page 409.

Steeple-chase—cross-country racing at Pau, with the field tackling a bank.

riders' knees. At Dieppe a succession of wide ditches running at an angle to the course have to be crossed. At Verrie-Saumur there are 'fences' (i.e., hedges) 1.70 m high and 3 m wide. At Pau the road crossing is 15 m wide, but flanked by two banks each 1.60 m high the second being just an upright. At Granville the course takes in the dunes by the seashore.

It should be pointed out that certain tracks possess only artificial courses, with purpose-built fences situated on uniformly flat ground, with no variations of terrain: these cannot really be considered courses across country.

A real cross-country course should wind its way along. No single fence is in itself ex-cessively severe, but the rise and fall of the ground is a challenge to the cleverness and condition of the horses, be they Throughbred, Part-bred (AQPS)? or Anglo-Arab, and the dash and balance of their riders.

In 1972, about a hundred 'cross-country' races were run in France, over about sixty courses. The most famous are in the west: Craon, Dieppe, Verrie-Saumur, Corlay, Le Pin-au-Haras, Le Pertre, Granville, Nuillé sur Vicoin, all of which have to the highest degree the stamp of the genuine, natural, countryside with all its variety.

The riders may be paofessional jockeys, 'gentlemen riders' or from the military.

In 1971, the 'Cross d'Habits Rouges' were started for bona fide amateurs riding their hunters or show jumpers. Re-designated 'Cross-Countries Spéciaux' in 1973, they now are under the aegis of the *Société des Steeple-Chases de France* and entries are confined to event horses.

Typically French, these cross-countries sometimes resemble horse trials courses. What is more, they often assisted in the training of French horses and riders selected for eventing at international level during the period when true outdoor equitation was highly esteemed in France. Captain Bernard Chevallier, Adjutants Guyon and Le Goff, and Major Guy Lefrant, for example, all competed in these cross-country races before winning Olympic honours in the three-day event.

The Taxis fence, with its huge ditch on the landing side, is one of the formidable obstacles to be jumped during the Pardubice steeplechase, held annually in Czechoslovakia.

The Grand Pardubice
Jean Froissard

The Grand Pardubice of Czechoslovakia must not be overlooked. On this racecourse, located about 90 km from Prague, one of the most world-famous jumping races is run in early October. Established in 1874 by Count Kinsky, this steeplechase has taken place annually ever since, except during the war, attracting over 50000 spectators. Set in woodlands, the course is made up chiefly of brush fences, ditches, brooks, and one Irish bank. As a steeplechase it differs from the Classic ones by the ground over which it is run: pastures, fields, ploughland, rough country. In fact, in character it is more evocative of the 'steeplechases – cross-countries' of France.

Since its inception, this race has undergone some changes; at present it is run over 6900 m with twenty-nine obstacles. One of the most fearsome is the 'Taxis', made up of a natural hedge 1.60 m high, 1.50 m wide, followed by a 5 m wide and 2 m deep ditch. The problem of taking this fence (no. 4) is further complicated by its being only 700 m from the starting line, a distance covered in less than one minute.

Trotting Races in Europe

Jean Delacourt

The trotting horse proper is a half-bred and has been extant in France since the beginning of the nineteenth century. The foundation stock in France consisted of Thoroughbred, and half-bred and Norfolk roadster stallions imported from England to Normandy by the Administration des Haras, which manages the national studs.

Their mating to Norman mares produced an animal notable for its robust constitution, and it was this that made the reputation of what is now called the French Trotter. Today international trotting depends on three breeds of harness racers: American Standardbred, Russian and French.

The Norman horse owes its transformation principally to the Thoroughbred sire Young Rattler, a son of Old Rattler out of a daughter of Snaps, dam unknown, foaled in 1811. Some thirty years later, another Thoroughbred foaled in England, The Heir of Linne, also contributed much improvement to harness racers, which were known thereafter as Anglo-Normans.

The names Young Rattler and The Heir of Linne are found again and again in pedigrees of Norman families and they were responsible for the establishment of a great line of half-bred trotters, the most famous being Conquérant, Lavater, Normand, Phaeton and Fuchsia. Almost ninety per cent of French Trotters trace back in some way to these 'big five'.

Although Normandy was the cradle of half-bred horse breeding, other regions, such as La Vendée, the centre of the country, etc., have also produced excellent stock. In France the main aim of trotting races has been to produce, through the infusions of the best blood, a horse possessed of strength and speed alike. The first trotting races in France date from 1806 on the Champ de Mars in Paris. Some were run in the provinces the following year at Saint-Brieuc, Nancy, at Tarbes, then, in 1820, at Aurillac, Strasbourg, Poitiers, and in 1835 at Nantes.

But the sport at that time was still in an embryonic stage, and the creation of a proper raceway, at Cherbourg, did not occur until 1836. This was largely due to the efforts of an officer in the State stud service named Ephrem Houel whose tireless work earned him the title of 'Father of French Trotting'.

Following the formation of the first racing society and the successful inauguration of Cherbourg, raceways appeared at Caen, Saint-Lô and, in 1839, Brittany. In 1840 racing societies were formed in Normandy, and there were meetings, three years later, at Le Pin and Rouen. Finally, an Imperial decree of 1861 lent official encouragement to the sport, leading to the foundation of the Société pour l'Amélioration du Cheval Français de Demi-Sang (which became the Société d'Encouragement à l'Élevage du Cheval Français in 1949). This society held its first meetings at Caen but later obtained the Vincennes track where the first races were run on 7 September 1879. At that time there were also harness events at Maisons-Laffitte and at the turn of the century another society, Le Trotting Club de Paris ran meetings at Neuilly-Levallois. This track looked like a cycle-racing track and disappeared in 1901 although races were run at Saint-Cloud until 1914.

Trotting under saddle: Bellino II, one of only four horses to have won both the driven and ridden French championships.

Thus the metropolitan region had become equipped with trotting tracks and the sport spread to the provinces: one may note in passing that there was once a track at Deauville.

Since World War One the only tracks functioning near Paris have been at Vincennes and Enghien, the latter a property of the Société Sportive d'Encouragement where trotting alternates with obstacle races and has done so since 1922.

The Vincennes raceway is unique. Its great cinder track measures 2000 m around, begins with a downhill slope and ends, in the last kilometre, with a particularly testing uphill stretch. Since 1852 floodlit races have been run on a smaller track of only 1200 m but some races take place on both tracks.

The sand track at Enghien, built around the inside of the steeplechase course, measures 1300 m. The surface of tracks varies from place to place, some being sand, some being turf tracks.

France is almost unique in having both harness and ridden races, though trotters are still ridden in Belgium and to some extent in Italy. At small meetings in the north of England there are also combined events on the card for trotters and pacers either ridden or driven, but it is in France that the most important races take place and this form of sport has been considered beneficial to Norman breeding, most of the great stallions having been champions under saddle.

Trotting goes on all the year round, the three most important meetings are at Vincennes from 15 November to 1 March, and from 16 August to 15 September, and the summer meeting at Enghien from 1 to 15 August.

In the country the most important fixtures are the winter (from mid-December to the end of March) and summer (July and August) meetings at Cagnes-sur-Mer.

The 2600 m Prix d'Amérique at Vincennes, which was first run in 1920, is France's premier driven race and is the richest trotting event in the world. The prize money amounts to some 800000 francs and the race, open to four- to ten-year-olds, attracts an international field.

Two other internationals, the Prix de France (350000 francs, over 2250 m) and the Prix de Paris (400000 francs, over 3150 m) are run on the two Sundays following.

In June, at one and the same meeting, the Prix René Ballière and the Prix du Président de la République are run. The former is held in memory of a great president of the SEECF who held the chair from 1935 to 1970 and died in 1972. Thanks to him French trotting reached great heights and achieved international status. He was also president of the European Trotting Union, and the race which bears his name is known as the Championnat Européen, worth a quarter of a million francs and run over 2350 m.

The Prix du Président de la République is for four-year-old ridden trotters (400000 francs, 2800 m) but the greatest race of this kind is the international Prix de Cornulier, run a week before the Prix d'Amérique. Like the latter, the Prix de Cornulier (450000 francs, 2600 m) is for four- to ten-year-olds and is the richest ridden trotting race in the world. Throughout the year the purse is very high at Vincennes.

Other major events in the harness racing calendar include the Critérium Continental (250000 francs, 2050 m) at the end of August, for four-year-olds; the international Prix de l'Atlantique (150000 francs, 2250 m) in May; the Prix d'Europe (200000 francs, 2800 m) in August; and the Grand Critérium de Vitesse (180000 francs, 1609 m), an international event run at Cagnes-sur-Mer in March and much coveted by the best European trotters.

The quality of trotters is measured by the time they take to run a kilometre. In order to appreciate the degree of improvement that selective breeding has achieved in France one must take a look at some of the records in the early days of the sport. In 1884 it was quite an event when a trotter did the kilometre in 1 minute and 40 seconds. In 1888 Hemine recorded a time of 1 minute and 38 seconds at Vincennes, and at the end of the century Képi trotted the distance in 1 minute and 27 seconds. One of the pre-1914 glories was the performance of Fred Leyburn, owned by Mr C. Rousseau. Foaled in 1905, Fred Leyburn was by Kalmia out of Helen Leyburn who was of American descent; in his time he set up a record that was the best in France: 1 minute and 21 4/10 seconds, winning in all 232408 gold francs at home and abroad. Mention of Helen Leyburn's American extraction reminds one that a ministerial order of 30 January 1937 closed the Trotteur Français Stud Book. Now it is undeniable that judicious crosses with the Standardbred have sharpened up the old Norman breed and served to bring French Trotter breeding to the front rank in the world. In 1973 there was a move, which may yet succeed, to re-open the stud book.

The first horse to record a time of under 1 minute and 20 seconds was Alfred Lefèvre's Feu Follet X. That was on New Year's Day of 1954 at Vincennes. Feu Follet X's time was 1 minute and 19 6/10 seconds. He subsequently won the Prix d'Amérique before being retired to stud. At present the best kilometre time is that recorded by the trotter Hairos II – 1 minute and 13 4/10 seconds. This was not in a race but in a trial at Enghien on 6 August 1959, when Hairos II was eight years old. He is now standing at stud. The French record in a public race is held by Jamin who, as a seven-year-old, on 20 February 1960 at Enghien trotted a kilometre in 1 minute and 14 4/10 seconds, without a mobile starting gate, while Tidalium Pelo recorded 1 minute 14 7/10 seconds at Argentan on 22 June 1969, behind a mobile starting gate. The records for mares are held by Infante II, 1 minute and 14 9/10 seconds, without a mobile starting gate, and Une de Mai, 1 minute and 15 1/10 seconds behind a mobile starting gate.

Trotting in harness: the great mare Une de Mai.

Among ridden trotters, male and female, records are held by Valmont (1 minute and 18 2/10 seconds) and Eringa (1 minute and 18 seconds), respectively. But the phenomenon of modern times trotting under saddle was Alphonse Martineau's Fandango whose best time was 1 minute and 20 seconds and who besides won thirty-eight consecutive races and also did well in harness. Foaled in 1949, Fandango has proved an outstanding sire.

The first French trotter to win a world championship in America was Jamin. Since then Hairos II, Roquepine and the mare Une de Mai also won this championship. Une de Mai, who was twice successful in this event, holds at the time of writing the world record for prize money won by a trotter, 8 829 478 francs. Equileo has since won a world championship in 1976.

Only a select handful of horses have proved versatile enough to win both the premier harness race, the Prix d'Amérique and the ridden equivalent, the Prix de Cornulier, namely Venutar, Masina, Tidalium Pelo and Bellino II.

France is, of all continental countries the one most committed to trotting races. But the importance of Italy should not be overlooked. There, as in most European countries, the tracks are usually 4 f. long. The most important races are the Gran Premio della Lotteria, run at Naples in the spring, and the Gran Premio dei Nazioni; the Premio d'Inverno, the Premio d'Europa and the Gran Premio della Feria are all run at Milan. Other important events include the Premio del Lido at Rome, the Côte d'Azur at Turin and the Premio dei Termi at Montecatini, and Bologna also stages important meetings.

In Germany the Grosser Preis von Hamburg is much coveted and at Munich there are two important races, the Grosser Preis von Bayern and the Preis der Besten, while Berlin stages the Preis der Matadoren and the Grosser Preis von Recklingshausen. There is also excellent racing at Gelsenkirchen.

There is much trotting in Belgium and Holland. Near Brussels, at Sterrebeek, there is a traditional race on Shrove Tuesday, the Grand Prix d'Hiver (harness), and also the Prix des Flandres (ridden), both good international events. The Kuurne raceway at Courtray is the venue for the Grand Prix Martini, while in Holland there is the Dutch Grand Prix, run at Duindigt.

The sport is also highly developed in Russia, and Moscow's Peace Prize is a particularly testing race. The Prix d'Élite Européen is run at Solvella in Sweden and the Aby Grand Prix at Göteborg. Austria has a raceway at Vienna which is rather longer than the conventional 800 m where the Graf Kalman Hunyadi Stakes, a rich international race, is run, and trotting is also popular in Finland, Norway, Denmark, Hungary and Romania.

Flat Racing and Steeplechasing in America

William Robertson

Horse racing has been one of the most popular sports in America since the very beginning of the country's recorded history. The Virginia colonists brought with them from England a love of horses, and a distinctly American form of racing – short dashes over narrow pathways through the dense forest – began during the first half of the seventeenth century. This form of racing has been perpetuated by the American Quarter horse, which today comprises the most numerous equine breed in the world.

Course racing in America originated in New York, where Governor Richard Nicolls laid out a racecourse on Hempstead Plain, Long Island, and, commencing in 1665, offered prizes for races. Nicolls, who was an emissary of Charles II, 'the father of the English turf', became known in his turn as 'the father of the American turf'. As cleared land became available in other colonies, course racing spread throughout the new country, subject to interruptions for political or religious reasons which have always played a prominent part in the history of American racing. The custom of laying out racetracks on land selected beforehand for this purpose has been preserved in America, in contrast to the mode of some older countries, where the conformation of tracks is dictated by the natural terrain and the going is as Nature made it. This has led to a certain monotony of appearance in American tracks – virtually all are elliptical and essentially flat – but the relative uniformity makes performances at different tracks more comparable with each other than would otherwise

be the case. Also, American tracks traditionally have been built with the accommodation of spectators and amenities for the public as major factors in the planning.

Prior to the Civil War (1861–5), Virginia was the principal breeding centre in America and vied with New York for leadership as a racing centre. After the war, during which Virginia was devastated and an appalling number of her horses lost, leadership in breeding passed to Kentucky, and New York became the undisputed racing centre. In modern times both racing and breeding have spread throughout the country, although, as of 1974, Pari-Mutuel racing is illegal in twenty of the fifty American states.

The 'community standing' of horse racing in America is difficult to evaluate on a nationwide basis. In some states the sport is wholeheartedly endorsed by the citizenry at large; in some states it is distinctly unpopular, but tolerated as a source of tax revenue; in others it is not permitted under any circumstances; and there are various combinations of these differing attitudes. It is an odd feature of American racing history that the great economic depression of the 1930s marked the period of greatest growth in the number of American racetracks, as state after state, desperately seeking an easy source of tax revenue, passed laws authorizing Pari-Mutuel wagering, most of them thereby repudiating previously held stands in opposition to gambling. This depiction of racing as a spawn of disaster, and a rather shady partner in a marriage of convenience, has persisted to the present day in the

Saratoga racecourse, the oldest in the United States, with its nine furlong dirt track and separate steeplechase and hurdle courses on the inside.

minds of many state politicians, much to the inconvenience of racing.

Notwithstanding its somewhat shaky socio-political status, American racing has grown into a veritable giant. Apart from numerous harness tracks, there are more than a hundred tracks in the United States devoted to Thoroughbred racing exclusively or to a combination of racing which includes Thoroughbred racing, and an even larger number of racing associations. Some racing associations do not own tracks but lease the tracks of other associations at which to hold their race meetings. (This practice is also followed by some associations which do own racetracks but prefer the facilities of another track.)

For the calendar year 1976, *Daily Racing Form* reported 103 flat race meetings conducted by 69 Thoroughbred racing associations at 56 different racetracks in the USA. Total USA attendance was 51 million, total Pari-Mutuel wagering was $5.4 billion, and a total of nearly $294 million in purse money was distributed. Statistics relating to horses – which included activity at seven Thoroughbred tracks in Canada and one at Agua Caliente, Mexico, in addition to the USA tracks – showed that 61089 horses participated in 69479 races during 1976. There were 7593 'days' (some of which actually were night programmes) of racing.

Within the wide scope of American racing there are enormous variations. Race tracks vary in circumference from approximately $\frac{1}{2}$ mi. to $1\frac{1}{2}$ mi., and in amenities from simple sheds which offer little more than protection from the weather to elegant palaces which include restaurants, infirmaries and other sophisticated facilities. The duration of a 'race meeting' varies from one day, as at a steeplechase meeting, to more than a hundred days. The typical race

While the majority of American races are run on dirt, the invitation Washington DC International takes place at the grass track at Laurel, Maryland. Here the French colt, Youth, is seen winning the 1976 race.

programme consists of nine or ten races run off at intervals of thirty minutes or less. Purses vary from token sums of less than $1000 to the $250 000 purse of the Marlboro Gold Cup, which is one of the very few commercially sponsored equine events in the USA. Night racing under electric lights, which was introduced during the nineteenth century but was discontinued, has made a comeback in recent years. Its popularity derives not from any special appeal peculiar to that form of sport, but rather from the larger number of spectators who are able to attend during evening hours. None of the major US tracks features night racing, but another recent innovation, Sunday racing, was adopted in 1973 by Santa Anita, one of the country's largest and most elegant tracks.

The Santa Anita grass course, incidentally, is one of the few courses in the USA that is not flat throughout. It begins outside the main (dirt) track and meanders over natural terrain, including a slight downhill section, before crossing the main track and entering the infield, where it thereafter follows the conventional pattern for grass courses: a concentric track inside the main track. The outside portion of the Santa Anita grass course is also unusual, for America, in that it entails a (very slight) turn to the right at one point. At all other tracks all turns are to the left, which in the opinion of some observers is liable to make horses one-sided and more prone to injury on the left side, although no accepted proof of this has ever been adduced.

Grass racing is popular in America, but dirt remains the most prevalent running surface. A grass surface would not withstand the pounding of ten races a day for a hundred days, not to mention the training activity. There are a few training centres in America, and some

Racing in Florida against a background of palm trees.

tracks maintain auxiliary tracks for training purposes only, but by and large training is accomplished on the same tracks that are used for racing. This entails close scheduling which has led to somewhat artificial daily routines. Because the track must be made ready for afternoon racing, training must be completed by mid-morning, so training commences at the earliest possible hour and feeding schedules are adjusted accordingly. American racehorses have no home yards as such. They are stabled at the tracks where they race (or at another nearby track). When one race meeting closes, the entire stable is moved to another track for the next meeting.

Because of their customary location, inside of the main track, grass courses are found only at the larger tracks, 1 mi. or more in circumference, and the turns on a grass course necessarily are tighter than those of the main track. Generally speaking, only one race per day on grass is scheduled, as a 'novelty' on the programme. At Calder Race Course in Florida, the main track is of a synthetic material designed to be impervious to weather, and there is an auxiliary grass course but no dirt course. Horsemen maintain that the synthetic surface has a tendency to 'grab' the horses' feet, so the Calder surface is sprinkled with sand. However, there are no sand race courses *per se* in the USA.

Maintenance of running surfaces has developed into quite an art, particularly since the racing 'season' has been extended into winter months in the northern latitudes. The track is packed tightly so as to repel any moisture overnight, then re-worked the next day to provide a proper cushion for the races.

Perhaps partially because of track running surfaces (and contour), and no doubt largely because of sheer number of opportunities, world time records are generally clustered in the United States – it stands to reason that 55 000 horses running in 63 000 races over carefully prepared, flat surfaces each year will produce faster times than a smaller number of horses running less frequently over undulating surfaces. American Thoroughbred races (as distinguished from Quarter horse races) are timed to the nearest fifth of a second, from a

running start, but the differences between American time records and time records of countries where timing is from a standing start are too great to be attributed to the running start.

On an average, the American Thoroughbred runs in ten races a year and there are nine runners per race. All flat races are started from the electric gate and, in general, the number of starters is limited to the number of stalls in the gate (usually twelve or fourteen). However, exceptions are made for stakes events, for which auxiliary gates sometimes are utilized, and the Kentucky Derby has been run with as many as twenty-two starters.

The average American horse earns approximately $4300 per season, although this figure is somewhat misleading in that it reflects huge purses of $100 000 and over which the truly average horse has no chance of winning. Median earnings are about $1800. On the other hand, the $4300 average also reflects earnings of horses which race only once or twice during a season; horses which race the 'normal' ten or more times average about $7500. At the extreme top of the earnings scale, ninety-one horses in 1973 earned $100 000 or more each, headed by Triple Crown winner

The start of New York's Aqueduct racecourse. New York's racing tradition began some three hundred years ago at Garden City, Long Island.

Secretariat who accumulated the record total for one season of $860 404, to bring his total for two seasons of racing up to $1 316 808. Of the thirteen American horses which have earned more than a million dollars each, Kelso is the leader with $1 977 896 which he earned during eight seasons of racing. Kelso is a gelding, but the fact that he failed to run in any of the Classics for three-year-olds was simply accidental since geldings are eligible to run in Classic races in America.

For many years America was known for the disproportionately large number of big purses that were allocated to two-year-olds. While this continues to be true to some extent, it is no longer so flagrantly the case. Of the seventy-five races in 1973 which had gross purses of $100 000 or more, eighteen were for two-year-olds, which comprises about one-sixth of the racing population.

America also has been known for its disproportionately large number of sprints, and this, unhappily, continues to be true. More than half the races are at 6 f. or less, and more than four-fifths are at 1 mi. or less. However, distance racing is encouraged in that the purses for stakes events over 1 mi. if. are substantially larger than purses for shorter races.

With few exceptions the first four finishers, at least, receive a share of the purse money, and at many tracks the fifth horse also gets an award. At a few tracks all starters receive some part of the purse regardless of their finishing position. As an overall national average purses are divided about sixty per cent to the winner, twenty per cent to second, eleven per cent to third, six per cent to fourth, two per cent to fifth, and one per cent to others. Some of the richer purses for futurity type events include awards for breeders and nominators of the first three or four finishers. The purses for such races frequently include large amounts (sometimes more than half the total purse) contributed by the owners of the competing horses in the form of stakes fees.

Steeplechasing in America is on the wane as a professional enterprise. With year-round flat racing, there is no special season for the jumpers and they must vie with the runners for public attention. Rightly or wrongly, the public appears to regard steeplechase races as poor betting propositions, and it is the income from Pari-Mutuel wagering that provides the purse money for horse racing. This public feeling was expressed by one racegoer as follows: 'When I bet, I don't like to see my money up in the air.' In any case, notwithstanding statistics which showed that form is as valid a factor in steeplechase races as in flat races, if not more so, when steeplechases were included on the programme of the metropolitan New York tracks they failed to generate what was deemed to be their proper share of wagering, and they were discontinued.

With the notable exception of the $100 000 Colonial Cup International Steeplechase Stakes, there are few lucrative opportunities for American steeplechasers – and the Colonial Cup owes its position to a generous subsidy by Mrs Marion DuPont Scott. The majority of steeplechase meetings are one-day affairs and most of them do not offer Pari-Mutuel wagering. Victory in some of the races entitles the winner to a trophy, but no money. There is little incentive to keep a steeplechaser in training as a business venture, but steeplechasing still survives as a sport among owners who are willing to risk the heavy financial odds.

Pari-Mutuel wagering is the only legal form of wagering in any of the United States except Nevada, and, more recently, New Jersey, which permit other forms of gambling. Because of its unique status – and its previously mentioned importance as a source of tax revenue (revenue to the states from Thoroughbred racing in 1975 amounted to more than $61 million) – racing is probably more carefully controlled than any other sport or business enterprise. Control is rather fragmented in that each of the racing states maintains its own racing commission and each commission maintains its own autonomy in writing rules of racing and administering the sport. There is a National Association of State Racing Commissioners which works toward

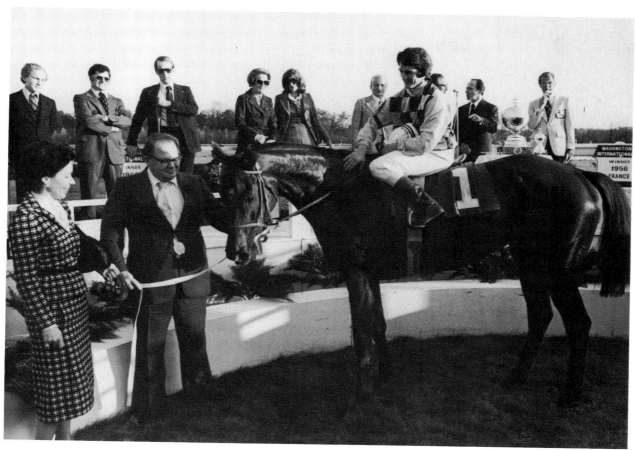

Mr and Mrs Nelson Bunker Hunt with their filly Nobiliary after she had been ridden to victory in the 1975 Washington International by jockey Sandy Hawley.

uniformity of rules among the various states and reciprocity among the states in honouring each other's rulings, but the NASRC has no power of fiat. In order for NASRC actions to become enforceable, the individual state racing commissions must adopt and implement them in each state.

Legal off-track Pari-Mutuel wagering was introduced in New York City in 1971 amidst considerable fanfare and considerable controversy. Apart from numerous setbacks associated with the complete newness of the enterprise, there was outright opposition from the racing industry because an insufficient portion of the revenue from off-track wagering was returned to the sport. The opposition was heightened when the introduction of off-track betting was accompanied by declines in attendance and Pari-Mutuel handle at the New York tracks. The formula for dividing revenues from off-track wagering has since been revised, and betting parlours have been opened elsewhere in New York State, but no arrangement satisfactory to all parties has been achieved. Connecticut has off-track betting based on New York racing, and other states have legislation pending (or approved) to implement off-track Pari-Mutuel betting, but the system in New York was the only one actually in operation at the time of writing.

The Story of Harness Racing in America

Philip A. Pines

Harness racing in America is as old as the country itself, though the term was not used until the end of the nineteenth century. 'Trotting' was the common name given to the sport that races both trotters and pacers. Both types are Standardbreds.

Beginning in 1879 a trotter or a pacer had to meet certain standards to be admitted to the official record of pedigrees. The National Association of Trotting Horse Breeders agreed upon the following:

In order to define what constitutes a trotting bred horse, and to establish a breed of trotters on a more intelligent basis, the following rules are adopted. When an animal meets the requirements of admission and is duly registered, it shall be accepted as a Standard trotting bred animal.

A long list followed, describing the qualifications necessary for a horse to be 'Standard'. Speed and breeding were the determinates.

The National Association of Trotting Horse Breeders had been organized in 1876. It was their job to fix a standard of admission to the official record of pedigrees. Other organizations followed but their purposes were to govern the activities of the sport. They included the National Trotting Association, the American Trotting Association, and the United Trotting Association. The three associations made their own rules and carried them out, often creating disunity among the three groups. In the meantime, a number of prominent breeders met in Chicago (1891) to form the American Trotting Register Association. They purchased the Register but the organi-zation floundered in the years to come. Finally the entire assets of the Register Associ-ation were purchased by the Trotting Horse Club of America (1927), under the leadership of E. Roland Harriman. Harriman assumed the presidency of the re-organized American Trotting Register Association. The Trotting Club also brought together the leadership of the three associations in 1939 and out of that meeting was organized the United States Trotting Association, with the NTA, ATA, and UTA disbanding. The Register was turned over to the newly formed USTA where it has remained since.

The reference only to 'trotters' in the Association's ruling resulted from the low esteem placed on pacers in those days. Pacers were a 'poor man's trotter'. However, when trotting blood was infused in pacing stock and the pacers began to record better times on the track than their trotting cousins, the harness horse world developed a more respectful attitude toward the pacer – gradually accepting him as an equal performer. Although some present-day horsemen still prefer the trotter (objecting to the pacers because the majority of them wear hobbles), most racing pro-grammes at harness tracks feature pacing contests. The hobbles hold the horse on gait, enabling him to finish the race without breaking stride. Trotters, who have no arti-ficial means to keep them on stride, often go off gait and the driver must take the horse to the outside and get him back on stride before he can continue to race. This necessary man-oeuvre delays the trotter and can cause him to

A field of trotters racing to the line. The lightweight bike wheel sulky has enabled the harness racer to achieve speeds comparable with those of the galloping Thoroughbred.

These pacers are equipped with hobbles, which are used to encourage the lateral gait.

lose the race. Pacers, though less apt to break, are subject to the same rules.

The sulky is a light two-wheel vehicle designed to carry one person. Some believe that it used to be 'so called from the owner's desire of riding alone'. Others claim a woman named the vehicle with a comment that 'only a sulky man would use it'. Less uncertain than its name, its history can be traced to before the American Revolution when it was constructed with heavy wooden wheels, iron axles and stout crossbars on which a driver placed his feet. It was driven where wagons and carriages feared to roll: over rough roads, across fields. Towards the middle of the nineteenth century high two-wheeled sulkies were introduced and tracks were constructed to permit trotters to test their speed and, at the same time, get them off the roads where their 'brushes' (brief races at top speed) were becoming a danger to pedestrians.

Two pacers in action at Goshen, New York. Pacers are marginally faster than trotters.

But originally trotters and pacers were ridden to saddle and not hitched to wagons until American streets and roadways improved. They were first used in transportation where they showed considerable speed. Conscious efforts to develop this aptitude resulted, decades later, in the creation of the Standardbred.

Because there were no uniform methods of keeping an account of significant events, official Standardbred records go back less than a century in the United States. A single-line newspaper reference in the *New York Commercial Advertiser*, for example, noted what actually became the first recorded mile of less than three minutes. Dated 11 June 1806, the story said, 'A horse named Yankee trotted a mile yesterday in 2:59 in Harlem, New York'. Not much is known of Yankee. He was a gelding from Boston and became the first trotter to go a mile in less than three minutes in order to win a wager. Nearly four decades later, the 'old gray mare', Lady Suffolk, went the mile in 2:30 in harness with a 2:29½ effort at Hoboken,

New Jersey. Speed being foremost in the minds of the mid-nineteenth century horsemen, a careful record has been kept of performances since Lady Suffolk's world mark. Another fifty-four years would go by before a really significant effort was recorded: the first two-minute mile by a trotter – Lou Dillon, in 1903. This huge reduction in recorded speed was due to improvement in breeding, better and faster tracks, and the introduction, eleven years earlier, of the low bike wheel sulky.

Long-distance tests were a popular way of determining a horse's endurance. At that time, gruelling distances of a hundred miles were sometimes specified to see if a trotter 'had it'. Some made it. Others did not. And when in 1853 a horse fell dead two days after completing a hundred-mile test, a public outcry eventually led horsemen to agree on a fifty mile maximum ruling. This in turn went down to twenty and eventually long distance racing was abandoned completely. Until the turn of the twentieth century, the best three out of five heats or five out of seven heats determined the winner of a race. A carry-over from these days still exists at some harness tracks today – The Hambletonian Stake, raced at DuQuoin, Illinois, is the most prominent race still using the best two in three system. Some events such as the Kentucky Futurity at Lexington, the Red Mile, carry on the traditional best two in three. But most tracks only call upon the horses to run in single dash events and the Standardbred is increasingly being trained for this kind of competition.

Steady Star has gone the fastest of all harness horses. With Joe O'Brien in the sulky, this pacer startled everyone in 1971 at Lexington, Kentucky, by clocking a mile in one minute, 52 seconds. Nevele Pride brought the trotting mark down to 1:54 4/5 at Indianapolis in 1969. Stanley Dancer, the colt's trainer-driver, was in the bike. Greyhound had held the trotting championship for thirty-one years prior to Nevele Pride's world-record performance.

Traditionally, harness racing has been a day-time sport, and during the first forty years of the twentieth century it experienced some very hard times. In 1940, with the introduction of night Pari-Mutuel harness racing at Roosevelt Raceway, Westbury, New York, a spirited revival began. Six years later, the first successful mobile starting gate was introduced, again at Roosevelt. It proved a boon to the sport by providing even starts every time, thus preventing the exasperating method of try and try again handed down from previous generations of horsemen. After World War Two, other tracks followed Roosevelt's lead and racecourses sprang up in metropolitan areas across America.

Today the sport is big business, as well as an international pastime. It is very popular in Canada, especially in the Toronto and Montreal areas, with little, if any, activity 'south of the border'. Nearly thirty million persons attend harness races at the large Pari-Mutuel and smaller country fair and state fair tracks in the United States each year. Over two billion dollars is wagered on these trotters and pacers, vast amounts going to state and local government treasuries.

The Roosevelt International Trot (worth $200000 at the time of writing) is raced at Roosevelt Raceway, Westbury, New York, in late summer. It welcomes horses from several countries. Winners have come from France, Holland, Canada, Sweden, as well as the United States. American horses compete annually in the Prix d'Amérique in Paris. An American entry, Delmonica Hanover, was a recent winner.

Several good Standardbreds have been sold abroad to race and upgrade foreign stock. Italy, Sweden, and France have been principal purchasers. Others have gone to New Zealand and Australia.

The Hall of Fame of the Trotter was opened in 1951 in Goshen, New York, to honour those people and horses who have contributed so much to this all-American sport. Their story is told in this museum.

Quarter Horse Racing

Don Essary

Short races over a straight course were undoubtedly the first form of horse racing where men mounted for sport and a possible wager. The most likely explanation for this is that the short sprints could be run through village streets or in any relatively small clearing. Such races were run in Asia and Europe hundreds of years before the American colonists bred horses of English blood to the native 'Chickasaw' horse and established the American Quarter horse. However, Quarter horse racing as it is known did not appear as a sport or pastime until the American colonies were well under way and the Quarter horse well established as a breed.

The first organized Quarter horse races in the

The Quarter horse, America's most popular breed. There has been a big revival in Quarter horse racing in recent times.

United States were recorded in Enrico County, Virginia, in 1674. Reports on the contemporary scene show that by 1690 large purses were being offered on Quarter horse races and plantations often changed hands on the outcome of one of those sprints down the straightaway. In colonial times any fallow field or thoroughfare served as a racetrack, which probably accounts for the dirt running surface which evolved in America.

J. F. D. Smith, who made a tour of the colonies prior to the Revolutionary War, said that the colonists were very much attached to Quarter racing, which was generally a match between two horses running not more than a quarter of a mile. He said that the colonists had a breed of horses that they called Quarter Pathers which performed with outstanding velocity.

In 1752, three-quarters of a century before the ultimate establishment of the Thoroughbred breed in America, a grandson of the Godolphin Barb was brought to Virginia from England, who was to play an extremely important role in Quarter horse racing. His name was Janus. He was described in the publication *The American Farmer* in this manner:

Although Janus partook of every cross in his pedigree calculated for the distance turf horse, yet his stock were more remarkable for speed than *bottom*. Janus, from his shoulders back, was considered the most perfect formed horse ever seen in Virginia, by the most skillful connoisseurs; he was remarkable for roundness of contour, strength of articulation, and indicated great power and stamina in his whole conformation. His stock partook of these qualities in an eminent degree, and for thirty or forty years they were considered as a peculiar stock, as they invariably exhibited even in the third and fourth generations from the old horse the same compactness of form, strength and the power.

Janus was the progenitor of a family of horses which had both the conformation and the short distance speed of the breed that has come to be known as the American Quarter horse.

As time passed and land became more settled, the difficulties of running long races vanished and by 1764 the popularity of Quarter horse racing gave way to the gruelling four-mile heats of the day. However, the loss of his pre-eminent position in the colonies did not affect the popularity of the Quarter horse on the frontier. He pulled wagons or carried cowboys during the week, but on Sunday he was once again a racehorse.

Quarter horse racing continued to grow in popularity as the breed grew. The speed, endurance, and versatility of the Quarter horse made him the choice of American frontiermen. Small tracks and weekend match races were common in the hundreds of small towns that sprang up along the way as the westward movement carried early settlers into the midwest, southwest and western areas of the present United States. Quarter racing continued on an informal basis for many years before being re-established formally in the western sections of the United States.

Modern-day Quarter racing began just after the turn of the present century at tracks in Tucson, Arizona, and King City and Corona, California. Soon new Quarter horse tracks were operating in most of the states west of the Mississippi. During that period of history Quarter horse breeders began breeding with an eye to speed since they no longer had to rely on their horse for work as they had in the past.

Present-day Quarter horses race on the straightaway, as opposed to the oval courses used in Thoroughbred racing. Otherwise, there is little difference in the two types of racing; the equipment or tack and the requirements for jockeys are the same. The emphasis in Quarter horse racing is on all-out speed.

Unlike Thoroughbred racing Quarter horses lunge from the gate and are at full speed after the first stride. They run the entire distance (220 to 440 yd) at full speed. There is no vying for position and no waiting until the right moment for the jockey to ask his horse to move for the lead; the race is on from the moment the gates open and each horse must run straight and true if he is to have any chance of winning.

The start of a Quarter horse race. Quarter horses are raced over short distances of up to two furlongs.

The American Quarter horse can carry 120 lbs. of rider and equipment down the straightaway at speeds in excess of forty-five miles per hour and cover a quarter of a mile in less than twenty-two seconds from a standing start.

With the advent of Pari-Mutuel betting, all horse racing flourished and the purses grew accordingly. The men who race Quarter horses held on to the idea of putting up their own money on behalf of their horse; it was that concept that gave birth to the $1 280 000 All American Quarter Horse Futurity, the richest horse race in the world. Four of the five richest races in the world are for Quarter horses.

Today Quarter horse racing is conducted at more than a hundred tracks throughout North America, and the popularity of the breed has spread to fifty-one countries outside the United States.

In most respects, Quarter horse racing is vastly different from its beginning of matched races down village streets. The village streets have been replaced by ultra-modern racing plants; however, the Quarter horse has changed very little. He has the same blood in his veins, and he is still the fastest horse in the world.

Gentlemen Riders

André Gareau

Racing has a long history. When in the eighteenth century it began seriously to attract the attention of the French, it had been part of the English way of life for more than a hundred years. But in fact there had been a certain taste for it in France for longer than that. The municipal archives of Semur-en-Auxois, on the Côte d'Or, record the accounts of Running at the Ring going back to 1639. And the wager between the Prince d'Harcourt and the Duc de Joyeuse was nothing but a match, as races with a field of two starters only used to be called in England: the stakes were a thousand écus, and were run for in 1651. One could quote other examples; and they all concerned amateurs only. Racing in France owes its genesis to amateurs.

Times have changed, professionalism has gained the upper hand, but amateurs still have the opportunity to compete in races on the flat, over fences or trotting. And this is just as well, for those who have actually competed on the course are best qualified to serve on committees of racing clubs; they are the best handicappers, the best judges at the finishing post, the best starters, and so on. Which means that racing clubs need to keep up events for gentlemen riders in order to ensure recruitment of racing officials with such experience.

Competitions for amateurs have thus stayed on the card at French courses. And since birds of a feather notoriously like to flock together, fifty such amateurs had the idea, in 1922, of forming the Club des Gentlemen-Riders which became an official body in January 1923 and since then has more than redoubled its efforts

to increase the number of races open to amateurs. It also serves as a channel of communication between the members of the club and the governing bodies of the mother-societies of racing and the management of individual courses.

This club owed its existence to the good offices of Count Greffulhe, first president of the Société de Sport de France. The Marquis de Jumilhac was the first president of the club. One of his successors, Georges Courtois, became the founder-president of FEGENTRI – the International Federation of Gentlemen Riders.

The federation came into being on 5 February 1955 at St Moritz in Switzerland. The founding countries were Germany, France, Italy, Sweden and Switzerland. Its avowed aim may be summarized in the following words: '. . . to establish among gentlemen riders of all countries ties of comradeship and sporting solidarity by favouring the creation of events reserved to amateurs'.

The efforts of the guiding spirits of FEGENTRI led to the creation in 1955 of an international championship at the end of which, annually, its 'Spurs' are awarded. These are in three categories: one for flat racing, another for steeplechasing and a third for achievement in the two together. The combined achievement is rewarded by 'The Golden Spur' for the winner, and 'The Vermilion Spur' for the runner-up. For flat racing and steeplechasing alone, 'The Silver Spur' is awarded to their respective winners.

Since 1955, FEGENTRI has made much

progress. Many other countries have joined the original five, thus justifying the remark of Georges Courtois when he said, 'The task I have undertaken is an arduous one, but it enchants me: I am building up Europe!' In 1977, FEGENTRI comprises thirteen national contingents: Germany, Austria, Belgium, Spain, France, Great Britain, Hungary, Holland, Ireland, Italy, Sweden, Switzerland and Czecho-slovakia. One may rest assured that others will come to swell this list. FEGENTRI is currently broadening its contacts with East European countries and with certain states in the Americas.

In 1976, the programme comprised 22 flat races and 11 steeplechases or hurdle races, which brought together over 122 amateurs belonging to the thirteen nations mentioned above. These meetings, apart from the pleasure which the participants derive from them, give the gentlemen riders of various countries the opportunity to get to know each other and appreciate each others' qualities.

The racing industry has become international, and here FEGENTRI has shown the way. International meetings have happily proliferated and enjoyed a well-deserved success. General de Saint-Didier, who succeeded Georges Courtois, contributed much to its development and expansion. Daniel Courtois, son of the founder, and in his turn president of the Club des Gentlemen-Riders de France and of FEGENTRI, has continued the good work.

Winners of 'The Golden Spur' since the foundation of FEGENTRI are: 1955/56/57, René Andretto, Switzerland; 1958, Christian Seguin, France; 1959, Rickwan von der Lanken, Germany; 1960, Jürg Zindel, Switzerland; 1962, Amadeo Tanzi, Italy; 1963, Erik Delaquis, Switzerland; 1964, Adolf Renk, Switzerland; 1965, Heinz Harzheim, Germany; 1966/67, Jacques de Chevigny, France; 1968, John Ciechanowski, Great Britain; 1969/70, the Duke of Albuquerque, Spain; 1971/72, Daniel Faillot, France; 1973, Patrick-Louis Biancone, France; 1974, Frank Turner, Italy;

1975, Gunter Rosenbusch, Germany; 1976/77 Pascal Adda, France.

The 'Golden Spur' is awarded according to rules that have acquired a certain patina over the years; thus, in 1961 no gentleman rider achieved the standard required for an award of this envied trophy, and by 1976, twenty-one 'Golden Spurs' had been awarded since the foundation of FEGENTRI. Seven were won by French horsemen, six by Swiss, three by Germans, two each by Italians and Spaniards, and one by a British rider.

We are in the century of Women's Lib and parity of sexes, and in most countries it is a legal offence to discriminate on grounds of gender. The female jockey is already a reality in England, and the Newmarket Town Plate has been open to lady riders since 1665. Now that women have attained the highest distinction in all spheres, why the devil should they not also ride races?

Races for women have existed in France since 1961. They appealed to the taste of the public, and since 1972, women have been allowed to ride in all races other than on the flat.

In 1972, Mlle Anny Kurtz was the first woman in France to win over hurdles. In 1973, Mme Janet Slade, an Englishwoman domiciled in France, was the first to win a steeplechase. Since this regulation came into force, 157 women have obtained a licence to ride in public (*licence de cavalière*). In 1974, they were allowed to ride on the flat, in certain races, against both male amateurs and professional jockeys.

Mlle Micheline Leurson, daughter of the ex-crack-jockey over the sticks, Raoul Leurson, has won 138 races since 1961 and has been top of the list eleven times. Mlles Béatrice Hardion and Elisabeth Loyen gained the other two 'Golden Whips'. Other countries which allowed women to ride in public before the French did are the Scandinavian kingdoms and Italy; and, more recently, Spain and Switzerland have followed suit. In Eastern Europe also women

One of Britain's leading lady riders on the flat, Miss Brooke Sanders, takes a horse down to the start.

are allowed to compete and some have entered the famous Grand Steeplechase at Pardubice in Czechoslovakia.

In 1972, FEGENTRI introduced an international grand championship for lady riders, under the name of Coupe Européenne des Cavalières. Mlle Micheline Leurson (France) was the first to win it, the victor the following year being Mme de Kat-Englebert of Holland. In this field, too, internationalization is the rule.

Part Six

Venery in France

Jean de Kermaingant

Venery (from Latin *venari*) is the art of hunting with hounds. Its origin goes back to remote antiquity, as witness such celebrated legends as those of Diana and Actaeon. In France, its rules were laid down in the Middle Ages and the technical vocabulary then current is still in use in France, while English stag hunters also employ it in only slightly anglicized form.

The object of hunting larger game was to control the numbers of animals that were harmful, even dangerous, to man, that lived in the forests which still covered large areas. Once the privilege of the monarch and the nobility, venery became democratized in the second half of the nineteenth century, but still kept intact the traditions bequeathed by the pre-Revolutionary era. It had reached its summit under Louis XV, himself a passionate hunting man. The Marquis de Dampierre, a contemporary of that king, devised the '*fanfares de circonstances*' and, in 1729, the type of hunting horn called 'Dauphine'. As modified in 1818, it became known as the 'Orléans'. It is by its rules and by its horn music that French hunting differs from other forms of hunting *par force*.

The literature of the subject has been abundant. The first work, *Le Livre du Roy Modus et de la Reine Ratio*, was written by Henry de Ferrières in 1375. The most notable, in chronological order, are *Le Livre de la Chasse* by Gaston Phoebus, Comte de Foix (1387), an English version of which, entitled *The Master of Game*, was made by Edward, Duke of York, who was killed in action at Agincourt in 1415. Fouilloux's treatise on venery, written in 1561; Salnova's *Vénerie Royale* written in 1655; and Yauville's written in 1788, considered a classic of its kind. The best-known English work published during the period, when English and French techniques were still practically identical, is Turberville's *Noble Art of Venery*, written in the reign of Elizabeth I and re-published under James I.

The hunting of the stag, the roebuck, the boar and the wolf (known in the older English traditions as Beasts of the Forest as opposed to Beasts of the Chase is called in French, *la Grande Vénerie*. The hunting of the hare, the rabbit and the fox is *la Petite Vénerie*. The hunt is directed by a Master; the establishment is known as an *équipage*, except where boar are hunted, when it is known as a *vautrait*. Every hunt has its uniform, and the buttons proper to it bear a device. The right to wear these buttons is only granted by the Master and a person so entitled is known as a *bouton*. Hunt servants are known collectively as *hommes* (men) and comprise the *piquers* (pronounced *piqueu*) somewhat, if not quite, similar to the English huntsman, and mounted or not, as occasion may require; the *valets de limiers*; and the *valets de chiens* (somewhat resembling the English whipper-in). Guests may join the hunt at the invitation of the Master. The pack of hounds is known as the *meute*.

Although the number of packs has decreased from 460 in 1867 to 75 today, the number of followers and of *boutons* has remained practically the same.

While in the beginning the object of hunting was the destruction of harmful animals, in our time it has become a sport: but for true hunting

A meet of the Rallye Valliae. The photograph shows the elaborate liveries which are typical of the stylized hunting practised in France.

men it is still an art. Packs were once the property of princes, of kings, of great lords, but today they are jointly owned and the expenses shared.

The Société de Vénerie (corresponding to the British MFHA) gives or refuses the right to hunt, in the form of a *Certificat de Meute*; it upholds among hunting men a sense of and respect for tradition, and represents them vis-à-vis the State and owners of private forests. (Hunting across agricultural lands is not such a factor in France as in Britain or Ireland.) The larger game is hunted in forests leased by the State and in private woodlands by invitation of the landowner. It is in the west, from north to south, and in the centre of France that these forests abound, and also to the southwest of Paris.

French forests are noted for their wide extent, their geographical distribution and their variety: remember that those of Fontainebleau, Rambouillet, Chantilly, Ermenonville, Orléans, are former Royal Forests and have been hunted over since medieval times.

It may often happen in the course of a hunt that a pack issues from its own territory and runs across country, through villages, over plains and arable land. Problems may thus arise (referred to as '*droit de suite*') which demand of the Master and his '*boutons*' a great sense of diplomacy and courtesy towards farmers and others. Despite such problems it is true to say that the country people love hunting and join in with pleasure.

We begin hunting in September to get into practice (much like English cub-hunting), but it is not until after the Feast of St Hubert (3 November) that the '*boutons*' turn out in full dress. On that day, St Hubert's Mass is celebrated with the magnificent fanfare created by the Marquis de Dampierre, and there follows the Blessing of the Hounds. The Master usually serves, and in the course of the mass the names of all defunct members of the hunt find their commemoration. The hunt becomes a festival which everyone strives to make more splendid, more triumphant, more traditional.

As everyone knows, the quality of a hunt depends on the quality of its hounds. They must be obedient and disciplined: they must love the chase and have keen noses; two indispensable qualities which alone can save the day in almost desperate situations. A good hound should be very deep-throated, recover himself quickly, and have a turn of speed. There are other qualities, of course, besides these essential ones, but it should always be kept in mind that hunting is not a matter of the individual hound but of the pack, and it is essential to have 'a good team, all going at the same pace, every hound working', for only thus will the stag be brought regularly to bay.

Hounds of the old French strains – *Grand Bleu de Gascogne, Gascon Saintongeais, Poitevin,*

Français Tricolore, Français Blanc et Noir, all have true noses and are accurate workers, but they are slower than English hounds; they are also more delicate in health and less easy to feed. Breeders have therefore been at pains to improve French hounds by an infusion of English blood. When the cross-breeding has been judicious, the result is a magnificent animal, uniting the swiftness of the English with the true nose of the French. Some seventy per cent of French packs are now made up of these hybrids, for which the term 'bastard' has been latterly replaced by the more polite '*Anglo-Français*'. For converse reasons, English Masters of Hounds have brought in French blood. Sir John Buchanan Jardine has done so with great success.

The three major wars which have swept over France in less than a century had a dire effect on hound breeding. In 1914 there were 160 packs with 7000 hounds. In 1939 there

Hunting in the Forest of Rambouillet.

were only 60, with 3000 hounds. But numbers have increased again, to the present 75 packs.

Unlike in British or Irish foxhunting, horses and hounds in France have to make a prolonged effort in the course of the day. Often 60 km of country are covered; it is not uncommon to take horse at noon and not quit the saddle until six or seven in the evening. If foxhunting takes place mostly in a varied landscape strewn with obstacles, and at a fast pace, it is far different with French hunting, where it is essential to spare hounds and horses in order to follow the game till nightfall. The first requires speed and jumping ability; the second, staying power. One is above all a sport, the other an art. Horses seldom have to jump and lose no opportunity of resting, waiting on hounds which themselves are doing a difficult job which takes time; for they have to stick to the hunted animal, recover from faults, and separate the quarry from other deer with which it may be running.

These considerations and the nature of the country hunted categorically dictate the choice of a horse; but, admittedly, personal preferences and aptitudes must play their part. People talk of the advantages and disadvantages of this breed and that, but it would be more accurate to speak of the *type* of horse, for it is recognized that type and character vary greatly within the breed. What must be sought after is a calm temperament and a horse that will not tire itself out needlessly, well balanced and well schooled to make an easy ride, attentive to the rider, of regular paces but keen: a horse that uses its natural resources to the maximum, with a minimum of effort.

Hunting proper may be divided into two quite distinct main parts: fixing on the animal to be hunted by discovering exactly where it lies, and the pursuit. If the second is more spectacular, more obvious, bringing into play a greater number of actors, the first is

Hounds and huntsmen leaving the Château de Fontainebleau after the traditional St Hubert's Day mass.

fundamental, if more arcane. It demands modest resources, a man or two and as many hounds, but their task is difficult and delicate. The huntsman must have a profound knowledge of the game and of its habits, as well as of the forest; the hound must have a keen nose and the ability to select and not give up the original scent if it encounters a fresh one. And at this stage he must be willing to run mute. This preparatory phase of the hunt is called in French *faire le bois*, and the hound used is a *limier* (in older English parlance a *limer*, in modern English staghunting called a *tufter*), and the hunt servant who works with him on a leash is the *valet de limier* whose function corresponds in part to that of the English harbourer.

The reconnaissance phase usually takes place on the morning of the hunt, at dawn. The tufter is held in leash, not by the collar but the *botte*, a sort of breast-plate which allows him to strain at the leash without choking himself. Work begins where the plain meets the woods, to find out where the stag has entered it: he will have been feeding at night in open country – called *faire sa nuit*. When the tufter crosses the stag's scent made on entering the covert, the man holding him in leash must let him go, proceeding cautiously so as not to rouse the stag or, worse, set him running. Before plunging into the woods he must mark the point of entry by breaking twigs, and mark his path in the same way (*briser*). This he may do 'high' or 'low', according to whether he leaves the not quite broken twigs still hanging on the branch or brings them to the ground. Perhaps after many, many attempts the tufter finds the stag's trail: now the man must find the footprints (*vol-ce-l'est*) which will inform him about the deer, as will his fewmets, or excrements. When by the aid of the tufter and the evidence of these traces he is certain that there is a deer in the covert, and what sort of deer it is, he makes for a prearranged point to report to the Master.

After taking stock of the various possibilities, the Master will decide which deer to hunt, and how to open the attack – whether with the *rapprocheurs* or with the *meute à mort*. In the first case, only a few old and tried hounds will be laid on in the covert, the rest of the pack being held up until the stag is set on foot, after which they will be let slip. In the second case, all the pack will be laid on at once. The choice depends greatly on what hounds the Master has available.

When the stag is afoot and the hounds on his scent, the chase proper begins, the second phase of the hunt. In this the horn plays a great part, and all the vicissitudes of the day's hunt are musically expressed by what are called *fanfares de circonstances*. Here are some of the main ones, most in use.

First the *Lancé*, followed most likely by the *Vue* when the followers catch sight of the

stag; the *Tête* which announces the age of the stag as apparent by his antlers. The *Bien-Allé* is sounded to indicate that all is well, and again every time the stag starts running. If the latter deceives the hounds by running with other deer, *Les Animaux en Compagnie* will be sounded. Or the hounds may be put at fault by his speed and cunning, when the *Défaut* will be sounded; if the pack has changed to another line, then the *Change* is sounded. Both the stag and the roebuck, unlike the boar, are attracted by water, especially when tired: the *Bat-l'Eau* announces the soiling stag, and another fanfare, the *Sortie de l'Eau*, when he quits the water. Trusting to his speed, the deer will break across open country, giving rise to the *Débuché*, and perhaps he will take refuge in another forest; for this, there is a call, *Changement de Forêt*.

In the end the quarry may or may not be hunted down, according to many factors; the

Hounds of the Équipage du Haut Poitou with their stag at bay.

quality of the pack, the experience of the Master and his men, the success or otherwise of the quarry's ruses, and finally the weather — scent is poor in cold or dry weather, for instance. When huntsman and hounds have tried in vain to overcome all the devices of their enemy, and night falls, then all hope of bringing him to bay must be abandoned, and the horn will sound the end of the long day by the *Retraite Manquée*. Sometimes, though brought to bay, the stag's life will be saved. In deference to his courage and skill, the hunters will spare his life and let him go; the signal for such quarter is the *Retraite de Grâce*. If, on the other hand, the stag is forced, broken with exhaustion, and has no more strength to flee, he will defy the hounds for a moment or two while *Hallali Debout* is sounded. When he is brought down, the horns wind the *Hallali par Terre*.

Having been stuck, the carcass is then gutted, and their portion given to hounds. This is a final ceremony called *La Curée*, also the name of a call. There follows the call, *Les Honneurs*, sounded while the huntsman presents on his hunt cap the right forefoot to the person whom the Master delights to honour this day. The last act of the drama is played out but still the horns will wind long in the forest, recalling the many events of the past day, in which all who have participated make their music, until at last the *Adieux des Maîtres* is echoed by the *Adieux des Piqueurs*.

And so the Great Venery may be likened to a play meticulously produced and skilfully acted, where everyone, however modest his part, contributes something to uphold the tradition. If the joy which an old hunting man feels at having brought his hounds to a kill when all hope of taking the stag seemed lost is not of the same order as that of the followers, at least the latter cannot but enjoy that sporting aspect of hunting, and certainly they will not be unmoved by the music of the horn, sometimes glad, sometimes plaintive, but always beautiful, waking the echoes of our magnificent immemorial forests.

Draghunting at Pau

Gen. Jean Herlem

In 1815, after the battle of Toulouse, Wellington's cavalry regiments were sent into rest billets in Béarn. The beauty and the climate of that countryside delighted them and many came back later in search of pleasure. This was the origin of an English colony around Pau which lasted until World War Two. They brought with them their native sports and those most suited to the land soon prospered. The first pack of foxhounds was established in 1840.

At first English practice was strictly followed, but foxhunting at Pau soon took on a flavour all its own which it preserves to this day.

Foxes began to get very scarce about 1850, so that the Master took to turning down a bag fox at the end of a drag which had been clandestinely laid.

The scent is imparted by a truss of straw which, having served as litter for kennelled foxes, is impregnated with their urine. This is towed at the end of two yards of rope by a 'dragman' (pl., 'dragmans') who goes across country simulating the line that a fox might take. He must know the country like the back of his hand because the entire course of the run depends on him. The line he takes must afford variety, presenting easy obstacles at the beginning, which get progressively more difficult, but he will avoid dangerous banks and those covered with briars. According to what kind of scenting day it is, he will start two to four hours before hounds are to be laid on. After he has gone as far as will take hounds some twenty-five minutes to run on the scent, he simulates a check by lifting the truss clear off the ground, for two or three hundred yards. He then begins to lay scent again, having provided for a 'breather' for hounds and horses, and for mounted stragglers to catch up. The second burst is also planned to last about twenty-five minutes. At the end of it, hounds ought to be only a few hundred yards behind him. A bag fox is then turned down. The cry of hounds as they change to the 'live' line is unmistakable to the ear of a hunting man. Mostly they run down and break up the fox very quickly.

In any case if they did not kill, no one would admit the fact, for the farmers are of the opinion that their fields are full enough of foxes without 'those hunting gentlemen' turning down more and then not catching them!

Another peculiarity of this hunt is the banks. There are so many in the country that no sooner has one been crossed than it is time to think of tackling the next. They have been there since the Middle Ages, having been first put up to mark boundaries, by labourers who came from the Landes. The regions in the Landes from which the diggers were drawn affected the dimensions of the banks. They all carried long rods to measure the height of the banks to be built, but the standard rod varied in length from region to region. Consequently a bank may be anything from 2ft 8in. to 6 ft 6 in. high. They were built up out of earth lifted from a ditch dug at their very foot. Some of them run along both sides of a lane. If the lane is wide enough for a horse to put down his feet before rising to the far bank, the obstacle is easy and pleasant to take. Otherwise, one leap must take the horse from bank to bank, for if he jumps down into the lane there is no room to jump up out again. As for the rider, he can only hope that the ditch beyond the second bank will not be too deep. The Pau draghunters have christened such obstacles 'tombs'.

It has been proved that any fit horse, even the most ordinary, provided it is of reasonable size, can do this job. Falls are hard, broken bones frequent; on the other hand, horses are seldom hurt.

Thus down the years the element of venery has been blurred in contrast to real foxhunting by the rugged sportsmanlike riding it calls forth. The drag has become a fast, exhilarating gallop across country, demanding from the horseman a willingness to take risks and a very firm seat.

During a good drag, lasting from an hour to ninety minutes, the field following behind the Master and Joint Master – who are responsible for the houndwork with fast, often over-excited hounds – will have to take, at speed, anything up to a hundred banks, some of them very severe, making one or two every minute.

The drag was for long the target of criticism and not recognized as a hunt until about 1860. But it is certain that without it no form of foxhunting would have survived at Pau. The expansion of arable farming has caused the extent of open moorland to shrink, and with it the number of banks. For a long time past a real foxhunt would have been impossible because of damage to crops. Moreover, for some years now the greatest enemy of horses and horsemen, barbed wire, has been gaining ground; visible to the eye or camouflaged by briars and brambles, it makes it impossible to follow a line not planned beforehand but simply dictated by the running of hounds. It is the skill and the thorough knowledge of the country evinced by the 'dragmans' which has enabled the pace to stay so fast, so that the field need only worry about keeping up with hounds and staying in the saddle.

This marvellous sport still has its ardent devotees as one of the boldest and most complete branches of horsemanship, and it would be unjust not to mention here among all the Masters who breathed life into the 'Pau Hunt Drag': Colonel White, Sir Henry Oxenden, and M. Corneval, who were the founders; M. Prince who was the last Master of the great pre-war era (there were ninety-nine horses in his stables); the Marquis du Vivier who revived the hunt after 1945, and the Baron d'Ariste who is in office at the time of writing.

The History of Foxhunting in Britain and Ireland

Charles Chenevix Trench

English sportsmen of the sixteenth and seventeenth centuries hunted the stag if they were of sufficiently exalted social status, and the hare if they were not. In Ireland wolves were still hunted. But the wolves were soon exterminated, and the wild deer disappeared from most of England as the forests were destroyed.* The fox was generally treated as vermin partly because (as Oscar Wilde remarked) he is uneatable, a matter of some importance when fresh meat was almost unobtainable in winter, though 200 years earlier the Duke of York, author of the first English book on hunting, had praised the fox's sporting qualities 'for he stinketh evermore'. And it was gradually discovered that the strong scenting, straight running fox gives better sport that the hare.

It is impossible to set a date for the beginning of foxhunting, but by the 1720s it was well established. It was the sport of the squirearchy rather than the aristocracy, and was emphatically not the sport of the Court, which still hunted the surviving deer. Foxhunting had about it a faint aura of country bumpkinism and opposition politics. Thus a French traveller writes of the ordinary country squire,

He drinks two favourite healths at his meals; the first is to all honest fox hunters in Great Britain, Protestant or Catholic without exception, the title of hunter reconciles them all. The second bumper is confusion to the Minister.

The ladies of the Court, coming home tired and sweating from a stag-hunt, 'with a red mark on the forehead from an uneasy hat', agreed disparagingly that 'all this may qualify them to make excellent wives for foxhunters, and bear abundance of ruddy complexioned children'. When the Duke of Grafton, who liked foxhunting, asked for a few days' leave from Court for this purpose, the irascible little George II, himself a keen staghunter, told him it was a pretty occupation for a man of quality, to spend all his time tormenting a poor fox, that was generally a much better beast than any of those which pursued him. . . . 'With your great corps of twenty stone weight,' added His Majesty, 'no horse, I am sure, can carry you within hearing, much less within sight, of your hounds.'

Hunting at that period was a dull occupation except for those who, impervious to fatigue, wind and weather, delighted in watching hounds work. They met at dawn, and picked up the 'drag' of a fox which was still heavy with his night's meal. Over several hours they virtually walked their fox to death or, more probably, to earth. To breed a hound with a good nose, irrespective of speed, they experimented, not always with the happiest results. The Master of a Galway pack, origin of the famous 'Blazers', crossed his hounds with bloodhound and mastiff. This made them so bold and fierce that when their old huntsman, somewhat fuddled with poteen, entered the kennels one night without a whip, they ate him.

It is not really possible to identify the first Master of true foxhounds: probably numerous

---

*Largely for shipbuilding. To construct an eighteenth-century ship of the time required 4000 mature oak trees.

The Prince of Wales, later Edward VII, out hunting with the Queen's staghounds. From the painting by G. D. Giles.

private packs, of which we have no record, hunted indifferently the fox and the hare, as do certain so-called harriers nowadays who much prefer hunting 'the long-tailed hare'. The claim is made for Thomas Boothby who probably hunted the Quorn country as early as 1697. The oldest packs of foxhounds in Ireland are said to be the Duhallow, founded well before 1745, and the Ormond.

Most hunting men of the seventeenth and early eighteenth centuries rode straight-legged, very much like the medieval knight, in a padded, high-pommelled, high cantled saddle. So much is clear from the writings of Gervase Markham, the Duke of Newcastle, and others; but the hunter had far more impulsion than the Great Horse, being trained (in Markham's words) to cover long distances at 'a continual loose sort of gallop', apparently bitted only with a snaffle. It is interesting, however, to note that Markham 'disliked much the custom of our northern riders who (at the gallop) stand up

straight upon their stirrup-leathers, so that, if you came up behind them, you may see day between their legs'.

Jumping was an exercise unknown to medieval and Renaissance horsemen. We first learn of it as enclosures became more common, towards the end of the seventeenth century. In one hunt the Duke of York, later James II, 'kept pretty close to the hounds, though the hedges were high and the ditches deep'. There is a reference to loyal Tory squires 'who have jumped hedge and ditch in all else', baulking at his political indiscretions. But still jumping was pretty rare, and seldom necessary, in the early days of foxhunting.

In the latter half of the eighteenth century a change was brought about by several inter-relating factors. There was a rapid increase in enclosures, so that anyone who wanted to follow hounds must be prepared to jump hedges, walls, ditches and timber. At first this was done at a slow pace, often from a walk, with the rider sometimes dismounting, but it was, of course, far more exciting to do it at a gallop. The famous Hugo Meynell, who took over the Quorn in 1753, started breeding hounds for speed as well as scent, and it was discovered that the faster the hounds, the faster ran the fox. His contemporary, Peter Beckford, author of *Thoughts upon Hare and Fox-hunting* (1782), systematized the science of hunting hounds, and much of what he wrote holds true today. Meynell and Beckford might well claim the joint paternity of foxhunting in its present form, the golden age of which was from about 1780 to 1820.

There were, and are, basically two kinds of foxhunters – those who ride in order to hunt, and those who hunt in order to ride. The former's pleasure is in the fascinating spectacle of hounds finding their fox and hunting a line. To them a horse is merely the most convenient vehicle for the purpose: they would almost as soon hunt on foot or with a bicycle. For the latter the pleasure of hunting is the supreme excitement, the single-minded exhilaration, of riding at speed across country when all is forgotten but the absolute necessity, transcending all other human ambitions, of keeping with hounds. Most foxhunters start by hunting to ride but learn eventually to ride to hunt, though some might as well be taking part in a paper-chase. One such confessed to me, 'All I ask of hounds is that they keep out of my way' – a point of view that is hardly popular with Masters.

The new style of hunting attracted the young, rich, dashing men-about-town. Their favourite hunting country was Leicestershire and the adjoining counties, known as the Shires, where there was very little plough and stiff fences to hold the large bullocks which were fattened there. The 'Corinthians', 'dashers' and 'plungers' who flocked to the Shires generally kept their horses at Melton Mowbray, and were known as Meltonians.

The most formidable obstacle in the Shires was the 'double-oxer' – a hedge with a drainage ditch on each side, each ditch being protected with a stiff timber rail to prevent bullocks from treading it down and pushing through the hedge. It is seldom if ever encountered nowadays, except in events and hunter trials. Unless it was grossly exaggerated, their country was 'bigger' than it is today, with double-oxers, five-foot walls and towering park railings abounding. The Irish speciality was – and is – an enormous bank, with wide and deep water on one or both sides. The theory in jumping was that, approaching a jump, one must lean well back to lighten the horse's forehand for his take-off, and lean even further back in landing. Here is Whyte Melville's description of a hard rider clearing four strong rails higher than a horse's withers (some 5 ft 4 in.) from a poached take-off to a drop-landing:

Leaning far back and sitting well down, he seemed to rouse, as it were, and concentrate the energies of the animal for the last half-stride when, rearing itself almost perpendicularly, it contrived to get safely over.

'Leaning far back', 'rearing itself almost perpendicularly' – to modern horsemen it seems a recipe for disaster. But that was how the contemporaries of Surtees, Nimrod and Whyte Melville did it. They considered it particularly elegant to raise right hand and whip on high, as though calling a cab. Nimrod laid down with authority that no gentleman would ride with a bent knee. It was not until about 1900 that foxhunters started to lean forward for the take-off, and not until after World War Two that most of them adopted some approximation to the 'forward seat'.

Except among Meltonians, who were notorious for snobbery, there was nothing exclusive about the hunting field. This was particularly so of provincial hunts, Irish hunts and those in the London region, where anyone was welcome to follow hounds, so long as he did not over-ride them, and horse ownership was more widespread than it is today. Not only squires and farmers, but business and professional men, naval and military officers, saddlers, millers, shopkeepers, barbers, tailors, blacksmiths, even 'the Badminton sweep wot 'unted with the Dukes' are recorded as foxhunters.

Many a tale illustrates this, including a favourite one told frequently by the Prince Regent.

There was a butcher out, God damn me, Ma'am, a great big fellow, six foot two inches and the bully of all Brighton. He over-rode my hounds several times. . . . At last, God Damn me, ma'am, he rode slap over my favourite bitch, Ruby. I could stand it no longer but, jumping off my horse, said, 'Get down, you damned rascal, pull off your coat, none shall interfere with us, but you or I shall go back to Brighton more dead than alive.' God damn me, ma'am, I threw off my coat, and the big ruffian, nothing loth, did the same by his. By God, ma'am, we fought for an hour and twenty minutes, my hunting field forming a ring round us, no one interfering; and at the end of it the big bully of Brighton was carried away senseless, while I had hardly a scratch.

Mr Jorrocks' *Hoisting himself on like a crate of earthenware*. An illustration by John Leech for Robert Smith Surtees's book, *Handley Cross*.

No doubt his respectful audience took His Royal Highness's story with a pinch of salt, but no one questioned the propriety of a butcher hunting.

Shooting, not hunting, was the snob-sport, a relic no doubt of the old Game Laws which prohibited the killing of game by all but those owning land worth more than £100 a year. When Lord Rosslyn's pheasant battu was interrupted by a pack of harriers whose Master was a grocer, he roared, 'Don't talk to me, sir! How dare you bring your hounds here? Go home, sir, and sand your sugar!'

Even Queen Victoria took the point, admonishing her eldest son to 'do away a little with the *exclusive* character of shooting. . . . With hunting (much as I dislike it on account of the danger) this is the case, and that is what makes it so popular'.

The same point is made in fiction. The immortal Jorrocks, Master of the Handley Cross, was a genial cockney grocer, to whom

'unting is all that's worth living for – all time is lost wot is not spent in 'unting – it's like the hair we breathe – if we have it not, we die – it's the sport of kings, the image of war without its guilt and only five and twenty per cent of the danger.

In Ireland the fields were, if possible, even more mixed, with peers of the realm and officers of the garrison riding alongside small farmers, squireens and 'half-sirs'.

Hunting was eminently the sport of the country clergy, many of whom not only followed but hunted hounds. 'Spurting Bullen', the eight stone vicar of Eastwall, hunted for over seventy years and, though he could afford only cheap screws, often led the Quorn field for the first half mile. Another hunting parson found that the objection to his taking a living far from his kennels was 'altogether frivolous', since he could easily 'hunt on Saturday and ride 110 miles to take Matins on Sunday. In Ireland, in the 1840s, when the gulf between the Protestant Ascendancy and the native Irish was, except on the hunting field, immeasurably wide, a parish priest, Father Dunne, whipped in for the (Protestant) Master of the Ormond. The official ecclesiastical view of foxhunting, expressed by a bishop, was that there was no harm in the clergy hunting 'so long as they did not tally-ho' – a very subtle distinction.

Nor was politics a bar in the hunting field. Daniel O'Connell, the Liberator, was a keen foxhunter; the Quorn's largest subscriber was an extreme radical Member of Parliament; and riding to hounds in Lancashire was, somewhat improbably, Friedrich Engels, collaborator of Karl Marx and co-author of *The Communist Manifesto*.

In the leisurely foxhunting of the early eighteenth century ladies, it seems, sometimes took part. But as the sport became fast and furious they dropped out of it. The side-saddle of the day was not suitable for jumping until the 'leaping-head' was invented, by a pro-

fessional huntsman prevented by injury from riding astride, during the Regency. This made it easier for ladies to ride across country, but long, trailing skirts still made it somewhat dangerous. Moreover foxhunters – not, one hopes, those in Holy Orders – had a reputation for hard drinking, hard swearing and destructive horse-play when in their cups; and Meltonian ménages were not infrequently irregular. So hunting was a male prerogative, save for a few female eccentrics such as the Countess of Salisbury, 'Old Sarum', who hunted her own hounds from 1777 to 1812.

The early years of Queen Victoria's reign saw

Henry Alken, sen. *The Whissendine Appears in View*. From a set of eight plates of the Quorn Hunt engraved by F. C. Lewis 1835. (Messrs Fores, London)

widespread change of moral climate, which affected foxhunters as well as others. 'The ostentation of vice at Melton' was felt to be bad form. Wives accompanied their husbands there in the 1840s, and even to meets, though they seldom rode beyond the first covert. Surtees was expressing a common view when he said that ladies were as much in place at the meet as out of it tearing across country.

This did not, of course, satisfy the more enterprising ladies who soon went further. Most were perfectly respectable, some were not. Lord Stamford, Master of the Quorn, married a circus equestrienne, the supposed model for Surtees's Lucy Glitters, 'beautiful and tolerably virtuous'. She naturally took it badly when the most popular and notorious courtesan of the day, known to one and all as 'Skittles', started going out with the Quorn too. Lord Stamford, under unrelenting domestic pressure, hinted to Skittles that she was unwelcome, so she took herself off to a neighbouring hunt, the Billesdon (later known as Mr Fernie's), firing a memorable parting shot: 'I don't know why Lady Stamford should object to me. She is not even the head of our profession. Lady Cardigan is.' W. W. Tailby, Master of the Billesdon, resisted all pressure to send her packing. He wrote:

I take my stand on the broad principle that the hunting field is open to all. . . . Nothing in the world would induce me to take hounds home merely because the unfortunate Skittles is out. . . . I never hear any complaints of her conduct in the hunting field, or that she is in any way objectionable to ladies who come out.

So Skittles enjoyed her hunting for many years, beautifully turned out, going uncommonly well and always in the first flight. Among her many friends was Jem Mason, the famous steeplechase jockey, always a favourite with his fellow foxhunters. 'What's it like, Jem?' he was asked as he prospected a very awkward jump. 'Eternal misery on this side,

my lord, and certain death on the other.'

Hunting ladies steadily increased in number, varying in social status from the Empress Elizabeth of Austria to 'old Smith's wife', to whom Tailby presented the brush one day in 1856. Now, perhaps, they form a majority of the field.

A common difficulty in the early days was shortage of foxes, and it was not uncommon to hunt a 'bagman', a practice now strictly forbidden by the Master of Foxhounds Association. But as more coverts were planted, and more landowners were persuaded to preserve foxes, the situation improved. By general consent the best country has always been the Shires, though many provincial hunts afforded almost as good sport. Irish foxhunters felt their country was particularly big and difficult. 'What's on the other side?' asked the Ormond's second whip, riding a nervous young horse and confronted by an enormous, hairy bank. 'I am, thank God,' the Master replied. Fields were about as big as they are now – as few as a dozen out in some provincial countries, as many as 300 in Leicestershire or 150 in Kildare.

It was always realized that hunting depended entirely on the goodwill and co-operation of the farmers. This was particularly so after the celebrated case of *Essex v. Capel* (1809)* disabused foxhunters of their ancient but erroneous belief that they had a legal right to ride over anyone's land in pursuit of vermin. Thereafter they realized that they could be warned off like other trespassers, and Masters took immense pains to propitiate farmers by, for instance, a gallon of gin to one difficult customer, a present of game to another, a silk dress to every farmer's wife in the Essex country. One MFH would always wait twenty minutes for a hunting farmer but only ten minutes for a hunting duke. Except for a few ignorant and selfish individuals, foxhunters took increasing care to shut gates, ride slowly past lambing ewes or in-calf heifers, avoid

---

*The Earl of Essex, a keen shooting man, sued his half-brother, the Honourable and Reverend William Capel, MFH, for trespass with his hounds.

riding over new grass leys or young corn. Compensation for damage by foxes, hounds or horses became an increasingly onerous item in hunt accounts, both in times of agricultural depression when farmers felt the pinch, and in times of agricultural prosperity when every acre was valuable. Generally, shooting landlords made more trouble than non-hunting farmers. They could not be made to understand that nesting pheasants positively enjoyed having a litter of foxes in their midst.

If one compares hunting and shooting of equal quality, hunting was, and is, much the cheaper. But not for the MFH. It was calculated in 1825 that it cost at least £1935 a year to hunt a provincial country four days a week, and anything up to £6000 a year in the Shires. As a result, during the agricultural depression which followed the Napoleonic Wars, private packs (Mr So-and-So's) generally gave way to subscription packs, subscribers paying from £5 to £50 a year. Subscription packs then, as now, attracted the occasional MFH who, like 'Facey Romford', managed to 'live off his hounds'. (I know one such who arrived at a meet on foot, having sold his horse en route.) But most Masters of subscription packs had to pay out a lot of money from their own pockets. Naturally men who were prepared to provide at such cost sport for anyone who cared to turn up enjoyed enormous prestige. It used to

be said (though I can find no confirmation of this) that an MFH in his own county took precedence after the Lord Lieutenant.

There is no doubt that 150 years ago foxhunters were able to ride much straighter than they can now. Then came railways, which they thought would be the ruination of sport, but in fact they made good use of railways, boxing their horses and so hunting over a much wider area than when they were dependent on galloping hacks to get them to meets. Plain wire, which first appeared in 1850, and barbed wire, which appeared a few years later, were a much greater menace, about which there was constant complaint from that day to this. Even the most co-operative farmer could hardly be expected to eschew the use of it when a fencing job which cost £100 with timber cost only £14 with wire. Only in a few favoured and very expensive counties was the wire taken down before the start of the season and replaced in the spring: elsewhere foxhunters had to build 'hunt jumps' or find a way round. Cars were the next menace: noisy, smelly, filling the air with noxious fumes and turning horses mad with fear. Now it is motorways, and a small but articulate minority who maintain that hunting is unkind to foxes. But somehow foxhunting, has survived them all, and there are far more foxhunters now than in the golden days of Hugo Meynell.

Hunting in Britain and Ireland

C. N. de Courcy-Parry

It is impossible to explain the complexities of foxhunting to those who have never taken part in it, nor had particular interest, and although a thousand and more large books have been written, they all tell the same thing only in slightly different phraseology. None face up to the direct question from the inquiring mind – why does it take place? or again, what is it?

The answer, briefly, is that it is a sport bringing out all that is best in human character, and as such, has remained unchanged, a part of the British countryside tradition down the years.

Hunting has been the greatest impulse, ever since the first man walked upon the earth, and early on he trained the wild dog to assist him in catching the quarry, so essential to his survival.

With increasing domesticity and the passing of the years, the necessity of hunting for food was replaced by the enjoyment in what was known as the 'chase', consisting, at that time, of watching their 'dogges' or 'houndes' in pursuit of game, this usually being deer. Those unable to follow on foot did so on horseback.

Later on, the fox, for so long accounted as 'vermin', replaced the stag as the first 'beast of the chase'.

The popularity of foxhunting increased and the people, being horse lovers, took great delight in riding after hounds.

Hunting, of course, had many critics condemning it; and the great sporting writer, Bromley-Davenport, in his parody on the poem 'Locksley Hall', wrote in all high humour:

What satisfaction on the morrow can his capture bring?
I'm ashamed through all my nature to have done so flat a thing. . . .
I'm an idiot for my pains.
Nature gave to every sportsman, an inferior set of brains.

Before the novice takes up this sport seriously, it is well that the less attractive aspects of it are considered, remembering the story of the foreign nobleman who, returning home from hunting with a famous pack in England, replied, to his host's enquiry as to whether he had enjoyed his day, that he had done so immensely but might he ask if anyone went out twice? And the evening occurs, frequently, to even the most determined devotee of this pastime, when he or she mutters between chattering teeth, 'Never again!'

Following hounds, however, in a car, voiture, or what you may, is very different from galloping across a strange and wet countryside, leaping tremendous obstacles upon a horse, apparently equipped with totally inadequate brakes, and with throttle jammed irrevocably wide open. In the car the hunting enthusiast can loll in comfort, reading the sporting papers, eating caviar and sipping wine; occasionally wiping the mist from the windows to glimpse, through the cigar smoke, what is going forward outside.

'*Tally ho,* Jenkins, a *check* I perceive, you have time to open another bottle.' That is the way to do it in this enlightened age, but if the heart beats high and the blood courses through the veins, then it must be the moment to re-echo the immortal words, 'To horse' and all that it implies; but first – and forgive me – I am presuming that you know nothing about it, excepting for a smattering picked up from friends who partake in it and with whom you have attended the Hunt Ball, the Hunt Dinner and the Hunt Races. Well, briefly, this is how this affair is conducted.

It has, of course, to have a boss, a top man, to be called the 'Master' and addressed as such. Lift the hat or bow the head demurely and say, 'Good morning, Master', even if he happens to be a Lady Master. This Master is elected or re-elected annually at a General Meeting of the subscribers to the Hunt, and appointed in his office by the members of the Hunt Committee, who represent the wishes of the local hunting community. It is then his duty to maintain a pack of hounds for the purpose of hunting foxes within the boundaries of the country, fixed rigidly by the Master of Foxhounds Association which is the governing body of everything connected with foxhunting, with a code of rules which must be obeyed.

The number of hounds and horses which the Master keeps depends upon the number of days in which the pack goes out to hunt in each week, and upon its social eminence. Hounds are hunted in pairs, called 'couples', and an invariable custom is to take out an uneven number, fifteen and a half couples being quite usual in a small hunt.

It is far better, at the outset of a hunting career, for a novice to remain dumb than to commit one of the many errors of speech which bestrew the path. To enquire of the huntsman, 'Say, chief, have you lost a dog?' might well ruin the chance of obtaining a ticket to the Hunt Ball for ever. . . . If you want the correct phrase and a reputation for taking an interest in hounds (What!!), then the words are, 'Excuse me, Master, but have you by any chance left half-a-couple back?'

We are supposing that the Master in this case is 'carrying the horn', that is, hunting the pack himself. When he does this he delegates his authority in controlling his followers to a 'Field Master' whose word is law, and some-times personal. The Master is open to criticism from everyone, and it is impossible for him to be right with so many, apparently, knowing better than himself. So we find that in many countries a 'professional huntsman' is employed by the Master, who now realizes that MFH may well mean 'More Fool He'. This is an experienced man who looks after hounds in kennels and out hunting, and is assisted by one or two whippers-in. Only one fox is hunted at the same time, and one of their duties is to assure that a 'fresh fox' does not take the pack 'off the line'. A small point here: the definite article is never used in connection with hounds – they are just 'hounds', never 'the' hounds; why, no one knows.

In Britain and Ireland, the hunting horn can only sound the one note. The huntsman explains his intentions to his hounds and his followers by blasts of varying lengths and intensity, unlike the melodic horn of 'venery' in France (see *Venery in France*).

A fox is not followed by sight, but by the scent which its body leaves lying on the ground as he passes over it. Hounds have been very carefully bred for generations just for the purpose of unravelling this unseen thread, whose volume depends upon atmospheric conditions, interferences, and upon the distance that the fox is ahead of hounds. Very often hounds are unable to 'own the line' (pick up the scent) and the hunt comes to a complete standstill. For this, it is usual to lay all the blame on the Master, and to murmur that the time has come to change him for a younger one. The speed at which hounds travel, 'the pace that puts the life into the chase' (as the old song, 'Drink, Puppy, Drink', puts it) is governed entirely by their ability to 'pick up the scent' or 'hold the line', and so come 'good' scenting days and 'bad' ones.

Thus, in the whole affair, a great deal of the glory lies in its uncertainty. For all that, it is most annoying to have gone to infinite trouble over attire and horse, and then endure a day which can only be described as an unhappy gap between two nights. The thrill lies in following hounds across the countryside, riding and jumping every type of obstacle on the way, and trying to keep as near to hounds as possible without 'over-riding them' and being soundly castigated by the Field Master for so doing; nothing ruins sport more than horse people being too close to hounds. Those following on foot and in cars enjoy watching hounds at work and listening to their 'music', the exciting cry which hounds give in varying crescendo as they grow closer to their fox. Once again, to draw comparison with French or any other woodland hunting, this 'music' plays the most important part in the chase, for the huntsman and the more experienced followers recognize each hound by his particular voice. Good hounds possess what is termed a 'great cry'. When no fox is found, the day is called a 'blank' one, and foxes are hard to 'find' as they lie up all day mostly in coverts (pronounced 'covers', without the 't').

If hounds lose the 'scent' for some reason, perhaps being 'headed' (and this is a crime in itself, meaning that someone has turned the fox from 'his point' or destination), then they 'check' and it is up to the huntsman to 'cast' them in an endeavour to 'hit off the line' and to 'lay hounds on to the scent' again. Since this is an invisible thread lying on the ground, which he can neither see nor smell, he has to possess great knowledge of the ways of a fox to 'pick him up' again.

Never has foxhunting in England and Ireland been so popular as it is today, when an affluent society has more money and leisure to enjoy sport formerly beyond their reach. This in turn creates an increasing problem for hunt establishments, as it is impossible to expect farmers to welcome crowds of strangers galloping across land which is becoming more precious and intensively farmed each year. Now, with farmers' children belonging to hunt pony clubs and loving hunting, the farmer himself may even buy a horse and be glad to welcome hounds on his land. Many hunts are compelled to forbid visitors to hunt with them on certain days in the week, and anyone wishing to hunt must write well in advance to the Hon. Secretary for permission so to do.

It seems that the end of the day for woodland hunting comes closer with each season, and the increase in forestry and woodland makes this inevitable; here advice on the way of it must be sought from France.

Many British packs are situated in less fashionable and wilder places where all are welcome and where sport is just as good, or better. For that matter, tremendous enjoyment can be had hunting hares with harriers, which are smaller than foxhounds and, unlike the smaller beagles, are followed on horseback. This is a grand, cheerful sport lacking foxhunting's formality, nor is there emphasis on the kill, and a hare, being far more cunning and elusive than a fox, more often wins the day. The chief enjoyment lies in watching the way in which hounds puzzle out the line. There is usually a great deal of jumping, and it is splendid schooling for young horses and young people, since hares mostly run large circles, often several miles wide. The hunt staff wear green coats and not scarlet, and the season, commencing on 1 October, ends on 1 March.

Fewer packs are found in England than formerly, but the famous 'White West Country' harrier blood has had a great influence on breeding foxhounds. Good harrier packs are still found hunting hares and occasionally foxes in Devonshire, Somerset and Cornwall.

In Scotland, hunting is extremely serious and orthodox, conducted with sound, well-run establishments, costing a great deal of money to follow, if you choose such splendid packs as the 'Bold Buccleuch'; but further southwards, near the English border, in rougher country with colder climate, the best genuine wild sport in Britain can be enjoyed at far less expense, in spite of dripping noses, frost-bitten ears and eyes almost blinded by blizzards. Here, beneath the Cheviot Hills, the College Valley Hounds have influenced hound breeders all the world over in their favour, being bred for over a quarter of a century by Sir Alfred Goodson, just to catch mountain foxes, from sires of the Lake District packs, which are followed only on foot in the steepest hunting country in the world.

All along this border country is hunting at its best, where hardy sportsmen are to be found hunting all day and, in the evening, drinking whisky as though it were milk. A strong man's country is this, and those who go there to hunt either stay for ever in the love of it or perish within a month of privation and hardship. For something different, for music and splendour in the chase, the Dumfriesshire black and tan hounds can have no equal, bred by the late Sir John Buchanan-Jardine of Castle Milk, and handed down to his son, Rupert, who carries them on in all the old glory.

'Jock' Jardine, whose chief love was boar hunting in France, spent a great deal of his time there, where this most charming of gentlemen and most forceful of characters endeared himself to French sporting circles. He was a breeder of hounds second to none, and his book on the subject is a classic. He introduced French blood into his pack and made them the most famous in pursuit, and for music, in the land. (The writer was told by a foxhunter, who had watched their performance in amazement, that they hunted like 'vacuum cleaners', travelling relentlessly forward.)

There is infinite choice on the English side of the border line, with the Tyndale (the Shires of the north) covering a wonderful country, and so down through countryside where it is not possible to go wrong, for all the packs are good, and into Yorkshire where a day on the Middleton Wolds must be as memorable as one amongst the bottomless, wide, Holderness ditches, a country this one which holds no attraction for any but the bravest of the bold; and these ditches and drains are to be found all down the east and into the great ploughlands of Lincolnshire.

Then Leicestershire, the 'Shires', Quorn, Pytchley, Cottesmore, Belvoir and Fernie; nowhere in all the wide world is its equal, nowhere can be found such horses, nor so many lovely well-turned-out women and brave men, too – in all elegance, riding across broad well-fenced acres, without a strand of wire to hinder them, galloping freely behind packs of hounds skimming like pigeons over the fairest country in Europe.

Then turn southwards to Badminton and all its glory and past the home of the greatest foxhunter of them all: His Grace, the Duke of Beaufort, Master of Her Majesty's Horse, and of his own hounds, as were his father and grandfather before him.

'Where are the folk like the folk in the West?' asks the singer of the old song. 'Where, indeed' we echo, for more packs of hounds are to be found all in friendship together in Devonshire and Somerset than anywhere else in Britain.

Staghounds are in abundance too, and these are tremendously popular with farmers and 'moor-men'. Here, on Exmoor, is an entirely different form of hunting, with very little jumping but with the most hazardous riding in a country of steep coombes or ravines of amazing fascination and delight, with great oak woods and rushing rivers, and miles of open moorland.

A stag fit to run, a 'warrantable stag', is chosen by the 'Harbourer' on the day before the hunt, and watched by him until he goes to rest at night, and on the morrow, as the poet Whyte Melville wrote:

> First came the Harbourer,
> The Harbourer, the Harbourer,
> Before the dawn was clear,
> And here he stopped, and here he stood,
> And round the Coombe he made it good,
> And harboured in the Lower Wood,
> A warrantable deer.

This warrantable deer can take hounds and horses across twenty and more miles of moorland and hill. The Quantock and the Tiverton packs hunt stag, too, and of the foxhounds, the Exmoor show wonderful sport in a country still quite unspoilt; nor will it ever be spoilt, for it is a national park.

Although the majority of packs now hunt the fox a few still hunt stag. Here the Devon and Somerset staghounds, with their huntsman, Dennis Boyles, are seen after a day's hunting on the moor.

Ireland's famous Scarteen (Black and Tans) hounds with their Master, Mr T. F. Ryan.

There is hunting for one and all in Ireland. It is the home of the horse, whence all the best in the world come, and hunting is a way of life; nor is any one thing talked of excepting horses, insomuch that some of us would like a 'horse-less day' established by law. Hunting takes place on Sundays after mass and holidays.

The many harrier packs hunt foxes in the same territory as do the established foxhound packs, working in perfect harmony with them and bringing hunting home to the whole countryside, who support them enthusiastically. One can jump 300 stone walls in a day's hunting with the Galway 'Blazers' and next door, in East Galway, one can jump those tremendous banks which divide one small field from another, often with a wide ditch on either side. It is all open to you from the Louth in the north-east, down to the 'Killing Kildares' and the great wide ditches of County Meath, with the foxhounds and the Ward Union Staghounds, down to Waterford and County Cork, with its pack at every crossroad. 'The long way to Tipperary' is well worth the journey. There are the legendary black and tan hounds of Scarteen, the family pack of the Ryans and, perhaps the best of all, Duhallow. It is all there for the 'brave and the bold' and here will foxhunting go on until the Archangel Gabriel sounds the last call . . . 'Home'.

Hunting in North America

W. Sidney Felton

Hunting with hounds started almost with the arrival of the English colonists who settled in the early seventeenth century in the area which is now Virginia and Maryland. England's initial contribution was not foxhunting, for that did not yet exist as a sport, but these were the men whose other hunting activities led colonists, a century later, to develop foxhunting in North America during the same period in which it was to develop in England.

To these early hunters, anything which crossed their path was fair game. Hunting provided an important addition to the family larder, was a defence against the hazard of marauding wild beasts, and incidentally provided sport. Contemporary accounts tell of hunting deer, bear, wolves, panther, wildcat, racoon, opossum and, of course, fox. Most of the country was heavily forested and not accessible to a mounted rider, so much of the hunting was on foot.

Hunting specifically in pursuit of the fox developed in both countries during the early years of the eighteenth century, but under quite different conditions. In England, foxhunting started as the sport of royalty, nobility, and the landed gentry, and in a relatively well-developed terrain. In America it started as an accepted sport at all social levels. Private packs were kept by wealthy plantation owners. At the other extreme, we find the 'fox chase', often organized and well advertised by a local tavern keeper, in which a bagged fox was released and quickly run down by a mixed pack assembled for the occasion. The sooner it was over, the more quickly the spectators

returned to patronize the establishment which had arranged this 'sporting' event.

The first 'organized' hunt was the Gloucester Foxhunting Club, founded on 13 December 1766 by colonists living in or near Philadelphia. It had for many years a fabulous whipper-in who went on foot but was reputed to be always present at the death. Hunting spread north into New Jersey and New York and south into the Carolinas and Georgia. Many new hunts were organized and flourished, though often only briefly. The trend was towards more formal hunting, especially in industrialized areas. This was the situation in 1860 at the start of the Civil War.

The end of the war marked the beginning of a new and different period. With devastation in the South and the accompanying ruin of the old aristocracy, hunting in that area for the moment came to an end. In the North, less affected by the war, interest quickly revived. One of the first to resume hunting was E. F. Bowditch, whose private pack was established in 1866 and four years later became the Millwood Hunt – a subscription pack. It hunted in and around Framingham, Massachusetts, until disbanded in 1969, having lost much of its country to housing developments. Many hunts sprang up throughout the north-east, and in due course hunting revived also in Virginia, largely through the efforts of sportsmen attracted to the area by its obvious suitability for the sport.

The latter half of the nineteenth century was a period of development and change, of trial and (not infrequently) of error. At first, the *dropped* or *bagged* fox was an all-too-important part of foxhunting. One less appealing activity was a drag leading to a point where a bagged fox was dropped just ahead of the hounds. Even the tavern keepers' fox-chase recurs from time to time. Not until well into the twentieth century did the growing disapproval of new generations of foxhunters bring into complete disrepute these once common practices.

During this same period foxhunters looked increasingly to England in accomplishing the transition to the more formal hunting of the present day. English hounds of many types were brought to North America. More carefully regulated breeding methods – long followed in England – led to the development of strains of American foxhound which many consider better suited to American conditions than even the best English hounds.

The Grafton-Middlesex Hound Match, held in the Piedmont Valley of Virginia, in November 1905, marked a new standard of achievement in developing the American fox-hound. It was intended to compare American and English hounds hunting under American conditions. Victory was awarded to the American hounds. Whatever the significance of the victory – as to which there were strong differences of opinion – the match clearly demonstrated the competence of a well-bred, well-trained pack of American hounds. Of equal importance, this well-publicized match between two northern packs (both from Massachusetts) brought forcible attention to Virginia and started an influx of sportsmen who were to make it the centre of North America's finest hunt country.

A significant milestone in North American foxhunting was the organization in 1907 of the Masters of Foxhounds Association of America. Its permanent office is at 112 Water Street in Boston, Massachusetts, where the clerk of the association is also the keeper of the stud book. In February 1974, it had in registered or recognized status a total of 142 hunts. The state of Virginia leads with twenty hunts, but the roster shows hunts in thirty-three states of

the United States and in three of the Canadian provinces. Fourteen hunts report draghunting only, and five report hunting coyote.

Dyed-in-the-wool foxhunters hold drag-hunting in low esteem, pointing out that galloping after hounds following an artificial scent is not hunting. In fairness to hunts in areas where terrain or other conditions do not permit the hunting of live fox, it is appropriate to point out that there are in North America draghunts which furnish sport of the highest standard. A well-controlled field following fast hounds over natural country with well-panelled and sometimes quite formidable fences can provide a challenging ride for the participant and a thrilling sight for the spectator. Many steeplechase riders have found in draghunting the perfect introduction to race riding.

But now, to our primary subject – the fox. There is considerable difference of opinion whether the red fox of North America is the same as the red fox of England. Naturalists say that there is no essential difference. However, one obvious difference is that the red fox of North America is wilder and has not adapted to living in close contact with people as has the apparently identical red fox of Great Britain.

Of more importance is the prevalence in North America of the grey fox which out-numbers the red in most of south-eastern North America. Although the red has recently been reported as far south as northern Florida, this is primarily grey fox country. From Pennsylvania north and north-west is red fox country. However, over a considerable area both may be found with the preponderance of one species or the other varying noticeably from time to time. The early colonial days were a period during which the grey was dominant. Some early Virginia colonists concluded that there were no red foxes in North America. This led to the importation of English red foxes, but these soon merged with the native red foxes.

The grey lacks the speed of his red cousin, and at first impressed some early settlers as clearly inferior. However, with the slow pace of the early hounds and the comparably slow

Hounds and hunt staff of the Iroquois Hunt Club in Lexington, Kentucky.

pace of the horses then in use, the grey fox soon became preferred. The grey tends to circle back at a relatively slow pace, whereas the red is apt to take off at a pace and in a direction which in early days was frequently too much for both hounds and horses. The foxhunting farmer, or even the more affluent plantation owner, rarely kept a horse solely for the purpose of hunting. The plantation owner might come out on the ambler or pacer which he had found best adapted for daily riding. The farmer might ride the same horse which hauled his wagon. A mule was an entirely acceptable and not uncommon mount. Even today, with faster hounds and Thoroughbred or near-Thoroughbred hunters, many Masters, whose primary interest is in houndwork, prefer to hunt the grey rather than the admittedly faster red. They accept without protest the ability of the grey to climb a tree and take refuge above ground rather than below.

Whether the grey is predominant or whether you are in red fox country, foxes are nowhere as plentiful as in the better foxhunting areas of England or Ireland. There is, therefore, little pressure to control the fox population, especially since most hunts are generous in compensating local farmers for loss of poultry. As elsewhere in the world, there is an increasing objection to blood sports. Accordingly, a kill by most North American packs is now looked upon as an unfortunate accident rather than a desired achievement. Earths are not stopped and terriers are not used. Master and field are both happy to have the hunted fox go to ground and survive for another day.

Rough uncleared wilderness which moulded the pattern of hunting in colonial days has long since disappeared. However, most areas suitable for hunting are still more heavily wooded and often more rugged than most hunt country in England. A covert is apt to be a wooded area of substantial size with irregular crooked wood rides. Getting a fox out of covert is often difficult. Outside the covert, there is, in most areas, excellent fly country where the horse gallops on firm turf. As a result, fences are in general jumped at a pace which would not be appropriate in the heavier going typical of England or Ireland.

A wide variety of obstacles is found in most hunt countries, but the one which is typical of North America is the post and rail fence. A classic example, constructed with locust posts and firmly-pegged chestnut rails – until old and rotten – is practically unbreakable. The Virginia snake fence is a rail fence with each set of rails placed at an angle to the next so as to be self-supporting. Other commonly used fences are the 'chicken coop' and the 'hog's back', both of which can be used as a panel over wire. The rocky pastures of New England abound with stone walls which are generally panelled with a firmly-supported rider, often an old telegraph pole. The English-type hedge and the Irish bank are exotic rarities.

In North America, as elsewhere, hunting is affected by climate. In the Deep South and on the Pacific Coast, hunting carries on throughout the winter without interruption. In the splendid hunting country in Virginia and Maryland, a hard freeze or heavy snow may force a disappointing interruption, but generally not for long. Further north, starting first in Canada, hunting stops with the arrival of frozen ground and snow, but these northern hunts do not surrender easily, and there is often good hunting on snow-covered ground. Some Masters hunt in the north during the first part of the season and then take their hounds south to a milder climate.

The horse has almost completely disappeared as a farm animal. Breeding costs have sky-rocketed. The heavyweight half-bred raised

The red and white hounds of the Orange County Hunt of Middleburg, Virginia, specially noted for their good noses and superb cry.

specifically as a hunter has become increasingly rare and expensive. Thoroughbreds which have proved too slow or otherwise unsuitable for racing are commonly used as hunters. With the constant increase in the size of the average Thoroughbred and the pleasantly obvious improvement in the skill of the younger riders, this conversion from track to hunting field is surprisingly successful. By comparison with top-grade English or Irish hunters, many race track Thoroughbreds seem lacking in substance. However, most hunting in North America is on firm, smooth turf, on top of rather than down into the ground. It is often said that a hunter can carry at least 14 lbs. more weight under American conditions than in England or Ireland. Accordingly, 'refugees' from the race track move at speeds and fly their fences in a manner which overseas visitors find pleasantly surprising. Not every rider should attempt to cope with a Thoroughbred in the hunting field. Also, there are areas where the rugged country is ill suited for a Thoroughbred, so many other breeds (sometimes mixed or unidentifiable) are used successfully in some areas.

Pigsticking

Charles Chenevix Trench

In the ancient world of Greece, Rome and Persia, men hunted the wild boar with spears. Besides being the oldest sport on horseback, pigsticking (or hoghunting) is probably the most dangerous, combining the perils of riding at full speed across very rough, blind country with those of fighting an animal which even tigers and leopards fear. A big boar can weigh 150 kg. and measure over a metre at the withers and can run for the first half mile as fast as a horse. He cunningly chooses his time and place for a fight, and when he charges, nothing but death will stop him; his razor-edged tushes can disembowel a man or a horse.

The theory of pigsticking is that – except under low-branched trees – where a boar can go, so can horse and rider. But the boar's

'The grave of the pigsticker is ever open'. (This is a travesty of the Arab proverb, 'The grave of the horseman is ever open'.) From *My Sketchbook in the Shiny* by Snaffles.

centre of gravity is much lower, so he can cross rough country with less risk of a fall.

The European boar is a forest animal and is generally hunted on foot. But in the eighteenth century British officers in India took to hunting the wild boar on horseback, and the sport is still practised by a few hard-riding Indians.

The hoghunter needs a bold, fast, handy horse, and a seven-foot spear with a tough bamboo shaft and a needle-sharp point. He finds his boar with the aid of beaters or by quietly riding round in the early morning and evening when the quarry is abroad. The hunters, known as 'spears', are best divided into 'heats' of three or four. Only one heat 'rides' one boar. A boar is sighted and allowed law until the leader of the nearest heat shouts, 'Ride!' Then it is a breakneck gallop on a loose rein, trusting the horse to keep his feet and balance over rocks and ravines, through soft sand and mud, rivers, head-high grass and tamarisk scrub. Ideally the heat rides in an arrowhead formation, one spear immediately behind the quarry, the others echeloned back to take the lead if the boar suddenly 'jinks' to right or left and the leader goes straight on.

Suddenly the boar disappears. Has he squatted in thick cover, changed direction or gone on? Now the expert's fieldcraft is needed. The spears separate and search, someone catches a glimpse of the boar bustling away, points with his spear and yells, 'On! On! On!'

The boar is tiring, the man on his tail lowers his spear and spurs on his horse. He may kill with a clean spear behind the shoulder, bowling the boar over as he runs, or the boar, especially if he is old and angry, short of breath and temper, may turn to fight. This is the moment of truth: his charge must be met at full gallop, for a standing or trotting horse may be hurled off his feet. The boar's head is as hard as iron, so he needs to be taken between the shoulder-blades. The spear is wrenched out and the rider gallops on; if he has missed this vital spot, someone will get hurt, rather badly.

In 3000 years horsemen have devised no sport more rough, tough and bloody.

Part Seven

Saddlery

E. Hartley Edwards
Jean Froissard

The word 'saddlery' covers the items of equipment, other than horse clothing, protective boots etc., used on the riding horse. 'Harness', on the other hand, refers to the equipment of the driving horse, and up to the turn of the century harness makers, particularly, perhaps, those engaged in heavy agricultural work, were considered socially inferior to the saddlers whose craft was concerned with the ridden horse. Indeed, the latter, in the two British centres of the leather industry, London and Walsall, were termed 'brown' saddlers, while the harness men were called 'black' saddlers. A further distinction between the two concerned the type of headgear favoured – 'browns' wearing silk top hats, whilst the 'blacks' affected the more humble bowler.

The colloquial English word used for both saddlery and harness is 'tack', an abbreviation of the word 'tackle'.

There is little doubt that the dominant influence in saddlery right into and through the nineteenth century, and indeed for much of the twentieth, was that of the English saddle-makers, whose craftsmanship and superlative materials made their firms household names in the equestrian circles of the world.

The saddle

Their principal output was the 'English hunting saddle', built on hand-shaped beech-wood trees, which sometimes gave a somewhat flat seat, and for many years fitted with a full serge-lined panel following the shape of the relatively straight-cut flap. Such a panel, though comfortable to the horse, prevented the rider from being in close contact with his mount, and in time an abbreviated panel was used which did away with the lower part lying directly under the rider's leg. Such panels were known as 'half' or 'Rugby' panels: 'Rugby' because it was at that town, a centre of polo at the turn of the century, that the design was first used.

The lining of saddle panels with serge allowed easy regulation of the stuffing wool by the saddler, as well as providing a soft surface, and the practice persisted up to twenty years ago. The disadvantage of the serge was its property of sweat absorption and the difficulty in keeping it clean. To overcome these problems, an over-lining of linen was often employed, but today the use of a leather lining for panels is almost universal.

Needless to say, the English hunting saddle is rarely seen in the 1970s.

From the beginning, the history of the saddle is closely allied to the history of riding, and changes in the former come about as a result of the differing requirements of increasing equestrian theory and practice.

The radical changes in design which have resulted in the modern saddles are, in no small part, due to the overturning of existing theory and, ultimately, of practice, brought about by the teachings of the Italian cavalry officer, Captain Federico Caprilli (1868–1908).

The first saddles seeking to conform to Caprilli's forward principle were those made by Pariani of Milan, and to this firm must be credited, in the early 1920s, the first saddles made with a 'spring' tree. A 'spring' is incorporated into an otherwise rigid tree by the introduction of two strips of tempered steel running from the head of the tree to the cantle. The effect is to give flexibility to the seat which allows it to 'give' with the movement of the horse's back and which also allows the rider's seat to exert a more direct driving influence. It will be appreciated that the influence of the rider's seat is largely negated by a 'rigid' tree which must, obviously, prevent the transmission of the exerted seat pressure.

Other attempts at producing a 'forward seat' saddle were, in the main, confined to Britain. This fact in itself is a surprising one, since in no country did the Caprilli seat find less acceptance. Indeed, many British riders, for the most part hunting people, were opposed to what they termed a 'monkey up a stick' type of riding.

None the less, it was in Britain that Piero Santini, a pupil of Caprilli, achieved the greatest success with his 'Santini' pattern saddle, which was, in fact, made to his specifications in the British Midlands town of Walsall. This saddle and the 'Distas Central Position', designed by Jack Hance, a leading British horseman, and F. E. Gibson, a horseman of almost equal experience who was also director of a saddlery concern, together with the French 'Danloux' pattern by Hermès of Paris, were the ones conforming most closely to the Caprilli seat in the pre-war years.

It was not, however, until after the Second World War, nearly half a century after the Caprilli revolution, that a saddle was made which fulfilled the needs of the modern jumping rider. This was the saddle designed by Count Ilias Toptani and marketed by George Parker and Sons of London at the instigation of F. E. Gibson. Toptani, a trainer of South American show jumpers, made the startling discovery that saddlers were virtually ignorant of the animal for which they made saddles and completely ignorant of the purposes for which the saddles were used. None of the South American saddlers with whom Toptani discussed his ideas had, in fact, ever ridden a horse, and the same was true of the English saddlers, with the exception of F. E. Gibson and possibly one or two others.

Toptani and Gibson re-designed the tree, the foundation of the saddle, narrowing the waist, so that the riders' thighs were not spread out; accentuating the dip in the seat that would ensure the rider's sitting in the deepest part of the saddle without effort; and, most importantly, altering the head of the tree, which had hitherto been vertical to the main body. The head, or pommel, of the tree in the Toptani saddle was sloped, so that the stirrup bars, attached to the arms and the points, were, in their turn, placed correspondingly further to the front. The effect, in conjunction with the seat and the forward cut of panel and flap, was to place the rider closest to the centre of balance of his horse. The latter was assisted by the supporting rolls incorporated in the front of the panel, which helped to fix the position of the lower leg. The spring trees used in these saddles were made from laminated strips of wood and produced in moulds. There was no variation, therefore, between one tree and the next.

From this saddle, originally intended for jumping, have been developed many more, as well as a less exaggerated form which has become known as a 'general' purpose or 'all-purpose' saddle. The third principal pattern of saddle today – apart from the race saddles, which do, in fact, accord entirely with the Caprilli doctrine – is that used for dressage.

In essence, the modern dressage saddle, the best of which are made in Germany, is no more than an up-to-date version of the Renaissance saddle. For perfection the seat is somewhat dipped and bars extend back so that the stirrup leather divides the virtually straight flap in equal parts, enabling the rider to sit centrally over the centre of balance dictated by the slower, more collected paces of the dressage horse.

The bridle

Although the invention of saddle and stirrup by our forebears would seem to have been an unduly protracted exercise, the same can hardly be said of bridle and bit. Snaffle bits, sometimes combined with studded nosebands, are commonplace in the pre-Christian era, and the Greek general, writer, philosopher, agriculturalist and horseman, Xenophon (430–355 BC), was clearly acquainted with bits of varying severity. 'Strong' bits, incorporating rollers and spiked mouthpieces, were known to the sixth-century Persians, although it would seem that the Celts of Gaul invented the curb bit in about 300 BC. The 'flying trench', forerunner of the bridoon, or snaffle, of the modern double bridle, did not come onto the equestrian scene until the time of the Renaissance riding masters. In the midst of this progression of forceful restraints it is pleasing to note that the Numidian cavalry, which accompanied Hannibal on his epic march, controlled their horses by a switch applied around the head.

The era that was undoubtedly the most prolific in bit design was the latter part of the nineteenth, and the early years of the twentieth century. Bits of every sort and shape were produced to satisfy the whims of the horseman, and their variety may well have been the cause of the comment made by Benjamin Latchford, the leading loriner (bridle-bit, stirrup and spur maker) of the time. In his treatise on bitting, *The Loriner*, published in 1880, Latchford wrote '. . . the horse's mouth and temper may be compared with a lock, so made that only one key will fit it . . .'. A little later in his foreword he makes this somewhat wry statement, ' . . . out of every twenty bits I make, nineteen are for men's heads and not more than one really for the horse's head'.

Fortunately, as far as the horse is concerned, modern equestrian thought encourages the use of the simplest of bitting arrangements and rejects the purely mechanical bitting approach in favour of the more humane and effective philosophy of 'legs before hands'.

None the less, whatever the period studied, it is true to say that every bit or bitting arrangement ever conceived belongs to one of five principal groups. These are: the snaffles, in endless permutations: the Weymouth or double

bridle; the Pelham; the gag; and that group which achieves its effects without recourse to the mouth, which may conveniently be labelled as 'the bitless bridle family'.

The snaffle, which may have numerous sub-divisions – for instance: jointed and mullen (half-moon) mouthpiece, eggbutt, T-cheek, or loose ring – is the simplest form of control available to the horseman. The action of the snaffle depends upon the degree of training of the horse and the corresponding head position. In the young horse, usually carrying its head low, the action is upwards against the corners of the lips; in the trained horse, with a higher head carriage, the action is across the lower jaw on the bars of the mouth (the area of gum between the molars and incisors). Conversely, the double bridle, employing both curb bit and bridoon, is the most sophisticated of the methods of control and allows a finesse in the placement of the head that is denied in other forms of bitting.

The bridoon, acting more upon the corners of the lips than otherwise in this arrangement, acts to raise the head. The curb and its curb chain, when held at an angle of 45° or more by the rein pressure, exerts a variety of more complex pressures. The mouthpiece, usually made with a tongue port to accommodate that organ and thus ensure that its bearing surfaces are in direct contact with the bars, acts downwards and to the rear. The curb chain, tightening in the curb groove, assists the action and also the relaxation of the lower jaw. The eye of the bit, to which are attached the cheekpieces of the bridle, produces a downward pressure on the poll (transmitted through the headpiece) when the eye is moved forwards, and consequently downwards, in response to rein pressure.

The Pelham bit, to all intents a curb to which has been added an additional rein loop to accommodate a bridoon rein, is the compromise bit, and like most compromises is an indefinite sort of arrangement. The bit can be made with a ported mouthpiece (Hartwell mouth), so that the bearing surfaces rest on the bars of the mouth, but more usually Pelhams are fitted with plain mullen mouths. The action of such mouthpieces is upon the tongue rather than the bars and is therefore less direct and, in the main, less effective. In theory, the curb action is brought into play by the use of the appropriate rein, and the snaffle action is produced similarly. In practice the curb action *tends* to predominate when the curb rein is carried outside the little finger, and the snaffle action when the opposite applies.

None the less, the very lack of definite action can be advantageous with some horses, and the bit is certainly useful for the short-jawed cob types whose mouths are unsuitably shaped to take the bit and bridoon of a double bridle. On the other hand, the Pelham is only rarely suitable for the Thoroughbred type of horse, the jaw formation of which tends to be long and fairly narrow. In these cases if the Pelham mouthpiece is fitted correctly, i.e. sufficiently high in the mouth, the curb chain will rest above the curb groove on the unprotected jaw bones, where it will, of course, cause chafing and considerable discomfort.

Occasionally Pelhams are worn with a single rein fastened to a leather rounding joining the curb and bridoon rings. There is then even less possibility of direct action being achieved, and it would be more sensible to use the Spanish type jumping bit, known also as the Kimblewick, which is, in fact, a member of the Pelham family.

The variety of gag bridles is very great, but all are associated with the restraint of an impetuous horse, or with the need to raise the head, or with both. The action of the gag is an accentuated upward one against the corners of the mouth, made possible by the rounded cheekpiece passing through holes in the centre of the bit ring and either being attached to, or continuing as, a rein to the hand.

In theory it could be argued that the gag exerts an opposite pressure of equal intensity on the poll, which would act to cancel out the upward pressure exerted by the bit. In practice, however, the gag may be taken to be an instrument by which the head can be raised, although it is difficult to justify the frequently

seen combination of standing martingale and gag bit.

Borrowed from the Western culture, or more correctly from the Spanish, is the bitless bridle, often called a hackamore, the name being a corruption of the Spanish word *jacema*. The action, which can be very severe, is upon the nose, and at the present time the device is popular with show jumpers.

Western bridles reflect the old horse culture of the Iberian Peninsular, and the mouthing of the Western horse, through the progression of bosal (a noseband weighted at the rear) to the ultimate spade bit operated by little more than the weight of the rein held in one hand, is a matter calling for an extremely skilled horseman.

Numerous items, which can be termed auxiliary aids to the bit, are used either to strengthen the action or to ensure its correctness. There are, for instance, nosebands of various designs, the most common being the ubiquitous drop noseband. This device fitted with the nosepiece some three inches above the nostrils and the rear strap secured beneath the bit effects a closure of the mouth and gives an extra degree of control to the rider. The closed mouth prevents any evasion of the bit and ensures its central action whilst the nosepiece, tightening on the nose in response to rein pressure, causes a slight interruption in the breathing which checks the horse and encourages him to drop his nose to an acceptable and more controllable level.

The most common martingales are the standing and the running types. The former, a single strap from the girth to the rear of a cavesson noseband, prevents any undue raising of the head. The running variety achieves the same result but, since the reins pass through the rings set at the end of the two branches, pressure is applied directly to the mouth. In both instances it used to be considered correct to adjust the martingales to a length corresponding with the height of the wither, but modern riders usually adjust considerably shorter in order to increase control.

Another martingale, no longer so fashionable as it was, is the 'Market Harborough', sometimes known as the 'German rein', and in Germany as the 'English rein'! The action, brought about only by the untoward raising of the horse's head, is, in fact, very much less severe than might be imagined. In rather a different class are the French schooling martingales, the rein Colbert, the Chambon and the logical extension of the latter, the Gogue. The last two, in particular, seek to improve the carriage by inducing a rounding of the outline, through a lowered head and actively engaged hocks (see p. 316).

In almost every country there will be devices of this type, some of which may be peculiar to a certain area or even to a particular individual. Design of various pieces of equipment may also vary from one country to another.

Among our illustrations of ingenious pieces of equipment we have included the Barnum, which is a most effective method of restraint when dealing with a fractious horse; a girth extension, which is used to bring into service a short girth on an over-fat horse; and a method of long-reining a horse in the French manner.

Fitting saddles and bridles

The basic principle concerned with the fitting of saddles to the backs of horses is that of one saddle to one horse. There is really no reason at all why a saddle should be expected to fit a variety of horses, any more than one would expect a pair of shoes to be a universal fit. In practice, however, saddles, like off-the-peg clothes, will fit horses of more or less the same conformation, more or less satisfactorily.

Ideally, the saddle should be made for the individual horse and rider, but where this is impractical, as it so often will be, then certain simple rules of fitting must be observed. In brief these are as follows:

1. The saddle tree must fit the back. If this is the case it follows that a properly made panel, built on the foundation of that tree, will follow suit.

If the tree is too narrow the points will pinch below the wither; if too broad the front arch will press directly on the wither. In either case soreness of the back will result.

2. The completed saddle must afford complete clearance of the wither and the backbone, both along the length and across the width of the latter. Any pressure on either of these areas inhibits the freedom of movement significantly.

3. The panel has to bear evenly upon the back in its entirety, so that the weight of the rider is distributed evenly over the whole of the area afforded by the panel's bearing surface. This entails the stuffing being absolutely even, so that the saddle rests level on the back.

4. The saddle, whilst conforming to the above rules, must fit as closely as possible. A saddle stuffed so that it is raised high off the back has a tendency to shift from side to side, and such friction between the panel and the back will cause galling.

5. The bearing surface must be resilient and free from any irregularity which might form a pressure point.

Additionally, a horse's back must be in hard condition before being subjected to anything but short periods of pressure from the saddle – non-compliance with this is the cause of the majority of sore backs.

The importance of a correctly fitting saddle of good design cannot be overemphasized since it contributes materially to the performance of both horse and rider.

A saddle that is uncomfortable for the horse will discourage his free movement, often causing the back to be hollowed and to stiffen. Similarly, a saddle that by its construction prevents the rider from positioning his body correctly in relationship to the movement, or is made so as to detract from his security, will have an adverse effect upon the overall performance of horse and rider.

The correct fitting of bridles is as important as the correct fitting of saddles. A badly fitting bridle, causing discomfort to the horse, detracts from his performance in the same way as a saddle that pinches the withers or otherwise restricts the movement of the back.

The adjustment and size of the bit is of paramount importance. The general rule is that the mouthpiece should project about $\frac{1}{2}$ in. each side of the mouth and should be adjusted in the case of a single mouthpiece, or the bridoon of a double bridle, sufficiently high to just wrinkle the corners of the lips. The curb bit of a double bridle should lie beneath the bridoon resting on the area of gum separating the incisor and molar teeth, i.e. the bars.

There is a further difficulty with a curb or Pelham bit connected with the 'eye' of the cheek, through which the cheekpiece of the bridle is passed. In most cases the part of the cheek above the mouthpiece, which includes the eye, is manufactured so as to form a vertical line with the mouth. In consequence the 'eyes' exert considerable pressure on the area of the jaw with which they come in contact. Indeed, it is quite possible for the teeth, and even the upper jaw, to become deformed as a result. The problem can be overcome by bending the eye outwards, an operation easily accomplished with the help of a vice.

For the rest of the bridle attention should be given to the following:

1.   The browband must be sufficiently large so as not to pull the headpiece up against the back of the ears, thus causing irritation and, very often, persistent head-tossing.
2.   The throatlatch should be fastened so as to allow the insertion of three fingers between it and the throat. A tight throatlatch is restricting and prevents proper flexion from the poll.
3.   Where a cavesson noseband is used it should be possible to insert two fingers between it and the jawbones. Drop nosebands should be adjusted so that the nosepiece lies about 3 in. above the nostrils so that the breathing cannot be restricted unduly. The rear strap of the drop noseband must be sufficiently long to allow it to rest in the curb groove and comfortably under the bit.

Obviously the cheekpiece should be checked to ensure equal adjustment on each side of the bridle.

Old Saddlery

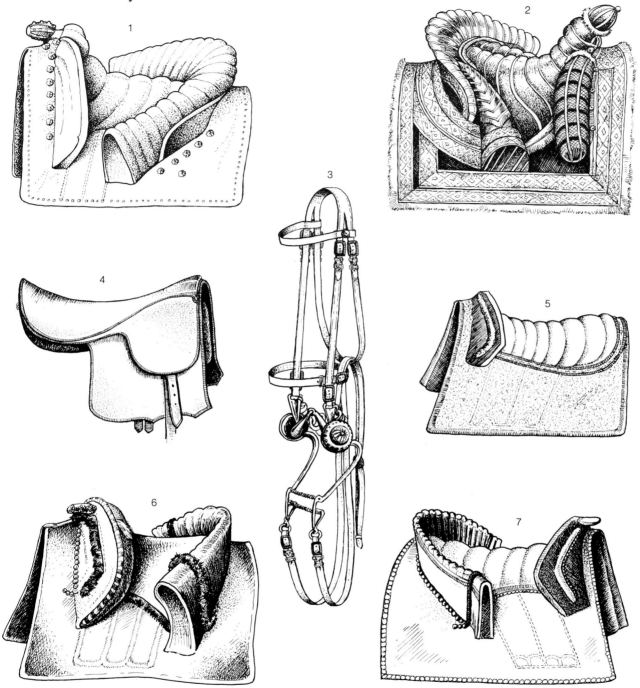

Some examples of early saddlery (seventeenth and eighteenth centuries):

1 A Newcastle saddle
2 A selle *à la Pluvinel*
3 An eighteenth-century bridle depicted in La Guérinière's *École de Cavalerie*

4 A selle *Angloise* from *École de Cavalerie*
5 A selle *Rase* from *École de Cavalerie*
6 *and* 7 Selles *à Picquer*

The Modern Saddle

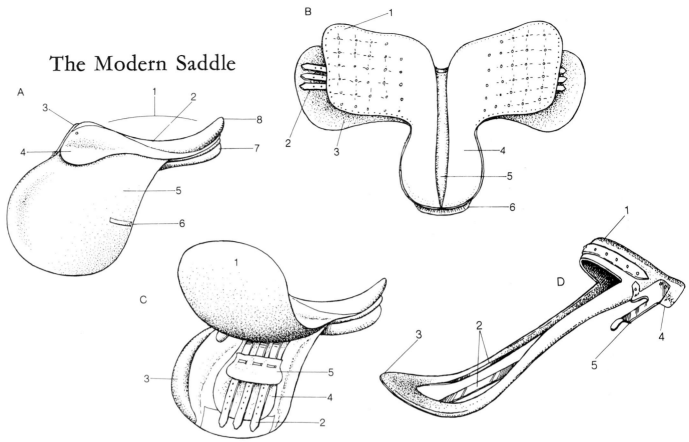

The parts of the saddle

A 1 Seat; 2 Twist; 3 Pommel; 4 Skirt; 5 Saddle flap;
6 Loop; 7 Panel; 8 Cantle
B 1 Sweat flap; 2 Girth straps or tabs; 3 Saddle flap;
4 Panel; 5 Channel; 6 Cantle
C 1 Saddle flap; 2 Girth straps or tabs; 3 Forward
roll; 4 Sweat flap; 5 Buckle guard
D The tree: 1 Head; 2 Springs; 3 Cantle; 4 Point;
5 Bars

Types of saddle

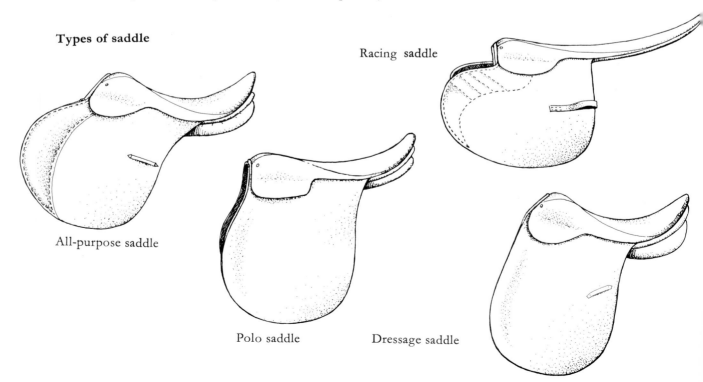

All-purpose saddle

Polo saddle

Dressage saddle

Racing saddle

The Bridle

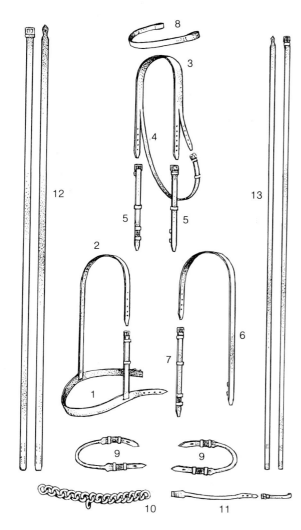

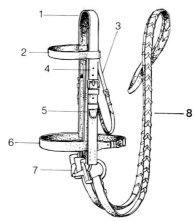

The Bridle

1 Headpiece; 2 Browband;
3 Throatlatch; 4 Cheekpieces; 5 Noseband cheek;
6 Plain noseband; 7 Dee cheek snaffle; 8 Laced reins

Nosebands

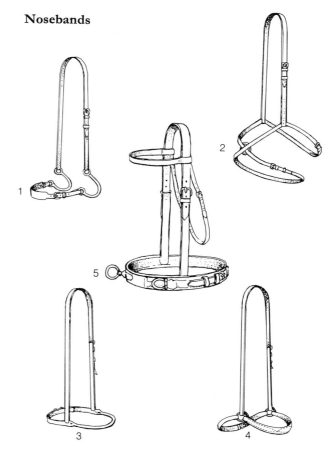

The parts of the bridle

1 Noseband; 2 Headstrap; 3 Headpiece; 4 Throatlatch
5 Cheekpieces; 6 Bridoon sliphead; 7 Bridoon
cheekpiece; 8 Browband; 9 Pelham roundings;
10 Curb chain with fly link for lip strap; 11 Lip strap;
12 Snaffle or bridoon reins; 13 Curb reins

1 Kineton noseband; 2 Grakle noseband; 3 Rounded
drop noseband; 4 Drop noseband; 5 Lunge cavesson

Martingales and Breast-plates

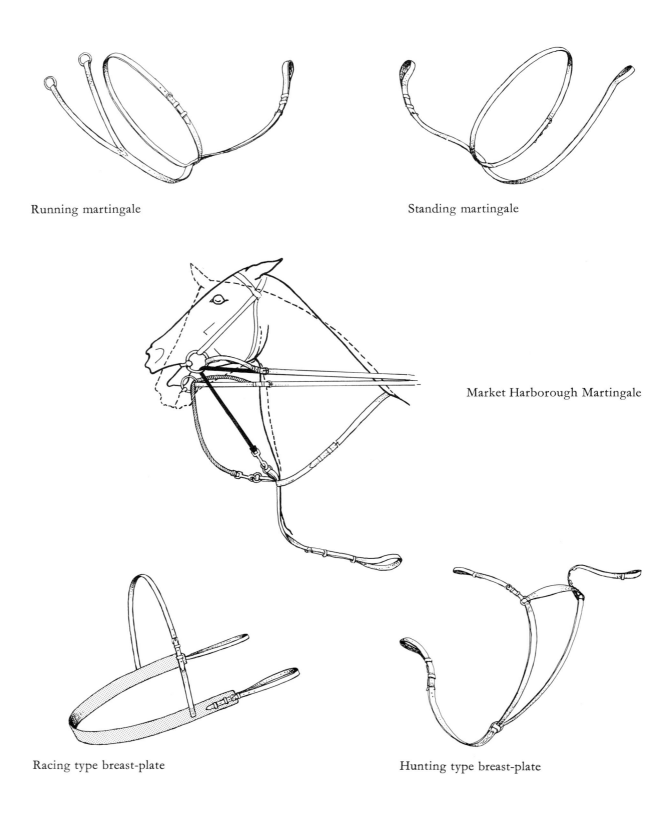

Running martingale

Standing martingale

Market Harborough Martingale

Racing type breast-plate

Hunting type breast-plate

Bits

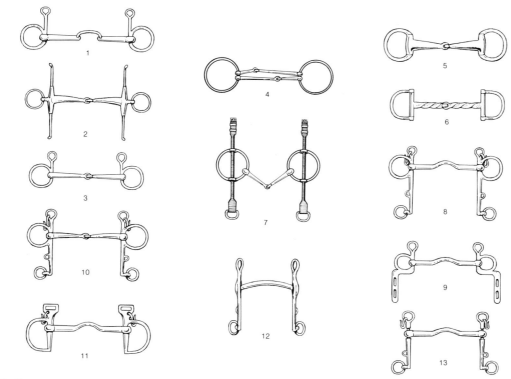

Snaffle, Pelham and curb bits

1 Fillis bridoon; 2 Australian loose ring cheek snaffle;
3 Baucher snaffle; 4 Y-mouth snaffle; 5 Eggbutt
German mouth snaffle; 6 Dee cheek twisted race
snaffle; 7 Balding gag; 8 Hartwell Pelham; 9 Angle
cheek Pelham; 10 Jointed Pelham; 11 Kimblewick;
12 Fixed cheek arch mouth curb; 13 Slide cheek
Weymouth with port

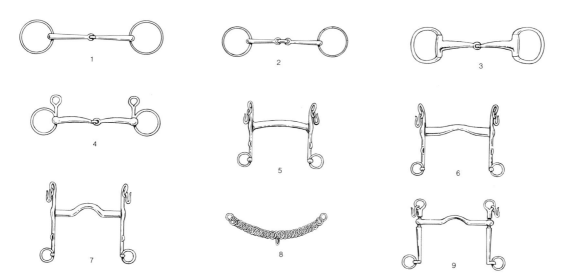

Bridoons and curb bits authorized by the FEI

1 Ordinary bridoon; 2 French bridoon;
3 Bridoon with eggbutt ring; 4 Baucher bridoon;
5 Fixed cheek arch mouth curb; 6 Curb bit with
incurved upper cheeks; 7 Curb bit with port; 8 Curb
chain; 9 Slide cheek Weymouth bit

Clothing and Fittings

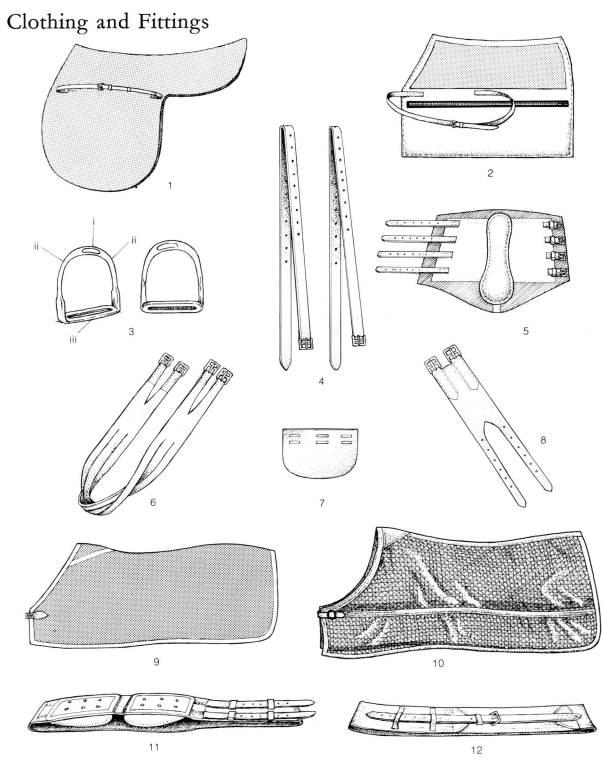

1 Numnah; 2 Weight cloth
3 Stirrup irons (Kournakoff or offset) (i) Eye;
(ii) Sides; (iii) Tread
4 Stirrup leathers; 5 Brushing boot; 6 Balding

girth; 7 Buckle guard or girth safe; 8 Girth
extension; 9 Woollen rug; 10 Anti-sweat rug;
11 Roller; 12 Surcingle

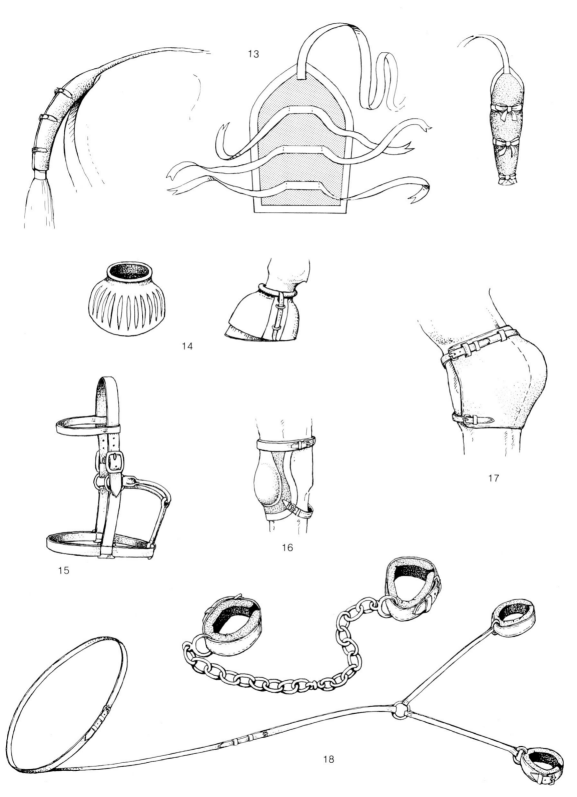

13 Tail guard; 14 Overreach boot; 15 Headcollar; 16 Knee cap; 17 Hock boot; 18 Hobbles

Training Equipment

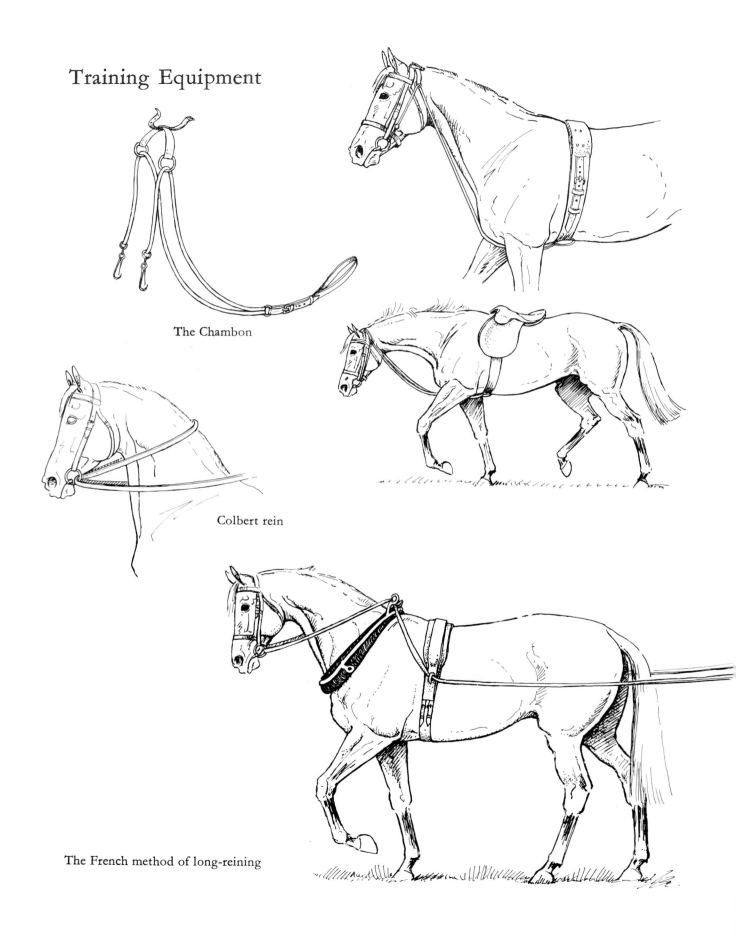

The Chambon

Colbert rein

The French method of long-reining

The Barnum (after the drawings of P. Chambry, *Encyclopédie du Cheval*)

Grooming Tools

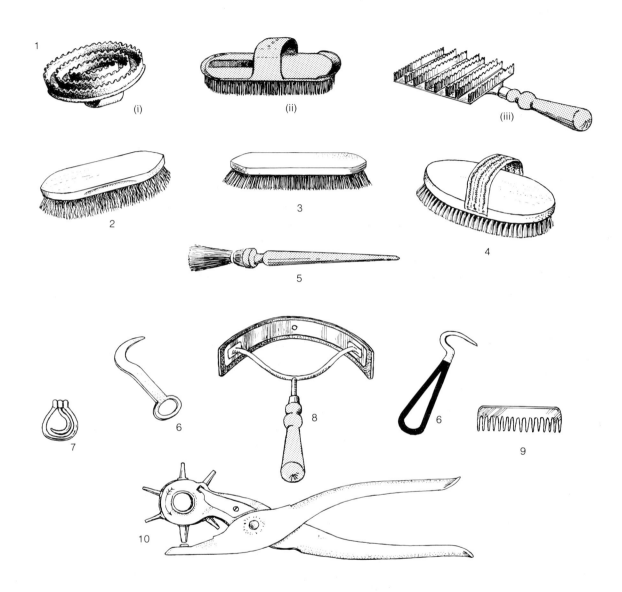

1 Curry combs (i) rubber, (ii) plastic, (iii) metal;
2 Dandy brush; 3 Water brush; 4 Body brush;
5 Hoof oil brush; 6 Hoof picks; 7 Folding hoof pick;
8 Sweat scraper; 9 Mane comb; 10 Revolving leather punch

Riding Horse and Harness Horse

Robert Dumas-Hermès

Saddlery

However far back in prehistory the first domestication of the horse may lie, it is not until the Bronze Age that we have the oldest tangible remains in the form of bits. But we should remember that the more primitive a stage in the horse culture, the greater is the amount of organic matter in the accoutrements. We may postulate, for instance, the existence of snaffles with mouthpieces of twisted rawhide and cheeks of wood or antler; but of these only the last-named material will have survived, and that only under special circumstances.

The saddle in Europe did not begin its most significant evolution until late in the history of the Roman Empire. Indeed, the Western Empire had ceased to exist before the introduction of stirrups, probably in the invasion of the Avars. From Byzantium, always open to Asiatic influence and a steady employer of oriental mercenaries, especially of cavalry, we have the first European pictures of saddles built on a tree, with pommel and cantle; and throughout Christendom, in what the French call the Middle Ages and the English the early Middle Ages, both men and women rode astride on such saddles. The change came in the fourteenth century with the introduction of the side-saddle.

Various types of saddlery arose for different purposes. Thus one can distinguish between saddlery for war, for the tourney, for hunting, and for ordinary travel, in the whole period during which the horse was an inseparable adjunct of human life.

In the sixteenth and seventeenth centuries, with the improvement of breeds, the horse by a sort of anthropomorphism became 'noble' in the sense of well-bred. It was left to the Romantic era, as part of the backwash of eighteenth-century sensibility à la Rousseau, to think of the horse as 'noble' in the ethical sense – the ultimate absurdity which we have not yet outgrown. Equitation became an art and the exercises of the high school (in Shakespeare's English, 'the manage') enjoyed royal patronage. Scientific refinements were applied to saddlery, and gentlemen riders of renown published books on breaking and riding; whole volumes were devoted to the fine points in which the mouthpiece of one bit differed from another – an inexhaustible, ever controversial theme.

Women's saddles, designed originally to afford the same seat on the mid-section of the horse as did the pillion on the hind quarters, were called in French, *sambues*, and had a back rail and a foot board or *planchette*. This model lasted all through the eighteenth century, while some men's saddles were enhanced by rich foot-cloths, housings, holsters and cruppers. It was not until the end of the eighteenth century that the true side-saddle with a pommel to support the right leg appeared. The back rail, by now vestigial, disappeared altogether. The saddle acquired a second pommel and a 'rocking' stirrup to lend security to the left leg. But English influence was already making itself felt and the English saddle (*la selle à l'anglaise*) was widely used, though it never

Late fifteenth-century lady's saddle with foot-board.

displaced the French saddle *à la Royale* for *haute école* purposes.

The nineteenth century firmly established the 'English saddle' for men, the side-saddle for women. The English saddle, since it had no high pommel or cantle, nor bolsters with a vertical wall, permitted rising to the trot which was impossible in the traditional French saddle and proved a revelation to the French.

Not until the twentieth century did French-women begin to ride astride and consequently to adopt the English saddle. It must be acknowledged that, by the angle at which the seat is set, it gives a perfectly balanced position, and we may regret the passing of the side-saddle, which lent inimitable grace and a very firm seat to the horsewoman.

The riding horse is equipped, briefly, with a saddle carrying the stirrups and a bridle with bit or bits; all the rest is merely accessory.

Early side-saddles (seventeenth and eighteenth centuries).

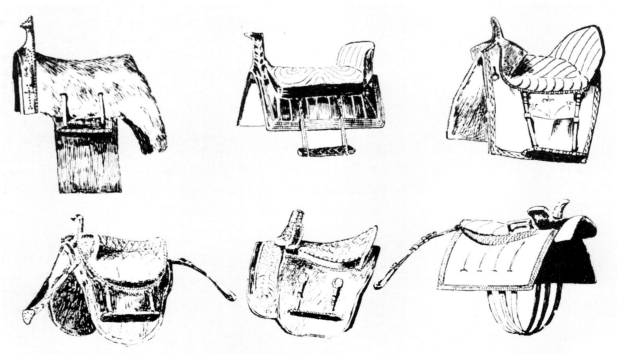

The saddle

The essence of the saddle is its tree which is made of iron-bound wood, lined with canvas and covered with leather. If well-suited to the conformation of the back – the prime requisite – it is the foundation of a well-made saddle. It must be capable of carrying the weight of the rider and the strain on the stirrups, transmitted through the stirrup leathers which are suspended from the bars.

The seat is made of thongs (webs) stretched across the tree, padded with wool and covered in pigskin. It must be comfortable for the rider, but even more so for the horse. The front end is the pommel, the rear end is the cantle, and it is kept on the horse by one or more girths.

In modern military saddles the tree is prolonged by two projections behind the cantle, to which a folded greatcoat or blanket may be secured.

On either side of the saddle are the skirts, covering the bars, and the flaps which prevent the rider's legs rubbing against the horse. These are often bulked out with knee-rolls to give a firmer seat. On the inside of the saddle are the panels, padded, but not so as to fill the entire space between the tree and the horse's back: there should be a tunnel all along the spine allowing passage of air.

We ought finally to mention the racing saddle, known as a pound saddle, perhaps because it can literally weigh as little as a pound, or perhaps because it once had pockets to contain handicapping weights of lead. Its sole function is to hold the stirrups firmly.

The stirrups

No saddle nowadays is without stirrups. At various times and places stirrups have been made of wood, iron, bronze, horn or leather. They have assumed the most diverse shapes. Their base, called floor or tread, might be round or flattened, horizontal or curved, fixed or pivoting, and sometimes slipper-shaped or comprising a cage or grill to protect the toes. Various safety patterns include hinged ones which open to release the foot. Some incorporate spurs, as did some Italian sixteenth-century models, and as do some in use today in Greece. Endless variants have been invented; for instance, one was designed like an old-fashioned laundry iron, and was heated by charcoal put in fresh at every stage. The same object was achieved more simply by hanging a lantern of one candle-power below it, thus at once lighting the way and warming the toes.

Bridles

These comprise a headpiece, two pairs of cheekpieces on which hang curb bit and bridoon, a browband, a noseband, a throatlatch and two pairs of reins. This is the double bridle, as opposed to the more simple snaffle bridle. Like the bit, the bridle has suffered much change over the centuries.

The bit

This is of prime importance. It is kept in place by the cheekpieces of the bridle and attached to the reins and is the chief means by which the rider transmits his signals to the horse. No other accoutrement has undergone so much change over the centuries.

The bit must be suited to the conformation of the horse. A horse may be hard- or soft-mouthed and is said to be well- or ill-bitted according to the bit chosen for it.

Modern bits are comprised of cheeks, mouthpiece, curb chain and its hooks. The cheeks, at right angles to the mouthpiece, act like levers, reinforced by the action of the curb chain.

The snaffle or bridoon is of much greater antiquity than the curb bit, and its design has varied less: in fact, snaffles of the Tène Gallic culture are indistinguishable from those in use now. Used, as it has now been for a long time, in conjunction with the curb bit, the bridoon acts on the corners of the mouth, while the curb bit acts on the bars. The use of both together permits great delicacy of touch, but the snaffle can be used alone for many purposes.

The spurs

This survey would not be complete without mention of the spur which, though not actually worn by the horse but by the rider, gives the rider the means to apply one of the aids with emphasis. Known in Europe since the Celtic Iron Age, spurs were at first of the 'prick' type, like those of a cock, and rowels did not appear until the fourteenth century. These were first placed at the end of a long neck, either straight or cranked, but by now they have been reduced to moderate length. For a long time the spur, as such, enjoyed a prestige hard to account for, apart from being the emblem of chivalry. A certain type of cavalier has always enjoyed making his spurs jangle, and at times the spur has been an essential decorative element in the horseman's costume, civilian or military. There are armies in which, even after total mechanization, the dress regulations decree the wearing of spurs by officers of a certain rank on certain occasions which have nothing remotely to do with equitation.

Accessories

The beautiful 'state' saddle of former times carried a crupper with saddle cloth and housing. More utilitarian versions of this once richly decorated item are still in common use, since they are pleasing to the eye, as well as protective against the horse's sweat. There is also the martingale which serves to control the movements of the horse's head.

Today's whip has a core of fibreglass replacing the former steel core, and the whalebone which preceded that.

Harness

The first coaches did not appear until the early sixteenth century. Previous to that, there had only been travelling carriages which were essentially wagons or chariots. At first, coach harness was very sketchy, consisting mostly of a simple bridle, a breast-collar, a cart saddle, breeching and a pair of traces; but all these items could be sumptuously ornamented.

In the seventeenth century, coaches became much more widespread, and new items were added to the harness, with the invention of blinkers and of the pad which is of lighter construction than the cart saddle. It is kept in place by the belly-band and has behind it a crupper which terminates in a dock piece. From it, the breeching hangs by the loin straps.

At the end of that century, many new vehicles came into use in France, besides coaches both public and private, postchaises, 'berlines coupées', calashes; but the road coach enjoyed even greater prestige. Teams were four- or six-in-hand and the harness was loaded with ornaments, lined with velvet and ringed with gold lace.

New heights were reached in the eighteenth century. The French tried hard to catch up with German, Belgian and English coachmakers who had a technical start on them. Light carriages, such as the phaeton, gig, and so on, made their appearance together with the curricle; and little by little differentiation between types of harness for different vehicles emerged.

In the nineteenth century, a whole new batch of vehicles hatched out: coupés, milords, victorias, tilburys, mail coaches. This was the day of the smart turn-out and fashion began to decree an elaborate code which laid down the precise makeup and style appropriate to every sort of carriage on every occasion. There were light or fancy harnesses for pairs, for four-in-hands, for single horses, for teams driven from

A mail coach.

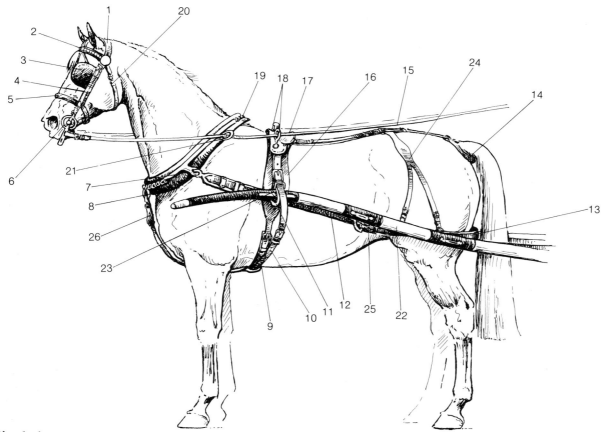

Single harness

1 Headpiece; 2 Browband; 3 Blinkers; 4 Cheekpiece; 5 Noseband; 6 Liverpool bit; 7 Hames; 8 Collar; 9 Girth; 10 Belly-band; 11 Tug; 12 Trace; 13 Breeching; 14 Crupper; 15 Rein; 16 Backband; 17 Pad; 18 Pad terret; 19 Hame strap; 20 Throat latch; 21 Hame terret; 22 Shaft; 23 Tug stop; 24 Loin strap; 25 Breeching strap; 26 False Martingale

the box and those ridden by postilions ('*à la Daumont*'), harness for going to the races, and many more. As a sample, we shall describe four sets, but note at the outset that all harness must fulfil these three requirements: to draw the carriage by means of breast-collar or the collar and traces; to prevent it overrunning by means of breeching and pole chains; to guide it, by means of bridle and reins.

The breast-plate

The breast-collar originated before the collar and is called in Old French *poitrail* and in Middle English *peytrel*, both from Latin *pectoralis* meaning 'worn on the chest'. Consist-

ing of a broad leather band, it is supported by the neck strap and is pushed forward by the breast. Whereas the hame collar is called in French, *à l'anglaise*, it is not an English invention. It appears, once again, to be a legacy of the Viking invasions; but in turn, the Norsemen seem to have taken it over from the Finns who adopted it from the Turkic peoples. In terms of French town harness, the hame collar steadily gained ground over the breast-collar, ultimately displacing it.

The collar

Unknown in European antiquity, the collar was a revolutionary invention multiplying the

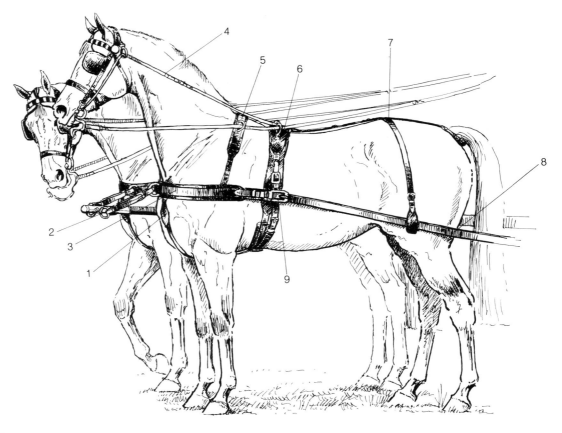

Pair harness

1 False martingale; 2 Pole chain; 3 Breast collar;
4 Bearing rein; 5 Neck strap; 6 Pad; 7 Loin strap;
8 Trace; 9 Trace buckle, joining trace to breast collar

efficiency of the draft horse by two at least, because it is the sole means whereby the drawing power of the shoulders can be exploited. But it is as smart and elegant as it is effective. Stuffed with straw, it has grooves into which the metallic hames fit for attaching the traces. It is also attached to the false martingale which passes down the breast and is fastened to the belly-band.

The traces

The traces join the splinter bar of the carriage to the collar, to draw directly; or else, they are joined to a swingle tree, a steel-bound wooden spar which serves to divide the tractive force equally between the two traces.

Breeching

This is a horizontal strap passing below the point of the buttocks and attached either to the pad or to the shafts. It is held up by a loin strap. It is the means whereby the horse is able to hold up the carriage going downhill, or to back it up.

Pole chains

Properly speaking, these are highly burnished steel links, but sometimes very strong straps. They join the collar to the head of the pole, and they exercise a braking effect on the pole. They are also the means of regulating the distance separating a pair of horses.

Bridles

As for riding, there is a headpiece, two cheek-pieces on which hang bit and/or bridoon, a browband, a noseband, a throatlatch, a curb chain, a lip strap (a little strap passing through the central link of the curb chain to the cheeks of the bit), a pair of blinkers, a pair of reins running through terrets on the hames and on the pad. Harness bits have long cheeks, the most common patterns in France being known as 'Ballon' or 'Wellington'. In England, where only a type of snaffle is called after the Duke of Wellington, the commonest driving bit is the 'Liverpool'. Mouthpieces come in all shapes. The bridoon is used in connection with bearing reins.

Simple bearing reins pass through rings on the collar to the pad. Their effect is to keep the head steady. By contrast, full bearing reins pass through runners (rings) at each side of the headpiece before leading back to the pad. Their action is progressive. The head is not fixed laterally but is forced to be held high. Though much in use in France, they are forbidden by law in some countries and their utility disputed in most, because it hinders the horse in all its movements and is harmful to his balance. It is worth noting that the most widely sold book about horses of all time, running to millions of copies and translated into scores of languages, was Anna Sewell's *Black Beauty* (1878), and the chief humanitarian plank in its platform was a polemic against the use of the bearing rein, then much used in England, especially by the richer classes.

The reins

These are most often of yellow leather. They run through the rings on the collar and the terret, there being two reins to each horse.

Harness pads and light pads

These are the central fixed point from which all other items of harness radiate. Depending on whether a single horse or two or four are driven, the pad is more or less light. At any rate, they either have terrets for the reins to slide through or a bearing rein hook or pillar. The pad is held in place by the belly-band. It is equipped with a strap (back-band) and the tugs. On the lighter model the back-band is replaced by tug hooks which secure at the same time stability of the traces, the collar and the breeching. To the back-strap is attached the crupper with its crupper dock and the loin straps which hold the breeching in place. The back-strap is attached to the back of the pad.

'Post' harness

This style owed its inspiration to the old-time postchaises and consisted of a breast-plate and a pad. It was used for important outings, for going to the meet, and for travelling. The larger turn-outs had pendants for sleigh bells attached to the bridle and were edged with badger skin. When going to the meet, each horse had a fox tail fixed to the bridle. Traces were of black rope, harness fittings and mountings of brass. One, two or four horses could be harnessed in this style.

Harness styles

There is no space here to list all the various styles of harness for one, two, four or five horses in the French, Hungarian, Russian or even American tradition. Our representative sample, of only four styles, must be drawn from the Anglo-French mainstream.

I *Classic single or pair harness.* One horse for very light carriages; one or two for coupés and victorias, according to weight. It consists of a double bridle with full bearing reins; chain-link browband with rosettes, with front-let pendant between the eyes; black patent leather collar and pad, plain back strap, with traces stitched in two or three lines. The owner's monogram in metal will appear on frontlet, pad and back strap.

II *Daumont and half-Daumont.* So called from the Duke d'Aumont, who brought this style back to France after his exile in England, in 1815. The full Daumont turn-out is for four horses. The front two are called leaders. The

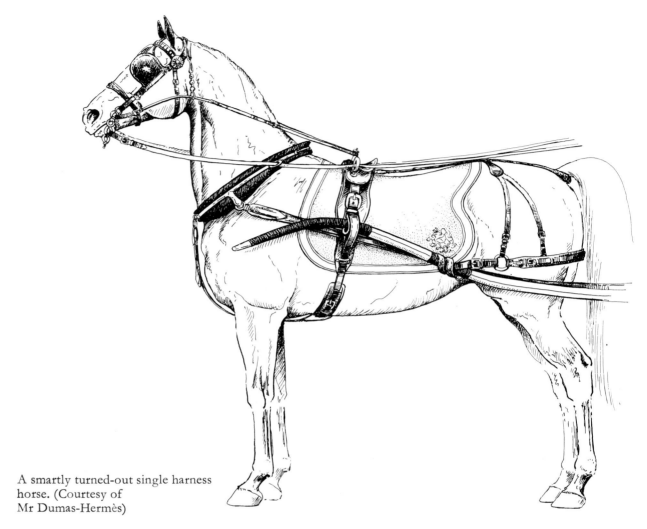

A smartly turned-out single harness
horse. (Courtesy of
Mr Dumas-Hermès)

rear pair (wheelers), like the former, comprise one (near) horse, ridden, and one (off) horse led in hand. Riders on the harnessed horses are termed postilions, and they are preceded by an outrider. There is no box and no coachman. This was the turn-out appropriate to very great houses, to the most distinguished personages using the most superior carriages, eight-springed calashes, landaus, state coaches, and so on.

The ridden horses are saddled, the saddles being of yellow leather, of light weight, with long flaps and yellow stirrup leathers. Each postilion carries a long whip, called a '*fouet de Daumont*'.

Harness on leaders: black patent leather collar, full bearing reins, patent leather blinkers. Near

horses have yellow leather reins, off horses do not have reins but a lead rope of plaited silk over the postilion's right arm, and a light pad in patent leather. There are plain cruppers and back straps on all horses, no breechings. The traces are stitched threefold, in sleeves, and joined to the traces of the wheelers by tug hooks or shackles.

Harness on wheelers: the same as on leaders, amplified by a breeching. The traces are the same, but they are coupled directly to the splinter bar of the fore-carriage. The pole chains are of steel links.

Throughout, there are frontlets and silk rosettes in the owner's colours. Owner's monogram is on blinkers, breast-collar, light pad, back strap and loin straps. The same team, reduced to the two wheelers, is known as a 'Half-Daumont'.

III Four-in-hand.

Less luxurious than the Daumont, this is, nevertheless, very elegant. It originates from England. It has neither outrider nor postilions but a skilled driver on the box, controlling the superbly harnessed horses by the 'ribbons': four pairs leading from his hands through running rings on the headpieces of the wheelers, then through the terrets on the leaders' light pads, then through rings on their collars to their bits.

Only the traces of the leaders are attached to a swingle tree which is coupled to the fore end of the pole, those of the wheelers being directly coupled to the splinter bar. The steel pole chains are attached to the pole. The rest of the harness has the same refinements as the foregoing, the light pads resting on a sumptuous cloth cut to their shape.

Teams so accoutred were particularly suitable for carriages with outside seats, such as mail coaches, road coaches or drags, for large calashes, and for brakes and chars-à-bancs.

IV Tandem.

More suitable for the road than for town work, this is a team of two, one before the other. Up to seven horses can be so harnessed. Its invention has been attributed to an eponymous Lord Tandem, of whom nothing else is known. (If he lived at all, he would have had to do so before 1340, since the Luttrell Psalter, illuminated before that date, shows a tandem of six horses.) We do not have to believe in him, however, since the *Oxford English Dictionary* explains the punning origin of the phrase. Harnessing one before another was once called, in English, 'at length'. The Latin word, *tandem*, means 'finally', for which 'at length' is a synonym. Tandem is a convenient shorthand first coined in the late eighteenth century, and glossed in 1795 as 'a two-wheeled vehicle drawn by two horses harnessed one before the other'. The French for this arrangement is '*en flèche*', although Frenchmen came to take over the English word.

A tandem is hard to drive, very sporting, characteristic of the dashing person, known as 'fast' in Edwardian parlance. The ostentatiously rich eschewed it because it was cheap. Most suitable to the gay but impecunious owner of a light carriage, it had a long run during the nineteenth century, but few drivers at any period were capable of handling it.

Harness is minimal. The traces of the leader (or leaders) are joined to those of the wheeler by tug hooks. Since there are no shafts or

A three-horse tandem.

another horse flanking him, the leader might wander at his own sweet will. So he has to be steady, for on him and on the skill of the whip depends the safety of the whole. The reins pass through the rings of the headpiece to get to the leader who, alone, needs no bearing reins to keep up his head.

The tandem enables the amateur whip, who cannot afford to set up a coach, to savour the delights of the ribbons.

Let us hope this short sketch will enable the reader to enjoy them, too, one day, as part of the flavour of those 'horse-drawn times' now past, but still so close.

The History and Practice of Coaching and Driving in Britain and Ireland

Sanders Watney

Although driving a horse was at one time a necessity for most people in England, it was not until the latter part of the eighteenth century that it came to be regarded as an art. Prior to this, the roads were extremely rough and mostly impassable in winter, and the vehicles were both heavy and clumsily built. Travelling, therefore, was slow and haphazard, and it was not until the road surfaces had been substantially improved that lighter vehicles came into being, speed was increased, and driving became a pleasurable pastime.

The author driving a team of piebalds to the Red Rover (London–Southampton) road coach.

Hyde Park Corner in Regency Days by James Pollard.
(John R. Freeman & Co.)

The fashion for driving reached its height during the Regency period, when members of the nobility vied with each other in the elegance of their vehicles and horses. In this flamboyant atmosphere carriage building flourished, and coach-builders competed against each other by constructing vehicles of exaggerated and extravagant designs – the products of the age being 'high-flyer' phaetons, cocking carts, curricles, and all types of gigs, and these were often used for taking part in road matches of all kinds, which were performed as the result of wagers. Glamorous as some of these races and feats of skill appear, they frequently involved ruthless over-driving and cruelty to the horses concerned which, rightly, would not be tolerated today.

The year 1784 saw the establishment of the mail coach service, which was to become the envy of the world. Fast mail and day coaches,

drawn by teams of four horses, began to travel the length and breadth of Britain, at speeds of up to twelve miles an hour. The coachmen became the heroes of the day, and the art of driving a four-in-hand the ambition of many young men about town, who succeeded in doing so by bribing the professional coachmen into allowing them to 'have a handful' which of course was not allowed for reasons of safety.

Soon after the inauguration of the coaching system in England, a similar service was begun in Ireland, where the roads had always been better maintained. But although a large number of coaches operated from Dublin, it was left to a young Italian emigrant, one Charles Bianconi, to produce a cross-country transport system which linked the coaching routes. This he started in 1815 with one jaunting, or outside, car, and it became so popular that within a few years he had built many more and larger vehicles capable of carrying up to twenty passengers each. Bianconi's cars operated in Ireland for many years, even after the arrival of the railways, since they provided the same service of linking up with them as they had with the coaches.

The invention of railways caused the total collapse of the coaching industry, and between 1830 and 1845, most coaches had disappeared from the roads in England, except in out of the way districts. In the second half of the century, however, there was a revival in the driving world, and coaches driven by sportsmen were put on some of the old coaching roads again. Numerous clubs were also formed at the instigation of such patrons of the art of driving as the Duke of Beaufort. The Four-in-Hand Club, founded in 1856, was followed by the Coaching Club in 1871, and many other driving clubs flourished, including the famous BDC, which had been founded as early as 1807. In towns, superbly matched carriage horses were still of course to be seen drawing all types of coachmen-driven vehicles such as landaus, barouches, broughams, and victorias, while owner-driven phaetons, dog-carts, and gigs of many different designs, were ever increasing in number. Wagers and matches against time were once again the order of the day, but of a less wild nature than in Georgian times.

In 1888, the famous coachman, Jim Selby, made road history by driving the 'Old Times' coach from London to Brighton and back – a distance of 108 miles, in the incredible time of seven hours and fifty minutes; while in 1891 Lord Lonsdale, the well-known sporting peer, drove twenty miles using four vehicles, in under one hour, using the five-mile stretch of the Brighton road between Reigate and Crawley.

In the early 1900s the advent of the motor-car dealt another blow to driving, and replaced the driving of horses for all but a few enthusiasts. Between the two world wars, however, another revival took place, and private driving and coaching classes were well filled at horse shows, and magnificent teams belonging to the late Mr Barron, Mr Claude Goddard, Mr Bertram Mills, and Mr H. J. Colebrook to name a few, will always be remembered.

After World War Two it seemed almost impossible that any enthusiasm for driving

horses would be revived, yet coaching classes were included in shows in 1947, and, from a small beginning, these increased to become a feature at most of the larger shows. The Coaching Club also became active, and is still in existence today with a satisfyingly growing membership, and at its centenary dinner in 1971, sixteen four-in-hand teams were shown.

Similarly, the driving of singles and pairs again became popular, and in 1956 the British Driving Society was formed in order to help people with this interest. From the 100 members enrolled at the start, this has grown to nearly 3000, while in 1973, HRH the Duke of Edinburgh paid the Society the supreme honour of agreeing to become its patron. Through the Society, many people from all walks of life have learned to appreciate the pleasure and relaxation to be found by driving a horse-drawn vehicle.

The art of driving consists of ninety per cent practice and ten per cent 'know-how'. Practice is of little use, however, and in fact can be definitely bad, unless the correct methods are carried out. No amount of study can take the place of personal instruction, and if fortunate enough to be able to learn from an expert 'whip', the beginner should start by watching the coachman's hands. The more experienced a whip is, the more imperceptible will be the movements of his hands and fingers, so that it takes a discerning eye to observe the movements which direct and control the horse, and thereby avoid any mishaps.

The basic principle of the English driving style is that the reins are always held permanently in the left hand, and all movements for directing the horse are made with the right hand. (Only in specialized branches of driving, such as trotting races, should a rein be held in each hand.) The right hand is also used for holding the whip, which should be carried at all times, and held loosely at the point of balance between the thumb and the forefinger. Except on rare occasions, when it might be necessary to punish a horse, the whip should only be used lightly in order to keep the horse

A single horse harnessed to a rallie cart.

up to his work, and applied by drawing it across the horse's shoulder – between the collar and the pad.

Before attempting to drive, the novice coachman should make himself conversant with each part of the harness, and see how it should be fitted, as not only does the horse's comfort depend on this, but the safety factor as well. Before getting up, therefore, the coachman should have a good look round, to make sure that the harness is not only fitted correctly, but also that it is in good condition.

No one should attempt to drive a pair, still less a team or tandem, until he has mastered the art of driving a single horse. As, however, the basic methods apply to all types of driving, it is only necessary to deal in detail with the correct way in which to drive a single.

Having therefore satisfied himself that the harness is correctly fitted, the coachman approaches the off side of the horse in order to

pick up the reins, which should have been temporarily slotted through the off side terret of the pad. These he takes in his *right* hand, by placing the near rein under the forefinger, and the off rein under the third finger. After mounting the vehicle, the reins should be immediately transferred to the *left* hand, with the near rein *over* the forefinger, and the off rein between the second and third fingers. He should then adjust the rug and sit down, keeping his back as straight as possible, his elbows into his side, and with his left forearm in a horizontal position with the wrist flexed inwards. In this position, he picks up the whip and is ready to move off.

The majority of harness horses are trained to walk on when told to do so, accompanied by a slight squeeze on the reins – which should then be relaxed immediately, although contact with the horse's mouth should be maintained at all times. Similarly, trotting is achieved by the voice and more pressure on the reins, although a light touch of the whip may also

Driving a pair.

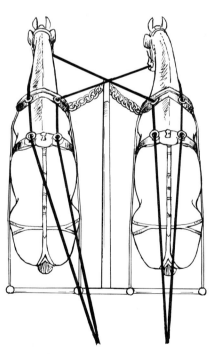

Arrangement of the reins for pair harness

be needed; while stopping requires a steady pull on the reins accompanied by the word 'Whoa'. Inclines to the right or left can be made by twisting the left wrist in the required direction, but if a definite turn is needed, then the right hand can be brought into play: in turning to the right, place the right hand on the off rein (holding it under the little finger) and pull as required. Similarly, when a turn to the left is wanted, take the near rein in the right hand, and draw it to the left.

When wishing to shorten or lengthen the reins, place the right hand the required distance in front of the left, and holding the reins firmly with the near rein under the index finger, and the off rein under the little finger, draw the left hand forward or back. With the right hand in this position, it can also be used to support the left in the case either of pulling up, or with a hard-mouthed horse. (From these directions, it can be seen that difficulties would ensue if the reins were to be split and held one in each hand.)

If it is required to drive on one rein (i.e., when turning) for any length of time, or if the right hand is needed, say, for giving a signal to traffic, then the appropriate rein can be held in position by looping the rein: in turning to the left, the near rein can be looped under the left thumb, or in turning to the right, the off rein can be looped under the left forefinger. When the turn has been completed, the loop should be slowly released.

Although looping, or 'making a point' as it is termed, is not often necessary when driving a pair, or a single, it is essential when driving a team or a tandem, where four reins are held in the left hand.

In driving a team or tandem, the near side *lead* rein is held *over* the forefinger; the off side *lead* rein *under* the forefinger; the near side *wheel* rein *over* the second finger; and the off side *wheel* rein *over* the third finger. Lengthening or shortening any, or all, of the reins is done in a similar manner to single driving, but major turns should be effected by looping the reins.

It is also often necessary to make a counter 'point' – that is to loop the leaders in one direc-

A tandem.

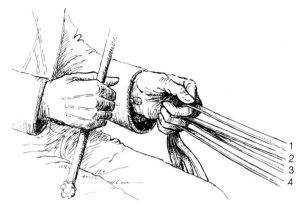

Holding the reins of a four-in-hand

1 Near leader; 2 Off leader; 3 Near wheeler; 4 Off wheeler

tion, and the wheelers in the opposite way. The reason for this is that in turning a corner, the wheelers, when they see the leading horses make the turn, will tend to follow, and if left to themselves will almost certainly cut the corner – causing the vehicle to hit the kerb – with perhaps disastrous results. Therefore, when turning to the right, the leaders should be looped to the right, but the wheelers looped to the *left*. When the leaders have completed the turn, their loop can be released, and the wheelers then looped to the right until they can also be straightened.

Of all forms of driving, tandem is the most difficult, the most dangerous, the most amusing, and the most unnecessary. The leader of a tandem is virtually only for show, and adds little to the pace, or the ease of draught – except perhaps, when going up a hill, or on heavy going, and unless in these circumstances he should be driven in such a way that his traces are loose. This gives the leader complete mobility, and he does not even have the steadying effect of another horse at his side – as in a team. A tandem leader therefore should be chosen for his ability to go forward under any circumstances, as a leader who hangs back is virtually un-drivable. Even so, the driver of a tandem has to anticipate every move, and be quick to correct it. It can, for instance, happen that a leader whips round to look the coachman in the face – an embarrassing as well as dangerous situation, with little remedy since the horse is beyond control by the reins. Unless therefore, help from the ground is at hand, the only procedure is to poke him in the face with the whip which is only sometimes effective!

Be it driving a single, pair, tandem, or team, there is no more pleasant and relaxing occupation. At a speed of 6 to 10 miles an hour, the countryside can be appreciated to the full. The rhythm of movement, the delight in watching the tell-tale signals from the horse's ears, and the feel of a good mouth are all experiences which can never be forgotten.

Driving Around the World

Tom Ryder

Holland

In this fertile land the horse has played an important role for many centuries, and not only in farming, for the Dutch trotters of the seventeenth century had a wide reputation. The style of harness and the manner of driving has followed the German pattern in most of the country, but in the northern province of Friesland there still survives the traditional Friesian chaise, a two-wheeled carriage of a type common in many countries of Western Europe in the eighteenth century. The body, with its ornamental carving and panels painted with classical scenes, is mounted on the carriage part by two longitudinal leather thoroughbraces. The driver sits on the left and there is room for one passenger beside him. The Friesian chaise has a pair of shafts for a single horse, or a pole can be fitted for two or more horses. The harness has a breast-collar with white rope traces and the reins are likewise made of white rope. No breeching is used, probably being thought unnecessary in that flat country. When a pair is used the pole is supported from the horses' saddles by a 'belly bugle', a curved metal stay fixed to the pole at right angles and fastened by straps to each side of the horses' saddles. The black Friesian horses have long manes and tails and are natural trotters with fairly high knee action.

Hungary

In Hungary, as in some other European countries, conditions were not dissimilar to those in

Arrangement of the reins for a multiple team (five-in-hand)

A Hungarian five-in-hand.

North America but the social order was very different. While fast horses and light carriages were wanted, driving was for the most part limited to certain classes, the land owners and military officers, among whom were many superb horsemen. Multiple teams of three, four or five horses driven to light four-wheeled carriages were common.

Hungarian harness is lightly made and decorated with strings of plaited leather and other ornaments of coloured leather and metal. A blinker bridle with straight or jointed double ring snaffle and no bearing rein is usual, as are breast-collars and light saddles with a crupper but no breeching.

The reins are the distinguishing feature of Hungarian harness together with the manner of handling them. The ends of both reins are buckled into a leather hand-piece, called a 'pretzel', and adjusted for length so that when the pretzel is held in the full left hand there is contact with the horses' mouths. The right hand carries a light and flexible drop-throng whip capable of making a resounding crack, and the right hand also assists the left in making turns and stopping. In four- or five-in-hand teams the ends of both wheel and lead reins are buckled together with a 'frog'. Hungarian sporting carriages do not have a high box-seat and the driver sits more or less on a level with his horses.

North America

Driving in North America developed under two prime influences which were, firstly, the long distances to be covered, and secondly, the state of the roads outside the big towns which were mostly of native earth. Even as late as 1915 no more than thirteen per cent of the roads in the United States had any kind of improved surface. These conditions brought about the evolution of a breed of fast trotting horses and the building of light but strong vehicles. In

American stage coach of the early nineteenth century.

colonial times the carriages used and the manner of driving them followed the contemporary European fashion but, by the early years of the ninteenth century, the use of wheeled vehicles for personal transportation had increased and the distinctive style of American driving began to emerge. After about 1850 Americans were talking about 'light' and 'heavy' harness, meaning not merely different kinds of harness but alluding to the complete turnout of harness, carriage and horse as well as the manner of driving: 'light' being the American style and 'heavy' the English.

American light harness should be black, with a single strap with horseshoe buckles which may be brass, gilt-plated or partly covered with hardened rubber. The bridle has square blinkers, and an 'overdraw' bearing rein, or check, consisting of a single rein passing through a loop in the centre of the crown-piece, down the horse's face between the eyes below which it divides to fasten to each side of the bearing rein bridoon. The usual driving bit is a jointed snaffle with half-cheeks. The breast-collar is fairly narrow, has a loop at the centre for a false martingale, and traces that may be round or flat. The saddle has a small housing and open shaft tugs with a 'tie-down' belly-strap. The back-strap has the crupper or dock stitched to it and there is a light breeching. The reins may be flat or round except for the hand-pieces. Pair-horse harness may have light, well-shaped collars and hames, or breast-collars. The pads are narrower than is usual with harness of English pattern and often have trace bearer loops on the side panels in place of trace-buckle tugs.

The overdraw check is used to encourage the horse to extend his neck, as he must, to achieve his best speed.

The reins are held in various ways but most commonly with a rein in each hand, the left rein passing over the index finger and down through the left hand while the right rein passes below the little finger of the right hand and upwards across the palm. Held thus it is quite easy to pass the right rein into the left when necessary. Because fast trotters driven in this way may at times take a firm hold of the bit the use of 'loops' or hand-holds, on the reins is quite common as are other means of preventing the reins from slipping.

The whip used with light harness is a flexible straight whip without a thong.

Tandem and four-in-hand driving for pleasure in North America today follows the European manner. The public stage coaches of former days were driven with the horses loosely coupled and wearing plain snaffles only. The drivers held the reins in two hands with the left reins coming upwards through the left hand and the right reins down through the right hand. A drop thong whip was carried.

The team of a cape cart.

A pair of trotters being driven to an American side-bar speed wagon.

South Africa

It is possible that the cape cart of South Africa is a development of the Friesian chaise. During the nineteenth century this two-wheeled carriage for a pair of horses became a common form of transport for the Boer farmers. The body of the cape cart was made to hold two or more persons and often had a rack behind for carrying goods or produce. The pole is supported by a 'neck-bugle', or yoke, made of some resilient wood, which has a loop of leather or metal at the centre through which the pole is passed. The yoke is hung in front of the horses' breasts by two straps fastened to the centre and passing over the neck of each horse close to the withers to be fastened to the outside ends of the yoke. The harness has light pads to carry the traces, leather traces and breechings. Snaffle bits and blinker bridles are usual. Cape carts were usually equipped with a tilt of white canvas and side curtains to protect the occupants from the strong sun.

A traditional Russian troika.

USSR

As in Hungary, driving was developed in Russia by the landowners who, if they travelled at all in winter, used sleighs to cover the long distances. The troika is the best known of the distinctly Russian teams, and is a word describing the team and the manner of driving rather than any particular conveyance, although the popular notion is of a sleigh speeding across the frozen wastes pursued by a pack of hungry wolves. A troika has three horses harnessed abreast, the centre horse being a trotter of a larger build than the outer two horses which gallop. The trotter is harnessed between a pair of shafts that have a high wooden bow, called a 'douga', connecting them across the horse's withers. The hames of the collar are fastened to this douga by short traces. The galloping horses wear breast collars with traces leading to swingletrees fastened to the carriage at each side of the shafts. The driver sits in the middle of the seat and guides the horses with a pair of reins to the centre horse and a rein each to the gallopers, this rein being fastened to the outer rings of their bits while the inner rings are fastened back to the pad of the centre horse by coupling reins or side-checks. Snaffles and open bridles are used on all three horses, blinker bridles being rarely seen in this country. Troika races take place at the Moscow Hippodrome and, presumably, at other sport centres in the USSR.

A tachanka is a team of four horses harnessed abreast, the centre pair being trotters and the two outer horses gallopers as with a troika.

The droshky is a four-wheeled carriage of a most primitive form, being merely two pairs of wheels and axles joined together by a flat board on which the driver sits straddle-legged. The single horse wears a full collar with hames and the shafts have a douga as does the troika. The reins do not pass through terrets on the pads as with other styles of driving but run at each side of the horse. Light single harness sleighs are harnessed in a similar way and are driven from the seat in the body rather than a small seat behind, as the sleigh of the Low Countries.

Part Eight

Polo

Lt. Col. J. A. Brau

The oldest records of polo are to be found in Persia, Tibet and Mongolia. There are those who say that the game began with the hunting of the musk-rat which took place only in winter. The animal has below its belly a sac containing the musk-glands. The Tibetans noticed that when the rat was tired with running to the point of exhaustion, this musk-gland became swollen and secreted more musk, making it a more valuable prize. During the summer months the hunters simulated a mounted hunt to keep in practice, using a ball covered with stretched yak-skin, called Pulu. Thus the first contests at this game were arranged between tribes. There are different transliterations – Pulu, Palas, Polo – but the last is the most suitable as now hallowed by custom.

Later the pastime spread to India, then carried by the Tartars to Korea, thence to China and Japan. The English brought it home to Europe, whence it spread to the Americas.

Old drawings, illuminations in Persian manuscripts and Chinese watercolours, such as are preserved in the Victoria and Albert Museum and the Bibliothèque Nationale, have stimulated scholars to make research in the literature of oriental countries concerning the origins of the game. Many historians and poets of the greatest antiquity accord it much importance in their writings. The Persian historian, Tabari, who was writing about AD 933, says that Darius the Great, learning that Alexander of Macedon was invading his dominions, sent him a ball and a stick, advising him to take up the game, as more in keeping with his youth and inexperience in war. It is said that Alexander thanked him, saying that in his eyes the ball stood for the world, and that he, Alexander, would wield the stick on it.

Michael Psellas, the Byzantine historian, relates that in the reign of Constantine IX the lords of Constantinople played the game, adopted from Persia. Later, Fazli Allani, Vizier to the Moghul Emperor Akbar, wrote in his *Ain-i-Akbari*, translated into English by Blackman, about the social and political manners and customs of his day. He devoted a special section to polo, in which he explained that the Emperor had a passion for the sport, as it enabled him to test the mettle of his courtiers.

He who watches a game of polo, coming on it by chance and with no knowledge of it, can only make a superficial judgement. But intelligent persons see in it a school in which one may learn rapidity of action and decision, in which manly valour is put to the test. Here horsemen really learn to ride and to become true experts.

In Tabari's day the game might be played by any number of horsemen, provided there were equal numbers each side. But an effort was made to keep the players down to ten a side.

Coming down to more recent times, the first polo club was formed in India in 1854 by Captain Stewart and Lieutenant Sherer of the 44th Bengal Regiment.

General principles

Polo is not only one of the most enthralling games to play, but it is one of the most com-

Play in progress at Cowdray Park. Polo, an Eastern game of ancient origin, was brought to Britain from India.

plete sports; for at one and the same time it brings out in the young horseman a taste for horses and riding ability, energy, a spirit of discipline and an appetite for risks which temper the heart and strengthen the body: *'Mens sana in corpore sano.'*

Polo is the king of sports, for it must be played at the fastest pace of which the horses are capable, and speed in our century is undoubtedly the aristocracy of sport.

Polo develops a taste for horses, in common with all other equestrian sports, of course. The horse is such a fascinating creature because it adds to all the joys of riding across country, over fences, or racing after the ball, the satisfaction and instinctive pride in having mastered, subjected and trained a well-bred animal.

It develops the spirit of discipline because polo is a team sport. So there must be harmony between the players, and with it, for every player, that element of self-denial which alone can bring victory to a team. Individuals, however brilliant, without discipline can only be opposed to each other instead of combining their efforts.

It develops an appetite for risk; by reason of its high speed it is the most dangerous of sports. For if some prudent rules forbid 'cutting-in' and ban certain forms of violence, hard jostling at full gallop, severe impacts, marking and hooking are not outlawed.

Polo is for the young, with its comradeship and social independence. Only at this sport could an ex-*vaquero*, who had become a champion at the game, use the familiar *tu* in addressing the King of Spain; and an ex-employee of the London Savoy Hotel, who had become captain of a team, afford to say to the Queen Mother of England: 'I wish Your Majesty would ask your son-in-law to go to bed earlier, for he is not in form just now.'

If you wield the stick with verve and have some human quality, such as generosity and good humour, you will be welcomed as a friend into this world reckoned so snobbish and aloof, yet which is free from any prejudice and certainly from egoism.

Some think well, some ill, of polo. Among those who know nothing about it, it gets bad marks for extravagance, a rich man's whim. Those who know something about it, as players or spectators, think highly of it. But there is not much critical study. Its public is too small to afford scope for social theorizing about it, in terms of the psychology of sport. When people talk about polo they only mention the scores, the difficulties, the danger and the expense.

The game – its rules

Polo closely resembles Association Football. The rulebook is only a few pages long. All the rules have but one aim: to avoid dangerous play and set such limits as are possible to the risk of accidents.

A player at full speed must not be 'cut out' by an opponent riding across his line; it is forbidden to zigzag in front of an opponent or to jostle him at too obtuse an angle, which might throw the pony off his balance or even bring him down. Hooking is not allowed unless you are on the same side of your opponent's horse as the ball, nor must the stick be passed over the croup, under the neck, or more particularly between his legs. Equipped with this information you may ride on to a polo ground without becoming a public danger. The line of the ball, with which the umpires are constantly preoccupied, is reserved to the player who hit it last, provided always that he keeps riding on a course parallel to that of the ball, which he should take on his off side.

But for the beginner it is not always easy to keep to the rules; carried away by the atmosphere of the game, he can see nothing but that little ball and in his frenzied pursuit is deaf to the yells of his opponent who is hurtling at thirty miles an hour on a line reserved to him, and not being able to stop his horse in time, crashes into him at an angle and sends horse and rider rolling on the grass; from such a fall one or both may not escape unscathed. Happily the most spectacular-looking falls are not always the most damaging, but they are often the result of the rashness or ignorance of an inexperienced player.

The umpire's task is a difficult and delicate one, for the play is fast. The penalties at his disposal can be severe, ranging from a free hit on the spot, to sending off the field a dangerous player or pony. That is why three umpires are required for a big match – two mounted umpires on the field and a referee on the touchline, who has the casting vote when the umpires disagree. When they appeal to him, his decision is final.

To make an interesting game, the sides must be well matched. To this end, the organizers of a tournament fix minimum and maximum handicaps. Every player is graded by his

This may happen when rules are ignored.

National Polo Federation with a personal handicap between 0 and 10. The handicap of a team is the sum of the handicaps of its four members. Nearly all the cups are played for under handicap, and by simple subtraction the number of goals which the weaker team will be allowed is determined. These handicaps are reckoned in terms of six chukkas. Games are divided into a certain number of chukkas each of seven and a half minute's duration, and the players change horses after each: a horse may only play two chukkas in any one game, and there must be a rest period between them, so that each team requires a considerable string of ponies. In every tournament, however, there is always an open cup, played without allowance of goals, and this is usually the high spot of the contest.

The horses

Although horses of any height can be played, they should preferably be 15 to 16 h.h.; that is, real horses able to carry a man hunting or for any other sport, for the expression 'polo pony' which was once literally exact has not been so for a long time. Close to the ground and short-coupled, with a well-set-on neck, well-balanced and handy, the polo pony should also have a calm and generous nature. Fast acceleration and a good turn of speed combined with great handiness should enable the polo pony to bound out from between his rider's legs. Most horses playing in Europe were born in Argentina. They are stocky, handy, durable, imbued with a spirit which makes them accept without reserve, if not with joy, a job which is often arduous. The legend created by Kipling in his charming story, *The Maltese Cat*, is purely a product of imagination; the pony is not playing the game, and, what is more, I do not think he appreciates it. Anyway, a horse playing off his own bat and constantly taking decisions not always identical with those of the rider would make perhaps a nice circus horse but a detestable polo pony.

The question of how much the horse counts is important. A great American player, Milburn Devereux, has said that the horse is a good sixty per cent of any man's game, but not forgetting that the horse does not play by himself, that the rider has to do all the thinking and that if his pony is capable of thought there inevitably will be differences of opinion.

The great polo pony, the dream-horse of us all, would have perfect balance, a light mouth, instant acceleration, efficient brakes, absolute calm, with weight and mass to mark an opponent, and speed to outstrip or escape from him.

Training the horse

Without entering into technical details, I will discuss what exercises and suppling routines will serve to turn a riding horse quite quickly into a good polo pony, provided of course that he has the right temperament and other qualities.

Assuming the horse is accustomed to the bridle, saddle, and the rider's weight, has learned the aids of hand and leg, has a pleasant mouth and is well-balanced at the gallop both on a straight line and on the turn, his trainer must prepare him for his new job by the appropriate exercises. He needs to learn to canter on a loose rein, with his head all but free, in shorter and shorter voltes. The rider accustoms him progressively to rapid changes of gait, halting abruptly and reining back, and then breaking into a gallop. Obedience should be instantly rewarded by making much of him, and all this work done on a loose rein held in the left hand. All changes of direction are done by means of neck-reining, with the hand high, light, though firm and authoritative.

All movements, particularly at the beginning, will be followed by an immediate return to calm, at the walk with long reins.

One suppling exercise which I cannot sufficiently recommend, and which has enabled me to achieve some spectacular results with young horses, consists of working at the canter in a riding hall or open arena, performing reversed half-voltes; the rider canters on the track which he leaves at an angle and, when at some distance from the wall, goes back to the track, on the opposite hand, making a half circle, regardless of which leg the horse is leading with. The half circles then become tighter and tighter, so that by the end of this work they are almost pirouettes. In this excellent suppling exercise, which is, however, hard to do well, the rider must take good care not to let his hands and above all his weight act contrary to the movement of the horse, and he must not impede impulsion after the pirouette when forward movement is resumed.

The horse should be broken to the stick as soon as training begins. He quickly learns to accept it whirling round him, provided of course that the rider takes great care not to hit him by mistake, especially at the outset. He will get the hang of it very quickly, just as his forebears did of whirling sabres and lances in cavalry squadrons.

When the horse is a bit settled, the rider dots a few balls around the practice ground and hits them, not hard at first even with a very calm horse, to right and to left, taking the greatest care not to let the bridle hand moved at the moment of striking. This is very important, otherwise the horse will associate the crack of stick on ball with a more or less violent jab in the mouth.

How to hit the ball

The following advice is derived from a booklet by the great polo player, Cyril R. Harrison.

Since the platform from which the player hits the ball is a galloping horse, any study of the subject must take into account the horse, its stride, and the movements of the player. The concurrence and timing of these different elements are difficult to achieve at the moment of striking. Correct timing involves controlling the horse so as to hit the ball at the exact moment when the horse's feet come to the ground after the phase of suspension. This ensures that the impact of the head of the stick on the ball is at its maximum.

The four basic strokes and their subdivisions
A Off-side forehander
B Off-side backhander
C Near-side forehander
D Near-side backhander
1 Drive; 2 Cut; 3 Pull

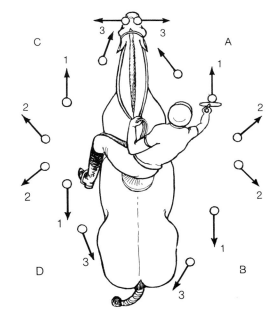

Because the body must twist in making the very best shot, the player has to stand in his stirrups, pivoting on his hips and supply bending towards the ball. Thus, right out of the saddle and leaning 'away from the horse', the player can strike the ball in many different directions. For a shot forward and to the left he pivots on his hips to the point where his shoulders are parallel to the horse. Thus he attacks the ball at right angles and at the beginning of his stroke is across his horse; his left knee pivots toward the right, and thereby his whole body moves with the stick at the moment of impact. In a shot straight ahead, the shoulder should remain back at the beginning of the swing, and when the stick hits the ball, arm and stick should form one straight line.

Length of shot does not depend on the stature or the strength of the player, nor on his weight, nor on the shape of the stick; but on the extent to which the player can combine his strength in action with that of the horse in perfect synchronization with the stride.

Tommy Hitchcock not only provided an example of the correct polo seat, but he was also a model striker of extreme strength and great accuracy. The combination of these factors earned him the reputation of being the best polo player in history.

The 'wooden horse' can be a great asset in helping the rider to acquire the technique and style which make great players. As its name suggests, the 'wooden horse' is like a gymnast's vaulting horse, its height and other proportions resembling as near as possible those of a real horse. It is placed in the middle of a great cage of netting with a bowl-shaped floor.

The wooden horse is saddled and bridled so as to place the rider in the most realistic position possible. Polo balls are thrown into the cage,

The layout of a polo ground

1 The goal; 2 The goal posts – ten feet high and eight yards apart; 3 Thirty yard line; 4 forty yard line; 5 Sixty yard line; 6 Width – 200 yards, grounds without boards; 7 Width – 160 yards, grounds with boards; 8 Length – 300 yards; 9 Limit of safety zone; 10 Side line of ground without boards; 11 Side boards, eleven inches high

and, thanks to the slope of the floor, they will always come back towards the rider at the bottom of the bowl after they are hit. The instructor outside the cage can correct his pupil's position and improve his style.

A polo team consists of four men, disposed in depth:

Number one is a forward, responsible for pressing home the attacks of his team. Off side, level with number four of the opposing side, he must seek to neutralize the latter and to come forward at the last moment to take a pass from one of his team-mates: if a ball comes too far out towards the touch-line, he has to centre it, and he shoots the goal when his team have brought the ball far enough up the field.

Number two is also a forward, his primary role being in the attack. He must be on the offensive but at the same time be prepared to take part in defence.

Number three is the linchpin of the team. It pivots round him as 'half-back', and it is up to him to ensure co-ordination between the forwards and the man behind him.

Number four, back and/or goalkeeper, has to

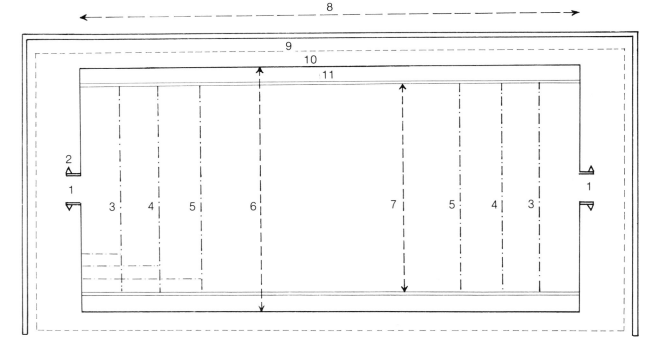

defend the goal and clear the ball with long passes to the forwards. He brings the ball back into play after a shot has gone wide of the goal, right or left.

Most of the time the players should be deployed in depth, *en échelon*. At all times the utmost concentration is necessary, since the game is so fast and of such unrelenting intensity; a single second lost in a single chukka due to a player's wandering attention could have disastrous results for the team. More than any other sport polo demands qualities of physical courage and constant forward-thinking. The player must anticipate not only the reactions of his own team but also, almost before they themselves do, those of his opponents, in order for him to take up the right tactical position from which to spoil the chances of a hostile attack from the outset.

Polo, which in Europe is a minority interest confined to its fanatical devotees, is the national sport of some Latin American countries. There it is not the prerequisite of the moneyed, leisured few who can afford to bear its heavy burden on time and purse. It is played in town and country, and on *haciendas* and *estancias*, when the cowhands have brought in the cattle in the evening, they may play polo.

That is the reason why many of us are wondering today whether, side by side with 'select' polo, it might not be wise to channel the enthusiasm of the thousands who have taken up riding for the love of horses, but who do not aspire to show jumping or dressage, towards a more accessible form of the game. Indoor polo or paddock polo is played three-a-side on less pretentious grounds and with a shorter string of ponies.

Polo at Vitel.

In the world as a whole riding has gained considerable ground since the war. Of the 200 000 people who ride in France, only about 15 000 or 20 000 take part in competition show-jumping, eventing or dressage. The rest, after elementary instruction, are often discouraged by boring hours in the riding school or by the daily hack on bridle paths they come to know by heart.

This 'mini-polo' would offer them a sporting objective quite as attractive as hacking or trek-king. It could become an admirable way of occupying the leisure time of all those who depend on the horse to bring joy into their lives by the practice of some form of mounted sport.

But it is up to us first to convince the riders and then to lobby managers and instructors of riding schools and clubs.

I hardly dare hope that after reading these lines the young rider will dash to get hold of a stick and ball to take a sample of the joys and emotions I promise him. But I beg him to be patient with me, considering that I have attempted to put into these few pages all my enthusiasm for, and all my faith in, a sport that I have loyally practised for forty-five years of my riding life.

The Circus

André Monteilhet

Despite the similarity of name, the ancient circuses offered quite a different spectacle from that of the modern kind which originated in England towards the middle of the eighteenth century. The ancient circus – Western or Eastern Roman – was chiefly a racecourse, inherited from Greece, where chariot, and sometimes ridden, races were held (such as the Circus Maximus rebuilt by Caesar for 150000 spectators), or an amphitheatre, the most famous being the Roman Colosseum, where the violent, yea bloody, programmes (fights between wild beasts, man against beast, gladiators, condemned men thrown to lions or crocodiles, etc.) were prohibited by the Christian emperors at the end of the fourth century AD. Acrobats and tightrope walkers continued to perform there, and chariot races continued to be run till the reigns of the Gothic kings (the last Games were held in 550 AD). Vaulting was practised there by men (*desultores*) or young women (*desultrices*), a tradition dating back to the 'Cavaliers of the Campagna', products of the conjunction, in the Neopolitan region, of the Etruscan aristocrats, issuing from Tuscany or Rome (the 'Tarquins') in the sixth century BC, and Greek colonists who were among the best horsemen of Hellas: the *hippobotoï* of Chalcis and Eritrea in Euboea. The *desultores* of the campagna, originally cavalrymen from areas such as Capua, Cumae and Neapolis, were swept along in Hannibal's defeat but subsisted as civilian circus riders.

Aside from the spectacular races which were held in Byzantine Constantinople, with their armed battles between 'Greens' and 'Blues' (which went so far as to massacre an emperor on the track), countless amphitheatres, some huge and some more modest, were built in every part of the Roman provinces, from Antioch or Alexandria to El Djem, from Syracuse, Arles or Nîmes to Lutetia and King Arthur's Welsh Caerleon. All of this disappeared from the West, at the latest, by the sixth century in the whirlwinds of Germanic, Arab or Scandinavian invasions.

The western Middle Ages knew only the jugglers, acrobats and exhibitors of animals, mostly paupers making a miserable living wandering from town to town, from castle to castle, humbled and often persecuted, as was the unfortunate Morio, burnt alive with his learned pony at Arles because the good people saw nothing but devilry in their feats.

Only by the end of the sixteenth century, when the Italian Renaissance spirit had gained the rest of Christendom, did one begin to see a few small wandering circuses, *romanis*, more or less mountebanks, such as the dynasty of the Chiarinis. They were 'travelling folk', who came from Italy to France when Henri IV had appeased the torments of the Wars of Religion. We shall find them again in the eighteenth century.

The modern circus

The modern circus made its appearance in the eighteenth century both in the England of George III, and also at the Hetz Theater in

Mary Chipperfield and her Lipizzaner horses.

Vienna, founded by the Frenchman Defraine, who offered such attractions as venery, animal fights, and brilliant horse parades accompanied by the sounding of flourishes .... Subsequently, the Colisée appeared in Paris and the Vauxhall in London, part circus, part ballroom, copied not only in Great Britain but on the Continent. In 1760, trick riding was practised at the Three Hats by Price and his modern *desultores*. Jacob Bates and Johnson showed at the same period, both as acrobatic and school riders, presenting for example, horses in tandem. This was when Astley came on to the scene.

Philip Astley (1742–1814), son of a cabinet maker from Newcastle-under-Lyme, enrolled at the age of seventeen in the 15th Regiment of Dragoons, taking part in Germany in the last campaigns of the Seven Years' War. He came back as quartermaster-sergeant, returned to civilian life in 1764, and met Johnson at Islington who showed him how easy (and spectacular) it was to stand on a horse cantering on a circle of a certain radius. Astley perfected his technique in London (1765), working with Sampson and Price. The following year, he married a young professional equestrienne and, with her, inaugurated in 1767 his first show at the Halfpenny Hatch at Lambeth. Businessman as well as trick rider, he created in 1769, on Westminster Bridge Road, under the name of Royal Grove, the first modern circus; its gates opened in 1770, and it was not to be demolished until 1893. The actual name of 'circus' appeared only in 1782, with the Royal Circus of Charles Hughes, ex-equestrian at Astley's and now his competitor. Astley was honoured with a visit of George III. In 1772, he performed in front of Louis XV and the Countess du Barry at Fontainebleau. In 1774, he published in London *The Modern Riding Master*, based on his personal experience. In 1780, he inaugurated the first covered circus and, in 1784, once more tasted success on the Continent: in the Holy Roman Empire and at the Great Stables (Grandes Écuries) at Versailles, this time in front of Louis XVI and Marie Antoinette, both great connoisseurs in matters equestrian. They applauded John Astley (1768–1821) whom the ladies at court nicknamed, 'The Rose of England'. At the same time, Philip Astley created in Paris, in the Faubourg du Temple, his Amphithéâtre Anglais, without abandoning the Royal Grove and fourteen other circuses in England and even one at Dublin.

At that time, Antonio Franconi (1738–1836), who was born at Udine and had had to leave Venice as a result of a duel, after making a living at Lyons as a bird exhibitor, was working at the Amphithéâtre Anglais leased from Philip Astley. The latter had gone to Paris at the time of the Peace of Amiens in 1802, after having taken up service again with his cherished 15th Regiment of Dragoons from 1793 to 1795, 'somewhere in Flanders'. He died on 26 October 1814 in his Paris dwelling close to the Amphithéâtre. His son, John, succeeded him. At the time the modern circus was firmly implanted both in Europe and in the United States where John W. Ricketts had started a first show in Philadelphia in 1793.

From the nineteenth century on, the overlordship of the English circus gave way to that of France and Germany.

The Franconis are a fine example of those dynasties of professional equestrians which in the nineteenth and twentieth centuries constituted the glory of the circus the world over. Laurent Franconi (1776–1849) and his brother, Henri (1779–1849), Antonio's sons, operated

At Drury Lane Theatre, 1853, Mlle Ella leaping over a flag nine feet wide. Mlle Ella was born of French parents in Louisiana, USA. In the foreground is Barry, the famous clown, who also played at Astley's Theatre.

the Cirque Olympique from 1808 to 1826, when it burned down. It was rebuilt and, in 1835, the Franconi brothers went into association with Jules-Charles Pellier and François Baucher (1796–1873) to create in Paris, on the Carré Marigny, the magnificent Cirque des Champs-Elysées. It was a stone construction (1840) and its name still echoes in the rue du Cirque, commemorated by a tablet affixed in 1975 on the wall of the present Théâtre Marigny. It was there that Baucher knew the most sparkling glory, the attendance being headed by the Tout-Paris, Jockey Club and Duc d'Orléans. Victor Franconi (1811–97), Laurent's son, managed the Cirque d'Hiver and the Cirque d'Été, where he taught and produced, among others, the Anglo-American equestrienne Adelina Price and the ill-starred Emilie Loisset who died in 1882, gutted by the pommel of her saddle under her overturned horse in an accident in the ring. Victor Franconi, all-round horseman (including steeplechase rider) has left behind a valuable book: *Le Cavalier et l'Écuyer* (Paris 1891). In 1907, his son Charles gave up the Cirque d'Hiver which was taken up by Desprez in 1923 and by the Bouglione brothers in 1934.

Another dynasty was the Chiarinis. In 1784, Angélique Chiarini was one of Astley's, then Franconi's, equestriennes. In 1847, Giuseppe Chiarini established a circus which toured the world, ending up in Brazil as personal equerry to the Emperor Dom Pedro.

In France, after Baucher's horrific accident in 1855 (though he continued to teach till 1870, he no longer performed in public), Louis Dejean, who bought the Cirque Olympique in 1835 from the Franconis, operated the Cirque des Champs-Elysées till 1870, the time of the Siege of Paris. The building was to be demolished in 1898. In 1875, he added the Cirque d'Hiver. His ringmaster was the famous Théodore Loyal who left his name, 'Monsieur Loyal', to his technical successors. The Nouveau Cirque of the rue Saint-Honoré was opened in 1886 by Joseph Oller and was demolished in 1926. In 1928, Jérôme Medrano bought out the old Cirque Fernando.

Le Salut by Toulouse-Lautrec.

Théodore Rancy (1818–92), a 'circus brat', but one of Baucher's pupils and married to Olive Loyal, opened his own circus at Rouen in 1856 and was applauded in Suez at the inauguration of the Canal in 1869. His sons, Alphonse and Napoléon (the latter dying in 1933), and his grandson Albert, operated the Nouveau Cirque des Champs-Elysées till its closure by the Occupation Forces in 1943. Finally, we must mention the unique example of Ernest Molier (1848–1934), nicknamed, 'the gentleman circus rider', since he was an amateur, as were all the members of high society who participated, from 1880 to 1914, in the festivities at his *manège* on the rue Bénouville, near the Bois de Boulogne. The grandest names of the Parisian Gotha exhibited themselves on horseback there, in the most difficult exercises, knee to knee with the theatrical and vaulting stars of the age. Molier eventually married, in 1914, the brilliant equestrian trapeze artist, Blanche Allarty. They continied to work together in *haute école* from 1919 till Molier's death; Blanche herself died only in 1967.

The grand age of the modern German circus began in the mid-nineteenth century. Yet, the

Spaniard Juan Porte (1740–1810), equerry to the Empress Maria Thérèse, had created in 1780, on the Mehlmarkt in Vienna, a circus where the English equestrian Hyam (d. 1845) was shining. In 1808, Christoph von Bach founded at the Prater the Circus Gymnasticus. Eventually, Brilloff, who opened a circus in 1825 and worked chiefly in Prussia, had the distinction of training the founder of a circus rider dynasty: Ernst Renz. Brilloff also trained the incomparable Charles-Magnus Hinné (d. 1890) who, in 1853, opened a circus at Königsberg which triumphed in Scandinavia, Moscow, St Petersburg, and in Warsaw where it burned down in 1859. In 1875, he gave up his circus to his brother-in-law, Gaetano Ciniselli.

The Renzs were for Germany what Astley was for England and the Franconis for France. Ernst Renz (1815–92), totally illiterate, succeeded in 1842 his master Brilloff who was killed by a kick from a horse. Renz found fame and fortune in Munich during the early 'reign' of Lola Montez, then triumphed in Berlin from 1860 on. His son, Franz, succeeded him till 1898. He was a rival to James Fillis in *haute école* training. His sister, Thérèse Renz, was honoured with the friendship of the Empress Elizabeth of Austria who was not

Liberty horses in a Russian circus. The circus is extremely popular in the Soviet Union and every major town has a 'big top'.

only 'the Queen of the Chase' in Ireland and at Gödölö but also able to train to *haute école* level, as she did with her Lipizzaner Maestoso, the greys Flick and Flock and the Thoroughbred Avolo. The sovereign also held in high esteem the equestrian Oscar Carré (d. 1911) whose father, Wilhelm Carré (1817–73), had founded, in 1865, the Royal Netherlands Circus. The German circus won honours through many other great names known all over Europe and America: Krone, Hagenbeck and, above all, the Knie dynasty whose founder, Friedrich Knie (1784–1850), made his début in 1806 and whose descendants shed their brilliant light on four generations.

In North America, after Bill Ricketts's circus (see above), there came around 1850 'Dr' Gilbert Spaulding's (1811–80) Floating Palace whose showboat was the stage of, let us say, spectacular spectacles. It was in the United States that circuses were first transported by rail, long before it became the custom in Europe.

But the greatest name of the American and even world circus is indubitably that of Barnum. In 1841, a native of Connecticut, Phineas T. Barnum (1810–91), who had begun by exhibiting an old Negress, allegedly George Washington's former wet nurse, had bought the Scudder's American Museum which he renamed Barnum's American Museum touring Europe and America from 1864 to 1865. In 1871, in

association with William C. Coup (1837–95) and Don Costello, he opened his new circus complete with menagerie at Madison Square: 'The Greatest Show on Earth', a jumbo enterprise which, in 1881, was joined by James A. Bailey to whom we owe the invention of enormous trailer vehicles opening behind and harnessed such as trains for parade. Wherever they went they were successful beyond precedent. After Barnum's death, the enterprise was sold, in 1907, to the Ringling Brothers.

Though the Russian circus tradition is ancient in Empire times, it was above all the German and French tours which earned the greatest applause. On the other hand, the Russian national circus was highly developed in the Soviet Union, chiefly since World War Two. Towards 1960, there were over a hundred tents throughout the country and the great Soviet circuses then started touring Eastern, later Central and Western Europe, while *haute école* riders, like Filatov, Kisimov and Petushkova, began to win Olympic medals in dressage.

The *Encyclopaedia Britannica** emphasizes the length of the equestrian predominance, since

*'Equestrian influence', vol. 5, p. 801.

Astley, in the fortunes of the modern circus. Astley, for example, was directly followed by Andrew Ducrow (1793–1842) whose *St Petersburg Courier* has been successful up to present times.

'During the first eighty years of its history', concludes the *Encyclopaedia Britannica*,

the circus was dominated by the horse. Many of the proprietors were riders and trainers who founded dynasties, such as Renz in Germany, Salamonsky in the Baltic States, Carré in the Netherlands and Schumann in Scandinavia. Other proprietors were also famous riders, the Cookes, Clarkes, Fossetts and Ginnetts in England and the Franconis, Loyals and Rancys in France. A number of the great US riders and trainers, such as Levi North, Charles Fisch, James Robinson, Robert Stickney and Spencer Q. Stokes, became proprietors or managers. When Richard Sands' circus visited England in 1842, the 'Company of American Horsemen' and the 'Stud of Highly Trained American Horses' topped the bill. . . . The Schumann family, directors of the permanent circus in Copenhagen, are excellent school riders and in the early 1960s were the greatest horse trainers in the world.

The Useful Horse

Anthony A. Dent

By reference to the article on the prehistoric horse, it will be seen that in the hunting economy which succeeded the most primitive food-gathering stage of human culture there were times and places when the horse was the principal quarry of the hunter and the principal food of his family. As witness the vast deposits of equine bones on the Old Stone Age site of Solutré. The keeping of horses, to the exclusion of other livestock, solely for meat and milk, is a phase of pastoralism peculiar to certain north-temperate regions: while some prehistorians regard this specialization as a change-over from an earlier, more varied exploitation of large herbivorous animals, arising in the New Stone Age, it is just possible that it is a more sophisticated version of the horse-hunting economy,

A harvester pulled by over thirty horses, *c.* 1927.

and so may go back to the Middle Stone Age or even earlier. It is hardly susceptible of proof, either way.

In Central Asia, where the earliest evidence for domesticated horses is found, this form of horse-farming is still practised, rationalized and on a large scale. In some Soviet republics such as Uzbekistan, there are large pastoral collectives for the production of mare's milk and foal meat. The milk is fermented (as kumiss) and the foal meat canned.

Because in the literate societies of the ancient Near East, from which the traditions of Mediterranean civilization derive, the horse appears only in a spectacular role, either as the adjunct of ceremonial or of formal warfare, there is a temptation to bring its first entry into the mundane sphere of economic life (transport) down to a recent era. So far as the use of horsedrawn vehicles for economic purposes goes, this view is justified. But outside the oriental/Mediterranean zone, the ass, and consequently the mule, did not exist, their original centre of domestication having been North Africa. Both Central Asia and Europe north of the Alps have a long history of pack-horse transport, and in the latter region the invention of the horseshoe itself arose out of this economic role of the horse. The chariot teams of antiquity went unshod, nor would they have performed any better with shoes on. But from Styria to Sweden the work of the pack-train proceeded in a damper climate than in the Mediterranean, over predominantly rocky tracks. The hoof softens the more it is exposed to damp, and is more readily abraded by stony surfaces. A dead weight of 220 lb., which has been the standard pack-horse load from time immemorial, is harder on the feet than most riders, and infinitely harder than work in harness.

The horseshoe is the product of the 'Celtic' material culture, specifically of its La Tène phase, beginning about 500 or 400 BC. But the dependence of metallurgy on horses is greater, and more ancient, than the dependence of working horses on shoeing-smiths. Ancient European mines were almost all in hilly country and could not be served by ox-wagons (the German for 'mine' is still *Bergwerk*). The mines of the Salzkammergut (especially Hall-statt which is the oldest industrial complex in Europe), the tin and copper mines of the British Isles and Iberia, were from their beginnings in the Bronze Age served by strings of pack-horses bringing fuel to the smelting-hearths and taking away the ingots of metal. The last pit-ponies of the Durham coal-field have only recently retired from service. Their employment underground only began in the nineteenth century, before which time there were no mechanical hoists capable of taking a horse down the shaft. But their employment at the pit-head and on the surface goes back much further than that. The passion of the Northum-brian miner for horses, nowadays expressed chiefly at the races on Newcastle Town Moor, derives in some measure from memory of a time when a mineral industry without horses could not exist. Apart from the deprivation of sunlight and grazing, the life of the pit-pony was not unenviable. Until very recent times, the owners took more care of them than of the men with whom they worked. The quality of stabling, fodder and bedding, and the standards of horsemastership, were far better than those enjoyed by most horses working above ground. So was the veterinary attendance.

The employment of horses in heavy draught work and in ploughing depends on the avail-ability of two competitors, both cheaper to keep than horses: these are the ox and the mule. The former was distributed throughout Europe, and rock drawings of the Bronze Age

In Scotland Highland ponies are still used to cart deer during the shooting season.

Horses carting hay during the Russian winter. There are still some four million horses working in agriculture in the Soviet Union.

in Scandinavia show oxen ploughing and drawing wagons in fashion identical with that of similar primitive art of the same period in Italy (Val Camonica). Yet it was in Scandinavia that the horse first replaced the ox before the plough. Horse ploughing in England before the Norman conquest was confined to regions heavily settled by Danish immigrants (e.g., East Anglia) while it seems to have begun earlier in France but for long to have been confined to the provinces of the Channel littoral: i.e., those most exposed to Scandinavian influence.

Outside the Mediterranean zone proper, where the heavy draught/agricultural horse hardly exists or has existed, France, and to some extent Switzerland, present a territorial partition as between the horse and the mule plough, the frontier being drawn at the latitude of the Loire. Tractorization notwithstanding, it is not yet time to employ the past tense. The gigantic Poitevin jackasses are still serving mares at the national stud of Tarbes, and colossal mules, foaled by *mulassier* mares from Deux Sèvres, may still be seen working in the south of France, while lighter mules plough the slopes of the Pyrenees.

Passenger transport by horse-drawn means reached its finest flower in the Napoleonic era, with the English mail-coach and its continental counterparts; shortly afterwards the railways killed the mail-coach – but that is all. In Western Europe and North America the greatest expansion of horse-drawn transport, the greatest advances in the breeding of 'utility' races for all kinds of harness work, the rationalization of transport undertakings which kept hundreds of horses on the road in superb condition and working to accurate timetables: all were a result of the railway revolution. Not only the General Omnibus Company of London, the Messageries Maritimes, and other companies, perfected the use and improved the working conditions of the heavy harness horse, but the railway companies themselves, in Britain and elsewhere, were among the largest operators of horse-drawn vehicles for collection and delivery to and from the railhead. The bell tolled after World War Two: the working horse and mule population of the USA reached its peak in 1925, since when decline has been as steep as the rise in the fortunes of the internal combustion engine everywhere.

Sporting Art

Stella A. Walker

Sporting art records not only pastimes concerned with field sports but is a genre which also reflects social and economic history and the country way of life. Therefore with the national addiction to outdoor recreations and to hunting and racing in particular it finds, understandably, its natural home in England with the horse playing the major role. Its roots, however, derive from the continent from such artists of the Low Countries as Fyt, Weenix, Wouwerman with their animal studies; from such French court painters as Desportes and Oudry with their savage and romantic hunting scenes; and from the Bohemian-born Wenceslaus Hollar who came to England in 1637 to influence in no small measure the work of Francis Barlow (*c.* 1626 – 1702), the first important name in British sporting art. For many years, however, several important painters in this sphere were to be of foreign descent – amongst them Tillemans, the Sartorius and Alken families, Herring, Chalon and the Barraud brothers – but all speedily became anglicized in style and outlook.

At the beginning of the eighteenth century the aim of every wealthy Englishman was to become a country gentleman with a stately home. Hunting and racing were the fashionable diversions and therefore the breeding of quality horses a major concern. It was the formative period in the development of the Thoroughbred; it was also an age of patronage. Racing became known as the 'Sport of Kings' and as a result animal painters never lacked for commissions.

British-born John Wootton (*c.* 1677–1765), a talented landscape artist and pupil of Jan Wyck, encouraged by the second Duke of Beaufort, began to paint hunting scenes, racehorses and portraits of the newly imported oriental stallions, forebears of the Thoroughbred and status symbols in themselves. His contemporary, a gifted amateur, James Seymour, made a speciality of the racing scene. The Sartorius family – John Sr., an émigré from Nuremberg, his son Francis and grandson John Nost – produced naïve, stiff pictures of long-legged English racehorses (height was often exaggerated for prestige reasons in this era when horses measured under 15 h.h.), and of titled landowners coursing and hunting on their estates. The Jockey Club became established in 1752 and royal commissions were received by Sawrey Gilpin (1733–1807) and James Ward (1769–1859), both of whom brought a touch of zest and fervour to the sporting picture. Ward's horse portraits and hunting groups must be considered works of art by any criterion.

In 1724 George Stubbs was born in Liverpool, a prolific animal painter of genius. Virtually self-taught and with an obsession for anatomical research (his *Anatomy of the Horse* still ranks as a classic), his aspirations were nevertheless anything but sporting. Yet with the patronage of the racing aristocracy, he became known as 'Mr Stubbs the horse painter'. His lifesize portraits of *Whistlejacket* and of *Hambletonian*, his brilliant scene *The Grosvenor Hunt* and his *Phaeton with Cream Ponies and a Stable Lad* would alone ensure his name for posterity, for Stubbs not only painted horses

James Ward, RA *Coursing in Sussex*, 1819. (Roy Miles Fine Painting, London)

George Stubbs, ARA. *Mares and Foals in a Landscape.* *c.* 1763–68. (The Tate Gallery, London)

with talented exactitude but also with the composure and assurance of a great artist.

Many lesser but highly competent sporting painters were working at the end of the eighteenth century. Ben Marshall (1767–1835), successful in hunting portraits, brought distinction to the racing scene, his human figures being as brilliantly depicted as his Thoroughbreds. Abraham Cooper, Harry Hall, Charles Towne were also important in this sphere. The most prolific was John F. Herring Sr. (1795–1865), of Dutch-American extraction, whose somewhat static and repetitive portraits of eighteen winners of the Derby and thirty-three consecutive winners of the St Leger provide a valuable record of the Thoroughbred. His galloping horses, elongated to the point of absurdity, illustrate the fact that length of back and speed were considered at that period to be complementary.

With the passing of the Enclosure Acts (the greatest number in the reign of George III) hunting became metamorphosed. Speed and the thrill of jumping the new fences and ditches became fashionable priorities: steeplechasing also became established. Sportsmen made the Shires their focal point and the Alken family, and Henry Alken Sr. (1785–1851) in particular, Dean Wolstenholme, William Shayer and many others produced a myriad of paintings depicting the excitements and disasters of this golden age of hunting. Most talented was John Ferneley (1782–1860), based at Melton Mowbray, whose pictures of the Leicestershire scene, its foxhunters and horses possess unique perception.

The years between 1815 and 1845 saw the heyday of the brief coaching era. Skilled road-makers had made possible the speeding-up of the royal mail coach services which ran with clockwork precision all over the country. At the same time the wealthy aristocracy formed

James Pollard. *The York-Edinburgh Mail at St Mary's Gate, York with Post Chaise Arriving*, 1826. (N. C. Selway, Esq.)

Robert Polhill Bevan. *Showing at Tattersalls. c.* 1919 (The Ashmolean Museum, Oxford)

driving clubs and also took to the road with elegantly appointed equipages and highly bred horses. Artists to find stimulating inspiration in this harness scene were, first and foremost, James Pollard (1792–1867) in meticulous, detailed scenes, and Charles Cooper Henderson (1803–77) in atmospheric studies of the Royal Mails. Prints after Pollard's pictures attained enormous popularity and a feature of English sporting art is the vogue during the first half of the nineteenth century for prints after the leading artists by such skilled engravers and aquatinters as Fuller, Harris, Reeve and Sutherland, with such activities as angling, shooting, cricket and pugilism also used as frequent subjects.

The mid-Victorian demand for exact pictorial representation fulfilled by such artists as Sir Edwin Landseer and Richard Ansdell later dissipated much of the robust vigorous qualities of British sporting art. In spite of this precision, however, the wooden convention of the rocking-horse gallop was to remain until the revealing instantaneous photographs of animal movement by Eadweard Muybridge in the 1870s. These new standards of realism brought little original inspiration until the turn of the century when French impressionism influenced two artists, Joseph Crawhall (1861–1913) with a unique economy of line in pictures of horses, hounds and other animals, and Robert Bevan (1865–1925) with masterly handling of crayon and colour washes in studies of the horse auction marts and seedy cabyards of

Sir Alfred Munnings, PRA. *Arrival at Epsom Downs*, 1920. (City Museum and Art Gallery, Birmingham)

London. Unfortunately, few other artists were influenced by their imaginative approach. Such men as Lynwood Palmer (1868–1939), painted splendid but derivative portraits of the contemporary racehorse; others like George Wright and Thomas Blinks produced competent conventional hunting scenes. Lionel Edwards (1878–1966), a prolific traditional sporting artist with a sensitive appreciation of the English landscape, gave instinctive quality to his sparkling studies of horse and hound. It was left to Sir Alfred Munnings (1878–1954), appointed president of the Royal Academy in 1944, using colour and form with verve and imagination, to bring to sporting art a brilliance not seen since the works of Stubbs.

Today several artists attempt a breakaway from the conventional approach, the most successful being Michael Lyne using thick oils in an impressionist style, and also John Skeaping R.A. in his fluid line studies in gouache of the modern Thoroughbred. Talented sculptor by profession, the latter's bronzes, often lifesize, of such giants of the turf as Hyperion, Mill Reef and Brigadier Gerard rely, however, on realism to present telling likenesses. Susan Crawford, talented, versatile and ambitious, breaks new ground in her use of colour and design in her studies of horses and jockeys; but patrons today, as in the eighteenth and nineteenth centuries, still demand representational portraits of their racehorses, hunters and hounds which finds fulfilment in the work of Peter Biegel, Richard Dupont, T. La Fontaine, John

King and of two women, Leesa Sandys-Lumsdaine and Madeleine Selfe, and many other exponents.

Great Britain alone possesses an established school of sporting art covering three centuries. France produced Victor Gerusez (1840–1906), known as 'Crafty', who in lively drawings recorded the equestrian scene in the style of Rowlandson. Géricault, of course, found his greatest inspiration in the horse; Degas, Manet, Toulouse-Lautrec and, more recently, Dufy have also used the racing panorama with evocative effect but can hardly be considered in the category of the sporting artist.

The United States has also evolved a true tradition of sporting art, first established by Edward Troye (1808–74), a Swiss who worked in England and emigrated to the States to become there the supreme portrayer of the Thoroughbred. Other American artists, such as Henry Still, W. Van Stadt and A. F. Tait, also became popular before the end of the nineteenth century. Today there is a flourishing sporting school and such artists as Milton Menesco, British-born Smithson Broadhead, R. Stone Reeves and Henry Koehler have made their name. Henry Haseltine, who died in 1962, established himself as one of the great international sculptors of the horse.

After World War One, Americans hunting in Leicestershire began their acquisition of British sporting pictures to form many fine collections across the Atlantic, the most extensive being owned by Mr Paul Mellon; as a result, during the past decade the rise in the value of sporting art has been phenomenal

John Skeaping RA. *Going Easily*. 1969.
(Messrs Arthur Ackermann & Son, London)

– £225 000 has been paid for a Stubbs and nearly £60 000 for a Ben Marshall – but happily many important pictures still remain in private hands in their native home.

In 1977 the British Sporting Art Trust was formed to establish a permanent collection in the Tate Gallery in London. The Trust is an independent body with charity status which is assembling sporting pictures for the Tate Gallery with funds from long-term loans, gifts and bequests, and it could be the means of saving many sporting pictures for the nation.

The Palette at the Pesage

Claude Ferdinand-Dreyfus

A thorough study of French horse painters would require a thick volume all to itself, but we shall not expatiate here on the very great number of French artists of the first rank whose names are household words, such as Géricault (1791–1824), Degas (1834–1917) and Toulouse-Lautrec (1864–1901) who, though not specialists in sporting art, have left us, among other works, pictures of great renown of horses, jockeys and racecourse scenes.

One of the greatest among the truly great painters of horses is undoubtedly Carle Vernet who was born at Bordeaux in 1758, the son of Joseph Vernet, a marine artist who also painted harbour scenes, and the father of Horace Vernet, also a great painter whose speciality was scenes of military life.

Carle was the pupil of Lepicie, and he won the Grand Prix de Rome at the age of twenty-one. When he died in 1836 he is said to have murmured: 'They will say of me what they said of the Great Dauphin – "Son of a king, father of a king, but never a king".'

How wrong he was, for he, too, was a marvellous painter; his oils and watercolours of horses, hunting and racing, not to mention his scenes of daily life during the French Revolution, the First Empire and the Restauration, are precious documents for the study of that important era in French history.

His original works, jealously guarded by private owners, seldom change hands commercially, but most of them have been engraved by Levachez–Coqueret and Debucourt. These engravings, at least those printed in the artist's lifetime, have now become very rare.

Another very great artist, a younger contemporary of Vernet, was Alfred de Dreux who was born in 1810 and died in 1860, the victim of a duel. His works circulated widely in lithograph editions and show a deep knowledge of horses. Unfortunately, he was so much copied that it is often very difficult to identify with certainty an authentic de Dreux.

Among his best paintings are his portraits of *Nautilus*, of *Quoniam*, and a remarkable study in oils of a race meeting on the Champ de Mars in 1842. His horsewomen and hunting scenes have also achieved a well-deserved reputation. His backgrounds and his trees are especially admirable, and his sunlight effects are particularly happy and enchanting in their use of colour.

Born some time later, in 1829, at Bordeaux (though of English stock), John-Lewis Brown

Horse Frightened by Lightning, by Géricault
(The National Gallery, London)

Rendez-vous de Chasse à Chantilly, by Alfred de Dreux
(Richard Green Galleries)

was also a painter of great quality whose work has retained its importance. Unfortunately, he made too great concessions to contemporary taste in painting horsemen in the style of the era of Louis XV; but his hunting pictures and his rarer racing scenes, as well as his portraits, bear witness to a great *maestria* and a perfect acquaintance with the horse.

The summit of prestige which René Princeteau (1843–1914) now enjoys seems well merited. He was born at Libourne and was a great friend of Toulouse-Lautrec; they worked in partnership and made a special study of the representation of movement. Princeteau had great success also in the portraiture of crack racers of his day, model works of their kind.

In 1965 there was an important exhibition in Paris of sporting art at which we were able to admire his portraits of *Semendria* and of *Dolma Bagtche,* both of which won the Grand Prix de Paris. This exhibition also showed other magnificent pictures by him, such as *The Duc d'Aumale's Pack of Hounds in the Chantilly Forest.*

Henri Delamarre was the owner of a very considerable string of racehorses and also a painter of great quality. He painted all his own big winners, as well as *Parade before the Grand Prix de Paris, 1864* which he won with *Vermout.* This picture hangs in the lounge of the Jockey Club of Paris.

Baron Finot (1826–1906), was another important owner and also an excellent painter. His gouaches, often on a small scale and given away liberally to his friends, are marvels of their kind and still greatly appreciated by connoisseurs.

Among professionals practising in that untroubled era we may note especially Paul Le More who taught drawing at the national stud, Haras du Pin, where his works are piously preserved; they represent stallions of his day, such as West Australian, as well as some very famous trotting sires.

'Semendria' Winning the Grand Prix de Paris in 1900, by Princeteau (Collection le Goupy)

Le Nail was a pupil of Corot and an artist much patronized by owners of big winners to immortalize their favourites. He had a large output which is still much prized today. It is interesting to note that he always signed pictures with a cross before his name, for Le Nail was very devout.

J. Audy was older than Le Nail and just as prolific, but chiefly in watercolour of which he was a master. However, he did paint with great skill in oils, though these are much rarer.

Mention should also be made of V. J. Cotlison, another Frenchman of English extraction, born at Maisons-Laffitte, Arsenius, Charles Detaille and Crafty, all excellent illustrators of the period. Also Theodore Fort and Olivier

Pichat, excellent artists; the weighing room at Longchamp contains a huge canvas by the latter, featuring Gladiateur at the canter in the Grand Prix de Paris.

Though not strictly speaking sporting artists, two other painters whose work is much sought after go to make up this illustrious galaxy: Jean Beraud (1849–1936) and Jacques-Emile Blanche (1861–1942), both pupils of Bonnat. The first, rather heavily specializing in scenes of smart Parisian life, painted among other works *Weighing-in at Auteuil in the Presidency of Jules Grévy*, as well as the *Arrival at Longchamp*, in which the horses, seen head-on, seem to be running right at the viewer. As for the second, who wrote as well as he painted, he was the author of many notable pictures showing scenes on the turf, especially steeplechasing.

Coming into a time much nearer our own,

Bressin, du Passage, Gouverneur, G. Busson, André Marchand, Frank Elim, Maurice Taquoy, all stand out above the throng of animal painters. And we must not forget Malaspina (1874–1942). He was a pupil of Edouard Detaille and may rightly be considered a post-impressionist with a method peculiarly his own of showing the action of a horse at all paces. He may best be compared to Princeteau, which is no mean compliment.

In our time, if we except the late Baron Karl Reille, and Xavier de Poret, a very fine draftsman, we have, to continue the tradition of sporting art, a young painter in Pierre Levé whose works bear a strikingly faithful likeness to the model. He has painted some of the great winners, such as Little Love and Jaazeiro, and more recently he has finished two canvases showing M. Mahmoud Fustok's two crack runners, Bilal and Malak El Hawa. His talents are undoubted and should succeed, in the near future, in reaching a level equal to that of the masters of the past.

'Auricula', Monté par Cassidy, Grand Steeple-chase de Dieppe, 1864, by J. Audy (Mr Desvignes)

Famous Mounted Troops

Lt. Col. M. A. Q. Darley
M. F. H. de Genellis
Col. Jaques Bois
Jean Froissard

The Household Cavalry

The Household Cavalry comprises the two senior regiments of the British Army, the Life Guards and the Blues and Royals (formally the Royal Horse Guards). Both regiments have traditions dating back over 300 years to the founding of the first regiments of horse of a new Regular Army authorized by Parliament after the Restoration in 1661.

These two cavalry regiments have by tradition always had a special role of guarding the sovereign, while at the same time one or both regiments have earned proud battle honours in all major wars on the European continent, in Egypt, South Africa and the Near East, since their foundation. In time of peace the traditional role of the Household Cavalry is maintained by keeping a squadron of each regiment in London on ceremonial duties such as internal security operations abroad, or part of NATO in Germany, or as a strategic reserve in England ready to move to any part of the world; as such they are an armoured car or armoured regiment.

It is the ceremonial duties in London which are most familiar to visitors, the Life Guards wearing red tunics with silver breast-plates and white plumes on their helmets, while the 'Blues' and 'Royals' wear the blue tunics with red plumes on their helmets.

The duties of these squadrons include escorts to the sovereign on all state occasions, escorting visiting Heads of State on their arrival in England, and the daily Guard Mounting at the ancient Palace of Whitehall in the heart of London. The squadrons are mounted on black chargers except for the trumpeters who ride greys.

The colonels of the regiments of Household Cavalry hold the Court Appointment of Gold Stick to the Sovereign.

Lt. Col. M.A.Q. Darley

The King's Troop — The Royal Horse Artillery

The first English use of artillery may have been in 1346, when bombards aided the victory of Edward III at Crécy; and in the Civil War Cromwell supported his cavalry with artillery.

The artillery was reorganized under the Duke of Marlborough, but the Royal Regiment of Artillery as such was founded in 1746.

We shall not elaborate on the battle honours of this corps which, during the period of horse-drawn warfare, had an evolution similar to that of other nations. We shall only mention here the King's Troop which, with the Household Cavalry, constitutes the only remaining mounted unit of the British Army today.

Every year at the Royal Tournament the Royal Horse Artillery puts on a show in which the gun-teams and the mounted gunners perform their drill at a gallop, which demands great skill on the part of drivers and riders.

The dark blue uniform with its frogged jacket has changed little in the past 150 years, though the bearskin of the Napoleonic wars has been replaced, first by a shako and later by the present busby.

The drum horses of the Household Cavalry. Note the reins attached to the musicians' stirrups.

Horses of the King's Troop, Royal Horse Artillery, being prepared for work.

This unit, which when wearing khaki normally handles the most up-to-date equipment, falls automatically into time-honoured traditions when it brings out its horses and its limbers and gun-carriages. On such occasions the officers all carry swords from which, according to an order of 1833, they should never be parted.

The King's Troop may be seen in all their glory going across London to Hyde Park to fire a royal salute of forty-one guns on the Queen's Birthday, on the anniversary of her accession or on some other ceremonial occasion.

The RHA is one of the seven regiments with the special privilege of marching through the City, drums beating and colours displayed; and of the seven it is the senior, belonging to the City. In fact, this right was conferred under Henry VIII on a company of archers which was the forerunner of the Royal Artillery – a special form of Freedom of the City.

The King's Troop therefore has every right to retain its place among the select few mounted troops which still occupy a unique position in British military annals.

M. F. H. de Genellis

The Cavalry Regiment of the Garde Républicaine de Paris

The Republican Guard of Paris is intimately linked to the history of the capital and actively participates in its present-day life. Its origin stems from the Royal Watch and from that Company of Constabulary of 120 men raised in 1666 which merged with the foot-archers to form one unit under the command of the Knight of the Watch. Since that date it has been a metropolitan unit, but since the days of the First Empire the Guard has made a glorious contribution on many a field of battle.

The Republican Guard has always contained mounted units; and today it constitutes the only surviving cavalry regiment in the French Army. It is commanded by a colonel and comprises two groups of squadrons, a motorcycle squadron, a mounted band and a training school.

Along with other police units it maintains law and order, but it also performs other functions, varied but all essentially Parisian: some of these serve purposes of prestige or pomp and circumstance in public buildings, on parade, escorting visiting dignitaries, forming an honour guard at official inaugurations and lending their presence to some of the great Parisian soirées. On these occasions the men

The fanfare of the Garde Républicaine.

wear the dress uniform as laid down in 1873, but embodying some sartorial features of eighteenth-century vintage. The troopers wear a crested helmet with a scarlet plume (the commander of the Corps wears a white aigrette and his staff tricolour plumes), a tunic with red trimmings and facings, red aiguillettes and epaulets, or gilt ones, according to rank, black boots with spurs and blue breeches – or white breeches if the president of the Republic is present.

They have honorific and security duties such as guards of honour at sessions of the Senate, the preservation of order at theatres and at Parisian racecourses. Also surveillance of State forests and parks in the metropolitan area and the provinces, in close liaison with the Gendarmerie of the departments.

Other prestige appearances include concerts by the band, demonstrations of horsemanship and participation in mounted competitive events.

In addition, as upholders of the army's equestrian traditions, the regiment represents the horseman's spirit wherever equestrian sports are popular. Its teams and special units appear in public and their efforts frequently meet with success in competition.

This, then, is the Republican Guard's mounted regiment, part and parcel of the Gendarmerie Nationale, at the same time faithful to the past and to the future, combining the traditions of the French Army with the sporting dynamism of the modern soldier.

Col. Jacques Bois

The Belgian Royal Horse Escort

The only mounted unit now remaining in Belgium is the Royal Escort which is part of the Gendarmerie, though greatly inferior in numbers to the motorized and foot branches.

The employment of gendarmes or other troops to escort the sovereign has varied greatly in the territory that now comprises Belgium, which over the centuries found itself under ever-changing foreign domination. Since 21 July 1831, when Leopold of Saxe-Coburg made his formal entry into Brussels as monarch of a newly independent Belgium, the Mounted Gendarmerie served as royal and official escorts. Subsequently these duties were passed on to the cavalry regiments – Guides, Lanciers, Chasseurs à Cheval.

In 1938 the demands of mechanization excluded the cavalry from duties of this nature and the Gendarmerie again took over, this time for good.

The Belgian Royal Escort is mounted on horses of one colour, the Standardbearer and his bodyguard alone being mounted on greys. Saddlery and accoutrements are the standard equipment once used by the cavalry. The uniform is that of the pre-1914 mounted gendarmes, which was chosen by Marshal Moncey under Napoleon I: a dark tunic, closely cut, white breeches, jack boots, bearskin with plume, belt in white buff leather and aiguillettes, and steel spurs. The squadron is 140 strong and embodies the traditions of the Belgian cavalry.

M. F. H. de Genellis

The Municipal Guard of Barcelona

This mounted troop was created by the Mayor of Barcelona in 1856 for a dual purpose: to ensure order and to provide a guard of honour. Quite naturally this came to include its participation in important equestrian events. Its riders presented their first carrousel in 1910 in front of King Alfonso XIII. The storms of the Civil War brought its activity to a temporary halt, but the corps was reconstituted and once more took up its presentations in 1947.

Mounted on Andalusian horses, its dress uniform consists of a red tunic, white breeches, black boots and a white-plumed steel helmet.

Jean Froissard

The Royal Canadian Mounted Police

Members of the Royal Canadian Mounted Police giving a display in London.

This police corps was founded in 1873 under the name of North-West Mounted Police; it took on its present name in 1920 and is more popularly known as 'The Mounties'. Its motto is, '*Maintiens le droit*' ('Maintain the law'), but there is another semi-official one, better known to outsiders, 'They always get their man'. Member of an elite corps, the Mountie is an all-purpose man; lost in the wilds with one or two companions, he keeps watch over hundreds of miles of country. In 1932, a Marine Division was created to guard the coasts, followed in 1935 by an Air Division. But only in 1944 did this corps acquire its own school, at Regina (Saskatchewan): the Canadian Police College whose headquarters is in Ottawa.

Although horses are no longer used on patrol, they are still present in their role of indispensable educators.

The Mountie uniform is still made up of the red tunic, dark-blue breeches with a yellow stripe, tan boots and the wide-brimmed hat.

Jean Froissard

Part Nine

The Arabian

Lady Anne Lytton

The Arabian horse – in Arabic Kehailan – is probably the most ancient of domestic breeds. He is also the original 'Thoroughbred' horse of the East, from whose example all Western ideas of thorough breeding in horse flesh was derived. He had been held in repute as of 'noble' blood for at least 1300 years and has been bred with fanatical reverence and pure from all foreign admixture in peninsular Arabia as far back as the records of that country go; that is to say, until the second century before Mohammed, the sixth of our era.

It is a matter of considerable dispute in modern science whether or not the Kehailan was indigenous to Arabia as an original breed. The Common Mohammedan tradition would make him a gift from Solomon to the Arabs, or, again, descended from mares ridden by the Prophet; but Western criticism rightly rejects these tales, nor are they in truth real Bedouin traditions local to Arabia itself. The local tradition is that the Kehailan is a separate wild breed kept pure in the desert from the time of his first capture and domestication; that his habitat was Nejd and the high plateaux of Yemen and that he owes his distinguishing qualities to the fact that his original blood has never been mixed with that of breeds of inferior type.

The above is a direct quotation from an article written by Wilfrid Scawen Blunt*. He goes on to say that the high plateaux of Yemen possessed some natural pasture but little water, therefore it is possible that the wild horse as well as the wild ass existed. There exists a certain fine grass called 'Nossi' which grows freely and is excellent pasture for horses.

All that we know positively is that in the fifth and sixth centuries of our era the bedouins of Nejd and Yemen were already possessed of a special breed of horses of which they boasted as an 'ancestral possession'. 'Are not these', say their poets of that date, 'an inheritance from our fathers? Shall not we to our sons in turn bequeath them?' It is clear, too, from their descriptions that the horse then possessed by them was identical in his chief characteristics with the modern Kehailan, as were the ideas of his owners concerning him.

I now continue by quoting from Wilfrid Blunt's article on the Arabian horse in the *Standard Cyclopaedia of Modern Agriculture*:

Like the Barb, his fellow progenitor of the English racehorse, the Kehailan would seem to have acquired his special characteristics of speed, sobriety and endurance with his fineness of coat and limb from the long isolation of his kind among desert surroundings.†

He continues by saying that these surroundings have imparted similar qualities to the hare, the fox, the gazelle and camel and to all desert mammals, and adds that they could not have been acquired under domestication. He then compares the Arabian to the Barb and says that it is not necessary to suppose a common ancestry between the two, the Arabian being probably an offshoot of the Asiatic, and the Barb from the European, wild stock, and notes they have marked differences in conformation.

The Encyclopaedia of Sport, ed. The Earl of Suffolk and Berkshire, Hedley Peek and F. G. Aflalo, published by Lawrence and Bullen Ltd. in 1897.
†Gresham Publishing Company, 1908.

The Darley Arabian (Messrs Fores, London)

Whereas the Barb is what the Arabs call 'ram-headed', that is to say with a convex profile line, the Arab has the upturned nostrils and slightly concave profile of the gazelle. He has the high wither which makes him pre-eminently a saddle horse; and above all his tail, instead of being set low and carried meanly between the hocks (the Barb characteristic), springs from the highest level of the quarters and is carried high. These are points of bone structure not to be overlooked and are important in the Arabian as an indication of pure breeding.

Later on he reminds us that the pure Kehail-an's introduction into Europe dates from the eighteenth century only. During the previous century racing had come into fashion in England and much Eastern blood had been imported, principally Spanish and Barb, but 'now for the first time stallions of authentic blood were procured from Aleppo and other towns on the desert's edge with immediate effect on the quality and speed of the English racehorse.' As we know, the most famous of these, and the best authenticated, was the Darley Arabian of the Managhi strain – one of the best breeds of the Anazeh Arabs.

Another almost equally famous, whose pedigree remains obscure, but who was said to be of the Jilfan strain, was the Godolphin – his original name 'Scham' (Arabic for Damascus) indicates from where he originated. Also in C. M. Prior's *The Royal Studs of the 16th and 17th Centuries*, he tells us that Lord Godolphin himself referred to him as The Arabian, and

The Byerley Turk (Messrs Fores, London)

foals by him were all entered as being by The Arabian and the others by The Barb (or Brown Barb). He had two of these at a later date. There were other well known Arabians mentioned in the early pedigrees such as the Byerley Turk, and Wilfrid Blunt goes on to say that it may be affirmed generally that at least three-fourths of the blood of the modern English Thoroughbred is derived from Arabia and that to the Kehailan he owes the initial quality of speed which two centuries of selection have developed into the perfected racehorse we now possess.

An article on the subject of strains by Lady Wentworth (daughter of Wilfrid Blunt) was published in the *American Horse News* in May 1950, and she says that it is wrong to designate Kehailan as a separate strain as it is the generic term common to all strains, just as we refer to the Thoroughbred racehorse, and the modern theory that some are inferior to others or that they each carry special characteristics is quite incorrect, and that all pure strains, uncrossed with non-Arabian blood are intrinsically of equal merit. Though she points out that individuals differ in perfection and size, and that different owners have varied greatly in their own talents for breeding the best, even out of the same original stock. She says that lately

Managhi, Jilfan and Hadban have come under an Algerian-sponsored suspicion on the false ground that Managhi is coarse, bony, heavy-headed, and ragged-hipped, though speedy. Jilfan is coarse-headed and common, Hadban coarse-coated, etc.

Every so often one strain became the fashion and at the time of the Blunts' visit to the Anazeh in 1878 the Managhi strain of Ibn Sbeyel had become little short of a craze. Then it was the Seglawis of Ibn Sudan.

Lady Wentworth also points out that the story of 'El Khamsa', the five mares of the Prophet, is a pious Islamic fairy tale. The Prophet had many more than five horses. She then adds that no Islamic writer ever mentions the same five. The main strains are not five but many, sub-strains being legion. All must admit that Hadban, Seglawi, Managhi, Nowak, Dahman, Krush, Abeyan, Wadnan, Jilfan, Jellabi and Hamdani are first-class main strains.

It is true that even in the desert many individuals have fallen short of perfection, and some have looked more like an English racehorse, with a longer head, deeper girth and more sloping quarters and lower set tail. The Blunts' famous mare, Hagar, who was a Kehilet Ajuz, answered this description. This leads one to suppose two types may once have existed.

Wilfrid Blunt again tells us in the *Encyclopaedia of Sport* that,

In Europe the oldest Arab studs are those of Prince Sanguscko and Count Joseph Potocki in Poland, both of high quality which date from the end of the last century – and of the Branicki family in the Ukraine, etc.

After two wars and a revolution many of these fine Arab horses were destroyed, scattered or looted, but enough of them remained to restart a national Stud. One stud, indeed, was taken to Germany where it was kept intact throughout the last war and eventually returned to Poland. Polish blood was introduced to Crabbet by Lady Wentworth when she acquired the imported Skowronek from Mr H. V. Musgrave Clark. He became the most famous of all Arabian sires and he refreshed the Crabbet blood which was becoming inbred. About 1960 Miss Patricia Lindsay imported a number of Polish-bred Arabs and some of these have blended well with the English stock and have been of great benefit to it.

Not until 1878 were Arabian horses imported

Son of Skowronek.

in any numbers to England and never before to found a pure Arabian stud. This was when Wilfrid and Lady Anne Blunt travelled in the spring of that year to Aleppo, Baghdad and Damascus when they visited all the great horse breeding tribes of the northern deserts and purchased from them mares and stallions of their best breeds. These visits were repeated in 1879 on a journey to Nejd, the central province of Arabia and once again, with the same object of procuring horses, in 1881 to the Hamad, or great desert, south of Palmyra. Twenty-five brood mares were collected thus and brought to England, the nucleus of what was to become the most famous stud in England, and probably of the western world. The only other considerable importation made by the Blunts was in 1896 when they purchased the remainder of the once celebrated stud of Abbas I, viceroy of Egypt, consisting of six first-class mares and four stallions which were added to the Crabbet stock. This stud, known as that of Ali Pasha Sherif, was the last of the great studs of purebred Arabs in the Arabian borderlands. It had been got together between 1850 and 1854, by the then viceroy, at an expense estimated at a quarter of a million sterling and had been carried on ever since at Cairo under bedouin superintendence. Wilfrid Blunt remarked that its removal to Sussex left Egypt without any first-class stud. However, when Lady Anne died in Egypt in 1917, the horses she had kept there at her Sheykh Obeyd Stud remained in Egypt. In 1920 Lady Wentworth exported eighteen Arabs to Egypt and Wilfrid Blunt also sold his favourite stallion, Rustem, to Egypt. In addition when an Englishman named Mr T. Trouncer, who lived in Egypt and bred Arab horses to race, and who introduced a stallion to his stock from Crabbet, died in the early 1950s, his horses also remained there. Egypt now has good studs and some very beautiful stock.

The Arab horse has also become very popular in the USA where it has been bred since the early part of the century from various importations, very largely from Crabbet, later from Poland and recently from Egypt, where it is used for many purposes.

The Arab has always been noted for his great endurance and in all the great tests for weight carrying over distance he has invariably won. He is well constructed for this purpose, having short cannon bones, powerful forearms and gaskins, and a very short back occasionally having one vertebra less than other horses. Such authorities as W. G. Palgrave and W. S. Blunt have said the back should be – to quote the former – 'a little, a very little saddle-backed, just the curve which indicates springiness without any weakness'. Wilfrid Blunt held to the ancient tradition in the desert that the best height of the Arabian Horse is about 14.3 h.h. and should not exceed 15 h.h., but neither he nor Lady Anne practised this entirely and used their Mahruss son Rijm, who was 15.3 h.h., quite extensively with the result that his blood is in most of our English stock. Many modern Arabs are 15 h.h. and over. Colours vary greatly, but the commonest today are chestnuts of all shades, greys, rarely bays, browns, and a very few of that pure white so highly admired in the desert. Some strains have had profuse white markings and occasional spots or splashes under the body or a lot of grey hairs in the coat, others with little white. Black is extremely uncommon.

An international body has been formed and the first conference was held in London in 1967 when the following countries were represented by delegates: Australia and New Zealand, the Netherlands, Poland, Portugal, Spain, South Africa, the United Kingdom, USA, USSR and West Germany. In addition the following countries sent observers; Denmark, Israel, Jordan and Sweden. This body has since been named The World Arabian Horse Organization, the main object being to have discussions and to come to a general agreement about the stud books of different countries. I was invited to speak at this first meeting on the type and standard of the Arab horse. I began by emphasizing the fact that he is a horse and not a pony – a small horse capable of siring offspring much larger than himself when crossed back to the Thoroughbred or hunter, the proof of this being that two first crosses have won such a testing competition as the Badminton Three-Day Event; and there are endless possibilities for him to develop.

The Barb

Jean-Paul Klein

Also known as 'the African breed with convex profile', the origins of this breed go far back in time and space. Ultimately it derives from Mongolia, having spread through Persia, Egypt and the Libyan desert in the course of invasions and migrations. The true Barb type presents the following characteristics: convex facial profile, narrow skull, arched neck, prominent withers, goose rump, flat thighs, short flanks, slender legs and narrow hoofs. Height varies from 14.2 to 15.2 h.h. The prevailing coat colour is grey but brown is often seen. It is a horse of great stamina and astonishing toughness.

In North Africa where the greatest numbers are found today, they often are crossed with pure-bred Arabians to make very good saddle horses. The Spahis (cavalry regiments) were all mounted on entire Barbs.

The Barb. (Messrs Fores, London)

The Thoroughbred

William Robertson

There are more elegant, and some quite poetic, definitions of a Thoroughbred, but a succinct and practical definition is that a Thoroughbred is a horse eligible for registration in a recognized stud book of the breed. The ideal Thoroughbred is, of course, much more – a finely-constructed animal of great beauty, surpassing speed and possessed of that intangible quality called 'heart' – but the Thorough-

bred is a work of nature as selected by man, and man continues to exercise his selective process with the result that some less-than-ideal

Eclipse (1764–89) who was unbeaten on the racecourse. As a sire he had a profound influence on the development of the modern Thoroughbred. From the original picture by George Stubbs. (Messrs. Fores, London)

The Godolphin Arabian also known as the Godolphin Barb (Messrs Fores, London).

offspring of Thoroughbred parents are not registered, and others which were registered but whose performance on the racecourse and/or at stud has been disappointing, are sold 'without papers', and thereby revert to being simply horses.

As is true of some other marvellous works of nature, the Thoroughbred required several centuries to develop, and its precise origin is somewhat shrouded since many generations had elapsed before the so-called foundation sires were determined, by hindsight, to have been such. Every modern Thoroughbred traces in the top (tail-male) lines of its pedigree to one of three stallions: Matchem, foaled in 1748; Herod (also called King Herod), 1758; Eclipse, 1764; who were, respectively, tail-male descen-

dants of the Godolphin Arabian, c. 1724; Byerley Turk, c. 1680; and Darley Arabian, c. 1700. The Godolphin Arabian is often described as a Barb, and whether the charger ridden in King William's wars by Captain Byerley (also spelled Byerly) was a Turk or a horse of some other kind which had been captured from the Turks has been questioned. In any case, the Thoroughbred breed evolved from mating horses imported into England from the Middle East with native stock, and while there are only three stallions whose tail-male lines survive today, the origin of the breed involved a considerably larger number of stallions whose male lines have died out but from whom modern Thoroughbreds descend in other lines of their pedigrees. In other than their direct male lines, Matchem, Herod and Eclipse all descend from D'Arcy's Yellow Turk and the Leedes Arabian, for example. If all lines in the pedigree are considered, Matchem and Herod descend from two of the three 'foundation sires', and Eclipse descends from all three. Today, representatives of the Eclipse male line are by far the most numerous, comprising perhaps ninety per cent of the Thoroughbred breed.

The blending of oriental blood with that of native English stock was found to produce a horse which exceeded either parental stock in speed. Horse racing was popular long before the advent of the foundation sires, but horses involved in the earliest races generally served some other utilitarian purpose, and the racing was a sideline. The original purpose behind the cross-breeding which led to development of the Thoroughbred probably also was utilitarian – to improve the cavalry or upgrade courier service – but the emphasis on pure speed soon led to the breeding of a special kind of horse, intended solely for sport. King John, who ruled England from 1199–1216, was said to have 'running horses' in his stables, which indicates that as far back as the twelfth century a distinction was made between 'running horses' and other kinds of horses. There is also evidence of professional race riders during the twelfth century.

The popularity of the 'English running horse' became such that a brisk market for it arose, and pedigrees were included in the documentation of sales. Owing to duplication of names, some natural confusion, and possibly some deliberate delusion, the pedigrees were not invariably accurate and in 1791 James Weatherby offered what he called *An Introduction to a General Stud Book* as a central source of pedigree information. There is no explicit evidence that Mr Weatherby intended that his work should become an equine *Almanach de Gotha*. He offered it simply as a collection of pedigrees which he had gleaned from records of races and of sales, as well as from private stud books. His original volume was revised several times over the course of many years, until it became Volume I of the *General Stud Book*.

In the latter part of the nineteenth century, an Australian researcher, Bruce Lowe, traced every mare in the *General Stud Book* of his era back in tail-female (bottom) line to her earliest recorded ancestress as listed in Volume I. He found that there were only forty-three 'tap-root' mares who still had surviving descendants – in tail-female line – although, of course, as in the case of stallions, the original pool from which the surviving mares descended comprised considerably more than forty-three mares, some of which had surviving descendants via other than the bottom lines of their pedigrees. Bruce Lowe numbered his female families according to the frequency with which members of each family had won the Epsom Derby, Oaks or St Leger, members of Family No. 1 having scored the most victories, and so forth. Families which were not represented by any winners of the designated Classic races were numbered according to Lowe's estimate of their general quality. For a time, breeding horses according to Bruce Lowe family numbers was a popular fad, but today the numbers are regarded chiefly as merely a convenient means of identification. Lowe's system embraced only mares whose 'tap-roots' were registered in Volume I of the *General Stud Book*, but the modern Thoroughbred breed includes additional English families plus families in other countries. *Family Tables of Racehorses*, compiled by Captain Kazimierz Bobinski and published by Count Etienne Zamoyski in 1953, does not purport to be a listing of all 'Thoroughbred' female families but, rather, a listing of those families of 'racehorses' whose members had won any one of 296 designated important races, scattered throughout the world.

This listing includes 173 female families, as follows: 49 of the Bruce Lowe classification, as expanded by subsequent research (these families actually are numbered 1 – 50, but subsequent research also indicated that family No. 50 was a branch of Family No. 3.); 24 English families, not traceable to a Bruce Lowe foundation mare, but eligible for registration in the *General Stud Book*; 26 English families not eligible for registration in the GSB; 37 American families;

33 Colonial (Australasian) families; 2 Argentine families; 2 Polish families.

As has been noted, long before the publication of Weatherby's first, rather tentative version of a stud book, the 'English running horse' was recognized as a distinct type. Breeding of these horses among themselves produced a distinct breed. Years before the word 'thoroughbred' *per se* came into use as applied to animals, there were references to horses as being 'full bred' or simply 'bred', as well as to fractional degrees of breeding such as seven-eighths, three-quarters and half-bred. It is highly probable that the American and Colonial families mentioned above were founded by 'bred' mares exported from England but concerning which adequate records were not kept, so they could not be traced back without interruption to animals recorded in the *General Stud Book*. It also is quite possible that the degree of 'breeding' of some of these mares was misinterpreted or misrepresented. Their descendants did not receive recognition as 'thoroughbreds' without contretemps.

In 1913, at the instigation of the Earl of Jersey, the Messrs Weatherby (tail-male descendants of the originator of the stud book) passed a rule that no horse could be registered in the *General Stud Book* unless it traced in all its lines to horses previously registered therein. The Jersey Act, as it was called, came at a time when racing in the United States was in the doldrums owing to repressive legislation, and North American horses were being shipped to other countries in increasing numbers, for racing and for sale. The effect of the Jersey Act, as construed by Americans, was to stigmatize the majority of American horses as being of 'tainted' blood. The English were accused of trying to protect the market for their own horses at the expense of foreignbreds. In some respects the Jersey Act was ambiguous, to say the least. An American-bred horse which had crossed the Atlantic and been registered in the *General Stud Book* prior to 1913 might have had full siblings which, subsequent to 1913, were not eligible for registry in the English book (although they could be regis-

tered in the *American Stud Book*). To the eternal credit of English sportsmanship, although their stud book was closed to outsiders, they left their races open. As horses ineligible for registration in the *General Stud Book* won a number of English Classic races (defeating registered horses), the English Jockey Club relented, and in 1949 requirements were eased so that a horse with eight or nine crosses of 'pure' blood became eligible for registration in the *GSB*. This action did not throw the book wide open, but it did serve to rescue a large number of American-breds from beyond the pale in a pedigree sense. (In a practical sense the Jersey Act was not all that terrifying; while it was in effect American racing grew by leaps and bounds, and some Europeans continued to breed horses that were not eligible for registration in the *GSB*. As it was in the beginning, they evidently believed that the merit of the horse should determine the merit of its pedigree, rather than vice versa.)

The modern Thoroughbred comes in a variety of sizes, shapes and colours (which reflects, perhaps, the fact that breeding is based on qualities that cannot be ascertained readily or easily). The height of mature Thoroughbreds varies from 14.2 to 17 h.h. although there are exceptions on either side of this range. Weight at maturity varies from 340 to 530 kg for a horse in training, up to 600 kg for a stallion. Although Thoroughbreds may begin racing as two-year-olds, they do not reach full physical maturity until the age of five, by which time many of them will have been retired. Regardless of individual foaling dates, ages of Thoroughbreds are reckoned from a common date, 1 January in the Northern Hemisphere and either 1 July or 1 August in the Southern. The common 'birthday', plus some practical considerations based on nature, serve to control the size of the Thoroughbred population. The period of gestation averages about eleven months, and a mating too soon after 1 January (in the Northern Hemisphere) entails the risk that the foal might be born prior to the next common birthday, in which case it would become a year old officially when only weeks

A modern Thoroughbred (Sir Ivor).

old chronologically, and hence at such a dis-advantage in comparison to other members of its official 'crop' of foals that it would be useless for racing purposes. The same consider-ation, to a lesser degree, applies to matings which take place too late in the year, with the consequence that breeding generally is confined to a period of about four and a half months (15 February to 30 June in the Northern Hemi-sphere). During this period a vigorous stallion might be bred one or more times to, say, forty mares, from which some twenty-five foals might result. Some stallions have had crops of more than forty foals although the most valuable stallions are not so heavily used.

Thoroughbreds are raised throughout the world, and are especially popular in England, France, Japan, the United States, New Zealand, Australia and other former British colonies. The United States/Canada combination leads in Thoroughbred production with an annual foal crop in excess of 24 000.

The most prevalent colour among Thorough-breds is bay, followed by chestnut, and other colours are brown, black, grey and roan – and as roans age, they turn grey. It is so difficult to distinguish between dark bay and brown that in some countries the designations 'dark bay or brown' or 'bay-brown' are used. In 1963, two white Thoroughbreds were registered – one in the US and one in France – there pre-viously having been only three of this colour in the history of the breed.

While some other animals are said to be

capable of quicker spurts over abbreviated distances, the Thoroughbred is capable of greater sustained speed than any other creature. A Thoroughbred can maintain absolute peak speed for only approximately a quarter of a mile (400 m), but it can run reasonably close to peak speed for surprisingly long distances. While carrying 57.3 kg the American Secretariat ran $1\frac{1}{2}$ miles in 2 minutes and 24 seconds, as a three-year-old. As a four-year-old, Dr Fager, under the respectable burden of 134 lb, ran a mile in 1 minute, $32\frac{1}{5}$ seconds. The listed world record for a quarter-mile is $20\frac{4}{5}$ seconds, established by Big Racket as a four-year-old in 1945. This is one of the oldest Thoroughbred time records on the books, since Thoroughbreds race at that short distance very, very rarely.

In addition to speed, stamina and weight-carrying capacity are factors considered in Thoroughbred breeding. While in flat racing weights in excess of 60 kg are seldom carried, in steeplechase racing, which usually involves longer distances, weights range up to 80 kg.

Some steeplechasers are not 'pure' Thoroughbreds, although the commonly used term, half-bred, often is a misnomer since many of the horses thus described are three-quarters, seven-eighths or even higher fractions of pure breeding. The purpose of such infusions of outside blood is to tone down the impetuosity associated with pure Thoroughbreds in order to make the horse more amenable to control. In days past, 'grade' Thoroughbreds were highly prized as cavalry mounts.

In other proportions, infusions of Thoroughbred blood with that of cold-blooded horses has been utilized to impart certain desired characteristics, including beauty, to the offspring. For instance, at one time it was estimated that nine-tenths of the light horses in America (not to mention some mules!) had some 'Thoroughbred' ancestry. Before the various stud books were originated in America it was not uncommon for the same stallion to serve as a sire of both 'running horses' (future Thoroughbreds) and trotting horses, and after the establishment of the American Stud Book many registered Thoroughbreds were used as sires of Quarter horses. Today, under certain, controlled circumstances it still is permissible to use Thoroughbreds in the breeding of Standardbred (trotting and pacing) and Quarter horses, but the reverse is not true.

The Criollo

Jean-Paul Klein

The Polo Pony

G. R. M. Kydd

The Criollo is the native horse of Argentina. Though not tall – between 14.2 and 15 h.h. – it has great endurance and willingness. It is descended from the Spanish horses of the *conquistadores*, many of which escaped and ran wild; feral bands of these horses or their descendants lived on the pampas in conditions identical with those of wild animals, exposed to a very harsh climate, with dry summers and cold winters. This brought about a natural selection whereby only the hardiest and most enduring survived. Of all the types brought over by the *conquistadores*, it is believed that the Andalusians, those with a strong dash of Barb blood, were the most successful in propagating themselves under these feral conditions, thanks to the toughness of their Barb ancestry. As with many other breeds, too great an infusion of foreign blood, derived from Spain and the United States, was almost the ruin of the breed, which gained speed and good looks at the expense of robustness. Perceiving this, breeders selected the best specimens of the old sort to breed from, since when the Criollo has had a new lease of life. A breed society was founded in 1918.

A noted instance of the Criollo's toughness and stamina was the famous journey which, forty years ago, the Swiss schoolmaster Tschiffely made with two horses from Buenos Aires to New York: 21 360 km, without a day's sickness or lameness.

This is not so much a breed as a type. Whatever its height, it is still called a pony. When the game was first played in the West, polo ponies were small but they were bred larger and larger by a gradual infusion of Thoroughbred blood. There are many requirements for a polo pony; but it must essentially be very fast, with lightning acceleration and the ability to stop dead instantly, able to turn on a sixpence, often at right angles, and be game for anything. Physically it must be a true athlete and have hocks of iron. It must also be kind. All these qualities, not always mutually compatible, mean that top-class specimens are scarce. The best are now bred in Argentina, from a blend of Criollo and Thoroughbred strains. The Argentinians are gradually succeeding in evolving a fixed polo 'breed' or at least type by keeping the best mares which have proved themselves in breeders' matches.

Life with Horses in Australia

Susan Edwards

Man's association with the horse in Australia has been no brief flirtation but an exciting affair that has survived progress. Horse and man made dangerous journeys of discovery together, afforded each other companionship on lonely bush tracks and won wars in distant lands. The horse's place is firmly entrenched in the hearts of all Australians. Urbanization has failed to make him redundant, and his popularity is confirmed by the thousands of spectators he attracts at sporting events around the country.

The first horses arrived in Australia after a gruelling seventy-seven-day voyage with ears pricked, eyes bright and spirits willing. And on that sunny day in Sydney Cove on 26 January 1788, the history of the horse in Australia began.

The number of horses that were taken aboard at Cape Hope by the First Fleet varies; some references note that four mares and two stallions were amongst the cargo, while other authorities put the total at three mares, one stallion, one colt and two fillies. But whatever their numbers, they were a small group. Ship surgeon Arthur Bowes, travelling aboard the *Lady Penrhyn*, jotted in his diary on 26 January, 'All the horses were landed in excellent condition.'

The precise breeding of these animals is not known, for the horse was no more indigenous to the Cape than he was to Australia. However. it could be assumed that they were a mixture of Arab and Barb imported from Java. The hardy Basuto pony had by then also evolved in the southern part of the African continent, so he, too, might have been aboard.

Very shortly after the discovery of Australia, ships began to make regular voyages between England and Australia, and each time the cargo would include a few more horses. The first blood horse arrived from South Africa in the latter part of the 1770s. He is referred to as both Rockingham and the Young Rockingham, but stud books show that about this period there was a stallion called Rockingham in England, so it is possible that the Australian import was sired by the English horse.

These early imports worked hard in their strange new country. Expeditions were made into deserts and mountain ranges on their backs, and they carried life-giving supplies to distant townships that were slowly being established. They pulled coaches and carts, lugged cleared timber and ploughed the land.

They also entertained the new settlers, and racing furnished relief from the hard working routine. There is no doubt that often when two horses met they were raced, but the first official meeting was in Sydney on Monday, 15 October 1810. The three-day meeting generated much excitement, a feeling that has stayed in the hearts of most Australians to the present day. Races were held on the Monday, Wednesday and Friday, and a silver cup and a purse of fifty guineas was presented. The favourite at this first meeting was a six-year-old grey gelding named Chase who won two of the major races. The new sport rapidly gained popularity and meetings began to be held in other parts of the huge continent. In Western Australia racing was established by 1833, in South Australia and Victoria in 1838, in Tasmania in 1814 and in Queensland by 1854.

This new interest did much to improve the bloodlines, and good Thoroughbreds and Arabs were now being imported from England with the sole purpose of breeding better and faster racehorses. This in turn led to the breeding of an improved working horse who was still required to deliver mail, transport passengers and herd cattle and sheep. This new equine settler slowly began to develop into a distinctive type. He was a light but hardy animal with boundless stamina, good feet and a kind and willing temperament. He could be ridden all day, covering many miles in hot dry conditions, be hobbled at night and left to forage for himself and yet step out keenly the next morning.

This was the working pattern for many horses in Australia, and it proved to be a valuable asset when there was a war to win. More than sixteen thousand horses went to the Boer War from Australia, and for the first time soldiers from other countries were introduced to the Waler – a war horse whose courage and stamina was to become famous.

The Waler stood between 15 and 16 h.h. was of 'dense bone' and capable of carrying 108 kg all day. He had good shoulders and quarters and well let down hocks. Nimble footed, with a good turn of speed, he could also jump (he was recorded as having cleared 8 ft. 4 in. in 1940).

This brave horse was called upon again in World War One and 121 324 were recruited. Probably his finest hour on the battlefield was the world-famous charge by the 4th Light Horse Brigade and the Anzacs upon Beersheba. They galloped fearlessly over unreconnoitred land, under intense machine-gun fire. The order went out to the Turks to bayonet the horses in their bellies, but they charged on right into the city of Beersheba in what must surely be one of the most daring cavalry charges in history. Sadly, the end of the war saw the end of the cavalry and the extinction of the Waler.

While climate and terrain play a part in the development of the horse in Australia, there can be no claims to a definite Australian breed.

Horse breeding is a multi-million dollar industry, and the Australian Thoroughbred is a high-quality product. He is finely bred, strong and able to withstand the rigorous training programme he faces. Because the majority of races in Australia are over short distances the Australian Thoroughbred tends to be much faster than his Northern Hemisphere counterparts.

The Thoroughbred trade is international and many stallions from England, Ireland, France and America are now covering mares in their own season, then flying to Australia for breeding in the Southern Hemisphere season. This traffic has given a great boost to the Thoroughbred breeders and products like Dayana and Vain are in the world class.

Today Australia has 1000 registered stallions and 22000 registered brood mares. These figures are increasing every year with the importation of overseas horses. There is no doubt that without the continued infusion of foreign blood the high quality associated with the Australian Thoroughbred could not have been achieved. Looking closely at the breeding of the champion Australian racehorse, Toy Show, one sees that she is the daughter of an English mare with French blood on the distaff side and some American blood. Her sire was Irish.

One of Australia's top studs, Queensland's Gainsborough Lodge (now sold), had stallions from England (Charlton), France (Rock Roi), and America (Beau Brummel).

One of the most beautiful studs is Colin Hayes's Lindsay Park stud in South Australia. During her Jubilee year visit, Elizabeth II requested a chance to look around Colin Hayes's stud. Australia's Jubilee gift to her was an offspring of the stud's top sire, Without Fear.

Australia is not populated by Thoroughbreds alone. The English and Irish native breeds are well established, and stallions from the respective breeds have a busy season as the popularity of these ponies grows.

The Welsh Mountain pony has been valuable in show pony breeding. Early records show that he was first imported by the Australian

Agricultural Company in 1826. Arabs, too, were imported about this time, many of them from India. The demand for these beautiful horses has never decreased and their value is rising. Arabs are used widely in equestrian sports – from endurance rides to show jumping.

The draught horse was quickly established in Australia, as much of the country's agricultural power came from the horse. (Bullocks and camels were also used, though not as widely.)

Weight was added to the heavy horse through the importation of English and Flemish sires and Australia's island state, Tasmania, can be credited with bringing out England's Shires.

Clydesdales were quickly established in Victoria and Suffolk Punches in New South Wales. Years ago these heavy breeds were crossed, though happily for purists this habit died out. The tough, and not particularly beautiful, Timor pony was imported from nearby islands, and this early strain did much for the stamina and toughness of many types.

Although ninety per cent of Australia's horses are bred 'to order', the wild horses of the desolate outback reproduce uncontrolled, provided they survive the harsh climate and the ruthless human. Many thousands of these wild horses (Brumbies) were killed purposely years ago when farmers felt they were eating too much grass. Despite the enormous loss of horseflesh after World War One (one horse returned to home shores), the Brumbies continued to be considered vermin. About this period some 4000 were shot on Glenormiston station, and a similar number on Clifton Hill, another large South Australian property. On a neighbouring property 9000 were slaughtered.

In many parts of Australia this slaughter continues today, and the Brumbie is trapped and killed by the unscrupulous for pet food. Some, however, find happy homes. The progeny of the Stock horse which has become feral, they are still suitable, for children's pets and as working horses.

The Stock horse is still the backbone of the agricultural industry, and despite modern advances in this area nothing has been found to replace him. The Australian Stock Horse Society had 11000 mares, 1000 stallions and 2000 geldings on its books in 1976. These horses are usually half Thoroughbred from proven mares who have proved to be hard workers. The Stock horse has a natural ability and many will swear their horses could 'work' cattle and sheep without human assistance. It has tremendous stamina and will work unflaggingly all day in blistering conditions. Most of the large stations breed from their own stallions, but with the recent forming of the society, property owners now have a wider choice from quality stallions.

The beauty, ability and characteristics of individual breeds captures the imagination of many Australians, and Arabs, Andalusians, Quarter horses and Shetlands are now being bred with enthusiasm by experts. However, as in other countries, many horses are regarded merely as pets and members of the family.

As previously noted, Australians are keen race-goers. Meetings are staged every day except Sunday on one or another of Australia's 464 racecourses. Indicative of the nation's participation in this sport is the public holiday given to those who live in Victoria on the day that the Melbourne Cup is run. The state's most prestigious race, it is staged on the first Tuesday in November. The Melbourne Cup along with the Sydney Gold Cup during the Easter Carnival are probably the racing calendar's major events.

Phar Lap – known affectionately as Big Red – was probably Australia's most internationally famous horse. Racing during the depression, he never let the public down, and they loved him. In more recent times a grey, Gunsynd – nicknamed 'the galloping grey' – was a brilliant horse and a high stakes winner. When he retired from his racing career he was given more presents and public tributes than any visiting movie star.

It is not just the neatly clipped lawn of the city racecourses that attract the race-goer. In the little bush towns, where the flies are thick and the air heavy with dust, the 'locals' from hundreds of miles away gather to watch the horses of their region race. Through the thick dust of the track it might be harder to distinguish the winner – but the cheers are just as loud.

Racing enthusiasts are not the only ones catered for. Each state has its major annual show which is staged in the heart of the city. During 'show week' the country people flood into town, and it is the horse events at these large agricultural shows that attract the crowds. The hotels, restaurants and pubs are filled with the talk of ribbons, champions and the day's events, and wide-brimmed hats and high-heeled boots are just as common during show week as the well tailored suit. Show jumping, hack and ridden pony classes attract many entries and are of a high standard. The premier awards are the championships at the Royal Melbourne in September and the Royal Sydney held during Easter.

Some Australian riders have international reputations: Bill Roycroft, Brian Crago, Laurie Morgan and Ern Barker have all done well overseas. At home, Kevin Bacon's name dominates the show jumping scene year after year.

Dressage was slow to establish itself in Australia and for a long time was confined to those who were attempting to qualify for the Olympics. Nowadays, however, it has a large number of devotees. Dressage competitions are included on the programmes of the larger shows, and dressage clubs, associations and societies stage their own events. It also is of course required for the three-day event, which is growing in popularity.

Sport that attracts almost the same number of spectators as racing is trotting. Mainly imported from the United States, the horses are known as Standardbreds. The 'trots', as they are known colloquially, are staged at night under floodlights. Betting is legal, and the excitement the sport arouses is enormous, with both trotting and pacing included on the programme. One of the most important events in the trotting calendar is the Interdominion

which was established in 1936 and is open to horses from New Zealand. The championships are held alternately in New Zealand or major Australian cities. The New Zealand-bred horse Cardigan Bay, who later competed in Australia and the United States, was one of the highest ever stakes winners, earning more than a million dollars in his brilliant career.

Driving classes have been attracting a wide following in recent years, though they cannot be compared to the classes held at English shows. However, Hackney stallions and foundation mares are being imported from England and societies are being formed to engender enthusiasm. The annual Harness Show in Victoria drew 235 entries in 1976. Three-day driving events (with dressage, cross-country and an obstacle course) are popular too.

An equestrian sport that grew naturally from the life-style of the Australian bushman is the rodeo. Today spectators gather to watch events like bronco riding, roping, cutting, and camp draughting while in the outback the horsebreaker still has to be able to ride the bucks of a newly broken horse, cattle still have to be cut out of the herd and calves have to be roped for branding.

Rodeos attract some of the most skilful riders in Australia. The events are hard on horses and men, and for some years the animal protection societies have been attempting to have rodeos banned. To celebrate the United States' bicentennial, eight rough-riders from Australia went to America to join the Professional Rodeo Cowboys Association. In 1975, Jim-Dix, an Australian rough-rider, won the famous Calgary Stampede.

Hunting, though practised by a dedicated group of horsemen and women, is not nearly as well supported as it is, for example, in the UK. The season is short, lasting from May to September, and hounds stay out for only three or four hours. Fox is the most common quarry, though kangaroo and dingo are hunted in Tasmania.

The unspoilt countryside that lies a few miles outside the cities and towns of Australia makes trail riding a pleasure and novice horsemen and women are beginning to take to this pastime. An extension of the trail rides are endurance rides, and these, too, are becoming popular. The 100-miles Tom Quilty Ride, organized by the Australian Endurance Riders' Association, is internationally known.

The national Equestrian Federation has permanent training grounds where instructional schools are held. This group does a grand job in raising money to send the Australian Olympic teams overseas.

The Royal Agricultural Societies in all states manage the massive organization that makes their major shows so successful.

The Pony Club was established in 1954 and is managed along the same guidelines as its parent body in England. Recognized as the most enthusiastic Pony Club nation, it boasts a membership of 25000. Rallies are well attended and camps fully booked. Each state manages its own affairs and, as in England, clubs are zoned.

Children are educated in the ways of the horse world by the Pony Club, while hunt clubs, dressage clubs, polo clubs and show jumping clubs organize events to bring riders together. Each state has a jockey, turf or racing body that oversees the many race meetings, while the breeding of racehorses is aided by the Bloodhorse Breeders Association. Every breed, colour and type has its society and all these hard-working people do much to generate enthusiasm and maintain standards in the horse world of Australia.

Principal breeds

The Australian Stock horse

In a largely agricultural country the Stock horse is invaluable. Bred along Thoroughbred lines he usually stands about 15.2 h.h. with strong quarters and good bone. His feet are excellent and able to withstand daily work over rough terrain for long months. Sure-footed, fast and with a great deal of stamina, he is valued more for his working capacity than his looks.

Australian pony

In the early days of the colony Exmoor, Shetland and Timorese ponies were interbred indiscriminately. In 1931 the pony stud book was opened and a standard type began to emerge. Though varying in height and showing Thoroughbred, Arab and British pony breed influences, it is now recognized as the Australian pony.

Life with Horses in Austria

Eva Podhajsky

Austria's history and rich tradition offer many points of interest to the horse lover. In Vienna one can see coaches and carriages, formerly used for galas and transportation at the Imperial Court from the seventeenth to the twentieth centuries, now exhibited in the Wagenburg (Coach Museum) established in the former riding hall of the Imperial palace of Schönbrunn. Trophies from the wars against the invading Turks and armour for horse and rider dating from the fifteenth and sixteenth centuries are on display in the Armament Museum (Neue Hofburg), and particularly fine examples of the art of armoury may be seen in Ambras Castle near Innsbruck (Tyrol). The Museum of Harness and Tack, as well as that of Shoeing and Hoof Care, may be visited in the Veterinary University in Vienna which is, incidentally, the third oldest in the world.

The bibliophile will find rare books and manuscripts at the National Library and that of the Veterinary University, and there is much fascinating reading matter at the Spanish Riding School. Austria has had a number of significant authors. The Imperial Equerry, Franz Holbein von Holbeinsberg, 1832–1910, in his *Directives* was the first to publish an outline of the training of horse and rider as practised at the Spanish Riding School where he was director from 1898 to 1901. Another famous member of this institute, Riding Master Max Ritter von Weyrother, in the early nineteenth century contributed to the *Regulations for Austrian Cavalry*. Instructor and second in command of the Military Equitation School in Salzburg, Christian Borries Freiherr von Oeynhausen, 1812–75, published several books and treatises on riding and training.

These books and manuscripts may be consulted at the Spanish Riding School, a visit to which is an absolute must for any tourist interested in horses and equitation. Daily training sessions and demonstrations of *haute école* are held on Sundays from March to December (July and August excepted) in Fischer von Erlach's beautiful riding hall, built from 1729 to 1735. The stables, with marble mangers, located in the sixteenth-century part of the Hofburg, may be visited throughout the year.

In the offices of the Spanish Riding School paintings of the Lipizzaners by Julius von Blaas (1845–1922) and Philip Ferdinand de Hamilton (1667–1750) are exhibited and more of their work may be seen in Schönbrunn, at the Museum of Art, and in the Austrian Gallery at the Belvedere. Ludwig Koch (1866–1934) was the first to represent correctly the sequence of the horse's movements. His theory of motion is compiled in his book *Die Reitkunst im Bilde*. His paintings of cavalry battles and army manoeuvres exhibited in the Army Museum, the Hofburg and the Museum of Art give a vivid picture of the grandeur of Austro-Hungarian cavalry.

Strolling through Vienna, the tourist's interest is arrested by a number of equestrian statues, the most outstanding of which are Anton Ritter von Fernkorn's (1813–78) statues of Prince Eugene of Savoy and of Archduke Charles on the lilac-studded Heldenplatz.

Although the Austrian cavalry school disappeared in 1938 and there is no longer a horse cavalry, the Military Academy in Wiener Neustadt maintains a small group of competitive (mainly three-day event) riders. International competitions are held regularly, such as the

CSI in Laab im Wald in May (Colonel Podhajsky Memorial Show), the CSI in Salzburg in early autumn and the CSI in Vienna (Stadthalle) in late autumn.

The National Federation (Bundesfachverband für Reiten und Fahren) controls the provincial federations which in turn control the riding clubs. Only members of clubs may participate in national competitions. To compete in international competitions they must be delegated by the National Federation. Within the Federation there are advisers for hacking and trekking, as well as for driving. Instead of regular pony clubs in the international sense there are junior groups aged ten to eighteen within the clubs, as well as vaulting groups. No federal control is exercised over the forty or so commercial riding schools and no teaching licences are required. There are some 200 riding clubs with about 12000 members. Although the clubs require no official teaching licences, eight of them are recognized by the National Federation and instruct apprentices to become teacher-trainers after three years of schooling.

Travel on horseback has become very popular in tourist regions where trekking excursions taking from one to several days are organized by the local tourist offices and riding clubs to which those interested may turn for information. The Burgenland, adjacent and leading up to the Hungarian plains, is particularly suited for trekking and offers much in the way of folkloric accents.

In the alpine provinces the indigenous breeds of Haflingers and Norikers are used for transportation, timber hauling, as pack-horses and for all agricultural work. Being part of daily life they play a role in folkloric events. There are processions on horseback, a mass and blessing of animals on St George's Day (23 April) and St Leonhard's Day (6 November), for a thanksgiving feast and on occasions of local importance. Contests of medieval origin are held, such as 'Ringelstechen' (running at the ring) where the rider, at full gallop, tries to catch a ring suspended on a pole. Haflingers are used for ski-jöring and sleigh competitions,

'Gasselfahren' being the Tyrol version of them. An unusual event is the Stallion Parade in Stadl-Paura which is held every autumn. In the nineteenth century Stadl-Paura provided quarters for horses that towed empty salt barges upstream. Later it was operated by the army as a station for stallions at stud and today is a government institution which provides all of Austria with sires. Here half-bred, Haflinger and Noriker stallions are selected and trained before they go to private breeders for the season. They are presented to the public in the Stallion Parade which includes demonstrations of riding and driving. Stadl-Paura is now developing into a training centre for riding and driving.

While driving was very popular in social, court and military circles during the Dual Monarchy the interest in this sport is only now reawakening.

Flat racing, including several international events, takes place on the Friedenau course in Vienna's Prater Park, the chief races being the Trial Stakes and the Austrian Derby, both held in late spring, and the St Leger in September. Harness racing is also popular in Austria, the leading course, the Krieau, also being in the Prater Park. Trotting takes place in Austria all the year round and important races include the national Trotters' Derby in June, and two international races in autumn. The racing societies are the Jockey Club and the Wiener Galopprennverein for flat racing and the Wiener Trabrennverein for trotting. There are also amateur and local associations which are dependent on these societies. There is no steeplechasing in Austria.

There are no packs of hounds in the country, but riding clubs organize hunts for their members and guests in which one rider takes the role of the fox.

Although probably chiefly remembered for his association with the Spanish Riding School, Alois Podhajsky achieved notable successes for Austria in competitive dressage with the Thoroughbred horse, Nero. This combination won the European Dressage Championship in Budapest in 1935 and went on to take the individual bronze medal at the 1936 Olympic Games in Berlin.

All horse breeding in Austria is government controlled, the Department of Agriculture supervising the official provincial stud organizations which control the National Breeding Societies. These maintain the stud books of their particular breeds, while the Jockey Club controls that of Thoroughbreds.

The total horse population is approximately 40000, comprising 500 Thoroughbreds, 4600 half-breds, 150 Arabs, 210 Lipizzaners, 2200 trotters, 1200 ponies, 17000 Norikers and 14000 Haflingers. All are bred by private breeders except for the Lipizzaners which are bred at the National Stud Farm at Piber, Styria. Half-breds are imported from Germany, Poland, Hungary and Czechoslovakia, generally as riding horses, plus Thoroughbred mares for breeding. Norikers are exported, mainly to Italy. Auctions are held for Haflinger colts in March and for foals in September in Ebbs in the Tyrol, and for Noriker stallions in Saalfelden in September and in Wels every four years. There are agricultural exhibitions every year, held alternately in Wels and Ried and within the Vienna Fair (March and September).

Principal breeds

The Haflinger

The Haflinger pony numbers the Arabian as one of its chief ancestors and was for many years employed as a pack, draught and general-purpose pony in southern and northern Tyrol. Today it is chiefly used as a saddle horse for leisure riding. Like most mountain-bred equines it is sure-footed, strong and long lived, with a docile temperament and adaptable nature. The Haflinger stands about 14 h.h. and is invariably chestnut in colour with a flaxen mane and tail.

The Lipizzaner

The Lipizzaner is descended from Andalusian horses imported by the Archdukes Maximilian II and Charles. Maximilian imported Spanish horses for the Imperial Stud of Kladrub in 1562. In 1580 Charles founded a stud at Lipizza in north-west Yugoslavia, from which the breed takes its name. Barb and Arabian blood was added to the Andalusian and the modern Lipizzaner is descended from fourteen female and six male lines, the latter being those of Maestoso, Favory, Pluto, Conversano, Neapolitano and Siglavy.

The Lipizzaner is a compact horse, standing about 15 to 15.2 h.h. with short, strong legs and strong back and quarters. Most Lipizzaners are grey although some bays occur. The greys are often born black or brown and may take as long as ten years to acquire their characteristic grey coats. Their intelligence, gentleness and longevity make them especially suitable for *haute école* work, and it is their association with the Spanish Riding School in Vienna which made them famous. Their principal studs are at Piber (Austria), Lipica (Yugoslavia), Farasabina (Italy) and Bábolna (Hungary). There are some minor studs in Czechoslovakia and in the USA.

The Noriker

The ancestor of this breed was the Roman charger which subsequently became the draught horse of the Alpine region. The name Noriker, derived from the state of Noricum, corresponded roughly in outline to present-day Austria and formed part of the Roman Empire. Infusions of Neapolitan and Andalusian blood increased the height of the breed and today it averages about 16 h.h. Having been bred and worked in mountain regions for so many years, the Noriker is a sure-footed horse and is much in demand as a work horse for hill country. It has a good temperament, is an economical feeder and is long lived. The principal colours are bay and chestnut, although some spotted horses are found too. There is a heavy type and a lighter one.

Life with Horses in Belgium

André Monteilhet
M. F. H. de Genellis

For a long time Belgium had a high reputation for her heavy draught horse, the Ardennais, a breed which is robust and resilient in the harshest climates, but since 1950 increasing mechanization has caused the numbers of horses to decline and by 1960 Belgium had only about 150000 horses left on her territory.

At present the riding horse is being bred most successfully under the control of two large institutions. The first of these, the Royal Society of the Belgian Half-Bred, was founded in 1920. Its 1800 members own about 100 stallions licensed to stand at public stud. Since 1960 it has registered about 8000 brood mares and 12000 riding horses. Every year it organizes about ten official shows, in addition to which another ten or so are organized by the local societies. The second institution, the National Association for Blood Horse Breeding (ANECS), was founded in 1955 by Canon A. de Mey and consisted in 1975 of 5390 breeders with 14000 brood mares. Since 1955 it has registered 27931 animals, 236 of which were Thoroughbred stallions; 104 stallions were admitted to stand at public stud in 1976. This association maintains an institute at Oud Heverlee offering seven-year training courses for students aspiring to a 'first class' instructor's degree, admitting about a thousand students every year. Its magazine, *Het Warmbloedpaard* (*Our Thoroughbred Horse*) is a Flemish-language publication because Thoroughbred breeding is concentrated in the Flemish provinces.

Belgium has taken an interest in the riding horse since her independence in 1830–1. As early as 1842 Leopold I instituted in Brussels a Practical Equitation Course, a strictly military organization which was transferred, in 1847, to Ypres. There it became the famous Cavalry School of Ypres, one of Europe's most brilliant until 1914. During the Belle Époque many distinguished horsemen were active there, such as Colonel Hagemans (commandant of the school), Lieutenants André de Meeus, de Blommaert, Terlinden and André Van Derton, and Ch. d'Orjo de Marchovelette who was champion of the Military on the eve of World War One and commanded the School of Brasschaet from 1931 to 1938.

In 1883 the Société Royale Hippique de Belgique (Royal Equestrian Society of Belgium), the first civilian riding club, was created. In 1884 it organized the first Belgian official horse show. In 1898 there appeared the Comité Central Hippique (Central Equestrian Committee) which in 1922 took on the name of Fédération Nationale Belge des Sports Équestres (Belgian National Federation of Equestrian Sports). Its first president, Mr Dupuich, collaborated in the foundation of the FEI (1921) which was located in Brussels and whose first president was Colonel du Teil of France. A Belgian general, Baron de Trannoy, was to preside over the FEI from 1946 to 1954.

On 27 August 1902 the long-distance ride from Brussels to Ostend, one of the first of its kind, was held over 135 km with Belgian, British, French, Dutch, Russian and Swedish officers taking part. The winner was the French Lieutenant of Dragoons Madamet on Courageux. A score of horses died of exhaustion or heat stroke.

An Institut de la Ferrure (a farriers' institute) was inaugurated in Brussels in 1904. This institute confers a State-recognized diploma and in 1975 was attended by 150 students.

In 1905 the first Belgian Military Championships were held. These championships, which became international in 1910, were the fore-runners of the *concours complet d'équitation*. Their success contributed to the admission of equestrian sports to the Stockholm Olympic Games in 1912, although, in fact, the Paris Olympics of 1900 had staged three equestrian events. The broad jump (6.10 m) was won by Lieutenant Van Langendonck and the show jumping by Captain Haegeman with Lieutenant Van der Poele in second place.

In 1912 at Stockholm Captain de Blommaert on Clonmore won the Olympic show jumping bronze medal.

Then came the war and the crushing of the unhappy town of Ypres whose ruins were preserved by the British soldiers for four years. The school, closed down in August 1914, was replaced by the Centre d'Instruction pour Sous-Lieutenants Auxiliaires de Cavalerie (Instruction Centre for Auxiliary Cavalry Second Lieutenants), first near Calais (1915–18), then at Tervueren (1919–21), prior to the opening of the new school at Brasschaet near Antwerp (1921–40). On 19 October 1918, at Burkel, two squadrons of the 1er Guides, led by Major Van Strydonck, conducted the last cavalry charge on the western front which pierced the defences of the surprised German machine gunners. The first commandant of the Brasschaet Cavalry School (1921) was the then Colonel Van Strydonck of Burkel fame.

From 1920 on Belgian riders met with spectacular success in Europe, North America and Egypt. This continued until the beginning of the mechanization of the army in 1937.

World War Two ended the School of Brasschaet (May 1940). After 1945 only the Gendarmerie Royale upheld the tradition of the military horse. But Captain Henri Laame (1891–1966), chief riding instructor at Brasschaet from 1933–40, wrote a valuable dressage treatise published in 1959.

The disappearance of the cavalry school was compensated for by the emergence in the fifties of a new generation of young civilian riders.

Eventually, in 1971, after over thirty years, a Belgian military team was once more set up by Colonel Pierre Francisse, chief of army sports, in collaboration with Colonel Lorgé, commandant of the Gendarmerie à Cheval. This team has revived the tradition of the Ypres and Brasschaet schools.

André Monteilhet

Principal breeds

The Ardennais

The Ardennais is native to the sandy soils of north-eastern Belgium and is a medium-heavy draught horse. As well as being popular as a farm and general transport horse it was, prior to mechanization, much used in the army. Throughout the nineteenth century and during the early half of the twentieth the Ardennais stallions were in demand in Germany and France as upgraders of the local heavy draught breeds. A stocky horse, the Ardennais stands between 15.1 and 15.3 h.h. Although it has a notably kind disposition it is a lively worker and is well suited to the hilly land of the Ardennes country. The usual colours are roan, sorrel, bay and chestnut and the breed is notable for being an economical feeder.

The Belgian Heavy Draught horse

The Belgian Heavy Draught horse is said to be descended from the diluvial horse of the quaternary era. The modern Heavy Draught horse is a powerful animal standing up to 16.3 h.h. The usual colours are red roan with black points, chestnut and sorrel, and it is one of the strongest of all draught breeds. The head, which is rather small and short, is set on a massive neck. The shoulders are very strong, the body compact and heavy, the legs short and very muscular, with abundant feather at the fetlocks. But despite these features the Heavy Draught horse is not without elegance.

The Ardennais.

The Belgian Saddle horse

The Saddle horse, far less well known than the draught breeds, has come much more to the fore recently and comprises two types: a riding horse and a trotter. Both are rather solid but neither has any striking physical characteristic. The Saddle horse is of mixed foreign origin, of which the principal contribution has been French blood.

M. F. H. de Genellis

Life with Horses in Canada

André Monteilhet
J. M. Draper

The French settlers of the mid-seventeenth century took with them the first horses ever seen in Canada. Later the British imported English and Irish horses, and Canadian horses have been renowned for their jumping since before 1914. During World War One draught horses were shipped from Canada to Europe by the thousands, their destinations the general transport and artillery branches of both the British and French armies.

In 1926 the Canadian Hunter and Light Horse Society was created, and in 1933 it opened, in Ottawa, a stud book for the Canadian hunter. But the provincial breeders have, over the years, created the Canadian Cutting horse, a cousin of the American Quarter horse, which, as its name implies, is used on the ranches or in open country for cutting cattle. The Cutting horse was the horse of the ranks of the Royal Canadian Mounted Police till 1940 when Commissioner Wood created around the venerable Fort Walsh (built in 1874) the private stud of the Mounties, a 15000-acre domain where Thoroughbred stallions cover half-bred and Canadian Cutting horse mares. (For a brief history of the Royal Canadian Mounted Police see the special article dealing with it.)

The 'empire of woods and wheat', which raises annually about a million head of beef cattle and 10 million sheep, still had, around 1970, half a million horses, many of which guarded the herds on the ranches of the West and were used in unloading logs in the forests or as pack animals in certain isolated districts of the Rocky Mountains. Increasing mechanization has caused horse breeders and users to turn towards the sports horse.

In Canada, which is still a free enterprise country, the official aid and premiums granted by so many European states to their breeders, individual riders or national teams, are largely unknown. In Canada it is the proprietors who select the young riders for training in private centres, the best known of which are near Cleveland and Toronto, the two Canadian 'stopovers' of the famous Fall Circuit (its other three being in the United States, at Harrisburg, Washington DC and New York). Toronto (Ontario) is considered to be Canada's equestrian sports capital. There the great CSIO takes place in November, coinciding with the opening of the Royal Agricultural Winter Fair, which was created in 1930 and is, according to A. Rockwell, one of the greatest exhibitions of horses in the world. Its international shows have since attracted, aside from Canadian riders, teams from Germany, Argentina, Belgium, Brazil, Chile, Cuba, Spain, the USA, France, Great Britain, Ireland, Mexico and the Netherlands.

The Canadian riders are true amateurs, holding all sorts of jobs. The three-day event team which won the team bronze medal in Stockholm in 1956 was a striking example of this. In the Technical Results section it can be seen that the Canadians have found themselves more than once in places of honour.

The 1976 Olympics took place in Montreal. The site chosen for the equestrian competitions – except for the Prix des Nations which is the ultimate competition before the closing ceremony and is traditionally held at the great Olympic stadium – was the vast equestrian stage at Bromont, 75 km from Montreal on the left bank of the St Lawrence. Bromont is the home of the Montreal Hunt, the dean, so it is said, of North American packs, dating back to 1826. At present there are about a dozen packs of hounds engaged in fox- and draghunting in Canada, all of them in Quebec and Ontario, in addition to the Rallye-Kebec, founded in 1969, which hunts the wolf, the fallow deer, the hare and the fox.

Canada has eleven flat racing tracks in the Montreal and Toronto regions and trotting races are also popular.

The country's principal equestrian journal is *Canada Rides*.

Life with Horses in Denmark

André Monteilhet
J. M. Draper

In the fourteenth century the Cistercians of Holstein (a Danish duchy until 1864) created on their vast domains stud farms, where they crossed the large mares of north Germany with Andalusian stallions, brought over from Spain at great expense. The modern Holstein and the Danish breeds have evolved from this early breeding policy.

In 1562 King Frederik II (1559–88) founded near his palace of Frederiksborg the famous stud farm of the same name. The stallion Pluto (1765), foundation sire of one of the present six lines of Lipizzaners, came from Frederiksborg. In 1840 the royal stud farm became a simple stallion station, finally disappearing in 1862. But the breed continues to be bred privately, specifically on the island of Bornholm.

In 1680 King Christian V (1670–99) created the Royal Riding School (Kongelig Rideskole) patterned after those of Vienna and the Great Stables installed by Louis XIV at Versailles in 1683. In 1771 it became the Royal Military Manège (Kgl. Militaere Manege).

A former pupil at the Royal Veterinary School of Lyons, Peter Chr. Abildgaard, founded in Copenhagen (Christianshavn) in 1773 the Royal Veterinary School (Kgl. Veterinaerskole) which served until 1852 as the Danish cavalry school. The latter was then transferred to Copenhagen proper and later (from 1923 to 1951) to Naestved where it was dissolved. By 1931 the Royal Manège of 1771 had disappeared and by 1932 the farrier's school had also closed. The remaining Danish cavalry consists of a squadron of Hussars of the Guard which is still garrisoned at Naestved from where it goes to Copenhagen for official functions and, occasionally, to perform abroad.

One of the most brilliant horsemen to emerge from Naestved was Capt. Peter Jensen (1897–1938) who, after a successful career in dressage in Scandinavia and Germany with his horse His Ex, died on horseback from a heart attack.

Despite its ancient equestrian tradition, Denmark entered the field of competitive sports rather late, i.e., not until the early years of the twentieth century. None the less in 1918 a National Equestrian Federation, Dansk Ride-Förbund, was created and affiliated with the FEI.

André Monteilhet

Principal breeds

The Frederiksborg

The Frederiksborg takes its name from the royal stud set up in 1562 by King Frederik II. Infusions of Neapolitan, British and Eastern blood were made in subsequent centuries, although the breed retains to this day the convex outline of the face indicative of its Spanish ancestry. The Frederiksborg was for many years much in demand as a charger as well as being a popular mount for *haute école* in the days of the great riding schools of Europe. It makes a good driving horse and, having a nice temperament, may be used in the dual roles of harness and saddle horse. Standing about 15.3 h.h., the Frederiksborg is a strong, active horse with a deep chest, powerful shoulders and good legs with plenty of bone. The usual colour is chestnut.

The Jutland

A heavy draught horse of enormous proportions, the Jutland is named after the island of the same name and is believed to have existed for about a thousand years. Although it carried armoured knights during the Middle Ages, it was and is mostly used as a draught horse, for which its gentle nature makes it particularly suitable. The present-day Jutland shows signs of Suffolk blood, a dark chestnut Suffolk stallion called Openheim LXII having been exported from Britain to Denmark in 1860 and crossed with Jutland mares. The exact origin is cloudy; the stallion may possibly have been a Shire. The Jutland stands up to about 16 h.h. and is massively built, with great depth through the chest and girth. The short, strong legs carry feather and the predominant colour is chestnut, but some roan, black, and bay also occur.

The Knabstrup

The Knabstrup is in essence a lighter version of the Frederiksborg. Its distinguishing feature is its spotted coat which it inherited from the spotted mare Flaebehoppen who was put to a Frederiksborg stallion in 1808, establishing a line of spotted horses. In more recent times the Knabstrup has been bred more for coat pattern than for type and the true Knabstrup breed may well have disappeared, although spotted horses of similar type are still found in Denmark, due to a crossing of the last true Knabstrups with a Frederiksborg. The average height of this breed is 15.3. h.h.

J. M. Draper

Life with Horses in France

Jean Froissard

For the past two decades equitation in France has been on the upswing. On the other hand it has also become highly state controlled. After passing through an administrative labyrinth, from the highest to the lowest level, it is now directed and supervised by an 'inter-Ministerial Committee' under the presidency of no less a person than the prime minister. If we add that horse breeding, except racehorses, is controlled by the Service of the National Studs, which in turn depends on the Ministry of Agriculture, and that the manège service of the Cavalry School of Saumur, the Cadre Noir, is dependent on the Superior Council of Equitation, itself an institution controlled by an office whose members are picked by the prime minister or by the State, it is easy to see that scant room is left for private initiative.

The official organization in charge of equitation is the Fédération Française des Sports Équestres (FFSE) whose head office is in Paris. Its principal task is to co-ordinate the efforts of the various institutions the Federation is dependent on and of those it controls. Under the initiative of its current president, Dr Edouard Pouret – all-round horseman, veterinarian of world renown (the Queen of England called on him to operate on her horse, Columbus), Thoroughbred breeder, racehorse owner, foxhunter in Ireland – French equitation has experienced a revival combining quantity with quality. Thanks particularly to his efforts, dressage has regained its place of honour. The technical aspects of the three Olympic disciplines are entrusted to a national technical director, assisted by an aide, on whom depend the three national coaches (dressage, CSO and CCE) who undertake the dual role of preparing riders and horses for international competition and training young riders eventually to take over. Parallel to this 'executive' body, the 'legislative' one is represented by a commission for each discipline.

France is divided into eighteen Regional Leagues, plus a nineteenth for the overseas territories. Each is headed by a president assisted by a regional technical counsellor. The latter combines the roles of judge and instructor of teachers at the clubs and riders alike. Such is, briefly, the organization of equitation in France where over 100000 people ride in one way or another.

Racing and polo alone escape governmental administration. While racing continues to grow – surely largely due to gambling (PMU) – polo has been in difficulty since the war and French polo players are rare despite the efforts of the old-timers. There are, however, still a few international matches held in May and June within the lovely setting of the Bois de Boulogne at the Paris Polo Club, and in July and August at Deauville.

The main flat racing courses are Longchamp, home of the Grand Prix de Paris and the Prix de l'Arc de Triomphe, Chantilly (Prix du Jockey Club and Prix de Diane), Saint-Cloud and Maisons-Laffitte. In winter there are meetings at Cagnes-sur-Mer on the Riviera and in August at Deauville.

Steeplechases and hurdle races are run at Auteuil, notably the Grand Steeple-chase and the Prix du Président de la République, and at

Enghien. In winter there is racing at Pau, at the foot of the Pyrenees and at Cagnes-sur-Mer. Trotting race meetings are held at Vincennes, near Paris, at Enghien and also at Cagnes-sur-Mer. 'Steeple-chases-Cross-countries' are held at Craon, Dieppe and Verrie-Saumur.

The 'chasse à courré' (comprising stag, roebuck, boar and some hare hunting) has many followers. There are at present 120 packs, most of which hunt stag. Staghunting is concentrated mainly in the Paris region, in the storied forests of Fontainebleau, Chantilly, Senlis, Rambouillet and Compiègne, in Normandy, Brittany and the centre of the country. South-eastern France lacks game, but the Pau region, in the south-west, is renowned for its foxhunts, or rather drag hunts, whose runs are profusely dotted with natural banks, the famous 'talus de Pau' throughout the Pau heaths (see *Venery in France* and *Draghunting at Pau*).

In addition there has been for some years past a great deal of trekking; and driving, which for years had fallen into total oblivion, except at the national studs, is coming into its own again.

Since 1968 the Cadre Noir has become, at least on paper, a civilian institution, although the great majority of its members remain commissioned and non-commissioned officers. As in the past it is in charge of training riding instructors at the École Nationale d'Équitation. But this is not its only function. It upholds national prestige by the continued presentation in France and abroad of the traditional *reprises* of the Cadre Noir, the essence of French equitation, and promotes competition by aiding the national coaches of the FFSE.

Equestrian instruction is entrusted to a body of instructors holding the state degrees of moniteur, instructeur or professeur. These diplomas are granted upon examination. Every year a nine-month course is held at the École Nationale d'Équitation for moniteurs getting ready for their instructor's examinations. Several times a year there are also shorter courses for teachers and riders in search of improvement. Besides the instructors' examinations, the ordinary riders have opportunities to check their progress through riding examinations, the easiest being the first degree, followed by a second and third.

Numerous dressage tests, horse shows and horse trials are held throughout France all through the season, both at regional and national levels; each of the three disciplines has its own senior and junior national championships.

The youngest of all institutions is Le Poney-Club de France. This nationwide organization comprises all Pony Clubs and it, too, depends on the Superior Council of Equitation. Young though they may be (b. 1970), these one hundred or so Pony Clubs have some 15 000 young members and are showing considerable vitality.

French breeding is directed by the service of the Haras Nationaux (National Studs), an agency of the Ministry of Agriculture. This service comprises a central administration including three offices – breeding, equitation, racing and Pari-Mutuel – as well as extension services divided into twenty-four conscriptions which, in turn, consist of two general inspection areas each. The four chief functions of this service are: 1) administrative supervision (racing associations); 2) control and technical assistance (orientation of breeding and the promotion of equestrian life); 3) organization of public covering services (utilization of the 1736 national stallions); 4) research for and publicizing of technical progress. This body presides over everything pertaining to the horse throughout the country. The funds provided by PMU betting are in part re-invested in the development of equitation. Moreover, the stud book commissions are presided over by the chief of the stud service. Those commissions are in charge of the following stud books: Thoroughbreds (French Stud Book), Trotters (Trotter Stud Book), Saddle horses (Saddle Horse Stud Book). Draught horse stud books are kept by the Syndicats of the respective breeds.

The Fédération Nationale des Associations d'Éleveurs et Propriétaires de Poneys (National Federation of Pony Breeders and Owners

Associations) is responsible for the stud books of the various pony breeds.

With its wealth of equestrian traditions, France has much to offer the foreign visitor interested in horses. Notable among the countless museums concerned with the horse are Le Musée du Cheval at the Château of Saumur overlooking the Loire; the Musée de l'Armée at the Hôtel des Invalides in Paris, which has a marvellous collection of armour for horse and rider; the Musée de la Vénerie at the Château of Senlis; and the carriage museums at the Château of Compiègne, Chantilly, and at the Grand Trianon in Versailles. Some of Napoleon's carriages can be seen at the Malmaison, and the Great and Small Stables at Versailles are well worth seeing, as are the Chantilly stables.

In addition, of course, one may attend at Saumur the *reprises* of the Cadre Noir which take place in the Manège des Écuyers. This is an eighteenth-century building which, before the Revolution, served the famous Carabineers of Monsieur, the king's brother. Its beauty resides in its simplicity and purity of lines. On a clear day this beauty is enhanced by most felicitous light effects created by the sun's rays shining through the tall windows to illuminate the interior. On Fridays the presentations are held in dress uniform.

French equestrian literature is particularly noteworthy, including as it does the works of Pluvinel, La Guérinière, Montfauçon de Rogles, Baucher, L'Hotte and Decarpentry (see *A History of Academic Equitation*). All such works are to be found at the Bibliothèque Nationale in Paris.

The Union Nationale Interprofessionnelle du Cheval in Paris, an organization which, although it is not a tourist agency as such, is able to offer a good deal of advice on matters equestrian, publishes two magazines, *L'Éperon* and *Courses et Élevage*, the former dealing with the saddle horse and the latter with racing and Thoroughbred breeding. Other magazines include *L'Information Hippique* and *Plaisirs Équestres*. For racegoers there are a number of weeklies, but the true racing enthusiast reads the daily *Paris-Turf – Sport Complet*.

Principal breeds

The Ardennais

The cradle of the breed is the Ardennes region of wooded hills on the borders of Belgium and north-east France. At one time whole regiments of cavalry were mounted on Ardennais and later, under the Empire, it was renowned as an artillery horse. Today, however, it is used as a heavy draught horse for which task its tractable nature and great stamina make it ideally suited. It varies in height from 16 to 16.3 h.h. and the usual colours are roan, chestnut and bay.

The Boulonnais

Originating in the north of France, the Boulonnais is a heavy draught horse which has been bred since before the time of the Crusades. Some oriental blood was introduced at the time of the Crusades but although the type has been modified over the centuries its qualities of stamina and docility have endured. Standing between 16 and 17 h.h., it is well proportioned and has a good walk and trot. The usual colours are grey, bay, roan or black. Like all heavy draught breeds, its future outside the horsemeat industry has long been threatened by mechanization.

The Breton

A hardy breed native to Brittany, the Breton can be traced back to the Middle Ages when there were two varieties: the Sommier (English *sumter* or *capul*) for ploughing, pack and cart work; and the Roussin (English *rouncy*), a lighter type used for riding. Over the centuries it was crossed with the Boulonnais, the Percheron and the Ardennais. The Norfolk Roadster Cross was used in the mid-nineteenth century to produce, with great success, the 'Postier Breton'. Until 1945 and later, three types were distinguishable: the heavy draught, the Postier and the mountain horse which was of more pronounced type than the first-named.

All these types have largely merged and now the breed is known simply as Breton Draught. It stands between 15 and 16 h.h. and colours are dun, bay, roan, chestnut, grey, or black. Chestnut roan is the most frequent, black the rarest.

The Camarguais

Considered a horse, not a pony, this breed, native to the Rhône delta, is one of the most ancient in France, but its origin is uncertain. Possibly it is related to the horses from the palaeolithic site of Solutré. A tough weight-carrier, it is ridden by the 'Gardians' when herding cattle. The chest is deep, the shoulder straight, the neck short, back and loins are short. The croup is sloping and rather short. It is a sure-footed animal with good limbs and great stamina. The predominant colour is grey and the mane and tail are abundant.

The French Anglo-Arab

The French Anglo-Arab today comprises what used to be called the pure-bred Anglo-Arab (resulting from the early nineteenth-century direct crossing of Thoroughbred and Arab stock), as well as local part-breds of the south generally and of Tarbes also known as the Navarrine breed, which over the centuries had itself acquired a considerable degree of Arab blood. The French Anglo-Arab shares a stud book with the pure-bred Arab which it greatly outnumbers; a minimum of twenty-five per cent of Arab blood is required for registration, and there must be no ancestors other than Arab, Anglo-Arab or Thoroughbred. This breed, which combines the docility, endurance and toughness of the Arab with the stature and speed of the Thoroughbred, cannot be regarded as fixed because sires and dams other than Anglo-Arab are still being used, but it has qualities peculiar to it.

It is a well-proportioned horse with a tapering head and broad brow, a long withers, a good back, well coupled at the loins, a long, level croup, sloping shoulder and good legs and feet. Height varies between 15 and 16 h.h. and is sometimes bigger. Fast, handy, thrifty, full of stamina, intelligent and good-natured, it is the perfect type of all-purpose riding horse for dressage, jumping, eventing, hunting and racing. The Anglo-Arab, along with the Thoroughbred, is officially recognized as an 'improver' and largely used in the breeding of the Selle Français.

The French Riding pony

The French Riding pony (Poney Français de Selle) is the result of crossing pony mares of the Landais or Pottok breeds with Welsh, Connemara, New Forest or even Arab sires, the object being to produce a pony of riding type up to a height of 14.2 h.h. However, the breeding scheme is at too early a stage for the results achieved to be adequately judged.

The French Trotter

The French Trotter, which is now fixed as a breed, is of mixed pedigree but derives principally from Norman mares crossed with Thoroughbred, Norfolk Roadster and American Standardbred stallions. Breeders even tried Arab blood at one time, but since the results were not satisfactory the experiment was abandoned. Today the French Trotter ranks among the best in the world, both in harness and under saddle. Of medium height, standing from 15.2 to 16.2 h.h., the Trotter has a straight facial profile, long ears, a broad chest and a good topline (long neck and withers, and a long, broad croup). The shoulder tends to be straight. The stud book, which was opened in 1922, was closed in 1941 and only foals by previously entered stallions can now be entered. The cross of Selle Français on Trotter mares has produced some notable show jumpers.

The Landais

Native to the Landes region of the south-west, the Landais is a very hardy breed of pony which nearly perished through lack of interest.

The gradual decline was halted when pony clubs were instituted in 1970, and since then the breed has been on the upgrade. The height may be anything between 11 and 14 h.h. The head is small but expressive, the legs rather slender, but strong, the tail long and well set on. Like all native ponies, the Landais is tough and an economical feeder. Its docile temperament makes it a good child's mount.

The Percheron

Perche is a district just to the south of Normandy which has always produced a breed of horses greatly admired not only in France but abroad. There is, for instance, a British Percheron Society, and there are breeders elsewhere outside France, notably in Canada, the USA and Japan. Before mechanization the chief employment of the Percheron was in agriculture and the transport of fish to Paris. The height is between 16 and 16.2 h.h., but despite its size the Percheron is a graceful, active horse. It has all the qualities of conformation desirable in a draught horse. The colour is usually grey, sometimes black.

The Pottok

Pottok is a Basque word given to the hill pony which comes from around Mont d'Aran and the ridges of Isparla in the Basque country. It is very tough and strong for its size, which varies from 11 to 14.2 h.h. Until World War Two it was much used by smugglers to carry packs across the Pyrenees. The herds live on the mountains all the year round and the ponies tend to be wild. Their chief use has been under pack-saddle but they are also harnessed to light carts.

The Selle Français

The Selle Français is the name now given collectively to half-breds derived from the crossing of regional light-horse breeds with Thoroughbreds and Anglo-Arabs for riding purposes. Basically mares of provincial breeds such as Charollais, Vendéen, Norman, etc., have been put to Thoroughbred stallions, but nowadays Anglo-Arabs and Selle Français stallions are also used. Being a pool of local types, each of which have their own characteristics, the Selle Français cannot be of uniform type. The object is to breed a type with a great deal of blood, and this is achieved by putting carefully selected mares of the old local breeds to Thoroughbred and Anglo-Arab stallions.

Selle Français horses which race do so under the designation AQPSA (Autre que pur sang), and there are several meetings for them alone. As a precaution against cheating, brood mares must have a pedigree proving their breeding, else they are classed as 'non-certified'. As such they cannot be covered by a Thoroughbred stallion, only by an Anglo-Arab or Selle Français, and the progeny of such a mare is registered as 'Selle' only.

Life with Horses in Great Britain

E. Hartley Edwards
G. R. M. Kydd

Riding is one of the major growth sports in Britain, and it is probable that a larger proportion of the population lists riding as a principal hobby than in any other country. As a result the number of horse activities, at all levels, in which riders can participate are many and varied. During the summer it is no exaggeration to say that there would be few, if any, areas of the country in which a rider would not have a choice of a number of competitive events within easy reach of his base on each and every weekend, and there would also be numerous mid-week competitions just as easily accessible.

The period of activity is greatest between the end of March and October, which is the 'season' for horse shows. These cater for the ridden classes for show and working hunters and ponies; for hacks and cobs; driving classes; and breed classes in-hand; and they also include jumping competitions. This is also the season for horse trials, long-distance and endurance riding and, of course, for polo and flat racing.

In 1976 the British Horse Society held seventy-three official horse trials (one-, two- and three-day events) with more entries than could be accepted. Additionally, there were probably two or three times that many 'unofficial' local events held by riding clubs and the branches of the Pony Club.

The hunting season proper opens on 1 November and finishes in April, but between September and the opening meet cub-hunting is carried out by the packs hunting fox. Some two hundred packs of foxhounds are listed in the 1976 edition of *Baily's Hunting Directory*, the bible of the hunting man, as well as twenty-six packs of harriers, nine of draghounds, three of bloodhounds and four of staghounds. In the West Country it is possible to hunt with the Devon and Somerset Staghounds for all but three months in the summer. Hunting in Britain is now possibly more popular than it has ever been and fields are so large, particularly on Saturdays, that many hunts are forced to restrict the number of followers.

Point-to-points, races over fences for amateurs, derive directly from hunting. Almost every hunt holds hunt races, from which the greater part of its income will be obtained, each year between February and May. The winter months of course, are also the season for the National Hunt steeplechases.

But hunting and racing are not the only sports open to horse owners and riders during the inclement British winter. Show jumping and dressage competitions are held increasingly in indoor schools, and outside there are hunter trials over cross-country courses similar to those used in evening, as well as cross-country races for hunt or club teams. The latter are a fairly recent innovation which is gaining rapidly in popularity.

Otherwise, for those who are not competitively minded, hacking about the countryside is something the British can do all the year round; and, of course, there are the numerous riding schools where instruction is given from one end of the year to the other.

The structure of the British horse world may appear to be somewhat fragmented in certain respects, particularly in the areas of horse and pony breeding, where no overall authority exists, but it is, none the less, highly developed and representative of all interests.

Outside racing, which is under the control of the Jockey Club, and polo, which also has its own governing body, the national authority is the British Equestrian Federation. It is an alliance of convenience between the British Horse Society, the body responsible for equitation in its widest sense, and the quite separate British Show Jumping Association, which governs only its own discipline.

The BEF was formed in recent years so that a single body, incorporating all facets of equestrian sport (with the exception of racing and polo) might represent British riding interests more effectively and conveniently at both national and international levels.

The BSJA is responsible for the formulation and maintenance of the rules of jumping, the appointment of judges and course builders, the selection of national teams and the grading of registered horses. The system of grading is based upon the amount of prize money won by a horse: Grade C, under £150; Grade B, £150–399; Grade A, over £400.

There is a junior membership for riders under sixteen years of age and a similar form of grading system is applied. To encourage novice horses, Foxhunter competitions, culminating in an annual championship, are held over courses designed to meet the requirements of horses in this category.

The BHS is obviously a far more complex organization, since its responsibilities cover the administration of all other riding interests, from the maintenance of bridleways to the disciplines of eventing and dressage, as well as the systems of training and examinations for riding instructors. For the latter there are four recognized qualifying grades: BHS Assistant Instructor, BHS Intermediate Instructor, BHS Instructor and the ultimate qualification, the Fellowship of the BHS. Certificates are also awarded for horsemastership and stable management for those wishing to work in stables but who have no ambition to teach riding.

The BHS also operates an approval scheme for privately owned riding schools. In Britain, however, there is no obligation for schools to seek such approval and the majority of the 3000 to 4000 establishments in the country, which may vary from small hiring stables to more sophisticated concerns, do not appear on the BHS approval list, though all, under the Riding Establishments Act, must be licensed by their local authority.

Perhaps the most unique feature of the British riding world and the base of the wide interest which exists in riding is the Pony Club, an autonomous organization incorporated into the BHS.

First formed in 1927, the Pony Club is really a club for young people under seventeen, with an associate membership up to the age of twenty-one. Originally its branches were attached to their local hunts and took their names from them, i.e., the Atherstone Hunt Branch of the Pony Club, and much emphasis was placed on hunting. Today the names are retained, but there is a notable shift of interest from hunting to competitive sports. Furthermore, as riding has become in Britain as much the sport of the urban dweller as of the countryman, numbers of urban-based branches have been formed without any relationship with the hunting field.

At present there are some 300 branches of the Pony Club, covering virtually all parts of Britain, with a membership exceeding 40000. The movement has also spread to other countries where there are in total no less than 1050 branches comprising some 48000 members. The Pony Club is organized in areas, each of which stages annual championships for horse trials, dressage, show jumping, mounted games, etc., which culminate each year in national championships. Individual branches organize their own programmes of instructional mounted and dismounted rallies and most of them have a yearly camp of a week's duration during the summer. It is interesting to note that British international riders, almost without exception, began their careers as members of a Pony Club branch.

The adult equivalent of the Pony Club is the Riding Clubs' movement, also under the jurisdiction of the BHS. Organized on the same lines as the Pony Club, the movement, principally for riders over seventeen, although some clubs may have facilities for juvenile membership as well, comprises over 400 clubs and has a membership almost as large as its junior counterpart.

It should be stressed that whilst the BHS, largely supported financially by its 30000 members, is the governing body centred at the National Equestrian Centre, at Stoneleigh, Warwickshire, it does not offer the facilities of a riding school. Numerous courses are held at the National Equestrian Centre, but its prime purpose is to act as a 'university' for instructors, and it is careful not to infringe upon the privately owned schools which provide much of its support.

Britain is perhaps as fortunate as any country in its ability to breed horses suitable for a variety of purposes, and even more so in having no less than nine indigenous pony breeds eminently suited, either in pure- or cross-bred form, for children and light adults.

There is, however, no equivalent in Britain of the large state studs that are to be found in so many parts of Europe. The breeding of riding horses and ponies, and even of blood-stock, is a matter of private enterprise and dependent more upon small, almost family, establishments than upon large concerns. The one exception is the National Stud at Newmarket, the headquarters of British racing, where leading sires are retained for use by the British bloodstock industry. It is supported largely by funds provided by the government's Horserace Betting Levy Board, but it can hardly be compared in size or influence with its overseas counterparts.

In Britain one may breed any sort of horse or pony, but stallions standing at stud (from age two and upward) must be inspected and subsequently licensed by the Ministry of Agriculture. Each breed has its own society dedicated to its furtherance and welfare. These societies all have stud books and registers and exert their influence by holding their own breed shows, defining the desirable type and characteristics of the horses and ponies with which they are concerned, and appointing panels of qualified judges.

Whilst the breeding of any type of horse is not the concern of government, the latter does give indirect support through the Horserace Betting Levy Board, which makes significant grants to many of the principal breed societies.

Such support is particularly evident in the case of the Hunters' Improvement and National Light Horse Breeding Society which operates, with the Board's assistance, a Premium Stallion scheme whereby some seventy Thoroughbred stallions are made available at much reduced fees to members of the Society and at slightly higher fees to breeders not belonging to the HIS.

The incorporation of the word 'hunter' in the Society's title is perhaps a little misleading. The primary object is indeed to encourage the breeding of quality hunters, but the term encompasses in reality Thoroughbred and half-bred horses whose activities are not necessarily confined to the hunting field, but who may go eventing, show jumping, point-to-pointing or steeplechasing.

Many such horses are bred privately, but there is no doubt that the HIS exerts the greatest single influence on British light horse breeding.

E. Hartley Edwards

Principal breeds

The Anglo-Arab and the Part-bred Arab

In Great Britain Arabian blood has been used on mares of every breed and type, in order to produce either a better animal of the same breed or type or a better or different type of animal. It was used in years past to create the Thoroughbred, the most famous product of Arabian blood in England. It has been used to improve conformation, action or overall quality in already existing breeds such as the Welsh Mountain pony, the Welsh pony, the Welsh

Cob, the Exmoor, the New Forest, the Connemara and the Hackney.

In the twentieth century, when all stud books for established breeds have gradually been closed to new blood from outside, its main use has been to produce individual horses suitable for performance in one sphere or another. This has been done generally by using Arabian stallions on pony, hunter, Thoroughbred or other mares and, more rarely, by using pony or Thoroughbred stallions on Arabian mares.

The performance horse in Britain, unless a Thoroughbred, usually contains a mixture of different kinds of blood, and it is the breeder's skill which discovers the best use of each.

The mixture of pure Arabian and pure Thoroughbred, the Anglo-Arab, produces high quality riding horses, show hacks, dressage and event horses. Provided the Arabian horses used are registered in the Arab Horse Stud Book and the Thoroughbred horses in the *General Stud Book*, Anglo-Arabs are eligible for registration in the Anglo-Arab Stud Book, whatever the relative proportions of Arabian and Thoroughbred blood.

Part-bred Arabs are horses, or ponies, containing a minimum of twenty-five per cent pure Arabian blood and any other blood, except exclusively Thoroughbred. The non-Arab element in Part-breds is often registered pony blood, and this mixture is used to produce show ponies and top-class working, jumping and hunting ponies. Bigger mares are put to Arabian stallions to produce show jumpers and hunter trials and event horses. Here the toughness, quality and speed of the Arab contribute to the ability of the Part-bred to compete effectively in these spheres. Provided the percentage of Arabian blood can be proved, such horses are registrable in the Part-bred Arab Register of the Arab Horse Society.

G. R. M. Kydd

The Cleveland Bay

The only British native horse, as opposed to the pony, that does not belong to the heavy horse category is the Cleveland Bay. Since medieval times the breed has been known in that part of Yorkshire from which it takes its name, where in days gone by it was used in a variety of roles, as a pack-horse, farm horse, in harness and under saddle as a hunter. Later it became the most popular of carriage horses. The Cleveland is usually bright bay in colour with black points and stands between 15.2 and 16 h.h. The body is large and well made with hard, short and clean legs displaying some nine inches of bone. The back, as befits a horse once used for pack work, is relatively long, but there is enormous strength in the loins. The head is fairly large and sometimes reminiscent of that of the Andalusian, whose blood played some part in the early foundation of the breed. The neck is long and the withers relatively unpronounced. Clevelands are usually good jumpers and have all the qualities of a heavyweight hunter, being particularly good, because of their inherent stamina, in heavy country.

When crossed with other breeds the Cleveland passes on its hardiness and strength of bone and is used very successfully crossed with the Thoroughbred to produce hunters and a lighter, faster type of carriage horse.

The Clydesdale

The Clydesdale is a heavy horse which originated in Scotland's Clyde Valley, an area regarded as that country's best horse-breeding land. Early stock was drawn from Flanders and Denmark in the reign of Edward I of England. In the late eighteenth century 'gig mares' of the south-west part of Scotland were crossed with Flanders stallions. By the time of the Industrial Revolution a century later the breed was established and stabilized as an active, quality draught horse of size, strength and stamina, which are characteristics apparent in the modern counterpart.

The Clydesdale stands about 17 h.h. The head is broad and flat-profiled, the back short, but the quarters are rather longer than is the case with other heavy breeds. A curious trait is a tendency to 'cow hocks' and this, combined with the shape of the quarters, can give a totally erroneous impression of a horse that is somewhat weak behind. Much emphasis is laid on the quality of the feet and legs, since the breed was used extensively for town haulage. Clydesdale colours are dark brown or black, often with prominent white stripes on the face and usually with pronounced white shanks. The legs carry heavy feather.

The Cob

Apart from the Welsh Cob, which is an established breed, there are others of mixed ancestry that are none the less of a clearly defined type. The word cob refers to a strong, stocky animal, big in the body and standing on powerful, short legs. Many very good cobs were, and to an extent still are, bred in Ireland out of Irish Draught mares or vanners put to Thoroughbred or polo stallions. Indeed, in the days before the car the cob was as much used in harness as under saddle and was ideally suited for this dual role. The cob is usually regarded as the mount for the heavy and elderly who want a comfortable ride without any displays of equine exuberance. It is not, however, a slug and in the show ring is expected to demonstrate that it can gallop with the best. Much emphasis is placed on manners and temperament. A good cob should come easily back to the hand and should not hot up.

Ideally the body should be deep through the girth and the back short and strong, whilst the head, set on a strong neck, should show as much quality as possible. The cob does not exceed 15.3 h.h. but, in fact, the limit set in British show classes is 15.1 h.h., and it is stipulated that the animal must be up to 14 st.

Until the Act of Parliament, introduced in 1949, which forbade the cruel practice of nicking and docking tails, cobs were frequently docked as a matter of course, and an undocked cob was not seen in the show ring. With 'a bottom like a cook and the head of a lady's maid', the docked cob with hogged mane certainly looked both sporty and jaunty. Today,

cobs have full tails, as they should, but the mane is still hogged, a fashion which suits the conformation of the neck very well, and to see a class of them in the ring is just as attractive a sight as it ever was.

The Dales pony

The Dales pony, which has been known for hundreds of years in the north of England, comes from the area to the east of the Pennines and was originally used as a pack-pony and trotter. The Dales is, in fact, still rather more suitable for driving than riding. The height should not exceed 14.1 h.h. and permissible colours are black and dark brown with an abundance of mane, tail and feather.

The Dartmoor pony

The Dartmoor, more graceful, perhaps, than the rugged Exmoor, is almost as old a breed, possibly originating in the 'little British horses' driven with their owners, the 'Walli', or Welsh, into the moorlands and forests of Wales, Exmoor and Dartmoor before the advancing Saxons. There have been, in the course of improving the breed, admixtures of other blood. Arab was certainly present from the earliest days, but possibly the most successful outcross was the Welsh Mountain stallion, Punchinello, in the early part of this century. The Dartmoor does not exceed 12.2 h.h. and may be bay, black or brown. There is, however, no colour bar, except in the case of pie- and skewbald. The pony has a small, quality head with small prick ears, strong hocks, back and quarters, a good shoulder and excellent feet. It is naturally sure-footed and a remarkably good performer under saddle.

The Exmoor pony

The Exmoor is the oldest and, it is argued, the purest of the British native breeds. Because of the harsh climatic conditions of its original habitat the Exmoor is incredibly tough. A very strong pony, well up to carrying a full-grown man on the moor, it has enormous stamina and courage. In height the Exmoor does not exceed 12.3 h.h. (The height for mares laid down by the Exmoor Pony Society is 12.2. h.h.) The pure-bred Exmoor has a mealy muzzle, the colour of oatmeal. The forehead, is wide, and the eyes prominent and beautiful, are often termed 'toad' eyes because the lids are slightly hooded. The ears are short, thick and pointed and the nostrils wide and generous. The ponies are bay, dun or brown without any white markings. The coat and tail are unusual: the former is harsh and springy to keep out the worst weather, but in summer it lies close and hard and shines; the Exmoor tail is an 'ice' tail, having a fanlike growth at the top.

The Fell pony

The Fell, originating from the opposite side of the Pennines from the Dales, was also formerly used as a pack-pony. Although it is strong and compact the Fell makes a fine riding pony and has a notably good shoulder. It is ideal for trekking and may be successfully crossed with the Thoroughbred to produce a hunter. The height limit is between 13 and 14 h.h. and permissible colours are bay, black, brown and sometimes grey. Preferably, there should be no white markings. Like the Dales, the Fell is distinguished by a full mane and tail and carries feather.

The Hack

A hundred years ago there were two distinct types of hack in Britain, the covert hack and the park hack. The former was up to more weight and was used to carry his master to the meet, often at a good, strong canter. The park hack, the type that has survived as a show horse up to the present day, was infinitely more elegant. This was the horse used for riding in the park under the appraising eye of the public. Consequently, to do its rider justice, the park hack had to be a beautiful horse of presence, moving with gaiety but having perfect manners.

This remains the objective for the hack exhibitor today.

Usually the show hack will be a Thoroughbred, or nearly so, but quite a number of great hacks have had some Arab blood as well. In the show ring the hack is expected to display a fairly high standard of training but is not expected to be a 'dressage' horse. Possibly the best definition of a hack is that, while being the most beautiful animal, balanced yet infinitely gay, one should be able to sit on it 'riding with one hand whilst flirting with the lovely companion who rides at your side'.

The Hackney

The modern Hackney came into being at about the same time as the Thoroughbred racehorse, oriental sires being used on native trotting (as opposed to running or galloping) mares. Such mares were to be found predominantly in the counties of Yorkshire, Lincolnshire and particularly in Norfolk. In the latter county the Norfolk Trotter, later known as the Norfolk Roadster, was well established in the eighteenth century and had been much improved by the great foundation sire Shales the Original, a son of the Thoroughbred Blaze by Flying Childers, a pillar of the British *General Stud Book*.

The early use of the Hackney was entirely utilitarian, these horses being used in harness and under saddle but always, in the last case, at the trot. Once, however, the railways and the car ousted the horse as a means of transport the role of the Hackney was confined almost entirely to the show ring, which from the 1870s up to the 1920s was dominated by harness classes. The show ring, with occasional excursions into coaching and even three-day event driving, remains the home of the modern Hackney.

In appearance the Hackney horse, standing between 14.3 and 15.3 h.h. is unmistakable, whether at rest or in action. The head is convex and may appear a shade large but without coarseness, the neck long and thick-set, the shoulders powerful, the body strong and compact, the legs short and the feet very well shaped with a fair slope and length to the pastern. But it is, of course, the action of the Hackney that is so eye-catching. It should be high and extravagant with enormous snap and thrust from the hocks, elastic and free-moving, so that at the trot it gives the impression of the horse floating, each stride having a moment of suspension. This action, allied to the fire and courage of the Hackney which give an overwhelming sense of 'presence', is what makes the breed the most spectacular of all.

There is, also, a smaller edition of the Hackney horse, the Hackney pony, full of real pony character, that stands under 14 h.h. The pony, treated almost as a separate breed by the Hackney Horse Society, dates from the Wilson ponies of the 1880s, a type developed by Christopher Wilson in Westmorland.

The Highland pony

Originating in northern Scotland and the Western Isles, the Highland pony is one of the larger British native breeds, standing between 13.2 and 14 h.h. The breed is of great antiquity and in the past had undoubtedly benefited from Arab blood. Originally bred for working the crofts and for carting deer, the present-day Highland is much used in Scotland's *trekking* industry. The ponies are very docile, exceptionally strong and hardy and most have attractive heads with wide-set eyes. The colouring of Highlands is especially notable and includes dun with a characteristic eel stripe, chestnut with silver mane and tail, as well as grey, bay and brown.

The Hunter

Since the hunter is not a breed but a type evolved for the express purpose of following hounds, the word could with justification be applied to any horse that is used in the hunting field. In theory the ideal hunter is the one exemplified by the exhibits in hunter classes that appear in the show rings. The purpose of such classes is, indeed, to encourage the breeding of horses best suited for carrying riders of various weights expeditiously and comfortably throughout a hunting season in the best of countries. Good conformation and action are, therefore, essential, along with complete soundness. Traditionally Ireland is the great source of hunter breeding although it is encouraged in England by the existence of the Hunters' Improvement and National Light Horse Breeding Society whose premium stallion scheme is responsible for providing considerable numbers of half- and three-quarter bred horses of good quality.

The New Forest pony

The New Forest pony has run in Hampshire's Forest area for possibly 1000 years, mention being made of large numbers in Canute's Royal Forest Law proclaimed at Winchester in 1016. It was not, however, until 1891 that a breed society, now the New Forest Pony Breeding and Cattle Society, was formed. Up to forty years ago the Forest ponies were subjected to a number of outcrosses: Arab, Thoroughbred, Welsh, Dartmoor, Exmoor, Highland and Fell. As a result there was, until recently, no very definite and recognizable type and even today there is a far greater variation in size than is to be found in other British pony breeds. New Forest ponies range between 12 and 14.2 h.h. and with the exception of piebald and skewbald may be of any colour. The modern New Forest is very much a riding pony with a good sloping shoulder. He makes an excellent family pony, being sound, tough and sure-footed.

The Riding pony

The British 'riding pony', now virtually a breed in its own right and certainly the most beautiful pony in the world, is based on native blood which causes it to retain pony type and character. These are not little horses but true ponies, mostly derived from Welsh and sometimes from Dartmoor blood, judiciously crossed with that of a small Thoroughbred of Arab, many containing a percentage of both.

The Shetland pony

The Shetland is the smallest of the British native ponies. Its original habitat was the islands of Shetland and Orkney. It stands between 38 and 42 in. at the withers but is possessed of a strength quite out of proportion to its size. Bred for working on the crofts, as well as for riding and driving, the breed thrives on the poorest keep. At one time Shetlands were in demand as pit ponies and were frequently very heavy in the head. However, a good modern Shetland has a much finer head and, if properly trained, is a good pony for a very small child and is excellent in harness. The Shetland is strong in the body, very deep-girthed and has short, hard legs showing plenty of bone. The breed may be of any colour. Unlike the other native breeds, the Shetland does not cross successfully.

The Shire

The Shire is the most massive of the heavy horses and is enormously powerful, sometimes standing as much as 18 h.h. and weighing upwards of a ton. The breed was founded on mares of the Old English Black horse bred on the east coast, to the north of East Anglia, and is claimed to be the purest survivor of the Great Horse. As its name implies the Shire was found originally in the 'shires' of England, particularly in the counties of Leicester, Stafford and Derby, but today it is more numerous in Wales, East Anglia and the northern counties. In appearance the Shire is majestic. The head shows quality, the girth is deep, the back broad, short and strong. The quarters are well let down and the legs and cannon bones comparatively short. The breed is characterized by white markings on legs carrying heavy feather against a body colour of black or bay, and grey Shires are also to be seen. The Shire is still used for draught work and is a popular attraction in the show rings.

The Suffolk Punch

The East Anglian county of Suffolk, as the name suggests, is the birthplace of the Suffolk Punch breed, but this impressive horse has for long been considered native to the whole of Britain's eastern counties. Camden's *Britannia* states that the breed can be dated back to 1506, but it also holds that the foundation stock could have been a legacy from the Viking invasions centuries earlier. There is a resemblance to the Jutland horse, and Flanders stallions are known to have been mated with Suffolk mares in the sixteenth and seventeenth centuries. Present-day representatives of the breed are said to trace back to one outstanding horse, Crisp's Horse of Offord, who was foaled in 1760.

Suffolks are always chestnut, there being seven acknowledged shades ranging from a dark to a bright colour. Unlike either the Clydesdale or Shire, the Suffolk is almost clean-legged with very little feather. The average height of these big-bodied horses is 16 h.h. and they rival the Shire in weight, often being well over a ton. The head is somewhat longer than that of the Shire but the Suffolk Punch is none the less very handsome and an exceptionally active, balanced horse with a noticeable depth of neck in collar. The Suffolk is also unusually long-lived and has, in addition to its other qualities, the ability to do well on a minimum of feed. Despite its enormous size and strength it is, like the other 'heavies', exceptionally docile and easy to handle.

The Welsh Cob

The Welsh Pony and Cob Society's Stud Book is divided into four main sections. Sections C and D of the book refer to the Welsh Cobs. Section C, with a height limit of 13.2 h.h. is termed 'Welsh pony of cob type' and is a smaller edition of the Welsh Cob, Section D, who may stand between 14.2 and 15.2 h.h.

Possibly the breed as we know it was founded on 'the old Welsh cart horse', whatever that was. No one is certain of the latter's origin, except that it had a background of Welsh pony blood. What is beyond doubt is that the Welsh Cob is the result of the Welshman's passion for a 'tremendous trotter'. The trot of the Cob is free, fast and forceful but quite unlike that of a Hackney. This is the pace for which the Cob is famed, but without his harness shoes he can gallop and jump with the best. He is, indeed, superb in harness, but in anything other than a grass country he also makes a first-rate hunter that is up to any weight.

The Welsh Mountain pony

The Welsh Mountain pony comes under the heading of section A in the stud book. He stands no more than 12 h.h. and may be chestnut, grey, brown, bay, black, cream or dun. In the improvement of the breed there have been infusions of Arab, Thoroughbred and Hackney blood, but the Welsh Mountain remains of unmistakable type and character. The head is fine with a slightly dished profile, a glorious eye and alert prick ears. The ponies are very sound and hardy and have exceptional feet, the horn being hard and often slate-coloured. The bone is flat and the action vigorous and true. Although these are riding ponies and ideal foundation stock for breeding the show riding pony, they are sufficiently versatile to be used in harness. Like all the Welsh breeds the mountain ponies have a distinctive fire and courage, but they never lose their most delightful character and temperament.

The Welsh pony, section B

The section B pony, described in the stud book as 'riding type', has all the attributes of section A but may stand as high as 13.2 h.h. This is the supreme riding pony of quality and many pure-bred Section B ponies are to be found in the show ring. Crossed with Arab or Thoroughbred the product is the 14.2 h.h. show pony.

E. Hartley Edwards

Life with Horses in Hungary

János Pál

The name Hungary conjures up in the foreign mind an image of horses and riders, for, not unreasonably, the world looks upon her as a nation of horsemen. The chroniclers report them storming on horseback into the Carpathian Basin, striking terror into its population. In a country where men and women rode equally well, their four-footed friends grew to be so much a part of them that the fallen hero was buried alongside his horse.

Even systematic horse breeding has been a tradition for over 1000 years; Prince Árpád (d. 907) founded the first known stud. The one on the Island of Csepel was run by Stud Manager Csepel and thus the isle on the Danube, just off Budapest, got its name. Stephan I, first king of Hungary, fostered horse breeding with equal enthusiasm, and soon the renown of the Hungarian horses' qualities crossed their native borders. Neighbouring countries bought them so eagerly for breeding purposes that later Hungarian kings forbade such 'exports' and in 1498 King Ulászlo II made it a crime equal to treason to defy this prohibition.

Hungarian horse breeding saw its second golden age under the Turkish overlordship. Up to the Battle of Mohács (1526) no foreign blood had entered the breed, which had been brought originally from east Russia. But the Turkish cavalry had oriental mounts. Many were captured and this booty was used to upgrade the native stock.

In the mid-eighteenth century horse breeding went into a slow decline. Though Marie Thérèse tried to promote breeding by means of premiums, her efforts were stymied by

lack of stallions. It was Josef II who resuscitated the breeding of horses by greatly increasing the premiums, establishing state covering depots, buying 500 selected stallions and employing supervisors for control and guidance. He founded Budapest's Veterinary College, and in 1784 decreed the construction of the stud farm of Mezöhegyes and in 1789 that of Bábolna (the former is still a state-owned farm, the latter is now co-operative). He was responsible for laying the foundations of the world-wide fame enjoyed by Hungarian horses in the nineteenth century, Hungary's outstanding era as a horse-breeding nation.

After World War Two, the state studs were rehabilitated with incredible speed. Private studs were expropriated and their stock integrated with that of the nearest state or co-operative farms. At the present time, experts on eighteen state and twenty-five co-operative farms are engaged in scientific breeding, having the use of 1200 brood mares.

Large scale industry and mechanization have greatly changed the horse's role, and it is the horses used for sport and recreation whose numbers are increasing. Breeding, sport and tourism go hand in hand. More people all over the world are becoming interested in equestrian sports. Nowadays the Hungarian Tourist Office and the State Supervisóry Council for Horse Breeding run fifty-four riding schools and associations. After World War Two it was Hungary which pioneered trekking, and this tourist pursuit is gaining in popularity each year. More and more foreign visitors are taking part in trekking through the most beautiful areas of the Hungarian countryside: Mátrabükk, the Donauknie, Balaton, Tokaj. Guests spend five or six days in the saddle, riding a daily thirty or thirty-five kilometres, or else go on daily excursions from centres such as Tata, Radiháza and Visegrád.

The annual Riders' Days of Hortobágy and Kiskunság-Apaj, the Herders' Days of Kiskunság, the historical Horsemanship Games in Nagyvázsony, in ancient Hungarian costumes, and the Riders' Days in Döbrente have become traditional events.

The most famous of all these games are those of the 'Csikós' horse herders in their traditional costumes: wide-sleeved shirts and baggy trousers, large black hats and short-handled whips. The Csikós saddle, the 'Patrac', has no girth and the rider is almost a part of his horse which obeys him unfailingly, lying down, sitting down, and doing whatever else its rider asks.

The Hungarian Post and the Puszta ötös, the latter immortalized by the famous Austrian painter Koch, are known throughout the world, and all horsemanship games programmes include displays by the traditional carriages drawn by teams of up to seven horses.

There is not much hunting in Hungary, there being no live game and no hounds. But hunt-like cross-country rides are organized for foreign guests in the autumn.

Among the museums of interest to the horseman are the Agricultural Museum in Budapest; the Carriage Museum in Parád; the Tack and Harness Museum in Szilvásvárad; and in Nagycenk the Museum in memory of Gr. István Szécheny, founder of the Hungarian Horse Breeding Society. In 1814 he became the first importer of English Thoroughbreds and the first to organize racing, in Pressburg in 1826 and in Pest in 1827. He and his companions also founded the Jockey Club.

An important landmark in Thoroughbred breeding was the establishment of the Kisbér Stud in 1853. In 1876 one of its stallions, appropriately named Kisbér, won the Epsom Derby and the Grand Prix de Paris.

Today's most important Thoroughbred stud farms are Dióspuszta, Kerteskö, Szenttamás,

Kisbér-Apáti, Szépalma and Orosháza. There are about 600 Thoroughbreds in the country, including 60 stallions. Some 400 horses are in training at the Budapest racetrack and there are over 50 race meetings every year. The first two-year-old races, including the Prix de Budapest, are run in May over 900 to 1400 m and there are several important races for three-year-olds, among them the Hungarian Derby over 2400 m and the Hungarian St Leger (2800 m). There are also hurdle and steeplechase races over distances ranging from 2400 to 3200 m.

The trotting horse, first bred in Hungary in the early twentieth century, virtually disappeared during World War Two, but in 1946 thirty-four trotters were imported and by 1947 race meetings were once again being organized.

The Hungarian show jumping team competes every year in one or two CSIOs, chiefly at Aachen and Olsztyn, and there is also always one club team competing in the CSIs of Austria, Yugoslavia and Czechoslovakia. And, of course, Hungary's famous drivers compete most successfully in international events, including the European and world championships.

A typical Hungarian phenomenon is that notwithstanding progress horses in Hungary still fulfil their ancient functions. On state and co-operative farms about 100000 of them – Hungarian Half-Breds, Nonius, Lipizzaners and Cold-Bloods – still bring in the crops and serve for transportation. Nor are horses yet lost in the field of industrial draught. Their more highly bred relatives, the Anglo-Arabs, English Thoroughbreds and some Hungarian Half-Breds, 2000 of them in all, are used under saddle in the riding schools.

Principal breeds

The Gidran

The Gidran is the Hungarian Anglo-Arab. The foundation sire was the Arab chestnut stallion Gidran Senior, imported from Arabia in 1816, and the breed was created at Mezöhegyes through the use of English Thoroughbred and Arab stallions. Today the Gidran is raised exclusively on the state farm of Dalmand where thirty brood mares are kept. But about thirty stallions stand at stud elsewhere in Hungary, mainly in the south between the Danube and Theiss. Research is being carried out into the possibilities of increasing Anglo-Arab breeding through the introduction of new Arab and Thoroughbred stock. The Gidran has a large frame and a great deal of bone, yet retains Arab characteristics. The typical colouring is chestnut. It is a sound horse, well suited to competitive sports.

The Hungarian Half-Bred

The best known types of Hungarian Half-Bred are the Mezöhegyes and the Kisbér, both named after the studs of their origin. The former, raised on the lush black soils of Mezöhegyes, is the result of crossing native mares with the inbred descendants of the two Thoroughbred stallions, Furioso (1842) and North Star (1853). The Kisbér, a light, show-jumping type, has been raised on the sandy soils of Kisbér since 1853, where much use has been made of Thoroughbred stallions. Some fifty-three per cent (95 000) of the country's total horse population are Half-Breds.

The Cold-Blood and the Muraközi

At the end of the last century the Austrian Noriker filtered across the western border of Hungary. The mares were bred to Arab stallions to develop a smaller, more mobile breed. This breeding programme began at Muraköz and the new breed became known as the Muraközi. More recently a good deal of new blood has been introduced: in 1948–9 fifty-eight Ardennes stallions were imported from Belgium and another fourteen stallions came from France. The Muraközi is a strong, active draught horse, particularly well suited to heavy farm work. The predominant colour is chestnut and the breed stands up to as much as 16 h.h.

The number of Cold-Bloods is 40 000. The large Cold-Bloods used in industrial transport are becoming extinct though they are still in use in agriculture. Cold-Bloods are exclusively draught horses and are popular because of their early maturity (at the age of two) and their calm temperament. Their massive flesh also makes them profitable meat animals.

The Nonius

The Nonius dates from 1816 when the stallion Nonius Senior, born in 1810 at the French stud of Rosières, arrived at Mezöhegyes. His sire was Orion, an English Thoroughbred, and his dam was the granddaughter of an English part-bred stallion. Arabs, Lipizzaners and Kladrubers played their part in developing the breed. More recently Thoroughbreds have been used for upgrading, and this practice has been intensified during the past decade. Chiefly a carriage horse and hunter, the Nonius constitutes about twenty-five per cent (40 000) of the country's horse population. It is bred in Hortobágy where there are sixty brood mares and in Mezöhegyes where there are thirty. Its regional breeding territory is the Komitat Hadju, Békés and the southern part of Bács-Kiskun.

Life with Horses in Ireland

André Monteilhet,
E. Hartley Edwards,
Lt. Col. M. A. Q. Darley

In 1972 the Irish Republic boasted a little over 200000 horses and ponies for three million inhabitants, i.e. one per fifteen inhabitants. A proportionate count in the United Kingdom would be three and a half million horses, in West Germany four million and in France or Italy a little over one million – which is far from the case. In fact, the Irish Republic still has the densest horse population of any European country, despite the inevitable dwindling of her draught horse population.

At the end of the seventeenth century and during the eighteenth, Ireland began to import her first English Thoroughbred sires, among them the celebrated foundation sire Byerley Turk. Like the hunter, the Thoroughbred flourishes on the country's mineral-rich soil and today there are several great foreign-owned Thoroughbred studs in the country.

In 1864 the Royal Dublin Society, founded in 1731 as an agricultural society, held the first Royal Horse Show at Dublin. This show was the earliest of all the international horse shows, and it is still one of the highlights of the international season, attracting huge entries in all classes.

Ireland is renowned for her hunting and, of course, for the production of quality hunters. Foxhunting is practised on a large scale all over the island, including the six northern counties and there are also two packs of staghounds (the Ward Union near Dublin and the County Down near Belfast), but, unlike in France and Belgium, the stag is not put to death. There are some harriers and beagles and, in Cork, otterhound packs, but the chief quarry is the fox. The oldest packs date back to the eighteenth century and include the Littlegrange (1723); the Westmeath (1740); the Muskerry (1742); the Duhallow (1745), and the Ormond (1778). Irish foxhunting is fast and bold. From 1877 to 1882 the Empress Elisabeth of Austria, that graceful and intrepid horsewoman who was known as the Queen of the Chase, often rode to hounds at Middleton where she was reminded of the hunts with the Emperor across the Hungarian puszta.

Punchestown, in the county of Dublin, is famous for its steeplechase course and is also the venue for international horse trials championships.

Along with Spain and Yugoslavia, Ireland is also one of the rare European states to have conserved a Military School of Equitation, at McKee Barracks (Dublin) where the renowned Russian Colonel Paul Rodzianko taught from 1928 to 1932. The civilian counterpart is the Herbertstown Riding Establishment at Herbertstown in Co. Meath. It is run by Captain Ian Dudgeon, the former international rider, and is one of the great civilian riding schools. Miss Iris Kellett, former European show-jumping champion and member of the Irish Horse Board, runs a school at Kill in Co. Kildare and bred the well-known show jumper Easter Light.

The Irish Horse Board promotes the development of breeding and equestrian sports, working in liaison with Aer Lingus and the Irish Tourist Office which maintains agencies in all the capitals and large cities of the world.

André Monteilhet

Principal breeds

The Connemara pony

The Connemara is an Irish product, having its origin on the western seaboard. It is possibly descended from imports of Andalusian and Galician stock made before and during the Roman occupation of Britain. More recently there have been introductions of Thoroughbred and Arabian blood to give added quality. A pony of excellent temperament, the Connemara is noted for its cleverness and jumping ability combined with good riding action and hereditary toughness. The main colours are black, bay, brown, grey and a very attractive dun. The height is between 13.2 and 14 h.h. Crosses with this breed have produced several famous show jumpers and eventers and at least one great dressage horse, the late Mrs V. D. S. Williams's Little Model. The breeding of Connemaras is widespread outside of Ireland, and this pony is so popular that there is now an English Connemara Society as well as the original Irish society.

E. Hartley Edwards

The Irish Draught horse

Limestone soil and the favourable climate of Ireland provide ideal conditions for rearing horses, and foxhunting seems to inspire them with natural boldness and jumping ability. The Irish clean-legged draught horse, a type rather than a specific breed, is the country's most significant contribution to the horse world, and the following description of mares of this type, laid down by the Irish Department of Agriculture during the 1930s, still pertains:

A broad mare of medium size standing 15.1 h.h. and upwards. Short of back and powerfully knit across the loins, with well developed hindquarters. Her general outline is of a low and roomy type standing close to the ground, very muscular in the forearm and with clean, flat bone below the knee. Her legs are devoid of anything in the nature of a *feather*. Her head is usually fine and clean cut in outline with long neck and shoulder well laid. Her withers are high and her ribs well sprung.

Classes for Irish draught stallions, mares and young stock are held by the Royal Dublin Society at their spring and summer shows. In 1968 the Irish Half-Bred Society was formed to protect the interests of Irish Draught mares and their progeny by Thoroughbred stallions, and a register of half-bred mares was started to form the basis of a stud book. In 1971 the function of this society was taken over by the Irish Horse Board and this organization now operates a half-bred stud book. An admixture of a half, three-quarters or seven-eighths Irish draught blood on the mare's side increases the substance, stamina and weight carrying capacity of the Thoroughbred horse and possibly tempers his impetuosity, thereby producing an ideal show jumper or event horse whose value has achieved world-wide recognition.

Lt. Col. M. A. Q. Darley

Life with Horses in Italy

André Monteilhet
J. M. Draper

In 1939 there were 781 000 horses in Italy; by 1971 this figure had dropped to 271 000. The 30.5 per cent was due, as elsewhere, to the mechanization of the army, civilian transport and agriculture. Agricultural mechanization brought with it an exodus from the rural areas which was aggravated by the disappearance of the latifundia and the consequent dwindling of pasture land.

At present continental Italy's regions richest in horse-breeding stock may be divided into three principal groups: Lombardy-Venezia-Emilia-Romagna; Tuscany-Latium; and Campania-Puglia-Lucania. The poorest regions are Piedmont-Liguria; Friuli (Venetia Giulia); Marche; and Calabria. Sicily is well stocked with horses and Sardinia reasonably well so.

Apart from the 'foreign' breeds (the English Thoroughbred, the Arabian, Anglo-Arab, Anglo-Norman, Bretons imported from France and Belgium, Trotters and Lipizzaners), the types of State or privately owned stallions standing at stud include the Italian Agricultural horse, the Avellignese, the Murgese, the Sardinian, the Maremmano, the Sicilian Sanfratellano, the Calabrian, the Pugliese, the Salernitano and the Noriker.

When the ex-Austrian, later Italian, Lipizzaner stud near Trieste was ceded to Yugoslavia in 1948, Italy obtained, from the body of the breed evacuated to Bohemia by the Germans, stallions of the six male lines and brood mares of thirteen lines. Today about fifty of these mares are kept at the Experimental Zootechnical Institute of Tor Mancina on the left bank of the Tiber, about thirty kilometres up-stream from Rome. Tor Mancina also produces an English-type saddle horse for sport, using two pure-bred Arabian stallions and Italian or Irish brood mares.

There are in Italy over three hundred Thoroughbred and about a thousand Trotter studs. Many studs, such as the Verona in Lombardy-Venezia in the heart of the Thoroughbred and Trotter breeding country, continue to improve their stock by importing new blood from the USA, France and Great Britain.

In Sicily, which has some 160 stallions and over 8000 brood mares, the Anglo-Arab saddle horse is being superseded by the Sanfratellano, while in Sardinia breeding is centred on the Sardinian Anglo-Arab which is based on the feral horse of Giara di Gesturi and has been refined by the regular introduction of French Anglo-Arab stock. It is a good riding horse which makes a first-class show jumper.

The first international horse shows in Italy were those held in Turin in 1902 and in Rome at Tor di Quinto in 1908 (subsequently transferred, in 1929, to the Piazza di Siena where it is attended by crowds in excess of 25 000).

Italian show jumping events are among the most brilliant in Europe, and Italian civilian and military riders have been among the best in the world since Federico Caprilli (1868–1907) brought back with him from Nola in Campania the revolutionary *sistema* which, between 1898 and 1902, was to raise the high jumping record from 1.40 m to 2.08 m. Caprillism spread progressively throughout the entire world and in Italy the chain is uninterrupted, stretching from Caprilli's companions, Ubertalli and Anselmi, via Alvisi, to the d'Inzeo brothers.

Harness racing is popular in Italy, the first official trotting track having been established at Prato Del Valle in 1808, and flat racing was also started in the early nineteenth century with regular meetings in Florence, Naples and Milan. Rome held her first organized meetings in 1868. Italy has produced some really great international horses, notably the mare Signorinetta who won the 1908 English Derby and Oaks, and, later, the unbeaten Nearco and Ribot, bred by Federico Tesio. Tesio's Dormello Stud, on the shores of Lake Maggiore, has had a significant influence on Thoroughbred breeding throughout the world since its inception in 1898, particularly through two of its greatest horses Donatello II and Nearco. Racing in Italy is centred round the great middle-distance races such as the Italian Derby ($1\frac{1}{2}$ mi.), the Gran Premio d'Italia ($1\frac{1}{2}$ mi.) and the Italian St Leger ($1\frac{3}{4}$ mi.) which constitute the Triple Crown, and the Gran Premio di Milano (1 mi. 7 f.).

Foxhunting is popular throughout the country and there are many very active hunts.

Italian trekking has its own School of Equestrian Travel, just outside southern Rome on the edge of the Appian Way.

André Monteilhet

Principal breeds

The Italian Heavy Draught horse

A medium-sized draught horse found throughout central and northern Italy, the Heavy Draught horse has Breton ancestry and was, prior to mechanization, much used for agricultural work. Nowadays, as its usefulness on the land dwindles, it is increasingly bred for meat. It is a deep-girthed, compact horse standing 15 to 16 h.h., and the most usual colour is liver chestnut with flaxen mane and tail.

The Maremmano

The Maremmano originates from Tuscany and was first bred at what is now the State stud of Grossetto. It is a heavy saddle or light draught horse and is used by the cattle herdsmen known as the *butteri*. An economical feeder that is noted for its hardiness, the Maremmano stands about 15.3 h.h. and may be of any solid colour.

The Murgese

The Murgese horse, which originates from the Orfano plain and the hill districts near Gravina, can be traced back at least to the fifteenth century. From 1494 to 1514 the Venetian Republic owned the port of Monopoli. Its governor kept a score of Murgese stallions and several hundred brood mares to provide remounts for the cavalry. Today the breed is of light draught or riding type and stands 15 to 16 h.h. with the predominant colour being chestnut. When put to an Arab or Thoroughbred stallion the Murgese mare produces a very good stamp of riding horse.

The Salerno

The breed known as the Salerno, a saddle horse and formerly the mount of the Italian cavalry, was evolved at what is now the State stud of Persano. Persano was a hunting reserve and was founded by Charles III of Bourbon, King of the Two Sicilies (1735–59). The Salerno has Neapolitan ancestry and is a horse of good conformation which, since the mechanization of the army, has become popular as an all-round riding horse, particularly as a jumper. It stands up to about 16 h.h. and may be of any solid colour. The champion show jumpers Pagoro and, later, Fiorello II, were both bred at Salerno.

André Monteilhet/J. M. Draper

Life with Horses in the Netherlands

André Monteilhet
J. M. Draper

Equitation in the Netherlands has successively followed the old French school – Gaspard de Saunier taught there from 1720 to 1748 – later, in the nineteenth century, the German school (Steinbrecht) and, from 1900 onwards, the contemporary French school (Saumur), as well as, from 1920, the *sistema* of Caprilli over fences and in horse trials.

The Netherlands also have a long tradition of cavalry schools, the last being that at Haarlem (1857) which was transferred to Venlo in 1859 and thence to Amersfoort (1886) where it was finally dissolved in 1946. There remains today a military equitation and driving school (Rijen Tractieschool) at Eindhoven and the Koninklijke Marechaussee (Royal Mounted Police) created in 1869, a part of which is still mounted. There is also the Veterinary School which was founded at Zutphen in 1807.

The draught horse is still popular in the Netherlands, and the Royal Netherlands Society of the Draught Horse (Koninklijke Vereiniging Het-Netherlandsche Trekpaard) regularly organizes international meets.

The Dutch farmer remains loyal to the farm horse which is an extremely useful animal. One of its ancillary services is the provision of dung for use in compost. At the instigation of Prince Bernhard, the Netherlands Federation of Equestrian Sports (Nederlandsche Hippische Sportbond) created in 1953 the International Championships of Rural Riders to further interest in the horse in rural areas.

Ponies of all breeds are popular, some are ridden by children and others driven in light harness. The main breeding centre is at Bemmel.

Despite their relatively modest stock of horses (about 170 000), the Netherlands achieve very creditable results in big international competitions, including the Olympic Games.

There have been no fewer than four (out of a total of nine) Dutch presidents of the FEI since its foundation in 1921, Colonel Maris (from 1927 to 1929), Major Quarles van Ufford (first from 1929 to 1931 and then again, as a colonel, from 1936 to 1942) and Prince Bernhard of the Netherlands (from 1954 to 1964).

André Monteilhet

Principal breeds

The Dutch Draught horse

The Dutch Draught horse is the result of crossing Zeeland-type mares with Brabant and Belgian Ardennais stallions and has been developed since World War One as an agricultural horse suitable for work on both sand and clay regions of Holland. Although it is a massive horse with a distinct resemblance to the Brabant, it has active paces and is by no means a sluggard. A kindly horse with a good deal of stamina, it stands up to 16.3 h.h. and is usually chestnut, bay or grey.

The Friesian

This attractive horse is of ancient origin and takes its name from Friesland where heavy horses have existed for nearly three thousand years. The descendants of this indigenous horse were crossed with oriental horses at the time of the Crusades and infusions of Andalusian blood were made during the eighty years when Spain was holding the Netherlands. Over the centuries the Friesian has been used as a draught horse, under saddle and, as a result of selective breeding, in trotting races during the nineteenth century. Today it is an all-round work horse standing about 15 h.h. Muscular and stocky, it has a fine head and a strong body set on short, strong legs which carry some feather. It is always black with no white markings and is an exceptionally good-natured animal.

The Gelderland

The popular Gelderland was developed in the nineteenth century by crossing the native mares of the Gelderland province with a variety of imported stallions, including the Arab and the Norfolk Roadster. Over the years Hackney, Oldenburg and Friesian blood have been added and, during this century, Anglo-Norman. The result is a first-rate carriage horse of great presence and good action which can also serve as a useful riding horse, often having a good deal of jumping ability. Standing about 15.2 h.h. it is usually chestnut or grey, although some skewbalds occur.

J. M. Draper

Life with Horses in New Zealand

Esperance Anderson

The horse was introduced into New Zealand by the early British settlers in the first half of the nineteenth century. Breeds flourishing at the present time include the Thoroughbred and the Clydesdale. The influence of both is to be seen in the excellent half- and three-quarter bred horses which are still used for mustering sheep and for sport, including hunting. There are large numbers of ponies throughout the country and pony clubs are very popular.

A number of hunt clubs are active in both islands. No native mammals exist, but the hare was introduced in the nineteenth century and provides sport for harriers. Drag hunting is popular on the outskirts of cities.

With large numbers of horses thus naturally schooled across country, steeplechasing flourishes and includes both professional meetings on regular courses and point-to-points run as far as possible over hunting country. Steeplechases, hurdle and flat races are often included in one meeting. Big cities and many small country towns have racecourses where at least one annual meeting is held. Harness racing for both trotters and pacers is generally conducted on different courses. Racing is often considered the national sport. New Zealand bloodstock has proved very successful abroad, and the annual yearling sales at Trentham attract many buyers from Australia, Japan and America.

Polo is played in some areas, mainly in the North Island.

New Zealand is primarily an agricultural country and agricultural and pastoral shows are held annually in most country towns as well as in cities. Classes are included for everything from farm animals to home preserves, and horses and ponies take a natural part. Jumping events attract big entries and crowds of spectators. The country's isolation and quarantine restrictions have largely prevented New Zealand horses from taking part in international competition, but in 1974 a New Zealand rider, John Cottell, took his own horses to Britain where he competed with credit in the Mens' World Championships at Hickstead.

Horsemen visiting Dunedin should not miss the Otago Museum whose Maori house contains a carved frieze depicting the famous New Zealand horse Phar Lap winning the Melbourne Cup. This modern subject is translated with great skill and humour into the traditional idiom of Maori art.

Esperance Anderson

Life with Horses in Poland

Patricia Lindsay

The horse has played an important role in Polish life for many centuries, a fact which is partly explained by geographical and historical conditions. Poland forms part of the north European plain which is open to invasion and ideal for mounted warfare. The land consists mainly of flat tracts of light arable soil where the ox has been little used and the dual roles played by the horse in farming and warfare have been vital.

The cavalry tradition – from the battles against the Teutonic Knights, the Polish Hussars under Jan Sobieski who beat back the Turks from the gates of Vienna, to the last tragic charges in 1939 by Polish cavalry against the German tanks – has endured to the present day. Polish remount horses are still in great demand in India and were, until recently, in Switzerland.

The agricultural role is equally enduring. After the break-up of the large private estates in 1944 the land was partly organized in big State and co-operative farms but, unlike in other East European countries, seventy-five per cent remained small, intensively cultivated family farms on which the horse is still the main source of motive power. The Ministry of Agriculture has played an enlightened part from the beginning. Instead of forcing through an expensive programme of wholesale mechanization, it has organized and encouraged the selective breeding of the best types of Polish horses. The State-owned studs, closely supervised by Ministry experts, aim to produce and test first-class horses, especially the stallions which go out to the villages and cover the peasants' mares at subsidized fees. As a result of this policy, Poland now has nearly two million horses, more than any other European country, and has regained her place as a major exporter of horses for sporting and breeding purposes.

The horse-breeding tradition is still an important part of Polish life, and it is the Arabian horse which is especially beloved. The best Polish horses have always shown much oriental blood, but it is in pure-bred Arab breeding that Poland has gained the most remarkable recent recognition. The numbers of Arab horses, decimated by war, have been built up again. The pure-bred studs, now three in number, have a world-wide reputation for producing horses of true type with quality and soundness and enjoy a very important export trade. In the USA and in Sweden, particularly, Polish Arabs have recently been taking more than their share of major show championships.

Racing, both flat and steeplechasing, is extremely popular in Poland and takes place at Warsaw, Poznan and Sopot. Income from the Totalizator is used to finance the breeding programme. Thoroughbred breeding is based on English, Italian and French bloodlines and regularly replenished by the purchase of stallions, mainly from England. There is also a complete programme of flat racing for pure-bred Arabs. This begins when the horses are three years old and is used as a test of soundness and temperament, rather than a means of selection for speed. Half-bred and Anglo-Arab horses are also tested in racing, mainly steeplechasing.

Enthusiasm for all horse sports is basic to Polish life and character. Up until the nineteenth century wolf, boar and bear hunting were popular in the eastern provinces. These are dramatically depicted in many paintings, for there is a long tradition of sporting art. Driving scenes are also numerous and include the extraordinary *Four-in-Hand* by Jozef Chelmonski, with horses harnessed abreast, which hangs in the Krakow Museum and makes an amazing impact as one enters the room. Especially famous are the pictures of Juliusz Kossak, who specializes in the twin themes of war and country life and shows us the beauty of the Polish oriental horse in all his roles. The country and people which we see in these paintings are recognizably the forerunners of the Poland of today: it is this strong sense of history and continuity with the past which makes Poland such a fascinating country for all horse lovers. Throughout the country one can see many horses, not simply sad relics of derelict areas, but busy at work on prosperous modern farms, while in many areas processions of decorated carts still carry the country brides to their weddings.

This sense of the past has led Polish filmmakers to produce some great historical epics, in which stallions and grooms from the main national studs, carefully selected for their suitability to the period, take part. No national celebration is complete without the horse. In 1966, when Poland celebrated her Millennium, there was an enormous procession through Warsaw of Polish Cavalry through the ages, all mounted on stallions. Once again the horses were carefully chosen to suit each epoch.

Both pleasure and competition riding are well catered for today. All studs and stallion stations have their own teams of riding horses, and there is a network of riding clubs, with their own horses, which run competitions at various levels. Young townspeople are encouraged to learn to ride and all horse establishments are asked to provide facilities and horses for teaching riders during the summer holidays.

Poland is very much a part of the international scene. She has been especially successful in show jumping and driving competitions, in three-day events and, to a lesser extent, in dressage. She has hosted many excellent international events, and a remarkable number of exported horses have gone right to the top for their new countries.

Riding holidays for foreigners are well organized in Poland and are usually centred on one of the beautifully restored castles or former stately homes. There are instructional courses in riding and driving, and also tours in the lake and forest country of the north and the mountains of the south. A number of sales cater for intending purchasers, sometimes with 'Try Your Own Horse' mock hunts or paperchases.

A typically Polish event was the opening ceremony of the Winter Biathlon at the ski resort of Zakopane when riders from the local club participated with the skiers and ski jumpers, carrying flaming torches down the snow slope in a series of frightening but effective patterns.

Indeed, in a severe winter the horse comes into his own, and even in this mechanized age the stranded traveller may hear the sound of sleigh bells and rejoice that Poland remains the land of the horse.

Principal breeds

The Hucul pony

The Hucul, who probably shares, in the Tarpan, a common ancestor with the Konik, is an 'improved' type of pony standing about 14 h.h. and is usually dun or bay. It is a useful pony for riding, pack work and for all jobs on the small hill farms.

The Konik pony

The Konik is a very hardy, primitive animal, about 13 h.h., whose colours include various shades of dun and mouse with an eel strip. Conformation is not always good, but the ponies are very intelligent and sure-footed.

The Malopolski

The Malopolski, whose homeland is southern and eastern Poland, is more of the traditional type of 'Polish horse'. Averaging about 15.3 h.h., it is based on the ancient strains of half-bred Arab and shows oriental quality and elegance allied to strength and endurance. These horses work on farms, especially in the hilly country, and make very attractive hacks, light-weight hunters and jumpers. Some strains contain a high percentage of Arab blood, while others, which have been influenced by the Gidran and the Furioso, are stronger and shorter in the leg.

The Slaski

The Slaski, tracing back to the Oldenburg and bred in Silesia, is said to be the largest clean-legged, warm-blooded breed in Europe and is a magnificent carriage horse type which is also capable of carrying great weights under saddle.

The Wielkopolski

The Wielkopolski, bred in central and western Poland, is a strong, handsome, warm-blooded hunter type, averaging about 16.2 h.h. with plenty of bone. His courage and good temperament make him a useful light harness horse, but he also has natural jumping ability and, because of his Thoroughbred ancestry, speed. The Wielkopolski also includes strains developed at the Trakehner Stud. Most of the jumpers and event horses exported from Poland are Wielkopolskis.

Patricia Lindsay

The following illustrations are arranged alphabetically according to country, in the same order as the text.

Breeds

Haflinger

Lipizzaner

Noriker

Ardennais

Canadian Cutting horse

Frederiksborg

Knapstrup

Boulonnais

Breton

French Anglo-Arab (36.20%)

French Trotter

Percheron

Selle Français

Cleveland Bay

Clydesdale

Cob

Dales pony

Dartmoor pony

Exmoor pony

Fell pony

Hack

Hackney horse

Highland pony

Heavyweight Hunter

New Forest pony

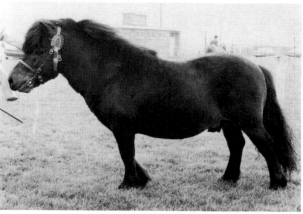

Shetland pony

Shire

Suffolk Punch

Welsh Mountain pony (Section A)

Welsh pony (Section B)

Welsh Cob (Section C)

Welsh Cob (Section D)

Hungarian Half-Bred

Murakozi

Nonius

Connemara pony

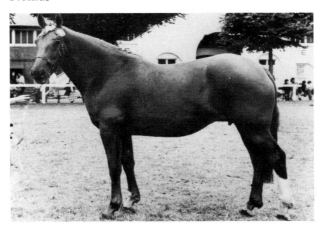

Irish Draught

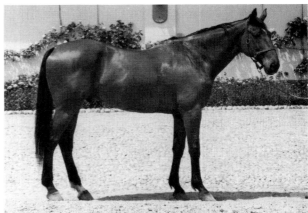

Salerno

Dutch Draught

Friesian

Gelderland

Hucul ponies

Konik pony

Wielkopolski

Andalusian

Swedish Warm Blood

Einsiedler

American Quarter horse

American Standardbred

Morgan

Tennessee Walking horse

Akhal-Teke

Budyony

Don

Karabair

Lithuanian Heavy Draught

Orlov Trotter

Tersk

Vladimir

Hanoverian

Holstein

Oldenburg

Schleswig

Trakehner

Life with Horses in Spain

Alvaro Domecq
Jean-Paul Klein

The horse population of Spain, which has always been closely linked with military requirements, has, not surprisingly, diminished considerably since World War Two. However, many of the popular horse sports are practised in Spain and horses of various types and breeds are bred to fulfil these requirements, in addition to draught animals and some ponies.

The national stud organization is run by cavalry officers specially appointed for this purpose and consists mainly of the stud at Vicos in Jerez de la Frontera, where pure-bred Andalusians, Arabs and Anglo-Arabs are bred, while Thoroughbreds are raised in Lore-Toki near San Sebastián. Stallions are kept in eight depots in Alcalá de Henares near Madrid, Zaragoza, Santander and León. These stallions are available to private studs at very low fees. However, there are few private studs. Thoroughbreds are bred by Antonio Blasco, Spain's leading breeder, at La Venta de la Rubia, near Madrid. Arabs, having reached a higher price than any other horse in Spain, thanks to the dedication to this breed of Mrs MariPaz de Heredia, are more and more appreciated and sought after, not only by domestic breeders, but also by foreigners. Andalusians, which have, after the Arab and the Thoroughbred, had more influence on the world's horse breeds than any other breed, are produced mainly in the south. They are much appreciated in Spanish American countries where they are regularly exported at high prices. Stud books are kept for Thoroughbreds, Arabs, Anglo-Arabs and Spanish horses (Andalusians) by the Government-run Jefatura de los Servicios de Cría Caballar.

Sales are held in Lore-Toki in mid-August and in Madrid in June and October, and every year in May in Jerez de la Frontera the famous Feria del Caballo takes place. Jerez is also the venue of a recently introduced show, Como Bailan los Caballos Andaluces (The Dancing Andalusian Horses) which is immensely popular.

Spain still has an Army Riding School which is known as the Escuela de Equitación y Aplicación del Ejército. It is situated in Madrid, as are several private schools such as the Escuela Española de Equitación de Somosaguas and the Club Ecuestre 'Las Lomas'. There are many other riding schools outside the capital, among them the Club Pineda in Seville and the Chapín in Jerez de la Frontera.

Racing in Spain is controlled by the Sociedad de Fomento de la Cría Caballar de España. Meetings are held in Madrid at La Zarzuela from February to July and from September to December. In the summer months the sport moves up to Lasarte which is San Sebastián's track. A winter meeting is held during the Christmas season at Pineda, Seville. Important races include the Grand Prix of Madrid which is held on Saint Peter's and Saint Paul's Day (29 June) with a purse of one million pesetas to the winner, and the Gold Cup of San Sebastian which carries a similar prize and is run in mid-August. These two races carry the biggest purses in national racing. Fegentri races are held on all three tracks.

Racing also takes place at Puerto de Santa María and Sanlucar de Barrameda during the summer. Sanlucar is unique in that racing is held on the beach.

There is also some hurdle racing, while steeplechasing, which was only started in 1973, is rapidly increasing in popularity. Trotting races are popular in Mallorca and Ibiza but pacing is completely unknown.

Endurance rides are held annually in Jerez de la Frontera to coincide with the Feria del Caballo, and elsewhere in the country.

Hunting is unknown in Spain, except for harriery where a team of two greyhounds are matched against each other. Jerez, Sevilla and Madrid are the main centres. The hunting circle in Spain is an exclusive one but guests are always welcome if they get in touch with the right people.

Spain possesses a surprising number of very fine carriages, notably in Jerez de la Frontera, where driving exhibitions are held during the Feria in May and the Sherry Vintage Festival in September. Many coaches can also be seen at the Seville Fair, in Córdoba, and at the Agricultural Show which is held every other year in Madrid. Visitors to Seville should not miss the Carriage and Coach Museum owned by the Marquis de Paradas y Salvatierra.

Polo is a sport enjoyed by only a select minority, the centres being Jerez de la Frontera, Barcelona, Sotogrande and Madrid. The main seasons are the spring in Madrid, the autumn in Barcelona and the winter in Jerez and Sotogrande in the south.

Horses are no longer used in transport, except in the northern provinces for farming on small properties, and the same applies to agricultural work. They are, however, indispensable in the cattle breeding world, especially in the rearing of the fighting bulls. The latter are tested in the fields as yearlings by a team of two men on horseback, using a pole called a *garrocha*, who chase the young bulls and try to fell them. Their quality can be judged by their reactions. The testing of the young bulls is a popular pastime especially when it is run on a competitive basis.

The most popular and widely circulated daily publication is *Marca* which deals exclusively with sport and gives good coverage of show jumping and racing. Other publications, which appear quarterly or weekly, include *Club de Jinetes* and *Deporte 2000*.

Alvaro Domecq

Principal breed

The Andalusian

The origins of the Andalusian horse date back to before the Roman colonization of the Iberian peninsula, since there exists at least one marble head of the Roman era of a type of horse that corresponds to that still found at present. Thus it seems that the Andalusian has not been significantly subject to the influence of the Barb horse, although it cannot be entirely ruled out. Any influence on the part of the Arab, on the other hand, remains quite an improbability, unless to a minimal degree, or else the pure-bred Arab strain dating very far back, for the head of the Andalusian is only slightly concave in profile. However this may be, it is a courageous horse, its conformation not lacking in harmony. Its size varies between 15 and 16 h.h.; its colour is grey or bay, rarely black. During the sixteenth, seventeenth and eighteenth centuries the Andalusian was greatly coveted for academic equitation and before the advent of the English Thoroughbred it was used as an upgrader for other breeds. The principal breeding grounds are Jerez, Seville and Cazallo.

Jean-Paul Klein

Life with Horses in Sweden

André Monteilhet
J. M. Draper

State studs existed as far back as the sixteenth century. In the 1550s Gustav I Vasa (1523–60) founded a brood mare stud on an island off the northern bank of Lake Mälar. Some sixty years later, in 1621, King Gustav Adolph opened the State stud of Strömsholm which, with its covered school, had been a centre of equitation from the end of the sixteenth century when the German riding master, Engelhardt von Löhneysen, disciple of the great Neapolitan masters, gave instruction there. Around 1660 Strömsholm was enlarged and in 1668 a castle was added. The famous White Riding School was built in 1855 and the spacious White Stables were completed in 1867. During the hundred years from 1868 to 1968 Strömsholm was the immutable and unique seat of the Swedish Cavalry School (Militär Central Ridskolan), created by Charles XV. It was succeeded by a civilian institution called Ridfrämjandet (for equestrian improvement). The brood mare stud had been dissolved in 1871 and the stallion station in 1956. In 1770 this latter had reached a peak of 360 stallions, but by the time it closed the number had been reduced to 80.

During the time that Strömsholm housed both the State studs and the cavalry school, the whole establishment was in the charge of one man, the *hovstallmastäre*. The first person to hold that post was Major Pehr P. W. Fischerström (1868–92). The student officers rode the stud's best stallions until the school came to own its own manège horses in 1923. A hunt pack for training riders across country was set up in 1880. At one time (1905–26) the establishment was run by Lieutenant-Colonel Mils Fischerström (no relation to P. P. W. Fischerström), one of the most famous horsemen of his time, and between the two world wars Strömsholm was managed by Lieutenant-Colonel Bertil Sandström who represented Sweden at the 1920 Olympic Games in Antwerp and the 1924 Games in Paris. The idea of equestrian events in the Olympics had been put forward in 1906 by Count Clarence von Rosen and the first actual events were held in Stockholm in 1912. The first Olympic equestrian panel of judges was under the presidency of the Swedish Colonel Nyblaeus and included Count von Rosen. Also in 1912 was the creation of the Swedish Federation of Equestrian Sports (Svenska Ridsportens Centralförbund) under the presidency of Prince Charles Bernadotte. Sweden has always shone in international competition, notably in dressage and eventing.

Sweden has created her own breed of horse, the Swedish Warm Blood, based on Danish, Trakehner, Norman, Hanoverian and Oldenburg blood and, in addition, breeds Thoroughbreds and Arabs. Oriental horses made their first, sporadic, appearance after the Napoleonic wars and Charles XV (1859–72) ran a pure-bred Arabian stud at Kungsör where half-bred stallions were used on Arab mares to produce remounts for the cavalry. In 1953 Dr Aby Ericsson brought over from Marbach the stallion Jäger, who was a descendant of the Egyptian Jasir and Cäsarea (Koheilan line) and one of the three pure-bred Arabian mares still at Marbach at that time.

In 1959 Countess Penelope Lewenhaupt

took Kariba Ox, which she had bred in Scotland, to Sweden. Breeders followed her example, buying pure-bred Arabians from Britain and Poland. In 1974 Count Lewenhaupt founded the Swedish Pure-bred Arabian Society which is affiliated to the World Arabian Horse Organization and which, since its foundation, has organized a biannual national show at the State stud of Flyinge. Anglo- and Part-bred Arabs are also bred. Arabian horses are doing well in Sweden and are adapting very successfully to the northern climate.

As well as Shetland and Norwegian ponies Sweden breeds a native pony, the Russ* which originated on the island of Gotland. The Swedish Pony Association was founded in 1954 for the protection of the Russ which for centuries had been exported to coal mining countries.

André Monteilhet

Principal breed

The Swedish Warm Blood

The origins of this horse date back about three centuries, to various crossings (Friesian, Arab, Spanish horses). Later, Trakehner, Hanoverian and Norman stallions were used. A royal stud was created at Strömsholm in 1621. Standing up to about 16.2 h.h., the Warm Blood possesses good conformation and an excellent temperament. This breed has produced distinguished dressage horses and, nowadays, through the gradual infusion of Thoroughbred blood, it is a horse 'with blood under the mass'.

J. M. Draper

*The word 'russe' was originally that of a Swedish tribe which crossed the Baltic Sea in the early Middle Ages.

Life with Horses in Switzerland

André Monteilhet
J. M. Draper

Up until a few years ago Switzerland maintained about 100000 horses, ten per cent of which were in the last Dragoon squadrons that were disbanded in 1973. The relatively small amount of horse breeding in Switzerland – except in the Jura Mountains – obliged the Military Department to import about 700 horses annually, half of them from West Germany, and the remainder from France, Poland and Sweden. These horses were acclimatized in Sand-Schönbühl, broken in at the Aarau equestrian centre, then partly re-sold to the Dragoons who assured their upkeep on the farm for ten years, whereafter the horses became their sole property. Each year the Dragoon and his faithful companion equipped themselves for a three-week period of man-oeuvres with their squadron. In three covered schools at the Federal Depot in Bern (1890–1975) the trainers (called *piqueux*) improved the schooling of about 1000 horses for riding and driving.

In 1874 a breeding station called the Régie fédérale had been created at Thun, transformed in 1890 into a military stallion station and was entrusted to the Federal Department of Public Economy. It was transferred in 1898 to Avenches and in 1924 a brood mare stud was added. At present Avenches is the great Federal (civilian) stud with 150 hectares in the plain of the Broye, near Lake Murten. The Avenches stud maintains a second establishment of 90 hectares at Peu-Claude in the neighbouring Jura Mountains, a few kilometres from the gorges of the Doubs which make up the border with France.

The robust horse of the Jura Mountains is the only representative of an essentially Swiss type of horse. Since the motorization of agriculture Avenches has been making systematic use of it for breeding a horse lighter than before, though of dual purpose, and recent imports have included Swedish, Hanoverian, Holsteiner and Trakehner mares. Since 1941 Avenches has submitted all State and privately owned stallions to speed and draught tests prior to registration as sires.

Every year, from November to March, the Federal stud organizes three five-week training sessions which in principle are reserved for the sons of farmers and breeders. All candidates must be sixteen years of age or over and the subjects studied include equitation, driving, grooming and veterinary first-aid. Since 1967 some of these training sessions have been open to girls.

In 1973 Switzerland finally lost the unique training opportunity – typical of the Federal militias – available to the young Dragoon through the presence of his 'Federal horse'. 'This horse', Colonel Pierre Mange wrote in 1975,

was the flesh and blood image of elegance and kindness, the companion-in-arms. . . . Sunday after Sunday the uniformed Dragoons would meet on horseback . . . at shows, at the races or Militaries. . . . And not to forget the important part played by the Federal horse on the farm . . . where it did hard work, as did man. . . . Our armed services branch was the symbol of the country where man and horse were at work together on one and the same land, ready to defend it together.

Despite a petition bearing 432 450 signatures (about ten per cent of the population!) the State and national councils voted to disband the last mounted squadrons.

Fortunately civilian interest in the horse was growing. Lucerne's first CHIO had been held in 1927 and was only preceded by Dublin (1864) and Turin (1902). Competitions in the three mounted disciplines, in driving and in ski-jöring have multiplied in such places as Geneva, St Gallen, Zürich, Basel, Thun, Schaffhausen, Davos, St Moritz and Frauenfeld. International Trekking Rallies are held in the Jura region and Swiss riders compete successfully in all disciplines at international level, most notably in dressage.

André Monteilhet

Principal breeds

The Einsiedler

The Einsiedler, also known as the Swiss Anglo-Norman, takes its name from the Kloster Einsiedel Stud which existed as far back as the eleventh century. The single most profound influence on the Einsiedler, as we know it today, is the Anglo-Norman which it closely resembles, although some Hackney blood may also run in its veins. The Swiss army used to purchase horses of this breed as remounts. Its principal stallion station is at present the Federal one at Avenches, and brood mares continue to be imported from Normandy. The conformation is usually good, particularly the shoulders and quarters, and the action is straight and true. Combining keenness with a tractable disposition, the Einsiedler makes an excellent riding horse capable of competing in all levels of competition, and also goes well in harness. It stands up to about 16.2 h.h. and may be of any whole colour, chestnut and bay being the most usual.

The Freiberger

Since the mechanization of agriculture the Avenches stud has been breeding a lighter type of horse based on the old Franches-Montagnes, the small draught horse of Switzerland's Jura mountain region. Infusions of warm blood such as Anglo-Norman, Trakehner, Swedish and Hanoverian have been used to produce a taller, dual-purpose riding and driving horse of good conformation and kind temperament. The modern Freiberger, stands up to 16 h.h. and combines good, active paces with the stamina and hardiness of its ancestors.

J. M. Draper

Life with Horses in the USA

Capt. Ed Bimberg
Don Essary
Elizabeth Anderson
Philip A. Pines

America is horse crazy.

In a nation that is perhaps the most mechanized in the world, the horse has re-assumed an importance in the hearts of Americans thought to have been lost almost a century ago. All over the country, in the big cities and suburbs, in the lonely farmlands, from the cold climates along the Canadian border to the semi-tropics of Florida and Southern California, the horse is king.

Racing, including Thoroughbred racing on the flat and Standardbred harness racing, is America's most popular spectator sport. Horse shows and horse trials take place every weekend. Rodeos are popular, not only throughout the western states where the sport originated, but in the east as well. Foxhunting is a sport enjoyed from border to border and coast to coast.

All this activity is, perhaps, the eventual result of America's heritage, for America was explored, settled, farmed and held together with the powerful assistance of the horse. The Spaniards conquered the south-west with their Barbs and Arabs and Andalusians – and these breeds formed the basis for the wild Mustangs that for so long roamed the western plains. Later colonists of English extraction imported Thoroughbreds which became the foundation stock for other breeds, such as the American Saddle horse, the Standardbred and the Quarter horse.

Necessity gave rise to other breeds and types as well. The Southern plantation owner, for instance, needed a soft-gaited, easy-to-ride horse from which he could oversee the work on his vast estates, and the Tennessee Walking horse was born. The Vermonter needed a workhorse for his rocky hills and the Morgan appeared on the scene.

But surely the greatest influence on life with horses in America was that period in history that is often called 'The Winning of the West'. For the West, with its tremendous grazing areas and its prosperous cattle industry, depended almost entirely on the horse, and for a century provided a background for the thundering hooves of the horses of cowboys, Indians, cavalrymen, stagecoach drivers and assorted adventurers.

The horse is very much a part of America's heritage even if only a small minority of the population actually does any serious riding.

The small minority that do become horsemen, do so in a variety of ways. In the country, many youngsters are introduced to horsemanship through '4–H' Clubs, a nation-wide organization originally just for farm boys and girls. More recently, as the farm population has declined, the interest has switched from agriculture to pleasure horses, and now many 4–H Clubs are simply riding clubs that sponsor both Western and English riding. The clubs are open to all, whether the prospective member owns his horse or not. While no formal riding instruction is provided, adult leaders help the children in horsemanship and horsemastership and aid in organizing horse shows and gymkhanas.

On a more sophisticated level are the pony clubs, where only English riding is encouraged. Here the member is expected to own his horse or pony and compete in rallies that test not only his practical ability but his theoretical knowledge as well. Pony clubbers are rated on four levels, from 'D' to 'A', and the rider who earns an 'A' rating is considered a very good young horseman indeed.

Those young riders who are not lucky enough to live in rural or suburban areas, where 4–H Clubs or pony clubs are available, have other outlets for their equestrian interests. Riding schools abound in the more populated areas. Unfortunately, riding instruction is neither standardized nor licensed or regulated in any way, so there is a wide range of expertise (or lack of it) in its application. Many so-called 'riding academies' are little more than livery stables of the worst sort, renting poor, under-fed nags to 'horsemen' whose only riding experience is watching Westerns on television. On the other hand, there are an ever-growing number of first-class riding establishments with superb facilities, including large indoor rings and excellent instruction. It is these that are providing a greater degree of educated riding in the United States than ever before.

As elsewhere in the world, the big problem in America is the lack of educated instructors, but that is a situation that is rapidly improving. The cavalry, with its school at Fort Riley, Kansas, once exchanged officers with other military riding schools throughout Europe, thus maintaining a standard of excellence that was not shared by civilian riding schools. Because there was little contact with the army, civilian standards remained low.

Strangely enough, with the disappearance of the cavalry and the closing of the Fort Riley school, civilian standards improved. Because the army had supplied equestrian teams for international competition and the Olympic Games, civilian instructors and trainers were not challenged to produce riders and horses of this calibre. When the army teams were disbanded after the 1948 Olympics, international competition was left to the civilians, and civilian horsemen rose to meet the challenge. Civilians learned, and over the years the standards of instruction rose as well. Today

there are numerous serious schools for riding instructors throughout the country and riding tnstruction is on a much higher plane than ever before. The ambitious young man or woman need only look through the pages of the leading horse magazines to find any number of courses available, lasting from several weeks to a year or more.

The goal of any gifted and ambitious rider is to be part, one day, of the United States Equestrian Team, representing the country on the international scene. The official headquarters of the USET is located at Gladstone, New Jersey, fifty miles from New York City. Once the property of a wealthy owner of Hackney horses, it features a great brick stable with luxurious box stalls, a spacious tack room decorated with the countless ribbons and trophies won by the team the world over. Complementing the stable, there is a large indoor ring, a huge jumping paddock and countryside with every type of obstacle for show jumping and event horses. The Gladstone centre used to shelter, indeed, both the CSO and CCE teams. The latter, which recently moved to New Hamilton, Massachusetts, near Boston, is coached by the Frenchman Jack Le Goff, himself an Olympic rider in this discipline. The CSO team, remaining at Gladstone, is coached by the Hungarian Bertalan de Nemethy. Under the leadership of these two coaches, American civilian riders have attained the very highest levels of international competition.

But all in the horse world is not competitive. Foxhunting was inherited from America's English ancestors and thrived in the new world. Hunting was popular in colonial times and George Washington himself was one of its most enthusiastic devotees. Today there are hunts all over the country, and although some of them have succumbed to urbanization, others have simply packed up and moved further from the cities. In some cases, when foxes became scarce, hunts became drags, with hounds chasing the scent of a fox dragged along the ground, rather than the animal itself. In some western states where foxes are rare, the game became coyotes, but aside from that the hunting remains the same, with pink coats, hunting horns, stirrup cups and the rest. Hunts have become centres for other types of riding, too, with hunt clubs sponsoring hunter trials, horse shows and, more recently, horse trials.

The rise of horse trials in America is itself a phenomenon. A sport unknown among any riders but the cavalry a scant twenty years ago, it has, within the past few years, grown immensely. The one-day event, particularly, appeals to the American amateur horseman for he can exhibit his skills at dressage, cross-country and show jumping with a fairly ordinary horse that he has trained himself. He doesn't need a fancy show hunter that costs a fortune or a proven show jumper which these days is even more expensive. The ordinary field hunter or pleasure horse, with proper training is up to the small obstacles and limited dressage requirements of the lower levels and will usually do well enough for the average rider just starting in the sport. Moreover, horse trials do not have the cut-throat win-or-else atmosphere of many of the larger American horse shows (and some of the smaller ones, too!).

Then, for those who, in the American tradition, prefer the more violent, body-contact sports, there is polo. This exciting game, once thought to be only for the very rich, has become popularized to the extent that Sunday polo games have become fairly commonplace in many parts of the country. The neophyte polo player may begin his career in college – several American universities have polo teams – or he may learn just by 'hanging around' stables where polo is played, exchanging lessons for work, walking hots and mucking out. He may end up playing 'indoor-outdoor' polo on a reduced-size playing field, using an inflated leather ball, similar to a small basketball. This slower type polo does not require a string of speedy, expensive ponies, and has become popular with the enthusiastic player without much ready cash.

For those with the wherewithal, polo can be found almost anywhere in the United States. The smack of mallet against ball and the thundering hooves of the ponies can be heard at exclusive and expensive clubs from New England to Florida (many players spend their winters at Palm Beach and Boca Raton), out through the west to California, and particularly in the south-west, where dry, sunny weather prevails all year.

Of course you do not have to be wealthy to enjoy horses in America. When it comes right down to it, the great majority of horse lovers ride 'backyard' horses, animals they keep in small stables on their own modest properties. These are used for a variety of purposes, not the least of which is 'trail riding', just quietly hacking through the countryside, enjoying the beauties of nature from the back of a horse.

More serious trail riders often graduate to endurance rides, long rides over difficult terrain, some as long as 100 miles, where the condition of the horse is judged, as well as the time in which the ride is completed.

And the list of equestrian pastimes could go on – hunt race steeplechasing for amateur and professional, bronc riding and calf roping for the rough and ready rodeo rider, the showing of the unique five-gaited American Saddle horse, high-level dressage for the very few, or just plain pleasure riding in the parks of our big cities. But whatever type of riding he does, the American horseman does it with gusto and enthusiasm and with a great feeling of satisfaction. Life with horses in America is good.

Captain Ed Bimberg

Principal breeds

The American Quarter horse

History records that in 1611 seventeen native English stallions and mares were imported to Virginia. The blood of those English horses was crossed with horses of pure-bred Spanish ancestry crossed with native stock and known as 'Chickasaws', so named because they were bred by the Chickasaw Indians of that region. The English blood crossed with the Chickasaws produced a compact and heavily muscled horse that could run short distances at great speed and was excellent in the every-day riding and work tasks of the early colonies. The colonists called their new breed Quarter Pathers and later they became known as 'The Illustrious Colonial Quarter of a Mile Running Horse'.

Hugh Jones, writing in 1724, described the Virginia horse of that day as being 'not very tall, but hardy, strong and fleet'. The modern day Quarter horse has much in common with his ancestors from Virginia. He usually stands about 15 to 15.2 h.h., is more heavily muscled than other breeds and shows more symmetry along with muscle definition, especially through the buttock, thigh, and gaskin. He has small ears set on a short head, the muzzle tapering back to strong prominent jaws and a neat, clean throat. The neck may be set slightly higher and is slightly shorter than other breeds; the withers are strong and the shoulders sloping. The legs are notable for their short and sturdy cannon bones. The thigh, buttock, gaskin, and forearm show more pronounced muscling.

The American Quarter Horse Association of Amarillo, Texas, became the keeper of the stud book in 1940; at the present time it is the largest breed registry in the world with more than 1 500 000 horses registered.

Don Essary

The American Saddle horse

The origins of this typically American breed can be traced to the time of the first settlers some four centuries ago. The type was developed by planters looking for easy and, above all, comfortable rides, to render the long inspection tours of their estates as little tiring as possible. The Saddle horse was developed by a policy of selective breeding using Spanish, Trotter and Thoroughbred blood. Among the stallions who had a decisive influence on the breed were the Thoroughbreds Denmark and Messenger and the Morgan Black Hawk. Lightly built, and standing about 15.2 to 16.2

h.h., the Saddlebred has a high, curved neck and a distinctive, high tail carriage which is artificially accentuated for competition. The shoulders tend to be straight and the withers are sunken. The action is characteristically lofty. The Saddlebred is possessed of considerable stamina and is usually of docile temperament.

Nowadays it is bred exclusively for the show ring where three types are admitted. The harness horse is shown harnessed to a light, four-wheeled vehicle; his gaits are the walk and a rather slow trot ('park trot'). The two other types, which are shown under saddle, are the three-gaited saddler and the five-gaited saddler. The former is shown at the walk, trot and canter; the latter, aside from these three gaits, shows the rack and the slow-gait. The rack is not a gait *per se* but a broken amble, a four-beat gait with each beat separated by a time of suspension where no foot is on the ground. The term 'slow-gait' defines, rather than the gait in itself, the shape and speed of a number of paces. Thus, the amble, the slow pace, the stepping pace, the running walk and the fox trot (a broken trot) are gaits apt to be used for the 'slow-gait'. In competition preference among all these gaits is given to the 'stepping pace', which is simply a slowed-down rack.

Elizabeth Anderson

The American Standardbred

The American Standardbred, as a distinct breed, is less than a hundred years old. The breed descends in direct male line from a pure Thoroughbred horse who did not race at the trot. His name was Messenger, and he was descended, through Flying Childers, from the Darley Arabian. He was a grandsire of Hambletonian, and from four outstanding sons of Hambletonian are traced nearly all present-day trotters and pacers racing in the United States.

Messenger (a grey son of Mambrino, one of the best racers of his day, himself a son of the famous stayer, Engineer), came to America from England in 1788 and was bred to mares of every type; after twenty seasons at stud his offspring produced at least 600 foals. One of his descendants, Lady Suffolk, became the first trotter to go a 2:30 mile in harness, and Messenger blood in trotters was in high demand. The roads and early speedways of New York, New Jersey and Pennsylvania saw their high-stepping action.

Two other bloodlines helped shape today's trotters and pacers: the Morgan horses and the Clays. They assisted in establishing a trotting gait best described as a round slashing front action, combined with the low-going, long-gaited action of the Messengers. Big and brawny, the Messengers were also known for substance and courage.

The term Standardbred was first adopted in 1879 by the National Association of Trotting Horse Breeders and appeared in Volume 4 of John H. Wallace's *American Trotting Register*. Volume 4 was published in 1882 and for the first time stallions were assigned numbers to provide identification. Abdallah was number one. His son was Hambletonian, a strapping bay foaled in 1849, and listed as number ten. With his sons and daughters Hambletonian so dominated the trotting sport that all other families died out and ninety-nine per cent of trotters and pacers racing today trace back to this prolific stallion.

Hambletonian's dam, known as the Charles Kent Mare, was by the imported Bellfounder, a descendant of the Norfolk trotters of England. Hambletonian's second and third dams were of Messenger blood and so was his sire. The four sons of Hambletonian who founded the sire lines that lead to nearly all trotting and pacing horses in America today were George Wilkes (1856), Dictator and Happy Medium (1863), and Electioneer (1868). Aside from what has already been described, much of the history of Standardbred breeding is still shrouded in mystery because there was no official record-keeping in the breed's earliest days.

Standardbreds have great endurance, energy and gameness. They stand anything from 14 to 16 h.h., and their weight varies from 900 to 1150 lbs. They are generally more rugged in conformation than the Thoroughbred.

Trotters and pacers tend to beget trotters and pacers. An example of how a sire passes on his gait is the late great pacer, Adios. Out of seventy-nine two-minute performers sired by Adios, seventy-eight were pacers, while the trotter, Star's Pride, produced twenty-four two-minute performers, twenty of them trotters.

Trotters are identified as line gaited or passing gaited. Viewed from the front or the rear, a line gaited horse's front and hind feet are in a direct line with each other when the trotter is in motion. A passing gait finds the trotter's hind feet landing outside the front feet. The pacer is easily identified by his side-swaying motion, a result of both feet on the same side of his body moving in the same direction at the same time. The pacer has almost always had the edge on speed over the trotter. He was the first to go a mile in two minutes or less (Star Pointer, 1:59 1/4 in 1897). And pacers are greater producers of speed than trotters, too.

Although a Standardbred may be distinguished by his conformation, there is the belief that a definite type of Standardbred has yet to be produced. Breeders envision trotters that never hit their shins and pacers that never crossfire, and horses of both gaits that will not touch their knees. To achieve these ends a longer barrelled trotter would be necessary and a wider-bodied pacer. Presumably time and careful breeding will produce such harness horses who are expected to attain a distinct, regal appearance.

Philip A. Pines

The Appaloosa

Although the exact origins of the Appaloosa are uncertain, we apparently owe this breed to the Nez Percé Indians in the Palouse region of Idaho as a war horse and, in more recent times, the distinctive spotted coat pattern has made the Appaloosa a popular circus horse. There are several types of coat patterns, ranging from all-over spots to spotting over the hips only. The basic coat is usually white with black or chocolate-coloured spots, but some horses show white spots on a dark background. The skin is usually pink, with grey mottling, and the hooves are usually parti-coloured. The Appaloosa stands between 14.2 and 15.2 h.h. and makes a good riding horse, having good shoulders and prominent withers. He is a hardy horse and often excels at jumping. His increasing popularity has placed him among America's Five 'Big Ones', the others being the Thoroughbred, the American Quarter horse, the Standardbred and the Shetland pony.

The Morgan

The Morgan horse is descended from one stallion, Justin Morgan, born in 1789 in Vermont and named after his second owner. Justin Morgan, who stood a mere 14 h.h., was probably based on Arab, Welsh and Thoroughbred blood. He was an incredibly tough little horse who excelled in weight-pulling competitions and was unbeaten in both ridden and driven races. In addition he was a prepotent sire and put his strong imprint upon his numerous progeny, The modern Morgan stands around 15 h.h. and is primarily a saddle horse, although he also goes well in harness and was used, prior to agricultural mechanization, as an all-purpose farm horse. The dscendants of Justin Morgan have retained his robustness and in endurance rides they often vie successfully with the pure-bred Arab.

The Palomino

The Palomino is not a breed as such but a colour type of ancient origin originating in the United States where it is also known as 'The Golden Horse of the West'. We know that Queen Isabella of Spain promoted the breeding of horses with the characteristic golden colour of the modern Palomino in the fifteenth century. A Palomino registry was opened in America in 1932 and in 1941 the Association of Palomino Horse Breeders of America was founded in California. Today the horse is found all over the USA and may be one of three types: the show horse, the bridle path

type and the stock horse. The Palomino's striking body coat colour is that of newly minted gold and the mane and tail are cream-coloured. Stars, stripes or blazes and socks or stockings are permitted, but no other markings are allowed. The height varies between 15.2 and 16.1 h.h.

The Pinto

The name Pinto is derived from the Spanish word, pintado (painted), hence the term 'paint' which is often used when referring to this horse. The Pinto was a favourite mount of the American Indians since his broken coat patterns blended into the landscape and afforded excellent camouflage. A colour type rather than a breed, the Pinto is any sort of horse with large areas of white coat. If the fundamental colour is black it is called *piebald*; otherwise it is termed *skewbald*. The Pinto is an intelligent, agile horse with great stamina. He is a fair jumper and hunter, docile enough for a child to ride and sufficiently handy to make an excellent cow pony.

The Pony of the Americas

This typically American breed is of recent origin and was created in 1956 by crossing a Shetland pony stallion with an Appaloosa mare. The result was an animal of pony size with many of the Appaloosa's characteristics, including skin colour and coat pattern. The success in the show ring of this first cross led to further experiments and a stud book was opened. To qualify for registration the ponies must stand from 11.2 to 13 h.h. and have the Appaloosa characteristics.

The Tennessee Walking horse

The Tennessee Walking horse might be called the first cousin of the American Saddle horse. Both breeds originated in the South (Kentucky, Tennessee, Missouri) and were developed for an identical purpose: to serve the planters as comfortable, swift, robust and docile mounts on tours of crop inspection. The Tennessee Walking horse is heavier and more powerful than the American Saddle horse and is perhaps a little more common, but he is renowned for his gentle disposition. The breed did not gain official recognition until 1935. The foundation sire was Black Allan, a Standardbred which had failed on the race track. Pacer, Thoroughbred, Arab and Morgan blood have also gone into the making of the Tennessee Walking horse. There are today 30000 horses in the stud book.

The breed shows three gaits: the flat-foot walk, the running walk and the canter, gaits which, through selective breeding, may be considered natural to this breed. The flat-foot walk is a four-beat gait in the same order as the walk (near fore, off hind, off fore, near hind), but the action of the forelegs is very lofty and the horse overstrides very strongly. The running walk resembles the former gait, with a difference in cadence (tempo). The canter, though its strides are the same as in the classical gait, is executed with a 'rocking chair' motion.

Elizabeth Anderson

Life with Horses in the USSR

Prof. Igor F. Bobylev
M. F. H. de Genellis

The vast expanses of the Soviet Union have been the home of horses and horsemen for countless centuries. Even today, when the horse is no longer required to carry the Russian soldier into battle or as the prime means of transportation, statistics show that there are an incredible four million horses still at work in the Soviet Union. Despite mechanization the horse has retained a role in agriculture, where he is able to perform some tasks more economically and efficiently than any machinery.

The basic laws of running and breeding horses in herds have been evolved and passed on to each successive generation over many centuries. This heritage has not been lost, for in Kirghizia, Kazakhstan, Yakutia, Buyatia and Bashkiria, horses are still run in herds and a policy of selective breeding has produced a supply of hardy horses particularly well adapted to extremes in climate. In these regions the horse is still an important part of everyday life. Not only is horsemeat eaten but great use is made of mare's milk, from which the beverage known as *kumis* is made. Many a farm in Bashkiria, Kazakhstan and elsewhere has gone into bottled *kumis* production on a large scale.

There are about fifty breeds or types of horse in the Soviet Union, more than in any other country. Some, such as the Akhal-Teke, are of ancient origin, others are the result of modern zootechnical skill. The second quarter of the twentieth century saw the creation, for specific purposes, of breeds such as the Budyony, the Tersk and the Russian Trotter, products of the combined skills of zootechnicians, ordinary horse breeders and stud personnel.

Horse breeding is the responsibility of the national studs, the *sovkhozzes* (State) and *kolkhozzes* (collective) farms. Many have an exciting history – the Khrenovsky National Stud, for instance, cradle of the Orlov Trotter, which celebrated its Bicentennial in 1975.

Every year the best products of the studs are sent to the permanent 'Exhibition of National Economic Achievements' in Moscow, and to other shows held at Union Republic, Regional and District levels throughout the country. Championship titles bring with them diplomas, cash premiums and trophies for their owner-studs.

The modern riding horse competes successfully in international competition and is increasingly exported to other parts of the world. The national studs now hold four sales a year, two at the Moscow, one at the Tersky and one at the Kirovsky studs.

During the past twenty-five years Soviet people have taken more and more interest in the horse for pleasure pursuits, exercise and relaxation. Racing is particularly popular and some sixty courses, and a number of trotting tracks, attract large crowds during the summer season. The most important are in Moscow, Pyatigorsk, Rostov, Tbilisi, Alma-Ata, Tashkent, Frunze, Krasnodar and Baku. All are governed by a common racing code ratified by the Ministry of Agriculture. The top Thoroughbred race for three-year-olds is the All-Union Grand Prix, run over 2400 m at the Moscow Hippodrome on or around the first Sunday in August. The trotting 'Derby' is also run at the Hippodrome, over a distance of 1600 m in or around July. These two meetings attract the country's finest racehorses both in harness and under saddle. Winning the Derby is the cherished dream of every stud, trainer and jockey.

The most famous Soviet racehorse of the sixties was Anilin (by Element out of Analogichnaya), who was an international star and the darling of the Moscow public. Anilin raced for five seasons, winning twenty-one times out of twenty-five starts. His jockey, Nikolai Nasibov, began his career as a lad and is now the highly respected trainer at the Voskhod National Stud.

More and more people take up riding in the Soviet Union every year and equitation is on the upswing. Its foundations, and some of the popular interest in it, probably date back to the time of the dashing cavalrymen of the First Mounted Army who fought so gallantly through the Civil War and Intervention, and who devoted much of their leisure time to mounted games. Many of those who fought in the fabled Red Cavalry during the Revolution and its aftermath retained their interest in horses, either in breeding or in riding and sometimes in both. The famous Marshal Budyony, for instance, who died aged ninety-one in October 1973, remained in the forefront of horse breeding and became a great promoter of Soviet equitation. Both the Budyony and the Tersk breeds were developed with his guidance and active participation.

Riding has become one of the chief sports accessible to all sectors of the population. In the 1920s there were only a few large riding schools in the country, but by the early 1940s the number had increased to twenty-two and today there are some eighty-five. Some, such as those in Moscow, Alma-Ata, Kiev, Novosibirsk, Tbilisi, Tashkent, Lugnask and Lvov, have excellent indoor schools, built within the last decade. There are more, better quality horses, too. In 1956 only 28.9 per cent of horses were Thoroughbreds. By 1974 this figures had risen to 44.4 per cent.

The principal competitive events are the Spartakiada of the USSR Nations, the Championships of the USSR, the All-Union Kolk-hozzes, Sovkhozzes and National Studs Riders Championships, the Village Riders Championships and the Republics Championships. There is also a nationwide championship event for agricultural students at both secondary and higher levels and numerous competitions are organized by the Central Soviets of sports societies, municipalities, etc.

Equestrian schools and clubs are run, not by individuals, but by the Veterinary Sports Society and high-level agricultural and veterinary schools, stud farms and hippodromes. Anyone wishing to take up equestrian sports can do so at these schools and clubs free of charge. Those who progress with their horsemanship and horsemastership gain successively third-class, second-class and first-class status as candidates for the Master of Sport degree. The Equestrian Federation of the USSR has control over the activities of schools and clubs.

Soviet riders made their first appearance in the Olympic Games at Helsinki in 1952 and since then have competed regularly at the Olympics and in international championships. Moscow, in 1965, and Kiev, in 1973, hosted the European three-day event championships. With long-distance travel no longer the problem it once was, Soviet riders such as Filatov, Kizimov, Petushkova and others have become well known outside the USSR.

Among the many mounted games which are so popular in the Soviet Union is *Kok-par*, the national equestrian game of Kazakh and Kirghiz peoples, in which two teams try to carry off a goat's carcass from centre field to the gates. Another typically Russian game is the hot pursuit of a horseman, carrying a fox brush on his sleeve, by two other riders trying to get at the brush. There is, in addition, a sort of mounted tennis; javelin-throwing games; archery at the gallop; another game where a 'fleeing' girl must be caught, or a cap taken away from a rider; mounted mock-battles, and so on.

These games are indeed an integral part of most championship events; they enhance the agricultural exhibition, enliven town and village feasts and festivals and, naturally, are popular leisure and holiday pastimes.

And, of course, there is driving. As far back as 1910, when nearly everyone was a fair whip and competition was accordingly stiff, Russian troikas won top honours in the Grand Prix at London's World Exhibition. And troika drives have remained strong favourites in Russia, both for pleasure and competition.

Troika bells still jingle down park lanes and raceways, and add sparkle to the Moscow festival called 'Russian Winter' which is held every year in February or March. Troikas also compete every winter at the National Economic Achievements Exhibition. There are black, bay, grey and light bay troika teams. Top honours in 1974 went to the splendid light greys from the Vladimir District, driven by Fomin, a great hand with a troika, whom you may have seen in New York, Washington, Leipzig or Budapest.

Just as everybody loves a troika, so everyone in the Soviet Union loves and has always loved a night at the circus. Horses have always been a major feature of the Russian circus and still perform daily to full houses in rings all over the country. The most famous riders are those of the Kantimirov circus dynasty who have toured the world and are the undisputed kings of circus riding in their country. They began in 1907 and their skills are carried on by their children, grandchildren and pupils today.

Notable among Soviet museums are the museum and library of the Timiryazyev Academy not far from Moscow, which is entirely devoted to the horse and possesses a truly unique collection of art and literature. In no other place, I am told, is there so much equestrian information to be found. It is, not surprisingly, a researcher's paradise.

Professor Igor F. Bobylev

Principal breeds

The Akhal-Teke

A breed of ancient origin, the Akhal-Teke is a strain of the Turkmene or Turcoman horse which can be traced back some 2500 years. Bred at the stud in the Akhal-Teke oasis, the breed is noted for its great hardiness and stamina. A typical desert horse, it is of light build, with a long, slender head and long neck. The body is long, the quarters sloping and the tail low-set. Although the legs are long, the tendons are very strong and the small feet are immensely hard. The mane and tail are sparse and of fine texture and the predominant colour is a striking shade of gold. Standing up to about 15.2 h.h. the Akhal-Teke is a good all-round riding horse.

The Budyony

The Budyony was developed by Marshal Budyony, a cavalry general and veteran of the Civil War, who held high command in 1941. It was bred as a cavalry horse and is based on Don and Thoroughbred blood. The best of the progeny of the first crosses were interbred and have produced an elegant, good-natured horse of good conformation and strong build. The usual colours are chestnut and bay and the average height 15.2 to 16 h.h. The Budyony makes an excellent competition horse and is much used in show jumping and steeple-chasing.

The Don

The Don horse, the mount of the Don Cossacks for centuries, was of Asiatic origin and was originally a wiry little horse. The original type has been improved by crossing with Karabair, Turkmene and Thoroughbred and the modern Don is taller, standing up to about 15.3 h.h., with a long but strong body, powerful neck and strong legs. It is exceptionally tough and thrives with a minimum of help from man. Don horses are bred in Rostov, Kirghizia and Kazakhstan and make excellent all-round work horses. The predominant colours are chestnut and bay.

The Jomud

The Jomud is a descendant of the ancient Turkmene, although there is evidence of Arabian influence. Standing up to about 15 h.h.

the Jomud is a wiry little horse possessed of great stamina – used in harness and a truly ideal mount for long-distance rides. The usual colour is grey; less so are bay and chestnut.

The Kabardin

The Kabardin is a mountain breed which has been known in the Caucasus for four hundred years. The mountain horses were crossed with Arabs and Turkmenes and today the Kabardin stands up to about 15 h.h. It has retained the sure-footedness common to all mountain breeds and is strongly built with tough tendons. The usual colours are bay or dark brown. The Kabardin is popular in many regions and is used for all-round riding purposes.

The Karabair

The Karabair is indigenous to Georgia and is of very ancient origin, the region which is now called Uzbekistan having been famous for its horses for two and a half thousand years. The modern Karabair horse comes in two distinct types: a saddle horse reminiscent of the Don horse and a light draught type. An exceptionally tough, sound horse, the Karabair shows signs of Arabian influence, being of similar height and conformation. The usual colours are bay, chestnut and grey.

The Lithuanian Heavy Draught horse

Breeding of the Lithuanian Heavy Draught horse began a hundred years ago to fulfil the need for a good, strong farm horse. Swedish Ardennais stallions were imported and crossed with Lithuania's Zhmud mares. Selective breeding over the years has produced the modern, medium-sized heavy draught horse which is possessed of a very active walk and trot and is a willing worker. The body is broad and strong, the legs short and the predominant colour chestnut.

The Orlov trotter

One of the world's great trotting horses, the Orlov was developed by Count Alexis Orlov at his Khrenov Stud, founded in 1778. Count Orlov based his trotter strain on Arabian and Dutch blood and by the beginning of the nineteenth century the breed had achieved great fame. Some Thoroughbred and Mecklenburg blood was also used. Today's trotter is a strong, upstanding horse, averaging about 16 h.h. with plenty of depth through the girth and strong legs. A long-lived horse of strong constitution, the Orlov is usually grey, bay, black or chestnut, and as well as being used as a racehorse (the first trotting races were held in Moscow in 1799) has been used as an all-round driving horse. The Orlov is crossed with the American Standardbred to produce the Russian Trotter, an improved performer on the racecourse.

The Przevalsky

The Przevalsky horse is the wild horse of Mongolia discovered by Colonel N. M. Przevalsky in 1881. All equines are believed to be descended from this primitive breed which has probably changed little since the Ice Age. Although it is still found on the borders of the USSR and Mongolia, the Przevalsky is now extremely rare, having been hunted to near extinction. However, the breed is being preserved through careful breeding in various zoos throughout the world. The body is heavy and compact, the neck thick, the shoulders strong, the legs short and muscular and the feet small and very hard. The coat colour varies between dark brown and red bay, the belly being cream-coloured and the legs having black stripes. Many Przevalskys have a dorsal stripe. The mane stands upright in summer and in winter, when the hairs are thicker, falls down both sides of the neck. The head is chunky, the ears small and the eyes large. The Przevalsky is an intractable animal and cannot be broken for riding.

The Russian Heavy Draught horse

The Russian Heavy Draught horse has been developed over the last hundred years by crossing country-bred mares with Percheron and Ardennais stallions and with Orlov trotters. The product has a powerful body set on short legs, giving it great tractive power. The small head is set on a strong, medium long neck, the shoulders are powerful, and the usual colour is chestnut. The breed is much used on farms in the Ukraine and in the Urals. Standing only about 14.2 h.h., the Heavy Draught horse shows an active walk and trot and possesses tough, strong feet.

The Tersk

The Tersk horse, which resembles the pure-bred Arab, was evolved at the Tersk and Stavropol studs in the Caucasus and was based on Strelets Arab blood. The Strelets Arab, which was the result of crossing pure-bred Arabs with Anglo-Arabs from the Orlov and Rastopchin studs, had almost died out by the end of World War One. The remaining Strelets were bred to pure- and and part-bred Arabs and after some thirty years the new Tersk type was fixed. Standing a little taller than the average pure-bred Arab, the Tersk is usually light grey in colour and is a very good-looking horse. It is used in the circus, for dressage and on the racecourse. It is bred at the Stavropcl stud, the Tersk stud being used for breeding pure Arabians only.

The Toric

A cobby-type horse much used in agriculture in Esthonia, the Toric was evolved at the end of the nineteenth century when the local Esthonian mares were mated to the imported Norfolk Roadster stallion Hatman. More Norfolk Roadster, and some Orlov, blood was added subsequently and the result is a medium-sized, active, light draught horse of good conformation standing about 15 to 15.2 h.h. The breed is noted for its good temperament and great stamina. Predominant colours are chestnut and bay.

The Viatka

The Viatka is a large breed of all-purpose pony from the Kazan region which is used for light agricultural work and is particularly adept at drawing sledges on snowbound roads in winter. Standing 13 to 14 h.h., it is a strongly-built pony, with a short back, powerful neck and quarters, deep girth and strong limbs and feet. The mane and tail are full and grey is the usual colour. It is an economical feeder and an active, willing worker. There are two types of Viatka, the Kazanski and the Ovinski, named after the localities from which they originate.

The Vladimir

The Vladimir, which comes from the district of that name, is a heavy draught horse of mixed ancestry, possessing Suffolk, Shire, Cleveland Bay, Percheron and Ardennais blood. It originated at the end of the last century and is bred today throughout the Ivanova and Vladimir regions. Standing about 16 h.h., the Vladimir is a powerfully built, active horse, usually bay in colour. It has great tractive power and is noted for its soundness.

M. F. H. de Genellis

Life with Horses in West Germany

André Monteilhet
Jean-Paul Klein

The Federal Republic of Germany which came into being in 1949 covers a territory of 248 000 km² with sixty million inhabitants and consists of eight states (Länder) with Bonn as the Federal capital. In 1970 some 400 000 horses and ponies lived there, practically all of them riding, light draught horses, or both.

Selective breeding has been practised for hundreds of years, one of the oldest centres being the famous stallion depot at Marbach in Württemberg. Founded in 1593 as a royal stud, Marbach still has an influence on breeding today. Stallion depots (Landgestüte) are still provided by the State, the riding horse depots being at Celle, Warendorf, Zweibrücken, Marbach, Dillenburg and Landshut. Marbach also houses a State stud which produces horses of various breeds, notably Württembergers and Arabians.

There are training centres in each State for horses and riders as well as riding instructors, and the National Training Centre, including the Olympic Games Committee, is located at Warendorf in Westphalia. Warendorf has taken over from the old Cavalry School of Hanover which had been transferred to Krampnitz in 1939 and was destroyed in 1945.

West German riders compete with great success in show jumping, eventing and dressage up to and including Olympic standard and, indeed, in post-war Olympics their record has been outstanding. There is also driving in West Germany and centres such as those at Dillenburg and Marbach provide instruction up to a high level. The Deutsche Reiterliche Vereinigung e.V. (German Federation of Equestrian Sports) runs an awards scheme in driving and candidates can take examinations for bronze, silver and gold grades.

Thoroughbred racing first took place in Germany in 1822 at Doberan in Mecklenburg and the first important Thoroughbred stud was located in Harzburg in the former duchy of Brunswick. The German Jockey Club, which became the Union Club in 1867, was founded in 1840 and the German Thoroughbred stud book was opened in 1847. Today there are thirty Thoroughbred studs, the most important being the Röttgen, Waldrun, Schlenderhan and Walfried. The Federal Republic runs five Classic races based on the English prototypes, namely the Derby, St Leger, Oaks, Henckel (2000 Guineas) and Schwarzgold (1000 Guineas), and a total of some 1500 races are run each season.

The first official trotting race was run in Hamburg (Altona) in 1874. To begin with Orlovs were used but in time they were superseded by American and French horses. The first breeding centres for trotters were set up at Mariahall in the Rhenish Palatinate (established in 1885) and Lilienhof, Baden (established in 1890) and a trotter stud book was opened in 1896.

Except for some draghunting (Schleppjagd) there is no hunting in Germany, but there are many hunting horn playing groups. Some of their fanfares are the same as in France, others are original.

Germany has only one native pony breed, the Dulmen, of which only a small number remain. Imported pony breeds, which are popular either as children's riding ponies or for draught and pack work, include the Norwegian Fjord, the Haflinger and the Shetland.

There are several museums of specific interest to horsemen, probably the most famous being that of the Wittelsbachs at Nymphenburg which houses one of the most impressive collections of carriages in Europe. Also of note are the Carriage Museum at Ratisbon in Bavaria, the Wilhelmsturm Museum in Dillenburg and the Hussard Museum in the castle of Vornholz near Warendorf. Vornholz is notable for its private stud, owned by Baron Clems von Nagel-Doornick who imports French Anglo-Arabs from Tarbes and Pau.

Contemporary German equestrian writings are impressive. First of all, there are the vast works by one of the greatest connoisseurs of European horses: Gustav Rau (1879–1954) who became inspector general of studs (Oberlandstallmeister). His writings published between 1907 and 1948 cover subjects beyond the German domain proper. Other equestrian authors include Felix Bürkner, Waldemar Seunig, Jasper Nissen, Von Zeeb-Guttman, Erika Schiele and Arnold Schlie.

The principal German equestrian publications are the monthly magazines *Sankt Georg* and *Reiter Revue*.

André Monteilhet

Principal breeds

The Hanoverian

The ancestry of this breed may be traced to the Great Horse of chivalry, but recorded origins go back to 1714, when the reigning Elector of Hanover and Duke of Brunswick became King George I of Great Britain and introduced Thoroughbred blood. George II founded the stud at Celle in 1735, which to this day is the official headquarters of the breed.

During the nineteenth century the infusion of Thoroughbred blood became too strong, and breeders turned back to native Hanoverian sires. After World War Two, when the need for agricultural horses (Wirtschaftstyp) was no longer felt, a lighter conformation was produced by a renewed Thoroughbred cross and also by the use of stallions from Trakehnen (East Prussia).

The breed existed in the Middle Ages, but the stud at Trakehnen was founded in 1732 by King Frederick William I of Prussia, the monarch with the sergeant-major's mind. Thereby he ensured the future of the breed. It may be said that the foundation stock was fifty per cent Thoroughbred, twenty-five per cent Arab and twenty-five per cent country-bred.

It is a handsome horse, well muscled-up, rather substantial, active, greatly esteemed for its staying power and kind temperament. Though some were bred for the plough and others for the carriage, the great majority were destined to be remounts.

Stallions are subjected to rigorous selection in order to maintain as far as possible the high standards of the breed. In fact, only those stallions that have been in training for a year, during which all their abilities have been tested, are sent to stud. World War Two was disastrous for the breed, and of the 25 000 horses registered in the Stud Book only 1200 were evacuated to West Germany where breeding has been resumed.

The Holstein

The Holstein is one of the oldest breeds in Germany and was evolved by putting native mares to oriental and Andalusian stallions. The resulting produce was so well thought of that as early as the sixteenth century exports were being made to several European countries, including Denmark, France and Italy. Infusions of Thoroughbred blood during the eighteenth century gave the Holstein more speed and improved conformation and gradually the breed became the model of a dual-purpose horse, ride or drive, and consequently also an artillery horse. The breed has been developed at the Traventhal stud in Schleswig-Holstein, founded by the Prussians in 1867. When the

Traventhal stallion depot was closed in 1961 responsibility for keeping the stud book and allocating approved stallions to districts was assumed by the Holstein Breeders Association at Elmshorn. Recent infusions of more Thoroughbred blood have produced a breed suitable for modern competitive sports, particularly show jumping and eventing and the modern Holstein is an intelligent, good-tempered horse of powerful build, with strong quarters and short legs with plenty of bone. The average height is between 15.3 and 16.2 h.h. and the usual colours are black, bay and brown.

The Oldenburg

The Oldenburg is the heaviest of the German warm-blood breeds and dates from the seventeenth century, being derived from the Friesian horse. In the second half of the eighteenth century, Spanish, Barb and English half-bred stallions were imported to add quality, and in the nineteenth century infusions of Thorough-bred, Norman, Cleveland and Hanoverian blood were added. The result was a harness horse (Karossierpferd) of great strength and early maturity, standing up to about 17 h.h. In the twentieth century the need for this type of harness horse, which was held in such esteem up to the time of World War One, has given place to the riding horse, and Thorough-bred, Hanoverian and Trakehner blood has been used to upgrade the breed. Today it is an all-purpose saddle horse, standing between 16.2 and 17.2 h.h. and is notable for its strong conformation and good bone. The usual colours are black, bay and brown.

The Schleswig

The Schleswig is a draught horse which originates from the province of that name situated between Holstein and Jutland. Indeed it traces back to the Jutland horse of Denmark and, like the Jutland, was formerly used for pulling omnibuses and trams. The breed society was founded in 1891 and up until 1938 infusions of Jutland blood were regularly made. After 1945 two French stallions, a Boulonnais and a Breton, were used to produce lighter conformation. Today's Schleswig is a compact horse, standing about 15.2 to 16 h.h., of placid disposition. The predominant colour is chestnut, with some bays and greys occurring.

The Trakehner

The Trakehner (or East Prussian) horse existed in the Middle Ages but was first bred systematically at the stud at Trakehnen, founded in 1732 by King Frederick William I of Prussia. The foundation stock was fifty per cent Thoroughbred, twenty-five per cent Arab and twenty-five per cent native. The Trakehner was bred princiaplly as a cavalry remount, although it was also capable of light agricultural work and was renowned for its great endurance. World War Two was disastrous for the breed and of the 25 000 horses registered in the East Prussian stud book only 1200 could be evacuated to the west. Today the Trakehner is found throughout West Germany and is bred on a large scale in Holstein, Hanover, the Rhineland and the Palatinate. Trakehner blood also influences a number of other studs, notably those at Dillenburg, Celle and Oldenburg. The Association of Breeders and Friends of the Trakehner has its headquarters in Hamburg. In order to maintain standards stallions are subjected to a rigorous selection programme before they can stand at stud. The Trakehner is a handsome horse, standing between 16 and 16.2 h.h., well muscled-up, active, and possessed of great staying power and kind temperament. Any solid colour is permissible.

The Württemberg

The Württemberg is still bred chiefly at Marbach, which has been a centre of horse breeding for nearly four hundred years. The foundation stock consisted of native mares who were crossed with Arab and, later, with East Prussian and Norman stallions. Oldenburg and

Suffolk blood was also used on occasion. The horse who had particular influence on the breed was the Norman stallion Faust. The Württemberg, which is noted for its docility and hardiness, is bred today as a sports horse, being suitable for use both under saddle and in harness. It stands up to about 16 h.h., has great depth through the girth, has good sound legs and is an economical feeder. The usual colours are brown, black, bay and chestnut. The stud book is kept by the Society of Horse Breeders of Württemberg in Stuttgart.

Jean-Paul Klein

Appendices

The History of the FEI

E. A. Sarasin

The first Equestrian Olympic Games, at Stockholm in 1912 and Antwerp in 1920, had demonstrated certain deficiencies in the rules. Baron Pierre de Coubertin, President of the International Olympic Committee, determined to take advantage of the International Congress at Lausanne to assemble the top personalities of the equestrian world and to try, with their skills, to work out a complete set of rules. Consequent to those meetings and on the initiative of France and Sweden the FEI – Fédération Équestrienne Internationale – was born in May 1921.

Its rules now in force were accepted in principle and with enthusiasm in the form worked out and presented by the French delegate, Major C. Hector.

These rules were debated again and definitively adopted at a Congress held in Paris, the 24th and 25th of November of that year, by the heads of delegates of the eight national Federations first joining. The first code was laid down then and came into force on the first day of 1922. Signatories were:

BELGIUM: M. Dupuich, President of the Fédération Nationale des Sports Équestres.

DENMARK: Capt. C. A. Kraft, President of Dansk Ridefozbund.

USA: Maj. Berkeley Merchant for General Harris, Adjutant-General of the US Army.

FRANCE: Baron du Teil, President of the Fédération Nationale des Sports Équestres.

ITALY: Gen. Bellotti for General Ajroldi, President of the Societa del Cavallo Italiano da Sella.

JAPAN: Col. Kaba for cavalry Colonel Tatekava, appointed by the Minister for War.

NORWAY: Maj. Chr.-F. Michelet, President of Nozges Ryttezfozbund.

SWEDEN: Count Clarence de Rosen, for HRH Prince Carl of Sweden, President of Svenska Ridsportens Centralforbund.

Since its foundation the FEI has developed widely and rapidly under the spirited impulse of successive chairmen: Baron du Teil, Col. Maris, Maj. Quarleg van Ufford, Gen. Guy Henry, Gen. Baron von Holzing-Berstett, Gen. Baron de Trannoy, and of its founder and Secretary-General, Maj. C. Hector, followed by M. Moezemans d'Emaus and the Chevalier H. de Menten de Horne, by HRH Prince Bernhard of the Netherlands and by the present President, HRH Prince Philip, Duke of Edinburgh.

In 1936 thirty-one national federations, representing thirty-one nations, went to make up the FEI.

From the beginning its assembly was concerned with regulating international competitions, but in fact it contented itself with establishing the rules for the three Olympic tests. Soon the need made itself felt for a more extensive code, tending in some measure to unify the basic principles of drawing up programmes for all international tests. Such a code was published in 1930.

By the creation in 1929 of an International Olympic Dressage Competition, and later the setting up of the Council of Judges and Judges-aspirant for Dressage, the FEI has given a new impetus to higher equitation which contemporary life styles had rather pushed into oblivion.

The first mention we find of a Horse Trials code appeared in the rules of 1938. The Three-Day Event Championship was initiated by the Congress of 1957.

Wishing to emphasize its interest in the promotion of equestrian sports for youth, the FEI in 1951 initiated the European Junior Championship for Show Jumping, recently supplemented by Junior Dressage and Junior Eventing Championships.

Three years ago there emerged, under the stimulus of its President, Prince Philip, Duke of Edinburgh, a code for driving events, this discipline of the sport being currently on the increase.

Aims

Among the aims pursued by the FEI is that of bringing under its sole control all international equestrian competitions, such as dressage, show jumping, eventing, driving, and any other form of horse sport, as the General Assembly shall determine.

It also has the aim of encouraging the teaching of horsemanship and horsemastership for recreational purposes.

Administration

The FEI is administered by a standing committee of thirteen members, comprising at least one from each continent, responsibilities being allotted among the different disciplines of the sport.

It is also constituted by a General Assembly comprising the delegates of the sixty-three National Federations affiliated, meeting at least once a year.

The study of different problems which may arise and of suggestions raised by various committees and authorities in each discipline of the sport is entrusted to various permanent commissions which have to report annually to the standing committee.

Relations with national federations

Throughout the world the FEI brings federations for equestrian sports together, giving them general assistance and uniting them by durable bonds of understanding and solidarity, in order to increase their sports potential.

While allowing the organizers the greatest freedom in drawing up their programmes, it intends to unify the rules applicable to international competitions and to watch over the enforcement of these rules.

It gives special assistance in the appointment of judges at international level, judges who have been present consistently at committee and council meetings.

It also assigns experts to national federations and nations requesting their presence. These experts have the task of teaching and educating, as well as studying the problems which confront national federations, and of finding the appropriate solutions.

The future

Organization and control of all international events must entail the training of new judges and technical delegates who will have to be picked from cadres replenished by new blood and equipped with adequate experience.

Health of horses and veterinary inspections, as well as restrictions placed on the movement of horses, will have to be studied with care and a solution found which will facilitate transport so as to resolve the problems raised by the differing quarantine regulations imposed by governments for the control of infectious equine diseases.

The FEI will also in future have to concern itself with tests for handicapped persons riding for therapeutic purposes, be concerned with such bodies as pony clubs, and possibly also with steeplechasing.

In so doing, the FEI will have to keep pace with an ever-expanding body of equestrian sports throughout the world, and through the medium of its own national federations face up to the problems encountered by horsemen.

The World Arabian Horse Organization

G. R. M. Kydd

Its objects are:

'To acquire and disseminate and promote and facilitate the acquisition and dissemination of knowledge or information in all or any countries directly or indirectly concerning horses of the Arabian breed and its derivatives.

'To promote throughout the world the welfare and safeguard the existence and interests of the breed of Arabian horses and its derivatives.

'To maintain throughout the world the purity of the blood of horses of the Arabian breed.'

Major Competition Results

OLYMPIC GAMES

1912 – Stockholm

DRESSAGE:

Individual	1 C. Bonde	Emperor	Sweden
	2 G. A. Boltenstern	Neptun	Sweden
	3 H. von Blixen-Finecke	Maggie	Sweden

No team competition

SHOW JUMPING:

Individual	1 J. Cariou	Mignon	France
	2 F. von Kröcher	Dohna	Germany
	3 E. de Blommaert de Soye	Clonmore	Belgium
Team	1 Sweden		
	2 France		
	3 Germany		

THREE-DAY EVENT:

Individual	1 A. Nordlander	Lady Artist	Sweden
	2 von Rochow	Idealist	Germany
	3 J. Cariou	Cocotte	France
Team	1 Sweden		
	2 Germany		
	3 USA		

1920 – Antwerp

DRESSAGE:

Individual	1 J. Lundblad	Uno	Sweden
	2 B. Sandström	Sabel	Sweden
	3 H. von Rosen	Running Sister	Sweden

No team competition

SHOW JUMPING:

Individual	1 T. Lequio	Trebecco	Italy
	2 A. Valerio	Cento	Italy
	3 G. Lewenhaupt	Mon Coeur	Sweden
Team	1 Sweden		
	2 Belgium		
	3 Italy		

THREE-DAY EVENT:

Individual	1 H. Helmer	Geria	Sweden
	2 A. Lundström	Yrsa	Sweden
	3 P. Caffarati	Traditore	Italy
Team	1 Sweden		
	2 Italy		
	3 Belgium		

1924 – Paris

DRESSAGE:

Individual	1 E. Linder	Piccolomini	Sweden
	2 B. Sandström	Sabel	Sweden
	3 X. Lesage	Plumarol	France

No team competition

SHOW JUMPING:

Individual	1 A. Gemuseus	Lucette	Switzerland
	2 T. Lequio	Trebecco	Italy
	3 A. Krolikiewicz	Picador	Poland
Team	1 Sweden		
	2 Switzerland		
	3 Portugal		

THREE-DAY EVENT:

Individual	1 V. van Zijp	Silver Piece	Netherlands
	2 F. Kirkebjerg	Metoo	Denmark
	3 S. Doak	Pathfinder	USA
Team	1 Netherlands		
	2 Sweden		
	3 Italy		

1928 – Amsterdam

DRESSAGE:

Individual	1 C. F. von Langen	Draufgänger	Germany
	2 C. L. P. Marion	Linon	France
	3 R. Olson	Günstling	Sweden
Team	1 Germany		
	2 Sweden		
	3 Netherlands		

SHOW JUMPING:

Individual	1 F. Ventura	Eliot	Czechoslo-vakia
	2 P. Bertran de Balanda	Papillon XIV	France
	3 C. Kuhn	Pepita	Switzerland
Team	1 Spain		
	2 Poland		
	3 Sweden		

THREE-DAY EVENT:

Individual	1 C. F. Pahud de Mortanges	Marcroix	Netherlands
	2 G. P. de Kruijff	Va-t-en	Netherlands
	3 B. Neumann	Ilja	Germany
Team	1 Netherlands		
	2 Norway		
	3 Poland		

1932 – Los Angeles

DRESSAGE:

Individual	1 X. Lesage	Taine	France
	2 C. Marion	Linon	France
	3 H. Tuttle	Olympic	USA
Team	1 France		
	2 Sweden		
	3 USA		

SHOW JUMPING:

Individual	1 T. Nishi	Uranus	Japan
	2 H. D. Chamberlin	Show Girl	USA
	3 C. von Rosen	Empire	Sweden

Since no team completed the course there were no team classifications

THREE-DAY EVENT:

Individual	1 C. Pahud de Mortanges	Marcroix	Netherlands
	2 E. F. Thomson	Jenny Camp	USA
	3 C. von Rosen, Jr.	Sunnyside Maid	Sweden
Team	1 USA		
	2 Netherlands		
	Only two teams finished		

1936 – Berlin

DRESSAGE:

Individual	1 H. Pollay	Kronos	Germany
	2 F. Gerhard	Absinth	Germany
	3 A. Podhajsky	Nero	Austria
Team	1 Germany		
	2 France		
	3 Sweden		

SHOW JUMPING:

Individual	1 K. Hasse	Tora	Germany
	2 H. Rang	Delphis	Rumania
	3 J. von Platthy	Sellö	Hungary
Team	1 Germany		
	2 Netherlands		
	3 Portugal		

THREE-DAY EVENT:

Individual	1 L. Stubbendorf	Nurmi	Germany
	2 E. F. Thomson	Jenny Camp	USA
	3 H. Lunding	Jason	Denmark
Team	1 Germany		
	2 Poland		
	3 Great Britain		

1948 – London

DRESSAGE:

Individual	1 H. Moser	Hummer	Switzerland
	2 A. Jousseaume	Harpagon	France
	3 G. Boltenstern	Trumpf	Sweden
Team	1 France		
	2 USA		
	3 Portugal		

SHOW JUMPING:

Individual	1 H. Marilés	Arete	Mexico
	2 R. Uriza	Hatvey	Mexico
	3 J. d'Orgeix	Sucre de Pomme	France
Team	1 Mexico		
	2 Spain		
	3 Great Britain		

THREE-DAY EVENT:

Individual	1 B. Chevallier	Aiglonne	France
	2 F. S. Henry	Swing Low	USA
	3 J. R. Selfet	Claque	Sweden
Team	1 USA		
	2 Sweden		
	3 Mexico		

1952 – Helsinki

DRESSAGE:

Individual	1 H. de Reverony Saint Cyr	Master Rufus	Sweden
	2 L. Hartel	Jubilee	Denmark
	3 A. Jousseaume	Harpagon	France
Team	1 Sweden		
	2 Switzerland		
	3 W. Germany		

SHOW JUMPING:

Individual	1 P. Jonquères d'Oriola	Ali Baba	France
	2 O. Cristi	Bambi	Chile
	3 F. Thiedemann	Meteor	W. Germany
Team	1 Great Britain		
	2 Chile		
	3 USA		

THREE-DAY EVENT:

Individual	1 H. von Blixen-Finecke	Jubal	Sweden
	2 G. Lefrant	Verdun	France
	3 W. Büsing	Hubertus	W. Germany
Team	1 Sweden		
	2 W. Germany		
	3 USA		

1956 – Stockholm

DRESSAGE:

Individual	1 H. de Reverony Saint Cyr	Juli XXX	Sweden
	2 L. Hartel	Jubilee	Denmark
	3 L. Linsenhoff	Adular	W. Germany
Team	1 Sweden		
	2 W. Germany		
	3 Switzerland		

SHOW JUMPING:

Individual	1 H. G. Winkler	Halla	W. Germany
	2 R. d'Inzeo	Merano	Italy
	3 P. d'Inzeo	Uruguay	Italy
Team	1 W. Germany		
	2 Italy		
	3 Great Britain		

THREE-DAY EVENT:

Individual	1 P. Kastenman	Illuster	Sweden
	2 A. Lütke-Westhues	Trux von Kamax	W. Germany
	3 F. Weldon	Kilbarry	Great Britain
Team	1 Great Britain		
	2 W. Germany		
	3 Canada		

1960 – Rome

DRESSAGE:

Individual	1 S. Filatov	Absent	USSR
	2 G. Fischer	Wald	Switzerland
	3 J. Neckermann	Asbach	W. Germany

No team competition

SHOW JUMPING:

Individual	1 R. d'Inzeo	Posillipo	Italy
	2 P. d'Inzeo	The Rock	Italy
	3 D. Broome	Sunsalve	Great Britain
Team	1 W. Germany		
	2 USA		
	3 Italy		

THREE-DAY EVENT

Individual	1 L. Morgan	Salad Days	Australia
	2 N. Lavis	Mirrabooka	Australia
	3 A. Bühler	Gay Spark	Switzerland
Team	1 Australia		
	2 Switzerland		
	3 France		

1964 – Tokyo

DRESSAGE:

Individual	1 H. Chammartin	Woermann	Switzerland
	2 H. Boldt	Remus	W. Germany
	3 S. Filatov	Absent	USSR
Team	1 W. Germany		
	2 Switzerland		
	3 USSR		

SHOW JUMPING:

Individual	1 P. Jonquères d'Oriola	Lutteur B	France
	2 H. Schridde	Dozent II	W. Germany
	3 P. D. Robeson	Firecrest	Great Britain
Team	1 W. Germany		
	2 France		
	3 Italy		

THREE-DAY EVENT:

Individual	1 M. Checcoli	Surbean	Italy
	2 C. Moratorio	Chalan	Argentina
	3 F. Ligges	Donkosak	W. Germany
Team	1 Italy		
	2 USA		
	3 W. Germany		

1968 – Mexico

DRESSAGE:

Individual	1 I. Kizimov	Ikhor	USSR
	2 J. Neckermann	Mariano	W. Germany
	3 R. Klimke	Dux	W. Germany
Team	1 W. Germany		
	2 USSR		
	3 Switzerland		

SHOW JUMPING:

Individual	1 W. Steinkraus	Snowbound	USA
	2 M. Coakes	Stroller	Great Britain
	3 D. Broome	Mister Softee	Great Britain
Team	1 Canada		
	2 France		
	3 W. Germany		

THREE-DAY EVENT:

Individual	1 J. Guyon	Pitou	France
	2 D. Allhusen	Lochinvar	Great Britain
	3 M. Page	Foster	USA
Team	1 Great Britain		
	2 USA		
	2 Australia		

1972 – Munich

DRESSAGE:

Individual	1 L. Linsenhoff	Piaff	W. Germany
	2 E. Petushkova	Pepel	USSR
	3 J. Neckermann	Venetia	W. Germany
Team	1 USSR		
	2 W. Germany		
	3 Sweden		

SHOW JUMPING:

Individual	1 G. Mancinelli	Ambassador	Italy
	2 A. Moore	Psalm	Great Britain
	3 N. Shapiro	Sloopy	USA
Team	1 W. Germany		
	2 USA		
	3 Italy		

THREE-DAY EVENT:

Individual	1 R. Meade	Laurieston	Great Britain
	2 A. Argenton	Woodland	Italy
	3 J. Jonsson	Sarajewo	Sweden
Team	1 Great Britain		
	2 USA		
	3 W. Germany		

1976 – Montreal

DRESSAGE:

Individual	1 C. Stückelberger	Granat	Switzerland
	2 H. Boldt	Woyceck	W. Germany
	3 R. Klimke	Mehmed	W. Germany
Team	1 W. Germany		
	2 Switzerland		
	3 USA		

SHOW JUMPING:

Individual	1 A. Schockemöhle	Warwick Rex	W. Germany
	2 M. Vaillancourt	Branch County	Canada
	3 F. Mathy	Gai Luron	Belgium
Team	1 France		
	2 W. Germany		
	3 Belgium		

THREE-DAY EVENT:

Individual	1 E. Coffin	Bally-Cor	USA
	2 J. Plumb	Better and Better	USA
	3 K. Schultz	Madrigal	W. Germany
Team	1 USA		
	2 W. Germany		
	3 Australia		

DRESSAGE – World Championships

1966 – Bern

Individual	1 J. Neckermann	Mariano	W. Germany
	2 H. Boldt	Remus	W. Germany
	3 R. Klimke	Dux	W. Germany
Team	1 W. Germany		
	2 Switzerland		
	3 USSR		

1970 – Aachen

Individual	1 E. Petushkova	Pepel	USSR
	2 L. Linsenhoff	Piaff	W. Germany
	3 I. Kizimov	Ikhor	USSR
Team	1 USSR		
	2 W. Germany		
	3 E. Germany		

1974 – Copenhagen

Individual	1 R. Klimke	Mehmed	W. Germany
	2 L. Linsenhoff	Piaff	W. Germany
	3 E. Petushkova	Pepel	USSR
Team	1 W. Germany		
	2 USSR		
	3 Switzerland		

1978 – Goodwood

Individual	1 C. Stückelberger	Granat	Switzerland
	2 U. Schulten-Baumer	Slibowitz	W. Germany
	3 J. Loriston-Clarke	Dutch Courage	Great Britain
Team	1 W. Germany		
	2 Switzerland		
	3 USSR		

European Championships

1967 – Aachen

Individual	1 R. Klimke	Dux	W. Germany
	2 I. Kizimov	Ikhor	USSR
	3 H. Boldt	Remus	W. Germany
Team	1 W. Germany		
	2 USSR		
	3 Switzerland		

1969 – Wolfsburg

Individual	1 L. Linsenhoff	Piaff	W. Germany
	2 I. Kizimov	Ikhor	USSR
	3 J. Neckermann	Mariano	W. Germany
Team	1 W. Germany		
	2 E. Germany		
	3 USSR		

1971 – Wolfsburg

Individual	1 L. Linsenhoff	Piaff	W. Germany
	2 J. Neckermann	Van Eick	W. Germany
	3 E. Petushkova	Pepel	USSR
Team	1 W. Germany		
	2 USSR		
	3 Sweden		

1973 – Aachen

Individual	1 R. Klimke	Mehmed	W. Germany
	2 E. Petushkova	Pepel	USSR
	3 I. Kalita	Tariph	USSR
Team	1 W. Germany		
	2 USSR		
	3 Switzerland		

1975 – Kiev

Individual	1 C. Stückelberger	Granat	Switzerland
	2 H. Boldt	Woyceck	W. Germany
	3 K. Schlüter	Liostro	W. Germany
Team	1 W. Germany		
	2 USSR		
	3 Switzerland		

1977 – St. Gallen

Individual	1 C. Stückelberger	Granat	Switzerland
	2 H. Boldt	Woyceck	W. Germany
	3 U. Schulten-Baumer	Slibovitz	W. Germany
Team	1 W. Germany		
	2 Switzerland		
	3 USSR		

1979 – Aarhus

Individual	1 E. Theurer	Mon Chérie	Austria
	2 C. Stückelberger	Granat	Switzerland
	3 H. Boldt	Woyceck	W. Germany
Team	1 W. Germany		
	2 USSR		
	3 Switzerland		

Junior European Championships

1973 – Aachen

Individual	M. Fassbender	Veneziano	W. Germany
Team	W. Germany		

1974 – Copenhagen

Individual	M. Fassbender	Veneziano	W. Germany
Team	W. Germany		

1975 – Fontainebleau

Individual	M. Fassbender	Veneziano	W. Germany
Team	W. Germany		

1976 – Deurne

Individual	M. Beck	Askan	W. Germany
Team	Netherlands		

1977 – Leverkusen

Individual	I. Schulze-Willbrenning	Don Benito	W. Germany
Team	West Germany		

1978 – Amstetten

Individual	I. Schultze-Wildrennig	Don Rentto	W. Germany
Team	W. Germany		

1979 – Strömsholm

Individual	T. Lösch	Flyinge	W. Germany
Team	W. Germany		

SHOW JUMPING

Men's World Championships

1953 – Paris

1 F. Goyoaga	Quorum	Spain
2 F. Thiedemann	Diamant	W. Germany
3 P. Jonquères d'Oriola	Ali Baba	France
4 P. d'Inzeo	Uruguay	Italy

1954 – Madrid

1 H. G. Winkler	Halla	W. Germany
2 P. Jonquères d'Oriola	Arlequin D	France
3 F. Goyoaga	Baden	Spain
4 S. Oppes	Pagoro	Italy

1955 – Aachen

1 H. G. Winkler	Orient	W. Germany
2 R. d'Inzeo	Merano	Italy
3 R. Dallas	Bones	Great Britain
4 P. Jonquères d'Oriola	Voulette	France

1956 – Aachen

1 R. d'Inzeo	Merano	Italy
2 F. Goyoaga	Fahnenkönig	Spain
3 F. Thiedemann	Meteor	W. Germany
4 C. Delia	Discutido	Argentina

1960 – Venice

1 R. d'Inzeo	Gowran Girl	Italy
2 C. Delia	Huipil	Argentina
3 D. Broome	Sunsalve	Great Britain
4 W. Steinkraus	Ksar d'Esprit	USA

1966 – Buenos Aires

1 P. Jonquères d'Oriola	Pomone B	France
2 J. Alrarez de Bohorques	Quizás	Spain
3 R. d'Inzeo	Bowjack	Italy
4 N. Pessoa	Huipil	Brazil

1970 – La Baule

1 D. Broome	Beethoven	Great Britain
2 G. Mancinelli	Fidux	Italy
3 H. Smith	Mattie Brown	Great Britain
4 A. Schockemöhle	Donald Rex	W. Germany

1974 – Hickstead

1 H. Steenken	Simona	W. Germany
2 E. Macken	Pele	Ireland
3 H. Simon	Lavendel	Austria
3 F. Chapot	Main Spring	USA

Women's World Championships

1965 – Hickstead

1 M. Coakes	Stroller	Great Britain
2 K. Kusner	Untouchable	USA
3 A. Westwood	The Maverick VII	Great Britain

1970 – Copenhagen

1 J. Lefebvre	Rocket	France
2 M. Mould	Stroller	Great Britain
3 A. Drummond-Hay	Merely-a-Monarch	Great Britain

1974 – La Baule (Final championship for women only)

1 J. Lefebvre-Tissot	Rocket	France
2 M. McEvoy	Mr Muskie	USA
3 B. Kerr	Magnor	Canada

World Championships (Men and Women)

1978 – Aachen

Individual	1 G. Wiltfang	Roman	W. Germany
	2 E. Macken	Boomerang	Ireland
	3 M. Matz	Jet Run	USA
Team	1 Great Britain		
	2 The Netherlands		
	3 USA		

Men's European Championships

1957 – Rotterdam

1 H. G. Winkler	Sonnenglanz	W. Germany
2 B. de Fombelle	Bucéphale	France
3 S. Oppes	Pagoro	Italy

1958 – Aachen

1 F. Thiedemann	Meteor	W. Germany
2 P. d'Inzeo	The Rock	Italy
3 H. G. Winkler	Halla	W. Germany

1959 – Paris

1 P. d'Inzeo	Uruguay	Italy
2 P. Jonquères d'Oriola	Virtuoso	France
3 F. Thiedemann	Godewind	W. Germany

1961 – Aachen

1 D. Broome	Sunsalve	Great Britain
2 P. d'Inzeo	Pioneer	Italy
3 H. G. Winkler	Romanus	W. Germany

1962 – London

1 C. D. Barker	Mister Softee	Great Britain
2 H. G. Winkler	Romanus	W. Germany
2 P. d'Inzeo	The Rock	Italy

1963 – Rome

1 G. Mancinelli	Rockette	Italy
2 A. Schockemöhle	Freiherr	W. Germany
3 H. Smith	O'Malley	Great Britain

1965 – Aachen

1 H. Schridde	Dozent	W. Germany
2 N. Pessoa	Gran Geste	Brazil
3 A. Schockemöhle	Exakt	W. Germany

1966– Lucerne

1 N. Pessoa	Gran Geste	Brazil
2 F. Chapot	San Lucas	USA
3 H. Arrambide	Chimbote	Argentina

1967 – Rotterdam

1 D. Broome	Mister Softee	Great Britain
2 H. Smith	Harvester	Great Britain
3 A. Schockemöhle	Donald Rex	W. Germany

1969 – Hickstead

1 D. Broome	Mister Softee	Great Britain
2 A. Schockemöhle	Donald Rex	W. Germany
3 H. G. Winkler	Enigk	W. Germany

1971 – Aachen

1 H. Steenken	Simona III	W. Germany
2 H. Smith	Evan Jones	Great Britain
3 P. Weier	Wulf	Switzerland

1973 – Hickstead (Final championship for men only)

1 P. MacMahon	Penwood Forge Mill	Great Britain
2 A. Schockemöhle	The Robber	W. Germany
3 H. Parot	Tic	France

Women's European Championships

1957 – Spa

1 P. Smythe	Flanagan	Great Britain
2 G. Serventi	Doly	Italy
3 M. d'Orgeix	Océane	France

1958 – Palermo

1 G. Serventi	Doly	Italy
2 A. Clement	Nico	W. Germany
3 I. Jansen	Adelbloom	Netherlands

1959 – Rotterdam

1 A. Townsend	Bandit IV	Great Britain
2 P. Smythe	Flanagan	Great Britain
3 A. Clement	Nico	W. Germany
3 G. Serventi	Doly	Italy

1960 – Copenhagen

1 S. Cohen	Clare Castle	Great Britain
2 D. Wofford	Hollandia	Great Britain
3 A. Clement	Nico	W. Germany

1961 – Deauville

1 P. Smythe	Flanagan	Great Britain
2 I. Jansen	Icare II	Netherlands
3 M. Cancre	Océane	France

1962 – Madrid

1 P. Smythe	Flanagan	Great Britain
2 H. Köhler	Cremona	W. Germany
3 P. Goyoaga	Kif-Kif	Spain

1963 – Hickstead

1 P. Smythe	Flanagan	Great Britain
2 A. Givaudan	Huipil	Brazil
3 A. Drummond-Hay	Merely-a-Monarch	Great Britain

1966 – Gijon

1 J. Lefebvre	Kenavo D	France
2 M. Bachmann	Sandro	Switzerland
3 L. Novo	Oxo Bob	Italy

1967 – Fontainebleau

1 K. Kusner	Untouchable	USA
2 L. Novo	Predestine	Italy
3 M. Bachmann	Erbach	Switzerland

1968 – Rome

1 A. Drummond-Hay	Merely-a-Monarch	Great Britain
2 G. Serventi	Gay Monarch	Italy
3 M. Coakes	Stroller	Great Britain

1969 – Dublin

1 I. Kellett	Morning Light	Ireland
2 A. Drummond-Hay	Xanthos	Great Britain
3 A. Westwood	The Maverick VII	Great Britain

1971 – St. Gallen

1 A. Moore	Psalm	Great Britain
2 A. Dawes	The Maverick VII	Great Britain
3 M. Leitenberger	Limbarro de Porto Conte	Austria

1973 – Vienna (final championship for women only)

1 A. Moore	Psalm	Great Britain
2 C. Bradley	True Lass	Great Britain
3 P. Weier	Erbach	Switzerland

European Championships (open to men and women)

1975 – Munich

Individual	1 A. Schockemöhle	Warwick	W. Germany
	2 H. Steenken	Erle	W. Germany
	3 S. Sönksen	Kwept	W. Germany
Team	1 W. Germany		
	2 Switzerland		
	3 France		

1977 – Vienna

Individual	1 J. Heins	Seven Valleys	Netherlands
	2 E. Macken	Kerrygold	Ireland
	3 A. Ebben	Jumbo Design	Netherlands
Team	1 Netherlands		
	2 Great Britain		
	3 W. Germany		

1979 – Rotterdam

Individual	1 G. Wiltfang	Roman	W. Germany
	2 P. Schockemöhle	Deister	W. Germany
	3 H. Simon	Gladstone	Austria
Team	1 Great Britain		
	2 W. Germany		
	3 Ireland		

World Team Championship for the President's Cup (each country's best six Nations Cup results to count)

1965

1 Great Britain
2 Italy
3 W. Germany

1966

1 USA
2 Spain
3 France

1967

1 Great Britain
2 W. Germany
3 Italy

1968

1 USA
2 Great Britain
3 Italy
3 W. Germany

1969

1 W. Germany
2 Great Britain
3 Italy

1970

1 Great Britain
2 W. Germany
3 USA

1971

1 W. Germany	
2 Great Britain	
3 USA	

1972

1 Great Britain	
2 W. Germany	
3 Italy	

1973

1 Great Britain	
2 W. Germany	
3 Switzerland	

1974

1 Great Britain	
2 W. Germany	
3 France	

1975

1 W. Germany	
2 Great Britain	
3 Italy	
3 Belgium	

1976

1 W. Germany	
2 France	
3 Ireland	

1977

1 Great Britain	
2 W. Germany	
3 Ireland	

Junior European Championships

1952 – Ostende

Individual	No classification
Team	Italy

1953 – Rome

Individual	No classification
Team	France

1954 – Rotterdam

Individual	No classification
Team	Italy

1955 – Bilbao

Individual	No classification		
Team	W. Germany		

1956 – Spa

Individual	J. White	Full Cry	Great Britain
Team	Great Britain		

1957 – London

Individual	R. Freitag	Freya	W. Germany
Team	Great Britain		

1958 – Hanover

Individual	G. Ravalo	Ballynool	Italy
Team	Great Britain		

1959 – London

Individual	S. FitzAlan-Howard	Oorskiet	Great Britain
Team	Great Britain		

1960 – Venice

Individual	G. Ravano	Prince Regent	Italy
Team	Great Britain		

1961 – Hickstead

Individual	S. Barnes	Sola	Great Britain
Team	W. Germany		

1962 – Berlin

Individual	J. Kidd	Manka	Great Britain
Team	Great Britain		

1963 – Rotterdam

Individual	F. Ghedini	Gengiskan	Italy
Team	Great Britain		

1964 – Budapest

Individual	L. Raper	Keewis	Great Britain
Team	Italy		

1965 – Milan

Individual	J. Baillie	Dominic	Great Britain
Team	Great Britain		

1966 – Copenhagen

Individual	R. Moller	Anzac	Denmark
Team	Italy		

1967 – Jesolo

Individual	zu Rantzau	Weintraube	W. Germany
Team	Great Britain		

1968 – Stoneleigh

Individual	A. Moore	Psalm	Great Britain
Team	Great Britain		

1969 – Dinard

Individual	B. Arles Dufour	Mounana	France
Team	Switzerland		

1970 – St Moritz

Individual	M. Fuchs	Famos II	Switzerland
Team	Great Britain		

1971 – Hickstead

Individual	M. Snoek	Janeau	W. Germany
Team	Ireland		

1972 – Cork

Individual	J. Notz	Serif	Switzerland
Team	Belgium		

1973 – Ekeren-Hoogboorn

Individual	D. Johnsey	Speculator	Great Britain
Team	Switzerland		

1974 – Lucerne

Individual	J. Kernan	Marcella	Ireland
Team	Austria		

1975 – Dornbirn

Individual	N. Skelton	Everest OK	Great Britain
Team	Belgium		

1976 – Brussels

Individual	B. McMahon	Heather Honey	Ireland
Team	Switzerland		

1977 – Tour-de-Peilz

Individual	E. Navet	Brooklyn	France
Team	Great Britain		

1978 – Stannington, Northumberland

Individual	L. Collard Bovy	Loecky	Belgium
Team	Great Britain		

1979 – Gijon

Individual	V. Gascoigne	McGinty	Great Britain
Team	Switzerland		

World Jumping Records

High Jump
1906 – Paris

Capt. Crousse	Conspirateur	France	2 m 35

1912 – Vittel

F. de Juge Montespieu	Biskra	France	2 m 36
R. Ricard	Montjoie III	France	

1933 – Paris

C. de Castries	Vol-au-Vent	France	2 m 38

1938 – Rome

A. Gutiérrez	Osoppo	Italy	2 m 44

1949 – Viña del Mar

A. Larraguibel	Huaso	Chile	2 m 47

Long Jump

1912 – Le Touquet

H. de Royer	Pick me up	France	7 m 50

1935 – Spa

C. de Castries	Tenace	France	7 m 60

1946 – Buenos Aires

J. Fraga Patrao	Guaraná	Argentina	7 m 70

1948 – Bilbao

N. Márquez	Bálcamo	Spain	7 m 80
F. Maestre Salinas	Faun	Spain	
N. Márquez	Bálcamo	Spain	8 m 00

1949 – La Haye

B. van der Woort, Jr.	Coeur Joli	Netherlands	8 m 10

1950 – Bilbao

N. Márquez	Bálcamo	Spain	8 m 20

1951 – Barcelona

F. López del Hierro	Amado Mío	Spain	8 m 30

1975 – Johannesburg

A. Ferreira	Something	South Africa	8 m 40

THREE-DAY EVENT
World Championships
1966 – Burghley

Individual	1 C. Moratorio	Chalan	Argentina
	2 R. Meade	Barberry	Great Britain
	3 V. Freeman-Jackson	Sam Weller	Ireland
Team	1 Ireland		
	2 Argentina		
	Only two finished		

1970 – Punchestown

Individual	1 M. Gordon-Watson	Cornishman V	Great Britain
	2 R. Meade	The Poacher	Great Britain
	3 J. C. Wofford	Kilkenny	USA
Team	1 Great Britain		
	2 France		
	Only two finished		

1974 – Burghley

Individual	1 B. Davidson	Irish Cap	USA
	2 M. Plumb	Good Mixture	USA
	3 H. Thomas	Playamar	Great Britain
Team	1 USA		
	2 Great Britain		
	3 W. Germany		

1978 – Lexington

Individual	1 B. Davidson	Might Tango	USA
	2 J. Watson	Cambridge Blue	Ireland
	3 H. Rethemeier	Ladalco	W. Germany
Team	1 Canada		
	2 W. Germany		
	3 USA		

European Championships
1953 – Badminton

Individual	1 L. Rook	Starlight XV	Great Britain
	2 F. Weldon	Kilbarry	Great Britain
	3 H. Schwarzenbach	Vae Victis	Switzerland
	1 Great Britain		
	Only one team finished		

1954 – Basle

Individual	1 A. E. Hill	Crispin	Great Britain
	2 F. Weldon	Kilbarry	Great Britain
	3 L. Rook	Starlight XV	Great Britain
Team	1 Great Britain		
	2 W. Germany		
	Only two finished		

1955 – Windsor

Individual	1 F. Weldon	Kilbarry	Great Britain
	2 J. Oram	Radar	Great Britain
	3 A. E. Hill	Countryman	Great Britain
Team	1 Great Britain		
	2 Switzerland		
	Only two finished		

1957 – Copenhagen

Individual	1 S. Willcox	High and Mighty	Great Britain
	2 A. Lütke-Westhues	Franko II	W. Germany
	3 J. Lindgren	Eldorado	Sweden
Team	1 Great Britain		
	2 W. Germany		
	3 Sweden		

1959 – Harewood

Individual	1 H. Schwarzenbach	Burn Trout	Switzerland
	2 F. Weldon	Samuel Johnson	Great Britain
	3 D. Allhusen	Laurien	Great Britain
Team	1 W. Germany		
	2 Great Britain		
	3 France		

1962 – Burghley

Individual	1 J. Templer	M'Lord Connolly	Great Britain
	2 G. Gazumov	Granj	USSR
	3 J. Wykeham-Musgrave	Ryebrooks	Great Britain
Team	1 USSR		
	2 Ireland		
	3 Great Britain		

1965 – Moscow

Individual	1 M. Babierecki	Volt	Poland
	2 L. Baklyshkin	Rulon	USSR
	3 H. Karsten	Condora	W. Germany
Team	1 USSR		
	2 Ireland		
	3 Great Britain		

1967 – Punchestown

Individual	1 E. Boylan	Durlas Eile	Ireland
	2 M. Whiteley	The Poacher	Great Britain
	3 D. Allhusen	Lochinvar	Great Britain
Team	1 Great Britain		
	2 Ireland		
	3 France		

1969 – Le Pin

Individual	1 M. Gordon-Watson	Cornishman V	Great Britain
	2 R. Walker	Pasha	Great Britain
	3 B. Messman	Windspiel	W. Germany
Team	1 Great Britain		
	2 USSR		
	3 W. Germany		

1971 – Burghley

Individual	1 HRH Princess Anne	Doublet	Great Britain
	2 D. West	Baccarat	Great Britain
	3 S. Stevens	Classic Chips	Great Britain
Team	1 Great Britain		
	2 USSR		
	3 Ireland		

1973 – Kiev

Individual	1 A. Evdokimov	Jeger	USSR
	2 H. Blöcker	Albrant	W. Germany
	3 H. Karsten	Sioux	W. Germany
Team	1 W. Germany		
	2 USSR		
	3 Great Britain		

1975 – Luhmühlen

Individual	1 L. Prior-Palmer	Be Fair	Great Britain
	2 HRH Princess Anne	Goodwill	Great Britain
	3 P. Gornuschko	Gusar	USSR
Team	1 USSR		
	2 Great Britain		
	3 W. Germany		

1977 – Burghley

Individual	1 L. Prior-Palmer	George	Great Britain
	2 K. Schultz	Madrigal	W. Germany
	3 H. Karsten	Sioux	W. Germany
Team	1 Great Britain		
	2 W. Germany		
	3 Ireland		

1979 – Luhmühlen

Individual	1 N. Haagensen	Monaco	Denmark
	2 R. Bayliss	Gurgle the Greek	Great Britain
	3 R. Schwarz	Power Game	W. Germany
Team	1 Ireland		
	2 Great Britain		
	3 France		

Junior European Championships

1967 – Eridge

Individual	A. Souchon	Roi d'Asturie	France

No team classifications

1968 – Craon

Individual	R. Walker	Pasha	Great Britain
Team	France		

1969 – Euskirchen

Individual	H. O. Bolten	Lausbub XIII	W. Germany
Team	USSR		

1970 – Holstebro

Individual	N. O. Barkander	Pegasus	Sweden
Team	W. Germany		

1971 – Wesel

Individual	C. Brooke	Olive Oyl	Great Britain
Team	Great Britain		

1972 – Eridge

Individual	B. Clément	Quel Pich	France
Team	Great Britain		

1973 – Pompadour

Individual	V. Holgate	Dubonnet	Great Britain
Team	Great Britain		

1974 – Pratoni del Vivaro

Individual	S. Kerr	Peer Gynt	Great Britain
Team	W. Germany		

1975

No official championships

1976 – Lage-Siekkrug

Individual	O. Depagne	Bobineau	France
Team	Great Britain		

1977 – Fontainebleau

Individual	M. Spehmann	Lorbass	W. Germany
Team	Ireland		

1978 – Burghley

Individual	D. Baumgart	Kurfurst	W. Germany
Team	W. Germany		

1979 – Punchestown

Individual	N. May	Commodore IV	Great Britain
Team	France		

DRIVING

World Championships

1972 – Munster

Individual	1 A. Dubey	Switzerland
	2 J. Miller	Great Britain
	3 D. Nicholson	Great Britain
Team	1 Great Britain	
	2 Switzerland	
	3 W. Germany	

1974 – Frauenfeld

Individual	1 S. Fülöp	Hungary
	2 C. Iseli	Switzerland
	3 G. Bowman	Great Britain
Team	1 Great Britain	
	2 Switzerland	
	3 Poland	

1976 – Apeldoorn

Individual	1 I. Abonyi	Hungary
	2 E. Jung	W. Germany
	3 Z. Waliszewski	Poland
Team	1 Hungary	
	2 W. Germany	
	3 Poland	

1978 – Kecskemét

Individual	1 G. Bárdos	Hungary
	2 S. Fülöp	Hungary
	3 F. Muity	Hungary
Team	1 Hungary	
	2 W. Germany	
	3 Great Britain	

European Championships

1971 – Budapest

Individual	1 I. Abonyi	Hungary
	2 S. Fülöp	Hungary
	3 J. Papp	Hungary
Team	1 Hungary	
	2 W. Germany	
	3 Switzerland	

1973 – Windsor

Individual	1 A. Dubey	Switzerland
	2 R. Doudin	Switzerland
	3 D. Nicholson	Great Britain
Team	1 Switzerland	
	2 W. Germany	
	3 Great Britain	

1975 – Sopot

Individual	1 I. Abonyi	Hungary
	2 G. Bárdos	Hungary
	3 F. Muity	Hungary
Team	1 Hungary	
	2 Poland	
	3 W. Germany	

1977 – Donaueschingen

Individual	1 G. Bardos	Hungary
	2 T. Velstra	Netherlands
	3 E. Jung	W. Germany
Team	1 Hungary	
	2 Poland	
	3 W. Germany	

1979 – Haras du Pin

Individual	1 G. Bardos	Hungary
	2 M. Balint	Hungary
	3 S. Waliszewski	Poland
Team	1 Hungary	
	2 Great Britain	
	3 Poland	

Dictionary of Technical Terms

afoot	*à pied*	bandage	*bandage, m.*
African horse sickness	*grippe ou peste africaine, f.*	bank, Irish	*banquette irlandaise, f.*
aids	*aides, f.pl.*	bank	*banquette, f.*
aids, lateral	*aides latérales, f.pl.*	bar	*barre, f. (obstacle) – barre,*
aids, diagonal	*aides diagonales, f.pl.*		*f. ou arc–boutant m. (pied)*
ailment	*maladie, f.*		*porte-étrivière, f.*
amble	*amble, m.*	bars	*barres, f.*
amble, to	*ambler, v.*	Barb	*cheval barbe, m.*
amble, broken	*amble rompu, m.*	bareback	*à cru*
ambler	*ambleur, adj.*	barley	*orge, f.*
American Saddle Horse	*American Saddle Horse, m.*	barnum	*longe Barnum, f.*
Andalusian	*andalou, adj.*	Barouche	*Barouche, f. ou calèche, f.*
angle cheek Pelham	*mors anglais*	barrel	*corps, m. (du cheval)*
angle of toe too steep	*pied à talons hauts*	barren	*stérile, adj. (iument stérile)*
angleberry	*papillome, m. verrue, f.*	Baucher bridoon	*filet Baucher, m. – utilisé avec*
Anglo-Arab	*Anglo-Arabe, m.*		*un mors de bride*
anti-sweat rug	*chemise à nids d'abeilles*	Baucher snaffle	*filet Baucher, m.*
aorta	*aorte, f.*	bay	*bai, adj.*
aortic valves	*valvules de l'aorte, f.pl.*	bay, at	*aux abois, m.pl.*
apex of the frog	*pointe de la fourchette, f.*	beagle	*beagle, m.*
Appaloosa	*Appaloosa, m.*	bearing rein	*enrênement*
approach	*abord, m. de l'obstacle*	beast of the chase	*animal de chasse, m.*
Arab, Arabian	*arabe, adj.*	beasts of the forest	*animaux, m. (de la forêt)*
Ardennais	*Ardennais, m.*	beat	*battue, f.*
arm	*bras, m.*	belly	*ventre, m. ou abdomen, m.*
arteritis (pinkeye)	*artérite à virus, f.*	belly-band	*sous-ventrière, f.*
astride	*à califourchon*	berline coupée	*berline coupée, f.*
at stud	*faire la monte, v.*	betting, off-track	*pari mutuel urbain, m.*
atrium	*oreillette, f.*		*(P.M.U.)*
Australian loose ring	*filet à aiguilles, m.*	bettor	*parieur, m.*
cheek snaffle		bevel	*affilure*
automatic starting gate	*autostart, m.*	bit	*mors. m.*
		bit, above the	*au-dessus de la main*
back	*dos, m.*	behind the	*derrière la main, en arrière de*
backband	*dossière, f.*		*la main,*
back chamber	*chambre postérieure, f.*		*sur la main*
back-strap	*dossière, f.*	on the	
balance	*équilibre, m.*	bit, curb	*mors de bride, m.*
balance strap	*contre-sangle, f. (selle*	bit, snaffle	*filet, m.*
	d'amazone)	black	*noir, adj.*
balding gag	*filet releveur, m.*	blacksmith	*maréchal-ferrant, m.*
balding girth	*sangle de polo, f.*	blank day	*un jour où l'on ne prend*
ball	*balle, f.*		*pas (vénerie)*

blaze	*liste, f. (large)*
blemish	*tare, f.*
blinker	*oeillère, f.*
blisters	*blister, m. vésicatoire, m.*
bloodline	*lignée, f.*
boar	*sanglier, m.*
boar-hunt	*chasse au sanglier, f.*
body brush	*brosse en soie, f.*
boldness	*perçant, m.*
bolster	*batte, f.*
bog spavin	*jarde*
bone spavin	*éparvin, m.*
boot	*botte, f. (du cavalier):* *guètre, f. (du cheval)*
Boulonnais	*Boulonnais, m.*
bounce strides	*saut de puce, m.*
bow legged	*membres cambrés, adj.*
box, or box seat	*siège, m. (du meneur)*
brake	*break, m.*
branches	*branches, f.pl.*
break across open country	*débucher, m.*
breaking or breaking in	*débourrage, m.*
break-up	*(terme équivalent à la curée dans la chasse au renard)*
breast	*poitrail, m.*
breast-collar	*collier (attelage), m.*
breast-plate	*collier de chasse, m. bricole, f. (pour une selle)*
bred, half	*demi-sang, m.*
bred, highly	*près du sang, très près du sang, cheval provenant de bonnes origines*
bred, part	*demi-sang, m.*
bred, pure	*de sang pur (cheval)*
breeching	*avaloire, m.; reculement, m.*
breeching strap	*courroie de reculement, f.*
breed	*race, f.*
breeder	*éleveur, m.*
breeder, shy	*mauvaise reproductrice, f. (élevage)*
breeding	*élevage, m.*
Breton	*Breton*
bridle	*bride, f.*
bridle, to	*brider, v.*
bridle hand	*main de bride, f.*
bridle path	*allée cavalière, f.*
bridle, double	*(en) bride, f.*
bridle, snaffle	*(en) filet simple, m.*
bridoon	*bridon, m.*
bridoon cheek piece	*montant de filet, m.*
bridoon sliphead	*tétière de filet, f.*
bridoon with eggbutt ring	*filet de mors de bride à olives, m.*
brisket	*passage de sangle, m.*
broken knee	*genou couronné, m.*
broken wind	*pousse, f.; emphysème pulmonaire, m.*
bronchitis	*bronchite, f.*
Brougham	*Brougham, m.*
brought to bay	*forcer l'animal de chasse*
browband	*frontal, m.*
brown	*bai brun, adj.*
brushing	*se faire des atteintes, v.*
brushing boot	*guètre de boulet et tendon*
buckjumping	*saut de mouton, m.*
bulbs of heel	*glomes, m.pl.*
buttock	*fesse, f.*
cadence	*cadence, f.*
calash	*calèche, f.*
calkin	*crampon, m.*
calkin, outside	*crampon à la branche externe, m.*
calf knees or back at the knees	*genou creux ou de mouton ou effacé*
call	*équivalent de la fanfare (vénerie)*
cane	*stick, m.*
cannon bone	*canon, m., os du canon, m.*
canter	*galop, m.*
canter, counter	*contre-galop, m. ou galop à faux*
canter, collected	*galop rassemblé, m.*
canter, departure at the	*départ au galop, m.*
canter, extended	*galop allongé, m.*
canter, medium	*galop moyen, m.*
canter, false	*galop à faux, m.*
cantle	*troussequin, m., arcade de derrière*
Cape cart	*charette du Cap, f. ou Cape cart, m.*
capped elbow	*éponge, f.*
capped hock	*capelet, m.*
carpal articular thoroughpin	*vessigon articulaire du genou, m.*
carpus	*carpe, m.*
carrousel	*carrousel, m.*
cart	*voiture à deux roues*
cast, to	*remettre les chiens sur la voie, v.*
cavalletti	*cavalletti, m.*
cavalry	*cavalerie, f. (militaire)*
cavalryman	*cavalier, m. (appartenant à la cavalerie)*
cavesson	*caveçon, m.*
central groove of the frog	*lacune médiane, f.*
centrals	*pinces, f.pl. (incisives)*
cervical vertebrae	*vertèbres cervicales, f.pl.*
Chambon	*Chambon, m.*
change to another line, to	*se mettre sur une autre voie, v.*

change of leg, flying	*changement de pied en l'air, m.*	coupe	*coupé, m.*
channel	*creux de panneaux*	coupled, short	*court de reins, adj.*
char-a-bancs	*char-à-bancs, m.*	couple	*couple, m. (de chiens)*
charger	*cheval d'armes, m.*	course	*parcours, m.*
Charolais	*Charolais, m.*	course-builder	*chef de piste, m.*
chase	*chasse à cheval f.*	course-building	*construction d'un parcours, f.*
check	*défaut, m. (vénerie)*	cover, to	*couvrir, v. (élevage)*
cheek	*joue, f. (du cheval)*	covering	*saillie, f.*
cheek	*branche, f. (du mors)*	covering season	*saison de monte, f.*
cheekpiece	*montant de bride, de filet, m.*	covert	*fourré servant d'abri au renard, m.*
chest	*poitrine, f.*		
chestnut	*alezan, adj., châtaigne, f.*	cow hocks	*jarrets clos ou crochus, m.pl.*
chin	*barbe, f. ou menton, m.*	coyote	*coyote, m.*
chin spot	*ladre au barbichet, m.*	crack	*champion, m.; crack, m.*
chukka	*période, f. ou chukka, f. (polo)*	crest	*bord supérior de l'encolure*
		crop	*production, f.; descendance, f. (élevage) ou fouet de chasse, m.*
Classic	*classiques, f.pl. (terme se référant à certaines courses)*		
Classic trial	*épreuve classique, f. (courses)*	cross, to	*croiser, v. (élevage)*
		cross-breeding	*croisement, m. (élevage)*
Classic winner	*un cheval gagnant d'épreuves classiques, m.*	cross-country	*cross, m.; cross-country, m.*
		crossed	*croisé, adj.*
clear, to	*sauter un obstacle sans faute, v.*	croup	*croupe, f.*
		crown-piece	*têtière, f.*
clear round	*parcours sans faute, m.*	crupper	*croupière, f.*
clip	*pinçon, m. (du fer)*	crystalline lens	*cristallin, m.*
close to the ground	*près de terre*	cub-hunting	*chasse d'entrainement, f.*
club foot	*pied bot, m.*	curb	*courbe f. ou mors, m.*
Clydesdale	*Clydesdale*	curb chain	*gourmette, f.*
coach	*carrosse, m.*	curb chain with fly link for lip strap	*gourmette avec l'anneau, pour la fausse gourmette*
coach, mail	*mail-coach, m.*		
coachmaker	*carrossier, m.*	curb reins	*rênes de bride, f.pl.*
coachman	*cocher, m.; bon meneur, m.*	curricle	*voiture légère*
coach, road	*carrosse, m.*	curry combs	*étrilles, f.*
coat colour	*robe, f.*	cut out, to be	*être coupé, v. (polo)*
cocking cart	*cocking-cart, m.*	cutting in	*coupé, m.*
coital exanthema	*exanthème du coit, m.*		
Colbert rein	*rêne Colbert, f.*	dam	*poulinière, f.*
colic	*colique, f.*	dandy brush	*bouchon chiendent, m.*
collar	*collier, m.*	Daumont, à la	*à la Daumont, ou, à la d'Aumont (attelage)*
collection	*rassembler, m.*		
colostrum	*colostrum m.*	death, the	*mort. f.; hallali, m. (vénerie)*
colt	*poulain, m.*		
combinations	*combinaisons, f.*	dee cheek snaffle	*filet verdun, m.*
competition	*compétition, f.*	dee cheek twisted race snaffle	*filet torsadé, m.*
competition horse	*cheval de compétition, m.*		
competitor	*concurrent, m.*	deep flexor tendon	*perforant*
condition, to	*mettre en condition, v.*	deep-throated	*bien gorgé (vénerie)*
conditioning	*mise en condition, f.*	deer	*cerf, m.*
co-ordination of the aids	*accord des aides, m.*	dentine	*ivoire, m. (dents)*
contact	*contact, m.*	destrier	*destrier, m.*
corium	*tissu velouté, m. (pied)*	diagonal	*bipède diagonal, m.*
cornea	*cornée transparente, f.*	direct female line	*lignée directe maternelle, f.*
corners	*coins, m. (incisives)*	direct male line	*lignée directe mâle, f.*
coronet	*couronne, f.*	dishing	*panard en marche, adj.*
counter-change of hand	*contre-changement de main, m.*	dismount, to	*mettre pied à terre, v.*
		disunited	*désuni, adj.*

ditch	*fossé, m.*
dividing septum	*ceinture de séparation, f.*
dock	*tronçon de la queue*
dock, to	*écourter, v. (une queue)*
dock piece	*culeron, m.*
dog-cart	*dog-cart, m.*
dorsal stripe	*raie de mulet, f.*
dorsal vertebrae	*vertèbres dorsales, f.pl.*
double-bank	*banquette double, f.*
double and treble	*double et triple, m.*
double jointed bridoon	*filet de mors de bride à double brisure, m.*
dovetail	*queue d'aronde, f.*
drag	*drag, m. (attelage)*
drag	*drag, m. (chasse à la trace,)*
draught	*animal de trait, m.*
drawing knife	*couteau anglais, m.*
dressage	*dressage, m.*
dressage test	*reprise de dressage, f.*
drive, to	*mener, v.*
driving	*menage, m.*
driving hammer	*mailloche, f.*
drop noseband	*muserole allemande, f.*
ear	*oreille, f.*
earth	*terrier, m.*
edges	*rives, f.pl.*
eggbutt German mouth snaffle	*filet Chantilly*
elbow	*coude, m.*
electric gate	*portail ou barrière électrique*
empty	*vide, adj.*
encephalomyelitis	*encéphalo-myélite, f.*
engagement	*engagement, m.*
equerry	*écuyer, m.*
equestrian	*équestre, adj.*
equine	*équin, adj.*
equitation, academic	*équitation académique, f.*
ergot	*ergot, m.*
event horses	*cheval de C.C.E., m.*
extension	*extension.; allongement, m.*
external enamel	*émail externe, m.*
eye	*oeil, m.*
false martingale	*fausse-martingale, f.*
false ribs	*côtes asternales, f.pl. ou fausses côtes*
fault	*défaut, m. (vénerie); faute, f. (concours de sauts d'obstacles)*
feather	*fanon, m.*
feet, hind	*pied postérieur, m.*
female line	*lignée maternelle, f.*
femur	*fémur, m.*
fence	*obstacle, m.*
fence, drop	*obstacle en contre-bas, m.*
fence, natural	*obstacle naturel, m.*
fence, post & rails	*barres superposées, f.pl. ou stationata*
fence, solid	*obstacle fixe, m.*
fence, fly their	*prendre un obstacle de volée, v.*
fence, Virginia snake	*obstacle américain, composé de groupes de barres formant des angles, et placées en zigzag*
fetlock	*boulet m.*
fewmets	*fumées, f.pl. (vénerie)*
field	*partants, m.pl. (courses); ensemble des cavaliers suivant une chasse au renard, m.*
Field Master	*adjoint du maitre d'équipage spécialment chargé de surveiller les cavaliers durant la chasse afin d'éviter qu'ils ne dérangent les chiens*
filly	*pouliche, f.*
Fillis bridoon	*filet Fillis, m.*
final straight	*ligne droite, f. (courses)*
firing	*feu, m. (vét.)*
fitness	*forme du cheval, f.*
fixed cheek arch mouth curb	*mors l'Hotte, mors cintré, m.*
fixed cheek Weymouth bit	*mors avec passage de langue, m.*
flag	*fanion, m.*
flanks	*flancs, m.pl.*
flap	*quartier, m. (de la selle)*
flat racing	*course de plat, f.*
flexion at the jaw	*cession de mâchoire, f.*
flexion	*flexion, f.*
flies, Bot	*oestre, m.*
flies, warble	*hypoderme, m.*
floor	*semelle de l'étrier, f.*
foal, to	*pouliner*
foal	*foal, m.*
foaling	*poulinage, m.*
foot	*pied, m.*
forage	*fourrage, m.*
force, to	*forcer, v. un animal*
forge, to	*forger, v.*
forearm	*avant-bras, m.*
forefoot	*pied antérieur, m.*
forehand	*avant-main, f.*
forehead	*front, m.*
forelegs	*antérieurs, m.pl.*
forelock	*toupet, m.*
form	*style, m. (du cheval)*
forward	*avant, m.; Polo, les joueurs 1 et 2 sont des avants*
forward movement	*mouvement en avant, m. (du cheval)*
forward roll	*taquet avant de la selle, m.*

foundation sire	*premier géniteur, m.*	groom, to	*panser, v.*
foundation stock	*base d'élevage, f.*	grooming	*pansage, m.*
fox	*renard, m.*		
getting a fox out of covert	*faire sortir le renard du bois, bosquet, v.*	hack	*promenade à cheval, f. – cheval de promenade, m.*
turn the fox from 'his point'	*détourner le renard de sa voie, v.*	hack, to	*faire une promenade à cheval, v.*
foxhound	*foxhound, m. (chien pour la chasse au renard)*	hackney	*hackney, m.*
		half-back	*joueur No. 3 au polo, m.*
foxhound pack	*meute pour la chasse au renard, f.*	half-bred	*demi-sang, m.*
		half-cheeks	*se dit d'un mors de filet possédant seulement des branches supérieures ou inférieures*
foxhunting	*chasse au renard, f.*		
fox, bag	*renard gardé en captivité en vue de l'utiliser pour la chasse ultérieurement, m.*		
		half-halt	*demi-arrêt, m.*
fox, bagged	*même signification*	half-pass	*appuyer, m.*
fox, to drop	*lâcher un renard, gardé en captivité, à la chasse, v.*	half-turn on the forehand	*demi-tour sur les épaules, m.*
		half-turn on the haunches	*demi-tour sur les hanches, m.*
fox, grey	*renard gris, m.*	half-volte	*demi-volte, f.*
fox, red	*renard rouge, m. (alezan foncé)*	halt, to	*arrêter*
		hames	*attelles, f.pl. du collier (attelage)*
foxtrot	*traquerenard, m.*		
frame	*corps, m. du cheval, cadre, m.*	hame strap	*courroie d'attelle, f.*
free handicap	*handicap libre, m.*	hame terret	*clés de collier*
free hit	*coup franc, m. (polo)*	hand	*à main gauche, à main droite – dans un manège, une carrière; – main, f. mesure anglo-saxonne pour mesurer la hauteur d'un cheval; une main est égale à 4 pouces, ou 10 cm.*
free range	*état sauvage, m.*		
French Trotter	*trotteur français, m.*		
Friesian Chaise	*chaise frisonne, f.*		
frog	*fourchette, f.*		
front chamber	*chambre antérieure, f.*		
frontlet	*plaque de front, f.*		
fullered iron	*fer rainé, m.*	hand, four in	*four in hand, m. ou en grandes guides*
gait	*allure, f.*	hand, six in	*attelage à 6 chevaux, m.*
gallop	*galop, m.*	handiness	*maniabilité, f.*
gallop, to	*galoper, v.*	hand-holds	*arrêtoirs, m.pl. sur les guides pour éviter qu'elles ne glissent des mains*
galloping race	*course de galop, f.*		
game	*gibier, m.*		
gaskin or 'second thigh'	*jambe, f.*	handicapper	*handicapeur, m.*
gelding	*hongre, m.*	handicaps	*handicap, m. (polo, les joueurs se voient attribuer un handicap, allant de 0 à 10)*
gentleman rider	*gentleman rider, m.*		
genuine	*honnête, adj. – un cheval honnête*		
gig	*cabriolet, m.*	hand-pieces	*voir 'hand-holds'*
girth	*sangle, f.*	hardy	*courageux, robuste, adj. (cheval)*
girth extension	*rallonge de sangle, f.*		
girth straps or tabs	*contre-sanglons, m.pl.*	hardy campaigner	*cheval régulier, m.*
glanders	*morve, f.*	hare	*lièvre, m.*
go to ground	*se terrer, v.*	harness	*harnais, m.*
goals	*buts, m.pl. (polo)*	harness, to	*atteler, v.*
grakle noseband	*muserolle croisée, f.*	harness horse	*cheval d'attelage, m.*
grandsire	*grand-père, m.*	harness racer	*trotteur, m. pour courses de trot attelé*
grandstand	*tribunes, f.pl.*		
great cry	*bien gorgé, adj. se dit d'un chien de chasse à courre qui peut être entendu de loin*	harrier	*harrier, m.*
		Hartwell Pelham	*Pelham, canon rigide, avec passage de langue, m.*
groom	*palefrenier, m.*	haunch	*hanche, f.*

haute école	*haute-école, f.*	humerus	*humérus, m.*
hay	*foin, m.*	hunt	*chasse, f.; l'équipage, m.*
head	*tête, f.*	hunter	*hunter, m.; cheval de*
headcollars	*licols, m.pl.*		*chasse, m.*
head	*voir 'point, to turn the fox*	hunt, to	*chasser, v.*
	from his'	hunting field	*l'ensemble des cavaliers*
headpiece	*têtière, f.*		*suivent une chasse au*
heart	*coeur, m.*		*renard, m.*
heel bug	*crevasse, f.*	hunting horn	*corne d'environ 25 cm. de*
heels	*talons m.pl.*		*long utilisée à la chasse*
h.h.	*paume, f. mesure égale à*		*au renard, f.*
	10 cm.	hunting a line	*suivre la voie du renard, v.*
high ringbone	*forme du paturon, f.*	hunting man	*veneur, m.*
hind foot	*pied postérieur, m.*	hunt servants	*piqueurs, m.pl.*
hind legs	*postérieurs, m.pl.*	hunting type breastplate	*collier de chasse, m.*
hind quarters, enagement	*engagement de l'arrière-main,*	huntsman	*maitre des chasses, m. (dans*
of the	*m.*		*les pays Anglo-Saxons).*
hit the line, to	*trouver la voie du renard*	hurdler	*cheval de haies, m.*
	chassé, v.	hygroma	*hygroma, m.*
hobbles	*entraves, f.pl.*		
hock	*jarret, m.*	ilium	*ilium, m.*
hock, bent	*jarret coudé, m.*	impulsion	*impulsion, f.*
hock boot	*protecteur de jarret, m.*	inbreeding	*inbreeding, m.*
hocks too straight	*jarrets droits, m.pl.*	inbreed, to	*faire de l'inbreeding, v.*
hocks well away from	*jarrets loin, m.pl.*	incisors	*incisives, f.pl.*
him		inclined plane	*plan incliné, m. (obstacles de*
honest	*honnête, adj. – cheval*		*volée)*
	honnête	infectious anaemia	*anémie infectieuse, f.*
hoof	*sabot, m.*	influenza	*grippe équine, f.*
hoof cutter	*tricoise, f.*	infundibulum	*cornet dentaire externe, f.*
hoof oil brush	*pinceau pour onguent de*	inside and outside toe	*mamelles (internes et*
	pied, m.		*externes), f.pl.*
hoof picks	*cure-pieds, m.pl.*	inside leg	*jambe intérieure, f.*
hoofprint	*empreinte, f.*	Intermediate Dressage	*Reprise Intermédiaire, f.*
hook	*queue d'aronde, fl.*	Test	
	(dentition)	iris	*iris, m.*
hooking	*accrochage, m. (polo, quand*	iron, fullered	*fer rainé, m.*
	un joueur accroche le	iron, plain	*fer ordinaire, m.*
	maillet d'un autre joueur)	ischium	*ischium, m.*
horn	*corne, f. (du sabot)*		
horn music	*fanfare, f. (trompe de chasse)*	Jacob's Ladder	*barre de Spa, f.*
horn tubes	*canaux cylindrique, m.pl.*	jaws	*mâchoires, f.pl.*
	(pied)	joint	*articulation, f.*
horse	*cheval, m.*	jointed Pelham	*Pelham, canon avec brisure*
horseman	*cavalier, m.; homme de*	judge at the finishing post	*juge à 'l'arrivée, m.*
	cheval, m.	jugular groove	*gouttière jugulaise, f.*
horse show	*concours, m.*	jump	*obstacle, m.*
horseback, on	*à cheval*	jump, to	*sauter*
horsemanship	*équitation, f.*	jumper	*cheval d'obstacle, m. jumper,*
horsemastership	*ensemble des connaissances*		*cheval de courses à*
	d'un homme de cheval, m.		*obstacles, m.*
horse racing	*course de chevaux, f.*	jumping	*concours de sauts d'obstacles,*
horse shoe	*fer à cheval, m.*		*m. C.S.O.*
horse trials	*concours complet, m. C.C.E.*	jump-off	*barrage, m.*
hounds	*chiens courants, m.pl.*	jump short	*départ de près, m. pour le*
hounds, to follow	*suivre les chiens, v.*		*saut*
houndwork	*travail des chiens, m.*	jump racing	*courses à obstacles, m.*

jumps, water	*rivière, f.*
high-jumping championships	*championnat de saut en hauteur, m.*
show jumps	*obstacles de jumping, de concours, m.pl.*
show jumping	*concours de sauts d'obstacles, jumping, m.*
keen	*avoir du perçant*
keeping with hounds	*à la queue des chiens*
kennel	*chenil, m.*
kill	*curée, f.*
Kimblewick	*mors espagnol*
kineton noseband	*muserolle à crochets*
Klebsiellosis	*Klebsiella, f.*
knee	*genou, m.*
knee cap	*genouillère, f.*
knee rolls	*taquets, m.pl. (de la selle)*
knock-kneed	*genou de boeuf*
laced reins	*rênes brédies, f.pl.*
laid on, to be	*mis sur la voie, chiens*
lame	*boiteux, adj.*
lameness	*boiterie, f.*
laminitis	*fourbure, f.*
Landau	*landau, m.*
large metacarpal bone or cannon bone	*métacarpien principal*
large metatarsal bone or cannon bone	*métatarsien principal*
lashing out behind	*ruer, v.*
lateral aids	*aides latérales, f.pl.*
lateral cartilages	*cartilages complémentaries, m.pl.*
lateral groove of the frog	*lacune latérale, f.*
lateral pair	*bipède latéral, m.*
laterals	*mitoyennes, f.pl. (dents)*
lay hounds onto the scent	*mettre les chiens sur la-voie, v.*
lay scent, to	*faire le tracé, v.*
lead at the canter	*pied sur lequel le cheval galope, m.*
leader	*cheval de volée, m.; leader, m.*
leaping-head	*fourche inférieure, f. d'une selle d'amazone, f.*
leggy	*cheval haut perché ou déguingardé*
leg, outside	*jambe extérieure, f. (du cavalier)*
legs	*membres, m.pl. (du cheval)*
leg-up	*prendre la jambe, v.*
let slip	*découpler, v.*
levade	*levade, f.*
ligament	*ligament, m.*
light	*léger, adj.*
lightness	*légèreté, f.*
limbs	*membres, m.pl. (du cheval)*

limer	*limier, m.*
line of the ball	*ligne de la balle, f. (Polo)*
line	*la voie, f.*
lips	*lèvres, f.pl.*
liver chestnut	*alezan brulé, adj.*
Liverpool bit	*mors Liverpool*
linseed	*graine de lin, f.*
loins	*rein, m. (région du rein)*
loin strap	*barre de fesse, f.*
long pastern bone	*os du paturon, m.*
loop, to	*boucler, v.; faire un boucle, f.; aux guides*
loop	*passe, f.; boucle, f.*
loose box	*box, m.*
lop-eared	*oreillard, adj.*
low ringbone	*forme coronaire, f.*
lower jaw	*mâchoire inférieure ou ganache, f.*
lumbar vertebrae	*vertèbres lombaires, f.pl.*
lunge, lunge line	*longe, f.*
lunge, to	*mettre à la longe, v.*
lungeing	*travail à la longe, m.*
lungeing whip	*chambrière, f.*
lymphangitis	*lymphangite, f.*
maiden filly	*maiden, f.; primiparde, adj.*
making a point	*faire un point, v. (menage)*
mallet	*maillet de polo, m.*
mane	*crinière, f.*
mane comb	*peigne crinière, m.*
mark, to	*marquer, v. un joueur, au polo*
Market Harborough martingale	*entrênement Howlett*
markings	*particularités, f.pl., d'une robe*
marking	*marquage, m. (polo)*
mass	*masse, f.*
Master	*voir 'Master of Hounds'*
Master of Hounds	*maitre d'équipage, m.*
match	*match (polo), m., ou course n'opposant que deux cavaliers, f.*
meconium	*meconium, m.*
meetings	*réunion, f., de courses*
meet	*rendez-vous, m. (chasse)*
melanomata	*tumeur mélanique, f.*
metritis	*métrite, f.*
miler	*miler, m.*
milord	*mylord, m.*
mise en main, the	*mise en main, f.*
mobile starting gate	*autostart, m.*
moon blindness	*fluxion périodique, f.*
Morgan horse	*Morgan, m.*
mount, to	*se mettre en selle, v.; monter, v.; remonter, v.; se remonter, v.*

mount	*monture, f.*
mounted	*à cheval, adj. (troupes à cheval)*
mouth	*bouche, f.*
mouthpiece	*canon, m.; d'une embouchure*
mouthpiece, two or three-piece jointed	*canon à une ou deux brisures, m.*
movements	*mouvements, m.pl.*
mucking out	*tirer le fumier des boxes, v.*
muscles	*muscles m.pl.*
nail	*clou, m.*
nail holes	*étampures, f.pl.*
nailing, coarse	*broché, trop haut, adj.*
nailing, fine	*broché trop bas, adj.*
nasal discharge	*jetage, m.*
navicular or 'shuttle bone'	*os naviculaire, m.; petit sésamoide, m.*
near	*gauche, adj.*
near leader	*cheval gauche de volée, m.*
near side	*côté gauche, côté montoir, m.*
near wheeler	*cheval gauche de timon, m.*
neat	*net, adj. (de tares)*
neck	*encolure, f.*
neck of the spur	*tige de l'éperon, f.*
neck strap	*dessus de cou on surcou, m.*
nervous influx	*influx nerveux, m.*
nick, to	*anglaiser, v.*
nominator	*propriétaire d'un cheval au moment de la course, m.; prête-nom sous lequel le cheval peut courir, m.*
Norfolk roadster	*Norfolk roadster, m.*
Norman	*normand, adj.*
nose	*chanfrein, m.*
noseband	*muserolle, f.*
noseband cheek	*montant de muserolle, m.*
noseband, drop	*muserolle allemande, f.*
nostril	*naseau, m.*
numnah	*tapis de selle, m.*
oats	*avoine, f.*
obstacle	*obstacle, m.*
obstacle race	*course à obstacles, f.*
off	*droit, adj.*
off leader	*cheval droit de volée, m.*
off-side	*côté hors-montoir, m.; côté droit, m.*
off wheeler	*cheval droit de timon, m.*
olecranon	*olécrane m.*
open ditch without guard rail	*fossé à bords francs, m.*
opossum	*opossum, m.*
optic nerve	*nerf optique, m.*

ordinary bridoon	*filet de mors de bride ordinaire, m.*
os calcis	*calcanéum, m.*
out of	*par, (préposition)*
over at the knees	*brassicourt*
overdraw bearing rein	*enrènement, m. (attelage)*
Overo	*overo*
overreach boot	*cloche en caoutchouc, f.*
over-ride (hounds)	*croiser les chiens, v.*
overtrack, to	*se méjuger, v.*
own the line	*sur la piste*
oxer	*oxer, m.*
pace	*train, m.*
pacer	*ambleur, m.*
paces	*allures, f.pl.*
paces, medium and extended	*allures, moyennes, allongées, f.pl.*
paces, working and collected	*allures de travail, rassemblées, f.pl.*
pack	*meute, f.; équipage, m.*
pack-animal	*animal de bât, m.*
pack of hounds	*meute, f.*
pad	*pad, m. mantelet, sellette, f. (attelage)*
pad terret	*clés de sellette*
paddock	*paddock, m.*
paddock, polo	*paddock, polo m.*
pairs	*attelage en paire, m.*
palfrey	*palefroit, m.*
Palomino	*polomino, m.*
panels	*panneaux, m.pl.*
parasites, internal	*parasites de l'intestin ou du sang, m.pl.*
Pari-Mutuel	*Pari-Mutuel, m.*
park trot	*park trot, m. (pace of the American Saddle Horse)*
pass	*passe, f.*
passage	*passage, m.*
pastern	*paturon, m.*
pasterns, sloping	*paturon, bas-jointé, m.*
patella	*rotule, f.*
pedal bone	*os du pied, m.; troisième phalange, f.*
pedigree	*pedigree, m.*
peg	*clou à glace, m.*
Pelham roundings	*alliances de Pelham, f.pl.*
pencilled	*biseauté adj. (fer à éponges biseautées)*
Percheron	*Percheron, adj.*
periople	*périople, m.*
perioplic ring	*bourrelet périoplique, m.*
peritonitis	*péritonite, f.*
peytrel	*poitrail, m.*
phaeton	*phaéton, m.*
piaffe	*piaffer, m.*
piebald	*pie noir, adj.*

pigeon-toed	*cagneux, adj.*	rabbit	*lapin, m.*
pillion, to ride	*monter à la fermière, v.*	raccoon	*raton laveur, m.*
pincers	*pinces, f.pl.*	race,	*course, f.*
Pinto	*Pinto, adj.*	racegoer	*turfiste, m.*
pirouette	*pirouette, f.*	racer	*cheval de courses, m.*
pirouette, reversed	*pirouette renversée, f.*	race over fences	*course à obstacles, f.*
pirouette, half-	*demi-pirouette, f.*	racing	*courses, les, f.pl.*
placer	*placer, m.*	racing, flat	*courses de plat, f.pl.*
plain iron	*fer ordinaire, m.*	racing type breastplate	*bricole, f.*
plain noseband	*muserolle ordinaire*	racecourse	*hippodrome, m.; champ de*
plantar cushion	*coussinet plantaire, m.*		*courses, m.*
pleurisy	*pleurésie, f.*	race horse	*cheval de courses, m.*
pneumonia	*pneumonie, f.*	race track	*hippodrome, m.; champ de*
point, to turn the fox from his	*détourner le renard de sa voie, v.*		*courses, m.*
point, to make a counter	*faire une opposition v. (attelage)*	raceway	*hippodrome de trot, m.*
		rack	*rack, ou traquenard, m. (allure des 'five-gaited horses')*
point of buttock	*pointe de la fesse, f.*		
point of hip	*hanche, f.*	radius	*radius*
point of hock	*pointe du jarret, f.*	rain scald	*teigne de boue, f.*
point of shoulders	*pointe de l'épaule, f.*	ramener	*ramener, m.*
point-to-point	*point-to-point, m.*	rangy	*étendu, adj.*
pole	*timon, m. (attelage)*	rasp	*râpe, f.*
pole, head of the	*bout de timon, m.*	rear, to	*se cabrer, pointer v.*
pole	*barre, f. (obstacle)*	recover himself	*rallier, v. (vénerie)*
pole chain	*chainette, f.*	red worms	*strongles, m.pl.*
poll	*nuque, f.*	referee	*referee, m. (polo), arbitre, m.*
polo	*polo, m.*	reins	*rênes, f.pl.; guides, f.pl.*
polo ground	*terrain, de polo, m.*	rein back, to	*reculer, v.*
polo pony	*poney de polo, m.*	contrary rein of opposition in front of the withers	*rêne contraire d'opposition en avant du garrot, f.*
polo, indoor	*indoor polo, m.*		
polo stick	*maillet de polo, m.*		
pommel	*pommeau, m.*	contrary rein of opposition behind the withers	*rêne contraire d'opposition en arrière du garrot, f.*
pony	*poney, m.*		
pony of the Americas, the	*poney d'Amérique, m.*		
position	*position, f.*	direct rein of opposition	*rêne directe d'opposition, f.*
postchaise	*chaise de poste, f.*	reins, bearing	*enrênement simple, m. (attelage)*
Postier Breton	*postier Breton, m.*		
postilion	*postillon, m.*	bearing rein hook	*croissant ou crochet d'enrênement, m.*
precocity	*précocité, f. (d'un cheval)*		
premier sire	*étalon dtête, m.*	bearing rein pillar	*id. id.*
present the brush, to	*en France: (vénerie) 'faire les honneurs du pied'*	full bearing reins	*enrênement à passages, m. (attelage)*
		rein, lead	*guide de volée, f.*
Prix St Georges	*Prix St Georges, m.*	rein, loose	*rênes en guirlande, f.pl.*
prize money	*allocation, f.*	rein, neck	*rêne d'appui, rêne contraire, f.*
puissance	*puissance, f.*		
pulling up	*arrêter, v. (attelage),*	long reins	*rênes longues, f.pl.*
pulmonary artery	*artère pulmonaire, f.*	rein, wheel	*guide de timon, f.*
pulmonary veins	*veines pulmonaires, f.pl.*	remove	*rassis, m.*
purse	*prix, m. (courses)*	report, to	*faire le rapport, v. (vénerie)*
put at fault	*tomber en défaut*	reproduction	*reproduction, f.*
		resistance, muscular	*résistance de force, f.*
quality	*distinction, f.*	resistance, weight	*résistance de poids, f.*
Quarter horse	*Quarter horse, m.*	retina	*rétine, f.*
quarters	*arrière-main, f.*	retired to stud	*enjoyé au haras, étalon, v.*
quarters (of the foot)	*mamelles et quartiers du piêd, f.pl.*	reversed half-volte	*demi-volte renversée, f.*

rhinopneumonitis	*rhino-pneumonie, f.*
ribs	*côtes, f. pl.*
ribbons	*flots, m. pl.; guides, f. pl. familiar*
ridden trotting race	*course de trot monté, f.*
ride, to	*monter, aller, se promener à cheval, v.*
ride, endurance	*épreuve ou course d'endurance*
ride to hounds	*chasser à courre, v.*
ride-off test	*reprise de rappel, f.*
rider	*cavalier, m.*
rig	*cheval monorchide, m.*
riding hall	*manège, m.*
riding horse	*cheval de selle, m.*
riding school	*école d'équitation, f.*
riding whip	*cravache, f.*
ringbone	*forme, f.*
ringworm	*teigne, f.*
road crossing	*passage de route, m.*
roan	*rouan, adj.*
roebuck	*chevreuil, m.*
roller	*surfaix d'écurie, m.*
rolling the toe	*tronqué en pince, adj.*
rosette	*cocarde, f. (menage)*
rounded drop noseband	*muserole italienne, f.*
rounsey	*roussin, m.*
rouse, to	*mettre sur pied, v. (vénerie)*
run, to	*courir, v.*
run mute, to	*secret, adj. chien secret, hunting*
runner	*concurrent, m. – cheval de plat, m.*
running start	*départ lancé, m.*
running walk	*'running walk', ou amble, m. (allure des 'five-gaited horses').*
sacral vertebrae	*vertèbres sacrées, f. pl.*
saddle	*selle, f.*
saddle, cart	*selle à piquer, f.*
saddle, pound	*selle de courses, f.*
saddle, to	*seller, v.*
saddle cloth	*tapis de selle, m.*
saddle flap	*quartier de selle*
five-gaited saddler	*'five-gaited horse', m. ou cheval à cinq allures*
three-gaited saddler	*'three-gaited horse', m. ou cheval à trois allures*
saddlery	*sellerie, f.*
side-saddle	*selle d'amazone, f. selle à fourches, f.*
safety catch	*sécurité, f. étrier à sécurité*
salmonellosis	*salmonellose, f.*
sand crack	*seime, f.*
saturated	*imprégné, adj.*
scapula	*scapulum, m.*

scent	*trace, f. suivie par les chiens de chasse (odorat); 'sur la voie de . . .'*
scent, to pick up the	*prendre la voie, v.*
school, high	*haute-école, f.*
school, low	*basse-école, f.*
school leaps	*sauts d'école, m. pl.*
school master	*maitre d'école, m.*
sclera	*sclérotique, f.*
scope	*étendue, f. cheval qui a de l'étendue*
score	*score, m.*
screw holes for studs	*mortaises pour crampons, f. pl.*
seat	*assiette, f., siege*
seat worm	*oxyure, m.*
seat, forward	*monte en avant, f.*
Selle Francais	*Selle Français, m.*
seller	*réclamer, une course à*
sensitive laminae	*tissu feuillété, m.*
service	*saillie, m. (d'un étalon)*
serve, to	*saillir, v.*
sesamoid bones	*grands sésamoïdes, m. pl.*
set on foot	*faire mettre debout, v. (vénerie)*
shafts	*brancards, m. pl.*
sharp gallop	*galop court mais rapide, m. ou 'Bout vite', m.*
shin	*partie antérieure du canon, f.*
shoes	*fers, m. pl.*
shoeing	*ferrure, f.*
shoeing, cold	*ferrure à froid, f.*
shoeing nail	*clou à ferrure, m.*
short coupled	*court dans son rein, adj.*
short-legged	*près de terre*
short pastern bone	*os de la couronne, m.*
shoulders	*épaules, f. pl.*
shoulder-in	*épaule en dedans, f.*
sickle hocks	*iarrets coudés, m. pl.*
sides	*branches, f. pl.*
side-saddle	*selle d'Amazone, f.*
single leg	*iambe isolée, f.*
sire, filly	*père de pouliches, m.*
sire, to	*produire, v.*
sire	*étalon, père, m.*
sire list	*liste des étalons, f.*
size	*taille, f.*
skewbald	*pie, adj. blanc avec tout autre couleur autre que le noir*
skin	*peau, f.*
skirt	*petit quartier recourant les porte-étrivières d'une selle, m.*
slab sides	*côtes plates, f. pl.*
sleigh	*trâineau, m.*
slide cheek Weymouth bit	*mors à pompe, m.*
slide cheek Weymouth with port	*mors à pompe avec passage de langue, m.*

sloping pastern	*long et bas jointé, adj.*	standing under in front	*sous lui du devant*
slow-downs	*ralentissements, m.pl.*	standing stretched in front	*campé du devant*
slow-gait	*allure lente, m.*	standing under behind	*sous lui du derrière*
slow-pace	*allure ralentie, f.*	standing stretched behind	*campé du derrière*
snaffle, jointed	*filet brisé, m.*	stands	*tribunes, f.pl.*
snaffle or bridoon reins	*rênes de filet, f.pl.*	star	*étoile, f.*
snip	*ladre, m.*	starters	*partants, m.pl. (courses)*
snotty nose	*naseaux souillés par de la*	starter	*starter, m.*
	sérosité, du pus, du sang, m.	stationnata	*stationnata, f.*
sock	*balzane, f.*	stay, to	*avoir de la tenue, v.*
soft ground	*terrain souple, élastique, m.*	stayer	*stayer, m.*
soil, to	*se mettre à l'eau, v.*	staying power	*tenue, f.*
	(vénerie)	steady pace	*allure soutenue, f.*
sole	*sole, f.*	steeplechase	*steeple-chase, m.*
sore shins	*sore-shins, m.pl.*	steeplechase-cross-country	*steeple-chase-cross-country, m.*
sore back	*gonfle, f. – plaie de dos*	stepping pace	*trot relevé*
sound	*cheval sain et exempt de tares,*	sternum or breast bone	*sternum, m.*
	m.	stifle (patella)	*grasset, m.*
spots	*plaques de poils, plus ou*	stirrup	*étrier, m.*
	moins étendues, d'une	stirrup leather	*étrivière, m.*
	teinte différente de la	stocking	*balzane, f.*
	robe, ou même d'une	straight	*ligne droite, f.*
	autre couleur	strain	*courant de sang, m.*
speed and endurance test	*épreuve de fond, f., C.C.E.*	strangles	*gourme, f.*
speed	*vitesse, f.*	straps, loin	*surdos, m. – barre de fesse, f.*
speed-ups	*allongements, m.pl.*	strap, lip	*fausse-gourmette, f.*
speedy cutting	*se couper, s'atteindre, v.*	stride	*foulée, f.*
splint	*suros, m.*	strip	*liste, f. (assez large)*
splint bone	*métacarpien ou métatarsien*	stud, at	*au haras, faire la monte*
	rudimentaire	stud	*haras, m.*
sprain	*claquage, m.*	studs	*crampons, m.pl.*
spread	*large, m. (jumping)*	stud groom	*étalonnier, m.; premier*
springs	*lames, f.pl.*		*garçon, m.*
sprint	*course de sprint, f.*	stud holes	*mortaises, f.pl.*
sprinter	*sprinter, m.*	stuffing	*matelassure, f.*
spur	*éperon, m.*	stumble, to	*broncher, trébucher, v.*
square oxer	*oxer au carré, m.*	style note	*note de style, f.*
squat	*compact, adj.*	substance	*masse, f.; trempe, f.*
stable	*écurie, f.*	sulky	*sulky, m.*
stable care	*soins d'écurie, m.pl.*	summer sheet	*chemise, f.*
stag	*cerf, m.*	summer pneumonia of	*pneumonie d'été des foals, f.*
staghounds	*chiens, courants pour la*	foals	
	chasse au cerf, m.pl.	superficial flexor tendon	*perforé*
stage coach	*diligence, f.*	suppling exercise	*exercise d'assouplissement, m.*
stag hunter	*veneur, m.*	surcingle	*surfaix, m.; sursangle, f.*
staghunt	*chasse au cerf, f.*	suspensory ligament	*suspenseur du boulet, m.*
stakes races	*courses principales,*	sweat scraper	*couteau de chaleur, m.*
	importantes, f.pl.	sweat flap	*faux-quartier, m.*
stallion-man	*étalonnier, m.*	sweepstakes	*sweepstakes, m.pl.*
stallion	*étalon, m.*	swing	*swing, m. (polo)*
stalls	*stalles, f.pl. (courses)*	swingle tree	*palonnier, m.*
stamina	*fond, m. ou tenue, f.*		
Standardbred	*Standardbred, trotteur*	table of the crown	*table dentaire, f.*
	american, m.	tachanka	*tachanca, f. (attelage russe)*
standing at stud	*faire la monte, f.*	tack	*harnachement, m.*
stand off, to	*partir de loin, v.*	tack room	*sellerie, f.*
standing start	*départ arrêté, m.*	tail-male line	*lignée male, f.*

tail	*queue, f.*	trainer	*dresseur, m.; entraîneur, m.*
tail guard	*fourreau de queue, m.*		*(courses)*
take off, to	*partir, v. ou prendre la battue,*	training	*dressage, m.; entraînement,*
	v. (obstacle)		*m. (courses)*
take the pack off the line	*arrêter les chiens, v.*	traveller, bad	*cheval voyageant mal, m.*
taken in the stride	*pris dans la foulée*	tread	*semelle de l'étrier, f.*
taking off close	*partir de près, v.*	treads	*atteintes, f.pl.*
tally ho	*halalli, m.*	tree	*arçon, m.*
tandem	*tandem, m.*	trekking	*tourisme équestre, m.*
tap-root, mare	*souche maternelle, f.*	trials, classic	*épreuves préparatoires pour*
tarsus	*tarse, m.*		*des classiques, f.pl.*
team	*équipe, f.; équipage à 4*	trim the hoof, to	*parer le pied, v.*
	chevaux, m.	Triple Crown	*Triple Couronne, f.*
teaser	*boute-en-train, m.*	troika	*troika, f.*
teeth	*dents, f.pl.*	trot	*trot, m.*
tendon	*tendon, m.*	trot, a broken	*trot rompu, traquenard, m.*
tendon, deep flexor	*tendon du fléchisseur profond*	trot, collected	*trot rassemblé, m.*
	des phalanges, m. ou	trot, fox	*trot rompu, traquenard, m.*
	perforant, m.	trot, rising or posting	*trot enlevé, m.; trot à*
tendon, superficial flexor	*tendon du fléchisseur*		*l'anglaise, m.*
	superficiel des phalanges,	trot, sitting	*trot, assis, m.; trot à la*
	m.; ou perforé, m.		*française, m.*
Tennessee Walking Horse	*Tennessee Walking Horse, m.*	trot, to	*trotter, v.*
test	*épreuve, f.*	trotteur	*trotteur, m.*
tetanus	*tétanos, m.*	trotting under saddle	*trot monté, m. (courses au*
thigh	*cuisse, f.*		*trot)*
thong	*mêche, f.*	true ribs	*côtes sternales, f.pl.*
Thoroughbred	*pur-sang, m. (P.S.A.)*	tuberculosis	*tuberculose, f.*
thoroughpin	*vessignon, m.*	tug hooks	*boucles à crampons, f.pl.*
three day event	*concours complet, m.*	tug	*porte-brancard, m.*
	(C.C.E.)	tug stop	*arrêtoirs de brancards, m.pl.*
throat	*gorge, f.*	turf track	*piste en gazon, f.*
throat latch	*auge, f.; sous-gorge, f.*	turn across the school	*doubler dans la largeur, m.*
tibia	*tibia, m.*	turn down the school	*doubler dans la longeur, m.*
Tilbury	*Tilbury, m.*	turn on the forehand	*pirouette renversée, f.*
toe	*pince, f. (du pied ou du fer)*	turn on the quarters	*pirouette, f.*
toe clip	*pinçon, m.*	turning down (a bag fox)	*lâcher, v. (le renard)*
toe too long	*pied à talons bas*	twist	*creux, m.*
toed out	*panard*	twisted mouthpiece	*canon torsadé, m.*
too narrow	*serré du devant*		
too wide	*trop ouvert du devant*	umpire	*arbitre, m. (polo)*
topline	*ligne du dessus, f.; dessus, m.*	undertrack, to	*se déjuger, v.*
top weighted	*top weight*	unhorsed	*désarçonné, adj.*
Tote	*P.M.U.*	unseated	*désarçonné, adj.*
touch-line	*ligne de touche, f.*	unsound	*atteint d'une affection; taré,*
trace-buckle	*boucle de boucleteau de*		*(cheval) adj.*
	trait, f.	unsoundness	*affection, f., tare, f.*
trace	*trait, m.*	upright	*vertical, m.*
track	*piste, f.*	upright pastern	*court et haut jointé*
track, cinder	*piste cendrée, f.*		
track, dirt	*piste en terre, f.*	vaulting	*voltige, f.*
track up, to	*se juger, v.*	vaulting surcingle	*surfaix de voltige, f.*
trail	*voie, f.*	valves	*valvules, f.pl.*
trail riding	*promenade, f. à cheval*	vena cava	*veine cave, f.*
train, to	*dresser, v.; entraîner, v.*	Vendeen	*Vendéen, adj.*
	(courses)	venery	*venerie, f.*
trailer	*remorque, f.*	ventricle	*ventricule, m.*

vertical	*vertical (obstacle)*	well set on	*bien greffé, adj.*
veterinary surgeon	*vétérinaire, m.*	wheeler	*cheval de timon, m.*
veterinary check	*contrôle vétérinaire, m.*	whip	*fouet, m.; meneur, m.*
Victoria	*Victoria, f.*	whip, drop thong	*fouet enroulé, m.*
volte	*volte, f.*	whip-in	*rallier les chiens*
volte, half	*demi-volte, f.*	whipper-in	*en France : le valet de chiens, m.*
wagering	*pari, m.*	white eye	*oeil cerclé, m.*
wagering, off-track Pari-Mutuel	*Pari Mutuel Urbain, P.M.U.*	white face	*belle face, adj.*
walk, collected	*pas rassemblé, m.*	white line	*ligne blanche, f.*
walk, extended	*pas allongé, m.*	white worms	*vers blancs, m.pl.; Ascaris equorum*
walk, flat-foot	*entre pas – pas défectueux*		
walk, medium	*pas moyen, m.*	wildcat	*chat sauvage, m.*
walking the course	*reconnaissance du parcours, f.*	wind	*souffle, m.*
wall	*mur, m.*	windgall	*molette f.*
wall (foot)	*paroi, (du pied)*	winner	*gagnant, m.*
warrantable stag	*cerf courable, m.*	withers	*garrot, m.*
wart	*verrue, f.*	wolf	*loup, m.*
water brush	*brosse à eau, f.*	wooden horse	*cheval de bois, m. (polo)*
way of going	*allure*	woollen rug	*couverture de laine, f.*
wedge inside	*mouche, f.*		
weighing in	*se peser*	Y mouth snaffle	*double filet, m.*
weighing room	*pesage, m. ou balances, f.pl.*	yearling	*yearling, m.*
weight cloth	*tapis plomb, m.*	yoke	*joug, m.*
well-coupled at the loins	*rein bien attaché, m.*	zig-zag	*ligne brisée, f.*

Metric Conversion Table

1 inch		2.54 cm
1 foot	12 inches	0.3048 m
1 yard	3 feet	0.914 m
1 furlong	220 yards	201 m
1 mile	1760 yards	1.609 m
1 hand	4 inches	10.16 cm
1 ounce		2.35 g
1 pound	16 ounces	0.4536 kg
1 centimetre		0.394 in.
1 metre		3.281 ft
1 kilometre		0.621 mi.
1 gramme		0.0353 oz.
1 kilogramme		2.205 lb.

For all practical purposes one may consider that:

$\frac{7}{16}$	1 cm
1″	2.50 cm
1 h.h.	10.00 cm
1 m	3ft 3in.
1 furlong	200 m
1 mile	1.600 m

cm = centimetre
m = metre
gr = gramme

h.h. = hands
f.   = furlong

Index

Photographic Acknowledgements

The publishers would like to thank the following organizations and individuals for permission to reproduce the photographs in this book:
Ackermans: 208, 286, 365; Agence P. Bertrand et Fils: 249, 251; Elizabeth Anderson: 145, 148; Animal Photography: 382, 400; Ashmolean Museum: 61 (1 &2), 363; City of Birmingham Museum and Gallery: 364; Photo Blanchard; 110, 144, 146; Prof. I. Bobylev: 92, 355, 358 (bottom); Col. Jacques Bois: 372; Muriel Bowen: 147, Col. J. A. Brau: 345, 349; The British Museum: 61(3), 63, 65(1), 68, 83; Cambridge University Press: 61(4); Musée de Cluny: 69; Collection le Goupy: 368; Country Life: 371 (bottom); R. Crawley (Association of Circus Proprietors): 352; Mr Desvignes: 369; Findlay Davidson: 129, 172; John Elliot: 127, 178, 181 (right), 191, 193; Elsa Mayo: 19 (bottom right); Don Essary: 264, 266; Fiona Forbes: 386; Fores: 378, 379, 383, 384; Fox Photos: 224, 225, 229, 230; Foxie Photo: 202; John R. Freeman: 330; Sir John Glubb: 76, 79; Mr Dumas Hermès: 320, 327; John Keene Studio: 196; Keystone: 223, 232, 234, 237, 238, 239, 243, 247, 254, 255, 256, 257, 259, 269, 275, 276, 297; Leslie Lane: 19 (top right), 125, 128, 133, 135, 143 (top), 160, 166, 168,

169, 174–5, 177, 180 (bottom), 181 (left), 182, 190, 192, 358 (top); C. E. Lea: 334; Jim Meads: 294; National Gallery; 366; Novosti: 19 (bottom left), 73; Philip A. Pines: 261, 262; Photo-news: 19 (top left); Photopress: 380, Planet News: 180 (top); Eva Podhajsky: 61 (bottom), 147; Politikens Presse Foto: 141; René Guilloux Photographe: 245; Richard Green Gallery: 367; Riding Magazine: 151, 154, 197, 285, 299, 353; Mike Roberts: 344, 371 (top); Peter Roberts: 124, 161; Dr Peter D. Rossdale: 42, 43, 44, 45, 46; W. W. Rouch: 216, 217, 218; Roy Miles Fine Paintings: 361 (top); Tom Ryder: 337, 338, 339, 340; Col. Jean de Saint-André: 123; François de la Sayette: 357; N. C. Selway Esq: 362; Société des Steeplechases de France: 241, 242; Studio Léo: 246; Peter Sweetman: 164, 175 (bottom), 177; The Tate Gallery: 361 (bottom); United Press International Limited: 374; Société de Venerie: 274, 278; Sanders Watney: 329, 332, 333; Western Americana Picture Library: 203, W. Wilkinson: 293.

For the breeds the publishers would like to thank the following: Lipizzaner (Werner Menzendorf); Noriker (Noriker Breed Society); French Trotter (P. Bertrand et Fils); Selle

Français (Y de la Fosse-David); Exmoor Pony (John Nestle); New Forest Pony (Photonews); Shire Horse, Heavyweight Hunter (Monty); Shetland Pony, Welsh Cob (Section D) (John Elliot); Cleveland Bay, Clydesdale, Cob, Dales pony, Hack, Hackney, Highland pony, Welsh Cob (Section C), Welsh pony (Section B), Connemara pony (Leslie Lane); Fell pony, Welsh Mountain pony (Section A), Suffolk Punch (Sport & General); Irish Draught (Ruth Rogers); Quarter horse, Morgan horse (US Department of Agriculture); Hungarian Half-Bred, Muraközi, Nonius, Salerno, Friesian, Gelderland, Hucul, Konik, Wielkopolski, Andalusian, Swedish Half-Bred, Einsiedler, Standardbred, Akhal-Teke, Budyony, Don, Karabair, Lithuanian Heavy Draught, Orlov Trotter, Hanoverian, Holstein, Oldenburg, Schleswig, Trakehner: Tersk, Vladimir, Dutch Draught, Tennessee Walking horse (Animal Photography)

And for the Colour Section: Spanish Riding School: (frontispiece), Roy Miles Fine Paintings: 1 (top), Yale Center for British Art: 1 (bottom), Gerry Cranham: 2–5, 7 (bottom), R. Crawley (Assoc. of Circus Proprietors): 6 (top), Leslie Lane: 6 (bottom), Mike Roberts: 7 (top), 8.